Book of Ezekiel

Ezekiel
God

King James Bible
Douay Rheims
American Standard Bible
Bible in Basic English
Webster Bible

Matthew Henry

ISBN-10: 1497368561
ISBN-13: 978-1497368569

"Again the word of the LORD came to me."

-Ezekiel 1:22.

CONTENTS

EZEKIEL

THE BOOK OF THE PROPHET EZEKIEL

KING JAMES BIBLE

1

1:1 Now it came to pass in the thirtieth year, in the fourth month, in the fifth day of the month, as I was
among the captives by the river of Chebar, that the heavens were opened, and I saw visions of God.
1:2 In the fifth day of the month, which was the fifth year of king Jehoiachin's captivity, 1:3 The word of
the LORD came expressly unto Ezekiel the priest, the son of Buzi, in the land of the Chaldeans by the
river Chebar; and the hand of the LORD was there upon him.
1:4 And I looked, and, behold, a whirlwind came out of the north, a great cloud, and a fire infolding
itself, and a brightness was about it, and out of the midst thereof as the colour of amber, out of the
midst of the fire.
1:5 Also out of the midst thereof came the likeness of four living creatures. And this was their
appearance; they had the likeness of a man.
1:6 And every one had four faces, and every one had four wings.
1:7 And their feet were straight feet; and the sole of their feet was like the sole of a calf's foot: and they
sparkled like the colour of burnished brass.
1:8 And they had the hands of a man under their wings on their four sides; and they four had their faces
and their wings.
1:9 Their wings were joined one to another; they turned not when they went; they went every one
straight forward.
1:10 As for the likeness of their faces, they four had the face of a man, and the face of a lion, on the
right side: and they four had the face of an ox on the left side; they four also had the face of an eagle.
1:11 Thus were their faces: and their wings were stretched upward; two wings of every one were joined
one to another, and two covered their bodies.
1:12 And they went every one straight forward: whither the spirit was to go, they went; and they turned
not when they went.
1:13 As for the likeness of the living creatures, their appearance was like burning coals of fire, and like
the appearance of lamps: it went up and down among the living creatures; and the fire was bright, and
out of the fire went forth lightning.
1:14 And the living creatures ran and returned as the appearance of a flash of lightning.
1:15 Now as I beheld the living creatures, behold one wheel upon the earth by the living creatures, with
his four faces.
1:16 The appearance of the wheels and their work was like unto the colour of a beryl: and they four had
one likeness: and their appearance and their work was as it were a wheel in the middle of a wheel.
1:17 When they went, they went upon their four sides: and they turned not when they went.
1:18 As for their rings, they were so high that they were dreadful; and their rings were full of eyes round
about them four.
1:19 And when the living creatures went, the wheels went by them: and when the living creatures were
lifted up from the earth, the wheels were lifted up.
1:20 Whithersoever the spirit was to go, they went, thither was their spirit to go; and the wheels were
lifted up over against them: for the spirit of the living creature was in the wheels.
1:21 When those went, these went; and when those stood, these stood; and when those were lifted up
from the earth, the wheels were lifted up over against them: for the spirit of the living creature was in
the wheels.
1:22 And the likeness of the firmament upon the heads of the living creature was as the colour of the
terrible crystal, stretched forth over their heads above.
1:23 And under the firmament were their wings straight, the one toward the other: every one had two,

which covered on this side, and every one had two, which covered on that side, their bodies.
1:24 And when they went, I heard the noise of their wings, like the noise of great waters, as the voice of the Almighty, the voice of speech, as the noise of an host: when they stood, they let down their wings.
1:25 And there was a voice from the firmament that was over their heads, when they stood, and had let down their wings.
1:26 And above the firmament that was over their heads was the likeness of a throne, as the appearance of a sapphire stone: and upon the likeness of the throne was the likeness as the appearance of a man above upon it.
1:27 And I saw as the colour of amber, as the appearance of fire round about within it, from the appearance of his loins even upward, and from the appearance of his loins even downward, I saw as it were the appearance of fire, and it had brightness round about.
1:28 As the appearance of the bow that is in the cloud in the day of rain, so was the appearance of the brightness round about. This was the appearance of the likeness of the glory of the LORD. And when I saw it, I fell upon my face, and I heard a voice of one that spake.

2

2:1 And he said unto me, Son of man, stand upon thy feet, and I will speak unto thee.
2:2 And the spirit entered into me when he spake unto me, and set me upon my feet, that I heard him that spake unto me.
2:3 And he said unto me, Son of man, I send thee to the children of Israel, to a rebellious nation that hath rebelled against me: they and their fathers have transgressed against me, even unto this very day.
2:4 For they are impudent children and stiffhearted. I do send thee unto them; and thou shalt say unto them, Thus saith the Lord GOD.
2:5 And they, whether they will hear, or whether they will forbear, (for they are a rebellious house,) yet shall know that there hath been a prophet among them.
2:6 And thou, son of man, be not afraid of them, neither be afraid of their words, though briers and thorns be with thee, and thou dost dwell among scorpions: be not afraid of their words, nor be dismayed at their looks, though they be a rebellious house.
2:7 And thou shalt speak my words unto them, whether they will hear, or whether they will forbear: for they are most rebellious.
2:8 But thou, son of man, hear what I say unto thee; Be not thou rebellious like that rebellious house: open thy mouth, and eat that I give thee.
2:9 And when I looked, behold, an hand was sent unto me; and, lo, a roll of a book was therein; 2:10 And he spread it before me; and it was written within and without: and there was written therein lamentations, and mourning, and woe.

3

3:1 Moreover he said unto me, Son of man, eat that thou findest; eat this roll, and go speak unto the house of Israel.
3:2 So I opened my mouth, and he caused me to eat that roll.
3:3 And he said unto me, Son of man, cause thy belly to eat, and fill thy bowels with this roll that I give thee. Then did I eat it; and it was in my mouth as honey for sweetness.
3:4 And he said unto me, Son of man, go, get thee unto the house of Israel, and speak with my words unto them.
3:5 For thou art not sent to a people of a strange speech and of an hard language, but to the house of Israel; 3:6 Not to many people of a strange speech and of an hard language, whose words thou canst not understand. Surely, had I sent thee to them, they would have hearkened unto thee.
3:7 But the house of Israel will not hearken unto thee; for they will not hearken unto me: for all the house of Israel are impudent and hardhearted.
3:8 Behold, I have made thy face strong against their faces, and thy forehead strong against their foreheads.
3:9 As an adamant harder than flint have I made thy forehead: fear them not, neither be dismayed at their looks, though they be a rebellious house.
3:10 Moreover he said unto me, Son of man, all my words that I shall speak unto thee receive in thine heart, and hear with thine ears.
3:11 And go, get thee to them of the captivity, unto the children of thy people, and speak unto them,

and tell them, Thus saith the Lord GOD; whether they will hear, or whether they will forbear.
3:12 Then the spirit took me up, and I heard behind me a voice of a great rushing, saying, Blessed be the glory of the LORD from his place.
3:13 I heard also the noise of the wings of the living creatures that touched one another, and the noise of the wheels over against them, and a noise of a great rushing.
3:14 So the spirit lifted me up, and took me away, and I went in bitterness, in the heat of my spirit; but the hand of the LORD was strong upon me.
3:15 Then I came to them of the captivity at Telabib, that dwelt by the river of Chebar, and I sat where they sat, and remained there astonished among them seven days.
3:16 And it came to pass at the end of seven days, that the word of the LORD came unto me, saying,
3:17 Son of man, I have made thee a watchman unto the house of Israel: therefore hear the word at my mouth, and give them warning from me.
3:18 When I say unto the wicked, Thou shalt surely die; and thou givest him not warning, nor speakest to warn the wicked from his wicked way, to save his life; the same wicked man shall die in his iniquity; but his blood will I require at thine hand.
3:19 Yet if thou warn the wicked, and he turn not from his wickedness, nor from his wicked way, he shall die in his iniquity; but thou hast delivered thy soul.
3:20 Again, When a righteous man doth turn from his righteousness, and commit iniquity, and I lay a stumbling-block before him, he shall die: because thou hast not given him warning, he shall die in his sin, and his righteousness which he hath done shall not be remembered; but his blood will I require at thine hand.
3:21 Nevertheless if thou warn the righteous man, that the righteous sin not, and he doth not sin, he shall surely live, because he is warned; also thou hast delivered thy soul.
3:22 And the hand of the LORD was there upon me; and he said unto me, Arise, go forth into the plain, and I will there talk with thee.
3:23 Then I arose, and went forth into the plain: and, behold, the glory of the LORD stood there, as the glory which I saw by the river of Chebar: and I fell on my face.
3:24 Then the spirit entered into me, and set me upon my feet, and spake with me, and said unto me, Go, shut thyself within thine house.
3:25 But thou, O son of man, behold, they shall put bands upon thee, and shall bind thee with them,
and thou shalt not go out among them: 3:26 And I will make thy tongue cleave to the roof of thy
mouth, that thou shalt be dumb, and shalt not be to them a reprover: for they are a rebellious house.
3:27 But when I speak with thee, I will open thy mouth, and thou shalt say unto them, Thus saith the Lord GOD; He that heareth, let him hear; and he that forbeareth, let him forbear: for they are a rebellious house.

4

4:1 Thou also, son of man, take thee a tile, and lay it before thee, and pourtray upon it the city, even
Jerusalem: 4:2 And lay siege against it, and build a fort against it, and cast a mount against it; set the
camp also against it, and set battering rams against it round about.
4:3 Moreover take thou unto thee an iron pan, and set it for a wall of iron between thee and the city: and set thy face against it, and it shall be besieged, and thou shalt lay siege against it. This shall be a sign to the house of Israel.
4:4 Lie thou also upon thy left side, and lay the iniquity of the house of Israel upon it: according to the number of the days that thou shalt lie upon it thou shalt bear their iniquity.
4:5 For I have laid upon thee the years of their iniquity, according to the number of the days, three hundred and ninety days: so shalt thou bear the iniquity of the house of Israel.
4:6 And when thou hast accomplished them, lie again on thy right side, and thou shalt bear the iniquity of the house of Judah forty days: I have appointed thee each day for a year.
4:7 Therefore thou shalt set thy face toward the siege of Jerusalem, and thine arm shall be uncovered, and thou shalt prophesy against it.
4:8 And, behold, I will lay bands upon thee, and thou shalt not turn thee from one side to another, till thou hast ended the days of thy siege.
4:9 Take thou also unto thee wheat, and barley, and beans, and lentiles, and millet, and fitches, and put them in one vessel, and make thee bread thereof, according to the number of the days that thou shalt lie upon thy side, three hundred and ninety days shalt thou eat thereof.

4:10 And thy meat which thou shalt eat shall be by weight, twenty shekels a day: from time to time shalt
thou eat it.
4:11 Thou shalt drink also water by measure, the sixth part of an hin: from time to time shalt thou drink.
4:12 And thou shalt eat it as barley cakes, and thou shalt bake it with dung that cometh out of man, in
their sight.
4:13 And the LORD said, Even thus shall the children of Israel eat their defiled bread among the
Gentiles, whither I will drive them.
4:14 Then said I, Ah Lord GOD! behold, my soul hath not been polluted: for from my youth up even
till now have I not eaten of that which dieth of itself, or is torn in pieces; neither came there abominable
flesh into my mouth.
4:15 Then he said unto me, Lo, I have given thee cow's dung for man's dung, and thou shalt prepare thy
bread therewith.
4:16 Moreover he said unto me, Son of man, behold, I will break the staff of bread in Jerusalem: and
they shall eat bread by weight, and with care; and they shall drink water by measure, and with
astonishment: 4:17 That they may want bread and water, and be astonied one with another, and
consume away for their iniquity.

5

5:1 And thou, son of man, take thee a sharp knife, take thee a barber's razor, and cause it to pass upon
thine head and upon thy beard: then take thee balances to weigh, and divide the hair.
5:2 Thou shalt burn with fire a third part in the midst of the city, when the days of the siege are fulfilled:
and thou shalt take a third part, and smite about it with a knife: and a third part thou shalt scatter in the
wind; and I will draw out a sword after them.
5:3 Thou shalt also take thereof a few in number, and bind them in thy skirts.
5:4 Then take of them again, and cast them into the midst of the fire, and burn them in the fire; for
thereof shall a fire come forth into all the house of Israel.
5:5 Thus saith the Lord GOD; This is Jerusalem: I have set it in the midst of the nations and countries
that are round about her.
5:6 And she hath changed my judgments into wickedness more than the nations, and my statutes more
than the countries that are round about her: for they have refused my judgments and my statutes, they
have not walked in them.
5:7 Therefore thus saith the Lord GOD; Because ye multiplied more than the nations that are round
about you, and have not walked in my statutes, neither have kept my judgments, neither have done
according to the judgments of the nations that are round about you; 5:8 Therefore thus saith the Lord
GOD; Behold, I, even I, am against thee, and will execute judgments in the midst of thee in the sight of
the nations.
5:9 And I will do in thee that which I have not done, and whereunto I will not do any more the like,
because of all thine abominations.
5:10 Therefore the fathers shall eat the sons in the midst of thee, and the sons shall eat their fathers; and
I will execute judgments in thee, and the whole remnant of thee will I scatter into all the winds.
5:11 Wherefore, as I live, saith the Lord GOD; Surely, because thou hast defiled my sanctuary with all
thy detestable things, and with all thine abominations, therefore will I also diminish thee; neither shall
mine eye spare, neither will I have any pity.
5:12 A third part of thee shall die with the pestilence, and with famine shall they be consumed in the
midst of thee: and a third part shall fall by the sword round about thee; and I will scatter a third part into
all the winds, and I will draw out a sword after them.
5:13 Thus shall mine anger be accomplished, and I will cause my fury to rest upon them, and I will be
comforted: and they shall know that I the LORD have spoken it in my zeal, when I have accomplished
my fury in them.
5:14 Moreover I will make thee waste, and a reproach among the nations that are round about thee, in
the sight of all that pass by.
5:15 So it shall be a reproach and a taunt, an instruction and an astonishment unto the nations that are
round about thee, when I shall execute judgments in thee in anger and in fury and in furious rebukes. I
the LORD have spoken it.
5:16 When I shall send upon them the evil arrows of famine, which shall be for their destruction, and
which I will send to destroy you: and I will increase the famine upon you, and will break your staff of
bread: 5:17 So will I send upon you famine and evil beasts, and they shall bereave thee: and pestilence

and blood shall pass through thee; and I will bring the sword upon thee. I the LORD have spoken it.

6

6:1 And the word of the LORD came unto me, saying, 6:2 Son of man, set thy face toward the mountains of Israel, and prophesy against them, 6:3 And say, Ye mountains of Israel, hear the word of the Lord GOD; Thus saith the Lord GOD to the mountains, and to the hills, to the rivers, and to the valleys; Behold, I, even I, will bring a sword upon you, and I will destroy your high places.
6:4 And your altars shall be desolate, and your images shall be broken: and I will cast down your slain men before your idols.
6:5 And I will lay the dead carcases of the children of Israel before their idols; and I will scatter your bones round about your altars.
6:6 In all your dwellingplaces the cities shall be laid waste, and the high places shall be desolate; that your altars may be laid waste and made desolate, and your idols may be broken and cease, and your images may be cut down, and your works may be abolished.
6:7 And the slain shall fall in the midst of you, and ye shall know that I am the LORD.
6:8 Yet will I leave a remnant, that ye may have some that shall escape the sword among the nations, when ye shall be scattered through the countries.
6:9 And they that escape of you shall remember me among the nations whither they shall be carried captives, because I am broken with their whorish heart, which hath departed from me, and with their eyes, which go a whoring after their idols: and they shall lothe themselves for the evils which they have committed in all their abominations.
6:10 And they shall know that I am the LORD, and that I have not said in vain that I would do this evil unto them.
6:11 Thus saith the Lord GOD; Smite with thine hand, and stamp with thy foot, and say, Alas for all the evil abominations of the house of Israel! for they shall fall by the sword, by the famine, and by the pestilence.
6:12 He that is far off shall die of the pestilence; and he that is near shall fall by the sword; and he that remaineth and is besieged shall die by the famine: thus will I accomplish my fury upon them.
6:13 Then shall ye know that I am the LORD, when their slain men shall be among their idols round about their altars, upon every high hill, in all the tops of the mountains, and under every green tree, and under every thick oak, the place where they did offer sweet savour to all their idols.
6:14 So will I stretch out my hand upon them, and make the land desolate, yea, more desolate than the wilderness toward Diblath, in all their habitations: and they shall know that I am the LORD.

7

7:1 Moreover the word of the LORD came unto me, saying, 7:2 Also, thou son of man, thus saith the Lord GOD unto the land of Israel; An end, the end is come upon the four corners of the land.
7:3 Now is the end come upon thee, and I will send mine anger upon thee, and will judge thee according to thy ways, and will recompense upon thee all thine abominations.
7:4 And mine eye shall not spare thee, neither will I have pity: but I will recompense thy ways upon thee, and thine abominations shall be in the midst of thee: and ye shall know that I am the LORD.
7:5 Thus saith the Lord GOD; An evil, an only evil, behold, is come.
7:6 An end is come, the end is come: it watcheth for thee; behold, it is come.
7:7 The morning is come unto thee, O thou that dwellest in the land: the time is come, the day of trouble is near, and not the sounding again of the mountains.
7:8 Now will I shortly pour out my fury upon thee, and accomplish mine anger upon thee: and I will judge thee according to thy ways, and will recompense thee for all thine abominations.
7:9 And mine eye shall not spare, neither will I have pity: I will recompense thee according to thy ways and thine abominations that are in the midst of thee; and ye shall know that I am the LORD that smiteth.
7:10 Behold the day, behold, it is come: the morning is gone forth; the rod hath blossomed, pride hath budded.
7:11 Violence is risen up into a rod of wickedness: none of them shall remain, nor of their multitude, nor of any of their's: neither shall there be wailing for them.
7:12 The time is come, the day draweth near: let not the buyer rejoice, nor the seller mourn: for wrath is

upon all the multitude thereof.
7:13 For the seller shall not return to that which is sold, although they were yet alive: for the vision is touching the whole multitude thereof, which shall not return; neither shall any strengthen himself in the iniquity of his life.
7:14 They have blown the trumpet, even to make all ready; but none goeth to the battle: for my wrath is upon all the multitude thereof.
7:15 The sword is without, and the pestilence and the famine within: he that is in the field shall die with the sword; and he that is in the city, famine and pestilence shall devour him.
7:16 But they that escape of them shall escape, and shall be on the mountains like doves of the valleys, all of them mourning, every one for his iniquity.
7:17 All hands shall be feeble, and all knees shall be weak as water.
7:18 They shall also gird themselves with sackcloth, and horror shall cover them; and shame shall be upon all faces, and baldness upon all their heads.
7:19 They shall cast their silver in the streets, and their gold shall be removed: their silver and their gold shall not be able to deliver them in the day of the wrath of the LORD: they shall not satisfy their souls, neither fill their bowels: because it is the stumblingblock of their iniquity.
7:20 As for the beauty of his ornament, he set it in majesty: but they made the images of their abominations and of their detestable things therein: therefore have I set it far from them.
7:21 And I will give it into the hands of the strangers for a prey, and to the wicked of the earth for a spoil; and they shall pollute it.
7:22 My face will I turn also from them, and they shall pollute my secret place: for the robbers shall enter into it, and defile it.
7:23 Make a chain: for the land is full of bloody crimes, and the city is full of violence.
7:24 Wherefore I will bring the worst of the heathen, and they shall possess their houses: I will also make the pomp of the strong to cease; and their holy places shall be defiled.
7:25 Destruction cometh; and they shall seek peace, and there shall be none.
7:26 Mischief shall come upon mischief, and rumour shall be upon rumour; then shall they seek a vision of the prophet; but the law shall perish from the priest, and counsel from the ancients.
7:27 The king shall mourn, and the prince shall be clothed with desolation, and the hands of the people of the land shall be troubled: I will do unto them after their way, and according to their deserts will I judge them; and they shall know that I am the LORD.

8

8:1 And it came to pass in the sixth year, in the sixth month, in the fifth day of the month, as I sat in mine house, and the elders of Judah sat before me, that the hand of the Lord GOD fell there upon me.
8:2 Then I beheld, and lo a likeness as the appearance of fire: from the appearance of his loins even downward, fire; and from his loins even upward, as the appearance of brightness, as the colour of amber.
8:3 And he put forth the form of an hand, and took me by a lock of mine head; and the spirit lifted me up between the earth and the heaven, and brought me in the visions of God to Jerusalem, to the door of the inner gate that looketh toward the north; where was the seat of the image of jealousy, which provoketh to jealousy.
8:4 And, behold, the glory of the God of Israel was there, according to the vision that I saw in the plain.
8:5 Then said he unto me, Son of man, lift up thine eyes now the way toward the north. So I lifted up mine eyes the way toward the north, and behold northward at the gate of the altar this image of jealousy in the entry.
8:6 He said furthermore unto me, Son of man, seest thou what they do? even the great abominations that the house of Israel committeth here, that I should go far off from my sanctuary? but turn thee yet again, and thou shalt see greater abominations.
8:7 And he brought me to the door of the court; and when I looked, behold a hole in the wall.
8:8 Then said he unto me, Son of man, dig now in the wall: and when I had digged in the wall, behold a door.
8:9 And he said unto me, Go in, and behold the wicked abominations that they do here.
8:10 So I went in and saw; and behold every form of creeping things, and abominable beasts, and all the idols of the house of Israel, pourtrayed upon the wall round about.
8:11 And there stood before them seventy men of the ancients of the house of Israel, and in the midst of them stood Jaazaniah the son of Shaphan, with every man his censer in his hand; and a thick cloud of

incense went up.
8:12 Then said he unto me, Son of man, hast thou seen what the ancients of the house of Israel do in the dark, every man in the chambers of his imagery? for they say, the LORD seeth us not; the LORD hath forsaken the earth.
8:13 He said also unto me, Turn thee yet again, and thou shalt see greater abominations that they do.
8:14 Then he brought me to the door of the gate of the LORD's house which was toward the north; and, behold, there sat women weeping for Tammuz.
8:15 Then said he unto me, Hast thou seen this, O son of man? turn thee yet again, and thou shalt see greater abominations than these.
8:16 And he brought me into the inner court of the LORD's house, and, behold, at the door of the temple of the LORD, between the porch and the altar, were about five and twenty men, with their backs toward the temple of the LORD, and their faces toward the east; and they worshipped the sun toward the east.
8:17 Then he said unto me, Hast thou seen this, O son of man? Is it a light thing to the house of Judah that they commit the abominations which they commit here? for they have filled the land with violence, and have returned to provoke me to anger: and, lo, they put the branch to their nose.
8:18 Therefore will I also deal in fury: mine eye shall not spare, neither will I have pity: and though they cry in mine ears with a loud voice, yet will I not hear them.

9

9:1 He cried also in mine ears with a loud voice, saying, Cause them that have charge over the city to draw near, even every man with his destroying weapon in his hand.
9:2 And, behold, six men came from the way of the higher gate, which lieth toward the north, and every man a slaughter weapon in his hand; and one man among them was clothed with linen, with a writer's inkhorn by his side: and they went in, and stood beside the brasen altar.
9:3 And the glory of the God of Israel was gone up from the cherub, whereupon he was, to the threshold of the house. And he called to the man clothed with linen, which had the writer's inkhorn by
his side; 9:4 And the LORD said unto him, Go through the midst of the city, through the midst of
Jerusalem, and set a mark upon the foreheads of the men that sigh and that cry for all the abominations that be done in the midst thereof.
9:5 And to the others he said in mine hearing, Go ye after him through the city, and smite: let not your
eye spare, neither have ye pity: 9:6 Slay utterly old and young, both maids, and little children, and
women: but come not near any man upon whom is the mark; and begin at my sanctuary. Then they began at the ancient men which were before the house.
9:7 And he said unto them, Defile the house, and fill the courts with the slain: go ye forth. And they went forth, and slew in the city.
9:8 And it came to pass, while they were slaying them, and I was left, that I fell upon my face, and cried, and said, Ah Lord GOD! wilt thou destroy all the residue of Israel in thy pouring out of thy fury upon
Jerusalem? 9:9 Then said he unto me, The iniquity of the house of Israel and Judah is exceeding great,
and the land is full of blood, and the city full of perverseness: for they say, The LORD hath forsaken the earth, and the LORD seeth not.
9:10 And as for me also, mine eye shall not spare, neither will I have pity, but I will recompense their way upon their head.
9:11 And, behold, the man clothed with linen, which had the inkhorn by his side, reported the matter, saying, I have done as thou hast commanded me.

10

10:1 Then I looked, and, behold, in the firmament that was above the head of the cherubims there appeared over them as it were a sapphire stone, as the appearance of the likeness of a throne.
10:2 And he spake unto the man clothed with linen, and said, Go in between the wheels, even under the cherub, and fill thine hand with coals of fire from between the cherubims, and scatter them over the city. And he went in in my sight.
10:3 Now the cherubims stood on the right side of the house, when the man went in; and the cloud filled the inner court.
10:4 Then the glory of the LORD went up from the cherub, and stood over the threshold of the house;

and the house was filled with the cloud, and the court was full of the brightness of the LORD's glory.
10:5 And the sound of the cherubims' wings was heard even to the outer court, as the voice of the Almighty God when he speaketh.
10:6 And it came to pass, that when he had commanded the man clothed with linen, saying, Take fire from between the wheels, from between the cherubims; then he went in, and stood beside the wheels.
10:7 And one cherub stretched forth his hand from between the cherubims unto the fire that was between the cherubims, and took thereof, and put it into the hands of him that was clothed with linen: who took it, and went out.
10:8 And there appeared in the cherubims the form of a man's hand under their wings.
10:9 And when I looked, behold the four wheels by the cherubims, one wheel by one cherub, and another wheel by another cherub: and the appearance of the wheels was as the colour of a beryl stone.
10:10 And as for their appearances, they four had one likeness, as if a wheel had been in the midst of a wheel.
10:11 When they went, they went upon their four sides; they turned not as they went, but to the place whither the head looked they followed it; they turned not as they went.
10:12 And their whole body, and their backs, and their hands, and their wings, and the wheels, were full of eyes round about, even the wheels that they four had.
10:13 As for the wheels, it was cried unto them in my hearing, O wheel.
10:14 And every one had four faces: the first face was the face of a cherub, and the second face was the face of a man, and the third the face of a lion, and the fourth the face of an eagle.
10:15 And the cherubims were lifted up. This is the living creature that I saw by the river of Chebar.
10:16 And when the cherubims went, the wheels went by them: and when the cherubims lifted up their wings to mount up from the earth, the same wheels also turned not from beside them.
10:17 When they stood, these stood; and when they were lifted up, these lifted up themselves also: for the spirit of the living creature was in them.
10:18 Then the glory of the LORD departed from off the threshold of the house, and stood over the cherubims.
10:19 And the cherubims lifted up their wings, and mounted up from the earth in my sight: when they went out, the wheels also were beside them, and every one stood at the door of the east gate of the LORD's house; and the glory of the God of Israel was over them above.
10:20 This is the living creature that I saw under the God of Israel by the river of Chebar; and I knew that they were the cherubims.
10:21 Every one had four faces apiece, and every one four wings; and the likeness of the hands of a man was under their wings.
10:22 And the likeness of their faces was the same faces which I saw by the river of Chebar, their appearances and themselves: they went every one straight forward.

11

11:1 Moreover the spirit lifted me up, and brought me unto the east gate of the LORD's house, which looketh eastward: and behold at the door of the gate five and twenty men; among whom I saw Jaazaniah the son of Azur, and Pelatiah the son of Benaiah, princes of the people.
11:2 Then said he unto me, Son of man, these are the men that devise mischief, and give wicked counsel
in this city: 11:3 Which say, It is not near; let us build houses: this city is the caldron, and we be the flesh.
11:4 Therefore prophesy against them, prophesy, O son of man.
11:5 And the Spirit of the LORD fell upon me, and said unto me, Speak; Thus saith the LORD; Thus have ye said, O house of Israel: for I know the things that come into your mind, every one of them.
11:6 Ye have multiplied your slain in this city, and ye have filled the streets thereof with the slain.
11:7 Therefore thus saith the Lord GOD; Your slain whom ye have laid in the midst of it, they are the flesh, and this city is the caldron: but I will bring you forth out of the midst of it.
11:8 Ye have feared the sword; and I will bring a sword upon you, saith the Lord GOD.
11:9 And I will bring you out of the midst thereof, and deliver you into the hands of strangers, and will execute judgments among you.
11:10 Ye shall fall by the sword; I will judge you in the border of Israel; and ye shall know that I am the LORD.
11:11 This city shall not be your caldron, neither shall ye be the flesh in the midst thereof; but I will
judge you in the border of Israel: 11:12 And ye shall know that I am the LORD: for ye have not walked
in my statutes, neither executed my judgments, but have done after the manners of the heathen that are

round about you.
11:13 And it came to pass, when I prophesied, that Pelatiah the son of Benaiah died. Then fell I down upon my face, and cried with a loud voice, and said, Ah Lord GOD! wilt thou make a full end of the remnant of Israel? 11:14 Again the word of the LORD came unto me, saying, 11:15 Son of man, thy brethren, even thy brethren, the men of thy kindred, and all the house of Israel wholly, are they unto whom the inhabitants of Jerusalem have said, Get you far from the LORD: unto us is this land given in possession.
11:16 Therefore say, Thus saith the Lord GOD; Although I have cast them far off among the heathen, and although I have scattered them among the countries, yet will I be to them as a little sanctuary in the countries where they shall come.
11:17 Therefore say, Thus saith the Lord GOD; I will even gather you from the people, and assemble you out of the countries where ye have been scattered, and I will give you the land of Israel.
11:18 And they shall come thither, and they shall take away all the detestable things thereof and all the abominations thereof from thence.
11:19 And I will give them one heart, and I will put a new spirit within you; and I will take the stony heart out of their flesh, and will give them an heart of flesh: 11:20 That they may walk in my statutes, and keep mine ordinances, and do them: and they shall be my people, and I will be their God.
11:21 But as for them whose heart walketh after the heart of their detestable things and their abominations, I will recompense their way upon their own heads, saith the Lord GOD.
11:22 Then did the cherubims lift up their wings, and the wheels beside them; and the glory of the God of Israel was over them above.
11:23 And the glory of the LORD went up from the midst of the city, and stood upon the mountain which is on the east side of the city.
11:24 Afterwards the spirit took me up, and brought me in a vision by the Spirit of God into Chaldea, to them of the captivity. So the vision that I had seen went up from me.
11:25 Then I spake unto them of the captivity all the things that the LORD had shewed me.

12

12:1 The word of the LORD also came unto me, saying, 12:2 Son of man, thou dwellest in the midst of a rebellious house, which have eyes to see, and see not; they have ears to hear, and hear not: for they are a rebellious house.
12:3 Therefore, thou son of man, prepare thee stuff for removing, and remove by day in their sight; and thou shalt remove from thy place to another place in their sight: it may be they will consider, though they be a rebellious house.
12:4 Then shalt thou bring forth thy stuff by day in their sight, as stuff for removing: and thou shalt go forth at even in their sight, as they that go forth into captivity.
12:5 Dig thou through the wall in their sight, and carry out thereby.
12:6 In their sight shalt thou bear it upon thy shoulders, and carry it forth in the twilight: thou shalt cover thy face, that thou see not the ground: for I have set thee for a sign unto the house of Israel.
12:7 And I did so as I was commanded: I brought forth my stuff by day, as stuff for captivity, and in the even I digged through the wall with mine hand; I brought it forth in the twilight, and I bare it upon my shoulder in their sight.
12:8 And in the morning came the word of the LORD unto me, saying, 12:9 Son of man, hath not the house of Israel, the rebellious house, said unto thee, What doest thou? 12:10 Say thou unto them, Thus saith the Lord GOD; This burden concerneth the prince in Jerusalem, and all the house of Israel that are among them.
12:11 Say, I am your sign: like as I have done, so shall it be done unto them: they shall remove and go into captivity.
12:12 And the prince that is among them shall bear upon his shoulder in the twilight, and shall go forth: they shall dig through the wall to carry out thereby: he shall cover his face, that he see not the ground with his eyes.
12:13 My net also will I spread upon him, and he shall be taken in my snare: and I will bring him to Babylon to the land of the Chaldeans; yet shall he not see it, though he shall die there.
12:14 And I will scatter toward every wind all that are about him to help him, and all his bands; and I will draw out the sword after them.
12:15 And they shall know that I am the LORD, when I shall scatter them among the nations, and disperse them in the countries.

12:16 But I will leave a few men of them from the sword, from the famine, and from the pestilence; that they may declare all their abominations among the heathen whither they come; and they shall know that I am the LORD.
12:17 Moreover the word of the LORD came to me, saying, 12:18 Son of man, eat thy bread with quaking, and drink thy water with trembling and with carefulness; 12:19 And say unto the people of the land, Thus saith the Lord GOD of the inhabitants of Jerusalem, and of the land of Israel; They shall eat their bread with carefulness, and drink their water with astonishment, that her land may be desolate from all that is therein, because of the violence of all them that dwell therein.
12:20 And the cities that are inhabited shall be laid waste, and the land shall be desolate; and ye shall know that I am the LORD.
12:21 And the word of the LORD came unto me, saying, 12:22 Son of man, what is that proverb that ye have in the land of Israel, saying, The days are prolonged, and every vision faileth? 12:23 Tell them therefore, Thus saith the Lord GOD; I will make this proverb to cease, and they shall no more use it as a proverb in Israel; but say unto them, The days are at hand, and the effect of every vision.
12:24 For there shall be no more any vain vision nor flattering divination within the house of Israel.
12:25 For I am the LORD: I will speak, and the word that I shall speak shall come to pass; it shall be no more prolonged: for in your days, O rebellious house, will I say the word, and will perform it, saith the Lord GOD.
12:26 Again the word of the LORD came to me, saying.
12:27 Son of man, behold, they of the house of Israel say, The vision that he seeth is for many days to come, and he prophesieth of the times that are far off.
12:28 Therefore say unto them, Thus saith the Lord GOD; There shall none of my words be prolonged any more, but the word which I have spoken shall be done, saith the Lord GOD.

13

13:1 And the word of the LORD came unto me, saying, 13:2 Son of man, prophesy against the prophets of Israel that prophesy, and say thou unto them that prophesy out of their own hearts, Hear ye the word of the LORD; 13:3 Thus saith the Lord GOD; Woe unto the foolish prophets, that follow their own spirit, and have seen nothing! 13:4 O Israel, thy prophets are like the foxes in the deserts.
13:5 Ye have not gone up into the gaps, neither made up the hedge for the house of Israel to stand in the battle in the day of the LORD.
13:6 They have seen vanity and lying divination, saying, The LORD saith: and the LORD hath not sent them: and they have made others to hope that they would confirm the word.
13:7 Have ye not seen a vain vision, and have ye not spoken a lying divination, whereas ye say, The LORD saith it; albeit I have not spoken? 13:8 Therefore thus saith the Lord GOD; Because ye have spoken vanity, and seen lies, therefore, behold, I am against you, saith the Lord GOD.
13:9 And mine hand shall be upon the prophets that see vanity, and that divine lies: they shall not be in the assembly of my people, neither shall they be written in the writing of the house of Israel, neither shall they enter into the land of Israel; and ye shall know that I am the Lord GOD.
13:10 Because, even because they have seduced my people, saying, Peace; and there was no peace; and one built up a wall, and, lo, others daubed it with untempered morter: 13:11 Say unto them which daub it with untempered morter, that it shall fall: there shall be an overflowing shower; and ye, O great hailstones, shall fall; and a stormy wind shall rend it.
13:12 Lo, when the wall is fallen, shall it not be said unto you, Where is the daubing wherewith ye have daubed it? 13:13 Therefore thus saith the Lord GOD; I will even rend it with a stormy wind in my fury; and there shall be an overflowing shower in mine anger, and great hailstones in my fury to consume it.
13:14 So will I break down the wall that ye have daubed with untempered morter, and bring it down to the ground, so that the foundation thereof shall be discovered, and it shall fall, and ye shall be consumed in the midst thereof: and ye shall know that I am the LORD.
13:15 Thus will I accomplish my wrath upon the wall, and upon them that have daubed it with untempered morter, and will say unto you, The wall is no more, neither they that daubed it; 13:16 To wit, the prophets of Israel which prophesy concerning Jerusalem, and which see visions of peace for her, and there is no peace, saith the Lord GOD.
13:17 Likewise, thou son of man, set thy face against the daughters of thy people, which prophesy out of their own heart; and prophesy thou against them, 13:18 And say, Thus saith the Lord GOD; Woe to the women that sew pillows to all armholes, and make kerchiefs upon the head of every stature to hunt souls! Will ye hunt the souls of my people, and will ye save the souls alive that come unto you? 13:19

And will ye pollute me among my people for handfuls of barley and for pieces of bread, to slay the souls that should not die, and to save the souls alive that should not live, by your lying to my people that hear your lies? 13:20 Wherefore thus saith the Lord GOD; Behold, I am against your pillows, wherewith ye there hunt the souls to make them fly, and I will tear them from your arms, and will let the souls go, even the souls that ye hunt to make them fly.
13:21 Your kerchiefs also will I tear, and deliver my people out of your hand, and they shall be no more in your hand to be hunted; and ye shall know that I am the LORD.
13:22 Because with lies ye have made the heart of the righteous sad, whom I have not made sad; and strengthened the hands of the wicked, that he should not return from his wicked way, by promising him life: 13:23 Therefore ye shall see no more vanity, nor divine divinations: for I will deliver my people out of your hand: and ye shall know that I am the LORD.

14

14:1 Then came certain of the elders of Israel unto me, and sat before me.
14:2 And the word of the LORD came unto me, saying, 14:3 Son of man, these men have set up their idols in their heart, and put the stumblingblock of their iniquity before their face: should I be enquired of at all by them? 14:4 Therefore speak unto them, and say unto them, Thus saith the Lord GOD; Every man of the house of Israel that setteth up his idols in his heart, and putteth the stumblingblock of his iniquity before his face, and cometh to the prophet; I the LORD will answer him that cometh according to the multitude of his idols; 14:5 That I may take the house of Israel in their own heart, because they are all estranged from me through their idols.
14:6 Therefore say unto the house of Israel, Thus saith the Lord GOD; Repent, and turn yourselves from your idols; and turn away your faces from all your abominations.
14:7 For every one of the house of Israel, or of the stranger that sojourneth in Israel, which separateth himself from me, and setteth up his idols in his heart, and putteth the stumblingblock of his iniquity before his face, and cometh to a prophet to enquire of him concerning me; I the LORD will answer him by myself: 14:8 And I will set my face against that man, and will make him a sign and a proverb, and I will cut him off from the midst of my people; and ye shall know that I am the LORD.
14:9 And if the prophet be deceived when he hath spoken a thing, I the LORD have deceived that prophet, and I will stretch out my hand upon him, and will destroy him from the midst of my people Israel.
14:10 And they shall bear the punishment of their iniquity: the punishment of the prophet shall be even as the punishment of him that seeketh unto him; 14:11 That the house of Israel may go no more astray from me, neither be polluted any more with all their transgressions; but that they may be my people, and I may be their God, saith the Lord GOD.
14:12 The word of the LORD came again to me, saying, 14:13 Son of man, when the land sinneth against me by trespassing grievously, then will I stretch out mine hand upon it, and will break the staff of the bread thereof, and will send famine upon it, and will cut off man and beast from it: 14:14 Though these three men, Noah, Daniel, and Job, were in it, they should deliver but their own souls by their righteousness, saith the Lord GOD.
14:15 If I cause noisome beasts to pass through the land, and they spoil it, so that it be desolate, that no man may pass through because of the beasts: 14:16 Though these three men were in it, as I live, saith the Lord GOD, they shall deliver neither sons nor daughters; they only shall be delivered, but the land shall be desolate.
14:17 Or if I bring a sword upon that land, and say, Sword, go through the land; so that I cut off man and beast from it: 14:18 Though these three men were in it, as I live, saith the Lord GOD, they shall deliver neither sons nor daughters, but they only shall be delivered themselves.
14:19 Or if I send a pestilence into that land, and pour out my fury upon it in blood, to cut off from it man and beast: 14:20 Though Noah, Daniel, and Job were in it, as I live, saith the Lord GOD, they shall deliver neither son nor daughter; they shall but deliver their own souls by their righteousness.
14:21 For thus saith the Lord GOD; How much more when I send my four sore judgments upon Jerusalem, the sword, and the famine, and the noisome beast, and the pestilence, to cut off from it man and beast? 14:22 Yet, behold, therein shall be left a remnant that shall be brought forth, both sons and daughters: behold, they shall come forth unto you, and ye shall see their way and their doings: and ye shall be comforted concerning the evil that I have brought upon Jerusalem, even concerning all that I have brought upon it.
14:23 And they shall comfort you, when ye see their ways and their doings: and ye shall know that I have

not done without cause all that I have done in it, saith the Lord GOD.

15

15:1 And the word of the LORD came unto me, saying, 15:2 Son of man, what is the vine tree more
than any tree, or than a branch which is among the trees of the forest? 15:3 Shall wood be taken thereof
to do any work? or will men take a pin of it to hang any vessel thereon? 15:4 Behold, it is cast into the
fire for fuel; the fire devoureth both the ends of it, and the midst of it is burned. Is it meet for any work?
15:5 Behold, when it was whole, it was meet for no work: how much less shall it be meet yet for any
work, when the fire hath devoured it, and it is burned? 15:6 Therefore thus saith the Lord GOD; As the
vine tree among the trees of the forest, which I have given to the fire for fuel, so will I give the
inhabitants of Jerusalem.
15:7 And I will set my face against them; they shall go out from one fire, and another fire shall devour
them; and ye shall know that I am the LORD, when I set my face against them.
15:8 And I will make the land desolate, because they have committed a trespass, saith the Lord GOD.

16

16:1 Again the word of the LORD came unto me, saying, 16:2 Son of man, cause Jerusalem to know her
abominations, 16:3 And say, Thus saith the Lord GOD unto Jerusalem; Thy birth and thy nativity is of
the land of Canaan; thy father was an Amorite, and thy mother an Hittite.
16:4 And as for thy nativity, in the day thou wast born thy navel was not cut, neither wast thou washed in water to supple thee; thou wast not salted at all, nor swaddled at all.
16:5 None eye pitied thee, to do any of these unto thee, to have compassion upon thee; but thou wast cast out in the open field, to the lothing of thy person, in the day that thou wast born.
16:6 And when I passed by thee, and saw thee polluted in thine own blood, I said unto thee when thou wast in thy blood, Live; yea, I said unto thee when thou wast in thy blood, Live.
16:7 I have caused thee to multiply as the bud of the field, and thou hast increased and waxen great, and thou art come to excellent ornaments: thy breasts are fashioned, and thine hair is grown, whereas thou wast naked and bare.
16:8 Now when I passed by thee, and looked upon thee, behold, thy time was the time of love; and I spread my skirt over thee, and covered thy nakedness: yea, I sware unto thee, and entered into a covenant with thee, saith the Lord GOD, and thou becamest mine.
16:9 Then washed I thee with water; yea, I throughly washed away thy blood from thee, and I anointed thee with oil.
16:10 I clothed thee also with broidered work, and shod thee with badgers' skin, and I girded thee about with fine linen, and I covered thee with silk.
16:11 I decked thee also with ornaments, and I put bracelets upon thy hands, and a chain on thy neck.
16:12 And I put a jewel on thy forehead, and earrings in thine ears, and a beautiful crown upon thine head.
16:13 Thus wast thou decked with gold and silver; and thy raiment was of fine linen, and silk, and broidered work; thou didst eat fine flour, and honey, and oil: and thou wast exceeding beautiful, and thou didst prosper into a kingdom.
16:14 And thy renown went forth among the heathen for thy beauty: for it was perfect through my comeliness, which I had put upon thee, saith the Lord GOD.
16:15 But thou didst trust in thine own beauty, and playedst the harlot because of thy renown, and pouredst out thy fornications on every one that passed by; his it was.
16:16 And of thy garments thou didst take, and deckedst thy high places with divers colours, and playedst the harlot thereupon: the like things shall not come, neither shall it be so.
16:17 Thou hast also taken thy fair jewels of my gold and of my silver, which I had given thee, and
madest to thyself images of men, and didst commit whoredom with them, 16:18 And tookest thy
broidered garments, and coveredst them: and thou hast set mine oil and mine incense before them.
16:19 My meat also which I gave thee, fine flour, and oil, and honey, wherewith I fed thee, thou hast even set it before them for a sweet savour: and thus it was, saith the Lord GOD.
16:20 Moreover thou hast taken thy sons and thy daughters, whom thou hast borne unto me, and these
hast thou sacrificed unto them to be devoured. Is this of thy whoredoms a small matter, 16:21 That thou
hast slain my children, and delivered them to cause them to pass through the fire for them? 16:22 And

in all thine abominations and thy whoredoms thou hast not remembered the days of thy youth, when thou wast naked and bare, and wast polluted in thy blood.
16:23 And it came to pass after all thy wickedness, (woe, woe unto thee! saith the LORD GOD;) 16:24
That thou hast also built unto thee an eminent place, and hast made thee an high place in every street.
16:25 Thou hast built thy high place at every head of the way, and hast made thy beauty to be abhorred, and hast opened thy feet to every one that passed by, and multiplied thy whoredoms.
16:26 Thou hast also committed fornication with the Egyptians thy neighbours, great of flesh; and hast increased thy whoredoms, to provoke me to anger.
16:27 Behold, therefore I have stretched out my hand over thee, and have diminished thine ordinary food, and delivered thee unto the will of them that hate thee, the daughters of the Philistines, which are ashamed of thy lewd way.
16:28 Thou hast played the whore also with the Assyrians, because thou wast unsatiable; yea, thou hast played the harlot with them, and yet couldest not be satisfied.
16:29 Thou hast moreover multiplied thy fornication in the land of Canaan unto Chaldea; and yet thou wast not satisfied therewith.
16:30 How weak is thine heart, saith the LORD GOD, seeing thou doest all these things, the work of an
imperious whorish woman; 16:31 In that thou buildest thine eminent place in the head of every way, and
makest thine high place in every street; and hast not been as an harlot, in that thou scornest hire; 16:32
But as a wife that committeth adultery, which taketh strangers instead of her husband! 16:33 They give
gifts to all whores: but thou givest thy gifts to all thy lovers, and hirest them, that they may come unto thee on every side for thy whoredom.
16:34 And the contrary is in thee from other women in thy whoredoms, whereas none followeth thee to commit whoredoms: and in that thou givest a reward, and no reward is given unto thee, therefore thou art contrary.
16:35 Wherefore, O harlot, hear the word of the LORD: 16:36 Thus saith the Lord GOD; Because thy
filthiness was poured out, and thy nakedness discovered through thy whoredoms with thy lovers, and with all the idols of thy abominations, and by the blood of thy children, which thou didst give unto
them; 16:37 Behold, therefore I will gather all thy lovers, with whom thou hast taken pleasure, and all them that thou hast loved, with all them that thou hast hated; I will even gather them round about against thee, and will discover thy nakedness unto them, that they may see all thy nakedness.
16:38 And I will judge thee, as women that break wedlock and shed blood are judged; and I will give thee blood in fury and jealousy.
16:39 And I will also give thee into their hand, and they shall throw down thine eminent place, and shall break down thy high places: they shall strip thee also of thy clothes, and shall take thy fair jewels, and leave thee naked and bare.
16:40 They shall also bring up a company against thee, and they shall stone thee with stones, and thrust thee through with their swords.
16:41 And they shall burn thine houses with fire, and execute judgments upon thee in the sight of many women: and I will cause thee to cease from playing the harlot, and thou also shalt give no hire any more.
16:42 So will I make my fury toward thee to rest, and my jealousy shall depart from thee, and I will be quiet, and will be no more angry.
16:43 Because thou hast not remembered the days of thy youth, but hast fretted me in all these things; behold, therefore I also will recompense thy way upon thine head, saith the Lord GOD: and thou shalt not commit this lewdness above all thine abominations.
16:44 Behold, every one that useth proverbs shall use this proverb against thee, saying, As is the mother, so is her daughter.
16:45 Thou art thy mother's daughter, that lotheth her husband and her children; and thou art the sister of thy sisters, which lothed their husbands and their children: your mother was an Hittite, and your father an Amorite.
16:46 And thine elder sister is Samaria, she and her daughters that dwell at thy left hand: and thy younger sister, that dwelleth at thy right hand, is Sodom and her daughters.
16:47 Yet hast thou not walked after their ways, nor done after their abominations: but, as if that were a very little thing, thou wast corrupted more than they in all thy ways.
16:48 As I live, saith the Lord GOD, Sodom thy sister hath not done, she nor her daughters, as thou hast done, thou and thy daughters.
16:49 Behold, this was the iniquity of thy sister Sodom, pride, fulness of bread, and abundance of idleness was in her and in her daughters, neither did she strengthen the hand of the poor and needy.
16:50 And they were haughty, and committed abomination before me: therefore I took them away as I saw good.

16:51 Neither hath Samaria committed half of thy sins; but thou hast multiplied thine abominations more than they, and hast justified thy sisters in all thine abominations which thou hast done.
16:52 Thou also, which hast judged thy sisters, bear thine own shame for thy sins that thou hast committed more abominable than they: they are more righteous than thou: yea, be thou confounded also, and bear thy shame, in that thou hast justified thy sisters.
16:53 When I shall bring again their captivity, the captivity of Sodom and her daughters, and the captivity of Samaria and her daughters, then will I bring again the captivity of thy captives in the midst
of them: 16:54 That thou mayest bear thine own shame, and mayest be confounded in all that thou hast done, in that thou art a comfort unto them.
16:55 When thy sisters, Sodom and her daughters, shall return to their former estate, and Samaria and her daughters shall return to their former estate, then thou and thy daughters shall return to your former estate.
16:56 For thy sister Sodom was not mentioned by thy mouth in the day of thy pride, 16:57 Before thy
wickedness was discovered, as at the time of thy reproach of the daughters of Syria, and all that are round about her, the daughters of the Philistines, which despise thee round about.
16:58 Thou hast borne thy lewdness and thine abominations, saith the LORD.
16:59 For thus saith the Lord GOD; I will even deal with thee as thou hast done, which hast despised the oath in breaking the covenant.
16:60 Nevertheless I will remember my covenant with thee in the days of thy youth, and I will establish unto thee an everlasting covenant.
16:61 Then thou shalt remember thy ways, and be ashamed, when thou shalt receive thy sisters, thine elder and thy younger: and I will give them unto thee for daughters, but not by thy covenant.
16:62 And I will establish my covenant with thee; and thou shalt know that I am the LORD: 16:63 That
thou mayest remember, and be confounded, and never open thy mouth any more because of thy shame, when I am pacified toward thee for all that thou hast done, saith the Lord GOD.

17

17:1 And the word of the LORD came unto me, saying, 17:2 Son of man, put forth a riddle, and speak a
parable unto the house of Israel; 17:3 And say, Thus saith the Lord GOD; A great eagle with great
wings, longwinged, full of feathers, which had divers colours, came unto Lebanon, and took the highest
branch of the cedar: 17:4 He cropped off the top of his young twigs, and carried it into a land of
traffick; he set it in a city of merchants.
17:5 He took also of the seed of the land, and planted it in a fruitful field; he placed it by great waters, and set it as a willow tree.
17:6 And it grew, and became a spreading vine of low stature, whose branches turned toward him, and the roots thereof were under him: so it became a vine, and brought forth branches, and shot forth sprigs.
17:7 There was also another great eagle with great wings and many feathers: and, behold, this vine did bend her roots toward him, and shot forth her branches toward him, that he might water it by the furrows of her plantation.
17:8 It was planted in a good soil by great waters, that it might bring forth branches, and that it might bear fruit, that it might be a goodly vine.
17:9 Say thou, Thus saith the Lord GOD; Shall it prosper? shall he not pull up the roots thereof, and cut off the fruit thereof, that it wither? it shall wither in all the leaves of her spring, even without great power or many people to pluck it up by the roots thereof.
17:10 Yea, behold, being planted, shall it prosper? shall it not utterly wither, when the east wind toucheth it? it shall wither in the furrows where it grew.
17:11 Moreover the word of the LORD came unto me, saying, 17:12 Say now to the rebellious house,
Know ye not what these things mean? tell them, Behold, the king of Babylon is come to Jerusalem, and
hath taken the king thereof, and the princes thereof, and led them with him to Babylon; 17:13 And hath
taken of the king's seed, and made a covenant with him, and hath taken an oath of him: he hath also
taken the mighty of the land: 17:14 That the kingdom might be base, that it might not lift itself up, but
that by keeping of his covenant it might stand.
17:15 But he rebelled against him in sending his ambassadors into Egypt, that they might give him horses and much people. Shall he prosper? shall he escape that doeth such things? or shall he break the
covenant, and be delivered? 17:16 As I live, saith the Lord GOD, surely in the place where the king
dwelleth that made him king, whose oath he despised, and whose covenant he brake, even with him in

the midst of Babylon he shall die.
17:17 Neither shall Pharaoh with his mighty army and great company make for him in the war, by casting up mounts, and building forts, to cut off many persons: 17:18 Seeing he despised the oath by breaking the covenant, when, lo, he had given his hand, and hath done all these things, he shall not escape.
17:19 Therefore thus saith the Lord GOD; As I live, surely mine oath that he hath despised, and my covenant that he hath broken, even it will I recompense upon his own head.
17:20 And I will spread my net upon him, and he shall be taken in my snare, and I will bring him to Babylon, and will plead with him there for his trespass that he hath trespassed against me.
17:21 And all his fugitives with all his bands shall fall by the sword, and they that remain shall be scattered toward all winds: and ye shall know that I the LORD have spoken it.
17:22 Thus saith the Lord GOD; I will also take of the highest branch of the high cedar, and will set it; I will crop off from the top of his young twigs a tender one, and will plant it upon an high mountain and eminent: 17:23 In the mountain of the height of Israel will I plant it: and it shall bring forth boughs, and bear fruit, and be a goodly cedar: and under it shall dwell all fowl of every wing; in the shadow of the branches thereof shall they dwell.
17:24 And all the trees of the field shall know that I the LORD have brought down the high tree, have exalted the low tree, have dried up the green tree, and have made the dry tree to flourish: I the LORD have spoken and have done it.

18

18:1 The word of the LORD came unto me again, saying, 18:2 What mean ye, that ye use this proverb concerning the land of Israel, saying, The fathers have eaten sour grapes, and the children's teeth are set on edge? 18:3 As I live, saith the Lord GOD, ye shall not have occasion any more to use this proverb in Israel.
18:4 Behold, all souls are mine; as the soul of the father, so also the soul of the son is mine: the soul that sinneth, it shall die.
18:5 But if a man be just, and do that which is lawful and right, 18:6 And hath not eaten upon the mountains, neither hath lifted up his eyes to the idols of the house of Israel, neither hath defiled his neighbour's wife, neither hath come near to a menstruous woman, 18:7 And hath not oppressed any, but hath restored to the debtor his pledge, hath spoiled none by violence, hath given his bread to the hungry, and hath covered the naked with a garment; 18:8 He that hath not given forth upon usury, neither hath taken any increase, that hath withdrawn his hand from iniquity, hath executed true judgment between man and man, 18:9 Hath walked in my statutes, and hath kept my judgments, to deal truly; he is just, he shall surely live, saith the Lord GOD.
18:10 If he beget a son that is a robber, a shedder of blood, and that doeth the like to any one of these things, 18:11 And that doeth not any of those duties, but even hath eaten upon the mountains, and defiled his neighbour's wife, 18:12 Hath oppressed the poor and needy, hath spoiled by violence, hath not restored the pledge, and hath lifted up his eyes to the idols, hath committed abomination, 18:13 Hath given forth upon usury, and hath taken increase: shall he then live? he shall not live: he hath done all these abominations; he shall surely die; his blood shall be upon him.
18:14 Now, lo, if he beget a son, that seeth all his father's sins which he hath done, and considereth, and doeth not such like, 18:15 That hath not eaten upon the mountains, neither hath lifted up his eyes to the idols of the house of Israel, hath not defiled his neighbour's wife, 18:16 Neither hath oppressed any, hath not withholden the pledge, neither hath spoiled by violence, but hath given his bread to the hungry, and hath covered the naked with a garment, 18:17 That hath taken off his hand from the poor, that hath not received usury nor increase, hath executed my judgments, hath walked in my statutes; he shall not die for the iniquity of his father, he shall surely live.
18:18 As for his father, because he cruelly oppressed, spoiled his brother by violence, and did that which is not good among his people, lo, even he shall die in his iniquity.
18:19 Yet say ye, Why? doth not the son bear the iniquity of the father? When the son hath done that which is lawful and right, and hath kept all my statutes, and hath done them, he shall surely live.
18:20 The soul that sinneth, it shall die. The son shall not bear the iniquity of the father, neither shall the father bear the iniquity of the son: the righteousness of the righteous shall be upon him, and the wickedness of the wicked shall be upon him.
18:21 But if the wicked will turn from all his sins that he hath committed, and keep all my statutes, and do that which is lawful and right, he shall surely live, he shall not die.

18:22 All his transgressions that he hath committed, they shall not be mentioned unto him: in his
righteousness that he hath done he shall live.
18:23 Have I any pleasure at all that the wicked should die? saith the Lord GOD: and not that he should
return from his ways, and live? 18:24 But when the righteous turneth away from his righteousness, and
committeth iniquity, and doeth according to all the abominations that the wicked man doeth, shall he
live? All his righteousness that he hath done shall not be mentioned: in his trespass that he hath
trespassed, and in his sin that he hath sinned, in them shall he die.
18:25 Yet ye say, The way of the LORD is not equal. Hear now, O house of Israel; Is not my way equal?
are not your ways unequal? 18:26 When a righteous man turneth away from his righteousness, and
committeth iniquity, and dieth in them; for his iniquity that he hath done shall he die.
18:27 Again, when the wicked man turneth away from his wickedness that he hath committed, and
doeth that which is lawful and right, he shall save his soul alive.
18:28 Because he considereth, and turneth away from all his transgressions that he hath committed, he
shall surely live, he shall not die.
18:29 Yet saith the house of Israel, The way of the LORD is not equal. O house of Israel, are not my
ways equal? are not your ways unequal? 18:30 Therefore I will judge you, O house of Israel, every one
according to his ways, saith the Lord GOD. Repent, and turn yourselves from all your transgressions; so
iniquity shall not be your ruin.
18:31 Cast away from you all your transgressions, whereby ye have transgressed; and make you a new
heart and a new spirit: for why will ye die, O house of Israel? 18:32 For I have no pleasure in the death
of him that dieth, saith the Lord GOD: wherefore turn yourselves, and live ye.

19

19:1 Moreover take thou up a lamentation for the princes of Israel, 19:2 And say, What is thy mother? A
lioness: she lay down among lions, she nourished her whelps among young lions.
19:3 And she brought up one of her whelps: it became a young lion, and it learned to catch the prey; it
devoured men.
19:4 The nations also heard of him; he was taken in their pit, and they brought him with chains unto the
land of Egypt.
19:5 Now when she saw that she had waited, and her hope was lost, then she took another of her
whelps, and made him a young lion.
19:6 And he went up and down among the lions, he became a young lion, and learned to catch the prey,
and devoured men.
19:7 And he knew their desolate palaces, and he laid waste their cities; and the land was desolate, and the
fulness thereof, by the noise of his roaring.
19:8 Then the nations set against him on every side from the provinces, and spread their net over him:
he was taken in their pit.
19:9 And they put him in ward in chains, and brought him to the king of Babylon: they brought him
into holds, that his voice should no more be heard upon the mountains of Israel.
19:10 Thy mother is like a vine in thy blood, planted by the waters: she was fruitful and full of branches
by reason of many waters.
19:11 And she had strong rods for the sceptres of them that bare rule, and her stature was exalted
among the thick branches, and she appeared in her height with the multitude of her branches.
19:12 But she was plucked up in fury, she was cast down to the ground, and the east wind dried up her
fruit: her strong rods were broken and withered; the fire consumed them.
19:13 And now she is planted in the wilderness, in a dry and thirsty ground.
19:14 And fire is gone out of a rod of her branches, which hath devoured her fruit, so that she hath no
strong rod to be a sceptre to rule. This is a lamentation, and shall be for a lamentation.

20

20:1 And it came to pass in the seventh year, in the fifth month, the tenth day of the month, that certain
of the elders of Israel came to enquire of the LORD, and sat before me.
20:2 Then came the word of the LORD unto me, saying, 20:3 Son of man, speak unto the elders of
Israel, and say unto them, Thus saith the Lord GOD; Are ye come to enquire of me? As I live, saith the
Lord GOD, I will not be enquired of by you.

20:4 Wilt thou judge them, son of man, wilt thou judge them? cause them to know the abominations of their fathers: 20:5 And say unto them, Thus saith the Lord GOD; In the day when I chose Israel, and lifted up mine hand unto the seed of the house of Jacob, and made myself known unto them in the land of Egypt, when I lifted up mine hand unto them, saying, I am the LORD your God; 20:6 In the day that I lifted up mine hand unto them, to bring them forth of the land of Egypt into a land that I had espied for them, flowing with milk and honey, which is the glory of all lands: 20:7 Then said I unto them, Cast ye away every man the abominations of his eyes, and defile not yourselves with the idols of Egypt: I am the LORD your God.

20:8 But they rebelled against me, and would not hearken unto me: they did not every man cast away the abominations of their eyes, neither did they forsake the idols of Egypt: then I said, I will pour out my fury upon them, to accomplish my anger against them in the midst of the land of Egypt.

20:9 But I wrought for my name's sake, that it should not be polluted before the heathen, among whom they were, in whose sight I made myself known unto them, in bringing them forth out of the land of Egypt.

20:10 Wherefore I caused them to go forth out of the land of Egypt, and brought them into the wilderness.

20:11 And I gave them my statutes, and shewed them my judgments, which if a man do, he shall even live in them.

20:12 Moreover also I gave them my sabbaths, to be a sign between me and them, that they might know that I am the LORD that sanctify them.

20:13 But the house of Israel rebelled against me in the wilderness: they walked not in my statutes, and they despised my judgments, which if a man do, he shall even live in them; and my sabbaths they greatly polluted: then I said, I would pour out my fury upon them in the wilderness, to consume them.

20:14 But I wrought for my name's sake, that it should not be polluted before the heathen, in whose sight I brought them out.

20:15 Yet also I lifted up my hand unto them in the wilderness, that I would not bring them into the land which I had given them, flowing with milk and honey, which is the glory of all lands; 20:16 Because they despised my judgments, and walked not in my statutes, but polluted my sabbaths: for their heart went after their idols.

20:17 Nevertheless mine eye spared them from destroying them, neither did I make an end of them in the wilderness.

20:18 But I said unto their children in the wilderness, Walk ye not in the statutes of your fathers, neither observe their judgments, nor defile yourselves with their idols: 20:19 I am the LORD your God; walk in my statutes, and keep my judgments, and do them; 20:20 And hallow my sabbaths; and they shall be a sign between me and you, that ye may know that I am the LORD your God.

20:21 Notwithstanding the children rebelled against me: they walked not in my statutes, neither kept my judgments to do them, which if a man do, he shall even live in them; they polluted my sabbaths: then I said, I would pour out my fury upon them, to accomplish my anger against them in the wilderness.

20:22 Nevertheless I withdrew mine hand, and wrought for my name's sake, that it should not be polluted in the sight of the heathen, in whose sight I brought them forth.

20:23 I lifted up mine hand unto them also in the wilderness, that I would scatter them among the heathen, and disperse them through the countries; 20:24 Because they had not executed my judgments, but had despised my statutes, and had polluted my sabbaths, and their eyes were after their fathers' idols.

20:25 Wherefore I gave them also statutes that were not good, and judgments whereby they should not live; 20:26 And I polluted them in their own gifts, in that they caused to pass through the fire all that openeth the womb, that I might make them desolate, to the end that they might know that I am the LORD.

20:27 Therefore, son of man, speak unto the house of Israel, and say unto them, Thus saith the Lord GOD; Yet in this your fathers have blasphemed me, in that they have committed a trespass against me.

20:28 For when I had brought them into the land, for the which I lifted up mine hand to give it to them, then they saw every high hill, and all the thick trees, and they offered there their sacrifices, and there they presented the provocation of their offering: there also they made their sweet savour, and poured out there their drink offerings.

20:29 Then I said unto them, What is the high place whereunto ye go? And the name whereof is called Bamah unto this day.

20:30 Wherefore say unto the house of Israel, Thus saith the Lord GOD; Are ye polluted after the manner of your fathers? and commit ye whoredom after their abominations? 20:31 For when ye offer your gifts, when ye make your sons to pass through the fire, ye pollute yourselves with all your idols, even unto this day: and shall I be enquired of by you, O house of Israel? As I live, saith the Lord GOD,

I will not be enquired of by you.
20:32 And that which cometh into your mind shall not be at all, that ye say, We will be as the heathen, as the families of the countries, to serve wood and stone.
20:33 As I live, saith the Lord GOD, surely with a mighty hand, and with a stretched out arm, and with fury poured out, will I rule over you: 20:34 And I will bring you out from the people, and will gather you out of the countries wherein ye are scattered, with a mighty hand, and with a stretched out arm, and with fury poured out.
20:35 And I will bring you into the wilderness of the people, and there will I plead with you face to face.
20:36 Like as I pleaded with your fathers in the wilderness of the land of Egypt, so will I plead with you, saith the Lord GOD.
20:37 And I will cause you to pass under the rod, and I will bring you into the bond of the covenant:
20:38 And I will purge out from among you the rebels, and them that transgress against me: I will bring them forth out of the country where they sojourn, and they shall not enter into the land of Israel: and ye shall know that I am the LORD.
20:39 As for you, O house of Israel, thus saith the Lord GOD; Go ye, serve ye every one his idols, and hereafter also, if ye will not hearken unto me: but pollute ye my holy name no more with your gifts, and with your idols.
20:40 For in mine holy mountain, in the mountain of the height of Israel, saith the Lord GOD, there shall all the house of Israel, all of them in the land, serve me: there will I accept them, and there will I require your offerings, and the firstfruits of your oblations, with all your holy things.
20:41 I will accept you with your sweet savour, when I bring you out from the people, and gather you out of the countries wherein ye have been scattered; and I will be sanctified in you before the heathen.
20:42 And ye shall know that I am the LORD, when I shall bring you into the land of Israel, into the country for the which I lifted up mine hand to give it to your fathers.
20:43 And there shall ye remember your ways, and all your doings, wherein ye have been defiled; and ye shall lothe yourselves in your own sight for all your evils that ye have committed.
20:44 And ye shall know that I am the LORD when I have wrought with you for my name's sake, not according to your wicked ways, nor according to your corrupt doings, O ye house of Israel, saith the Lord GOD.
20:45 Moreover the word of the LORD came unto me, saying, 20:46 Son of man, set thy face toward the south, and drop thy word toward the south, and prophesy against the forest of the south field; 20:47 And say to the forest of the south, Hear the word of the LORD; Thus saith the Lord GOD; Behold, I will kindle a fire in thee, and it shall devour every green tree in thee, and every dry tree: the flaming flame shall not be quenched, and all faces from the south to the north shall be burned therein.
20:48 And all flesh shall see that I the LORD have kindled it: it shall not be quenched.
20:49 Then said I, Ah Lord GOD! they say of me, Doth he not speak parables? 21:1 And the word of the LORD came unto me, saying, 21:2 Son of man, set thy face toward Jerusalem, and drop thy word toward the holy places, and prophesy against the land of Israel, 21:3 And say to the land of Israel, Thus saith the LORD; Behold, I am against thee, and will draw forth my sword out of his sheath, and will cut off from thee the righteous and the wicked.

21

21:4 Seeing then that I will cut off from thee the righteous and the wicked, therefore shall my sword go forth out of his sheath against all flesh from the south to the north: 21:5 That all flesh may know that I the LORD have drawn forth my sword out of his sheath: it shall not return any more.
21:6 Sigh therefore, thou son of man, with the breaking of thy loins; and with bitterness sigh before their eyes.
21:7 And it shall be, when they say unto thee, Wherefore sighest thou? that thou shalt answer, For the tidings; because it cometh: and every heart shall melt, and all hands shall be feeble, and every spirit shall faint, and all knees shall be weak as water: behold, it cometh, and shall be brought to pass, saith the Lord GOD.
21:8 Again the word of the LORD came unto me, saying, 21:9 Son of man, prophesy, and say, Thus saith the LORD; Say, A sword, a sword is sharpened, and also furbished: 21:10 It is sharpened to make a sore slaughter; it is furbished that it may glitter: should we then make mirth? it contemneth the rod of my son, as every tree.
21:11 And he hath given it to be furbished, that it may be handled: this sword is sharpened, and it is furbished, to give it into the hand of the slayer.

21:12 Cry and howl, son of man: for it shall be upon my people, it shall be upon all the princes of Israel: terrors by reason of the sword shall be upon my people: smite therefore upon thy thigh.
21:13 Because it is a trial, and what if the sword contemn even the rod? it shall be no more, saith the Lord GOD.
21:14 Thou therefore, son of man, prophesy, and smite thine hands together. and let the sword be doubled the third time, the sword of the slain: it is the sword of the great men that are slain, which entereth into their privy chambers.
21:15 I have set the point of the sword against all their gates, that their heart may faint, and their ruins be multiplied: ah! it is made bright, it is wrapped up for the slaughter.
21:16 Go thee one way or other, either on the right hand, or on the left, whithersoever thy face is set.
21:17 I will also smite mine hands together, and I will cause my fury to rest: I the LORD have said it.
21:18 The word of the LORD came unto me again, saying, 21:19 Also, thou son of man, appoint thee
two ways, that the sword of the king of Babylon may come: both twain shall come forth out of one land: and choose thou a place, choose it at the head of the way to the city.
21:20 Appoint a way, that the sword may come to Rabbath of the Ammonites, and to Judah in Jerusalem the defenced.
21:21 For the king of Babylon stood at the parting of the way, at the head of the two ways, to use divination: he made his arrows bright, he consulted with images, he looked in the liver.
21:22 At his right hand was the divination for Jerusalem, to appoint captains, to open the mouth in the slaughter, to lift up the voice with shouting, to appoint battering rams against the gates, to cast a mount, and to build a fort.
21:23 And it shall be unto them as a false divination in their sight, to them that have sworn oaths: but he will call to remembrance the iniquity, that they may be taken.
21:24 Therefore thus saith the Lord GOD; Because ye have made your iniquity to be remembered, in that your transgressions are discovered, so that in all your doings your sins do appear; because, I say, that ye are come to remembrance, ye shall be taken with the hand.
21:25 And thou, profane wicked prince of Israel, whose day is come, when iniquity shall have an end,
21:26 Thus saith the Lord GOD; Remove the diadem, and take off the crown: this shall not be the same: exalt him that is low, and abase him that is high.
21:27 I will overturn, overturn, overturn, it: and it shall be no more, until he come whose right it is; and I will give it him.
21:28 And thou, son of man, prophesy and say, Thus saith the Lord GOD concerning the Ammonites, and concerning their reproach; even say thou, The sword, the sword is drawn: for the slaughter it is
furbished, to consume because of the glittering: 21:29 Whiles they see vanity unto thee, whiles they
divine a lie unto thee, to bring thee upon the necks of them that are slain, of the wicked, whose day is come, when their iniquity shall have an end.
21:30 Shall I cause it to return into his sheath? I will judge thee in the place where thou wast created, in the land of thy nativity.
21:31 And I will pour out mine indignation upon thee, I will blow against thee in the fire of my wrath, and deliver thee into the hand of brutish men, and skilful to destroy.
21:32 Thou shalt be for fuel to the fire; thy blood shall be in the midst of the land; thou shalt be no more remembered: for I the LORD have spoken it.

22

22:1 Moreover the word of the LORD came unto me, saying, 22:2 Now, thou son of man, wilt thou
judge, wilt thou judge the bloody city? yea, thou shalt shew her all her abominations.
22:3 Then say thou, Thus saith the Lord GOD, The city sheddeth blood in the midst of it, that her time may come, and maketh idols against herself to defile herself.
22:4 Thou art become guilty in thy blood that thou hast shed; and hast defiled thyself in thine idols which thou hast made; and thou hast caused thy days to draw near, and art come even unto thy years: therefore have I made thee a reproach unto the heathen, and a mocking to all countries.
22:5 Those that be near, and those that be far from thee, shall mock thee, which art infamous and much vexed.
22:6 Behold, the princes of Israel, every one were in thee to their power to shed blood.
22:7 In thee have they set light by father and mother: in the midst of thee have they dealt by oppression with the stranger: in thee have they vexed the fatherless and the widow.
22:8 Thou hast despised mine holy things, and hast profaned my sabbaths.

22:9 In thee are men that carry tales to shed blood: and in thee they eat upon the mountains: in the midst of thee they commit lewdness.
22:10 In thee have they discovered their fathers' nakedness: in thee have they humbled her that was set apart for pollution.
22:11 And one hath committed abomination with his neighbour's wife; and another hath lewdly defiled his daughter in law; and another in thee hath humbled his sister, his father's daughter.
22:12 In thee have they taken gifts to shed blood; thou hast taken usury and increase, and thou hast greedily gained of thy neighbours by extortion, and hast forgotten me, saith the Lord GOD.
22:13 Behold, therefore I have smitten mine hand at thy dishonest gain which thou hast made, and at thy blood which hath been in the midst of thee.
22:14 Can thine heart endure, or can thine hands be strong, in the days that I shall deal with thee? I the LORD have spoken it, and will do it.
22:15 And I will scatter thee among the heathen, and disperse thee in the countries, and will consume thy filthiness out of thee.
22:16 And thou shalt take thine inheritance in thyself in the sight of the heathen, and thou shalt know that I am the LORD.
22:17 And the word of the LORD came unto me, saying, 22:18 Son of man, the house of Israel is to me become dross: all they are brass, and tin, and iron, and lead, in the midst of the furnace; they are even the dross of silver.
22:19 Therefore thus saith the Lord GOD; Because ye are all become dross, behold, therefore I will gather you into the midst of Jerusalem.
22:20 As they gather silver, and brass, and iron, and lead, and tin, into the midst of the furnace, to blow the fire upon it, to melt it; so will I gather you in mine anger and in my fury, and I will leave you there, and melt you.
22:21 Yea, I will gather you, and blow upon you in the fire of my wrath, and ye shall be melted in the midst therof.
22:22 As silver is melted in the midst of the furnace, so shall ye be melted in the midst thereof; and ye shall know that I the LORD have poured out my fury upon you.
22:23 And the word of the LORD came unto me, saying, 22:24 Son of man, say unto her, Thou art the land that is not cleansed, nor rained upon in the day of indignation.
22:25 There is a conspiracy of her prophets in the midst thereof, like a roaring lion ravening the prey; they have devoured souls; they have taken the treasure and precious things; they have made her many widows in the midst thereof.
22:26 Her priests have violated my law, and have profaned mine holy things: they have put no difference between the holy and profane, neither have they shewed difference between the unclean and the clean, and have hid their eyes from my sabbaths, and I am profaned among them.
22:27 Her princes in the midst thereof are like wolves ravening the prey, to shed blood, and to destroy souls, to get dishonest gain.
22:28 And her prophets have daubed them with untempered morter, seeing vanity, and divining lies unto them, saying, Thus saith the Lord GOD, when the LORD hath not spoken.
22:29 The people of the land have used oppression, and exercised robbery, and have vexed the poor and needy: yea, they have oppressed the stranger wrongfully.
22:30 And I sought for a man among them, that should make up the hedge, and stand in the gap before me for the land, that I should not destroy it: but I found none.
22:31 Therefore have I poured out mine indignation upon them; I have consumed them with the fire of my wrath: their own way have I recompensed upon their heads, saith the Lord GOD.

23

23:1 The word of the LORD came again unto me, saying, 23:2 Son of man, there were two women, the daughters of one mother: 23:3 And they committed whoredoms in Egypt; they committed whoredoms in their youth: there were their breasts pressed, and there they bruised the teats of their virginity.
23:4 And the names of them were Aholah the elder, and Aholibah her sister: and they were mine, and they bare sons and daughters. Thus were their names; Samaria is Aholah, and Jerusalem Aholibah.
23:5 And Aholah played the harlot when she was mine; and she doted on her lovers, on the Assyrians her neighbours, 23:6 Which were clothed with blue, captains and rulers, all of them desirable young men, horsemen riding upon horses.
23:7 Thus she committed her whoredoms with them, with all them that were the chosen men of Assyria,

and with all on whom she doted: with all their idols she defiled herself.
23:8 Neither left she her whoredoms brought from Egypt: for in her youth they lay with her, and they bruised the breasts of her virginity, and poured their whoredom upon her.
23:9 Wherefore I have delivered her into the hand of her lovers, into the hand of the Assyrians, upon whom she doted.
23:10 These discovered her nakedness: they took her sons and her daughters, and slew her with the sword: and she became famous among women; for they had executed judgment upon her.
23:11 And when her sister Aholibah saw this, she was more corrupt in her inordinate love than she, and in her whoredoms more than her sister in her whoredoms.
23:12 She doted upon the Assyrians her neighbours, captains and rulers clothed most gorgeously, horsemen riding upon horses, all of them desirable young men.
23:13 Then I saw that she was defiled, that they took both one way, 23:14 And that she increased her whoredoms: for when she saw men pourtrayed upon the wall, the images of the Chaldeans pourtrayed with vermilion, 23:15 Girded with girdles upon their loins, exceeding in dyed attire upon their heads, all of them princes to look to, after the manner of the Babylonians of Chaldea, the land of their nativity:
23:16 And as soon as she saw them with her eyes, she doted upon them, and sent messengers unto them into Chaldea.
23:17 And the Babylonians came to her into the bed of love, and they defiled her with their whoredom, and she was polluted with them, and her mind was alienated from them.
23:18 So she discovered her whoredoms, and discovered her nakedness: then my mind was alienated from her, like as my mind was alienated from her sister.
23:19 Yet she multiplied her whoredoms, in calling to remembrance the days of her youth, wherein she had played the harlot in the land of Egypt.
23:20 For she doted upon their paramours, whose flesh is as the flesh of asses, and whose issue is like the issue of horses.
23:21 Thus thou calledst to remembrance the lewdness of thy youth, in bruising thy teats by the Egyptians for the paps of thy youth.
23:22 Therefore, O Aholibah, thus saith the Lord GOD; Behold, I will raise up thy lovers against thee, from whom thy mind is alienated, and I will bring them against thee on every side; 23:23 The Babylonians, and all the Chaldeans, Pekod, and Shoa, and Koa, and all the Assyrians with them: all of them desirable young men, captains and rulers, great lords and renowned, all of them riding upon horses.
23:24 And they shall come against thee with chariots, wagons, and wheels, and with an assembly of people, which shall set against thee buckler and shield and helmet round about: and I will set judgment before them, and they shall judge thee according to their judgments.
23:25 And I will set my jealousy against thee, and they shall deal furiously with thee: they shall take away thy nose and thine ears; and thy remnant shall fall by the sword: they shall take thy sons and thy daughters; and thy residue shall be devoured by the fire.
23:26 They shall also strip thee out of thy clothes, and take away thy fair jewels.
23:27 Thus will I make thy lewdness to cease from thee, and thy whoredom brought from the land of Egypt: so that thou shalt not lift up thine eyes unto them, nor remember Egypt any more.
23:28 For thus saith the Lord GOD; Behold, I will deliver thee into the hand of them whom thou hatest, into the hand of them from whom thy mind is alienated: 23:29 And they shall deal with thee hatefully, and shall take away all thy labour, and shall leave thee naked and bare: and the nakedness of thy whoredoms shall be discovered, both thy lewdness and thy whoredoms.
23:30 I will do these things unto thee, because thou hast gone a whoring after the heathen, and because thou art polluted with their idols.
23:31 Thou hast walked in the way of thy sister; therefore will I give her cup into thine hand.
23:32 Thus saith the Lord GOD; Thou shalt drink of thy sister's cup deep and large: thou shalt be laughed to scorn and had in derision; it containeth much.
23:33 Thou shalt be filled with drunkenness and sorrow, with the cup of astonishment and desolation, with the cup of thy sister Samaria.
23:34 Thou shalt even drink it and suck it out, and thou shalt break the sherds thereof, and pluck off thine own breasts: for I have spoken it, saith the Lord GOD.
23:35 Therefore thus saith the Lord GOD; Because thou hast forgotten me, and cast me behind thy back, therefore bear thou also thy lewdness and thy whoredoms.
23:36 The LORD said moreover unto me; Son of man, wilt thou judge Aholah and Aholibah? yea, declare unto them their abominations; 23:37 That they have committed adultery, and blood is in their hands, and with their idols have they committed adultery, and have also caused their sons, whom they

bare unto me, to pass for them through the fire, to devour them.
23:38 Moreover this they have done unto me: they have defiled my sanctuary in the same day, and have profaned my sabbaths.
23:39 For when they had slain their children to their idols, then they came the same day into my sanctuary to profane it; and, lo, thus have they done in the midst of mine house.
23:40 And furthermore, that ye have sent for men to come from far, unto whom a messenger was sent; and, lo, they came: for whom thou didst wash thyself, paintedst thy eyes, and deckedst thyself with ornaments, 23:41 And satest upon a stately bed, and a table prepared before it, whereupon thou hast set mine incense and mine oil.
23:42 And a voice of a multitude being at ease was with her: and with the men of the common sort were brought Sabeans from the wilderness, which put bracelets upon their hands, and beautiful crowns upon their heads.
23:43 Then said I unto her that was old in adulteries, Will they now commit whoredoms with her, and she with them? 23:44 Yet they went in unto her, as they go in unto a woman that playeth the harlot: so went they in unto Aholah and unto Aholibah, the lewd women.
23:45 And the righteous men, they shall judge them after the manner of adulteresses, and after the manner of women that shed blood; because they are adulteresses, and blood is in their hands.
23:46 For thus saith the Lord GOD; I will bring up a company upon them, and will give them to be removed and spoiled.
23:47 And the company shall stone them with stones, and dispatch them with their swords; they shall slay their sons and their daughters, and burn up their houses with fire.
23:48 Thus will I cause lewdness to cease out of the land, that all women may be taught not to do after your lewdness.
23:49 And they shall recompense your lewdness upon you, and ye shall bear the sins of your idols: and ye shall know that I am the Lord GOD.

24

24:1 Again in the ninth year, in the tenth month, in the tenth day of the month, the word of the LORD came unto me, saying, 24:2 Son of man, write thee the name of the day, even of this same day: the king of Babylon set himself against Jerusalem this same day.
24:3 And utter a parable unto the rebellious house, and say unto them, Thus saith the Lord GOD; Set on a pot, set it on, and also pour water into it: 24:4 Gather the pieces thereof into it, even every good piece, the thigh, and the shoulder; fill it with the choice bones.
24:5 Take the choice of the flock, and burn also the bones under it, and make it boil well, and let them seethe the bones of it therein.
24:6 Wherefore thus saith the Lord GOD; Woe to the bloody city, to the pot whose scum is therein, and whose scum is not gone out of it! bring it out piece by piece; let no lot fall upon it.
24:7 For her blood is in the midst of her; she set it upon the top of a rock; she poured it not upon the ground, to cover it with dust; 24:8 That it might cause fury to come up to take vengeance; I have set her blood upon the top of a rock, that it should not be covered.
24:9 Therefore thus saith the Lord GOD; Woe to the bloody city! I will even make the pile for fire great.
24:10 Heap on wood, kindle the fire, consume the flesh, and spice it well, and let the bones be burned.
24:11 Then set it empty upon the coals thereof, that the brass of it may be hot, and may burn, and that the filthiness of it may be molten in it, that the scum of it may be consumed.
24:12 She hath wearied herself with lies, and her great scum went not forth out of her: her scum shall be in the fire.
24:13 In thy filthiness is lewdness: because I have purged thee, and thou wast not purged, thou shalt not be purged from thy filthiness any more, till I have caused my fury to rest upon thee.
24:14 I the LORD have spoken it: it shall come to pass, and I will do it; I will not go back, neither will I spare, neither will I repent; according to thy ways, and according to thy doings, shall they judge thee, saith the Lord GOD.
24:15 Also the word of the LORD came unto me, saying, 24:16 Son of man, behold, I take away from thee the desire of thine eyes with a stroke: yet neither shalt thou mourn nor weep, neither shall thy tears run down.
24:17 Forbear to cry, make no mourning for the dead, bind the tire of thine head upon thee, and put on thy shoes upon thy feet, and cover not thy lips, and eat not the bread of men.
24:18 So I spake unto the people in the morning: and at even my wife died; and I did in the morning as I

was commanded.
24:19 And the people said unto me, Wilt thou not tell us what these things are to us, that thou doest so?
24:20 Then I answered them, The word of the LORD came unto me, saying, 24:21 Speak unto the house of Israel, Thus saith the Lord GOD; Behold, I will profane my sanctuary, the excellency of your strength, the desire of your eyes, and that which your soul pitieth; and your sons and your daughters whom ye have left shall fall by the sword.
24:22 And ye shall do as I have done: ye shall not cover your lips, nor eat the bread of men.
24:23 And your tires shall be upon your heads, and your shoes upon your feet: ye shall not mourn nor weep; but ye shall pine away for your iniquities, and mourn one toward another.
24:24 Thus Ezekiel is unto you a sign: according to all that he hath done shall ye do: and when this cometh, ye shall know that I am the Lord GOD.
24:25 Also, thou son of man, shall it not be in the day when I take from them their strength, the joy of their glory, the desire of their eyes, and that whereupon they set their minds, their sons and their daughters, 24:26 That he that escapeth in that day shall come unto thee, to cause thee to hear it with thine ears? 24:27 In that day shall thy mouth be opened to him which is escaped, and thou shalt speak, and be no more dumb: and thou shalt be a sign unto them; and they shall know that I am the LORD.

25

25:1 The word of the LORD came again unto me, saying, 25:2 Son of man, set thy face against the Ammonites, and prophesy against them; 25:3 And say unto the Ammonites, Hear the word of the Lord GOD; Thus saith the Lord GOD; Because thou saidst, Aha, against my sanctuary, when it was profaned; and against the land of Israel, when it was desolate; and against the house of Judah, when they went into captivity; 25:4 Behold, therefore I will deliver thee to the men of the east for a possession, and they shall set their palaces in thee, and make their dwellings in thee: they shall eat thy fruit, and they shall drink thy milk.
25:5 And I will make Rabbah a stable for camels, and the Ammonites a couching place for flocks: and ye shall know that I am the LORD.
25:6 For thus saith the Lord GOD; Because thou hast clapped thine hands, and stamped with the feet, and rejoiced in heart with all thy despite against the land of Israel; 25:7 Behold, therefore I will stretch out mine hand upon thee, and will deliver thee for a spoil to the heathen; and I will cut thee off from the people, and I will cause thee to perish out of the countries: I will destroy thee; and thou shalt know that I am the LORD.
25:8 Thus saith the Lord GOD; Because that Moab and Seir do say, Behold, the house of Judah is like unto all the heathen; 25:9 Therefore, behold, I will open the side of Moab from the cities, from his cities which are on his frontiers, the glory of the country, Bethjeshimoth, Baalmeon, and Kiriathaim, 25:10 Unto the men of the east with the Ammonites, and will give them in possession, that the Ammonites may not be remembered among the nations.
25:11 And I will execute judgments upon Moab; and they shall know that I am the LORD.
25:12 Thus saith the Lord GOD; Because that Edom hath dealt against the house of Judah by taking vengeance, and hath greatly offended, and revenged himself upon them; 25:13 Therefore thus saith the Lord GOD; I will also stretch out mine hand upon Edom, and will cut off man and beast from it; and I will make it desolate from Teman; and they of Dedan shall fall by the sword.
25:14 And I will lay my vengeance upon Edom by the hand of my people Israel: and they shall do in Edom according to mine anger and according to my fury; and they shall know my vengeance, saith the Lord GOD.
25:15 Thus saith the Lord GOD; Because the Philistines have dealt by revenge, and have taken vengeance with a despiteful heart, to destroy it for the old hatred; 25:16 Therefore thus saith the Lord GOD; Behold, I will stretch out mine hand upon the Philistines, and I will cut off the Cherethims, and destroy the remnant of the sea coast.
25:17 And I will execute great vengeance upon them with furious rebukes; and they shall know that I am the LORD, when I shall lay my vengeance upon them.

26

26:1 And it came to pass in the eleventh year, in the first day of the month, that the word of the LORD came unto me, saying, 26:2 Son of man, because that Tyrus hath said against Jerusalem, Aha, she is

broken that was the gates of the people: she is turned unto me: I shall be replenished, now she is laid
waste: 26:3 Therefore thus saith the Lord GOD; Behold, I am against thee, O Tyrus, and will cause
many nations to come up against thee, as the sea causeth his waves to come up.
26:4 And they shall destroy the walls of Tyrus, and break down her towers: I will also scrape her dust from her, and make her like the top of a rock.
26:5 It shall be a place for the spreading of nets in the midst of the sea: for I have spoken it, saith the Lord GOD: and it shall become a spoil to the nations.
26:6 And her daughters which are in the field shall be slain by the sword; and they shall know that I am the LORD.
26:7 For thus saith the Lord GOD; Behold, I will bring upon Tyrus Nebuchadrezzar king of Babylon, a king of kings, from the north, with horses, and with chariots, and with horsemen, and companies, and much people.
26:8 He shall slay with the sword thy daughters in the field: and he shall make a fort against thee, and cast a mount against thee, and lift up the buckler against thee.
26:9 And he shall set engines of war against thy walls, and with his axes he shall break down thy towers.
26:10 By reason of the abundance of his horses their dust shall cover thee: thy walls shall shake at the noise of the horsemen, and of the wheels, and of the chariots, when he shall enter into thy gates, as men enter into a city wherein is made a breach.
26:11 With the hoofs of his horses shall he tread down all thy streets: he shall slay thy people by the sword, and thy strong garrisons shall go down to the ground.
26:12 And they shall make a spoil of thy riches, and make a prey of thy merchandise: and they shall break down thy walls, and destroy thy pleasant houses: and they shall lay thy stones and thy timber and thy dust in the midst of the water.
26:13 And I will cause the noise of thy songs to cease; and the sound of thy harps shall be no more heard.
26:14 And I will make thee like the top of a rock: thou shalt be a place to spread nets upon; thou shalt be built no more: for I the LORD have spoken it, saith the Lord GOD.
26:15 Thus saith the Lord GOD to Tyrus; Shall not the isles shake at the sound of thy fall, when the
wounded cry, when the slaughter is made in the midst of thee? 26:16 Then all the princes of the sea shall
come down from their thrones, and lay away their robes, and put off their broidered garments: they shall clothe themselves with trembling; they shall sit upon the ground, and shall tremble at every moment, and be astonished at thee.
26:17 And they shall take up a lamentation for thee, and say to thee, How art thou destroyed, that wast
inhabited of seafaring men, the renowned city, which wast strong in the sea, she and her inhabitants,
which cause their terror to be on all that haunt it! 26:18 Now shall the isles tremble in the day of thy fall;
yea, the isles that are in the sea shall be troubled at thy departure.
26:19 For thus saith the Lord GOD; When I shall make thee a desolate city, like the cities that are not
inhabited; when I shall bring up the deep upon thee, and great waters shall cover thee; 26:20 When I
shall bring thee down with them that descend into the pit, with the people of old time, and shall set thee
in the low parts of the earth, in places desolate of old, with them that go down to the pit, that thou be
not inhabited; and I shall set glory in the land of the living; 26:21 I will make thee a terror, and thou
shalt be no more: though thou be sought for, yet shalt thou never be found again, saith the Lord GOD.

27

27:1 The word of the LORD came again unto me, saying, 27:2 Now, thou son of man, take up a
lamentation for Tyrus; 27:3 And say unto Tyrus, O thou that art situate at the entry of the sea, which art
a merchant of the people for many isles, Thus saith the Lord GOD; O Tyrus, thou hast said, I am of
perfect beauty.
27:4 Thy borders are in the midst of the seas, thy builders have perfected thy beauty.
27:5 They have made all thy ship boards of fir trees of Senir: they have taken cedars from Lebanon to make masts for thee.
27:6 Of the oaks of Bashan have they made thine oars; the company of the Ashurites have made thy benches of ivory, brought out of the isles of Chittim.
27:7 Fine linen with broidered work from Egypt was that which thou spreadest forth to be thy sail; blue and purple from the isles of Elishah was that which covered thee.
27:8 The inhabitants of Zidon and Arvad were thy mariners: thy wise men, O Tyrus, that were in thee, were thy pilots.

27:9 The ancients of Gebal and the wise men thereof were in thee thy calkers: all the ships of the sea with their mariners were in thee to occupy thy merchandise.
27:10 They of Persia and of Lud and of Phut were in thine army, thy men of war: they hanged the shield and helmet in thee; they set forth thy comeliness.
27:11 The men of Arvad with thine army were upon thy walls round about, and the Gammadims were in thy towers: they hanged their shields upon thy walls round about; they have made thy beauty perfect.
27:12 Tarshish was thy merchant by reason of the multitude of all kind of riches; with silver, iron, tin, and lead, they traded in thy fairs.
27:13 Javan, Tubal, and Meshech, they were thy merchants: they traded the persons of men and vessels of brass in thy market.
27:14 They of the house of Togarmah traded in thy fairs with horses and horsemen and mules.
27:15 The men of Dedan were thy merchants; many isles were the merchandise of thine hand: they brought thee for a present horns of ivory and ebony.
27:16 Syria was thy merchant by reason of the multitude of the wares of thy making: they occupied in thy fairs with emeralds, purple, and broidered work, and fine linen, and coral, and agate.
27:17 Judah, and the land of Israel, they were thy merchants: they traded in thy market wheat of Minnith, and Pannag, and honey, and oil, and balm.
27:18 Damascus was thy merchant in the multitude of the wares of thy making, for the multitude of all riches; in the wine of Helbon, and white wool.
27:19 Dan also and Javan going to and fro occupied in thy fairs: bright iron, cassia, and calamus, were in thy market.
27:20 Dedan was thy merchant in precious clothes for chariots.
27:21 Arabia, and all the princes of Kedar, they occupied with thee in lambs, and rams, and goats: in these were they thy merchants.
27:22 The merchants of Sheba and Raamah, they were thy merchants: they occupied in thy fairs with chief of all spices, and with all precious stones, and gold.
27:23 Haran, and Canneh, and Eden, the merchants of Sheba, Asshur, and Chilmad, were thy merchants.
27:24 These were thy merchants in all sorts of things, in blue clothes, and broidered work, and in chests of rich apparel, bound with cords, and made of cedar, among thy merchandise.
27:25 The ships of Tarshish did sing of thee in thy market: and thou wast replenished, and made very glorious in the midst of the seas.
27:26 Thy rowers have brought thee into great waters: the east wind hath broken thee in the midst of the seas.
27:27 Thy riches, and thy fairs, thy merchandise, thy mariners, and thy pilots, thy calkers, and the occupiers of thy merchandise, and all thy men of war, that are in thee, and in all thy company which is in the midst of thee, shall fall into the midst of the seas in the day of thy ruin.
27:28 The suburbs shall shake at the sound of the cry of thy pilots.
27:29 And all that handle the oar, the mariners, and all the pilots of the sea, shall come down from their
ships, they shall stand upon the land; 27:30 And shall cause their voice to be heard against thee, and shall
cry bitterly, and shall cast up dust upon their heads, they shall wallow themselves in the ashes: 27:31 And
they shall make themselves utterly bald for thee, and gird them with sackcloth, and they shall weep for
thee with bitterness of heart and bitter wailing.
27:32 And in their wailing they shall take up a lamentation for thee, and lament over thee, saying, What
city is like Tyrus, like the destroyed in the midst of the sea? 27:33 When thy wares went forth out of the
seas, thou filledst many people; thou didst enrich the kings of the earth with the multitude of thy riches
and of thy merchandise.
27:34 In the time when thou shalt be broken by the seas in the depths of the waters thy merchandise and all thy company in the midst of thee shall fall.
27:35 All the inhabitants of the isles shall be astonished at thee, and their kings shall be sore afraid, they shall be troubled in their countenance.
27:36 The merchants among the people shall hiss at thee; thou shalt be a terror, and never shalt be any more.

28

28:1 The word of the LORD came again unto me, saying, 28:2 Son of man, say unto the prince of
Tyrus, Thus saith the Lord GOD; Because thine heart is lifted up, and thou hast said, I am a God, I sit

in the seat of God, in the midst of the seas; yet thou art a man, and not God, though thou set thine heart as the heart of God: 28:3 Behold, thou art wiser than Daniel; there is no secret that they can hide from thee: 28:4 With thy wisdom and with thine understanding thou hast gotten thee riches, and hast gotten gold and silver into thy treasures: 28:5 By thy great wisdom and by thy traffick hast thou increased thy riches, and thine heart is lifted up because of thy riches: 28:6 Therefore thus saith the Lord GOD; Because thou hast set thine heart as the heart of God; 28:7 Behold, therefore I will bring strangers upon thee, the terrible of the nations: and they shall draw their swords against the beauty of thy wisdom, and they shall defile thy brightness.

28:8 They shall bring thee down to the pit, and thou shalt die the deaths of them that are slain in the midst of the seas.

28:9 Wilt thou yet say before him that slayeth thee, I am God? but thou shalt be a man, and no God, in the hand of him that slayeth thee.

28:10 Thou shalt die the deaths of the uncircumcised by the hand of strangers: for I have spoken it, saith the Lord GOD.

28:11 Moreover the word of the LORD came unto me, saying, 28:12 Son of man, take up a lamentation upon the king of Tyrus, and say unto him, Thus saith the Lord GOD; Thou sealest up the sum, full of wisdom, and perfect in beauty.

28:13 Thou hast been in Eden the garden of God; every precious stone was thy covering, the sardius, topaz, and the diamond, the beryl, the onyx, and the jasper, the sapphire, the emerald, and the carbuncle, and gold: the workmanship of thy tabrets and of thy pipes was prepared in thee in the day that thou wast created.

28:14 Thou art the anointed cherub that covereth; and I have set thee so: thou wast upon the holy mountain of God; thou hast walked up and down in the midst of the stones of fire.

28:15 Thou wast perfect in thy ways from the day that thou wast created, till iniquity was found in thee.

28:16 By the multitude of thy merchandise they have filled the midst of thee with violence, and thou hast sinned: therefore I will cast thee as profane out of the mountain of God: and I will destroy thee, O covering cherub, from the midst of the stones of fire.

28:17 Thine heart was lifted up because of thy beauty, thou hast corrupted thy wisdom by reason of thy brightness: I will cast thee to the ground, I will lay thee before kings, that they may behold thee.

28:18 Thou hast defiled thy sanctuaries by the multitude of thine iniquities, by the iniquity of thy traffick; therefore will I bring forth a fire from the midst of thee, it shall devour thee, and I will bring thee to ashes upon the earth in the sight of all them that behold thee.

28:19 All they that know thee among the people shall be astonished at thee: thou shalt be a terror, and never shalt thou be any more.

28:20 Again the word of the LORD came unto me, saying, 28:21 Son of man, set thy face against Zidon, and prophesy against it, 28:22 And say, Thus saith the Lord GOD; Behold, I am against thee, O Zidon; and I will be glorified in the midst of thee: and they shall know that I am the LORD, when I shall have executed judgments in her, and shall be sanctified in her.

28:23 For I will send into her pestilence, and blood into her streets; and the wounded shall be judged in the midst of her by the sword upon her on every side; and they shall know that I am the LORD.

28:24 And there shall be no more a pricking brier unto the house of Israel, nor any grieving thorn of all that are round about them, that despised them; and they shall know that I am the Lord GOD.

28:25 Thus saith the Lord GOD; When I shall have gathered the house of Israel from the people among whom they are scattered, and shall be sanctified in them in the sight of the heathen, then shall they dwell in their land that I have given to my servant Jacob.

28:26 And they shall dwell safely therein, and shall build houses, and plant vineyards; yea, they shall dwell with confidence, when I have executed judgments upon all those that despise them round about them; and they shall know that I am the LORD their God.

29

29:1 In the tenth year, in the tenth month, in the twelfth day of the month, the word of the LORD came unto me, saying, 29:2 Son of man, set thy face against Pharaoh king of Egypt, and prophesy against him, and against all Egypt: 29:3 Speak, and say, Thus saith the Lord GOD; Behold, I am against thee, Pharaoh king of Egypt, the great dragon that lieth in the midst of his rivers, which hath said, My river is mine own, and I have made it for myself.

29:4 But I will put hooks in thy jaws, and I will cause the fish of thy rivers to stick unto thy scales, and I will bring thee up out of the midst of thy rivers, and all the fish of thy rivers shall stick unto thy scales.

29:5 And I will leave thee thrown into the wilderness, thee and all the fish of thy rivers: thou shalt fall upon the open fields; thou shalt not be brought together, nor gathered: I have given thee for meat to the beasts of the field and to the fowls of the heaven.
29:6 And all the inhabitants of Egypt shall know that I am the LORD, because they have been a staff of reed to the house of Israel.
29:7 When they took hold of thee by thy hand, thou didst break, and rend all their shoulder: and when they leaned upon thee, thou brakest, and madest all their loins to be at a stand.
29:8 Therefore thus saith the Lord GOD; Behold, I will bring a sword upon thee, and cut off man and beast out of thee.
29:9 And the land of Egypt shall be desolate and waste; and they shall know that I am the LORD: because he hath said, The river is mine, and I have made it.
29:10 Behold, therefore I am against thee, and against thy rivers, and I will make the land of Egypt utterly waste and desolate, from the tower of Syene even unto the border of Ethiopia.
29:11 No foot of man shall pass through it, nor foot of beast shall pass through it, neither shall it be inhabited forty years.
29:12 And I will make the land of Egypt desolate in the midst of the countries that are desolate, and her cities among the cities that are laid waste shall be desolate forty years: and I will scatter the Egyptians among the nations, and will disperse them through the countries.
29:13 Yet thus saith the Lord GOD; At the end of forty years will I gather the Egyptians from the people whither they were scattered: 29:14 And I will bring again the captivity of Egypt, and will cause them to return into the land of Pathros, into the land of their habitation; and they shall be there a base kingdom.
29:15 It shall be the basest of the kingdoms; neither shall it exalt itself any more above the nations: for I will diminish them, that they shall no more rule over the nations.
29:16 And it shall be no more the confidence of the house of Israel, which bringeth their iniquity to remembrance, when they shall look after them: but they shall know that I am the Lord GOD.
29:17 And it came to pass in the seven and twentieth year, in the first month, in the first day of the month, the word of the LORD came unto me, saying, 29:18 Son of man, Nebuchadrezzar king of Babylon caused his army to serve a great service against Tyrus: every head was made bald, and every shoulder was peeled: yet had he no wages, nor his army, for Tyrus, for the service that he had served against it: 29:19 Therefore thus saith the Lord GOD; Behold, I will give the land of Egypt unto Nebuchadrezzar king of Babylon; and he shall take her multitude, and take her spoil, and take her prey; and it shall be the wages for his army.
29:20 I have given him the land of Egypt for his labour wherewith he served against it, because they wrought for me, saith the Lord GOD.
29:21 In that day will I cause the horn of the house of Israel to bud forth, and I will give thee the opening of the mouth in the midst of them; and they shall know that I am the LORD.

30

30:1 The word of the LORD came again unto me, saying, 30:2 Son of man, prophesy and say, Thus saith the Lord GOD; Howl ye, Woe worth the day! 30:3 For the day is near, even the day of the LORD is near, a cloudy day; it shall be the time of the heathen.
30:4 And the sword shall come upon Egypt, and great pain shall be in Ethiopia, when the slain shall fall in Egypt, and they shall take away her multitude, and her foundations shall be broken down.
30:5 Ethiopia, and Libya, and Lydia, and all the mingled people, and Chub, and the men of the land that is in league, shall fall with them by the sword.
30:6 Thus saith the LORD; They also that uphold Egypt shall fall; and the pride of her power shall come down: from the tower of Syene shall they fall in it by the sword, saith the Lord GOD.
30:7 And they shall be desolate in the midst of the countries that are desolate, and her cities shall be in the midst of the cities that are wasted.
30:8 And they shall know that I am the LORD, when I have set a fire in Egypt, and when all her helpers shall be destroyed.
30:9 In that day shall messengers go forth from me in ships to make the careless Ethiopians afraid, and great pain shall come upon them, as in the day of Egypt: for, lo, it cometh.
30:10 Thus saith the Lord GOD; I will also make the multitude of Egypt to cease by the hand of Nebuchadrezzar king of Babylon.
30:11 He and his people with him, the terrible of the nations, shall be brought to destroy the land: and

they shall draw their swords against Egypt, and fill the land with the slain.
30:12 And I will make the rivers dry, and sell the land into the hand of the wicked: and I will make the land waste, and all that is therein, by the hand of strangers: I the LORD have spoken it.
30:13 Thus saith the Lord GOD; I will also destroy the idols, and I will cause their images to cease out of Noph; and there shall be no more a prince of the land of Egypt: and I will put a fear in the land of Egypt.
30:14 And I will make Pathros desolate, and will set fire in Zoan, and will execute judgments in No.
30:15 And I will pour my fury upon Sin, the strength of Egypt; and I will cut off the multitude of No.
30:16 And I will set fire in Egypt: Sin shall have great pain, and No shall be rent asunder, and Noph shall have distresses daily.
30:17 The young men of Aven and of Pibeseth shall fall by the sword: and these cities shall go into captivity.
30:18 At Tehaphnehes also the day shall be darkened, when I shall break there the yokes of Egypt: and the pomp of her strength shall cease in her: as for her, a cloud shall cover her, and her daughters shall go into captivity.
30:19 Thus will I execute judgments in Egypt: and they shall know that I am the LORD.
30:20 And it came to pass in the eleventh year, in the first month, in the seventh day of the month, that
the word of the LORD came unto me, saying, 30:21 Son of man, I have broken the arm of Pharaoh
king of Egypt; and, lo, it shall not be bound up to be healed, to put a roller to bind it, to make it strong to hold the sword.
30:22 Therefore thus saith the Lord GOD; Behold, I am against Pharaoh king of Egypt, and will break his arms, the strong, and that which was broken; and I will cause the sword to fall out of his hand.
30:23 And I will scatter the Egyptians among the nations, and will disperse them through the countries.
30:24 And I will strengthen the arms of the king of Babylon, and put my sword in his hand: but I will break Pharaoh's arms, and he shall groan before him with the groanings of a deadly wounded man.
30:25 But I will strengthen the arms of the king of Babylon, and the arms of Pharaoh shall fall down; and they shall know that I am the LORD, when I shall put my sword into the hand of the king of Babylon, and he shall stretch it out upon the land of Egypt.
30:26 And I will scatter the Egyptians among the nations, and disperse them among the countries; and they shall know that I am the LORD.

31

31:1 And it came to pass in the eleventh year, in the third month, in the first day of the month, that the
word of the LORD came unto me, saying, 31:2 Son of man, speak unto Pharaoh king of Egypt, and to
his multitude; Whom art thou like in thy greatness? 31:3 Behold, the Assyrian was a cedar in Lebanon
with fair branches, and with a shadowing shroud, and of an high stature; and his top was among the thick boughs.
31:4 The waters made him great, the deep set him up on high with her rivers running round about his plants, and sent her little rivers unto all the trees of the field.
31:5 Therefore his height was exalted above all the trees of the field, and his boughs were multiplied, and his branches became long because of the multitude of waters, when he shot forth.
31:6 All the fowls of heaven made their nests in his boughs, and under his branches did all the beasts of the field bring forth their young, and under his shadow dwelt all great nations.
31:7 Thus was he fair in his greatness, in the length of his branches: for his root was by great waters.
31:8 The cedars in the garden of God could not hide him: the fir trees were not like his boughs, and the chestnut trees were not like his branches; nor any tree in the garden of God was like unto him in his beauty.
31:9 I have made him fair by the multitude of his branches: so that all the trees of Eden, that were in the garden of God, envied him.
31:10 Therefore thus saith the Lord GOD; Because thou hast lifted up thyself in height, and he hath
shot up his top among the thick boughs, and his heart is lifted up in his height; 31:11 I have therefore
delivered him into the hand of the mighty one of the heathen; he shall surely deal with him: I have driven him out for his wickedness.
31:12 And strangers, the terrible of the nations, have cut him off, and have left him: upon the mountains and in all the valleys his branches are fallen, and his boughs are broken by all the rivers of the land; and all the people of the earth are gone down from his shadow, and have left him.
31:13 Upon his ruin shall all the fowls of the heaven remain, and all the beasts of the field shall be upon

his branches: 31:14 To the end that none of all the trees by the waters exalt themselves for their height,
neither shoot up their top among the thick boughs, neither their trees stand up in their height, all that
drink water: for they are all delivered unto death, to the nether parts of the earth, in the midst of the
children of men, with them that go down to the pit.
31:15 Thus saith the Lord GOD; In the day when he went down to the grave I caused a mourning: I
covered the deep for him, and I restrained the floods thereof, and the great waters were stayed: and I
caused Lebanon to mourn for him, and all the trees of the field fainted for him.
31:16 I made the nations to shake at the sound of his fall, when I cast him down to hell with them that
descend into the pit: and all the trees of Eden, the choice and best of Lebanon, all that drink water, shall
be comforted in the nether parts of the earth.
31:17 They also went down into hell with him unto them that be slain with the sword; and they that
were his arm, that dwelt under his shadow in the midst of the heathen.
31:18 To whom art thou thus like in glory and in greatness among the trees of Eden? yet shalt thou be
brought down with the trees of Eden unto the nether parts of the earth: thou shalt lie in the midst of the
uncircumcised with them that be slain by the sword. This is Pharaoh and all his multitude, saith the Lord
GOD.

32

32:1 And it came to pass in the twelfth year, in the twelfth month, in the first day of the month, that the
word of the LORD came unto me, saying, 32:2 Son of man, take up a lamentation for Pharaoh king of
Egypt, and say unto him, Thou art like a young lion of the nations, and thou art as a whale in the seas:
and thou camest forth with thy rivers, and troubledst the waters with thy feet, and fouledst their rivers.
32:3 Thus saith the Lord GOD; I will therefore spread out my net over thee with a company of many
people; and they shall bring thee up in my net.
32:4 Then will I leave thee upon the land, I will cast thee forth upon the open field, and will cause all the
fowls of the heaven to remain upon thee, and I will fill the beasts of the whole earth with thee.
32:5 And I will lay thy flesh upon the mountains, and fill the valleys with thy height.
32:6 I will also water with thy blood the land wherein thou swimmest, even to the mountains; and the
rivers shall be full of thee.
32:7 And when I shall put thee out, I will cover the heaven, and make the stars thereof dark; I will cover
the sun with a cloud, and the moon shall not give her light.
32:8 All the bright lights of heaven will I make dark over thee, and set darkness upon thy land, saith the
Lord GOD.
32:9 I will also vex the hearts of many people, when I shall bring thy destruction among the nations, into
the countries which thou hast not known.
32:10 Yea, I will make many people amazed at thee, and their kings shall be horribly afraid for thee,
when I shall brandish my sword before them; and they shall tremble at every moment, every man for his
own life, in the day of thy fall.
32:11 For thus saith the Lord GOD; The sword of the king of Babylon shall come upon thee.
32:12 By the swords of the mighty will I cause thy multitude to fall, the terrible of the nations, all of
them: and they shall spoil the pomp of Egypt, and all the multitude thereof shall be destroyed.
32:13 I will destroy also all the beasts thereof from beside the great waters; neither shall the foot of man
trouble them any more, nor the hoofs of beasts trouble them.
32:14 Then will I make their waters deep, and cause their rivers to run like oil, saith the Lord GOD.
32:15 When I shall make the land of Egypt desolate, and the country shall be destitute of that whereof it
was full, when I shall smite all them that dwell therein, then shall they know that I am the LORD.
32:16 This is the lamentation wherewith they shall lament her: the daughters of the nations shall lament
her: they shall lament for her, even for Egypt, and for all her multitude, saith the Lord GOD.
32:17 It came to pass also in the twelfth year, in the fifteenth day of the month, that the word of the
LORD came unto me, saying, 32:18 Son of man, wail for the multitude of Egypt, and cast them down,
even her, and the daughters of the famous nations, unto the nether parts of the earth, with them that go
down into the pit.
32:19 Whom dost thou pass in beauty? go down, and be thou laid with the uncircumcised.
32:20 They shall fall in the midst of them that are slain by the sword: she is delivered to the sword: draw
her and all her multitudes.
32:21 The strong among the mighty shall speak to him out of the midst of hell with them that help him:
they are gone down, they lie uncircumcised, slain by the sword.

32:22 Asshur is there and all her company: his graves are about him: all of them slain, fallen by the
sword: 32:23 Whose graves are set in the sides of the pit, and her company is round about her grave: all
of them slain, fallen by the sword, which caused terror in the land of the living.
32:24 There is Elam and all her multitude round about her grave, all of them slain, fallen by the sword, which are gone down uncircumcised into the nether parts of the earth, which caused their terror in the land of the living; yet have they borne their shame with them that go down to the pit.
32:25 They have set her a bed in the midst of the slain with all her multitude: her graves are round about him: all of them uncircumcised, slain by the sword: though their terror was caused in the land of the living, yet have they borne their shame with them that go down to the pit: he is put in the midst of them that be slain.
32:26 There is Meshech, Tubal, and all her multitude: her graves are round about him: all of them uncircumcised, slain by the sword, though they caused their terror in the land of the living.
32:27 And they shall not lie with the mighty that are fallen of the uncircumcised, which are gone down to hell with their weapons of war: and they have laid their swords under their heads, but their iniquities shall be upon their bones, though they were the terror of the mighty in the land of the living.
32:28 Yea, thou shalt be broken in the midst of the uncircumcised, and shalt lie with them that are slain with the sword.
32:29 There is Edom, her kings, and all her princes, which with their might are laid by them that were slain by the sword: they shall lie with the uncircumcised, and with them that go down to the pit.
32:30 There be the princes of the north, all of them, and all the Zidonians, which are gone down with the slain; with their terror they are ashamed of their might; and they lie uncircumcised with them that be slain by the sword, and bear their shame with them that go down to the pit.
32:31 Pharaoh shall see them, and shall be comforted over all his multitude, even Pharaoh and all his army slain by the sword, saith the Lord GOD.
32:32 For I have caused my terror in the land of the living: and he shall be laid in the midst of the uncircumcised with them that are slain with the sword, even Pharaoh and all his multitude, saith the Lord GOD.

33

33:1 Again the word of the LORD came unto me, saying, 33:2 Son of man, speak to the children of thy
people, and say unto them, When I bring the sword upon a land, if the people of the land take a man of
their coasts, and set him for their watchman: 33:3 If when he seeth the sword come upon the land, he
blow the trumpet, and warn the people; 33:4 Then whosoever heareth the sound of the trumpet, and
taketh not warning; if the sword come, and take him away, his blood shall be upon his own head.
33:5 He heard the sound of the trumpet, and took not warning; his blood shall be upon him. But he that taketh warning shall deliver his soul.
33:6 But if the watchman see the sword come, and blow not the trumpet, and the people be not warned; if the sword come, and take any person from among them, he is taken away in his iniquity; but his blood will I require at the watchman's hand.
33:7 So thou, O son of man, I have set thee a watchman unto the house of Israel; therefore thou shalt hear the word at my mouth, and warn them from me.
33:8 When I say unto the wicked, O wicked man, thou shalt surely die; if thou dost not speak to warn the wicked from his way, that wicked man shall die in his iniquity; but his blood will I require at thine hand.
33:9 Nevertheless, if thou warn the wicked of his way to turn from it; if he do not turn from his way, he shall die in his iniquity; but thou hast delivered thy soul.
33:10 Therefore, O thou son of man, speak unto the house of Israel; Thus ye speak, saying, If our
transgressions and our sins be upon us, and we pine away in them, how should we then live? 33:11 Say
unto them, As I live, saith the Lord GOD, I have no pleasure in the death of the wicked; but that the
wicked turn from his way and live: turn ye, turn ye from your evil ways; for why will ye die, O house of
Israel? 33:12 Therefore, thou son of man, say unto the children of thy people, The righteousness of the
righteous shall not deliver him in the day of his transgression: as for the wickedness of the wicked, he
shall not fall thereby in the day that he turneth from his wickedness; neither shall the righteous be able
to live for his righteousness in the day that he sinneth.
33:13 When I shall say to the righteous, that he shall surely live; if he trust to his own righteousness, and commit iniquity, all his righteousnesses shall not be remembered; but for his iniquity that he hath committed, he shall die for it.

33:14 Again, when I say unto the wicked, Thou shalt surely die; if he turn from his sin, and do that which is lawful and right; 33:15 If the wicked restore the pledge, give again that he had robbed, walk in the statutes of life, without committing iniquity; he shall surely live, he shall not die.
33:16 None of his sins that he hath committed shall be mentioned unto him: he hath done that which is lawful and right; he shall surely live.
33:17 Yet the children of thy people say, The way of the Lord is not equal: but as for them, their way is not equal.
33:18 When the righteous turneth from his righteousness, and committeth iniquity, he shall even die thereby.
33:19 But if the wicked turn from his wickedness, and do that which is lawful and right, he shall live thereby.
33:20 Yet ye say, The way of the Lord is not equal. O ye house of Israel, I will judge you every one after his ways.
33:21 And it came to pass in the twelfth year of our captivity, in the tenth month, in the fifth day of the month, that one that had escaped out of Jerusalem came unto me, saying, The city is smitten.
33:22 Now the hand of the LORD was upon me in the evening, afore he that was escaped came; and had opened my mouth, until he came to me in the morning; and my mouth was opened, and I was no more dumb.
33:23 Then the word of the LORD came unto me, saying, 33:24 Son of man, they that inhabit those wastes of the land of Israel speak, saying, Abraham was one, and he inherited the land: but we are many; the land is given us for inheritance.
33:25 Wherefore say unto them, Thus saith the Lord GOD; Ye eat with the blood, and lift up your eyes toward your idols, and shed blood: and shall ye possess the land? 33:26 Ye stand upon your sword, ye work abomination, and ye defile every one his neighbour's wife: and shall ye possess the land? 33:27 Say thou thus unto them, Thus saith the Lord GOD; As I live, surely they that are in the wastes shall fall by the sword, and him that is in the open field will I give to the beasts to be devoured, and they that be in the forts and in the caves shall die of the pestilence.
33:28 For I will lay the land most desolate, and the pomp of her strength shall cease; and the mountains of Israel shall be desolate, that none shall pass through.
33:29 Then shall they know that I am the LORD, when I have laid the land most desolate because of all their abominations which they have committed.
33:30 Also, thou son of man, the children of thy people still are talking against thee by the walls and in the doors of the houses, and speak one to another, every one to his brother, saying, Come, I pray you, and hear what is the word that cometh forth from the LORD.
33:31 And they come unto thee as the people cometh, and they sit before thee as my people, and they hear thy words, but they will not do them: for with their mouth they shew much love, but their heart goeth after their covetousness.
33:32 And, lo, thou art unto them as a very lovely song of one that hath a pleasant voice, and can play well on an instrument: for they hear thy words, but they do them not.
33:33 And when this cometh to pass, (lo, it will come,) then shall they know that a prophet hath been among them.

34

34:1 And the word of the LORD came unto me, saying, 34:2 Son of man, prophesy against the shepherds of Israel, prophesy, and say unto them, Thus saith the Lord GOD unto the shepherds; Woe be to the shepherds of Israel that do feed themselves! should not the shepherds feed the flocks? 34:3 Ye eat the fat, and ye clothe you with the wool, ye kill them that are fed: but ye feed not the flock.
34:4 The diseased have ye not strengthened, neither have ye healed that which was sick, neither have ye bound up that which was broken, neither have ye brought again that which was driven away, neither have ye sought that which was lost; but with force and with cruelty have ye ruled them.
34:5 And they were scattered, because there is no shepherd: and they became meat to all the beasts of the field, when they were scattered.
34:6 My sheep wandered through all the mountains, and upon every high hill: yea, my flock was scattered upon all the face of the earth, and none did search or seek after them.
34:7 Therefore, ye shepherds, hear the word of the LORD; 34:8 As I live, saith the Lord GOD, surely because my flock became a prey, and my flock became meat to every beast of the field, because there was no shepherd, neither did my shepherds search for my flock, but the shepherds fed themselves, and

fed not my flock; 34:9 Therefore, O ye shepherds, hear the word of the LORD; 34:10 Thus saith the Lord GOD; Behold, I am against the shepherds; and I will require my flock at their hand, and cause them to cease from feeding the flock; neither shall the shepherds feed themselves any more; for I will deliver my flock from their mouth, that they may not be meat for them.

34:11 For thus saith the Lord GOD; Behold, I, even I, will both search my sheep, and seek them out.

34:12 As a shepherd seeketh out his flock in the day that he is among his sheep that are scattered; so will I seek out my sheep, and will deliver them out of all places where they have been scattered in the cloudy and dark day.

34:13 And I will bring them out from the people, and gather them from the countries, and will bring them to their own land, and feed them upon the mountains of Israel by the rivers, and in all the inhabited places of the country.

34:14 I will feed them in a good pasture, and upon the high mountains of Israel shall their fold be: there shall they lie in a good fold, and in a fat pasture shall they feed upon the mountains of Israel.

34:15 I will feed my flock, and I will cause them to lie down, saith the Lord GOD.

34:16 I will seek that which was lost, and bring again that which was driven away, and will bind up that which was broken, and will strengthen that which was sick: but I will destroy the fat and the strong; I will feed them with judgment.

34:17 And as for you, O my flock, thus saith the Lord GOD; Behold, I judge between cattle and cattle, between the rams and the he goats.

34:18 Seemeth it a small thing unto you to have eaten up the good pasture, but ye must tread down with your feet the residue of your pastures? and to have drunk of the deep waters, but ye must foul the residue with your feet? 34:19 And as for my flock, they eat that which ye have trodden with your feet; and they drink that which ye have fouled with your feet.

34:20 Therefore thus saith the Lord GOD unto them; Behold, I, even I, will judge between the fat cattle and between the lean cattle.

34:21 Because ye have thrust with side and with shoulder, and pushed all the diseased with your horns, till ye have scattered them abroad; 34:22 Therefore will I save my flock, and they shall no more be a prey; and I will judge between cattle and cattle.

34:23 And I will set up one shepherd over them, and he shall feed them, even my servant David; he shall feed them, and he shall be their shepherd.

34:24 And I the LORD will be their God, and my servant David a prince among them; I the LORD have spoken it.

34:25 And I will make with them a covenant of peace, and will cause the evil beasts to cease out of the land: and they shall dwell safely in the wilderness, and sleep in the woods.

34:26 And I will make them and the places round about my hill a blessing; and I will cause the shower to come down in his season; there shall be showers of blessing.

34:27 And the tree of the field shall yield her fruit, and the earth shall yield her increase, and they shall be safe in their land, and shall know that I am the LORD, when I have broken the bands of their yoke, and delivered them out of the hand of those that served themselves of them.

34:28 And they shall no more be a prey to the heathen, neither shall the beast of the land devour them; but they shall dwell safely, and none shall make them afraid.

34:29 And I will raise up for them a plant of renown, and they shall be no more consumed with hunger in the land, neither bear the shame of the heathen any more.

34:30 Thus shall they know that I the LORD their God am with them, and that they, even the house of Israel, are my people, saith the Lord GOD.

34:31 And ye my flock, the flock of my pasture, are men, and I am your God, saith the Lord GOD.

35

35:1 Moreover the word of the LORD came unto me, saying, 35:2 Son of man, set thy face against mount Seir, and prophesy against it, 35:3 And say unto it, Thus saith the Lord GOD; Behold, O mount Seir, I am against thee, and I will stretch out mine hand against thee, and I will make thee most desolate.

35:4 I will lay thy cities waste, and thou shalt be desolate, and thou shalt know that I am the LORD.

35:5 Because thou hast had a perpetual hatred, and hast shed the blood of the children of Israel by the force of the sword in the time of their calamity, in the time that their iniquity had an end: 35:6 Therefore, as I live, saith the Lord GOD, I will prepare thee unto blood, and blood shall pursue thee: sith thou hast not hated blood, even blood shall pursue thee.

35:7 Thus will I make mount Seir most desolate, and cut off from it him that passeth out and him that

returneth.
35:8 And I will fill his mountains with his slain men: in thy hills, and in thy valleys, and in all thy rivers, shall they fall that are slain with the sword.
35:9 I will make thee perpetual desolations, and thy cities shall not return: and ye shall know that I am the LORD.
35:10 Because thou hast said, These two nations and these two countries shall be mine, and we will possess it; whereas the LORD was there: 35:11 Therefore, as I live, saith the Lord GOD, I will even do according to thine anger, and according to thine envy which thou hast used out of thy hatred against them; and I will make myself known among them, when I have judged thee.
35:12 And thou shalt know that I am the LORD, and that I have heard all thy blasphemies which thou hast spoken against the mountains of Israel, saying, They are laid desolate, they are given us to consume.
35:13 Thus with your mouth ye have boasted against me, and have multiplied your words against me: I have heard them.
35:14 Thus saith the Lord GOD; When the whole earth rejoiceth, I will make thee desolate.
35:15 As thou didst rejoice at the inheritance of the house of Israel, because it was desolate, so will I do unto thee: thou shalt be desolate, O mount Seir, and all Idumea, even all of it: and they shall know that I am the LORD.

36

36:1 Also, thou son of man, prophesy unto the mountains of Israel, and say, Ye mountains of Israel, hear the word of the LORD: 36:2 Thus saith the Lord GOD; Because the enemy hath said against you, Aha, even the ancient high places are ours in possession: 36:3 Therefore prophesy and say, Thus saith the Lord GOD; Because they have made you desolate, and swallowed you up on every side, that ye might be a possession unto the residue of the heathen, and ye are taken up in the lips of talkers, and are an infamy of the people: 36:4 Therefore, ye mountains of Israel, hear the word of the Lord GOD; Thus saith the Lord GOD to the mountains, and to the hills, to the rivers, and to the valleys, to the desolate wastes, and to the cities that are forsaken, which became a prey and derision to the residue of the heathen that are round about; 36:5 Therefore thus saith the Lord GOD; Surely in the fire of my jealousy have I spoken against the residue of the heathen, and against all Idumea, which have appointed my land into their possession with the joy of all their heart, with despiteful minds, to cast it out for a prey.
36:6 Prophesy therefore concerning the land of Israel, and say unto the mountains, and to the hills, to the rivers, and to the valleys, Thus saith the Lord GOD; Behold, I have spoken in my jealousy and in my fury, because ye have borne the shame of the heathen: 36:7 Therefore thus saith the Lord GOD; I have lifted up mine hand, Surely the heathen that are about you, they shall bear their shame.
36:8 But ye, O mountains of Israel, ye shall shoot forth your branches, and yield your fruit to my people of Israel; for they are at hand to come.
36:9 For, behold, I am for you, and I will turn unto you, and ye shall be tilled and sown: 36:10 And I will multiply men upon you, all the house of Israel, even all of it: and the cities shall be inhabited, and the wastes shall be builded: 36:11 And I will multiply upon you man and beast; and they shall increase and bring fruit: and I will settle you after your old estates, and will do better unto you than at your beginnings: and ye shall know that I am the LORD.
36:12 Yea, I will cause men to walk upon you, even my people Israel; and they shall possess thee, and thou shalt be their inheritance, and thou shalt no more henceforth bereave them of men.
36:13 Thus saith the Lord GOD; Because they say unto you, Thou land devourest up men, and hast bereaved thy nations: 36:14 Therefore thou shalt devour men no more, neither bereave thy nations any more, saith the Lord GOD.
36:15 Neither will I cause men to hear in thee the shame of the heathen any more, neither shalt thou bear the reproach of the people any more, neither shalt thou cause thy nations to fall any more, saith the Lord GOD.
36:16 Moreover the word of the LORD came unto me, saying, 36:17 Son of man, when the house of Israel dwelt in their own land, they defiled it by their own way and by their doings: their way was before me as the uncleanness of a removed woman.
36:18 Wherefore I poured my fury upon them for the blood that they had shed upon the land, and for their idols wherewith they had polluted it: 36:19 And I scattered them among the heathen, and they were dispersed through the countries: according to their way and according to their doings I judged them.
36:20 And when they entered unto the heathen, whither they went, they profaned my holy name, when they said to them, These are the people of the LORD, and are gone forth out of his land.

36:21 But I had pity for mine holy name, which the house of Israel had profaned among the heathen, whither they went.
36:22 Therefore say unto the house of Israel, thus saith the Lord GOD; I do not this for your sakes, O house of Israel, but for mine holy name's sake, which ye have profaned among the heathen, whither ye went.
36:23 And I will sanctify my great name, which was profaned among the heathen, which ye have profaned in the midst of them; and the heathen shall know that I am the LORD, saith the Lord GOD, when I shall be sanctified in you before their eyes.
36:24 For I will take you from among the heathen, and gather you out of all countries, and will bring you into your own land.
36:25 Then will I sprinkle clean water upon you, and ye shall be clean: from all your filthiness, and from all your idols, will I cleanse you.
36:26 A new heart also will I give you, and a new spirit will I put within you: and I will take away the stony heart out of your flesh, and I will give you an heart of flesh.
36:27 And I will put my spirit within you, and cause you to walk in my statutes, and ye shall keep my judgments, and do them.
36:28 And ye shall dwell in the land that I gave to your fathers; and ye shall be my people, and I will be your God.
36:29 I will also save you from all your uncleannesses: and I will call for the corn, and will increase it, and lay no famine upon you.
36:30 And I will multiply the fruit of the tree, and the increase of the field, that ye shall receive no more reproach of famine among the heathen.
36:31 Then shall ye remember your own evil ways, and your doings that were not good, and shall lothe yourselves in your own sight for your iniquities and for your abominations.
36:32 Not for your sakes do I this, saith the Lord GOD, be it known unto you: be ashamed and confounded for your own ways, O house of Israel.
36:33 Thus saith the Lord GOD; In the day that I shall have cleansed you from all your iniquities I will also cause you to dwell in the cities, and the wastes shall be builded.
36:34 And the desolate land shall be tilled, whereas it lay desolate in the sight of all that passed by.
36:35 And they shall say, This land that was desolate is become like the garden of Eden; and the waste and desolate and ruined cities are become fenced, and are inhabited.
36:36 Then the heathen that are left round about you shall know that I the LORD build the ruined places, and plant that that was desolate: I the LORD have spoken it, and I will do it.
36:37 Thus saith the Lord GOD; I will yet for this be enquired of by the house of Israel, to do it for them; I will increase them with men like a flock.
36:38 As the holy flock, as the flock of Jerusalem in her solemn feasts; so shall the waste cities be filled with flocks of men: and they shall know that I am the LORD.

37

37:1 The hand of the LORD was upon me, and carried me out in the spirit of the LORD, and set me
down in the midst of the valley which was full of bones, 37:2 And caused me to pass by them round
about: and, behold, there were very many in the open valley; and, lo, they were very dry.
37:3 And he said unto me, Son of man, can these bones live? And I answered, O Lord GOD, thou knowest.
37:4 Again he said unto me, Prophesy upon these bones, and say unto them, O ye dry bones, hear the word of the LORD.
37:5 Thus saith the Lord GOD unto these bones; Behold, I will cause breath to enter into you, and ye
shall live: 37:6 And I will lay sinews upon you, and will bring up flesh upon you, and cover you with
skin, and put breath in you, and ye shall live; and ye shall know that I am the LORD.
37:7 So I prophesied as I was commanded: and as I prophesied, there was a noise, and behold a shaking, and the bones came together, bone to his bone.
37:8 And when I beheld, lo, the sinews and the flesh came up upon them, and the skin covered them above: but there was no breath in them.
37:9 Then said he unto me, Prophesy unto the wind, prophesy, son of man, and say to the wind, Thus saith the Lord GOD; Come from the four winds, O breath, and breathe upon these slain, that they may live.
37:10 So I prophesied as he commanded me, and the breath came into them, and they lived, and stood

up upon their feet, an exceeding great army.
37:11 Then he said unto me, Son of man, these bones are the whole house of Israel: behold, they say,
Our bones are dried, and our hope is lost: we are cut off for our parts.
37:12 Therefore prophesy and say unto them, Thus saith the Lord GOD; Behold, O my people, I will
open your graves, and cause you to come up out of your graves, and bring you into the land of Israel.
37:13 And ye shall know that I am the LORD, when I have opened your graves, O my people, and
brought you up out of your graves, 37:14 And shall put my spirit in you, and ye shall live, and I shall
place you in your own land: then shall ye know that I the LORD have spoken it, and performed it, saith
the LORD.
37:15 The word of the LORD came again unto me, saying, 37:16 Moreover, thou son of man, take thee
one stick, and write upon it, For Judah, and for the children of Israel his companions: then take another
stick, and write upon it, For Joseph, the stick of Ephraim and for all the house of Israel his companions:
37:17 And join them one to another into one stick; and they shall become one in thine hand.
37:18 And when the children of thy people shall speak unto thee, saying, Wilt thou not shew us what
thou meanest by these? 37:19 Say unto them, Thus saith the Lord GOD; Behold, I will take the stick of
Joseph, which is in the hand of Ephraim, and the tribes of Israel his fellows, and will put them with him,
even with the stick of Judah, and make them one stick, and they shall be one in mine hand.
37:20 And the sticks whereon thou writest shall be in thine hand before their eyes.
37:21 And say unto them, Thus saith the Lord GOD; Behold, I will take the children of Israel from
among the heathen, whither they be gone, and will gather them on every side, and bring them into their
own land: 37:22 And I will make them one nation in the land upon the mountains of Israel; and one
king shall be king to them all: and they shall be no more two nations, neither shall they be divided into
two kingdoms any more at all.
37:23 Neither shall they defile themselves any more with their idols, nor with their detestable things, nor
with any of their transgressions: but I will save them out of all their dwellingplaces, wherein they have
sinned, and will cleanse them: so shall they be my people, and I will be their God.
37:24 And David my servant shall be king over them; and they all shall have one shepherd: they shall
also walk in my judgments, and observe my statutes, and do them.
37:25 And they shall dwell in the land that I have given unto Jacob my servant, wherein your fathers
have dwelt; and they shall dwell therein, even they, and their children, and their children's children for
ever: and my servant David shall be their prince for ever.
37:26 Moreover I will make a covenant of peace with them; it shall be an everlasting covenant with
them: and I will place them, and multiply them, and will set my sanctuary in the midst of them for
evermore.
37:27 My tabernacle also shall be with them: yea, I will be their God, and they shall be my people.
37:28 And the heathen shall know that I the LORD do sanctify Israel, when my sanctuary shall be in the
midst of them for evermore.

38

38:1 And the word of the LORD came unto me, saying, 38:2 Son of man, set thy face against Gog, the
land of Magog, the chief prince of Meshech and Tubal, and prophesy against him, 38:3 And say, Thus
saith the Lord GOD; Behold, I am against thee, O Gog, the chief prince of Meshech and Tubal: 38:4
And I will turn thee back, and put hooks into thy jaws, and I will bring thee forth, and all thine army,
horses and horsemen, all of them clothed with all sorts of armour, even a great company with bucklers
and shields, all of them handling swords: 38:5 Persia, Ethiopia, and Libya with them; all of them with
shield and helmet: 38:6 Gomer, and all his bands; the house of Togarmah of the north quarters, and all
his bands: and many people with thee.
38:7 Be thou prepared, and prepare for thyself, thou, and all thy company that are assembled unto thee,
and be thou a guard unto them.
38:8 After many days thou shalt be visited: in the latter years thou shalt come into the land that is
brought back from the sword, and is gathered out of many people, against the mountains of Israel,
which have been always waste: but it is brought forth out of the nations, and they shall dwell safely all of
them.
38:9 Thou shalt ascend and come like a storm, thou shalt be like a cloud to cover the land, thou, and all
thy bands, and many people with thee.
38:10 Thus saith the Lord GOD; It shall also come to pass, that at the same time shall things come into
thy mind, and thou shalt think an evil thought: 38:11 And thou shalt say, I will go up to the land of

unwalled villages; I will go to them that are at rest, that dwell safely, all of them dwelling without walls, and having neither bars nor gates, 38:12 To take a spoil, and to take a prey; to turn thine hand upon the desolate places that are now inhabited, and upon the people that are gathered out of the nations, which have gotten cattle and goods, that dwell in the midst of the land.

38:13 Sheba, and Dedan, and the merchants of Tarshish, with all the young lions thereof, shall say unto thee, Art thou come to take a spoil? hast thou gathered thy company to take a prey? to carry away silver and gold, to take away cattle and goods, to take a great spoil? 38:14 Therefore, son of man, prophesy and say unto Gog, Thus saith the Lord GOD; In that day when my people of Israel dwelleth safely, shalt thou not know it? 38:15 And thou shalt come from thy place out of the north parts, thou, and many people with thee, all of them riding upon horses, a great company, and a mighty army: 38:16 And thou shalt come up against my people of Israel, as a cloud to cover the land; it shall be in the latter days, and I will bring thee against my land, that the heathen may know me, when I shall be sanctified in thee, O Gog, before their eyes.

38:17 Thus saith the Lord GOD; Art thou he of whom I have spoken in old time by my servants the prophets of Israel, which prophesied in those days many years that I would bring thee against them? 38:18 And it shall come to pass at the same time when Gog shall come against the land of Israel, saith the Lord GOD, that my fury shall come up in my face.

38:19 For in my jealousy and in the fire of my wrath have I spoken, Surely in that day there shall be a great shaking in the land of Israel; 38:20 So that the fishes of the sea, and the fowls of the heaven, and the beasts of the field, and all creeping things that creep upon the earth, and all the men that are upon the face of the earth, shall shake at my presence, and the mountains shall be thrown down, and the steep places shall fall, and every wall shall fall to the ground.

38:21 And I will call for a sword against him throughout all my mountains, saith the Lord GOD: every man's sword shall be against his brother.

38:22 And I will plead against him with pestilence and with blood; and I will rain upon him, and upon his bands, and upon the many people that are with him, an overflowing rain, and great hailstones, fire, and brimstone.

38:23 Thus will I magnify myself, and sanctify myself; and I will be known in the eyes of many nations, and they shall know that I am the LORD.

39

39:1 Therefore, thou son of man, prophesy against Gog, and say, Thus saith the Lord GOD; Behold, I am against thee, O Gog, the chief prince of Meshech and Tubal: 39:2 And I will turn thee back, and leave but the sixth part of thee, and will cause thee to come up from the north parts, and will bring thee upon the mountains of Israel: 39:3 And I will smite thy bow out of thy left hand, and will cause thine arrows to fall out of thy right hand.

39:4 Thou shalt fall upon the mountains of Israel, thou, and all thy bands, and the people that is with thee: I will give thee unto the ravenous birds of every sort, and to the beasts of the field to be devoured.

39:5 Thou shalt fall upon the open field: for I have spoken it, saith the Lord GOD.

39:6 And I will send a fire on Magog, and among them that dwell carelessly in the isles: and they shall know that I am the LORD.

39:7 So will I make my holy name known in the midst of my people Israel; and I will not let them pollute my holy name any more: and the heathen shall know that I am the LORD, the Holy One in Israel.

39:8 Behold, it is come, and it is done, saith the Lord GOD; this is the day whereof I have spoken.

39:9 And they that dwell in the cities of Israel shall go forth, and shall set on fire and burn the weapons, both the shields and the bucklers, the bows and the arrows, and the handstaves, and the spears, and they shall burn them with fire seven years: 39:10 So that they shall take no wood out of the field, neither cut down any out of the forests; for they shall burn the weapons with fire: and they shall spoil those that spoiled them, and rob those that robbed them, saith the Lord GOD.

39:11 And it shall come to pass in that day, that I will give unto Gog a place there of graves in Israel, the valley of the passengers on the east of the sea: and it shall stop the noses of the passengers: and there shall they bury Gog and all his multitude: and they shall call it The valley of Hamongog.

39:12 And seven months shall the house of Israel be burying of them, that they may cleanse the land.

39:13 Yea, all the people of the land shall bury them; and it shall be to them a renown the day that I shall be glorified, saith the Lord GOD.

39:14 And they shall sever out men of continual employment, passing through the land to bury with the

passengers those that remain upon the face of the earth, to cleanse it: after the end of seven months shall they search.
39:15 And the passengers that pass through the land, when any seeth a man's bone, then shall he set up a sign by it, till the buriers have buried it in the valley of Hamongog.
39:16 And also the name of the city shall be Hamonah. Thus shall they cleanse the land.
39:17 And, thou son of man, thus saith the Lord GOD; Speak unto every feathered fowl, and to every beast of the field, Assemble yourselves, and come; gather yourselves on every side to my sacrifice that I do sacrifice for you, even a great sacrifice upon the mountains of Israel, that ye may eat flesh, and drink blood.
39:18 Ye shall eat the flesh of the mighty, and drink the blood of the princes of the earth, of rams, of lambs, and of goats, of bullocks, all of them fatlings of Bashan.
39:19 And ye shall eat fat till ye be full, and drink blood till ye be drunken, of my sacrifice which I have sacrificed for you.
39:20 Thus ye shall be filled at my table with horses and chariots, with mighty men, and with all men of war, saith the Lord GOD.
39:21 And I will set my glory among the heathen, and all the heathen shall see my judgment that I have executed, and my hand that I have laid upon them.
39:22 So the house of Israel shall know that I am the LORD their God from that day and forward.

39:23 And the heathen shall know that the house of Israel went into captivity for their iniquity: because they trespassed against me, therefore hid I my face from them, and gave them into the hand of their enemies: so fell they all by the sword.
39:24 According to their uncleanness and according to their transgressions have I done unto them, and hid my face from them.
39:25 Therefore thus saith the Lord GOD; Now will I bring again the captivity of Jacob, and have mercy upon the whole house of Israel, and will be jealous for my holy name; 39:26 After that they have borne their shame, and all their trespasses whereby they have trespassed against me, when they dwelt safely in their land, and none made them afraid.
39:27 When I have brought them again from the people, and gathered them out of their enemies' lands, and am sanctified in them in the sight of many nations; 39:28 Then shall they know that I am the LORD their God, which caused them to be led into captivity among the heathen: but I have gathered them unto their own land, and have left none of them any more there.
39:29 Neither will I hide my face any more from them: for I have poured out my spirit upon the house of Israel, saith the Lord GOD.

40

40:1 In the five and twentieth year of our captivity, in the beginning of the year, in the tenth day of the month, in the fourteenth year after that the city was smitten, in the selfsame day the hand of the LORD was upon me, and brought me thither.
40:2 In the visions of God brought he me into the land of Israel, and set me upon a very high mountain, by which was as the frame of a city on the south.
40:3 And he brought me thither, and, behold, there was a man, whose appearance was like the appearance of brass, with a line of flax in his hand, and a measuring reed; and he stood in the gate.
40:4 And the man said unto me, Son of man, behold with thine eyes, and hear with thine ears, and set thine heart upon all that I shall shew thee; for to the intent that I might shew them unto thee art thou brought hither: declare all that thou seest to the house of Israel.
40:5 And behold a wall on the outside of the house round about, and in the man's hand a measuring reed of six cubits long by the cubit and an hand breadth: so he measured the breadth of the building, one reed; and the height, one reed.
40:6 Then came he unto the gate which looketh toward the east, and went up the stairs thereof, and measured the threshold of the gate, which was one reed broad; and the other threshold of the gate, which was one reed broad.
40:7 And every little chamber was one reed long, and one reed broad; and between the little chambers were five cubits; and the threshold of the gate by the porch of the gate within was one reed.
40:8 He measured also the porch of the gate within, one reed.
40:9 Then measured he the porch of the gate, eight cubits; and the posts thereof, two cubits; and the

porch of the gate was inward.

40:10 And the little chambers of the gate eastward were three on this side, and three on that side; they three were of one measure: and the posts had one measure on this side and on that side.

40:11 And he measured the breadth of the entry of the gate, ten cubits; and the length of the gate, thirteen cubits.

40:12 The space also before the little chambers was one cubit on this side, and the space was one cubit on that side: and the little chambers were six cubits on this side, and six cubits on that side.

40:13 He measured then the gate from the roof of one little chamber to the roof of another: the breadth was five and twenty cubits, door against door.

40:14 He made also posts of threescore cubits, even unto the post of the court round about the gate.

40:15 And from the face of the gate of the entrance unto the face of the porch of the inner gate were fifty cubits.

40:16 And there were narrow windows to the little chambers, and to their posts within the gate round about, and likewise to the arches: and windows were round about inward: and upon each post were palm trees.

40:17 Then brought he me into the outward court, and, lo, there were chambers, and a pavement made for the court round about: thirty chambers were upon the pavement.

40:18 And the pavement by the side of the gates over against the length of the gates was the lower pavement.

40:19 Then he measured the breadth from the forefront of the lower gate unto the forefront of the inner court without, an hundred cubits eastward and northward.

40:20 And the gate of the outward court that looked toward the north, he measured the length thereof, and the breadth thereof.

40:21 And the little chambers thereof were three on this side and three on that side; and the posts thereof and the arches thereof were after the measure of the first gate: the length thereof was fifty cubits, and the breadth five and twenty cubits.

40:22 And their windows, and their arches, and their palm trees, were after the measure of the gate that looketh toward the east; and they went up unto it by seven steps; and the arches thereof were before them.

40:23 And the gate of the inner court was over against the gate toward the north, and toward the east; and he measured from gate to gate an hundred cubits.

40:24 After that he brought me toward the south, and behold a gate toward the south: and he measured the posts thereof and the arches thereof according to these measures.

40:25 And there were windows in it and in the arches thereof round about, like those windows: the length was fifty cubits, and the breadth five and twenty cubits.

40:26 And there were seven steps to go up to it, and the arches thereof were before them: and it had palm trees, one on this side, and another on that side, upon the posts thereof.

40:27 And there was a gate in the inner court toward the south: and he measured from gate to gate toward the south an hundred cubits.

40:28 And he brought me to the inner court by the south gate: and he measured the south gate
according to these measures; 40:29 And the little chambers thereof, and the posts thereof, and the
arches thereof, according to these measures: and there were windows in it and in the arches thereof
round about: it was fifty cubits long, and five and twenty cubits broad.

40:30 And the arches round about were five and twenty cubits long, and five cubits broad.

40:31 And the arches thereof were toward the utter court; and palm trees were upon the posts thereof: and the going up to it had eight steps.

40:32 And he brought me into the inner court toward the east: and he measured the gate according to these measures.

40:33 And the little chambers thereof, and the posts thereof, and the arches thereof, were according to these measures: and there were windows therein and in the arches thereof round about: it was fifty cubits long, and five and twenty cubits broad.

40:34 And the arches thereof were toward the outward court; and palm trees were upon the posts thereof, on this side, and on that side: and the going up to it had eight steps.

40:35 And he brought me to the north gate, and measured it according to these measures; 40:36 The
little chambers thereof, the posts thereof, and the arches thereof, and the windows to it round about: the
length was fifty cubits, and the breadth five and twenty cubits.

40:37 And the posts thereof were toward the utter court; and palm trees were upon the posts thereof, on this side, and on that side: and the going up to it had eight steps.

40:38 And the chambers and the entries thereof were by the posts of the gates, where they washed the

burnt offering.
40:39 And in the porch of the gate were two tables on this side, and two tables on that side, to slay thereon the burnt offering and the sin offering and the trespass offering.
40:40 And at the side without, as one goeth up to the entry of the north gate, were two tables; and on the other side, which was at the porch of the gate, were two tables.
40:41 Four tables were on this side, and four tables on that side, by the side of the gate; eight tables, whereupon they slew their sacrifices.
40:42 And the four tables were of hewn stone for the burnt offering, of a cubit and an half long, and a cubit and an half broad, and one cubit high: whereupon also they laid the instruments wherewith they slew the burnt offering and the sacrifice.
40:43 And within were hooks, an hand broad, fastened round about: and upon the tables was the flesh of the offering.
40:44 And without the inner gate were the chambers of the singers in the inner court, which was at the side of the north gate; and their prospect was toward the south: one at the side of the east gate having the prospect toward the north.
40:45 And he said unto me, This chamber, whose prospect is toward the south, is for the priests, the keepers of the charge of the house.
40:46 And the chamber whose prospect is toward the north is for the priests, the keepers of the charge of the altar: these are the sons of Zadok among the sons of Levi, which come near to the LORD to minister unto him.
40:47 So he measured the court, an hundred cubits long, and an hundred cubits broad, foursquare; and the altar that was before the house.
40:48 And he brought me to the porch of the house, and measured each post of the porch, five cubits on this side, and five cubits on that side: and the breadth of the gate was three cubits on this side, and three cubits on that side.
40:49 The length of the porch was twenty cubits, and the breadth eleven cubits, and he brought me by the steps whereby they went up to it: and there were pillars by the posts, one on this side, and another on that side.

41

41:1 Afterward he brought me to the temple, and measured the posts, six cubits broad on the one side, and six cubits broad on the other side, which was the breadth of the tabernacle.
41:2 And the breadth of the door was ten cubits; and the sides of the door were five cubits on the one side, and five cubits on the other side: and he measured the length thereof, forty cubits: and the breadth, twenty cubits.
41:3 Then went he inward, and measured the post of the door, two cubits; and the door, six cubits; and the breadth of the door, seven cubits.
41:4 So he measured the length thereof, twenty cubits; and the breadth, twenty cubits, before the temple: and he said unto me, This is the most holy place.
41:5 After he measured the wall of the house, six cubits; and the breadth of every side chamber, four cubits, round about the house on every side.
41:6 And the side chambers were three, one over another, and thirty in order; and they entered into the wall which was of the house for the side chambers round about, that they might have hold, but they had not hold in the wall of the house.
41:7 And there was an enlarging, and a winding about still upward to the side chambers: for the winding about of the house went still upward round about the house: therefore the breadth of the house was still upward, and so increased from the lowest chamber to the highest by the midst.
41:8 I saw also the height of the house round about: the foundations of the side chambers were a full reed of six great cubits.
41:9 The thickness of the wall, which was for the side chamber without, was five cubits: and that which was left was the place of the side chambers that were within.
41:10 And between the chambers was the wideness of twenty cubits round about the house on every side.
41:11 And the doors of the side chambers were toward the place that was left, one door toward the north, and another door toward the south: and the breadth of the place that was left was five cubits round about.
41:12 Now the building that was before the separate place at the end toward the west was seventy cubits

broad; and the wall of the building was five cubits thick round about, and the length thereof ninety cubits.
41:13 So he measured the house, an hundred cubits long; and the separate place, and the building, with the walls thereof, an hundred cubits long; 41:14 Also the breadth of the face of the house, and of the separate place toward the east, an hundred cubits.
41:15 And he measured the length of the building over against the separate place which was behind it, and the galleries thereof on the one side and on the other side, an hundred cubits, with the inner temple, and the porches of the court; 41:16 The door posts, and the narrow windows, and the galleries round about on their three stories, over against the door, cieled with wood round about, and from the ground up to the windows, and the windows were covered; 41:17 To that above the door, even unto the inner house, and without, and by all the wall round about within and without, by measure.
41:18 And it was made with cherubims and palm trees, so that a palm tree was between a cherub and a cherub; and every cherub had two faces; 41:19 So that the face of a man was toward the palm tree on the one side, and the face of a young lion toward the palm tree on the other side: it was made through all the house round about.
41:20 From the ground unto above the door were cherubims and palm trees made, and on the wall of the temple.
41:21 The posts of the temple were squared, and the face of the sanctuary; the appearance of the one as the appearance of the other.
41:22 The altar of wood was three cubits high, and the length thereof two cubits; and the corners thereof, and the length thereof, and the walls thereof, were of wood: and he said unto me, This is the table that is before the LORD.
41:23 And the temple and the sanctuary had two doors.
41:24 And the doors had two leaves apiece, two turning leaves; two leaves for the one door, and two leaves for the other door.
41:25 And there were made on them, on the doors of the temple, cherubims and palm trees, like as were made upon the walls; and there were thick planks upon the face of the porch without.
41:26 And there were narrow windows and palm trees on the one side and on the other side, on the sides of the porch, and upon the side chambers of the house, and thick planks.

42

42:1 Then he brought me forth into the utter court, the way toward the north: and he brought me into the chamber that was over against the separate place, and which was before the building toward the north.
42:2 Before the length of an hundred cubits was the north door, and the breadth was fifty cubits.
42:3 Over against the twenty cubits which were for the inner court, and over against the pavement which was for the utter court, was gallery against gallery in three stories.
42:4 And before the chambers was a walk to ten cubits breadth inward, a way of one cubit; and their doors toward the north.
42:5 Now the upper chambers were shorter: for the galleries were higher than these, than the lower, and than the middlemost of the building.
42:6 For they were in three stories, but had not pillars as the pillars of the courts: therefore the building was straitened more than the lowest and the middlemost from the ground.
42:7 And the wall that was without over against the chambers, toward the utter court on the forepart of the chambers, the length thereof was fifty cubits.
42:8 For the length of the chambers that were in the utter court was fifty cubits: and, lo, before the temple were an hundred cubits.
42:9 And from under these chambers was the entry on the east side, as one goeth into them from the utter court.
42:10 The chambers were in the thickness of the wall of the court toward the east, over against the separate place, and over against the building.
42:11 And the way before them was like the appearance of the chambers which were toward the north, as long as they, and as broad as they: and all their goings out were both according to their fashions, and according to their doors.
42:12 And according to the doors of the chambers that were toward the south was a door in the head of the way, even the way directly before the wall toward the east, as one entereth into them.
42:13 Then said he unto me, The north chambers and the south chambers, which are before the

separate place, they be holy chambers, where the priests that approach unto the LORD shall eat the most holy things: there shall they lay the most holy things, and the meat offering, and the sin offering, and the trespass offering; for the place is holy.
42:14 When the priests enter therein, then shall they not go out of the holy place into the utter court, but there they shall lay their garments wherein they minister; for they are holy; and shall put on other garments, and shall approach to those things which are for the people.
42:15 Now when he had made an end of measuring the inner house, he brought me forth toward the gate whose prospect is toward the east, and measured it round about.
42:16 He measured the east side with the measuring reed, five hundred reeds, with the measuring reed round about.
42:17 He measured the north side, five hundred reeds, with the measuring reed round about.
42:18 He measured the south side, five hundred reeds, with the measuring reed.
42:19 He turned about to the west side, and measured five hundred reeds with the measuring reed.
42:20 He measured it by the four sides: it had a wall round about, five hundred reeds long, and five hundred broad, to make a separation between the sanctuary and the profane place.

43

43:1 Afterward he brought me to the gate, even the gate that looketh toward the east: 43:2 And, behold, the glory of the God of Israel came from the way of the east: and his voice was like a noise of many waters: and the earth shined with his glory.
43:3 And it was according to the appearance of the vision which I saw, even according to the vision that I saw when I came to destroy the city: and the visions were like the vision that I saw by the river Chebar; and I fell upon my face.
43:4 And the glory of the LORD came into the house by the way of the gate whose prospect is toward the east.
43:5 So the spirit took me up, and brought me into the inner court; and, behold, the glory of the LORD filled the house.
43:6 And I heard him speaking unto me out of the house; and the man stood by me.
43:7 And he said unto me, Son of man, the place of my throne, and the place of the soles of my feet, where I will dwell in the midst of the children of Israel for ever, and my holy name, shall the house of Israel no more defile, neither they, nor their kings, by their whoredom, nor by the carcases of their kings in their high places.
43:8 In their setting of their threshold by my thresholds, and their post by my posts, and the wall between me and them, they have even defiled my holy name by their abominations that they have committed: wherefore I have consumed them in mine anger.
43:9 Now let them put away their whoredom, and the carcases of their kings, far from me, and I will dwell in the midst of them for ever.
43:10 Thou son of man, shew the house to the house of Israel, that they may be ashamed of their iniquities: and let them measure the pattern.
43:11 And if they be ashamed of all that they have done, shew them the form of the house, and the fashion thereof, and the goings out thereof, and the comings in thereof, and all the forms thereof, and all the ordinances thereof, and all the forms thereof, and all the laws thereof: and write it in their sight, that they may keep the whole form thereof, and all the ordinances thereof, and do them.
43:12 This is the law of the house; Upon the top of the mountain the whole limit thereof round about shall be most holy. Behold, this is the law of the house.
43:13 And these are the measures of the altar after the cubits: The cubit is a cubit and an hand breadth; even the bottom shall be a cubit, and the breadth a cubit, and the border thereof by the edge thereof round about shall be a span: and this shall be the higher place of the altar.
43:14 And from the bottom upon the ground even to the lower settle shall be two cubits, and the breadth one cubit; and from the lesser settle even to the greater settle shall be four cubits, and the breadth one cubit.
43:15 So the altar shall be four cubits; and from the altar and upward shall be four horns.
43:16 And the altar shall be twelve cubits long, twelve broad, square in the four squares thereof.
43:17 And the settle shall be fourteen cubits long and fourteen broad in the four squares thereof; and the border about it shall be half a cubit; and the bottom thereof shall be a cubit about; and his stairs shall look toward the east.
43:18 And he said unto me, Son of man, thus saith the Lord GOD; These are the ordinances of the altar

in the day when they shall make it, to offer burnt offerings thereon, and to sprinkle blood thereon.
43:19 And thou shalt give to the priests the Levites that be of the seed of Zadok, which approach unto me, to minister unto me, saith the Lord GOD, a young bullock for a sin offering.
43:20 And thou shalt take of the blood thereof, and put it on the four horns of it, and on the four corners of the settle, and upon the border round about: thus shalt thou cleanse and purge it.
43:21 Thou shalt take the bullock also of the sin offering, and he shall burn it in the appointed place of the house, without the sanctuary.
43:22 And on the second day thou shalt offer a kid of the goats without blemish for a sin offering; and they shall cleanse the altar, as they did cleanse it with the bullock.
43:23 When thou hast made an end of cleansing it, thou shalt offer a young bullock without blemish, and a ram out of the flock without blemish.
43:24 And thou shalt offer them before the LORD, and the priests shall cast salt upon them, and they shall offer them up for a burnt offering unto the LORD.
43:25 Seven days shalt thou prepare every day a goat for a sin offering: they shall also prepare a young bullock, and a ram out of the flock, without blemish.
43:26 Seven days shall they purge the altar and purify it; and they shall consecrate themselves.
43:27 And when these days are expired, it shall be, that upon the eighth day, and so forward, the priests shall make your burnt offerings upon the altar, and your peace offerings; and I will accept you, saith the Lord GOD.

44

44:1 Then he brought me back the way of the gate of the outward sanctuary which looketh toward the east; and it was shut.
44:2 Then said the LORD unto me; This gate shall be shut, it shall not be opened, and no man shall enter in by it; because the LORD, the God of Israel, hath entered in by it, therefore it shall be shut.
44:3 It is for the prince; the prince, he shall sit in it to eat bread before the LORD; he shall enter by the way of the porch of that gate, and shall go out by the way of the same.
44:4 Then brought he me the way of the north gate before the house: and I looked, and, behold, the glory of the LORD filled the house of the LORD: and I fell upon my face.
44:5 And the LORD said unto me, Son of man, mark well, and behold with thine eyes, and hear with thine ears all that I say unto thee concerning all the ordinances of the house of the LORD, and all the laws thereof; and mark well the entering in of the house, with every going forth of the sanctuary.
44:6 And thou shalt say to the rebellious, even to the house of Israel, Thus saith the Lord GOD; O ye
house of Israel, let it suffice you of all your abominations, 44:7 In that ye have brought into my
sanctuary strangers, uncircumcised in heart, and uncircumcised in flesh, to be in my sanctuary, to pollute it, even my house, when ye offer my bread, the fat and the blood, and they have broken my covenant because of all your abominations.
44:8 And ye have not kept the charge of mine holy things: but ye have set keepers of my charge in my sanctuary for yourselves.
44:9 Thus saith the Lord GOD; No stranger, uncircumcised in heart, nor uncircumcised in flesh, shall enter into my sanctuary, of any stranger that is among the children of Israel.
44:10 And the Levites that are gone away far from me, when Israel went astray, which went astray away from me after their idols; they shall even bear their iniquity.
44:11 Yet they shall be ministers in my sanctuary, having charge at the gates of the house, and ministering to the house: they shall slay the burnt offering and the sacrifice for the people, and they shall stand before them to minister unto them.
44:12 Because they ministered unto them before their idols, and caused the house of Israel to fall into iniquity; therefore have I lifted up mine hand against them, saith the Lord GOD, and they shall bear their iniquity.
44:13 And they shall not come near unto me, to do the office of a priest unto me, nor to come near to any of my holy things, in the most holy place: but they shall bear their shame, and their abominations which they have committed.
44:14 But I will make them keepers of the charge of the house, for all the service thereof, and for all that shall be done therein.
44:15 But the priests the Levites, the sons of Zadok, that kept the charge of my sanctuary when the children of Israel went astray from me, they shall come near to me to minister unto me, and they shall
stand before me to offer unto me the fat and the blood, saith the Lord GOD: 44:16 They shall enter

into my sanctuary, and they shall come near to my table, to minister unto me, and they shall keep my charge.
44:17 And it shall come to pass, that when they enter in at the gates of the inner court, they shall be clothed with linen garments; and no wool shall come upon them, whiles they minister in the gates of the inner court, and within.
44:18 They shall have linen bonnets upon their heads, and shall have linen breeches upon their loins; they shall not gird themselves with any thing that causeth sweat.
44:19 And when they go forth into the utter court, even into the utter court to the people, they shall put off their garments wherein they ministered, and lay them in the holy chambers, and they shall put on other garments; and they shall not sanctify the people with their garments.
44:20 Neither shall they shave their heads, nor suffer their locks to grow long; they shall only poll their heads.
44:21 Neither shall any priest drink wine, when they enter into the inner court.
44:22 Neither shall they take for their wives a widow, nor her that is put away: but they shall take maidens of the seed of the house of Israel, or a widow that had a priest before.
44:23 And they shall teach my people the difference between the holy and profane, and cause them to discern between the unclean and the clean.
44:24 And in controversy they shall stand in judgment; and they shall judge it according to my judgments: and they shall keep my laws and my statutes in all mine assemblies; and they shall hallow my sabbaths.
44:25 And they shall come at no dead person to defile themselves: but for father, or for mother, or for son, or for daughter, for brother, or for sister that hath had no husband, they may defile themselves.
44:26 And after he is cleansed, they shall reckon unto him seven days.
44:27 And in the day that he goeth into the sanctuary, unto the inner court, to minister in the sanctuary, he shall offer his sin offering, saith the Lord GOD.
44:28 And it shall be unto them for an inheritance: I am their inheritance: and ye shall give them no possession in Israel: I am their possession.
44:29 They shall eat the meat offering, and the sin offering, and the trespass offering: and every dedicated thing in Israel shall be theirs.
44:30 And the first of all the firstfruits of all things, and every oblation of all, of every sort of your oblations, shall be the priest's: ye shall also give unto the priest the first of your dough, that he may cause the blessing to rest in thine house.
44:31 The priests shall not eat of any thing that is dead of itself, or torn, whether it be fowl or beast.

45

45:1 Moreover, when ye shall divide by lot the land for inheritance, ye shall offer an oblation unto the LORD, an holy portion of the land: the length shall be the length of five and twenty thousand reeds, and the breadth shall be ten thousand. This shall be holy in all the borders thereof round about.
45:2 Of this there shall be for the sanctuary five hundred in length, with five hundred in breadth, square round about; and fifty cubits round about for the suburbs thereof.
45:3 And of this measure shalt thou measure the length of five and twenty thousand, and the breadth of ten thousand: and in it shall be the sanctuary and the most holy place.
45:4 The holy portion of the land shall be for the priests the ministers of the sanctuary, which shall come near to minister unto the LORD: and it shall be a place for their houses, and an holy place for the sanctuary.
45:5 And the five and twenty thousand of length, and the ten thousand of breadth shall also the Levites, the ministers of the house, have for themselves, for a possession for twenty chambers.
45:6 And ye shall appoint the possession of the city five thousand broad, and five and twenty thousand long, over against the oblation of the holy portion: it shall be for the whole house of Israel.
45:7 And a portion shall be for the prince on the one side and on the other side of the oblation of the holy portion, and of the possession of the city, before the oblation of the holy portion, and before the possession of the city, from the west side westward, and from the east side eastward: and the length shall be over against one of the portions, from the west border unto the east border.
45:8 In the land shall be his possession in Israel: and my princes shall no more oppress my people; and the rest of the land shall they give to the house of Israel according to their tribes.
45:9 Thus saith the Lord GOD; Let it suffice you, O princes of Israel: remove violence and spoil, and execute judgment and justice, take away your exactions from my people, saith the Lord GOD.

45:10 Ye shall have just balances, and a just ephah, and a just bath.

45:11 The ephah and the bath shall be of one measure, that the bath may contain the tenth part of an homer, and the ephah the tenth part of an homer: the measure thereof shall be after the homer.

45:12 And the shekel shall be twenty gerahs: twenty shekels, five and twenty shekels, fifteen shekels, shall be your maneh.

45:13 This is the oblation that ye shall offer; the sixth part of an ephah of an homer of wheat, and ye shall give the sixth part of an ephah of an homer of barley: 45:14 Concerning the ordinance of oil, the bath of oil, ye shall offer the tenth part of a bath out of the cor, which is an homer of ten baths; for ten baths are an homer: 45:15 And one lamb out of the flock, out of two hundred, out of the fat pastures of Israel; for a meat offering, and for a burnt offering, and for peace offerings, to make reconciliation for them, saith the Lord GOD.

45:16 All the people of the land shall give this oblation for the prince in Israel.

45:17 And it shall be the prince's part to give burnt offerings, and meat offerings, and drink offerings, in the feasts, and in the new moons, and in the sabbaths, in all solemnities of the house of Israel: he shall prepare the sin offering, and the meat offering, and the burnt offering, and the peace offerings, to make reconciliation for the house of Israel.

45:18 Thus saith the Lord GOD; In the first month, in the first day of the month, thou shalt take a young bullock without blemish, and cleanse the sanctuary: 45:19 And the priest shall take of the blood of the sin offering, and put it upon the posts of the house, and upon the four corners of the settle of the altar, and upon the posts of the gate of the inner court.

45:20 And so thou shalt do the seventh day of the month for every one that erreth, and for him that is simple: so shall ye reconcile the house.

45:21 In the first month, in the fourteenth day of the month, ye shall have the passover, a feast of seven days; unleavened bread shall be eaten.

45:22 And upon that day shall the prince prepare for himself and for all the people of the land a bullock for a sin offering.

45:23 And seven days of the feast he shall prepare a burnt offering to the LORD, seven bullocks and seven rams without blemish daily the seven days; and a kid of the goats daily for a sin offering.

45:24 And he shall prepare a meat offering of an ephah for a bullock, and an ephah for a ram, and an hin of oil for an ephah.

45:25 In the seventh month, in the fifteenth day of the month, shall he do the like in the feast of the seven days, according to the sin offering, according to the burnt offering, and according to the meat offering, and according to the oil.

46

46:1 Thus saith the Lord GOD; The gate of the inner court that looketh toward the east shall be shut the six working days; but on the sabbath it shall be opened, and in the day of the new moon it shall be opened.

46:2 And the prince shall enter by the way of the porch of that gate without, and shall stand by the post of the gate, and the priests shall prepare his burnt offering and his peace offerings, and he shall worship at the threshold of the gate: then he shall go forth; but the gate shall not be shut until the evening.

46:3 Likewise the people of the land shall worship at the door of this gate before the LORD in the sabbaths and in the new moons.

46:4 And the burnt offering that the prince shall offer unto the LORD in the sabbath day shall be six lambs without blemish, and a ram without blemish.

46:5 And the meat offering shall be an ephah for a ram, and the meat offering for the lambs as he shall be able to give, and an hin of oil to an ephah.

46:6 And in the day of the new moon it shall be a young bullock without blemish, and six lambs, and a ram: they shall be without blemish.

46:7 And he shall prepare a meat offering, an ephah for a bullock, and an ephah for a ram, and for the lambs according as his hand shall attain unto, and an hin of oil to an ephah.

46:8 And when the prince shall enter, he shall go in by the way of the porch of that gate, and he shall go forth by the way thereof.

46:9 But when the people of the land shall come before the LORD in the solemn feasts, he that entereth in by the way of the north gate to worship shall go out by the way of the south gate; and he that entereth by the way of the south gate shall go forth by the way of the north gate: he shall not return by the way of the gate whereby he came in, but shall go forth over against it.

46:10 And the prince in the midst of them, when they go in, shall go in; and when they go forth, shall go forth.
46:11 And in the feasts and in the solemnities the meat offering shall be an ephah to a bullock, and an ephah to a ram, and to the lambs as he is able to give, and an hin of oil to an ephah.
46:12 Now when the prince shall prepare a voluntary burnt offering or peace offerings voluntarily unto the LORD, one shall then open him the gate that looketh toward the east, and he shall prepare his burnt offering and his peace offerings, as he did on the sabbath day: then he shall go forth; and after his going forth one shall shut the gate.
46:13 Thou shalt daily prepare a burnt offering unto the LORD of a lamb of the first year without blemish: thou shalt prepare it every morning.
46:14 And thou shalt prepare a meat offering for it every morning, the sixth part of an ephah, and the third part of an hin of oil, to temper with the fine flour; a meat offering continually by a perpetual ordinance unto the LORD.
46:15 Thus shall they prepare the lamb, and the meat offering, and the oil, every morning for a continual burnt offering.
46:16 Thus saith the Lord GOD; If the prince give a gift unto any of his sons, the inheritance thereof shall be his sons'; it shall be their possession by inheritance.
46:17 But if he give a gift of his inheritance to one of his servants, then it shall be his to the year of liberty; after it shall return to the prince: but his inheritance shall be his sons' for them.
46:18 Moreover the prince shall not take of the people's inheritance by oppression, to thrust them out of their possession; but he shall give his sons inheritance out of his own possession: that my people be not scattered every man from his possession.
46:19 After he brought me through the entry, which was at the side of the gate, into the holy chambers of the priests, which looked toward the north: and, behold, there was a place on the two sides westward.
46:20 Then said he unto me, This is the place where the priests shall boil the trespass offering and the sin offering, where they shall bake the meat offering; that they bear them not out into the utter court, to sanctify the people.
46:21 Then he brought me forth into the utter court, and caused me to pass by the four corners of the court; and, behold, in every corner of the court there was a court.
46:22 In the four corners of the court there were courts joined of forty cubits long and thirty broad: these four corners were of one measure.
46:23 And there was a row of building round about in them, round about them four, and it was made with boiling places under the rows round about.
46:24 Then said he unto me, These are the places of them that boil, where the ministers of the house shall boil the sacrifice of the people.

47

47:1 Afterward he brought me again unto the door of the house; and, behold, waters issued out from under the threshold of the house eastward: for the forefront of the house stood toward the east, and the waters came down from under from the right side of the house, at the south side of the altar.
47:2 Then brought he me out of the way of the gate northward, and led me about the way without unto the utter gate by the way that looketh eastward; and, behold, there ran out waters on the right side.
47:3 And when the man that had the line in his hand went forth eastward, he measured a thousand cubits, and he brought me through the waters; the waters were to the ankles.
47:4 Again he measured a thousand, and brought me through the waters; the waters were to the knees. Again he measured a thousand, and brought me through; the waters were to the loins.
47:5 Afterward he measured a thousand; and it was a river that I could not pass over: for the waters were risen, waters to swim in, a river that could not be passed over.
47:6 And he said unto me, Son of man, hast thou seen this? Then he brought me, and caused me to return to the brink of the river.
47:7 Now when I had returned, behold, at the bank of the river were very many trees on the one side and on the other.
47:8 Then said he unto me, These waters issue out toward the east country, and go down into the desert, and go into the sea: which being brought forth into the sea, the waters shall be healed.
47:9 And it shall come to pass, that every thing that liveth, which moveth, whithersoever the rivers shall come, shall live: and there shall be a very great multitude of fish, because these waters shall come thither: for they shall be healed; and every thing shall live whither the river cometh.

47:10 And it shall come to pass, that the fishers shall stand upon it from Engedi even unto Eneglaim; they shall be a place to spread forth nets; their fish shall be according to their kinds, as the fish of the great sea, exceeding many.
47:11 But the miry places thereof and the marishes thereof shall not be healed; they shall be given to salt.
47:12 And by the river upon the bank thereof, on this side and on that side, shall grow all trees for meat, whose leaf shall not fade, neither shall the fruit thereof be consumed: it shall bring forth new fruit according to his months, because their waters they issued out of the sanctuary: and the fruit thereof shall be for meat, and the leaf thereof for medicine.
47:13 Thus saith the Lord GOD; This shall be the border, whereby ye shall inherit the land according to the twelve tribes of Israel: Joseph shall have two portions.
47:14 And ye shall inherit it, one as well as another: concerning the which I lifted up mine hand to give it unto your fathers: and this land shall fall unto you for inheritance.
47:15 And this shall be the border of the land toward the north side, from the great sea, the way of Hethlon, as men go to Zedad; 47:16 Hamath, Berothah, Sibraim, which is between the border of Damascus and the border of Hamath; Hazarhatticon, which is by the coast of Hauran.
47:17 And the border from the sea shall be Hazarenan, the border of Damascus, and the north northward, and the border of Hamath. And this is the north side.
47:18 And the east side ye shall measure from Hauran, and from Damascus, and from Gilead, and from the land of Israel by Jordan, from the border unto the east sea. And this is the east side.
47:19 And the south side southward, from Tamar even to the waters of strife in Kadesh, the river to the great sea. And this is the south side southward.
47:20 The west side also shall be the great sea from the border, till a man come over against Hamath. This is the west side.
47:21 So shall ye divide this land unto you according to the tribes of Israel.
47:22 And it shall come to pass, that ye shall divide it by lot for an inheritance unto you, and to the strangers that sojourn among you, which shall beget children among you: and they shall be unto you as born in the country among the children of Israel; they shall have inheritance with you among the tribes of Israel.
47:23 And it shall come to pass, that in what tribe the stranger sojourneth, there shall ye give him his inheritance, saith the Lord GOD.

48

48:1 Now these are the names of the tribes. From the north end to the coast of the way of Hethlon, as one goeth to Hamath, Hazarenan, the border of Damascus northward, to the coast of Hamath; for these are his sides east and west; a portion for Dan.
48:2 And by the border of Dan, from the east side unto the west side, a portion for Asher.
48:3 And by the border of Asher, from the east side even unto the west side, a portion for Naphtali.
48:4 And by the border of Naphtali, from the east side unto the west side, a portion for Manasseh.
48:5 And by the border of Manasseh, from the east side unto the west side, a portion for Ephraim.
48:6 And by the border of Ephraim, from the east side even unto the west side, a portion for Reuben.
48:7 And by the border of Reuben, from the east side unto the west side, a portion for Judah.
48:8 And by the border of Judah, from the east side unto the west side, shall be the offering which ye shall offer of five and twenty thousand reeds in breadth, and in length as one of the other parts, from the east side unto the west side: and the sanctuary shall be in the midst of it.
48:9 The oblation that ye shall offer unto the LORD shall be of five and twenty thousand in length, and of ten thousand in breadth.
48:10 And for them, even for the priests, shall be this holy oblation; toward the north five and twenty thousand in length, and toward the west ten thousand in breadth, and toward the east ten thousand in breadth, and toward the south five and twenty thousand in length: and the sanctuary of the LORD shall be in the midst thereof.
48:11 It shall be for the priests that are sanctified of the sons of Zadok; which have kept my charge, which went not astray when the children of Israel went astray, as the Levites went astray.
48:12 And this oblation of the land that is offered shall be unto them a thing most holy by the border of the Levites.
48:13 And over against the border of the priests the Levites shall have five and twenty thousand in length, and ten thousand in breadth: all the length shall be five and twenty thousand, and the breadth ten

thousand.
48:14 And they shall not sell of it, neither exchange, nor alienate the firstfruits of the land: for it is holy unto the LORD.
48:15 And the five thousand, that are left in the breadth over against the five and twenty thousand, shall be a profane place for the city, for dwelling, and for suburbs: and the city shall be in the midst thereof.
48:16 And these shall be the measures thereof; the north side four thousand and five hundred, and the south side four thousand and five hundred, and on the east side four thousand and five hundred, and the west side four thousand and five hundred.
48:17 And the suburbs of the city shall be toward the north two hundred and fifty, and toward the south two hundred and fifty, and toward the east two hundred and fifty, and toward the west two hundred and fifty.
48:18 And the residue in length over against the oblation of the holy portion shall be ten thousand eastward, and ten thousand westward: and it shall be over against the oblation of the holy portion; and the increase thereof shall be for food unto them that serve the city.
48:19 And they that serve the city shall serve it out of all the tribes of Israel.
48:20 All the oblation shall be five and twenty thousand by five and twenty thousand: ye shall offer the holy oblation foursquare, with the possession of the city.
48:21 And the residue shall be for the prince, on the one side and on the other of the holy oblation, and of the possession of the city, over against the five and twenty thousand of the oblation toward the east border, and westward over against the five and twenty thousand toward the west border, over against the portions for the prince: and it shall be the holy oblation; and the sanctuary of the house shall be in the midst thereof.
48:22 Moreover from the possession of the Levites, and from the possession of the city, being in the midst of that which is the prince's, between the border of Judah and the border of Benjamin, shall be for the prince.
48:23 As for the rest of the tribes, from the east side unto the west side, Benjamin shall have a portion.
48:24 And by the border of Benjamin, from the east side unto the west side, Simeon shall have a portion.
48:25 And by the border of Simeon, from the east side unto the west side, Issachar a portion.
48:26 And by the border of Issachar, from the east side unto the west side, Zebulun a portion.
48:27 And by the border of Zebulun, from the east side unto the west side, Gad a portion.
48:28 And by the border of Gad, at the south side southward, the border shall be even from Tamar unto the waters of strife in Kadesh, and to the river toward the great sea.
48:29 This is the land which ye shall divide by lot unto the tribes of Israel for inheritance, and these are their portions, saith the Lord GOD.
48:30 And these are the goings out of the city on the north side, four thousand and five hundred measures.
48:31 And the gates of the city shall be after the names of the tribes of Israel: three gates northward; one gate of Reuben, one gate of Judah, one gate of Levi.
48:32 And at the east side four thousand and five hundred: and three gates; and one gate of Joseph, one gate of Benjamin, one gate of Dan.
48:33 And at the south side four thousand and five hundred measures: and three gates; one gate of Simeon, one gate of Issachar, one gate of Zebulun.
48:34 At the west side four thousand and five hundred, with their three gates; one gate of Gad, one gate of Asher, one gate of Naphtali.
48:35 It was round about eighteen thousand measures: and the name of the city from that day shall be, The LORD is there.

THE PROPHECY OF EZECHIEL

DOUAY RHEIMS BIBLE

EZECHIEL, whose name signifies the STRENGTH OF GOD, was of the priestly race; and of the number of captives that were carried away to Babylon with king JOACHIN. He was contemporary with JEREMIAS, and prophesied to the same effect in Babylon, as JEREMIAS did in Jerusalem; and is said to have ended his days in like manner, by martyrdom.

Ezechiel Chapter 1

The time of Ezechiel's prophecy: he sees a glorious vision.

1:1. Now it came to pass in the thirtieth year, in the fourth month, on the fifth day of the month, when I was in the midst of the captives by the river Chobar, the heavens were opened, and I saw the visions of God.
The thirtieth year... Either of the age of Ezechiel; or, as others will have it, from the solemn covenant made in the eighteenth year of the reign of Josias. 4 Kings 23.
1:2. On the fifth day of the month, the same was the fifth year of the captivity of king Joachin,
1:3. The word of the Lord came to Ezechiel the priest the son of Buzi in the land of the Chaldeans, by the river Chobar: and the hand of the Lord was there upon him.
1:4. And I saw, and behold a whirlwind came out of the north: and a great cloud, and a fire infolding it, and brightness was about it: and out of the midst thereof, that is, out of the midst of the fire, as it were the resemblance of amber:
1:5. And in the midst thereof the likeness of four living creatures: and this was their appearance: there was the likeness of a man in them.
Living creatures... Cherubims (as appears from Ecclesiasticus 49.10) represented to the prophet under these mysterious shapes, as supporting the throne of God, and as it were drawing his chariot. All this chapter appeared so obscure, and so full of mysteries to the ancient Hebrews, that, as we learn from St. Jerome, (Ep. ad Paulin.,) they suffered none to read it before they were thirty years old.
1:6. Every one had four faces, and every one four wings.
1:7. Their feet were straight feet, and the sole of their foot was like the sole of a calf's foot, and they sparkled like the appearance of glowing brass.
1:8. And they had the hands of a man under their wings on their four sides: and they had faces, and wings on the four sides,
1:9. And the wings of one were joined to the wings of another. They turned not when they went: but every one went straight forward.
1:10. And as for the likeness of their faces: there was the face of a man, and the face of a lion on the right side of all the four: and the face of an ox, on the left side of all the four: and the face of an eagle over all the four.
1:11. And their faces, and their wings were stretched upward: two wings of every one were joined, and two covered their bodies:
1:12. And every one of them went straight forward: whither the impulse of the spirit was to go, thither they went: and they turned not when they went.
1:13. And as for the likeness of the living creatures, their appearance was like that of burning coals of fire, and like the appearance of lamps. This was the vision running to and fro in the midst of the living creatures, a bright fire, and lightning going forth from the fire.
1:14. And the living creatures ran and returned like flashes of lightning.
1:15. Now as I beheld the living creatures, there appeared upon the earth by the living creatures one wheel with four faces.
1:16. And the appearance of the wheels, and the work of them was like the appearance of the sea: and

the four had all one likeness: and their appearance and their work was as it were a wheel in the midst of a wheel.
1:17. When they went, they went by their four parts: and they turned not when they went.
When they went, they went by their four parts... That is, indifferently to any of their sides either forward or backward: to the right or to the left.
1:18. The wheels had also a size, and a height, and a dreadful appearance: and the whole body was full of eyes round about all the four.
1:19. And, when the living creatures went, the wheels also went together by them: and when the living creatures were lifted up from the earth, the wheels also were lifted up with them.
1:20. Withersoever the spirit went, thither as the spirit went the wheels also were lifted up withal, and followed it: for the spirit of life was in the wheels.
1:21. When those went these went, and when those stood these stood, and when those were lifted up from the earth, the wheels were lifted up together, and followed them: for the spirit of life was in the wheels.
1:22. And over the heads of the living creatures was the likeness of the firmament, the appearance of crystal terrible to behold, and stretched out over their heads above.
1:23. And under the firmament were their wings straight, the one toward the other, every one with two wings covered his body, and the other was covered in like manner.
1:24. And I heard the noise of their wings, like the noise of many waters, as it were the voice of the most high God: when they walked, it was like the voice of a multitude, like the noise of an army, and when they stood, their wings were let down.
1:25. For when a voice came from above the firmament, that was over their heads, they stood, and let down their wings.
1:26. And above the firmament that was over their heads, was the likeness of a throne, as the appearance of the sapphire stone, and upon the likeness of the throne, was the likeness of the appearance of a man above upon it.
1:27. And I saw as it were the resemblance of amber as the appearance of fire within it round about: from his loins and upward, and from his loins downward, I saw as it were the resemblance of fire shining round about.
1:28. As the appearance of the rainbow when it is in a cloud on a rainy day: this was the appearance of the brightness round about.

Ezechiel Chapter 2

The prophet receives his commission.

2:1. This was the vision of the likeness of the glory of the Lord, and I saw, and I fell upon my face, and I heard the voice of one that spoke, and he said to me: Son of man, stand upon thy feet, and I will speak to thee.
2:2. And the spirit entered into me after that he spoke to me, and he set me upon my feet: and I heard him speaking to me,
2:3. And saying: Son of man, I send thee to the children of Israel, to a rebellious people, that hath revolted from me, they, and their fathers, have transgressed my covenant even unto this day.
2:4. And they to whom I send thee are children of a hard face, and of an obstinate heart: and thou shalt say to them: Thus saith the Lord God:
2:5. If so be they at least will hear, and if so be they will forbear, for they are a provoking house: and they shall know that there hath been a prophet in the midst of them.
2:6. And thou, O son of man, fear not, neither be thou afraid of their words: for thou art among unbelievers and destroyers, and thou dwellest with scorpions. Fear not their words, neither be thou dismayed at their looks: for they are a provoking house.
2:7. And thou shalt speak my words to them, if perhaps they will hear, and forbear: for they provoke me to anger.
2:8. But thou, O son of man, hear all that I say to thee: and do not thou provoke me, as that house provoketh me: open thy mouth, and eat what I give thee.
2:9. And I looked, and behold, a hand was sent to me, wherein was a book rolled up: and he spread it before me, and it was written within and without: and there were written in it lamentations, and canticles, and woe.

Ezechiel Chapter 3

The prophet eats the book, and receives further instructions: the office of a watchman.

3:1. And he said to me: Son of man, eat all that thou shalt find: eat this book, and go speak to the children of Israel.
Eat this book, and go speak to the children of Israel... By this eating of the book was signified the diligent attention and affection with which we are to receive, and embrace the word of God; and to let it, as it were, sink into our interior by devout meditation.
3:2. And I opened my mouth, and he caused me to eat that book:
3:3. And he said to me: Son of man, thy belly shall eat, and thy bowels shall be filled with this book, which I give thee, and I did eat it: and it was sweet as honey in my mouth.
3:4. And he said to me: Son of man, go to the house of Israel, and thou shalt speak my words to them.
3:5. For thou art not sent to a people of a profound speech, and of an unknown tongue, but to the house of Israel:
3:6. Nor to many nations of a strange speech, and of an unknown tongue, whose words thou canst not understand: and if thou wert sent to them, they would hearken to thee.
3:7. But the house of Israel will not hearken to thee: because they will not hearken to me: for all the house of Israel are of a hard forehead and an obstinate heart.
3:8. Behold I have made thy face stronger than their faces: and thy forehead harder than their foreheads.
3:9. I have made thy face like an adamant and like flint: fear them not, neither be thou dismayed at their presence: for they are a provoking house.
3:10. And he said to me: Son of man, receive in thy heart, and hear with thy ears, all the words that I speak to thee:
3:11. And go get thee in to them of the captivity, to the children of thy people, and thou shalt speak to them, and shalt say to them: Thus saith the Lord: If so be they will hear, and will forbear.
3:12. And the spirit took me up, and I heard behind me the voice of a great commotion, saying: Blessed be the glory of the Lord, from his place.
3:13. The noise of the wings of the living creatures striking one against another, and the noise of the wheels following the living creatures, and the noise of a great commotion.
3:14. The spirit also lifted me, and took me up: and I went away in bitterness in the indignation of my spirit: for the hand of the Lord was with me, strengthening me.
3:15. And I came to them of the captivity, to the heap of new corn, to them that dwelt by the river Chobar, and I sat where they sat: and I remained there seven days mourning in the midst of them.
The heap of new corn... It was the name of a place: in Hebrew, tel abib.
3:16. And at the end of seven days the word of the Lord came to me, saying:
3:17. Son of man, I have made thee a watchman to the house of Israel: and thou shalt hear the word out of my mouth, and shalt tell it them from me.
3:18. If, when I say to the wicked, Thou shalt surely die: thou declare it not to him, nor speak to him, that he may be converted from his wicked way, and live: the same wicked man shall die in his iniquity, but I will require his blood at thy hand.
3:19. But if thou give warning to the wicked, and he be not converted from his wickedness, and from his evil way: he indeed shall die in his iniquity, but thou hast delivered thy soul.
3:20. Moreover if the just man shall turn away from his justice, and shall commit iniquity: I will lay a stumblingblock before him, he shall die, because thou hast not given him warning: he shall die in his sin, and his justices which he hath done, shall not be remembered: but I will require his blood at thy hand.
3:21. But if thou warn the just man, that the just may not sin, and he doth not sin: living he shall live, because thou hast warned him, and thou hast delivered thy soul.
3:22. And the hand of the Lord was upon me, and he said to me: Rise and go forth into the plain, and there I will speak to thee.
3:23. And I rose up, and went forth into the plain: and behold the glory of the Lord stood there, like the glory which I saw by the river Chobar: and I fell upon my face.
3:24. And the spirit entered into me, and set me upon my feet: and he spoke to me, and said to me: Go in; and shut thyself up in the midst of thy house.
3:25. And thou, O son of man, behold they shall put bands upon thee, and they shall bind thee with them: and thou shalt not go forth from the midst of them.
3:26. And I will make thy tongue stick fast to the roof of thy mouth, and thou shalt be dumb, and not as a man that reproveth: because they are a provoking house.
3:27. But when I shall speak to thee, I will open thy mouth, and thou shalt say to them: Thus saith the Lord God: He that heareth, let him hear: and he that forbeareth, let him forbear: for they are a

provoking house.

Ezechiel Chapter 4

A prophetic description of the siege of Jerusalem, and the famine that shall reign there.

4:1. And thou, O son of man, take thee a tile, and lay it before thee: and draw upon it the plan of the city of Jerusalem.
4:2. And lay siege against it, and build forts, and cast up a mount, and set a camp against it, and place battering rams round about it.
4:3. And take unto thee an iron pan, and set it for a wall of iron between thee and the city: and set thy face resolutely against it, and it shall be besieged, and thou shalt lay siege against it: it is a sign to the house of Israel.
4:4. And thou shalt sleep upon thy left side, and shalt lay the iniquities of the house of Israel upon it, according to the number of the days that thou shalt sleep upon it, and thou shalt take upon thee their iniquity.
4:5. And I have laid upon thee the years of their iniquity, according to the number of the days three hundred and ninety days: and thou shalt bear the iniquity of the house of Israel.
4:6. And when thou hast accomplished this, thou shalt sleep again upon thy right side, and thou shalt take upon thee the iniquity of the house of Juda forty days: a day for a year, yea, a day for a year I have appointed to thee.
4:7. And thou shalt turn thy face to the siege of Jerusalem and thy arm shall be stretched out: and thou shalt prophesy against it.
4:8. Behold I have encompassed thee with bands: and thou shalt not turn thyself from one side to the other, till thou hast ended the days of thy siege.
4:9. And take to thee wheat and barley, and beans, and lentils, and millet, and fitches, and put them in one vessel, and make thee bread thereof according to the number of the days that thou shalt lie upon thy side: three hundred and ninety days shalt thou eat thereof.
4:10. And thy meat that thou shalt eat, shall be in weight twenty staters a day: from time to time thou shalt eat it.
4:11. And thou shalt drink water by measure, the sixth part of a hin: from time to time thou shalt drink it,
Hin... That is, a measure of liquids containing about ten pints.
4:12. And thou shalt eat it as barley bread baked under the ashes: and thou shalt cover it, in their sight, with the dung that cometh out of a man.
4:13. And the Lord said: So shall the children of Israel eat their bread all filthy among the nations whither I will cast them out.
4:14. And I said: Ah, ah, ah, O Lord God, behold my soul hath not been defiled, and from my infancy even till now, I have not eaten any thing that died of itself, or was torn by beasts, and no unclean flesh hath entered into my mouth.
4:15. And he said to me: Behold I have given thee neat's dung for man's dung, and thou shalt make thy bread therewith.
4:16. And he said to me: Son of man: Behold, I will break in pieces the staff of bread in Jerusalem: and they shall eat bread by weight, and with care: and they shall drink water by measure, and in distress.
4:17. So that when bread and water fail, every man may fall against his brother, and they may pine away in their iniquities.

Ezechiel Chapter 5

The judgments of God upon the Jews are foreshewn under the type of the prophet's hair.

5:1. And thou, son of man, take thee a sharp knife that shaveth the hair: and cause it to pass over thy head, and over thy beard: and take thee a balance to weigh in, and divide the hair.
5:2. A third part thou shalt burn with fire in the midst of the city, according to the fulfilling of the days of the siege: and thou shalt take a third part, and cut it in pieces with the knife all round about: and the other third part thou shalt scatter in the wind, and I will draw out the sword after them.
5:3. And thou shalt take thereof a small number: and shalt bind them in the skirt of thy cloak.
5:4. And thou shalt take of them again, and shalt cast them in the midst of the fire, and shalt burn them with fire: and out of it shall come forth a fire into all the house of Israel.

5:5. Thus saith the Lord God: This is Jerusalem, I have set her in the midst of the nations, and the countries round about her.
5:6. And she hath despised my judgments, so as to be more wicked than the Gentiles; and my commandments, more than the countries that are round about her: for they have cast off my judgments, and have not walked in my commandments.
5:7. Therefore thus saith the Lord God: Because you have surpassed the Gentiles that are round about you, and have not walked in my commandments, and have not kept my judgments, and have not done according to the judgments of the nations that are round about you:
5:8. Therefore thus saith the Lord God: Behold I come against thee, and I myself will execute judgments in the midst of thee in the sight of the Gentiles.
5:9. And I will do in thee that which I have not done: and the like to which I will do no more, because of all thy abominations.
5:10. Therefore the fathers shall eat the sons in the midst of thee, and the sons shall eat their fathers: and I will execute judgments in thee, and I will scatter thy whole remnant into every wind.
5:11. Therefore as I live, saith the Lord God: Because thou hast violated my sanctuary with all thy offences, and with all thy abominations: I will also break thee in pieces, and my eye shall not spare, and I will not have any pity.
5:12. A third part of thee shall die with the pestilence, and shall be consumed with famine in the midst of thee: and a third part of thee shall fall by the sword round about thee: and a third part of thee will I scatter into every wind, and I will draw out a sword after them.
5:13. And I will accomplish my fury, and will cause my indignation to rest upon them, and I will be comforted: and they shall know that I the Lord have spoken it in my zeal, when I shall have accomplished my indignation in them.
5:14. And I will make thee desolate, and a reproach among the nations that are round about thee, in the sight of every one that passeth by.
5:15. And thou shalt be a reproach, and a scoff, an example, and an astonishment amongst the nations that are round about thee, when I shall have executed judgments in thee in anger, and in indignation, and in wrathful rebukes.
5:16. I the Lord have spoken it: When I shall send upon them the grievous arrows of famine, which shall bring death, and which I will send to destroy you: and I will gather together famine against you: and I will break among you the staff of bread.
5:17. And I will send in upon you famine, and evil beasts unto utter destruction: and pestilence, and blood shall pass through thee, and I will bring in the sword upon thee. I the Lord have spoken it.

Ezechiel Chapter 6

The punishment of Israel for their idolatry: a remnant shall be saved.

6:1. And the word of the Lord came to me, saying:
6:2. Son of man set thy face towards the mountains of Israel, and prophesy against them.
6:3. And say: Ye mountains of Israel, hear the word of the Lord God: Thus saith the Lord God to the mountains, and to the hills, and to the rocks, and the valleys: Behold, I will bring upon you the sword, and I will destroy your high places.
6:4. And I will throw down your altars, and your idols shall be broken in pieces: and I will cast down your slain before your idols.
6:5. And I will lay the dead carcasses of the children of Israel before your idols: and I will scatter your bones round about your altars,
6:6. In all your dwelling places. The cities shall be laid waste, and the high places shall be thrown down, and destroyed, and your altars shall be abolished, and shall be broken in pieces: and your idols shall be no more, and your temples shall be destroyed, and your works shall be defaced.
6:7. And the slain shall fall in the midst of you: and you shall know that I am the Lord.
6:8. And I will leave in you some that shall escape the sword among the nations, when I shall have scattered you through the countries.
6:9. And they that are saved of you shall remember me amongst the nations, to which they are carried captives: because I have broken their heart that was faithless, and revolted from me: and their eyes that went a fornicating after their idols: and they shall be displeased with themselves because of the evils which they have committed in all their abominations.
6:10. And they shall know that I the Lord have not spoken in vain that I would do this evil to them.
6:11. Thus saith the Lord God: Strike with thy hand and stamp with thy foot, and say: Alas, for all the

abominations of the evils of the house of Israel: for they shall fall by the sword, by the famine, and by the pestilence.
6:12. He that is far off shall die of the pestilence: and he that is near, shall fall by the sword: and he that remaineth, and is besieged, shall die by the famine: and I will accomplish my indignation upon them.
6:13. And you shall know that I am the Lord, when your slain shall be amongst your idols, round about your altars, in every high hill, and on all the tops of mountains, and under every woody tree, and under every thick oak, the place where they burnt sweet smelling frankincense to all their idols.
6:14. And I will stretch forth my hand upon them: and I will make the land desolate, and abandoned from the desert of Deblatha in all their dwelling places: and they shall know that I am the Lord.

Ezechiel Chapter 7

The final desolation of Israel: from which few shall escape.
7:1. And the word of the Lord came to me, saying:
7:2. And thou son of man, thus saith the Lord God to the land of Israel: The end is come, the end is come upon the four quarters of the land.
7:3. Now is an end come upon thee, and I will send my wrath upon thee, and I will judge thee according to thy ways: and I will set all thy abominations against thee.
7:4. And my eye shall not spare thee, and I will shew thee no pity: but I will lay thy ways upon thee, and thy abominations shall be in the midst of thee: and you shall know that I am the Lord.
7:5. Thus saith the Lord God: One affliction, behold an affliction is come.
7:6. An end is come, the end is come, it hath awaked against thee: behold it is come.
7:7. Destruction is come upon thee that dwellest in the land: the time is come, the day of slaughter is near, and not of the joy of mountains.
7:8. Now very shortly I will pour out my wrath upon thee, and I will accomplish my anger in thee: and I will judge thee according to thy ways, and I will lay upon thee all thy crimes.
7:9. And my eye shall not spare, neither will I shew mercy: but I will lay thy ways upon thee, and thy abominations shall be in the midst of thee: and you shall know that I am the Lord that strike.
7:10. Behold the day, behold it is come: destruction is gone forth, the rod hath blossomed, pride hath budded.
7:11. Iniquity is risen up into a rod of impiety: nothing of them shall remain, nor of their people, nor of the noise of them: and there shall be no rest among them.
7:12. The time is come, the day is at hand: let not the buyer rejoice: nor the seller mourn: for wrath is upon all the people thereof.
7:13. For the seller shall not return to that which he hath sold, although their life be yet among the living. For the vision which regardeth all the multitude thereof, shall not go back: neither shall man be strengthened in the iniquity of his life.
7:14. Blow the trumpet, let all be made ready, yet there is none to go to the battle: for my wrath shall be upon all the people thereof.
7:15. The sword without: and the pestilence, and the famine within: he that is in the field shall die by the sword: and they that are in the city, shall be devoured by the pestilence, and the famine.
7:16. And such of them as shall flee shall escape: and they shall be in the mountains like doves of the valleys, all of them trembling, every one for his iniquity.
7:17. All hands shall be made feeble, and all knees shall run with water.
7:18. And they shall gird themselves with haircloth, and fear shall cover them and shame shall be upon every face, and baldness upon all their heads.
7:19. Their silver shall be cast forth, and their gold shall become a dunghill. Their silver and their gold shall not be able to deliver them in the day of the wrath of the Lord. They shall not satisfy their soul, and their bellies shall not be filled: because it hath been the stumblingblock of their iniquity.
7:20. And they have turned the ornament of their jewels into pride, and have made of it the images of their abominations, and idols: therefore I have made it an uncleanness to them.
7:21. And I will give it into the hands of strangers for spoil, and to the wicked of the earth for a prey, and they shall defile it.
7:22. And I will turn away my face from them, and they shall violate my secret place: and robbers shall enter into it, and defile it.
Secret place, etc... Viz., the inward sanctuary, the holy of holies.
7:23. Make a shutting up: for the land is full of the judgment of blood, and the city is full of iniquity.
Make a shutting up... In Hebrew, a chain, viz., for imprisonment and captivity.
7:24. And I will bring the worst of the nations, and they shall possess their houses: and I will make the

pride of the mighty to cease, and they shall possess their sanctuary.
7:25. When distress cometh upon them, they will seek for peace and there shall be none.
7:26. Trouble shall come upon trouble, and rumour upon rumour, and they shall seek a vision of the prophet, and the law shall perish from the priest, and counsel from the ancients.
7:27. The king shall mourn, and the prince shall be clothed with sorrow, and the hands of the people of the land shall be troubled. I will do to them according to their way, and will judge them according to their judgments: and they shall know that I am the Lord.

Ezechiel Chapter 8

The prophet sees in a vision the abominations committed in Jerusalem; which determine the Lord to spare them no longer.

8:1. And it came to pass in the sixth year, in the sixth month, in the fifth day of the month, as I sat in my house, and the ancients of Juda sat before me, that the hand of the Lord God fell there upon me.
8:2. And I saw, and behold a likeness as the appearance of fire: from the appearance of his loins, and downward, fire: and from his loins, and upward, as the appearance of brightness, as the appearance of amber.
8:3. And the likeness of a hand was put forth and took me by a lock of my head: and the spirit lifted me up between the earth and the heaven, and brought me in the vision of God into Jerusalem, near the inner gate, that looked toward the north, where was set the idol of jealousy to provoke to jealousy.
8:4. And behold the glory of the God of Israel was there, according to the vision which I had seen in the plain.
8:5. And he said to me: Son of man, lift up thy eyes towards the way of the north, and I lifted up my eyes towards the way of the north: and behold on the north side of the gate of the altar the idol of jealousy in the very entry.
8:6. And he said to me: Son of man, dost thou see, thinkest thou, what these are doing, the great abominations that the house of Israel committeth here, that I should depart far off from my sanctuary? and turn thee yet again and thou shalt see greater abominations.
8:7. And he brought me in to the door of the court: and I saw, and behold a hole in the wall.
8:8. And he said to me: Son of man, dig in the wall, and when I had digged in the wall, behold a door.
8:9. And he said to me: Go in, and see the wicked abominations which they commit here.
8:10. And I went in and saw, and behold every form of creeping things, and of living creatures, the abominations, and all the idols of the house of Israel, were painted on the wall all round about.
8:11. And seventy men of the ancients of the house of Israel, and Jezonias the son of Saaphan stood in the midst of them, that stood before the pictures: and every one had a censer in his hand: and a cloud of smoke went up from the incense.
8:12. And he said to me: Surely thou seest, O son of man, what the ancients of the house of Israel do in the dark, every one in private in his chamber: for they say: The Lord seeth us not, the Lord hath forsaken the earth.
8:13. And he said to me: If thou turn thee again, thou shalt see greater abominations which these commit.
8:14. And he brought me in by the door of the gate of the Lord's house, which looked to the north: and behold women sat there mourning for Adonis.
Adonis... The favourite of Venus, slain by a wild boar, as feigned by the heathen poets, and which being here represented by an idol, is lamented by the female worshippers of that goddess. In the Hebrew, the name is Tammuz.
8:15. And he said to me: Surely thou hast seen, O son of man: but turn thee again, thou shalt see greater abominations than these.
8:16. And he brought me into the inner court of the house of the Lord: and behold at the door of the temple of the Lord, between the porch and the altar, were about five and twenty men having their backs towards the temple of the Lord, in their faces to the east: and they adored towards the rising of the sun.
8:17. And he said to me: Surely thou hast seen, O son of man: is this a light thing to the house of Juda, that they should commit these abominations which they have committed here: because they have filled the land with iniquity, and have turned to provoke me to anger? and behold they put a branch to their nose.
8:18. Therefore I also will deal with them in my wrath: my eye shall not spare them, neither will I shew mercy: and when they shall cry to my ears with a loud voice, I will not hear them.

Ezechiel Chapter 9

All are ordered to be destroyed that are not marked in their foreheads. God will not be entreated for them.

9:1. And he cried in my ears with a loud voice, saying: The visitations of the city are at hand, and every one hath a destroying weapon in his hand.
9:2. And behold six men came from the way of the upper gate, which looketh to the north: and each one had his weapon of destruction in his hand: and there was one man in the midst of them clothed with linen, with a writer's inkhorn at his reins: and they went in, and stood by the brazen altar.
9:3. And the glory of the Lord of Israel went up from the cherub, upon which he was, to the threshold of the house: and he called to the man that was clothed with linen, and had a writer's inkhorn at his loins.
9:4. And the Lord said to him: Go through the midst of the city, through the midst of Jerusalem: and mark Thau upon the foreheads of the men that sigh, and mourn for all the abominations that are committed in the midst thereof.
Mark Thau... Thau, or Tau, is the last letter in the Hebrew alphabet, and signifies a sign, or a mark; which is the reason why some translators render this place set a mark, or mark a mark without specifying what this mark was. But St. Jerome, and other interpreters, conclude it was the form of the letter Thau, which in the ancient Hebrew character, was the form of a cross.
9:5. And to the others he said in my hearing: Go ye after him through the city, and strike: let not your eyes spare, nor be ye moved with pity.
9:6. Utterly destroy old and young, maidens, children and women: but upon whomsoever you shall see Thau, kill him not, and begin ye at my sanctuary. So they began at the ancient men who were before the house.
9:7. And he said to them: Defile the house, and fill the courts with the slain: go ye forth. And they went forth, and slew them that were in the city.
9:8. And the slaughter being ended I was left; and I fell upon my face, and crying, I said: Alas, alas, alas, O Lord God, wilt thou then destroy all the remnant of Israel, by pouring out thy fury upon Jerusalem?
9:9. And he said to me: The iniquity of the house of Israel, and of Juda, is exceeding great, and the land is filled with blood, and the city is filled with perverseness: for they have said: The Lord hath forsaken the earth, and the Lord seeth not.
9:10. Therefore neither shall my eye spare, nor will I have pity: I will requite their way upon their head.
9:11. And behold the man that was clothed with linen, that had the inkhorn at his back, returned the word, saying: I have done as thou hast commanded me.

Ezechiel Chapter 10

Fire is taken from the midst of the wheels under the cherubims, and scattered over the city. A description of the cherubims.

10:1. And I saw and behold in the firmament that was over the heads of the cherubims, there appeared over them as it were the sapphire stone, as the appearance of the likeness of a throne.
10:2. And he spoke to the man, that was clothed with linen, and said: Go in between the wheels that are under the cherubims and fill thy hand with the coals of fire that are between the cherubims, and pour them out upon the city. And he went in, in my sight:
10:3. And the cherubims stood on the right side of the house, when the man went in, and a cloud filled the inner court.
10:4. And the glory of the Lord was lifted up from above the cherub to the threshold of the house: and the house was filled with the cloud, and the court was filled with the brightness of the glory of the Lord.
10:5. And the sound of the wings of the cherubims was heard even to the outward court as the voice of God Almighty speaking.
10:6. And when he had commanded the man that was clothed with linen, saying: Take fire from the midst of the wheels that are between the cherubims: he went in and stood beside the wheel.
10:7. And one cherub stretched out his arm from the midst of the cherubims to the fire that was between the cherubims: and he took, and put it into the hands of him that was clothed with linen: who took it and went forth.
10:8. And there appeared in the cherubims the likeness of a man's hand under their wings.
10:9. And I saw, and behold there were four wheels by the cherubims: one wheel by one cherub, and

another wheel by another cherub: and the appearance of the wheels was to the sight like the chrysolite stone:
10:10. And as to their appearance, all four were alike: as if a wheel were in the midst of a wheel.
10:11. And when they went, they went by four ways: and they turned not when they went: but to the place whither they first turned, the rest also followed, and did not turn back.
By four ways... That is, by any of the four ways, forward, backward, to the right or to the left.
10:12. And their whole body, and their necks, and their hands, and their wings, and the circles were full of eyes, round about the four wheels.
10:13. And these wheels he called voluble, in my hearing.
Voluble... That is, rolling wheels, galgal.
10:14. And every one had four faces: one face was the face of a cherub, and the second face, the face of a man: and in the third was the face of a lion: and in the fourth the face of an eagle.
10:15. And the cherubims were lifted up: this is the living creature that I had seen by the river Chobar.
10:16. And when the cherubims went, the wheels also went by them: and when the cherubims lifted up their wings, to mount up from the earth, the wheels stayed not behind, but were by them.
10:17. When they stood, these stood: and when they were lifted up, these were lifted up: for the spirit of life was in them.
10:18. And the glory of the Lord went forth from the threshold of the temple: and stood over the cherubims.
10:19. And the cherubims lifting up their wings, were raised from the earth before me: and as they went out, the wheels also followed: and it stood in the entry of the east gate of the house of the Lord: and the glory of the God of Israel was over them.
10:20. This is the living creature, which I saw under the God of Israel by the river Chobar: and I understood that they were cherubims.
10:21. Each one had four faces, and each one had four wings: and the likeness of a man's hand was under their wings.
10:22. And as to the likeness of their faces, they were the same faces which I had seen by the river Chobar, and their looks, and the impulse of every one to go straight forward.

Ezechiel Chapter 11

A prophecy against the presumptuous assurance of the great ones. A remnant shall be saved, and receive a new spirit, and a new heart.

11:1. And the spirit lifted me up, and brought me into the east gate of the house of the Lord, which looketh towards the rising of the sun: and behold in the entry of the gate five and twenty men: and I saw in the midst of them Jezonias the son of Azur, and Pheltias the son of Banaias, princes of the people.
11:2. And he said to me: Son of man, these are the men that study iniquity, and frame a wicked counsel in this city,
11:3. Saying: Were not houses lately built? This city is the caldron, and we the flesh.
Were not houses lately built, etc... These men despised the predictions and threats of the prophets; who declared to them from God, that the city should be destroyed, and the inhabitants carried into captivity: and they made use of this kind of argument against the prophets, that the city, so far from being like to be destroyed, had lately been augmented by the building of new houses; from whence they further inferred, by way of a proverb, using the similitude of a cauldron, out of which the flesh is not taken, till it is thoroughly boiled, and fit to be eaten, that they should not be carried away out of their city, but there end their days in peace.
11:4. Therefore prophesy against them, prophesy, thou son of man.
11:5. And the spirit of the Lord fell upon me, and said to me: Speak: Thus saith the Lord: Thus have you spoken, O house of Israel, for I know the thoughts of your heart.
11:6. You have killed a great many in this city, and you have filled the streets thereof with the slain.
11:7. Therefore thus saith the Lord God: Your slain, whom you have laid in the midst thereof, they are the flesh, all this is the caldron: and I will bring you forth out of the midst thereof.
11:8. You have feared the sword, and I will bring the sword upon you, saith the Lord God.
11:9. And I will cast you out of the midst thereof, and I will deliver you into the hand of the enemies, and I will execute judgments upon you.
11:10. You shall fall by the sword: I will judge you in the borders of Israel, and you shall know that I am the Lord.
In the borders of Israel... They pretended that they should die in peace in Jerusalem; God tells them it

should not be so; but that they should be judged and condemned, and fall by the sword in the borders of Israel: viz., in Reblatha in the land of Emath, where all their chief men were put to death by Nabuchodonosor. 4 Kings 25., and Jer. 52.10, 27.
11:11. This shall not be as a caldron to you, and you shall not be as flesh in the midst thereof: I will judge you in the borders of Israel.
11:12. And you shall know that I am the Lord: because you have not walked in my commandments, and have not done my judgments, but you have done according to the judgments of the nations that are round about you.
11:13. And it came to pass, when I prophesied, that Pheltias the son of Banaias died: and I fell down upon my face, and I cried with a loud voice: and said: Alas, alas, alas, O Lord God: wilt thou make an end of all the remnant of Israel?
11:14. And the word of the Lord came to me, saying:
11:15. Son of man, thy brethren, thy brethren, thy kinsmen, and all the house of Israel, all they to whom the inhabitants of Jerusalem have said: Get ye far from the Lord, the land is given in possession to us.
Thy brethren, etc... He speaks of them that had been carried away captives before; who were despised by them that remained in Jerusalem: but as the prophet here declares to them from God, should be in a more happy condition than they, and after some time return from their captivity.
11:16. Therefore thus saith the Lord God: Because I have removed them far off among the Gentiles, and because I have scattered them among the countries: I will be to them a little sanctuary in the countries whither they are come.
11:17. Therefore speak to them: Thus saith the Lord God: I will gather you from among the peoples, and assemble you out of the countries wherein you are scattered, and I will give you the land of Israel.
11:18. And they shall go in thither, and shall take away all the scandals, and all the abominations thereof from thence.
11:19. And I will give them one heart, and will put a new spirit in their bowels: and I will take away the stony heart out of their flesh, and will give them a heart of flesh:
11:20. That they may walk in my commandments, and keep my judgments, and do them: and that they may be my people, and I may be their God.
11:21. But as for them whose heart walketh after their scandals and abominations, I will lay their way upon their head, saith the Lord God.
11:22. And the cherubims lifted up their wings, and the wheels with them: and the glory of the God of Israel was over them.
11:23. And the glory of the Lord went up from the midst of the city, and stood over the mount that is on the east side of the city.
11:24. And the spirit lifted me up, and brought me into Chaldea, to them of the captivity, in vision, by the spirit of God: and the vision which I had seen was taken up from me.
11:25. And I spoke to them of the captivity all the words of the Lord, which he had shewn me.

Ezechiel Chapter 12

The prophet forsheweth, by signs, the captivity of Sedecias, and the desolation of the people: all which shall quickly come to pass.
12:1. And the word of the Lord came to me, saying:
12:2. Son of man, thou dwellest in the midst of a provoking house: who have eyes to see, and see not: and ears to hear, and hear not: for they are a provoking house.
12:3. Thou, therefore, O son of man, prepare thee all necessaries for removing, and remove by day into their sight: and thou shalt remove out of thy place to another place in their sight, if so be they will regard it: for they are a provoking house.
12:4. And thou shalt bring forth thy furniture as the furniture of one that is removing by day in their sight: and thou shalt go forth in the evening in their presence, as one goeth forth that removeth his dwelling.
12:5. Dig thee a way through the wall before their eyes: and thou shalt go forth through it.
12:6. In their sight thou shalt be carried out upon men's shoulders, thou shalt be carried out in the dark: thou shalt cover thy face, and shalt not see the ground: for I have set thee for a sign of things to come to the house of Israel.
12:7. I did therefore as he had commanded me: I brought forth my goods by day, as the goods of one that removeth: and in the evening I digged through the wall with my hand, and I went forth in the dark, and was carried on men's shoulders in their sight.
12:8. And the word of the Lord came to me in the morning, saying:

12:9. Son of man, hath not the house of Israel, the provoking house, said to thee: What art thou doing?
12:10. Say to them: Thus saith the Lord God: This burden concerneth my prince that is in Jerusalem, and all the house of Israel, that are among them.
12:11. Say: I am a sign of things to come to you: as I have done, so shall it be done to them: they shall be removed from their dwellings, and go into captivity.
12:12. And the prince that is in the midst of them, shall be carried on shoulders, he shall go forth in the dark: they shall dig through the wall to bring him out: his face shall be covered, that he may not see the ground with his eyes.
12:13. And I will spread my net over him, and he shall be taken in my net: and I will bring him into Babylon, into the land of the Chaldeans, and he shall not see it, and there he shall die.
He shall not see it... Because his eyes shall be put out by Nabuchodonosor.
12:14. And all that are about him, his guards, and his troops I will scatter into every wind: and I will draw out the sword after them.
12:15. And they shall know that I am the Lord, when I shall have dispersed them among the nations, and scattered them in the countries.
12:16. And I will leave a few men of them from the sword, and from the famine, and from the pestilence: that they may declare all their wicked deeds among the nations whither they shall go: and they shall know that I am the Lord.
12:17. And the word of the Lord came to me, saying:
12:18. Son of man, eat thy bread in trouble and drink thy water in hurry and sorrow.
12:19. And say to the people of the land: Thus saith the Lord God to them that dwell in Jerusalem in the land of Israel: They shall eat their bread in care, and drink their water in desolation: that the land may become desolate from the multitude that is therein, for the iniquity of all that dwell therein.
12:20. And the cities that are now inhabited shall be laid waste, and the land shall be desolate: and you shall know that I am the Lord.
12:21. And the word of the Lord came to me, saying:
12:22. Son of man, what is this proverb that you have in the land of Israel? saying: The days shall be prolonged, and every vision shall fail.
12:23. Say to them therefore: Thus saith the Lord God: I will make this proverb to cease, neither shall it be any more a common saying in Israel: and tell them that the days are at hand, and the effect of every vision.
12:24. For there shall be no more any vain visions, nor doubtful divination in the midst of the children of Israel.
12:25. For I the Lord will speak: and what word soever I shall speak, it shall come to pass, and shall not be prolonged any more: but in your days, ye provoking house, I will speak the word, and will do it, saith the Lord God.
12:26. And the word of the Lord came to me, saying:
12:27. Son of man, behold the house of Israel, they that say: The visions that this man seeth, is for many days to come: and this man prophesieth of times afar off.
12:28. Therefore say to them: Thus saith the Lord God: not one word of mine shall be prolonged any more: the word that I shall speak shall be accomplished, saith the Lord God.

Ezechiel Chapter 13

God declares against false prophets and prophetesses, that deceive the people with lies.
13:1. And the word of the Lord came to me, saying:
13:2. Son of man, prophesy thou against the prophets of Israel that prophesy: and thou shalt say to them that prophesy out of their own heart: Hear ye the word of the Lord:
13:3. Thus saith the Lord God: Woe to the foolish prophets that follow their own spirit, and see nothing.
13:4. Thy prophets, O Israel, were like foxes in the deserts.
13:5. You have not gone up to face the enemy, nor have you set up a wall for the house of Israel, to stand in battle in the day of the Lord.
13:6. They see vain things, and they foretell lies, saying: The Lord saith: whereas the Lord hath not sent them: and they have persisted to confirm what they have said.
13:7. Have you not seen a vain vision and spoken a lying divination: and you say: The Lord saith: whereas I have not spoken.
13:8. Therefore thus saith the Lord God: Because you have spoken vain things, and have seen lies: therefore behold I come against you, saith the Lord God.

13:9. And my hand shall be upon the prophets that see vain things, and that divine lies: they shall not be in the council of my people, nor shall they be written in the writing of the house of Israel, neither shall they enter into the land of Israel, and you shall know that I am the Lord God.
13:10. Because they have deceived my people, saying: Peace, and there is no peace: and the people built up a wall, and they daubed it with dirt without straw.
13:11. Say to them that daub without tempering, that it shall fall: for there shall be an overflowing shower, and I will cause great hailstones to fall violently from above, and a stormy wind to throw it down.
13:12. Behold, when the wall is fallen: shall it not be said to you: Where is the daubing wherewith you have daubed it?
13:13. Therefore thus saith the Lord God: Lo, I will cause a stormy wind to break forth in my indignation, and there shall be an overflowing shower in my anger: and great hailstones in my wrath to consume.
13:14. And I will break down the wall that you have daubed with untempered mortar: and I will make it even with the ground, and the foundation thereof shall be laid bare: and it shall fall, and shall be consumed in the midst thereof: and you shall know that I am the Lord.
13:15. And I will accomplish my wrath upon the wall, and upon them that daub it without tempering the mortar, and I will say to you: The wall is no more, and they that daub it are no more.
13:16. Even the prophets of Israel that prophesy to Jerusalem, and that see visions of peace for her: and there is no peace, saith the Lord God.
13:17. And thou, son of man, set thy face against the daughters of thy people that prophesy out of their own heart: and do thou prophesy against them,
13:18. And say: Thus saith the Lord God: Woe to them that sew cushions under every elbow: and make pillows for the heads of persons of every age to catch souls: and when they caught the souls of my people, they gave life to their souls.
Sew cushions, etc... Viz., by making people easy in their sins, and promising them impunity.-Ibid. They gave life to their souls... That is, they flattered them with promises of life, peace, and security.
13:19. And they violated me among my people, for a handful of barley, and a piece of bread, to kill souls which should not die, and to save souls alive which should not live, telling lies to my people that believe lies.
Violated me... That is, dishonoured and discredited me. Ibid. To kill souls, etc... That is, to sentence souls to death, which are not to die; and to promise life to them who are not to live.
13:20. Therefore thus saith the Lord God: Behold I declare against your cushions, wherewith you catch flying souls: and I will tear them off from your arms: and I will let go the soul that you catch, the souls that should fly.
13:21. And I will tear your pillows, and will deliver my people out of your hand, neither shall they be any more in your hands to be a prey: and you shall know that I am the Lord.
13:22. Because with lies you have made the heart of the just to mourn, whom I have not made sorrowful: and have strengthened the hands of the wicked, that he should not return from his evil way, and live.
13:23. Therefore you shall not see vain things, nor divine divinations any more, and I will deliver my people out of your hand: and you shall know that I am the Lord.

Ezechiel Chapter 14

God suffers the wicked to be deceived in punishment of their wickedness.
The evils that shall come upon them for their sins: for which they shall not be delivered by the prayers of Noe, Daniel, and Job. But a remnant shall be preserved.
14:1. And some of the ancients of Israel came to me, and sat before me.
14:2. And the word of the Lord came to me, saying:
14:3. Son of man, these men have placed their uncleannesses in their hearts, and have set up before their face the stumblingblock of their iniquity: and shall I answer when they inquire of me?
Uncleanness... That is, their filthy idols, upon which they have set their hearts: and which are a stumblingblock to their souls.
14:4. Therefore speak to them, and say to them: Thus saith the Lord God: Man, man of the house of Israel that shall place his uncleannesses in his heart, and set up the stumblingblock of his iniquity before his face, and shall come to the prophet inquiring of me by him: I the Lord will answer him according to the multitude of his uncleannesses:
Man, man... That is, every man, an Hebrew expression.

14:5. That the house of Israel may be caught in their own heart, with which they have departed from me through all their idols.
14:6. Therefore say to the house of Israel: Thus saith the Lord God: Be converted, and depart from your idols, and turn away your faces from all your abominations.
14:7. For every man of the house of Israel, and every stranger among the proselytes in Israel, if he separate himself from me, and place his idols in his heart, and set the stumblingblock of his iniquity before his face, and come to the prophet to inquire of me by him: I the Lord will answer him by myself.
14:8. And I will set my face against that man, and will make him an example, and a proverb, and will cut him off from the midst of my people: and you shall know that I am the Lord.
14:9. And when the prophet shall err, and speak a word: I the Lord have deceived that prophet: and I will stretch forth my hand upon him, and will cut him off from the midst of my people Israel.
The prophet shall err, etc... He speaks of false prophets, answering out of their own heads and according to their own corrupt inclinations.
Ibid. I have deceived that prophet... God Almighty deceives false prophets, partly by withdrawing his light from them; and abandoning them to their own corrupt inclinations, which push them on to prophesy such things as are agreeable to those who consult them: and partly by disappointing them, and causing all thing to happen contrary to what they have said.
14:10. And they shall bear their iniquity: according to the iniquity of him that inquireth, so shall the iniquity of the prophet be.
14:11. That the house of Israel may go no more astray from me, nor be polluted with all their transgressions: but may be my people, and I may be their God, saith the Lord of hosts.
14:12. And the word of the Lord came to me, saying:
14:13. Son of man, when a land shall sin against me, so as to transgress grievously, I will stretch forth my hand upon it, and will break the staff of the bread thereof: and I will send famine upon it, and will destroy man and beast out of it.
14:14. And if these three men, Noe, Daniel, and Job, shall be in it: they shall deliver their own souls by their justice, saith the Lord of hosts.
14:15. And if I shall bring mischievous beasts also upon the land to waste it, and it be desolate, so that there is none that can pass because of the beasts:
14:16. If these three men shall be in it, as I live, saith the Lord, they shall deliver neither sons nor daughters: but they only shall be delivered, and the land shall be made desolate.
14:17. Or if I bring the sword upon that land, and say to the sword: Pass through the land: and I destroy man and beast out of it:
14:18. And these three men be in the midst thereof: as I live, saith the Lord God, they shall deliver neither sons nor daughters, but they themselves alone shall be delivered.
14:19. Or if I also send the pestilence upon that land, and pour out my indignation upon it in blood, to cut off from it man and beast:
14:20. And Noe, and Daniel, and Job be in the midst thereof: as I live, saith the Lord God, they shall deliver neither son nor daughter: but they shall only deliver their own souls by their justice.
14:21. For thus saith the Lord: Although I shall send in upon Jerusalem my four grievous judgments, the sword, and the famine, and the mischievous beasts, and the pestilence, to destroy out of it man and beast,
14:22. Yet there shall be left in it some that shall be saved, who shall bring away their sons and daughters: behold they shall come among you, and you shall see their way, and their doings: and you shall be comforted concerning the evil that I have brought upon Jerusalem, in all things that I have brought upon it.
14:23. And they shall comfort you, when you shall see their ways, and their doings: and you shall know that I have not done without cause all that I have done in it, saith the Lord God.

Ezechiel Chapter 15

As a vine cut down is fit for nothing but the fire; so it shall be with Jerusalem, for her sins.

15:1. And the word of the Lord came to me, saying:
15:2. Son of man, what shall be made of the wood of the vine, out of all the trees of the woods that are among the trees of the forests?
15:3. Shall wood be taken of it, to do any work, or shall a pin be made of it for any vessel to hang thereon?
15:4. Behold it is cast into the fire for fuel: the fire hath consumed both ends thereof, and the midst

thereof is reduced to ashes: shall it be useful for any work?
15:5. Even when it was whole it was not fit for work: how much less, when the fire hath devoured and consumed it, shall any work be made of it?
15:6. Therefore thus saith the Lord God: As the vine tree among the trees of the forests which I have given to the fire to be consumed, so will I deliver up the inhabitants of Jerusalem.
15:7. And I will set my face against them: they shall go out from fire, and fire shall consume them: and you shall know that I am the Lord, when I shall have set my face against them.
15:8. And I shall have made their land a wilderness, and desolate, because they have been transgressors, saith the Lord God.

Ezechiel Chapter 16

Under the figure of an unfaithful wife, God upbraids Jerusalem with her ingratitude and manifold disloyalties: but promiseth mercy by a new covenant.
16:1. And the word of the Lord came to me, saying:
16:2. Son of man, make known to Jerusalem her abominations.
Make known to Jerusalem... That is, by letters, for the prophet was then in Babylon.
16:3. And thou shalt say: Thus saith the Lord God to Jerusalem: Thy root, and thy nativity is of the land of Chanaan, thy father was an Amorrhite, and thy mother a Cethite.
16:4. And when thou wast born, in the day of thy nativity thy navel was not cut, neither wast thou washed with water for thy health, nor salted with salt, nor swaddled with clouts.
16:5. No eye had pity on thee to do any of these things for thee, out of compassion to thee: but thou wast cast out upon the face of the earth in the abjection of thy soul, in the day that thou wast born.
16:6. And passing by thee, I saw that thou wast trodden under foot in thy own blood: and I said to thee when thou wast in thy blood: Live: I have said to thee: Live in thy blood.
16:7. I caused thee to multiply as the bud of the field: and thou didst increase and grow great, and advancedst, and camest to woman's ornament: thy breasts were fashioned, and thy hair grew: and thou was naked, and full of confusion.
16:8. And I passed by thee, and saw thee: and behold thy time was the time of lovers: and I spread my garment over thee, and covered thy ignominy and I swore to thee, and I entered into a covenant with thee, saith the Lord God: and thou becamest mine.
16:9. And I washed thee with water, and cleansed away thy blood from thee: and I anointed thee with oil.
16:10. And I clothed thee with embroidery, and shod thee with violet coloured shoes: and I girded thee about with fine linen, and clothed thee with fine garments.
16:11. I decked thee also with ornaments, and put bracelets on thy hands, and a chain about thy neck.
I decked thee also with ornaments, etc... That is, with spiritual benefits, giving you a law with sacrifices, sacraments, and other holy rites.
16:12. And I put a jewel upon thy forehead and earrings in thy ears, and a beautiful crown upon thy head.
16:13. And thou wast adorned with gold, and silver, and wast clothed with fine linen, and embroidered work, and many colours: thou didst eat fine flour, and honey, and oil, and wast made exceeding beautiful: and wast advanced to be a queen.
16:14. And thy renown went forth among the nations for thy beauty: for thou wast perfect through my beauty, which I had put upon thee, saith the Lord God.
16:15. But trusting in thy beauty, thou playedst the harlot because of thy renown, and thou hast prostituted thyself to every passenger, to be his.
16:16. And taking of thy garments thou hast made thee high places sewed together on each side: and hast played the harlot upon them, as hath not been done before, nor shall be hereafter.
16:17. And thou tookest thy beautiful vessels, of my gold, and my silver, which I gave thee, and thou madest thee images of men, and hast committed fornication with them.
16:18. And thou tookest thy garments of divers colours, and coveredst them: and settest my oil and my sweet incense before them.
16:19. And my bread which I gave thee, the fine flour, and oil, and honey, wherewith I fed thee, thou hast set before them for a sweet odour; and it was done, saith the Lord God.
16:20. And thou hast taken thy sons, and thy daughters, whom thou hast borne to me: and hast sacrificed the same to them to be devoured. Is thy fornication small?
16:21. Thou hast sacrificed and given my children to them, consecrating them by fire.
Thou hast sacrificed, etc... As there is nothing more base and abominable than the crimes mentioned

throughout this chapter; so the infidelities of the Israelites in forsaking God, and sacrificing even their children to idols, are strongly figured by these allegories.
16:22. And after all thy abominations, and fornications, thou hast not remembered the days of thy youth, when thou wast naked, and full of confusion, trodden under foot in thy own blood.
16:23. And it came to pass after all thy wickedness (woe, woe to thee, saith the Lord God)
16:24. That thou didst also build thee a common stew, and madest thee a brothel house in every street.
16:25. At every head of the way thou hast set up a sign of thy prostitution: and hast made thy beauty to be abominable: and hast prostituted thyself to every one that passed by, and hast multiplied thy fornications.
16:26. And thou hast committed fornication with the Egyptians thy neighbours, men of large bodies, and hast multiplied thy fornications to provoke me.
16:27. Behold, I will stretch out my hand upon thee, and will take away thy justification: and I will deliver thee up to the will of the daughters of the Philistines that hate thee, that are ashamed of thy wicked way.
16:28. Thou hast also committed fornication with the Assyrians, because thou wast not yet satisfied: and after thou hadst played the harlot with them, even so thou wast not contented.
16:29. Thou hast also multiplied thy fornications in the land of Chanaan with the Chaldeans: and neither so wast thou satisfied.
16:30. Wherein shall I cleanse thy heart, saith Lord God: seeing thou dost all these the works of a shameless prostitute?
16:31. Because thou hast built thy brothel house at the head of every way, and thou hast made thy high place in every street: and wast not as a harlot that by disdain enhanceth her price,
16:32. But is an adulteress, that bringeth in strangers over her husband.
16:33. Gifts are given to all harlots: but thou hast given hire to all thy lovers, and thou hast given them gifts to come to thee from every side, to commit fornication with thee.
16:34. And it hath happened in thee contrary to the custom of women in thy fornications, and after thee there shall be no such fornication, for in that thou gavest rewards, and didst not take rewards, the contrary hath been done in thee.
16:35. Therefore, O harlot, hear the word of the Lord.
16:36. Thus saith the Lord God: Because thy money hath been poured out, and thy shame discovered through thy fornications with thy lovers, and with the idols of thy abominations, by the blood of thy children whom thou gavest them:
16:37. Behold, I will gather together all thy lovers with whom thou hast taken pleasure, and all whom thou hast loved, with all whom thou hast hated: and I will gather them together against thee on every side, and will discover thy shame in their sight, and they shall see all thy nakedness.
16:38. And I will judge thee as adulteresses, and they that shed blood are judged: and I will give thee blood in fury and jealousy.
16:39. And I will deliver thee into their hands, and they shall destroy thy brothel house, and throw down thy stews: and they shall strip thee of thy garments, and shall take away the vessels of thy beauty: and leave thee naked, and full of disgrace.
16:40. And they shall bring upon thee a multitude, and they shall stone thee with stones, and shall slay thee with their swords.
16:41. And they shall burn thy houses with fire, and shall execute judgments upon thee in the sight of many women: and thou shalt cease from fornication, and shalt give no hire any more.
16:42. And my indignation shall rest in thee: and my jealousy shall depart from thee, and I will cease and be angry no more.
16:43. Because thou hast not remembered the days of thy youth, but hast provoked me in all these things: wherefore I also have turned all thy ways upon thy head, saith the Lord God, and I have not done according to thy wicked deeds in all thy abominations.
16:44. Behold every one that useth a common proverb, shall use this against thee, saying: As the mother was, so also is her daughter.
16:45. Thou art thy mother's daughter, that cast off her husband, and her children: and thou art the sister of thy sisters, who cast off their husbands, and their children: your mother was a Cethite, and your father an Amorrhite.
16:46. And thy elder sister is Samaria, she and her daughters that dwell at thy left hand: and thy younger sister that dwelleth at thy right hand is Sodom, and her daughters.
16:47. But neither hast thou walked in their ways, nor hast thou done a little less than they according to their wickednesses: thou hast done almost more wicked things than they in all thy ways.
16:48. As I live, saith the Lord God, thy sister Sodom herself, and her daughters, have not done as thou

hast done, and thy daughters.
16:49. Behold this was the iniquity of Sodom thy sister, pride, fulness of bread, and abundance, and the idleness of her, and of her daughters: and they did not put forth their hand to the needy, and the poor.
This was the iniquity of Sodom, etc... That is, these were the steps by which the Sodomites came to fall into those abominations for which they were destroyed. For pride, gluttony, and idleness are the highroad to all kinds of lust; especially when they are accompanied with a neglect of the works of mercy.
16:50. And they were lifted up, and committed abominations before me: and I took them away as thou hast seen.
16:51. And Samaria committed not half thy sins: but thou hast surpassed them with thy crimes, and hast justified thy sisters by all thy abominations which thou hast done.
16:52. Therefore do thou also bear thy confusion, thou that hast surpassed thy sisters with thy sins, doing more wickedly than they: for they are justified above thee, therefore be thou also confounded, and bear thy shame, thou that hast justified thy sisters.
16:53. And I will bring back and restore them by bringing back Sodom, with her daughters, and by bringing back Samaria, and her daughters: and I will bring those that return of thee in the midst of them.
I will bring back, etc... This relates to the conversion of the Gentiles out of all nations, and of many of the Jews, to the church of Christ.
16:54. That thou mayest bear thy shame, and mayest be confounded in all that thou hast done, comforting them.
16:55. And thy sister Sodom and her daughters shall return to their ancient state: and Samaria and her daughters shall return to their ancient state: and thou and thy daughters shall return to your ancient state.
Ancient state... That is, to their former state of liberty, and their ancient possessions. In the spiritual sense, to the true liberty, and the happy inheritance of the children of God, through faith in Christ.
16:56. And Sodom thy sister was not heard of in thy mouth, in the day of thy pride,
16:57. Before thy malice was laid open: as it is at this time, making thee a reproach of the daughters of Syria, and of all the daughters of Palestine round about thee, that encompass thee on all sides.
16:58. Thou hast borne thy wickedness, and thy disgrace, saith the Lord God.
16:59. For thus saith the Lord God: I will deal with thee, as thou hast despised the oath, in breaking the covenant:
16:60. And I will remember my covenant with thee in the days of thy youth: and I will establish with thee an everlasting covenant.
16:61. And thou shalt remember thy ways, and be ashamed: when thou shalt receive thy sisters, thy elder and thy younger: and I will give them to thee for daughters, but not by thy covenant.
16:62. And I will establish my covenant with thee: and thou shalt know that I am the Lord,
16:63. That thou mayest remember, and be confounded, and mayest no more open thy mouth because of thy confusion, when I shall be pacified toward thee for all that thou hast done, saith the Lord God.

Ezechiel Chapter 17

The parable of the two eagles and the vine. A promise of the cedar of Christ and his church.

17:1. And the word of the Lord came to me, saying:
17:2. Son of man, put forth a riddle, and speak a parable to the house of Israel,
17:3. And say: Thus saith the Lord God; A large eagle with great wings, long-limbed, full of feathers, and of variety, came to Libanus, and took away the marrow of the cedar.
A large eagle... Nabuchodonosor, king of Babylon.-Ibid. Came to Libanus... That is, to Jerusalem.-Ibid. Took away the marrow of the cedar... King Jechonias.
17:4. He cropped off the top of the twigs thereof: and carried it away into the land of Chanaan, and he set it in a city of merchants.
Chanaan... This name, which signifies traffic, is not taken here for Palestine, but for Chaldea: and the city of merchants here mentioned is Babylon.
17:5. And he took of the seed of the land, and put it in the ground for seed, that it might take a firm root over many waters: he planted it on the surface of the earth.
Of the seed of the land, etc... Viz., Sedecias, whom he made king.
17:6. And it sprung up and grew into a spreading vine of low stature, and the branches thereof looked towards him: and the roots thereof were under him. So it became a vine, and grew into branches, and shot forth sprigs.
Towards him... Nabuchodonosor, to whom Sedecias swore allegiance.

17:7. And there was another large eagle, with great wings, and many feathers: and behold this vine, bending as it were her roots towards him, stretched forth her branches to him, that he might water it by the furrows of her plantation.
Another large eagle... Viz., the king of Egypt.
17:8. It was planted in a good ground upon many waters, that it might bring forth branches, and bear fruit, that it might become a large vine.
17:9. Say thou: Thus saith the Lord God: Shall it prosper then? shall he not pull up the roots thereof, and strip off its fruit, and dry up all the branches it hath shot forth, and make it wither: and this without a strong arm, or many people to pluck it up by the root?
17:10. Behold, it is planted: shall it prosper then? shall it not be dried up when the burning wind shall touch it, and shall it not wither in the furrows where it grew?
17:11. And the word of the Lord came to me, saying:
17:12. Say to the provoking house: Know you not what these things mean? Tell them: Behold the king of Babylon cometh to Jerusalem: and he shall take away the king and the princes thereof and carry them with him to Babylon.
Shall take away... Or, hath taken away, etc., for all this was now done.
17:13. And he shall take one of the king's seed, and make a covenant with him, and take an oath of him. Yea, and he shall take away the mighty men of the land,
17:14. That it may be a low kingdom and not lift itself up, but keep his covenant and observe it.
17:15. But he hath revolted from him and sent ambassadors to Egypt, that it might give him horses, and much people. And shall he that hath done thus prosper, or be saved? and shall he escape that hath broken the covenant?
17:16. As I live, saith the Lord God: In the place where the king dwelleth that made him king, whose oath he hath made void, and whose covenant he broke, even in the midst of Babylon shall he die.
17:17. And not with a great army, nor with much people shall Pharao fight against him: when he shall cast up mounts, and build forts, to cut off many souls.
17:18. For he had despised the oath, breaking his covenant, and behold he hath given his hand: and having done all these things, he shall not escape.
17:19. Therefore thus saith the Lord God: As I live, I will lay upon his head the oath he hath despised, and the covenant he hath broken.
17:20. And I will spread my net over him, and he shall be taken in my net: and I will bring him into Babylon, and will judge him there for the transgression by which he hath despised me.
17:21. And all his fugitives with all his bands shall fall by the sword: and the residue shall be scattered into every wind: and you shall know that I the Lord have spoken.
17:22. Thus saith the Lord God: I myself will take of the marrow of the high cedar, and will set it: I will crop off a tender twig from the top of the branches thereof, and I will plant it on a mountain high and eminent.
Of the marrow of the high cedar, etc... Of the royal stock of David.
Ibid. A tender twig... Viz., Jesus Christ, whom God hath planted in mount Sion, that is, the high mountain of his church, to which all nations flow.
17:23. On the high mountains of Israel will I plant it, and it shall shoot forth into branches and shall bear fruit, and it shall become a great cedar: and all birds shall dwell under it, and every fowl shall make its nest under the shadow of the branches thereof.
17:24. And all the trees of the country shall know that I the Lord have brought down the high tree, and exalted the low tree: and have dried up the green tree, and have caused the dry tree to flourish. I the Lord have spoken and have done it.

Ezechiel Chapter 18

One man shall not bear the sins of another, but every one his own; if a wicked man truly repent, he shall be saved; and if a just man leave his justice, he shall perish.
18:1. And the word of the Lord came to me, saying: What is the meaning?
18:2. That you use among you this parable as a proverb in the land of Israel, saying: The fathers have eaten sour grapes, and the teeth of the children are set on edge.
18:3. As I live, saith the Lord God, this parable shall be no more to you a proverb in Israel.
18:4. Behold all souls are mine: as the soul of the father, so also the soul of the son is mine: the soul that sinneth, the same shall die.
18:5. And if a man be just, and do judgment and justice,
18:6. And hath not eaten upon the mountains, nor lifted up his eyes to the idols of the house of Israel:

and hath not defiled his neighbour's wife, nor come near to a menstruous woman:
Not eaten upon the mountains... That is, of the sacrifices there offered to idols.
18:7. And hath not wronged any man: but hath restored the pledge to the debtor, hath taken nothing away by violence: hath given his bread to the hungry, and hath covered the naked with a garment:
18:8. Hath not lent upon usury, nor taken any increase: hath withdrawn his hand from iniquity, and hath executed true judgment between man and man:
18:9. Hath walked in my commandments, and kept my judgments, to do truth: he is just, he shall surely live, saith the Lord God.
To do truth... That is, to act according to truth; for the Hebrews called everything that was just, truth.
18:10. And if he beget a son that is a robber, a shedder of blood, and that hath done some one of these things:
18:11. Though he doth not all these things, but that eateth upon the mountains, and that defileth his neighbour's wife:
18:12. That grieveth the needy and the poor, that taketh away by violence, that restoreth not the pledge, and that lifteth up his eyes to idols, that comitteth abomination:
18:13. That giveth upon usury, and that taketh an increase: shall such a one live? he shall not live. Seeing he hath done all these detestable things, he shall surely die, his blood shall be upon him.
18:14. But if he beget a son, who, seeing all his father's sins, which he hath done, is afraid, and shall not do the like to them:
18:15. That hath not eaten upon the mountains, nor lifted up his eyes to the idols of the house of Israel, and hath not defiled his neighbour's wife:
18:16. And hath not grieved any man, nor withholden the pledge, nor taken away with violence, but hath given his bread to the hungry, and covered the naked with a garment:
18:17. That hath turned away his hand from injuring the poor, hath not taken usury and increase, but hath executed my judgments, and hath walked in my commandments: this man shall not die for the iniquity of his father, but living he shall live.
18:18. As for his father, because he oppressed and offered violence to his brother, and wrought evil in the midst of his people, behold he is dead in his own iniquity.
18:19. And you say: Why hath not the son borne the iniquity of his father? Verily, because the son hath wrought judgment and justice, hath kept all my commandments, and done them, living, he shall live.
18:20. The soul that sinneth, the same shall die: the son shall not bear the iniquity of the father, and the father shall not bear the iniquity of the son: the justice of the just shall be upon him, and the wickedness of the wicked shall be upon him.
18:21. But if the wicked do penance for all his sins which he hath committed, and keep all my commandments, and do judgment, and justice, living he shall live, and shall not die.
18:22. I will not remember all his iniquities that he hath done: in his justice which he hath wrought, he shall live.
18:23. Is it my will that a sinner should die, saith the Lord God, and not that he should be converted from his ways, and live?
18:24. But if the just man turn himself away from his justice, and do iniquity according to all the abominations which the wicked man useth to work, shall he live? all his justices which he hath done, shall not be remembered: in the prevarication, by which he hath prevaricated, and in his sin, which he hath committed, in them he shall die.
18:25. And you have said: The way of the Lord is not right. Hear ye, therefore, O house of Israel: Is it my way that is not right, and are not rather your ways perverse?
18:26. For when the just turneth himself away from his justice, and comitteth iniquity, he shall die therein: in the injustice that he hath wrought he shall die.
18:27. And when the wicked turneth himself away from his wickedness, which he hath wrought, and doeth judgment, and justice: he shall save his soul alive.
18:28. Because he considereth and turneth away himself from all his iniquities which he hath wrought, he shall surely live, and not die.
18:29. And the children of Israel say: The way of the Lord is not right.
Are not my ways right, O house of Israel, and are not rather your ways perverse?
18:30. Therefore will I judge every man according to his ways, O house of Israel, saith the Lord God. Be converted, and do penance for all your iniquities: and iniquity shall not be your ruin.
18:31. Cast away from you all your transgressions, by which you have transgressed, and make to yourselves a new heart, and a new spirit: and why will you die, O house of Israel?
18:32. For I desire not the death of him that dieth, saith the Lord God, return ye and live.

Ezechiel Chapter 19

The parable of the young lions, and of the vineyard that is wasted.
19:1. Moreover take thou up a lamentation for the princes of Israel,
19:2. And say: Why did thy mother the lioness lie down among the lions, and bring up her whelps in the midst of young lions?
Thy mother the lioness... Jerusalem.
19:3. And she brought out one of her whelps, and he became a lion: and he learned to catch the prey, and to devour men.
One of her whelps... Viz., Joachaz, alias Sellum.
19:4. And the nations heard of him, and took him, but not without receiving wounds: and they brought him in chains into the land of Egypt.
19:5. But she seeing herself weakened, and that her hope was lost, took one of her young lions, and set him up for a lion.
One of her young lions... Joakim.
19:6. And he went up and down among the lions, and became a lion: and he learned to catch the prey, and to devour men.
19:7. He learned to make widows, and to lay waste their cities: and the land became desolate, and the fulness thereof by the noise of his roaring.
19:8. And the nations came together against him on every side out of the provinces, and they spread their net over him, in their wounds he was taken.
19:9. And they put him into a cage, they brought him in chains to the king of Babylon: and they cast him into prison, that his voice should no more be heard upon the mountains of Israel.
19:10. Thy mother is like a vine in thy blood planted by the water: her fruit and her branches have grown out of many waters.
19:11. And she hath strong rods to make sceptres for them that bear rule, and her stature was exalted among the branches: and she saw her height in the multitude of her branches.
19:12. But she was plucked up in wrath, and cast on the ground, and the burning wind dried up her fruit: her strong rods are withered, and dried up: the fire hath devoured her.
19:13. And now she is transplanted into the desert, in a land not passable, and dry.
19:14. And a fire is gone out from a rod of her branches, which hath devoured her fruit: so that she now hath no strong rod, to be a sceptre of rulers. This is a lamentation, and it shall be for a lamentation.

Ezechiel Chapter 20

God refuses to answer the ancients of Israel inquiring by the prophet: but by him setteth his benefits before their eyes, and their heinous sins: threatening yet greater punishments: but still mixed with mercy.
20:1. And it came to pass in the seventh year, in the fifth month, the tenth day of the month: there came men of the ancients of Israel to inquire of the Lord, and they sat before me.
20:2. And the word of the Lord came to me, saying:
20:3. Son of man, speak to the ancients of Israel and say to them: Thus saith the Lord God: Are you come to inquire of me? As I live, I will not answer you, saith the Lord God.
20:4. If thou judgest them, if thou judgest, O son of man, declare to them the abominations of their fathers.
If thou judgest them... Or, if thou wilt enter into the cause and plead against them.
20:5. And say to them: Thus saith the Lord God: In the day when I chose Israel, and lifted up my hand for the race of the house of Jacob: and appeared to them in the land of Egypt, and lifted up my hand for them, saying: I am the Lord your God:
20:6. In that day I lifted up my hand for them to bring them out of the land of Egypt, into a land which I had provided for them, flowing with milk and honey, which excelled amongst all lands.
20:7. And I said to them: Let every man cast away the scandals of his eyes, and defile not yourselves with the idols of Egypt: I am the Lord your God.
Scandals, etc... Offensiones. That is, the abominations or idols, to the worship of which they were allured by their eyes.
20:8. But they provoked me, and would not hearken to me: they did not every man cast away the abominations of his eyes, neither did they forsake the idols of Egypt: and I said I would pour out my indignation upon them, and accomplish my wrath against them in the midst of the land of Egypt.
20:9. But I did otherwise for my name's sake, that it might not be violated before the nations, in the midst of whom they were, and among whom I made myself known to them, to bring them out of the

land of Egypt.
20:10. Therefore I brought them out from the land of Egypt, and brought them into the desert.
20:11. And I gave them my statutes, and I shewed them my judgments, which if a man do, he shall live in them.
20:12. Moreover I gave them also my sabbaths, to be a sign between me and them: and that they might know that I am the Lord that sanctify them.
20:13. But the house of Israel provoked me in the desert: they walked not in my statutes, and they cast away my judgments, which if a man do he shall live in them: and they grievously violated my sabbaths. I said therefore that I would pour out my indignation upon them in the desert, and would consume them.
20:14. But I spared them for the sake of my name, lest it should be profaned before the nations, from which I brought them out, in their sight.
20:15. So I lifted up my hand over them in the desert, not to bring them into the land which I had given them flowing with milk and honey, the best of all lands.
20:16. Because they cast off my judgments, and walked not in my statutes, and violated my sabbaths: for their heart went after idols.
20:17. Yet my eye spared them, so that I destroyed them not: neither did I consume them in the desert.
20:18. And I said to their children in the wilderness: Walk not in the statutes of your fathers, and observe not their judgments, nor be ye defiled with their idols:
20:19. I am the Lord your God: walk ye in my statutes, and observe my judgments, and do them.
20:20. And sanctify my sabbaths, that they may be a sign between me and you: and that you may know that I am the Lord your God.
20:21. But their children provoked me, they walked not in my commandments, nor observed my judgments to do them: which if a man do, he shall live in them: and they violated my sabbaths: and I threatened to pour out my indignation upon them, and to accomplish my wrath in them in the desert.
20:22. But I turned away my hand, and wrought for my name's sake, that it might not be violated before the nations, out of which I brought them forth in their sight.
20:23. Again I lifted up my hand upon them in the wilderness, to disperse them among the nations, and scatter them through the countries:
20:24. Because they had not done my judgments, and had cast off my statutes, and had violated my sabbaths, and their eyes had been after the idols of their fathers.
20:25. Therefore I also gave them statutes that were not good, and judgments, in which they shall not live.
Statutes that were not good, etc... Viz., the laws and ordinances of their enemies; or those imposes upon them by that cruel tyrant the devil, to whose power they were delivered up for their sins.
20:26. And I polluted them in their own gifts, when they offered all that opened the womb, for their offences: and they shall know that I am the Lord.
I polluted them, etc... That is, I gave them up to such blindness in punishment of their offences, as to pollute themselves with the blood of all their firstborn, whom they offered up to their idols in compliance with their wicked devices.
20:27. Wherefore speak to the house of Israel, O son of man, and say to them: Thus saith the Lord God: Moreover in this also your fathers blaspheme me, when they had despised and contemned me;
20:28. And I had brought them into the land, for which I lifted up my hand to give it them: they saw every high hill, and every shady tree, and there they sacrificed their victims: and there they presented the provocation of their offerings, and there they set their sweet odours, and poured forth their libations.
20:29. And I said to them: What meaneth the high place to which you go? and the name thereof was called High-place even to this day.
20:30. Wherefore say to the house of Israel: Thus saith the Lord God: Verily, you are defiled in the way of your fathers, and you commit fornication with their abominations.
20:31. And you defile yourselves with all your idols unto this day, in the offering of your gifts, when you make your children pass through the fire: and shall I answer you, O house of Israel? As I live, saith the Lord God, I will not answer you.
20:32. Neither shall the thought of your mind come to pass, by which you say: We will be as the Gentiles, and as the families of the earth, to worship stocks and stones.
20:33. As I live, saith the Lord God, I will reign over you with a strong hand, and with a stretched out arm, and with fury poured out.
20:34. And I will bring you out from the people, and I will gather you out of the countries, in which you are scattered, I will reign over you with a strong hand and with a stretched out arm, and with fury poured out.
20:35. And I will bring you into the wilderness of people, and there will I plead with you face to face.

The wilderness of people... That is, a desert in which there are no people.
20:36. As I pleaded against your fathers in the desert of the land of Egypt; even so will I judge you, saith the Lord God.
20:37. And I will make you subject to my sceptre, and will bring you into the bands of the covenant.
20:38. And I will pick out from among you the transgressors, and the wicked, and will bring them out of the land where they sojourn, and they shall not enter into the land of Israel: and you shall know that I am the Lord.
20:39. And as for you, O house of Israel: thus saith the Lord God: Walk ye every one after your idols, and serve them. But if in this also you hear me not, but defile my holy name any more with your gifts, and with your idols;
Walk ye every one, etc... It is not an allowance, much less a commandment to serve idols; but a figure of speech, by which God would have them to understand that if they would walk after their idols, they must not pretend to serve him at the same time: for that he would by no means suffer such a mixture of worship.
20:40. In my holy mountain, in the high mountain of Israel, saith the Lord God, there shall all the house of Israel serve me; all of them I say, in the land in which they shall please me, and there will I require your firstfruits, and the chief of your tithes with all your sanctifications.
In my holy mountain, etc... The foregoing verse, to make the sense complete, must be understood so as to condemn and reject that mixture of worship which the Jews then followed. In this verse, God promises to the true Israelites, especially to those of the Christian church, that they shall serve him in another manner, in his holy mountain, the spiritual Sion: and shall by accepted of by him.
20:41. I will accept of you for an odour of sweetness, when I shall have brought you out from the people, and shall have gathered you out of the lands into which you are scattered, and I will be sanctified in you in the sight of the nations.
20:42. And you shall know that I am the Lord, when I shall have brought you into the land of Israel, into the land for which I lifted up my hand to give it to your fathers.
20:43. And there you shall remember your ways, and all your wicked doings with which you have been defiled; and you shall be displeased with yourselves in your own sight, for all your wicked deeds which you committed.
20:44. And you shall know that I am the Lord, when I shall have done well by you for my own name's sake, and not according to your evil ways, nor according to your wicked deeds, O house of Israel, saith the Lord God.
20:45. And the word of the Lord came to me, saying:
20:46. Son of man, set thy face against the way of the south, and drop towards the south, and prophesy against the forest of the south field.
Of the south... Jerusalem lay towards the south of Babylon, (where the prohet then was,) and is here called the forest of the south field, and is threatened with utter desolation.
20:47. And say to the south forest: Hear the word of the Lord: Thus saith the Lord God: Behold I will kindle a fire in thee, and will burn in thee every green tree, and every dry tree: the flame of the fire shall not be quenched: and every face shall be burned in it, from the south even to the north.
20:48. And all flesh shall see, that I the Lord have kindled it, and it shall not be quenched.
20:49. And I said: Ah, ah, ah, O Lord God: they say of me: Doth not this man speak by parables?

Ezechiel Chapter 21

The destruction of Jerusalem by the sword is further described: the ruin also of the Ammonites is forshewn. And finally Babylon, the destroyer of others, shall be destroyed.
21:1. And the word of the Lord came to me, saying:
21:2. Son of man, set thy face toward Jerusalem, and let thy speech flow towards the holy places, and prophesy against the land of Israel:
21:3. And say to the land of Israel, Thus saith the Lord God: Behold I come against thee, and I will draw forth my sword out of its sheath, and will cut off in thee the just, and the wicked.
21:4. And forasmuch as I have cut off in thee the just and the wicked, therefore shall my sword go forth out of its sheath against all flesh, from the south even to the north.
21:5. That all flesh may know that I the Lord have drawn my sword out of its sheath not to be turned back.
21:6. And thou, son of man, mourn with the breaking of thy loins, and with bitterness sigh before them.
21:7. And when they shall say to thee: Why mournest thou? thou shalt say: For that which I hear: because it cometh, and every heart shall melt, and all hands shall be made feeble, and every spirit shall

faint, and water shall run down every knee: behold it cometh, and it shall be done, saith the Lord God.
21:8. And the word of the Lord came to me, saying:
21:9. Son of man, prophesy, and say: Thus saith the Lord God: Say: The sword, the sword is sharpened, and furbished.
21:10. It is sharpened to kill victims: it is furbished that it may glitter: thou removest the sceptre of my son, thou hast cut down every tree.
Thou removest the sceptre of my son... He speaks (according to St.
Jerome) to the sword of Nabuchodonosor: which was about to remove the sceptre of Israel, whom God here calls his son.
21:11. And I have given it to be furbished, that it may be handled: this sword is sharpened, and it is furbished, that it may be in the hand of the slayer.
21:12. Cry, and howl, O son of man, for this sword is upon my people, it is upon all the princes of Israel, that are fled: they are delivered up to the sword with my people, strike therefore upon thy thigh,
21:13. Because it is tried: and that when it shall overthrow the sceptre, and it shall not be, saith the Lord God.
21:14. Thou therefore, O son of man, prophesy, and strike thy hands together, and let the sword be doubled, and let the sword of the slain be tripled: this is the sword of a great slaughter, that maketh them stand amazed,
21:15. And languish in heart, and that multiplieth ruins. In all their gates I have set the dread of the sharp sword, the sword that is furbished to glitter, that is made ready for slaughter.
21:16. Be thou sharpened, go to the right hand, or to the left, which way soever thou hast a mind to set thy face.
21:17. And I will clap my hands together, and will satisfy my indignation: I the Lord have spoken.
21:18. And the word of the Lord came to me, saying:
21:19. And thou son of man, set thee two ways, for the sword of the king of Babylon to come: both shall come forth out of one land: and with his hand he shall draw lots, he shall consult at the head of the way of the city.
21:20. Thou shalt make a way that the sword may come to Rabbath of the children of Ammon, and to Juda unto Jerusalem the strong city.
21:21. For the king of Babylon stood in the highway, at the head of two ways, seeking divination, shuffling arrows: he inquired of the idols, and consulted entrails.
21:22. On his right hand was the divination for Jerusalem, to set battering rams, to open the mouth in slaughter, to lift up the voice in howling, to set engines against the gates, to cast up a mount, to build forts.
21:23. And he shall be in their eyes as one consulting the oracle in vain, and imitating the leisure of sabbaths: but he will call to remembrance the iniquity that they may be taken.
21:24. Therefore thus saith the Lord God: Because you have remembered your iniquity, and have discovered your prevarications, and your sins have appeared in all your devices: because, I say, You have remembered, you shall be taken with the hand.
21:25. But thou profane wicked prince of Israel, whose day is come that hath been appointed in the time of iniquity:
Thou profane, etc... He speaks to king Sedecias, who had broken his oath, and was otherwise a wicked prince.
21:26. Thus saith the Lord God: Remove the diadem, take off the crown: is it not this that hath exalted the low one, and brought down him that was high?
Is it not this that hath exalted the low one... The royal crown of Juda had exalted Sedecias from a private state and condition to the sovereign power, as the loss of it had brought down Jechonias, etc.
21:27. I will shew it to be iniquity, iniquity, iniquity: but this was not done till he came to whom judgment belongeth, and I will give it him.
I will shew it to be iniquity, etc... Or, I will overturn it, viz., the crown of Juda for the manifold iniquities of the kings: but it shall not be utterly removed, till Christ come whose right it is: and who shall reign in the spiritual house of Jacob, that is, in his church, for evermore.
21:28. And thou son of man, prophesy, and say: Thus saith the Lord God concerning the children of Ammon, and concerning their reproach, and thou shalt say: O sword, O sword, come out of the scabbard to kill, be furbished to destroy, and to glitter,
Concerning their reproach... By which they had reproached and insulted over the Jews, at the time of the destruction of Jerusalem.
21:29. Whilst they see vain things in thy regard, and they divine lies: to bring thee upon the necks of the wicked that are wounded, whose appointed day is come in the time of iniquity.

21:30. Return into thy sheath. I will judge thee in the place wherein thou wast created, in the land of thy nativity.
Return into thy sheath, etc... The sword of Babylon, after raging against many nations, was shortly to be judged and destroyed at home by the Medes and Persians.
21:31. And I will pour out upon thee my indignation: in the fire of my rage will I blow upon thee, and will give thee into the hands of men that are brutish and contrive thy destruction.
21:32. Thou shalt be fuel for the fire, thy blood shall be in the midst of the land, thou shalt be forgotten: for I the Lord have spoken it.

Ezechiel Chapter 22

The general corruption of the inhabitants of Jerusalem: for which God will consume them as dross in his furnace.

22:1. And the word of the Lord came to me, saying:
22:2. And thou son of man, dost thou not judge, dost thou not judge the city of blood?
22:3. And thou shalt shew her all her abominations, and shalt say: Thus saith the Lord God: This is the city that sheddeth blood in the midst of her, that her time may come: and that hath made idols against herself, to defile herself.
22:4. Thou art become guilty in thy blood which thou hast shed: and thou art defiled in thy idols which thou hast made: and thou hast made thy days to draw near, and hast brought on the time of thy years: therefore have I made thee a reproach to the Gentiles, and a mockery to all countries.
22:5. Those that are near, and those that are far from thee, shall triumph over thee: thou filthy one, infamous, great in destruction.
22:6. Behold the princes of Israel, every one hath employed his arm in thee to shed blood.
22:7. They have abused father and mother in thee, they have oppressed the stranger in the midst of thee, they have grieved the fatherless and widow in thee.
22:8. Thou hast despised my sanctuaries, and profaned my sabbaths.
22:9. Slanderers have been in thee to shed blood, and they have eaten upon the mountains in thee, they have committed wickedness in the midst of thee.
22:10. They have discovered the nakedness of their father in thee, they have humbled the uncleanness of the menstruous woman in thee.
22:11. And every one hath committed abomination with his neighbour's wife, and the father in law hath wickedly defiled his daughter in law, the brother hath oppressed his sister the daughter of his father in thee.
22:12. They have taken gifts in thee to shed blood: thou hast taken usury and increase, and hast covetously oppressed thy neighbours: and thou hast forgotten me, saith the Lord God.
22:13. Behold, I have clapped my hands at thy covetousness, which thou hast exercised: and at the blood that hath been shed in the midst of thee.
22:14. Shall thy heart endure, or shall thy hands prevail in the days which I will bring upon thee: I the Lord have spoken, and will do it.
22:15. And I will disperse thee in the nations, and will scatter thee among the countries, and I will put an end to thy uncleanness in thee.
22:16. And I will possess thee in the sight of the Gentiles, and thou shalt know that I am the Lord.
22:17. And the word of the Lord came to me, saying:
22:18. Son of man, the house of Israel is become dross to me: all these are brass, and tin, and iron, and lead, in the midst of the furnace: they are become the dross of silver.
22:19. Therefore thus saith the Lord God: Because you are all turned into dross, therefore behold I will gather you together in the midst of Jerusalem.
22:20. As they gather silver, and brass, and tin, and iron, and lead in the midst of the furnace: that I may kindle a fire in it to melt it: so will I gather you together in my fury and in my wrath, and will take my rest, and I will melt you down.
22:21. And will gather you together, and will burn you in the fire of my wrath, and you shall be melted in the midst thereof.
22:22. As silver is melted in the midst of the furnace, so shall you be in the midst thereof: and you shall know that I am the Lord, when I have poured out my indignation upon you.
22:23. And the word of the Lord came to me, saying:
22:24. Son of man, say to her: Thou art a land that is unclean, and not rained upon in the day of wrath.
22:25. There is a conspiracy of prophets in the midst thereof: like a lion that roareth and catcheth the

prey, they have devoured souls, they have taken riches and hire, they have made many widows in the midst thereof.
22:26. Her priests have despised my law, and have defiled my sanctuaries: they have put no difference between holy and profane: nor have distinguished between the polluted and the clean: and they have turned away their eyes from my sabbaths, and I was profaned in the midst of them.
22:27. Her princes in the midst of her, are like wolves ravening the prey to shed blood, and to destroy souls, and to run after gains through covetousness.
22:28. And her prophets have daubed them without tempering the mortar, seeing vain things, and divining lies unto them, saying: Thus saith the Lord God: when the Lord hath not spoken.
22:29. The people of the land have used oppression, and committed robbery: they afflicted the needy and poor, and they oppressed the stranger by calumny without judgment.
22:30. And I sought among them for a man that might set up a hedge, and stand in the gap before me in favour of the land, that I might not destroy it: and I found none.
22:31. And I poured out my indignation upon them, in the fire of my wrath I consumed them: I have rendered their way upon their own head, saith the Lord God.

Ezechiel Chapter 23

Under the names of the two harlots, Oolla and Ooliba, are described the manifold disloyalties of Samaria and Jerusalem, with the punishment of them both.

23:1. And the word of the Lord came to me, saying:
23:2. Son of man, there were two women, daughters of one mother.
23:3. And they committed fornication in Egypt, in their youth they committed fornication: there were their breasts pressed down, and the teats of their virginity were bruised.
Committed fornication... That is, idolatry.
23:4. And their names were Oolla the elder, and Ooliba her younger sister: and I took them, and they bore sons and daughters. Now for their names, Samaria is Oolla, and Jerusalem is Ooliba.
Oolla and Ooliba... God calls the kingdom of Israel Oolla, which signifies their own habitation, because they separated themselves from his temple: and the kingdom of Juda, Ooliba, which signifies his habitation in her, because of his temple among them in Jerusalem.
23:5. And Oolla committed fornication against me, and doted on her lovers, on the Assyrians that came to her,
On the Assyraians, etc... That is, the idols of the Assyrians: for all that is said in this chapter of the fornications of Israel and Juda, is to be understood in a spiritual sense, of their disloyalty to the Lord, by worshipping strange gods.
23:6. Who were clothed with blue, princes, and rulers, beautiful youths, all horsemen, mounted upon horses.
23:7. And she committed her fornications with those chosen men, all sons of the Assyrians: and she defiled herself with the uncleanness of all them on whom she doted.
23:8. Moreover also she did not forsake her fornications which she had committed in Egypt: for they also lay with her in her youth, and they bruised the breasts of her virginity, and poured out their fornication upon her.
23:9. Therefore have I delivered her into the hands of her lovers, into the hands of the sons of the Assyrians, upon whose lust she doted.
23:10. They discovered her disgrace, took away her sons and daughters, and slew her with the sword: and they became infamous women, and they executed judgments in her.
23:11. And when her sister Ooliba saw this, she was mad with lust more than she: and she carried her fornication beyond the fornication of her sister.
23:12. Impudently prostituting herself to the children of the Assyrians, the princes, and rulers that came to her, clothed with divers colours, to the horsemen that rode upon horses, and to young men all of great beauty.
23:13. And I saw that she was defiled, and that they both took one way.
23:14. And she increased her fornications: and when she had seen men painted on the wall, the images of the Chaldeans set forth in colours,
23:15. And girded with girdles about their reins, and with dyed turbans on their heads, the resemblance of all the captains, the likeness of the sons of Babylon, and of the land of the Chaldeans wherein they were born,
23:16. She doted upon them with the lust of her eyes, and she sent messengers to them into Chaldea.

23:17. And when the sons of Babylon were come to her to the bed of love, they defiled her with their fornications, and she was polluted by them, and her soul was glutted with them.
23:18. And she discovered her fornications, and discovered her disgrace: and my soul was alienated from her, as my soul was alienated from her sister.
23:19. For she multiplied her fornications, remembering the days of her youth, in which she played the harlot in the land of Egypt.
23:20. And she was mad with lust after lying with them whose flesh is as the flesh of asses: and whose issue as the issue of horses.
23:21. And thou hast renewed the wickedness of thy youth, when thy breasts were pressed in Egypt, and the paps of thy virginity broken.
23:22. Therefore, Ooliba, thus saith the Lord God: Behold I will raise up against thee all thy lovers with whom thy soul hath been glutted: and I will gather them together against thee round about.
23:23. The children of Babylon, and all the Chaldeans, the nobles, and the kings, and princes, all the sons of the Assyrians, beautiful young men, all the captains, and rulers, the princes of princes, and the renowned horsemen.
23:24. And they shall come upon thee well appointed with chariot and wheel, a multitude of people: they shall be armed against thee on every side with breastplate, and buckler, and helmet: and I will set judgment before them, and they shall judge thee by their judgments.
23:25. And I will set my jealousy against thee, which they shall execute upon thee with fury: they shall cut off thy nose and thy ears: and what remains shall fall by the sword: they shall take thy sons, and thy daughters, and thy residue shall be devoured by fire.
23:26. And they shall strip thee of thy garments, and take away the instruments of thy glory.
23:27. And I will put an end to thy wickedness in thee, and thy fornication brought out of the land of Egypt: neither shalt thou lift up thy eyes to them, nor remember Egypt any more.
23:28. For thus saith the Lord God: Behold, I will deliver thee into the hands of them whom thou hatest, into their hands with whom thy soul hath been glutted.
23:29. And they shall deal with thee in hatred, and they shall take away all thy labours, and shall let thee go naked, and full of disgrace, and the disgrace of thy fornication shall be discovered, thy wickedness, and thy fornications.
23:30. They have done these things to thee, because thou hast played the harlot with the nations among which thou wast defiled with their idols.
23:31. Thou hast walked in the way of thy sister and I will give her cup into thy hand.
23:32. Thus saith the Lord God: Thou shalt drink thy sister's cup, deep and wide: thou shalt be had in derision and scorn, which containeth very much.
23:33. Thou shalt be filled with drunkenness, and sorrow: with the cup of grief and sadness, with the cup of thy sister Samaria.
23:34. And thou shalt drink it, and shalt drink it up even to the dregs, and thou shalt devour the fragments thereof, thou shalt rend thy breasts: because I have spoken it, saith the Lord God.
23:35. Therefore thus saith the Lord God: Because thou hast forgotten me, and hast cast me off behind thy back, bear thou also thy wickedness, and thy fornications.
23:36. And the Lord spoke to me, saying: Son of man, dost thou judge Oolla, and Ooliba, and dost thou declare to them their wicked deeds?
23:37. Because they have committed adultery, and blood is in their hands, and they have committed fornication with their idols: moreover also their children, whom they bore to me, they have offered to them to be devoured.
23:38. Yea, and they have done this to me. They polluted my sanctuary on the same day, and profaned my sabbaths.
23:39. And when they sacrificed their children to their idols, and went into my sanctuary the same day to profane it: they did these things even in the midst of my house.
23:40. They sent for men coming from afar, to whom they had sent a messenger: and behold they came: for whom thou didst wash thyself, and didst paint thy eyes, and wast adorned with women's ornaments.
23:41. Thou sattest on a very fine bed, and a table was decked before thee: whereupon thou didst set my incense, and my ointment.
23:42. And there was in her the voice of a multitude rejoicing: and to some that were brought of the multitude of men, and that came from the desert, they put bracelets on their hands, and beautiful crowns on their heads.
23:43. And I said to her that was worn out in her adulteries: Now will this woman still continue in her fornication.
23:44. And they went in to her, as to a harlot: so went they in unto Oolla, and Ooliba, wicked women.

23:45. They therefore are just men: these shall judge them as adulteresses are judged, and as shedders of blood are judged: because they are adulteresses, and blood is in their hands.
23:46. For thus saith the Lord God: Bring a multitude upon them, and deliver them over to tumult and rapine:
23:47. And let the people stone them with stone, and let them be stabbed with their swords: they shall kill their sons and daughters, and their houses they shall burn with fire.
23:48. And I will take away wickedness out of the land: and all women shall learn, not to do according to the wickedness of them.
23:49. And they shall render your wickedness upon you, and you shall bear the sins of your idols: and you shall know that I am the Lord God.

Ezechiel Chapter 24

Under the parable of a boiling pot is shewn the utter destruction of Jerusalem: for which the Jews at Babylon shall not dare to mourn.

24:1. And the word of the Lord came to me in the ninth year, in the tenth month, the tenth day of the month, saying:
24:2. Son of man, write thee the name of this day, on which the king of Babylon hath set himself against Jerusalem to day.
24:3. And thou shalt speak by a figure a parable to the provoking house, and say to them: Thus saith the Lord God: Set on a pot, set it on, I say, and put water in it.
24:4. Heap together into it the pieces thereof, every good piece, the thigh and the shoulder, choice pieces and full of bones.
24:5. Take the fattest of the flock, and lay together piles of bones under it: the seething thereof is boiling hot, and the bones thereof are thoroughly sodden in the midst of it.
24:6. Therefore thus saith the Lord God: Woe to the bloody city, to the pot whose rust is in it, and its rust is not gone out of it: cast it out piece by piece, there hath no lot fallen upon it.
24:7. For her blood is in the midst of her, she hath shed it upon the smooth rock: she hath not shed it upon the ground, that it might be covered with dust.
24:8. And that I might bring my indignation upon her, and take my vengeance: I have shed her blood upon the smooth rock, that it should not be covered.
24:9. Therefore thus saith the Lord God: Woe to the bloody city, of which I will make a great bonfire.
24:10. Heap together the bones, which I will burn with fire: the flesh shall be consumed, and the whole composition shall be sodden, and the bones shall be consumed.
24:11. Then set it empty upon burning coals, that it may be hot, and the brass thereof may be melted: and let the filth of it be melted in the midst thereof, and let the rust of it be consumed.
24:12. Great pains have been taken, and the great rust thereof is not gone out, not even by fire.
24:13. Thy uncleanness is execrable: because I desired to cleanse thee, and thou art not cleansed from thy filthiness: neither shalt thou be cleansed, before I cause my indignation to rest in thee.
24:14. I the Lord have spoken: it shall come to pass, and I will do it: I will not pass by, nor spare, nor be pacified: I will judge thee according to thy ways, and according to thy doings, saith the Lord.
24:15. And the word of the Lord came to me, saying:
24:16. Son of man, behold I take from thee the desire of thy eyes with a stroke, and thou shall not lament, nor weep; neither shall thy tears run down.
24:17. Sigh in silence, make no mourning for the dead: let the tire of thy head be upon thee, and thy shoes on thy feet, and cover not thy face, nor eat the meat of mourners.
24:18. So I spoke to the people in the morning, and my wife died in the evening: and I did in the morning as he had commanded me.
24:19. And the people said to me: Why dost thou not tell us what these things mean that thou doest?
24:20. And I said to them: The word of the Lord came to me, saying:
24:21. Speak to the house of Israel: Thus saith the Lord God: Behold I will profane my sanctuary, the glory of your realm, and the thing that your eyes desire, and for which your soul feareth: your sons, and your daughters, whom you have left, shall fall by the sword.
24:22. And you shall do as I have done: you shall not cover your faces, nor shall you eat the meat of mourners.
24:23. You shall have crowns on your heads, and shoes on your feet: you shall not lament nor weep, but you shall pine away for your iniquities, and every one shall sigh with his brother.
24:24. And Ezechiel shall be unto you for a sign of things to come: according to all that he hath done, so

shall you do, when this shall come to pass: and you shall know that I am the Lord God.
24:25. And thou, O son of man, behold in the day wherein I will take away from them their strength, and the joy of their glory, and the desire of their eyes, upon which their souls rest, their sons and their daughters.
24:26. In that day when he that escapeth shall come to thee, to tell thee:
24:27. In that day, I say, shall thy mouth be opened to him that hath escaped, and thou shalt speak, and shalt be silent no more: and thou shalt be unto them for a sign of things to come, and you shall know that I am the Lord.

Ezechiel Chapter 25

A prophecy against the Ammonites, Moabites, Edomites, and Philistines, for their malice against the Israelites.

25:1. And the word of the Lord came to me, saying:
25:2. Son of man, set thy face against the children of Ammon, and thou shalt prophesy of them.
25:3. And thou shalt say to the children of Ammon: Hear ye the word of the Lord God: Thus saith the Lord God: Because thou hast said: Ha, ha, upon my sanctuary, because it was profaned: and upon the land of Israel, because it was laid waste: and upon the house of Juda, because they are led into captivity:
25:4. Therefore will I deliver thee to the men of the east for an inheritance, and they shall place their sheepcotes in thee, and shall set up their tents in thee: they shall eat thy fruits: and they shall drink thy milk.
25:5. And I will make Rabbath a stable for camels, and the children of Ammon a couching place for flocks: and you shall know that I am the Lord.
Rabbath... The capital city of the Ammonites: it was afterwards called Philadelphia.
25:6. For thus saith the Lord God: Because thou hast clapped thy hands and stamped with thy foot, and hast rejoiced with all thy heart against the land of Israel:
25:7. Therefore behold I will stretch forth my hand upon thee, and will deliver thee to be the spoil of nations, and will cut thee off from among the people, and destroy thee out of the lands, and break thee in pieces: and thou shalt know that I am the Lord.
25:8. Thus saith the Lord God: Because Moab and Seir have said: Behold the house of Juda is like all other nations:
25:9. Therefore behold I will open the shoulder of Moab from the cities, from his cities, I say, and his borders, the noble cities of the land of Bethiesimoth, and Beelmeon, and Cariathaim,
25:10. To the people of the east with the children of Ammon, and I will give it them for an inheritance: that there may be no more any remembrance of the children of Ammon among the nations.
25:11. And I will execute judgments in Moab: and they shall know that I am the Lord.
25:12. Thus saith the Lord God: Because Edom hath taken vengeance to revenge herself of the children of Juda, and hath greatly offended, and hath sought revenge of them:
25:13. Therefore thus saith the Lord God: I will stretch forth my hand upon Edom, and will take away out of it man and beast, and will make it desolate from the south: and they that are in Dedan shall fall by the sword.
25:14. And I will lay my vengeance upon Edom by the hand of my people Israel: and they shall do in Edom according to my wrath, and my fury: and they shall know my vengeance, saith the Lord God.
25:15. Thus saith the Lord God: Because the Philistines have taken vengeance, and have revenged themselves with all their mind, destroying and satisfying old enmities:
25:16. Therefore thus saith the Lord God: Behold I will stretch forth my hand upon the Philistines, and will kill the killers, and will destroy the remnant of the sea coast.
25:17. And I will execute great vengeance upon them, rebuking them in fury: and they shall know that I am the Lord, when I shall lay my vengeance upon them.

Ezechiel Chapter 26

A prophecy of the destruction of the famous city of Tyre by Nabuchodonosor.
26:1. And it came to pass in the eleventh year, the first day of the month, that the word of the Lord came to me, saying:
26:2. Son of man, because Tyre hath said of Jerusalem: Aha, the gates of the people are broken, she is turned to me: I shall be filled, now she is laid waste.
26:3. Therefore thus saith the Lord God: Behold I come against thee, O Tyre, and I will cause many

nations to come up to thee, as the waves of the sea rise up.
26:4. And they shall break down the walls of Tyre, and destroy the towers thereof: and I will scrape her dust from her, and make her like a smooth rock.
26:5. She shall be a drying place for nets in the midst of the sea, because I have spoken it, saith the Lord God: and she shall be a spoil to the nations.
26:6. Her daughters also that are in the field, shall be slain by the sword: and they shall know that I am the Lord.
26:7. For thus saith the Lord God: Behold I will bring against Tyre Nabuchodonosor king of Babylon, the king of kings, from the north, with horses, and chariots, and horsemen, and companies, and much people.
26:8. Thy daughters that are in the field, he shall kill with the sword: and he shall compass thee with forts, and shall cast up a mount round about: and he shall lift up the buckler against thee.
26:9. And he shall set engines of war and battering rams against thy walls, and shall destroy thy towers with his arms.
26:10. By reason of the multitude of his horses, their dust shall cover thee: thy walls shall shake at the noise of the horsemen, and wheels, and chariots, when they shall go in at thy gates, as by the entrance of a city that is destroyed.
26:11. With the hoofs of his horses he shall tread down all thy streets, thy people he shall kill with the sword, and thy famous statues shall fall to the ground.
26:12. They shall waste thy riches, they shall make a spoil of thy merchandise: and they shall destroy thy walls, and pull down thy fine houses: and they shall lay thy stones and thy timber, and thy dust in the midst of the waters.
26:13. And I will make the multitude of thy songs to cease, and the sound of thy harps shall be heard no more.
26:14. And I will make thee like a naked rock, thou shalt be a drying place for nets, neither shalt thou be built any more: for I have spoken it, saith the Lord God.
26:15. Thus saith the Lord God to Tyre: Shall not the islands shake at the sound of thy fall, and the groans of thy slain when they shall be killed in the midst of thee?
26:16. Then all the princes of the sea shall come down from their thrones: and take off their robes, and cast away their broidered garments, and be clothed with astonishment: they shall sit on the ground, and with amazement shall wonder at thy sudden fall.
26:17. And taking up a lamentation over thee, they shall say to thee: How art thou fallen, that dwellest in the sea, renowned city that wast strong in the sea, with thy inhabitants whom all did dread?
26:18. Now shall the ships be astonished in the day of thy terror: and the islands in the sea shall be troubled because no one cometh out of thee.
26:19. For thus saith the Lord God: When I shall make thee a desolate city like the cities that are not inhabited: and shall bring the deep upon thee, and many waters shall cover thee:
26:20. And when I shall bring thee down with those that descend into the pit to the everlasting people, and shall set thee in the lowest parts of the earth, as places desolate of old, with them that are brought down into the pit, that thou be not inhabited: and when I shall give glory in the land of the living,
26:21. I will bring thee to nothing, and thou shalt not be, and if thou be sought for, thou shalt not be found any more for ever, saith the Lord God.

Ezechiel Chapter 27

A description of the glory and riches of Tyre: and of her irrecoverable fall.

27:1. And the word of the Lord came to me, saying:
27:2. Thou therefore, O son of man, take up a lamentation for Tyre:
27:3. And say to Tyre that dwelleth at the entry of the sea, being the mart of the people for many islands: Thus saith the Lord God: O Tyre, thou hast said: I am of perfect beauty,
27:4. And situate in the heart of the sea. Thy neighbours, that built thee, have perfected thy beauty:
27:5. With fir trees of Sanir they have built thee with all sea planks: they have taken cedars from Libanus to make thee masts.
Sea planks... That is, timber brought by sea to build the city.
27:6. They have cut thy oars out of the oaks of Basan: and they have made thee benches of Indian ivory and cabins with things brought from the islands of Italy.
27:7. Fine broidered linen from Egypt was woven for thy sail, to be spread on thy mast: blue and purple from the islands of Elisa, were made thy covering.

27:8. The inhabitants of Sidon, and the Arabians were thy rowers: thy wise men, O Tyre, were thy pilots.
27:9. The ancients of Gebal, and the wise men thereof furnished mariners for the service of thy various furniture: all the ships of the sea, and their mariners were thy factors.
27:10. The Persians, and Lydians, and the Libyans were thy soldiers in thy army: they hung up the buckler and the helmet in thee for thy ornament.
27:11. The men of Arad were with thy army upon thy walls round about: the Pygmeans also that were in thy towers, hung up their quivers on thy walls round about: they perfected thy beauty.
Pygmeans... That is, strong and valiant men. In Hebrew, Gammadim.
27:12. The Carthaginians thy merchants supplied thy fairs with a multitude of all kinds of riches, with silver, iron, tin, and lead,
27:13. Greece, Thubal, and Mosoch, they were thy merchants, they brought to thy people slaves and vessels of brass.
27:14. From the house of Thogorma they brought horses, and horsemen, and mules to thy market.
27:15. The men of Dedan were thy merchants: many islands were the traffic of thy hand, they exchanged for thy price teeth of ivory and ebony.
27:16. The Syrian was thy merchant: by reason of the multitude of thy works, they set forth precious stories, and purple, and broidered works, and fine linen, and silk, and chodchod in thy market.
Chodchod... It is the Hebrew name for some precious stone; but of what kind in particular interpreters are not agreed.
27:17. Juda and the land of Israel, they were thy merchants with the best corn: they set forth balm, and honey, and oil and rosin in thy fairs.
27:18. The men of Damascus were thy merchants in the multitude of thy works, the multitude of divers riches, in rich wine, in wool of the best colour.
27:19. Dan, and Greece, and Mosel have set forth in thy marts wrought iron: stacte, and calamus were in thy market.
27:20. The men of Dedan were thy merchants in tapestry for seats.
27:21. Arabia, and all the princes of Cedar, they were the merchants of thy hand: thy merchants came to thee with lambs, and rams, and kids.
27:22. The sellers of Saba, and Reema, they were thy merchants: with all the best spices, and precious stones, and gold, which they set forth in thy market.
27:23. Haran, and Chene, and Eden were thy merchants; Saba, Assur, and Chelmad sold to thee.
27:24. They were thy merchants in divers manners, with bales of blue cloth, and of embroidered work, and of precious riches, which were wrapped up and bound with cords: they had cedars also in thy merchandise.
27:25. The ships of the sea, were thy chief in thy merchandise: and thou wast replenished, and glorified exceedingly in the heart of the sea.
27:26. Thy rowers have brought thee into great waters: the south wind hath broken thee in the heart of the sea.
27:27. Thy riches, and thy treasures, and thy manifold furniture, thy mariners, and thy pilots, who kept thy goods, and were chief over thy people: thy men of war also, that were in thee, with all thy multitude that is in the midst of thee: shall fall in the heart of the sea in the day of thy ruin.
27:28. Thy fleets shall be troubled at the sound of the cry of thy pilots.
27:29. And all that handled the oar shall come down from their ships: the mariners, and all the pilots of the sea shall stand upon the land:
27:30. And they shall mourn over thee with a loud voice and shall cry bitterly: and they shall cast up dust upon their heads and shall be sprinkled with ashes.
27:31. And they shall shave themselves bald for thee, and shall be girded with haircloth: and they shall weep for thee with bitterness of soul, with most bitter weeping.
27:32. And they shall take up a mournful song for thee, and shall lament thee: What city is like Tyre, which is become silent in the midst of the sea?
27:33. Which by thy merchandise that went from thee by sea didst fill many people: which by the multitude of thy riches, and of thy people didst enrich the kings of the earth.
27:34. Now thou art destroyed by the sea, thy riches are in the bottom of the waters, and all the multitude that was in the midst of thee is fallen.
27:35. All the inhabitants of the islands are astonished at thee: and all their kings being struck with the storm have changed their countenance.
27:36. The merchants of people have hissed at thee: thou art brought to nothing, and thou shalt never be any more.

Ezechiel Chapter 28

The king of Tyre, who affected to be like to God, shall fall under the like sentence with Lucifer. The judgment of Sidon. The restoration of Israel.

28:1. And the word of the Lord came to me, saying:
28:2. Son of man, say to the prince of Tyre: Thus saith the Lord God: Because thy heart is lifted up, and thou hast said: I am God, and I sit in the chair of God in the heart of the sea: whereas thou art a man, and not God: and hast set thy heart as if it were the heart of God.
28:3. Behold thou art wiser than Daniel: no secret is hid from thee.
Thou art wiser than Daniel... Viz., in thy own conceit. The wisdom of Daniel was so much celebrated in his days, that it became a proverb amongst the Chaldeans, when any one would express an extraordinary wisdom, to say he was as wise as Daniel.
28:4. In thy wisdom and thy understanding thou hast made thyself strong: and hast gotten gold an silver into thy treasures.
28:5. By the greatness of thy wisdom, and by thy traffic thou hast increased thy strength: and thy heart is lifted up with thy strength.
28:6. Therefore, thus saith the Lord God: Because thy heart is lifted up as the heart of God:
28:7. Therefore behold, I will bring upon thee strangers: the strongest of the nations: and they shall draw their swords against the beauty of thy wisdom, and they shall defile thy beauty.
28:8. They shall kill thee, and bring thee down: and thou shalt die the death of them that are slain in the heart of the sea.
28:9. Wilt thou yet say before them that slay thee: I am God; whereas thou art a man, and not God, in the hand of them that slay thee?
28:10. Thou shalt die the death of the uncircumcised by the hand of strangers: for I have spoken it, saith the Lord God.
28:11. And the word of the Lord came to me, saying: Son of man, take up a lamentation upon the king of Tyre:
28:12. And say to him: Thus saith the Lord God: Thou wast the seal of resemblance, full of wisdom, and perfect in beauty.
Thou wast the seal of resemblance... The king of Tyre, by his dignity and his natural perfections, bore in himself a certain resemblance to God, by reason of which he might be called the seal of resemblance, etc.
But what is here said to him is commonly understood of Lucifer, the king over all the children of pride.
28:13. Thou wast in the pleasures of the paradise of God: every precious stone was thy covering: the sardius, the topaz, and the jasper, the chrysolite, and the onyx, and the beryl, the sapphire, and the carbuncle, and the emerald: gold the work of thy beauty: and thy pipes were prepared in the day that thou wast created.
28:14. Thou a cherub stretched out, and protecting, and I set thee in the holy mountain of God, thou hast walked in the midst of the stones of fire.
A cherub stretched out... That is, thy wings extended. This alludes to the figure of the cherubims in the sanctuary, which with stretched out wings covered the ark.-Ibid. The stones of fire... That is, bright and precious stones which sparkle like fire.
28:15. Thou wast perfect in thy ways from the day of thy creation, until iniquity was found in thee.
28:16. By the multitude of thy merchandise, thy inner parts were filled with iniquity, and thou hast sinned: and I cast thee out from the mountain of God, and destroyed thee, O covering cherub, out of the midst of the stones of fire.
28:17. And thy heart was lifted up with thy beauty: thou hast lost thy wisdom in thy beauty, I have cast thee to the ground: I have set thee before the face of kings, that they might behold thee.
28:18. Thou hast defiled thy sanctuaries by the multitude of thy iniquities, and by the iniquity of thy traffic: therefore I will bring forth a fire from the midst of thee, to devour thee, and I will make thee as ashes upon the earth in the sight of all that see thee.
28:19. All that shall see thee among the nations, shall be astonished at thee: thou art brought to nothing, and thou shalt never be any more.
28:20. And the word of the Lord came to me, saying:
28:21. Son of man, set thy face against Sidon: and thou shalt prophesy of it,
28:22. And shalt say: Thus saith the Lord God: Behold I come against thee, Sidon, and I will be glorified in the midst of thee: and they shall know that I am the Lord, when I shall execute judgments in her, and shall be sanctified in her.

28:23. And I will send into her pestilence, and blood in her streets: and they shall fall being slain by the sword on all sides in the midst thereof: and they shall know that I am the Lord.
28:24. And the house of Israel shall have no more a stumblingblock of bitterness, nor a thorn causing pain on every side round about them, of them that are against them: and they shall know that I am the Lord God.
28:25. Thus saith the Lord God: When I shall have gathered together the house of Israel out of the people among whom they are scattered: I will be sanctified in them before the Gentiles: and they shall dwell in their own land, which I gave to my servant Jacob.
28:26. And they shall dwell therein secure, and they shall build houses, and shall plant vineyards, and shall dwell with confidence, when I shall have executed judgments upon all that are their enemies round about: and they shall know that I am the Lord their God.

Ezechiel Chapter 29

The king of Egypt shall be overthrown, and his kingdom wasted: it shall be given to Nabuchodonosor for his service against Tyre.

29:1. In the tenth year, the tenth month, the eleventh day of the month, the word of the Lord came to me, saying:
29:2. Son of man, set thy face against Pharao king of Egypt: and thou shalt prophesy of him, and of all Egypt:
29:3. Speak, and say: Thus saith the Lord God: Behold, I come against thee, Pharao king of Egypt, thou great dragon that liest in the midst of thy rivers, and sayest: The river is mine, and I made myself.
29:4. But I will put a bridle in thy jaws: and I will cause the fish of thy rivers to stick to thy scales: and I will draw thee out of the midst of thy rivers, and all thy fish shall stick to thy scales.
29:5. And I will cast thee forth into the desert, and all the fish of thy river: thou shalt fall upon the face of the earth, thou shalt not be taken up, nor gathered together: I have given thee for meat to the beasts of the earth, and to the fowls of the air.
29:6. And all the inhabitants of Egypt shall know that I am the Lord: because thou hast been a staff of a reed to the house of Israel.
29:7. When they took hold of thee with the hand thou didst break, and rent all their shoulder: and when they leaned upon thee, thou brokest, and weakenest all their loins.
29:8. Therefore thus saith the Lord God: Behold, I will bring the sword upon thee: and cut off man and beast out of thee.
29:9. And the land of Egypt shall become a desert, and a wilderness: and they shall know that I am the Lord, because thou hast said: The river is mine, and I made it.
29:10. Therefore, behold I come against thee, and thy rivers: and I will make the land of Egypt utterly desolate, and wasted by the sword, from the tower of Syene, even to the borders of Ethiopia.
29:11. The foot of man shall not pass through it, neither shall the foot of beasts go through it: nor shall it be inhabited during forty years.
29:12. And I will make the land of Egypt desolate in the midst of the lands that are desolate, and the cities thereof in the midst of the cites that are destroyed, and they shall be desolate for forty years: and I will scatter the Egyptians among the nations, and will disperse them through the countries.
29:13. For thus saith the Lord God: At the end of forty years I will gather the Egyptians from the people among whom they had been scattered.
29:14. And I will bring back the captivity of Egypt, and will place them in the land of Phatures, in the land of their nativity, and they shall be there a low kingdom:
29:15. It shall be the lowest among other kingdoms, and it shall no more be exalted over the nations, and I will diminish them that they shall rule no more over the nations.
29:16. And they shall be no more a confidence to the house of Israel, teaching iniquity, that they may flee, and follow them: and they shall know that I am the Lord God.
29:17. And it came to pass in the seven and twentieth year in the first month, in the first of the month: that the word of the Lord came to me, saying:
29:18. Son of man, Nabuchodonosor king of Babylon hath made his army to undergo hard service against Tyre: every head was made bald, and every shoulder was peeled and there hath been no reward given him, nor his army for Tyre, for the service that he rendered me against it.
29:19. Therefore thus saith the Lord God: Behold, I will set Nabuchodonosor the king of Babylon in the land of Egypt: and he shall take her multitude, and take the booty thereof for a prey, and rifle the spoils thereof: and it shall be wages for his army.

29:20. And for the service that he hath done me against it: I have given him the land of Egypt, because he hath laboured for me, saith the Lord God.
29:21. In that day a horn shall bud forth to the house of Israel, and I will give thee an open mouth in the midst of them: and they shall know that I am the Lord.

Ezechiel Chapter 30

The desolation of Egypt and her helpers: all her cities shall be wasted.
30:1. And the word of the Lord came to me, saying:
30:2. Son of man prophesy, and say: Thus saith the Lord God: Howl ye, Woe, woe to the day:
30:3. For the day is near, yea the day of the Lord is near: a cloudy day, it shall be the time of the nations.
30:4. And the sword shall come upon Egypt: and there shall be dread in Ethiopia, when the wounded shall fall in Egypt, and the multitude thereof shall be taken away, and the foundations thereof shall be destroyed.
30:5. Ethiopia, and Libya, and Lydia, and all the rest of the crowd, and Chub, and the children of the land of the covenant, shall fall with them by the sword.
30:6. Thus saith the Lord God: They also that uphold Egypt shall fall, and the pride of her empire shall be brought down: from the tower of Syene shall they fall in it by the sword, saith the Lord the God of hosts.
30:7. And they shall be desolate in the midst of the lands that are desolate, and the cities thereof shall be in the midst of the cities that are wasted.
30:8. And they shall know that I am the Lord: when I shall have set a fire in Egypt, and all the helpers thereof shall be destroyed.
30:9. In that day shall messengers go forth from my face in ships to destroy the confidence of Ethiopia, and there shall be dread among them in the day of Egypt: because it shall certainly come.
30:10. Thus saith the Lord God: I will make the multitude of Egypt to cease by the hand of Nabuchodonosor the king of Babylon.
30:11. He and his people with him, the strongest of nations, shall be brought to destroy the land: and they shall draw their swords upon Egypt: and shall fill the land with the slain.
30:12. And I will make the channels of the rivers dry, and will deliver the land into the hand of the wicked: and will lay waste the land and all that is therein by the hands of strangers, I the Lord have spoken it.
30:13. Thus saith the Lord God: I will also destroy the idols, and I will make an end of the idols of Memphis: and there shall: be no more a prince of the land of Egypt and I will cause a terror in the land of Egypt.
30:14. And I will destroy the land of Phatures, and will make a fire in Taphnis, and will execute judgments in Alexandria.
Alexandria... In the Hebrew, No: which was the ancient name of that city, which was afterwards rebuilt by Alexander the Great, and from his name called Alexandria.
30:15. And I will pour out my indignation upon Pelusium the strength of Egypt, and will cut off the multitude of Alexandria.
30:16. And I will make a fire in Egypt: Pelusium shall be in pain like a woman in labour, and Alexandria shall be laid waste, and in Memphis there shall be daily distresses.
30:17. The young men of Heliopolis, and of Bubastus shall fall by the sword, and they themselves shall go into captivity.
30:18. And in Taphnis the day shall be darkened, when I shall break there the sceptres of Egypt, and the pride of her power shall cease in her: a cloud shall cover her, and her daughters shall be led into captivity.
30:19. And I will execute judgments in Egypt: and they shall know that I am the Lord.
30:20. And it came to pass in the eleventh year, in the first month, in the seventh day of the month, that the word of the Lord came, me, saying:
30:21. Son of man, I have broken the arm of Pharao king of Egypt: and behold it is not bound up, to be healed, to be tied up with clothes, and swathed with linen, that it might recover strength, and hold the sword.
30:22. Therefore, thus saith the Lord God: Behold, I come against Pharao king of Egypt, and I will break into pieces his strong arm, which is already broken: and I will cause the sword to fall out of his hand:
30:23. And I will disperse Egypt among the nations, and scatter them through the countries.
30:24. And I will strengthen the arms of the king of Babylon, and will put my sword in his hand: and I

will break the arms of Pharao, and they shall groan bitterly being slain before his face.
30:25. And I will strengthen the arms of the king of Babylon, and the arms of Pharao shall fall: and they shall know that I am the Lord, when I shall have given my sword into the hand of the king of Babylon, and he shall have stretched it forth upon the land of Egypt.
30:26. And I will disperse Egypt among the nations, and will scatter them through the countries, and they shall know that I am the Lord.

Ezechiel Chapter 31

The Assyrian empire fell for their pride: the Egyptian shall fall in like manner.

31:1. And it came to pass, in the eleventh year, the third month the first day of the month, that the word of the Lord came to me, saying:
31:2. Son of man, speak to Pharao king of Egypt, and to his people: To whom art thou like in thy greatness?
31:3. Behold, the Assyrian like a cedar in Libanus, with fair branches, and full of leaves, of a high stature, and his top was elevated among the thick boughs.
31:4. The waters nourished him, the deep set him tip on high, the streams thereof ran round about his roots, and it sent, forth its rivulets to all the trees of the country.
31:5. Therefore was his height exalted above all the trees of the country and his branches were multiplied, and his boughs were elevated because of many waters.
31:6. And when he had spread forth his shadow, all the fowls of the air made their nests in his boughs, and all the beasts of the forest brought forth their young under his branches, and the assembly of many nations dwelt under his shadow.
31:7. And he was most beautiful for his greatness, and for the spreading of his branches: for his root was near great waters.
31:8. The cedars in the paradise of God were not higher than he, the fir trees did not equal his top, neither were the plane trees to be compared with him for branches: no tree in the paradise of God was like him in his beauty.
31:9. For I made him beautiful and thick set with many branches: and all the trees of pleasure, that were in the paradise of God, envied him.
31:10. Therefore thus saith the Lord God: Because he was exalted in height, and shot up his top green and thick, and his heart was lifted up in his height:
31:11. I have delivered him into the hands of the mighty one of the nations, he shall deal with him: I have cast him out according to his wickedness.
I have delivered... Here the time past is put for the future, i. e., I shall deliver.--Ibid. The mighty one, etc... Viz., Nabuchodonosor, who conquered both the Assyrians and Egyptians.
31:12. And strangers, and the most cruel of the nations shall cut him down, and cast him away upon the mountains, and his boughs shall fall in every valley, and his branches shall be broken on every rock of the country: and all the people of the earth shall depart from his shadow, and leave him.
31:13. All the fowls of the air dwelt upon his ruins, and all the beasts of the field were among his branches.
31:14. For which cause none of the trees by the waters shall exalt themselves for their height: nor shoot up their tops among the thick branches and leaves, neither shall any of them that are watered stand up in their height: for they are all delivered unto death to the lowest parts of the earth, in the midst of the children of men, with them that go down into the pit.
31:15. Thus saith the Lord God: In the day when he went down to hell, I brought in mourning, I covered him with the deep: and I withheld its rivers, and restrained the many waters: Libanus grieved for him, and all the trees of the field trembled.
31:16. I shook the nations with the sound of his fall, when I brought him down to hell with them that descend into the pit: and all the trees of pleasure, the choice and best in Libanus, all that were moistened with waters, were comforted in the lowest parts of the earth.
31:17. For they also shall go down with him to hell to them that are slain by the sword; and the arm of every one shall sit down under his shadow in the midst of the nations.
31:18. To whom art thou like, O thou that art famous and lofty among the trees of pleasure? Behold, thou art brought down with the trees of pleasure to the lowest parts of the earth: thou shalt sleep in the midst of the uncircumcised, with them that are slain by the sword: this is Pharao, and all his multitude, saith the Lord God.

Ezechiel Chapter 32

The prophet's lamentation for the king of Egypt.

32:1. And it came to pass in the twelfth year, in the twelfth month, in the first day of the month, that the word of the Lord came to me, saying:
32:2. Son of man, take up a lamentation for Pharao the king of Egypt, and say to him: Thou art like the lion of the nations, and the dragon that is in the sea: and thou didst push with the horn in thy rivers, and didst trouble the waters with thy feet, and didst trample upon their streams.
32:3. Therefore, thus saith the Lord God: I will spread out my net over thee with the multitude of many people, and I will draw thee up in my net.
32:4. And I will throw thee out on the land, I will cast thee away into the open field and I will cause all the fowls of the air to dwell upon thee, and I will fill the beasts of all the earth with thee.
32:5. And I will lay thy flesh upon the mountains, and will fill thy hills with thy corruption,
32:6. And I will water the earth with thy stinking blood upon the mountains, and the valleys shall be filled with thee.
32:7. And I will cover the heavens, when thou shalt be put out, and I will make the stars thereof dark: I will cover the sun with a cloud, and the moon shall not give her light.
32:8. I will make all the lights of heaven to mourn over thee and I will cause darkness upon thy land, saith the Lord God, when thy wounded shall fall in the midst of the land, saith the Lord God.
32:9. And I shall provoke to anger the heart of many people, when I shall have brought in thy destruction among the nations upon the lands, which thou knowest not.
32:10. And I will make many people to be amazed at thee, and their kings shall be horribly afraid for thee, when my sword shall begin to fly upon their faces: and they shall be astonished on a sudden, every one for his own life, in the day of their ruin.
32:11. For thus saith the Lord God: The sword of the king of Babylon shall come upon thee,
32:12. By the swords of the mighty I will overthrow thy multitude: all these nations are invincible: and they shall waste the pride of Egypt, and the multitude thereof shall be destroyed.
32:13. I will destroy also all the beasts thereof that were beside the great waters: and the foot of man shall trouble them no more, neither shall the hoof of beasts trouble them.
32:14. Then will I make their waters clear, and cause their rivers to run like oil, saith the Lord God:
32:15. When I shall have made the land of Egypt desolate: and the land shall be destitute of her fulness, when I shall have struck all the inhabitants thereof and they shall know that I am the Lord.
32:16. This is the lamentation, and they shall lament therewith: the daughters of the nations shall lament therewith for Egypt, and for the multitude thereof they shall lament therewith, saith the Lord God.
32:17. And it came to pass in the twelfth year, in the fifteenth day of the month, that the word of the Lord came to me saying:
32:18. Son of man, sing a mournful song for the multitude of Egypt: and cast her down, both her, and the daughters of the mighty nations to the lowest part of the earth, with them that go down into the pit.
32:19. Whom dost thou excel in beauty? go down and sleep with the uncircumcised.
32:20. They shall fall in the midst of them that are slain with the sword: the sword is given, they have drawn her down, and all her people.
32:21. The most mighty among the strong ones shall speak to him from the midst of hell, they that went down with his helpers and slept uncircumcised, slain by the sword.
32:22. Assur is there, and all his multitude: their graves are round about him, all of them slain, and that fell by the sword.
32:23. Whose graves are set in the lowest parts of the pit: and his multitude lay round about his grave: all of them slain, and fallen by the sword, they that heretofore spread terror in the land of the living.
32:24. There is Elam and all his multitude round about his grave, all of them slain, and fallen by the sword; that went down uncircumcised to the lowest parts of the earth: that caused their terror in the land of the living, and they have borne their shame with them that go down into the pit.
32:25. In the midst of the slain they have set him a bed among all his people: their graves are round about him: all these are uncircumcised, and slain by the sword: for they spread their terror in the land of the living, and have borne their shame with them that descend into the pit: they are laid in the midst of the slain.
32:26. There is Mosoch, and Thubal, and all their multitude: their graves are round about him: all of them uncircumcised and slain, and fallen by the sword: though they spread their terror in the land of the living.
32:27. And they shall not sleep with the brave, and with them that fell uncircumcised, that went down to

hell with their weapons, and laid their swords under their heads, and their iniquities were in their bones, because they were the terror of the mighty in the land of the living.
32:28. So thou also shalt be broken in the midst of the uncircumcised, and shalt sleep with them that are slain by the sword.
32:29. There is Edom, and her kings, and all her princes, who with their army are joined with them that are slain by the sword: and have slept with the uncircumcised, and with them that go down into the pit.
32:30. There are all the princes of the north, and all the hunters: who were brought down with the slain, fearing, and confounded in their strength: who slept uncircumcised with them that are slain by the sword, and have borne their shame with them that go down into the pit.
32:31. Pharao saw them, and he was comforted concerning all his multitude, which was slain by the sword: Pharao, and all his army, saith the Lord God:
32:32. Because I have spread my terror in the land of the living, and he hath slept in the midst of the uncircumcised with them that are slain by the sword: Pharao and all his multitude, saith the Lord God.

Ezechiel Chapter 33

The duty of the watchman appointed by God: the justice of God's ways: his judgments upon the Jews.

33:1. And the word of the Lord came to me, saying:
33:2. Son of man, speak to the children of thy people, and say to them: When I bring the sword upon a land, if the people of the land take a man, one of their meanest, and make him a watchman over them:
33:3. And he sees the sword coming upon the land, and sound the trumpet, and tell the people:
33:4. Then he that heareth the sound of the trumpet, whosoever he be, and doth not look to himself, if the sword come, and cut him off: his blood shall be upon his own head.
33:5. He heard the sound of the trumpet, and did not look to himself, his blood shall be upon him: but if he look to himself, he shall save his life.
33:6. And if the watchman see the sword coming, and sound not the trumpet: and the people look not to themselves, and the sword come, and cut off a soul from among them: he indeed is taken away in his iniquity, but I will require his blood at the hand of the watchman.
33:7. So thou, O son of man, I have made thee a watchman to the house of Israel: therefore thou shalt hear the word from my mouth, and shalt tell it them from me.
33:8. When I say to the wicked: O wicked man, thou shalt surely die: if thou dost not speak to warn the wicked man from his way: that wicked man shall die in his iniquity, but I will require his blood at thy hand.
33:9. But if thou tell the wicked man, that he may be converted from his ways, and he be not converted from his way he shall die in his iniquity: but thou hast delivered thy soul.
33:10. Thou therefore, O son of man, say to the house of Israel: Thus you have spoken, saying: Our iniquities, and our sins are upon us, and we pine away in them: how then can we live?
33:11. Say to them: As I live, saith the Lord God, I desire not the death of the wicked, but that the wicked turn from his way, and live.
Turn ye, turn ye from your evil ways: and why will you die, O house of Israel?
33:12. Thou therefore, O son of man, say to the children of thy people: The justice of the just shall not deliver him, in what day soever he shall sin: and the wickedness of the wicked shall not hurt him, in what day soever he shall turn from his wickedness: and the just shall not be able to live in his justice, in what day soever he shall sin.
33:13. Yea, if I shall say to the just that he shall surely live, and he, trusting in his justice, commit iniquity: all his justices shall be forgotten, and his iniquity, which he hath committed, in the same shall he die.
33:14. And it I shall say to the wicked: Thou shalt surely die: and he do penance for his sin, and do judgment and justice,
33:15. And if that wicked man restore the pledge, and render what he had robbed, and walk in the commandments of life, and do no unjust thing: he shall surely live, and shall not die.
33:16. None of his sins, which he hath committed, shall be imputed to him: he hath done judgment and justice, he shall surely live.
33:17. And the children of thy people have said: The way of the Lord is not equitable: whereas their own way is unjust.
33:18. For when the just shall depart from his justice, and commit iniquities, he shall die in them.
33:19. And when the wicked shall depart from his wickedness, and shall do judgments, and justice, he shall live in them.

33:20. And you say: The way of the Lord is not right, I will judge every one of you according to his ways, O house of Israel.
33:21. And it came to pass in the twelfth year of our captivity, in the tenth month, in the fifth day of the month, that there came to me one that was fled from Jerusalem, saying: The city is laid waste.
33:22. And the hand of the Lord had been upon me in the evening, before he that was fled came: and he opened my mouth till he came to me in the morning, and my mouth being opened, I was silent no more.
33:23. And the word of the Lord came to me, saying:
33:24. Son of man, they that dwell in these ruinous places in the land of Israel, speak, saying: Abraham was one, and he inherited the land, but we are many, the land is given us in possession.
33:25. Therefore say to them: Thus saith the Lord God: You that eat with the blood and lift up your eyes to your uncleannesses, and that shed blood: shall you possess the land by inheritance?
33:26. You stood on your swords, you have committed abominations, and every one hath defiled his neighbours wife; and shall you possess the land by inheritance?
33:27. Say thou thus to them: Thus saith the Lord God: As I live, they that dwell in the ruinous places, shall fall by the sword: and he that is in the field, shall be given to the beasts to be devoured: and they that are in holds, and caves, shall die of the pestilence.
33:28. And I will make the land a wilderness, and a desert, and the proud strength thereof shall fail, and the mountains of Israel shall be desolate, because there is none to pass by them,
33:29. And they shall know that I am the Lord, when I shall have made their land waste and desolate, for all their abominations which they have committed.
33:30. And thou son of man: the children of thy people, that talk of thee by the walls, and in the doors of the houses, and speak one to another each man to his neighbour, saying: Come, and let us hear what is the word that cometh forth from the Lord.
33:31. And they come to thee, as if people were coming in, and my people sit before thee: and hear thy words, and do them not: for they turn them into a song of their mouth, and their heart goeth after their covetousness.
33:32. And thou art to them as a musical song which is sung with a sweet and agreeable voice: and they hear thy words, and do them not.
33:33. And when that which was foretold shall come to pass, for behold it is coming, then shall they know that a prophet hath been among them.

Ezechiel Chapter 34

Evil pastors are reproved. Christ the true pastor shall come, and gather together his flock from all parts of the earth, and preserve it for ever.

34:1. And the word of the Lord came to me, it saying:
34:2. Son of man, prophesy concerning the shepherds of Israel: prophesy, and say to the shepherds: Thus saith the Lord God: Woe to the shepherds of Israel, that fed themselves: should not the flocks be fed by the shepherds?
Shepherds... That is, princes, magistrates, chief priests, and scribes.
34:3. You ate the milk, and you clothed yourselves with the wool, and you killed that which was fat: but my flock you did not feed.
34:4. The weak you have not strengthened, and that which was sick you have not healed, that which was broken you have not bound up, and that which was driven away you have not brought again, neither have you sought that which was lost: but you ruled over them with rigour, and with a high hand.
34:5. And my sheep were scattered, because there was no shepherd and they became the prey of all the beasts of the field, and were scattered.
34:6. My sheep have wandered in every mountain, and in every high hill: and my flocks were scattered upon the face of the earth, and there was none that sought them, there was none, I say, that sought them.
34:7. Therefore, ye shepherds, hear the word of the Lord:
34:8. As I live, saith the Lord God, forasmuch as my flocks have been made a spoil, and my sheep are become a prey to all the beasts of the field, because there was no shepherd: for my shepherds did not seek after my flock, but the shepherds fed themselves, and fed not my flocks:
34:9. Therefore, ye shepherds, hear the word of the Lord:
34:10. Thus saith the Lord God: Behold I myself come upon the shepherds, I will require my flock at their hand, and I will cause them to cease from feeding the flock any more, neither shall the shepherds feed themselves any more: and I will deliver my flock from their mouth, and it shall no more be meat

for them.
34:11. For thus saith the Lord God: Behold I myself will seek my sheep, and will visit them.
34:12. As the shepherd visiteth his flock in the day when he shall be in the midst of his sheep that were scattered, so will I visit my sheep, and will deliver them out of all the places where they have been scattered in the cloudy and dark day.
34:13. And I will bring them out from the peoples, and will gather them out of the countries, and will bring them to their own land: and I will feed them in the mountains of Israel, by the rivers, and in all the habitations of the land.
34:14. I will feed them in the most fruitful pastures, and their pastures shall be in the high mountains of Israel: there shall they rest on the green grass, and be fed in fat pastures upon the mountains of Israel.
34:15. I will feed my sheep: and I will cause them to lie down, saith the Lord God.
34:16. I will seek that which was lost: and that which was driven away, I will bring again: and I will bind up that which was broken, and I will strengthen that which was weak, and that which was fat and strong I will preserve, and I will feed them in judgment.
34:17. And as for you, O my flocks, thus saith the Lord God: Behold I judge between cattle and cattle, of rams and of he goats.
34:18. Was it not enough for you to feed upon good pastures? but you must also tread down with your feet the residue of your pastures: and when you drank the clearest water, you troubled the rest with your feet.
34:19. And my sheep were fed with that which you had trodden with your feet: and they drank what your feet had troubled.
34:20. Therefore thus saith the Lord God to you: Behold, I myself will judge between the fat cattle and the lean.
34:21. Because you thrusted with sides and shoulders, and struck all the weak cattle with your horns, till they were scattered abroad:
34:22. I will save my flock, and it shall be no more a spoil, and I will judge between cattle and cattle.
34:23. And I WILL SET UP ONE SHEPHERD OVER THEM, and he shall feed them, even my servant David: he shall feed them, and he shall be their shepherd.
David... Christ, who is of the house of David.
34:24. And I the Lord will be their God: and my servant David the prince in the midst of them: I the Lord have spoken it.
34:25. And I will make a covenant of peace with them, and will cause the evil beasts to cease out of the land: and they that dwell in the wilderness shall sleep secure in the forests.
34:26. And I will make them a blessing round about my hill: and I will send down the rain in its season, there shall be showers of blessing.
34:27. And the tree of the field shall yield its fruit, and the earth shall yield her increase, and they shall be in their land without fear: and they shall know that I am the Lord, when I shall have broken the bonds of their yoke, and shall have delivered them out of the hand of those that rule over them.
34:28. And they shall be no more for a spoil to the nations, neither shall the beasts of the earth devour them: but they shall dwell securely without, any terror.
34:29. And I will raise up for them a bud of renown: and they shall be no more consumed with famine in the land, neither shall they bear any more the reproach of the Gentiles.
A bud of renown... Germen nominatum. He speaks of Christ our Lord, the illustrious bud of the house of David, renowned over all the earth. See Jer. 33.15.
34:30. And they shall know that I the Lord their God am with them, and that they are my people the house of Israel: saith the Lord God.
34:31. And you my flocks, the flocks of my pasture are men: and I am the Lord your God, saith the Lord God.

Ezechiel Chapter 35

The judgment of mount Seir, for their hatred of Israel.

35:1. And the word of the Lord came to me, saying:
35:2. Son of man, set thy face against mount Seir, and prophesy concerning it, and say to it:
35:3. Thus saith the Lord God: Behold I come against thee, mount Seir, and I will stretch forth my hand upon thee, and I will make thee desolate and waste.
35:4. I will destroy thy cities, and thou shalt be desolate: and thou shalt know that I am the Lord.
35:5. Because thou hast been an everlasting enemy, and hast shut up the children of Israel in the hands

of the sword in the time of their affliction, in the time of their last iniquity.
35:6. Therefore as I live, saith the Lord God, I will deliver thee up to blood, and blood shall pursue thee: and whereas thou hast hated blood, blood shall pursue thee.
35:7. And I will make mount Seir waste and desolate: and I will take away from it him that goeth and him that returneth.
35:8. And I will fill his mountains with his men that are slain: in thy hills, and in thy valleys, and in thy torrents they shall fall that are slain with the sword.
35:9. I will make thee everlasting desolations, and thy cities shall not be inhabited: and thou shalt know that I am the Lord God.
35:10. Because thou hast said: The two nations, and the two lands shall be mine, and I will possess them by inheritance: whereas the Lord was there.
35:11. Therefore as I live, saith the Lord God, I will do according to thy wrath, and according to thy envy, which thou hast exercised in hatred to them: and I will be made known by them, when I shall have judged thee.
35:12. And thou shalt know that I the Lord have heard all thy reproaches, that thou hast spoken against the mountains of Israel, saying. They are desolate, they are given to us to consume.
35:13. And you rose up against me with your mouth, and have derogated from me by your words: I have heard them.
35:14. Thus saith the Lord God: When the whole earth shall rejoice, I will make thee a wilderness.
35:15. As thou hast rejoiced over the inheritance of the house of Israel, because it was laid waste, so will I do to thee: thou shalt be laid waste, O mount Seir, and all Idumea: and they shall know that I am the Lord.

Ezechiel Chapter 36

The restoration of Israel, not for their merits, but by God's special grace. Christ's baptism.

36:1. And thou son of man, prophesy to the mountains of Israel, and say: Ye mountains of Israel, hear the word of the Lord:
36:2. Thus saith the Lord God: Because the enemy hath said to you: Aha, the everlasting heights are given to us for an inheritance.
36:3. Therefore prophesy, and say: Thus saith the Lord God: Because you have been desolate, and trodden under foot on every side, and made an inheritance to the rest of the nations, and are become the subject of the talk, and the reproach of the people:
36:4. Therefore, ye mountains of Israel, hear the word of the Lord God: Thus saith the Lord God to the mountains, and to the hills, to the brooks, and to the valleys, and to desolate places, and ruinous walls, and to the cities that are forsaken, that are spoiled, and derided by the rest of the nations round about.
36:5. Therefore thus saith the Lord God: In the fire of my zeal I have spoken of the rest of the nations, and of all Edom, who have taken my land to themselves, for an inheritance with joy, and with all the heart, and with the mind: and have cast it out to lay it waste.
36:6. Prophesy therefore concerning the land of Israel, and say to the mountains, and to the hills, to the ridges, and to the valleys: Thus saith the Lord God: Behold I have spoken in my zeal, and in my indignation, because you have borne the shame of the Gentiles.
36:7. Therefore thus saith the Lord God: I have lifted up my hand, that the Gentiles who are round about you, shall themselves bear their shame.
36:8. But as for you, O mountains of Israel, shoot ye forth your branches, and yield your fruit to my people of Israel: for they are at hand to come.
36:9. For I, I am for you, and I will turn to you, and you shall be ploughed and sown.
36:10. And I will multiply men upon you, and all the house of Israel: and the cities ball be inhabited, and the ruinous places shall be repaired.
36:11. And I will make you abound with men and with beasts: and they shall be multiplied, and increased: and I will settle you as from the beginning, and will give you greater gifts, than you had from the beginning: and you shall know that I am the Lord.
36:12. And I will bring men upon you, my people Israel, and they shall possess thee for their inheritance: and thou shalt be their inheritance, and shalt no more henceforth be without them.
36:13. Thus saith the Lord God: Because thy say of you: Thou art a devourer of men, and one that suffocatest thy nation:
36:14. Therefore thou shalt devour men no more nor destroy thy nation any more, saith the Lord God.
36:15. Neither will I cause men to hear in thee the shame of the nations any more, nor shalt thou bear

the reproach of the people, nor lose thy nation any more, saith the Lord God.
Nor lose thy nation any more... This whole promise principally relates to the church of Christ, and God's perpetual protection of her: for as to the carnal Jews, they have been removed out of their land these sixteen hundred years.
36:16. And the word of the Lord came to me, saying:
36:17. Son of man, when the house of Israel dwelt in their own land, they defiled it with their ways, and with their doings: their way was before me like the uncleanness of a menstruous woman.
36:18. And I poured out my indignation upon them for the blood which they had shed upon the land, and with their idols they defiled it.
36:19. And I scattered them among the nations, and they are dispersed through the countries: I have judged them according to their ways, and their devices.
36:20. And when they entered among the nations whither they went, they profaned my holy name, when it was said of them: This is the people of the Lord, and they are come forth out of his land.
36:21. And I have regarded my own holy name, which the house of Israel hath profaned among the nations to which they went in.
36:22. Therefore thou shalt say to the house of Israel: Thus saith the Lord God: It is not for your sake that I will do this, O house of Israel, but for my holy name's sake, which you have profaned among the nations whither you went.
36:23. And I will sanctify my great name, which was profaned among the Gentiles, which you have profaned in the midst of them: that the Gentiles may know that I am the Lord, saith the Lord of hosts, when I shall be sanctified in you before their eyes.
36:24. For I will take you from among the Gentiles, and will gather you together out of all the countries, and will bring you into your own land.
36:25. And I will pour upon you clean water, and you shall be cleansed from all your filthiness, and I will cleanse you from all your idols.
36:26. And I will give you a new heart, and put a new spirit within you: and I will take away the stony heart out of your flesh, and will give you a heart of flesh.
36:27. And I will put my spirit in the midst of you: and I will cause you to walk in my commandments, and to keep my judgments, and do them.
36:28. And you shall dwell in the land which I gave to your fathers, and you shall be my people, and I will be your God.
36:29. And I will save you from all your uncleannesses: and I will call for corn, and will multiply it, and will lay no famine upon you.
36:30. And I will multiply the fruit of the tree, and the increase of the field, that you bear no more the reproach of famine among the nations.
36:31. And you shall remember your wicked ways, and your doings that were not good: and your iniquities, and your wicked deeds shall displease you.
36:32. It is not for your sakes that I will do this, saith the Lord God, be it known to you: be confounded, and ashamed at your own ways, O house of Israel.
36:33. Thus saith the Lord God: In the day that I shall cleanse you from all your iniquities, and shall cause the cities to be inhabited, and shall repair the ruinous places,
36:34. And the desolate land shall be tilled, which before was waste in the sight of all that passed by,
36:35. They shall say: This land that was untilled is become as a garden of pleasure: and the cities that were abandoned, and desolate, and destroyed, are peopled and fenced.
36:36. And the nations, that shall be left round about you, shall know that I the Lord have built up what was destroyed, and planted what was desolate, that I the Lord have spoken and done it.
36:37. Thus saith the Lord God: Moreover in this shall the house of Israel find me, that I will do it for them: I will multiply them as a flock of men,
36:38. As a holy flock, as the flock of Jerusalem in her solemn feasts: so shall the waste cities be full of flocks of men: and they shall know that I am the Lord.

Ezechiel Chapter 37

A vision of the resurrection of dry bones, foreshewing the deliverance of the people from their captivity. Juda and Israel shall be all one kingdom under Christ. God's everlasting covenant with the church.

37:1. The hand of the Lord was upon me, and brought me forth in the spirit of the Lord: and set me down in the midst of a plain that was full of bones.
37:2. And he led me about through them on every side: now they were very many upon the face of the

plain, and they were exceeding dry.
37:3. And he said to me: Son of man, dost thou think these bones shall live and I answered: O Lord God, thou knowest.
37:4. And he said to me: Prophesy concerning these bones; and say to them: Ye dry bones, hear the word of the Lord.
37:5. Thus saith the Lord God to these bones: Behold, I will send spirit into you, and you shall live.
Spirit... That is, soul, life, and breath.
37:6. And I will lay sinews upon you, and will cause flesh to grow over you, and will cover you with skin: and I will give you spirit and you shall live, and you shall know that I am the Lord.
37:7. And I prophesied as he had commanded me: and as I prophesied there was a noise, and behold a commotion: and the bones came together, each one, its joint.
37:8. And I saw, and behold the sinews, and the flesh came up upon them: and the skin was stretched out over them, but there was no spirit in them.
37:9. And he said to me: Prophesy to the spirit, prophesy, O son of man, and say to the spirit: Thus saith the Lord God: Come, spirit, from the four winds, and blow upon these slain, and let them live again.
37:10. And I prophesied as he had commanded me: and the spirit came into them, and they lived: and they stood up upon their feet, an exceeding great army.
37:11. And he said to me: Son of man: All these bones are the house of Israel: they say: Our bones are dried up, and our hope is lost, and we are cut off.
37:12. Therefore prophesy, and say to them: Thus saith the Lord God: Behold I will open your graves, and will bring you out of your sepulchres, O my people: and will bring you into the land of Israel.
37:13. And you shall know that I am the Lord, when I shall have opened your sepulchres, and shall have brought you out of your graves, O my people:
37:14. And shall have put my spirit in you, and you shall live, and I shall make you rest upon your own land: and you shall know that I the Lord have spoken, and done it, saith the Lord God:
37:15. And the word of the Lord came to me, saying:
37:16. And thou son of man, take thee a stick: and write upon it: Of Juda, and of the children of Israel his associates: and take another stick and write upon it: For Joseph the stick of Ephraim, and for all the house of Israel, and of his associates.
37:17. And join them one to the other into one stick, and they shall become one in thy hand.
37:18. And when the children of thy people shall speak to thee, saying: Wilt thou not tell us what thou meanest by this?
37:19. Say to them: Thus saith the Lord God: Behold, I will take the stick of Joseph, which is in the hand of Ephraim, and the tribes of Israel that are associated with him, and I will put them together with the stick of Juda, and will make them one stick: and they shall be one in his hand.
37:20. And the sticks whereon thou hast written, shall be in thy hand, before their eyes.
37:21. And thou shalt say to them: Thus saith the Lord God: Behold, I will take of the children of Israel from the midst of the nations whither they are gone: and I will gather them on every side, and will bring them to their own land.
37:22. And I will make them one nation in the land on the mountains of Israel, and one king shall be king over them all: and they shall no more be two nations, neither shall they be divided any more into two kingdoms.
37:23. Nor shall they be defiled any more with their idols, nor with their abominations, nor with all their iniquities: and I will save them out of all the places in which they have sinned, and I will cleanse them: and they shall be my people, and I will be their God.
37:24. And my servant David shall be king over them, and they shall have one shepherd: they shall walk in my judgments, and shall keep my commandments, and shall do them.
37:25. And they shall dwell in the land which I gave to my servant Jacob, wherein your fathers dwelt, and they shall dwell in it, they and their children, and their children's children, for ever: and David my servant shall be their prince for ever.
37:26. And I will make a covenant of peace with them, it shall be an everlasting covenant with them: and I will establish them, and will multiply them, and will set my sanctuary in the midst of them for ever.
37:27. And my tabernacle shall be with them: and I will be their God, and they shall be my people.
37:28. And the nations shall know that I am the Lord the sanctifier of Israel, when my sanctuary shall be in the midst of them for ever.

Ezechiel Chapter 38

Gog shall persecute the church in the latter days. He shall be overthrown.
38:1. And the word of the Lord came to me, saying:
38:2. Son of man, set thy face against Gog, the land of Magog, the chief prince of Mosoch and Thubal: and prophesy of him,
Gog... This name, which signifies hidden or covered, is taken in this place, either for the persecutors of the church of God in general, or some arch-persecutor in particular: such as Antichrist shall be in the latter days. See Apoc. 20.8. And what is said of the punishment of Gog, is verified by the unhappy ends of persecutors.-Ibid. Magog... Scythia or Tartary, from whence the Turks, and other enemies of the church of Christ, originally sprung.
38:3. And say to him: Thus saith the Lord God: Behold, I come against thee, O Gog, the chief prince of Mosoch and Thubal.
38:4. And I will turn thee about, and I will put a bit in thy jaws: and I will bring thee forth, and all thy army, horses and horsemen all clothed with coats of mail, a great multitude, armed with spears and shields and swords.
38:5. The Persians, Ethiopians, and Libyans with them, all with shields and helmets.
38:6. Gomer, and all his bands, the house of Thogorma, the northern parts and all his strength, and many peoples with thee.
38:7. Prepare and make thyself ready, and all thy multitude that is assembled about thee, and be thou commander over them.
38:8. After many days thou shalt be visited: at the end of years thou shalt come to the land that is returned from the sword, and is gathered out of many nations, to the mountains of Israel which have been continually waste: but it hath been brought forth out of the nations, and they shall all of them dwell securely in it.
38:9. And thou shalt go up and come like a storm, and like a cloud to cover the land, thou and all thy bands and many people with thee.
38:10. Thus saith the Lord God: In that day projects shall enter into thy heart, and thou shalt conceive a mischievous design.
38:11. And thou shalt say: I will go up to the land which is without a wall, I will come to them that are at rest, and dwell securely: all these dwell without a wall, they have no bars nor gates:
38:12. To take spoils, and lay hold on the prey, to lay thy hand upon them that had been wasted, and afterwards restored, and upon the people that is gathered together out of the nations, which hath begun to possess and to dwell in the midst of the earth.
38:13. Saba, and Dedan, and the merchants of Tharsis, and all the lions thereof shall say to thee: Art thou come to take spoils? behold, thou hast gathered thy multitude to take a prey, to take silver, and gold, and to carry away goods and substance, and to take rich spoils.
38:14. Therefore, thou son of man, prophesy and say to Gog: Thus saith the Lord God: Shalt thou not know, in that day, when my people of Israel shall dwell securely?
38:15. And thou shalt come out of thy place from the northern parts, thou and many people with thee, all of them riding upon horses, a great company and a mighty army.
38:16. And thou shalt come upon my people of Israel like a cloud, to cover the earth. Thou shalt be in the latter days, and I will bring thee upon my land: that the nations may know me, when I shall be sanctified in thee, O Gog, before their eyes.
38:17. Thus saith the Lord God: Thou then art he, of whom I have spoken in the days of old, by my servants the prophets of Israel, who prophesied in the days of those times that I would bring thee upon them.
38:18. And it shall come to pass in that day, in the day of the coming of Gog upon the land of Israel, saith the Lord God, that my indignation shall come up in my wrath.
38:19. And I have spoken in my zeal, and in the fire of my anger, that in that day there shall be a great commotion upon the land of Israel:
38:20. So that the fishes of the sea, and the birds of the air, and the beasts of the field, and every creeping thing that creepeth upon the ground, and all men that are upon the face of the earth, shall be moved at my presence: and the mountains shall be thrown down, and the hedges shall fall, and every wall shall fall to the ground.
38:21. And I will call in the sword against him in all my mountains, saith the Lord God: every man's sword shall be pointed against his brother.
38:22. And I will judge him with pestilence, and with blood, and with violent rain, and vast hailstones: I will rain fire and brimstone upon him, and upon his army, and upon the many nations that are with him.
38:23. And I will be magnified, and I will be sanctified: and I will be known in the eyes of many nations and they shall know that I am the Lord.

Ezechiel Chapter 39

God's judgments upon Gog. God's people were punished for their sins: but shall be favoured with everlasting kindness.

39:1. And thou, son of man, prophesy against Gog, and say: Thus saith the Lord God: Behold, I come against thee, O Gog, the chief prince of Mosoch and Thubal.
39:2. And I will turn thee round, and I will lead thee out, and will make thee go up from the northern parts: and will bring thee upon the mountains of Israel.
39:3. And I will break thy bow in thy left hand, and I will cause thy arrows to fall out of thy right hand.
39:4. Thou shalt fall upon the mountains of Israel, thou and all thy bands, and thy nations that are with thee: I have given thee to the wild beasts, to the birds, and to every fowl, and to the beasts of the earth to be devoured.
39:5. Thou shalt fall upon the face of the field: for I have spoken it, saith the Lord God.
39:6. And I will send a fire on Magog, and on them that dwell confidently in the islands: and they shall know that I am the Lord.
39:7. And I will make my holy name known in the midst of my people Israel, and my holy name shall be profaned no more: and the Gentiles shall know that I am the Lord, the Holy One of Israel.
39:8. Behold it cometh, and it is done, saith the Lord God: this is the day whereof I have spoken.
39:9. And the inhabitants shall go forth of the cities of Israel, and shall set on fire and burn the weapons, the shields, and the spears, the bows and the arrows, and the handstaves and the pikes: and they shall burn them with fire seven years.
39:10. And they shall not bring wood out of the countries, nor cut down out of the forests: for they shall burn the weapons with fire, and shall make a prey of them to whom they had been a prey, and they shall rob those that robbed them, saith the Lord God.
39:11. And it shall come to pass in that day, that I will give Gog a noted place for a sepulchre in Israel: the valley of the passengers on the east of the sea, which shall cause astonishment in them that pass by: and there shall they bury Gog, and all his multitude, and it shall be called the valley of the multitude of Gog.
39:12. And the house of Israel shall bury them for seven months to cleanse the land.
39:13. And all the people of the land shall bury him, and it shall be unto them a noted day, wherein I was glorified, saith the Lord God.
39:14. And they shall appoint men to go continually about the land, to bury and to seek out them that were remaining upon the face of the earth, that they may cleanse it: and after seven months they shall begin to seek.
39:15. And they shall go about passing through the land: and when they shall see the bone of a man, they shall set up sign by it, till the buriers bury it in the valley, of the multitude of Gog.
39:16. And the name of the city shall be Amona, and they shall cleanse the land.
39:17. And thou, O son of man, saith the Lord God, say to every fowl, and to all the birds, and to all the beasts of the field: Assemble yourselves, make haste, come together from every side to my victim, which I slay for you, a great victim upon the mountains of Israel: to eat flesh, and drink blood.
39:18. You shall eat the flesh of the mighty, and you shall drink the blood of the princes of the earth, of rams, and of lambs, and of he goats, and bullocks, and of all that are well fed and fat.
39:19. And you shall eat the fat till you be full, and shall drink blood till you be drunk of the victim which I shall slay for you.
39:20. And you shall be filled at my table with horses, and mighty horsemen, and all the men of war, saith the Lord God.
39:21. And I will set my glory among the nations: and all nations shall see my judgment that I have executed, and my hand that I have laid upon them.
39:22. And the house of Israel shall know that I am the Lord their God from that day and forward.
39:23. And the nations shall know that the house of Israel were made captives for their iniquity, because they forsook me, and I hid my face from them: and I delivered them into the hands of their enemies, and they fell all by the sword.
39:24. I have dealt with them according to their uncleanness, and wickedness, and hid my face from them.
39:25. Therefore, thus saith the Lord God: Now will I bring back the captivity of Jacob, and will have mercy on all the house of Israel and I will be jealous for my holy name.
39:26. And they shall bear their confusion, and all the transgressions wherewith they have transgressed

against me, when they shall dwell in their land securely fearing no man:
39:27. And I shall have brought them back from among the nations, and shall have gathered them together out of the lands of their enemies, and shall be sanctified in them, in the sight of many nations.
39:28. And they shall know that I am the Lord their God, because I caused them to be carried away among the nations; and I have gathered them together unto their own land, and have not left any of them there.
39:29. And I will hide my face no more from them, for I have poured out my spirit upon all the house of Israel, saith the Lord God.

Ezechiel Chapter 40

The prophet sees in a vision the rebuilding of the temple: the dimensions of several parts thereof.

40:1. In the five and twentieth year of our captivity, in the beginning of the year, the tenth day of the month, the fourteenth year after the city was destroyed: in the selfsame day the hand of the Lord was upon me, and he brought me thither.
40:2. In the visions of God he brought me into the land of Israel, and set me upon a very high mountain: upon which there was as the building of a city, bending towards the south.
40:3. And he brought me in thither, and behold a man, whose appearance was like the appearance of brass, with a line of flax in his hand, and a measuring reed in his hand, and he stood in the gate.
40:4. And this man said to me: Son of man, see with thy eyes, and hear with thy ears, and set thy heart upon all that I shall shew thee: for thou art brought hither that they may be shewn to thee: declare all that thou seest, to the house of Israel.
40:5. And behold there was a wall on the outside of the house round about, and in the man's hand a measuring reed of six cubits and a handbreadth: and he measured the breadth of the building one reed, and the height one reed.
40:6. And he came to the gate that looked toward the east, and he went up the steps thereof: and he measured the breadth of the threshold of the gate one reed, that is, one threshold was one reed broad;
40:7. And every little chamber was one reed long, and one reed broad: and between the little chambers were five cubits:
40:8. And the threshold of the gate by the porch of the gate within, was one reed.
40:9. And he measured the porch of the gate eight cubits, and the front thereof two cubits: and the porch of the gate was inward.
40:10. And the little chambers of the gate that looked eastward were three on this side, and three on that side: all three were of one measure, and the fronts of one measure, on both parts.
40:11. And he measured the breadth of the threshold of the gate ten cubits: and the length of the gate thirteen cubits:
40:12. And the border before the little chambers one cubit: and one cubit was the border on both sides: and the little chambers were six cubits on this side and that side.
40:13. And he measured the gate from the roof of one little chamber to the roof of another, in breadth five and twenty cubits: door against door.
40:14. He made also fronts of sixty cubits: and to the front the court of the gate on every side round about.
40:15. And before the face of the gate which reached even to the face of the porch of the inner gate, fifty cubits.
40:16. And slanting windows in the little chambers, and in their fronts, which were within the gate on every side round about: and in like manner there were also in the porches windows round about within, and before the fronts the representation of palm trees.
40:17. And he brought me into the outward court, and behold there were chambers, and a pavement of stone in the court round about: thirty chambers encompassed the pavement.
There were chambers... Gazophylacia, so called, because the priests and Levites kept in them the stores and vessels that belonged to the temple.
40:18. And the pavement in the front of the gates according to the length of the gates was lower.
40:19. And he measured the breadth from the face of the lower gate to the front of the inner court without, a hundred cubits to the east, and to the north.
40:20. He measured also both the length and the breadth of the gate of the outward court, which looked northward.
40:21. And the little chambers thereof three on this side, and three on that side: and the front thereof, and the porch thereof according to the measure of the former gate, fifty cubits long, and five and twenty

cubits broad.
40:22. And the windows thereof, and the porch, and the gravings according to the measure of the gate that looked to the east, and they went up to it by seven steps, and a porch was before it.
40:23. And the gate of the inner court was over against the gate of the north, and that of the east: and he measured from gate to gate a hundred cubits.
40:24. And he brought me out to the way of the south, and behold the gate that looked to the south: and he measured the front thereof, and the porch thereof according to the former measures.
40:25. And the windows thereof, and the porches round about, as the other windows: the length was fifty cubits, and the breadth five and twenty cubits.
40:26. And there were seven steps to go up to it: and a porch before the doors thereof: and there were graven palm trees, one on this side, and another on that side in the front thereof.
40:27. And there was a gate of the inner court towards the south: and he measured from gate to gate towards the south, a hundred cubits.
40:28. And he brought me into the inner court at the south gate: and he measured the gate according to the former measures.
40:29. The little chamber thereof, and the front thereof, and the porch thereof with the same measures: and the windows thereof, and the porch thereof round about it was fifty cubits in length, and five and twenty cubits in breadth.
40:30. And the porch round about was five and twenty cubits long, and five cubits broad.
40:31. And the porch thereof to the outward court, and the palm trees thereof in the front: and there were eight steps to go up to it.
40:32. And he brought me into the inner court by the way of the east: and he measured the gate according to the former measures.
40:33. The little chamber thereof, and the front thereof, and the porch thereof as before: and the windows thereof, and the porches thereof round about it was fifty cubits long, and five and twenty cubits broad.
40:34. And the porch thereof, that is, of the outward court: and the graven palm trees in the front thereof on this side and on that side: and the going up thereof was by eight steps.
40:35. And he brought me into the gate that looked to the north: and he measured according to the former measures.
40:36. The little chamber thereof, and the front thereof, and the porch thereof, and the windows thereof round about it was fifty cubits long, and five and twenty cubits broad.
40:37. And the porch thereof looked to the outward court: and the graving of palm trees in the front thereof was on this side and on that side: and the going up to it was by eight steps.
40:38. And at every chamber was a door in the forefronts of the gates: there they washed the holocaust.
40:39. And in the porch of the gate were two tables on this side, and two tables on that side: that the holocaust, and the sin offering, and the trespass offering might be slain thereon.
40:40. And on the outward side, which goeth up to the entry of the gate that looketh toward the north, were two tables: and at the other side before the porch of the gate were two tables,
40:41. Four tables were on this side, and four tables on that side at the sides of the gate were eight tables, upon which they slew the victims.
40:42. And the four tables for the holocausts were made of square stones: one cubit and a half long, and one cubit and a half broad, and one cubit high: to lay the vessels upon, in which the holocaust and the victim is slain.
40:43. And the borders of them were of one handbreadth, turned inwards round about: and upon the tables was the flesh of the offering.
40:44. And without the inner gate were the chambers of the singing men in the inner court, which was on the side of the gate that looketh to the north: and their prospect was towards the south, one at the side of the east gate, which looketh toward the north.
40:45. And he said to me: This chamber, which looketh toward the south shall be for the priests that watch in the wards of the temple.
40:46. But the chamber that looketh towards the north shall be for the priests that watch over the ministry of the altar. These are the sons of Sadoc, who among the sons of Levi, come near to the Lord, to minister to him.
40:47. And he measured the court a hundred cubits long, and a hundred cubits broad foursquare: and the altar that was before the face of the temple.
40:48. And he brought me into the porch of the temple: and he measured the porch five cubits on this side, and five cubits on that side: and the breadth of the gate three cubits on this side, and three cubits on that side.

40:49. And the length of the porch was twenty cubits, and the breadth eleven cubits, and there were eight steps to go up to it. And there were pillars in the fronts: one on this side, and another on that side.

Ezechiel Chapter 41

A description of the temple, and of all the parts of it.

41:1. And he brought me into the temple, and he measured the fronts six cubits broad on this side, and six cubits on that side, the breadth of the tabernacle.
The temple... This plan of a temple, which was here shewn to the prophet in a vision, partly had relation to the material temple, which was to be rebuilt: and partly, in a mystical sense, to the spiritual temple of God, the church of Christ.
41:2. And the breadth of the gate was ten cubits: and the sides of the gate five cubits on this side, and five cubits on that side: and he measured the length thereof forty cubits, and the breadth twenty cubits.
41:3. Then going inward he measured the front of the gate two cubits: and the gate six cubits, and the breadth of the gate seven cubits.
41:4. And he measured the length thereof twenty cubits, and the breadth twenty cubits, before the face of the temple: and he said to me: This is the holy of holies.
41:5. And he measured the wall of the house six cubits: and the breadth of every side chamber four cubits round about the house on every side.
41:6. And the side chambers one by another, were twice thirty-three: and they bore outwards, that they might enter in through the wall of the house in the sides round about, to hold in, and not to touch the wall of the temple.
One by another... Or one over another; literally, side to side, or side upon side.
41:7. And there was a broad passage round about, going up by winding stairs, and it led into the upper loft of the temple all round: therefore was the temple broader in the higher parts: and so from the lower parts they went to the higher by the midst.
41:8. And I saw in the house the height round about, the foundations of the side chambers which were the measure of a reed the space of six cubits:
41:9. And the thickness of the wall for the side chamber without, which was five cubits: and the inner house was within the side chambers of the house,
And the inner house was within the side chambers of the house... Because these side chambers were in the very walls of the temple all round. Or, it may also be rendered (more agreeably to the Hebrew) so as to signify that the thickness of the wall for the side chamber within, was the same as that of the wall without; that is, equally five cubits.
41:10. And between the chambers was the breadth of twenty cubits round about the house on every side.
41:11. And the door of the side chambers was turned towards the place of prayer: one door was toward the north, and another door was toward the south: and the breadth of the place for prayer, was five cubits round about.
41:12. And the building that was separate, and turned to the way that looked toward the sea, was seventy cubits broad and the wall of the building, five cubits thick round about: and ninety cubits long.
41:13. And he measured the length of the house, a hundred cubits: and the separate building, and the walls thereof, a hundred cubits in length.
41:14. And the breadth before the face of the house, and of the separate place toward the east, a hundred cubits.
41:15. And he measured the length of the building over against it, which was separated at the back of it: and the galleries on both sides a hundred cubits: and the inner temple, and the porches of the court.
41:16. The thresholds, and the oblique windows, and the galleries round about on three sides, over against the threshold of every one, and floored with wood all round about: and the ground was up to the windows, and the windows were shut over the doors.
41:17. And even to the inner house, and without all the wall round about within and without, by measure.
41:18. And there were cherubims and palm trees wrought, so that a palm tree was between a cherub and a cherub, and every cherub had two faces.
41:19. The face of a man was toward the palm tree on one side, and the face of a lion was toward the palm tree on the other side: set forth through all the house round about.
41:20. From the ground even to the upper parts of the gate, were cherubims and palm trees wrought in the wall of the temple.

41:21. The threshold was foursquare, and the face of the sanctuary sight to sight.
The threshold was foursquare... That is, the gate of the temple was foursquare: and so placed as to answer the gate of the sanctuary within.
41:22. The altar of wood was three cubits high: and the length thereof was two cubits: and the corners thereof, aid the length thereof, and the walls thereof, were of wood. And he said to me: This is the table before the Lord.
41:23. And there were two doors in the temple, and in the sanctuary.
41:24. And in the two doors on both sides were two little doors, which were folded within each other: for there were two wickets on both sides of the doors.
41:25. And there were cherubims also wrought in the doors of the temple, and the figures of palm trees, like as were made on the walls: for which cause also the planks were thicker in the front of the porch without.
41:26. Upon which were the oblique windows, and the representation of palm trees on this side, and on that side in the sides of the porch, according to the sides of the house, and the breadth of the walls.

Ezechiel Chapter 42

A description of the courts, chambers, and other places belonging to the temple.

42:1. And he brought me forth into the outward court by the way that leadeth to the north, and he brought me into the chamber that was over against the separate building, and over against the house toward the north.
42:2. In the face of the north door was the length of hundred cubits, and the breadth of fifty cubits.
42:3. Over against the twenty cubits of the inner court, and over against the pavement of the outward court that was paved with stone, where there was a gallery joined to a triple gallery.
42:4. And before the chambers was a walk ten cubits broad, looking to the inner parts of a way of one cubit. And their doors were toward the north.
42:5. Where were the store chambers lower above: because they bore up the galleries, which appeared above out of them from he lower parts, and from the midst of the building.
42:6. For they were of three stories, and had not pillars, as the pillars of the courts: therefore did they appear above out of the lower places, and out of the middle places, fifty cubits from the ground.
42:7. And the outward wall that went about by the chambers, which were towards the outward court on the forepart of the chambers, was fifty cubits long.
42:8. For the length of the chambers of the outward court was fifty cubits: and the length before the face of the temple, a hundred cubits.
42:9. And there was under these chambers, an entrance from the east, for them that went into them out of the outward court.
42:10. In the breadth of the outward wall of the court that was toward the east, over against the separate building, and there were chambers before the building.
42:11. And the way before them was like the chambers which were toward the north: they were as long as they, and as broad as they: and all the going in to them, and their fashions, and their doors were alike.
42:12. According to the doors of the chambers that were towards the south: there was a door in the head of the way, which way was before the porch, separated towards the east as one entereth in.
42:13. And he said to me: The chambers of the north, and the chambers of the south, which are before the separate building: they are holy chambers, in which the priests shall eat, that approach to the Lord into the holy of holies: there they shall lay the most holy things, and the offering for sin, and for trespass: for it is a holy place.
42:14. And when the priests shall have entered in, they shall not go out of the holy places into the outward court: but there they shall lay their vestments, wherein they minister, for they are holy: and they shall put on other garments, and so they shall go forth to the people.
42:15. Now when he had made an end of measuring the inner house, he brought me out by the way of the gate that looked toward the east: and he measured it on every side round about.
42:16. And he measured toward the east with the measuring reed, five hundred reeds with the measuring reed round about.
42:17. And he measured toward the north five hundred reeds with the measuring reed round about.
42:18. And towards the south he measured five hundred reeds with the measuring reed round about.
42:19. And toward the west he measured five hundred reeds, with the measuring reed.
42:20. By the four winds he measured the wall thereof on every side round about, five hundred cubits and five hundred cubits broad, making a separation between the sanctuary and the place of the people.

Ezechiel Chapter 43

The glory of God returns to the new temple. The Israelites shall no more profane God's name by idolatry: the prophet is commanded to shew them the dimensions, and form of the temple, and of the altar, with the sacrifices to be offered thereon.

43:1. And he brought me to the gate that looked towards the east.
43:2. And behold the glory of the God of Israel came in by the way of the east: and his voice was like the noise of many waters, and the earth shone with his majesty.
43:3. And I saw the vision according to the appearance which I had seen when he came to destroy the city: and the appearance was according to the vision which I had seen by the river Chobar: and I fell upon my face.
43:4. And the majesty of the Lord went into the temple by the way of the gate that looked to the east.
43:5. And the spirit lifted me up and brought me into the inner court: and behold the house was filled with the glory of the Lord.
43:6. And I heard one speaking to me out of the house, and the man that stood by me,
43:7. Said to me: Son of man, the place of my throne, and the place of the soles of my feet, where I dwell in the midst of the children of Israel for ever: and the house of Israel shall no more profane my holy name, they and their kings by their fornications, and by the carcasses of their kings, and by the high places.
43:8. They who have set their threshold by my threshold, and their posts by my posts: and there was but a wall between me, and them: and they profaned my holy name by the abominations which they committed: for which reason I consumed them in my wrath.
43:9. Now therefore let them put away their fornications, and the carcasses of their kings far from me: and I will dwell in the midst of them for ever.
43:10. But thou, son of man, shew to the house of Israel the temple, and let them be ashamed of their iniquities, and let them measure the building:
43:11. And be ashamed of all that they have done. Shew them the form of the house, and of the fashion thereof, the goings out and the comings in, and the whole plan thereof, and all its ordinances, and all its order, and all its laws, and thou shalt write it in their sight: that they may keep the whole form thereof, and its ordinances, and do them.
43:12. This is the law of the house upon the top of the mountain: All its border round about; most holy: this then is the law of the house.
43:13. And these are the measures of the altar by the truest cubit, which is a cubit and a handbreadth: the bottom thereof was a cubit, and the breadth a cubit: and the border thereof unto its edge, and round about, one handbreadth: and this was the trench of the altar.
43:14. And from the bottom of the ground to the lowest brim two cubits, and the breadth of one cubit: and from the lesser brim to the greater brim four cubits, and the breadth of one cubit.
43:15. And the Ariel itself was four cubits: and from the Ariel upward were four horns.
The Ariel... That is, the altar itself, or rather the highest part of it, upon which the burnt offerings were laid. In the Hebrew it is Harel, that is, the mountain of God: but in the following verse Haariel, that is, the lion of God; a figure, from its consuming, and as it were devouring the sacrifices, as a lion devours its prey.
43:16. And the Ariel was twelve cubits long, and twelve cubits broad, foursquare, with equal sides.
43:17. And the brim was fourteen cubits long, and fourteen cubits broad in the four corners thereof: and the crown round about it was half a cubit, and the bottom of it one cubit round about: and its steps turned toward the east.
43:18. And he said to me: Son of man, thus saith the Lord God: These are the ceremonies of the altar, in what day soever it shall be made: that holocausts may be offered upon it, and blood poured out.
43:19. And thou shalt give to the priests, and the Levites, that are of the race of Sadoc, who approach to me, saith the Lord God, to offer to me a calf of the herd for sin.
43:20. And thou shalt take of his blood, and shalt put it upon the four horns thereof, and upon the four corners of the brim, and upon the crown round about: and thou shalt cleanse, and expiate it.
43:21. And thou shalt take the calf, that is offered for sin: and thou shalt burn him in a separate place of the house without the sanctuary.
43:22. And in the second day thou shalt offer a he goat without blemish for sin: and they shall expiate the altar, as they expiated it with the calf.
43:23. And when thou shalt have made an end of the expiation thereof, thou shalt offer a calf of the

herd without blemish, and a ram of the flock without blemish.
43:24. And thou shalt offer them in the sight of the Lord, and the priests shall put salt upon them, and shall offer them a holocaust to the Lord.
43:25. Seven days shalt thou offer a he goat for sin daily: they shall offer also a calf of the herd, and a ram of the flock without blemish.
43:26. Seven days shall they expiate the altar, and shall cleanse it: and they shall consecrate it.
Consecrate it... Literally, fill its hand, that is, dedicate and apply it to holy service.
43:27. And the days being expired, on the eighth day and thenceforward, the priests shall offer your holocausts upon the altar, and the peace offerings: and I will be pacified towards you, saith the Lord God.

Ezechiel Chapter 44

The east gate of the sanctuary shall be always shut. The uncircumcised shall not enter into the sanctuary: nor the Levites that have served idols: but the sons of Sadoc shall do the priestly functions, who stood firm in the worst of times.

44:1. And he brought me back to the way of the gate of the outward sanctuary, which looked towards the east: and it was shut.
44:2. And the Lord said to me: This gate shall be shut, it shall not be opened, and no man shall pass through it: because the Lord the God of Israel hath entered in by it, and it shall be shut
44:3. For the prince. The prince himself shall sit in it, to eat bread before the Lord: he shall enter in by the way of the porch of the gate, and shall go out by the same way.
44:4. And he brought me by the way of the north gate, in the sight of the house: and I saw, and behold the glory of the Lord filled the house of the Lord: and I fell on my face.
44:5. And the Lord said to me: Son of man, attend with thy heart and behold with thy eyes, and hear with thy ears, all that I say to thee concerning all the ceremonies of the house of the Lord, and concerning all the laws thereof: and mark well the ways of the temple, with all the goings out of the sanctuary.
44:6. And thou shalt say to the house of Israel that provoketh me: Thus saith the Lord God: Let all your wicked doings suffice you, O house of Israel:
44:7. In that you have brought in strangers uncircumcised in heart, and uncircumcised in flesh, to be in my sanctuary, and to defile my house: and you offer my bread, the fat, and the blood: and you have broken my covenant by all your wicked doings.
44:8. And you have not kept the ordinances of my sanctuary: but you have set keepers of my charge in my sanctuary for yourselves.
44:9. Thus saith the Lord God: No stranger uncircumcised in heart, and uncircumcised in flesh, shall enter into my sanctuary, no stranger that is in the midst of the children of Israel.
44:10. Moreover the Levites that went away far from me, when the children of Israel went astray, and have wandered from me after their idols, and have borne their iniquity:
44:11. They shall be officers in my sanctuary, and doorkeepers of the gates of the house, and ministers to the house: they shall slay the holocausts, and the victims of the people: and they shall stand in their sight, to minister to them.
44:12. Because they ministered to them before their idols, and were a stumblingblock of iniquity to the house of Israel: therefore have I lifted up my hand against them, saith the Lord God, and they shall bear their iniquity:
44:13. And they shall not come near to me, to do the office of priest to me, neither shall they come near to any of my holy things that are by the holy of holies: but they shall bear their shame, and their wickednesses which they have committed.
44:14. And I will make them doorkeepers of the house, for all the service thereof, and for all that shall be done therein.
44:15. But the priests, and Levites, the sons of Sadoc, who kept the ceremonies of my sanctuary, when the children of Israel went astray from me, they shall come near to me, to minister to me: and they shall stand before me, to offer me the fat, and the blood, saith the Lord God.
44:16. They shall enter into my sanctuary, and they shall come near to my table, to minister unto me, and to keep my ceremonies.
44:17. And when they shall enter in at the gates of the inner court, they shall be clothed with linen garments: neither shall any woollen come upon them, when they minister in the gates of the inner court and within.

44:18. They shall have linen mitres on their heads, and linen breeches on their loins, and they shall not be girded with any thing that causeth sweat.
44:19. And when they shall go forth to the outward court to the people, they shall put off their garments wherein they ministered, and lay them up in the store chamber of the sanctuary, and they shall clothe themselves with other garments: and they shall not sanctify the people with their vestments.
Shall not sanctify the people with their vestments... By exposing them to the danger of touching the sacred vestments, which none were to touch but they that were sanctified.
44:20. Neither shall they shave their heads, nor wear long hair: but they shall only poll their heads.
44:21. And no priest shall drink wine when he is to go into the inner court.
44:22. Neither shall they take to wife a widow, nor one that is divorced, but they shall take virgins of the seed of the house of Israel: but they may take a widow also, that is, the widow of a priest.
44:23. And they shall teach my people the difference between holy and profane, and shew them how to discern between clean and unclean.
44:24. And when there shall be a controversy, they shall stand in my judgments, and shall judge: they shall keep my laws, and my ordinances in all my solemnities, and sanctify my sabbaths.
44:25. And they shall come near no dead person, lest they be defiled, only their father and mother, and son and daughter, and brother and sister, that hath not had another husband: for whom they may become unclean.
44:26. And after one is cleansed, they shall reckon unto him seven days.
44:27. And in the day that he goeth into the sanctuary, to the inner court, to minister unto me in the sanctuary, he shall offer for his sin, saith the Lord God.
44:28. And they shall have no inheritance, I am their inheritance: neither shall you give them any possession in Israel, for I am their possession.
44:29. They shall eat the victim both for sin and for trespass: and every vowed thing in Israel shall be theirs.
30. And the firstfruits of all the firstborn, and all the libations of all things that are offered, shall be the priest's: and you shall give the firstfruits of your meats to the priest, that he may return a blessing upon thy house.
44:31. The priests shall not eat of any thing that is dead of itself or caught by a beast, whether it be fowl or cattle.

Ezechiel Chapter 45

Portions of land for the sanctuary, for the city, and for the prince. Ordinances for the prince.

45:1. And when you shall begin to divide the land by lot, separate ye firstfruits to the Lord, a portion of the land to be holy, in length twenty-five thousand and in breadth ten thousand: it shall be holy in all the borders thereof round about.
Twenty-five thousand... Viz., reeds or cubits.
45:2. And there shall be for the sanctuary on every side five hundred by five hundred, foursquare round about: and fifty cubits for the suburbs thereof round about.
45:3. And with this measure thou shalt measure the length of five and twenty thousand, and the breadth of ten thousand, and in it shall be the temple and the holy of holies.
45:4. The holy portion of the land shall be for the priests the ministers of the sanctuary, who come near to the ministry of the Lord: and it shall be a place for their houses, and for the holy place of the sanctuary.
45:5. And five and twenty thousand of length, and ten thousand of breadth shall be for the Levites, that minister in the house: they shall possess twenty store chambers.
45:6. And you shall appoint the possession of the city five thousand broad, and five and twenty thousand long, according to the separation of the sanctuary, for the whole house of Israel.
45:7. For the prince also on the one side and on the other side, according to the separation of the sanctuary, and according to the possession of the city, over against the separation of the sanctuary, and over against the possession of the city: from the side of the sea even to the sea, and from the side of the east even to the east. And the length according to every part from the west border to the east border.
45:8. He shall have a portion of the land in Israel: and the princes shall no more rob my people: but they shall give the land to the house of Israel according to their tribes:
45:9. Thus saith the Lord God: Let it suffice you, O princes of Israel: cease from iniquity and robberies, and execute judgment and justice, separate your confines from my people, saith the Lord God.
45:10. You shall have just balances, and a just ephi, and a just bate.

45:11. The ephi and the bate shall be equal, and of one measure: that the bate may contain the tenth part of a core, and the ephi the tenth part of a core: their weight shall be equal according to the measure of a core.
The ephi and the bate... These measures were of equal capacity, but the bate served for liquids, and the ephi for dry things.
45:12. And the sicle hath twenty obols. Now twenty sicles, and five and twenty sicles, and fifteen sicles, make a mna,
45:13. And these are the firstfruits, which you shall take: the sixth part of an ephi of a core of wheat, and the sixth part of an ephi of a core of barley.
45:14. The measure of oil also, a bate of oil is the tenth part of a core: and ten bates make a core: for ten bates fill a core.
45:15. And one ram out of a flock of two hundred, of those that Israel feedeth for sacrifice, and for holocausts, and for peace offerings, to make atonement for them, saith the Lord God.
45:16. All the people of the land shall be bound to these firstfruits for the prince in Israel.
45:17. And the prince shall give the holocaust, and the sacrifice, and the libations on the feasts, and on the new moons, and on the sabbaths, and on all the solemnities of the house of Israel: he shall offer the sacrifice for sin, and the holocaust, and the peace offerings to make expiation for the house of Israel.
45:18. Thus saith the Lord God: In the first month, the first of the month, thou shalt take a calf of the herd without blemish, and thou shalt expiate the sanctuary.
45:19. And the priest shall take of the blood of the sin offering: and he shall put it on the posts of the house, and on the four corners of the brim of the altar, and oil the posts of the gate of the inner court.
45:20. And so shalt thou do in the seventh day of the month, for every one that hath been ignorant, and hath been deceived by error, and thou shalt make expiation for the house.
45:21. In the first month, the fourteenth day of the month, you shall observe the solemnity of the pasch: seven days unleavened bread shall be eaten.
45:22. And the prince on that day shall offer for himself, and for all the people of the land, a calf for sin.
45:23. And in the solemnity of the seven days he shall offer for a holocaust to the Lord, seven calves, and seven rams without blemish daily for seven days: and for sin a he goat daily.
45:24. And he shall offer the sacrifice of an ephi for every calf, and an ephi for every ram: and a hin of oil for every ephi.
45:25. In the seventh month, in the fifteenth day of the month, in the solemn feast, he shall do the like for the seven days: as well in regard to the sin offering, as to the holocaust, and the sacrifice, and the oil.

Ezechiel Chapter 46

Other ordinances for the prince and for the sacrifices.

46:1. Thus saith the Lord God: The gate of the inner court that looketh toward the east, shall be shut the six days, on which work is done; but on the sabbath day it shall be opened, yea and on the day of the new moon it shall be opened.
46:2. And the prince shall enter by the way of the porch of the gate from without, and he shall stand at the threshold of the gate: and the priests shall offer his holocaust, and his peace offerings: and he shall adore upon the threshold of the gate, and shall go out: but the gate shall not be shut till the evening.
46:3. And the people of the land shall adore at the door of that gate before the Lord on the sabbaths, and on the new moons.
46:4. And the holocaust that the prince shall offer to the Lord on the sabbath day, shall be six lambs without blemish, and a ram without blemish.
46:5. And the sacrifice of all ephi for a ram: but for the lambs what sacrifice his hand shall allow: and a hin of oil for every ephi.
46:6. And on the day of the new moon a calf of the herd without blemish: and the six lambs, and the rams shall be without blemish.
46:7. And he shall offer in sacrifice an ephi for calf, an ephi also for a ram: but for the lambs, as his hand shall find: and a hin of oil for every ephi.
46:8. And when the prince is to go in, let him go in by the way of the porch of the gate, and let him go out the same way.
46:9. But when the people of the land shall go in before the Lord in the solemn feasts, he that goeth in by the north gate to adore, shall go out by the way of the south gate; and he that goeth in by the way of the south gate, shall go out by the way of the north gate: he shall not return by the way of the gate whereby he came in, but shall go out at that over against it.

46:10. And the prince in the midst of them, shall go in when they go in, and go out when they go out.
46:11. And in the fairs, and in the solemnities there shall be the sacrifice of an ephi to a calf, and an ephi to a ram: and to the lambs, the sacrifice shall be as his hand shall find: and a hin of oil to every ephi.
46:12. But when the prince shall offer a voluntary holocaust, or voluntary peace offering to the Lord: the gate that looketh towards the east shall be opened to him, and he shall offer his holocaust, and his peace offerings, as it is wont to be done on the sabbath day: and he shall go out, and the gate shall be shut after he is gone forth.
46:13. And he shall offer every day for a holocaust to the Lord, a lamb of the same year without blemish: he shall offer it always in the morning.
46:14. And he shall offer the sacrifice for it morning by morning, the sixth part of an ephi: and the third part of a hin of oil to be mingled with the fine flour: a sacrifice to the Lord by ordinance continual and everlasting.
46:15. He shall offer the lamb, and the sacrifice, and the oil morning by morning: an everlasting holocaust.
46:16. Thus saith the Lord God: If the prince give a gift to any of his sons: the inheritance of it shall go to his children, they shall possess it by inheritance.
46:17. But if he give a legacy out of his inheritance to one of his servants, it shall be his until the year of release, and it shall return to the prince: but his inheritance shall go to his sons.
46:18. And the prince shall not take of the people's inheritance by violence, nor of their possession: but out of his own possession he shall give an inheritance to his sons: that my people be not dispersed every man from his possession.
46:19. And he brought me in by the entry that was at the side of the gate, into the chambers of the sanctuary that were for the priests, which looked toward the north. And there was a place bending to the west.
46:20. And he said to me: This is the place where the priests shall boil the sin offering, and the trespass offering: where they shall dress the sacrifice, that they may not bring it out into the outward court, and the people be sanctified.
46:21. And he brought me into the outward court, and he led me about by the four corners of the court: and behold there was a little court in the corner of the court, to every corner of the court there was a little court.
46:22. In the four corners of the court were little courts disposed, forty cubits long, and thirty broad, all the four were of one measure.
46:23. And there was a wall round about compassing the four little courts, and there were kitchens built under the rows round about.
46:24. And he said to me: This is the house of the kitchens wherein the ministers of the house of the Lord shall boil the victims of the people.

Ezechiel Chapter 47

The vision of the holy waters issuing out from under the temple: the borders of the land to be divided among the twelve tribes.

47:1. And he brought me again to the gate of the house, and behold waters issued out from under the threshold of the house toward the east: for the forefront of the house looked toward the east: but the waters came down to the right side of the temple to the south part of the altar.
Waters... These waters are not to be understood literally (for there were none such that flowed from the temple); but mystically, of the baptism of Christ, and of his doctrine and his grace: the trees that grow on the banks are Christian virtues: the fishes are Christians, that spiritually live in and by these holy waters, the fishermen are the apostles, and apostolic preachers: the fenny places, where there is no health, are such as by being out of the church are separated from these waters of life.
47:2. And he led me out by the way of the north gate, and he caused me to turn to the way without the outward gate to the way that looked toward the east: and behold there ran out waters on the right side.
47:3. And when the man that had the line in his hand went out towards the east, he measured a thousand cubits: and he brought me through the water up to the ankles.
47:4. And again he measured a thousand, and he brought me through the water up to the knees.
47:5. And he measured a thousand, and he brought me through the water up to the loins. And he measured a thousand, and it was a torrent, which I could not pass over: for the waters were risen so as to make a deep torrent, which could not be passed over.
47:6. And he said to me: Surely thou hast seen, O son of man. And he brought me out, and he caused

me to turn to the bank of the torrent.
47:7. And when I had turned myself, behold on the bank of the torrent were very many trees on both sides.
47:8. And he said to me: These waters that issue forth toward the hillocks of sand to the east, and go down to the plains of the desert, shall go into the sea, and shall go out, and the waters shall be healed.
47:9. And every living creature that creepeth whithersoever the torrent shall come, shall live: and there shall be fishes in abundance after these waters shall come thither, and they shall be healed, and all things shall live to which the torrent shall come.
47:10. And the fishers shall stand over these waters, from Engaddi even to Engallim there shall be drying of nets: there shall be many sorts of the fishes thereof, as the fishes of the great sea, a very great multitude:
47:11. But on the shore thereof, and in the fenny places they shall not be healed, because they shall be turned into saltpits.
47:12. And by the torrent on the banks thereof on both sides shall grow all trees that bear fruit: their leaf shall not fall off, and their fruit shall not fail: every month shall they bring forth firstfruits, because the waters thereof shall issue out of the sanctuary: and the fruits thereof shall be for food, and the leaves thereof for medicine.
47:13. Thus saith the Lord God: This is the border, by which you shall possess the land according to the twelve tribes of Israel: for Joseph hath a double portion.
47:14. And you shall possess it, every man in like manner as his brother: concerning which I lifted up my hand to give it to your fathers: and this land shall fall unto you for a possession.
47:15. And this is the border of the land: toward the north side, from the great sea by the way of Hethalon, as men go to Sedada,
47:16. Emath, Berotha, Sabarim, which is between the border of Damascus and the border of Emath the house of Tichon, which is by the border of Auran.
47:17. And the border from the sea even to the court of Enan, shall be the border of Damascus, and from the north to the north: the border of Emath, this is the north side.
47:18. And the east side is from the midst of Auran, and from the midst of Damascus, and from the midst of Galaad, and from the midst of the land of Israel, Jordan making the bound to the east sea, and thus you shall measure the east side.
47:19. And the south side southward is, from Thamar even to the waters of contradiction of Cades: and, the torrent even to the great sea: and this is the south side southward.
47:20. And the side toward the sea, is the great sea from the borders straight on, till thou come to Emath: this is the side of the sea.
47:21. And you shall divide this land unto you by the tribes of Israel:
47:22. And you shall divide it by lot for an inheritance to you, and to the strangers that shall come over to you, that shall beget children among you: and they shall be unto you as men of the same country born among the children of Israel: they shall divide the possession with you in the midst of the tribes of Israel.
47:23. And in what tribe soever the stranger shall be, there shall you give him possession, saith the Lord God.

Ezechiel Chapter 48

The portions of the twelve tribes, of the sanctuary, of the city, and of the prince. The dimensions and gates of the city.

48:1. And these are the names of the tribes from the borders of the north, by the way of Hethalon, as they go to Emath, the court of Enan the border of Damascus northward, by the way off Emath. And from the east side thereof to the sea shall be one portion for Dan.
48:2. And by the border of Dan, from the east side even to the side of the sea, one portion for Aser:
48:3. And by the border of Aser, from the east side even to the side of the sea one portion for Nephthali.
48:4. And by the border of Nephthali, from the east side even to the side of the one portion for Manasses.
48:5. And by the border of Manasses, from the east side even to the side of the sea, one portion for Ephraim.
48:6. And by the border of Ephraim, from the east side even to the side of the sea, one portion for Ruben.

48:7. And by the border of Ruben, from the east side even to the side of the sea, one portion for Juda.
48:8. And by the border of Juda, from the east side even to the side of the sea, shall be the firstfruits which you shall set apart, five and twenty thousand in breadth, and length, as every one of the portions from the east side to the side of the sea: and the sanctuary shall be in the midst thereof.
48:9. The firstfruits which you shall set apart for the Lord will be the length of five and twenty thousand, and the breadth of ten thousand.
48:10. And these shall be the firstfruits of the sanctuary for the priests: toward the north five and twenty thousand in length, and toward the sea ten thousand in breadth, and toward the east also ten thousand in breadth, and toward the south five and twenty thousand in length: and the sanctuary of the Lord shall be in the midst thereof.
48:11. The sanctuary shall be for the priests of the sons of Sadoc, who kept my ceremonies, and went not astray when the children of Israel went astray, as the Levites also went astray.
48:12. And for them shall be the firstfruits of the firstfruits of the land holy of holies, by the border of the Levites,
48:13. And the Levites in like manner shall have by the borders of the priests five and twenty thousand in length, and ten thousand in breadth.
All the length shall be five and twenty thousand, and the breadth ten thousand.
48:14. And they shall not sell thereof, nor exchange, neither shall the firstfruits of the land be alienated, because they are sanctified to the Lord.
48:15. But the five thousand that remain in the breadth over against the five and twenty thousand, shall be a profane place for the city for dwelling, and for suburbs and the city shall be in the midst thereof.
48:16. And these are the measures thereof: on the north side four thousand and five hundred: and on the south side four thousand and five hundred: and on the east side four thousand and five hundred: and on the west side four thousand and five hundred.
48:17. And the suburbs of the city shall be to the north two hundred and fifty, and the south two hundred and fifty, and to the east two hundred and fifty, and to the sea two hundred and fifty.
48:18. And the residue in length by the firstfruits of the sanctuary, ten thousand toward the east, and ten thousand toward the west, shall be as the firstfruits of the sanctuary: and the fruit thereof shall be for bread to them that serve the city.
48:19. And they that serve the city, shall serve it out of all the tribes of Israel.
48:20. All the firstfruits, of five and twenty thousand, by five and twenty thousand foursquare, shall be set apart for the firstfruits of the sanctuary, and for the possession of the city.
48:21. And the residue shall be for the prince on every side of the firstfruits of the sanctuary, and of the possession of the city over against the five and twenty thousand of the firstfruits unto the east border: toward the sea also over against the five and twenty thousand, unto the border of the sea, shall likewise be the portion of the prince: and the firstfruits of the sanctuary, and the sanctuary of the temple shall be in the midst thereof.
48:22. And from the possession of the Levites, and from the possession of the city which are in the midst of the prince's portions: what shall be to the border of Juda, and to the border of Benjamin, shall also belong to the prince.
48:23. And for the rest of the tribes: from the east side to the west side, one portion for Benjamin.
48:24. And over against the border of Benjamin, from the east side to the west side, one portion for Simeon.
48:25. And by the border of Simeon, from the east side to the west side, one portion for Issachar.
48:26. And by the border of Issachar, from the east side to the west side, one portion for Zabulon.
48:27. And by the border of Zabulon, from the east side to the side of the sea, one portion for Gad.
48:28. And by the border of Gad, the south side southward: and the border shall be from Thamar, even to the waters of contradiction of Cades, the inheritance over against the great sea.
48:29. This is the land which you shall divide by lot to the tribes of Israel: and these are the portions of them, saith the Lord God.
48:30. And these are the goings out of the city: on the north side thou shalt measure four thousand and five hundred.
48:31. And the gates of the city according to the name, of the tribes of Israel, three gates on the north side, the gate of Ruben one, the gate of Juda one, the gate of Levi one.
48:32. And at the east side, four thousand and five hundred: and three gates, the gate of Joseph one, the gate of Benjamin one, the gate of Dan one.
48:33. And at the south side, thou shalt measure four thousand and five hundred and three gates, the gate of Simeon one, the gate of Issachar one, the gate of Zabulon one.
48:34. And at the west side, four thousand and five hundred, and their three gates, the gate of Gad one,

the gate of Aser one, the gate of Nephthali one.
48:35. Its circumference was eighteen thousand: and the name of the city from that day, The Lord is there.
The Lord is there.... This name is here given to the city, that is, to the church of Christ: because the Lord is always with her till the end of the world. Matt. 28.20.

THE BOOK OF THE PROPHET EZEKIEL

AMERICAN STANDARD BIBLE

Chapter 1

1 Now it came to pass in the thirtieth year, in the fourth [month], in the fifth [day] of the month, as I
was among the captives by the river Chebar, that the heavens were opened, and I saw visions of God.
2 In the fifth [day] of the month, which was the fifth year of king Jehoiachin's captivity,
3 the word of Jehovah came expressly unto Ezekiel the priest, the son of Buzi, in the land of the
Chaldeans by the river Chebar; and the hand of Jehovah was there upon him.
4 And I looked, and, behold, a stormy wind came out of the north, a great cloud, with a fire infolding
itself, and a brightness round about it, and out of the midst thereof as it were glowing metal, out of the
midst of the fire.
5 And out of the midst thereof came the likeness of four living creatures. And this was their appearance:
they had the likeness of a man.
6 And every one had four faces, and every one of them had four wings.
7 And their feet were straight feet; and the sole of their feet was like the sole of a calf's foot; and they
sparkled like burnished brass.
8 And they had the hands of a man under their wings on their four sides; and they four had their faces
and their wings [thus]:
9 their wings were joined one to another; they turned not when they went; they went every one straight
forward.
10 As for the likeness of their faces, they had the face of a man; and they four had the face of a lion on
the right side; and they four had the face of an ox on the left side; they four had also the face of an eagle.
11 And their faces and their wings were separate above; two [wings] of every one were joined one to
another, and two covered their bodies.
12 And they went every one straight forward: whither the spirit was to go, they went; they turned not
when they went.
13 As for the likeness of the living creatures, their appearance was like burning coals of fire, like the
appearance of torches: [the fire] went up and down among the living creatures; and the fire was bright,
and out of the fire went forth lightning.
14 And the living creatures ran and returned as the appearance of a flash of lightning.
15 Now as I beheld the living creatures, behold, one wheel upon the earth beside the living creatures,
for each of the four faces thereof.
16 The appearance of the wheels and their work was like unto a beryl: and they four had one likeness;
and their appearance and their work was as it were a wheel within a wheel.
17 When they went, they went in their four directions: they turned not when they went.
18 As for their rims, they were high and dreadful; and they four had their rims full of eyes round about.
19 And when the living creatures went, the wheels went beside them; and when the living creatures were
lifted up from the earth, the wheels were lifted up.
20 Whithersoever the spirit was to go, they went; thither was the spirit to go: and the wheels were lifted
up beside them; for the spirit of the living creature was in the wheels.
21 When those went, these went; and when those stood, these stood; and when those were lifted up
from the earth, the wheels were lifted up beside them: for the spirit of the living creature was in the
wheels.
22 And over the head of the living creature there was the likeness of a firmament, like the terrible crystal
to look upon, stretched forth over their heads above.
23 And under the firmament were their wings straight, the one toward the other: every one had two
which covered on this side, and every one had two which covered on that side, their bodies.
24 And when they went, I heard the noise of their wings like the noise of great waters, like the voice of

the Almighty, a noise of tumult like the noise of a host: when they stood, they let down their wings.
25 And there was a voice above the firmament that was over their heads: when they stood, they let down their wings.
26 And above the firmament that was over their heads was the likeness of a throne, as the appearance of a sapphire stone; and upon the likeness of the throne was a likeness as the appearance of a man upon it above.
27 And I saw as it were glowing metal, as the appearance of fire within it round about, from the appearance of his loins and upward; and from the appearance of his loins and downward I saw as it were the appearance of fire, and there was brightness round about him.
28 As the appearance of the bow that is in the cloud in the day of rain, so was the appearance of the brightness round about. This was the appearance of the likeness of the glory of Jehovah. And when I saw it, I fell upon my face, and I heard a voice of one that spake.

Chapter 2

1 And he said unto me, Son of man, stand upon thy feet, and I will speak with thee.
2 And the Spirit entered into me when he spake unto me, and set me upon my feet; and I heard him that spake unto me.
3 And he said unto me, Son of man, I send thee to the children of Israel, to nations that are rebellious, which have rebelled against me: they and their fathers have transgressed against me even unto this very day.
4 And the children are impudent and stiffhearted: I do sent thee unto them; and thou shalt say unto them, Thus saith the Lord Jehovah.
5 And they, whether they will hear, or whether they will forbear, (for they are a rebellious house,) yet shall know that there hath been a prophet among them.
6 And thou, son of man, be not afraid of them, neither be afraid of their words, though briers and thorns are with thee, and thou dost dwell among scorpions: be not afraid of their words, nor be dismayed at their looks, though they are a rebellious house.
7 And thou shalt speak my words unto them, whether they will hear, or whether they will forbear; for they are most rebellious.
8 But thou, son of man, hear what I say unto thee; be not thou rebellious like that rebellious house: open thy mouth, and eat that which I give thee.
9 And when I looked, behold, a hand was put forth unto me; and, lo, a roll of a book was therein;
10 And he spread it before me: and it was written within and without; and there were written therein lamentations, and mourning, and woe.

Chapter 3

1 And he said unto me, Son of man, eat that which thou findest; eat this roll, and go, speak unto the house of Israel.
2 So I opened my mouth, and he caused me to eat the roll.
3 And he said unto me, Son of man, cause thy belly to eat, and fill thy bowels with this roll that I give thee. Then did I eat it; and it was in my mouth as honey for sweetness.
4 And he said unto me, Son of man, go, get thee unto the house of Israel, and speak with my words unto them.
5 For thou art not sent to a people of a strange speech and of a hard language, but to the house of Israel;
6 not to many peoples of a strange speech and of a hard language, whose words thou canst not understand. Surely, if I sent thee to them, they would hearken unto thee.
7 But the house of Israel will not hearken unto thee; for they will not hearken unto me: for all the house of Israel are of hard forehead and of a stiff heart.
8 Behold, I have made thy face hard against their faces, and thy forehead hard against their foreheads.
9 As an adamant harder than flint have I made thy forehead: fear them not, neither be dismayed at their looks, though they are a rebellious house.
10 Moreover he said unto me, Son of man, all my words that I shall speak unto thee receive in thy heart, and hear with thine ears.
11 And go, get thee to them of the captivity, unto the children of thy people, and speak unto them, and tell them, Thus saith the Lord Jehovah; whether they will hear, or whether they will forbear.
12 Then the Spirit lifted me up, and I heard behind me the voice of a great rushing, [saying], Blessed be

the glory of Jehovah from his place.
13 And [I heard] the noise of the wings of the living creatures as they touched one another, and the noise of the wheels beside them, even the noise of a great rushing.
14 So the Spirit lifted me up, and took me away; and I went in bitterness, in the heat of my spirit; and the hand of Jehovah was strong upon me.
15 Then I came to them of the captivity at Tel-abib, that dwelt by the river Chebar, and to where they dwelt; and I sat there overwhelmed among them seven days.
16 And it came to pass at the end of seven days, that the word of Jehovah came unto me, saying,
17 Son of man, I have made thee a watchman unto the house of Israel: therefore hear the word at my mouth, and give them warning from me.
18 When I say unto the wicked, Thou shalt surely die; and thou givest him not warning, nor speakest to warn the wicked from his wicked way, to save his life; the same wicked man shall die in his iniquity; but his blood will I require at thy hand.
19 Yet if thou warn the wicked, and he turn not from his wickedness, nor from his wicked way, he shall die in his iniquity; but thou hast delivered thy soul.
20 Again, when a righteous man doth turn from his righteousness, and commit iniquity, and I lay a stumblingblock before him, he shall die: because thou hast not given him warning, he shall die in his sin, and his righteous deeds which he hath done shall not be remembered; but his blood will I require at thy hand.
21 Nevertheless if thou warn the righteous man, that the righteous sin not, and he doth not sin, he shall surely live, because he took warning; and thou hast delivered thy soul.
22 And the hand of Jehovah was there upon me; and he said unto me, Arise, go forth into the plain, and I will there talk with thee.
23 Then I arose, and went forth into the plain: and, behold, the glory of Jehovah stood there, as the glory which I saw by the river Chebar; and I fell on my face.
24 Then the Spirit entered into me, and set me upon my feet; and he spake with me, and said unto me, Go, shut thyself within thy house.
25 But thou, son of man, behold, they shall lay bands upon thee, and shall bind thee with them, and thou shalt not go out among them:
26 and I will make thy tongue cleave to the roof of thy mouth, that thou shalt be dumb, and shalt not be to them a reprover; for they are a rebellious house.
27 But when I speak with thee, I will open thy mouth, and thou shalt say unto them, Thus saith the Lord Jehovah: He that heareth, let him hear; and he that forbeareth, let him forbear: for they are a rebellious house.

Chapter 4

1 Thou also, son of man, take thee a tile, and lay it before thee, and portray upon it a city, even Jerusalem:
2 and lay siege against it, and build forts against it, and cast up a mound against it; set camps also against it, and plant battering rams against it round about.
3 And take thou unto thee an iron pan, and set it for a wall of iron between thee and the city: and set thy face toward it, and it shall be besieged, and thou shalt lay siege against it. This shall be a sign to the house of Israel.
4 Moreover lie thou upon thy left side, and lay the iniquity of the house of Israel upon it; [according to] the number of the days that thou shalt lie upon it, thou shalt bear their iniquity.
5 For I have appointed the years of their iniquity to be unto thee a number of days, even three hundred and ninety days: so shalt thou bear the iniquity of the house of Israel.
6 And again, when thou hast accomplished these, thou shalt lie on thy right side, and shalt bear the iniquity of the house of Judah: forty days, each day for a year, have I appointed it unto thee.
7 And thou shalt set thy face toward the siege of Jerusalem, with thine arm uncovered; and thou shalt prophesy against it.
8 And, behold, I lay bands upon thee, and thou shalt not turn thee from one side to the other, till thou hast accomplished the days of thy siege.
9 Take thou also unto thee wheat, and barley, and beans, and lentils, and millet, and spelt, and put them in one vessel, and make thee bread thereof; [according to] the number of the days that thou shalt lie upon thy side, even three hundred and ninety days, shalt thou eat thereof.
10 And thy food which thou shalt eat shall be by weight, twenty shekels a day: from time to time shalt thou eat it.

11 And thou shalt drink water by measure, the sixth part of a hin: from time to time shalt thou drink.
12 And thou shalt eat it as barley cakes, and thou shalt bake it in their sight with dung that cometh out
of man.
13 And Jehovah said, Even thus shall the children of Israel eat their bread unclean, among the nations
whither I will drive them.
14 Then said I, Ah Lord Jehovah! behold, my soul hath not been polluted; for from my youth up even
till now have I not eaten of that which dieth of itself, or is torn of beasts; neither came there abominable
flesh into my mouth.
15 Then he said unto me, See, I have given thee cow's dung for man's dung, and thou shalt prepare thy
bread thereon.
16 Moreover he said unto me, Son of man, behold, I will break the staff of bread in Jerusalem: and they
shall eat bread by weight, and with fearfulness; and they shall drink water by measure, and in dismay:
17 that they may want bread and water, and be dismayed one with another, and pine away in their
iniquity.

Chapter 5

1 And thou, son of man, take thee a sharp sword; [as] a barber's razor shalt thou take it unto thee, and
shalt cause it to pass upon thy head and upon thy beard: then take thee balances to weigh, and divide the
hair.
2 A third part shalt thou burn in the fire in the midst of the city, when the days of the siege are fulfilled;
and thou shalt take a third part, and smite with the sword round about it; and a third part thou shalt
scatter to the wind, and I will draw out a sword after them.
3 And thou shalt take thereof a few in number, and bind them in thy skirts.
4 And of these again shalt thou take, and cast them into the midst of the fire, and burn them in the fire;
therefrom shall a fire come forth into all the house of Israel.
5 Thus saith the Lord Jehovah: This is Jerusalem; I have set her in the midst of the nations, and
countries are round about her.
6 And she hath rebelled against mine ordinances in doing wickedness more than the nations, and against
my statutes more than the countries that are round about her; for they have rejected mine ordinances,
and as for my statutes, they have not walked in them.
7 Therefore thus saith the Lord Jehovah: Because ye are turbulent more than the nations that are round
about you, and have not walked in my statutes, neither have kept mine ordinances, neither have done
after the ordinances of the nations that are round about you;
8 therefore thus saith the Lord Jehovah: Behold, I, even I, am against thee; and I will execute judgments
in the midst of thee in the sight of the nations.
9 And I will do in thee that which I have not done, and whereunto I will not do any more the like,
because of all thine abominations.
10 Therefore the fathers shall eat the sons in the midst of thee, and the sons shall eat their fathers; and I
will execute judgments on thee; and the whole remnant of thee will I scatter unto all the winds.
11 Wherefore, as I live, saith the Lord Jehovah, surely, because thou hast defiled my sanctuary with all
thy detestable things, and with all thine abominations, therefore will I also diminish [thee]; neither shall
mine eye spare, and I also will have no pity.
12 A third part of thee shall die with the pestilence, and with famine shall they be consumed in the midst
of thee; and a third part shall fall by the sword round about thee; and a third part I will scatter unto all
the winds, and will draw out a sword after them.
13 Thus shall mine anger be accomplished, and I will cause my wrath toward them to rest, and I shall be
comforted; and they shall know that I, Jehovah, have spoken in my zeal, when I have accomplished my
wrath upon them.
14 Moreover I will make thee a desolation and a reproach among the nations that are round about thee,
in the sight of all that pass by.
15 So it shall be a reproach and a taunt, an instruction and an astonishment, unto the nations that are
round about thee, when I shall execute judgments on thee in anger and in wrath, and in wrathful
rebukes; (I, Jehovah, have spoken it;)
16 when I shall send upon them the evil arrows of famine, that are for destruction, which I will send to
destroy you: and I will increase the famine upon you, and will break your staff of bread;
17 and I will send upon you famine and evil beasts, and they shall bereave thee; and pestilence and
blood shall pass through thee; and I will bring the sword upon thee: I, Jehovah, have spoken it.

Chapter 6

1 And the word of Jehovah came unto me, saying,
2 Son of man, set thy face toward the mountains of Israel, and prophesy unto them,
3 and say, Ye mountains of Israel, hear the word of the Lord Jehovah: Thus saith the Lord Jehovah to the mountains and to the hills, to the watercourses and to the valleys: Behold, I, even I, will bring a sword upon you, and I will destroy your high places.
4 And your altars shall become desolate, and your sun-images shall be broken; and I will cast down your slain men before your idols.
5 And I will lay the dead bodies of the children of Israel before their idols; and I will scatter your bones round about your altars.
6 In all your dwelling-places the cities shall be laid waste, and the high places shall be desolate; that your altars may be laid waste and made desolate, and your idols may be broken and cease, and your sun-images may be hewn down, and your works may be abolished.
7 And the slain shall fall in the midst of you, and ye shall know that I am Jehovah.
8 Yet will I leave a remnant, in that ye shall have some that escape the sword among the nations, when ye shall be scattered through the countries.
9 And those of you that escape shall remember me among the nations whither they shall be carried captive, how that I have been broken with their lewd heart, which hath departed from me, and with they eyes, which play the harlot after their idols: and they shall loathe themselves in their own sight for the evils which they have committed in all their abominations.
10 And they shall know that I am Jehovah: I have not said in vain that I would do this evil unto them.
11 Thus saith the Lord Jehovah: Smite with thy hand, and stamp with thy foot, and say, Alas! because of all the evil abominations of the house of Israel; for they shall fall by the sword, by the famine, and by the pestilence.
12 He that is far off shall die of the pestilence; and he that is near shall fall by the sword; and he that remaineth and is besieged shall die by the famine: thus will I accomplish my wrath upon them.
13 And ye shall know that I am Jehovah, when their slain men shall be among their idols round about their altars, upon every high hill, on all the tops of the mountains, and under every green tree, and under every thick oak, the places where they offered sweet savor to all their idols.
14 And I will stretch out my hand upon them, and make the land desolate and waste, from the wilderness toward Diblah, throughout all their habitations: and they shall know that I am Jehovah.

Chapter 7

1 Moreover the word of Jehovah came unto me, saying,
2 And thou, son of man, thus saith the Lord Jehovah unto the land of Israel, An end: the end is come upon the four corners of the land.
3 Now is the end upon thee, and I will send mine anger upon thee, and will judge thee according to thy ways; and I will bring upon thee all thine abominations.
4 And mine eye shall not spare thee, neither will I have pity; but I will bring thy ways upon thee, and thine abominations shall be in the midst of thee: and ye shall know that I am Jehovah.
5 Thus saith the Lord Jehovah: An evil, an only evil; behold, it cometh.
6 An end is come, the end is come; it awaketh against thee; behold, it cometh.
7 Thy doom is come unto thee, O inhabitant of the land: the time is come, the day is near, [a day of] tumult, and not [of] joyful shouting, upon the mountains.
8 Now will I shortly pour out my wrath upon thee, and accomplish mine anger against thee, and will judge thee according to thy ways; and I will bring upon thee all thine abominations.
9 And mine eye shall not spare, neither will I have pity: I will bring upon thee according to thy ways; and thine abominations shall be in the midst of thee; and ye shall know that I, Jehovah, do smite.
10 Behold, the day, behold, it cometh: thy doom is gone forth; the rod hath blossomed, pride hath budded.
11 Violence is risen up into a rod of wickedness; none of them [shall remain], nor of their multitude, nor of their wealth: neither shall there be eminency among them.
12 The time is come, the day draweth near: let not the buyer rejoice, nor the seller mourn; for wrath is upon all the multitude thereof.
13 For the seller shall not return to that which is sold, although they be yet alive: for the vision is touching the whole multitude thereof, none shall return; neither shall any strengthen himself in the iniquity of his life.

14 They have blown the trumpet, and have made all ready; but none goeth to the battle; for my wrath is upon all the multitude thereof.
15 The sword is without, and the pestilence and the famine within: he that is in the field shall die with the sword: and he that is in the city, famine and pestilence shall devour him.
16 But those of them that escape shall escape, and shall be on the mountains like doves of the valleys, all of them moaning, every one in his iniquity.
17 All hands shall be feeble, and all knees shall be weak as water.
18 They shall also gird themselves with sackcloth, and horror shall cover them; and shame shall be upon all faces, and baldness upon all their heads.
19 They shall cast their silver in the streets, and their gold shall be as an unclean thing; their silver and their gold shall not be able to deliver them in the day of the wrath of Jehovah: they shall not satisfy their souls, neither fill their bowels; because it hath been the stumblingblock of their iniquity.
20 As for the beauty of his ornament, he set it in majesty; but they made the images of their abominations [and] their detestable things therein: therefore have I made it unto them as an unclean thing.
21 And I will give it into the hands of the strangers for a prey, and to the wicked of the earth for a spoil; and they shall profane it.
22 My face will I turn also from them, and they shall profane my secret [place]; and robbers shall enter into it, and profane it.
23 Make the chain; for the land is full of bloody crimes, and the city is full of violence.
24 Wherefore I will bring the worst of the nations, and they shall possess their houses: I will also make the pride of the strong to cease; and their holy places shall be profaned.
25 Destruction cometh; and they shall seek peace, and there shall be none.
26 Mischief shall come upon mischief, and rumor shall be upon rumor; and they shall seek a vision of the prophet; but the law shall perish from the priest, and counsel from the elders.
27 The king shall mourn, and the prince shall be clothed with desolation, and the hands of the people of the land shall be troubled: I will do unto them after their way, and according to their deserts will I judge them; and they shall know that I am Jehovah.

Chapter 8

1 And it came to pass in the sixth year, in the sixth [month], in the fifth [day] of the month, as I sat in my house, and the elders of Judah sat before me, that the hand of the Lord Jehovah fell there upon me.
2 Then I beheld, and, lo, a likeness as the appearance of fire; from the appearance of his loins and downward, fire; and from his loins and upward, as the appearance of brightness, as it were glowing metal.
3 And he put forth the form of a hand, and took me by a lock of my head; and the Spirit lifted me up between earth and heaven, and brought me in the visions of God to Jerusalem, to the door of the gate of the inner [court] that looketh toward the north; where was the seat of the image of jealousy, which provoketh to jealousy.
4 And, behold, the glory of the God of Israel was there, according to the appearance that I saw in the plain.
5 Then said he unto me, Son of man, lift up thine eyes now the way toward the north. So I lifted up mine eyes the way toward the north, and behold, northward of the gate of the altar this image of jealousy in the entry.
6 And he said unto me, Son of man, seest thou what they do? even the great abominations that the house of Israel do commit here, that I should go far off from my sanctuary? but thou shalt again see yet other great abominations.
7 And he brought me to the door of the court; and when I looked, behold, a hole in the wall.
8 Then said he unto me, Son of man, dig now in the wall: and when I had digged in the wall, behold, a door.
9 And he said unto me, Go in, and see the wicked abominations that they do here.
10 So I went in and saw; and behold, every form of creeping things, and abominable beasts, and all the idols of the house of Israel, portrayed upon the wall round about.
11 And there stood before them seventy men of the elders of the house of Israel; and in the midst of them stood Jaazaniah the son of Shaphan, every man with his censer in his hand; and the odor of the cloud of incense went up.
12 Then said he unto me, Son of man, hast thou seen what the elders of the house of Israel do in the dark, every man in his chambers of imagery? for they say, Jehovah seeth us not; Jehovah hath forsaken

the land.
13 He said also unto me, Thou shalt again see yet other great abominations which they do.
14 Then he brought me to the door of the gate of Jehovah's house which was toward the north; and
behold, there sat the women weeping for Tammuz.
15 Then said he unto me, Hast thou seen [this], O son of man? thou shalt again see yet greater
abominations than these.
16 And he brought me into the inner court of Jehovah's house; and behold, at the door of the temple of
Jehovah, between the porch and the altar, were about five and twenty men, with their backs toward the
temple of Jehovah, and their faces toward the east; and they were worshipping the sun toward the east.
17 Then he said unto me, Hast thou seen [this], O son of man? Is it a light thing to the house of Judah
that they commit the abominations which they commit here? for they have filled the land with violence,
and have turned again to provoke me to anger: and, lo, they put the branch to their nose.
18 Therefore will I also deal in wrath; mine eye shall not spare, neither will I have pity; and though they
cry in mine ears with a loud voice, yet will I not hear them.

Chapter 9

1 Then he cried in mine ears with a loud voice, saying, Cause ye them that have charge over the city to
draw near, every man with his destroying weapon in his hand.
2 And behold, six men came from the way of the upper gate, which lieth toward the north, every man
with his slaughter weapon in his hand; and one man in the midst of them clothed in linen, with a writer's
inkhorn by his side. And they went in, and stood beside the brazen altar.
3 And the glory of the God of Israel was gone up from the cherub, whereupon it was, to the threshold
of the house: and he called to the man clothed in linen, who had the writer's inkhorn by his side.
4 And Jehovah said unto him, Go through the midst of the city, through the midst of Jerusalem, and set
a mark upon the foreheads of the men that sigh and that cry over all the abominations that are done in
the midst thereof.
5 And to the others he said in my hearing, Go ye through the city after him, and smite: let not your eye
spare, neither have ye pity;
6 slay utterly the old man, the young man and the virgin, and little children and women; but come not
near any man upon whom is the mark: and begin at my sanctuary. Then they began at the old men that
were before the house.
7 And he said unto them, Defile the house, and fill the courts with the slain: go ye forth. And they went
forth, and smote in the city.
8 And it came to pass, while they were smiting, and I was left, that I fell upon my face, and cried, and
said, Ah Lord Jehovah! wilt thou destroy all the residue of Israel in thy pouring out of thy wrath upon
Jerusalem?
9 Then said he unto me, The iniquity of the house of Israel and Judah is exceeding great, and the land is
full of blood, and the city full of wrestling [of judgment]: for they say, Jehovah hath forsaken the land,
and Jehovah seeth not.
10 And as for me also, mine eye shall not spare, neither will I have pity, but I will bring their way upon
their head.
11 And behold, the man clothed in linen, who had the inkhorn by his side, reported the matter, saying, I
have done as thou hast commanded me.

Chapter 10

1 Then I looked, and behold, in the firmament that was over the head of the cherubim there appeared
above them as it were a sapphire stone, as the appearance of the likeness of a throne.
2 And he spake unto the man clothed in linen, and said, Go in between the whirling [wheels], even
under the cherub, and fill both thy hands with coals of fire from between the cherubim, and scatter
them over the city. And he went in in my sight.
3 Now the cherubim stood on the right side of the house, when the man went in; and the cloud filled
the inner court.
4 And the glory of Jehovah mounted up from the cherub, [and stood] over the threshold of the house;
and the house was filled with the cloud, and the court was full of the brightness of Jehovah's glory.
5 And the sound of the wings of the cherubim was heard even to the outer court, as the voice of God
Almighty when he speaketh.
6 And it came to pass, when he commanded the man clothed in linen, saying, Take fire from between

the whirling wheels, from between the cherubim, that he went in, and stood beside a wheel.
7 And the cherub stretched forth his hand from between the cherubim unto the fire that was between
the cherubim, and took [thereof], and put it into the hands of him that was clothed in linen, who took it
and went out.
8 And there appeared in the cherubim the form of a man's hand under their wings.
9 And I looked, and behold, four wheels beside the cherubim, one wheel beside one cherub, and
another wheel beside another cherub; and the appearance of the wheels was like unto a beryl stone.
10 And as for their appearance, they four had one likeness, as if a wheel have been within a wheel.
11 When they went, they went in their four directions: they turned not as they went, but to the place
whither the head looked they followed it; they turned not as they went.
12 And their whole body, and their backs, and their hands, and their wings, and the wheels, were full of
eyes round about, [even] the wheels that they four had.
13 As for the wheels, they were called in my hearing, the whirling [wheels].
14 And every one had four faces: the first face was the face of the cherub, and the second face was the
face of a man, and the third face the face of a lion, and the fourth the face of an eagle.
15 And the cherubim mounted up: this is the living creature that I saw by the river Chebar.
16 And when the cherubim went, the wheels went beside them; and when the cherubim lifted up their
wings to mount up from the earth, the wheels also turned not from beside them.
17 When they stood, these stood; and when they mounted up, these mounted up with them: for the
spirit of the living creature was in them.
18 And the glory of Jehovah went forth from over the threshold of the house, and stood over the
cherubim.
19 And the cherubim lifted up their wings, and mounted up from the earth in my sight when they went
forth, and the wheels beside them: and they stood at the door of the east gate of Jehovah's house; and
the glory of the God of Israel was over them above.
20 This is the living creature that I saw under the God of Israel by the river Chebar; and I knew that
they were cherubim.
21 Every one had four faces, and every one four wings; and the likeness of the hands of a man was
under their wings.
22 And as for the likeness of their faces, they were the faces which I saw by the river Chebar, their
appearances and themselves; they went every one straight forward.

Chapter 11

1 Moreover the Spirit lifted me up, and brought me unto the east gate of Jehovah's house, which
looketh eastward: and behold, at the door of the gate five and twenty men; and I saw in the midst of
them Jaazaniah the son of Azzur, and Pelatiah the son of Benaiah, princes of the people.
2 And he said unto me, Son of man, these are the men that devise iniquity, and that give wicked counsel
in this city;
3 that say, [The time] is not near to build houses: this [city] is the caldron, and we are the flesh.
4 Therefore prophesy against them, prophesy, O son of man.
5 And the Spirit of Jehovah fell upon me, and he said unto me, Speak, Thus saith Jehovah: Thus have ye
said, O house of Israel; for I know the things that come into your mind.
6 Ye have multiplied your slain in this city, and ye have filled the streets thereof with the slain.
7 Therefore thus saith the Lord Jehovah: Your slain whom ye have laid in the midst of it, they are the
flesh, and this [city] is the caldron; but ye shall be brought forth out of the midst of it.
8 Ye have feared the sword; and I will bring the sword upon you, saith the Lord Jehovah.
9 And I will bring you forth out of the midst thereof, and deliver you into the hands of strangers, and
will execute judgments among you.
10 Ye shall fall by the sword; I will judge you in the border of Israel; and ye shall know that I am
Jehovah.
11 This [city] shall not be your caldron, neither shall ye be the flesh in the midst thereof; I will judge you
in the border of Israel;
12 and ye shall know that I am Jehovah: for ye have not walked in my statutes, neither have ye executed
mine ordinances, but have done after the ordinances of the nations that are round about you.
13 And it came to pass, when I prophesied, that Pelatiah the son of Benaiah died. Then fell I down
upon my face, and cried with a loud voice, and said, Ah Lord Jehovah! wilt thou make a full end of the
remnant of Israel?
14 And the word of Jehovah came unto me, saying,

15 Son of man, thy brethren, even thy brethren, the men of thy kindred, and all the house of Israel, all of them, [are they] unto whom the inhabitants of Jerusalem have said, Get you far from Jehovah; unto us is this land given for a possession.
16 Therefore say, Thus saith the Lord Jehovah: Whereas I have removed them far off among the nations, and whereas I have scattered them among the countries, yet will I be to them a sanctuary for a little while in the countries where they are come.
17 Therefore say, Thus saith the Lord Jehovah: I will gather you from the peoples, and assemble you out of the countries where ye have been scattered, and I will give you the land of Israel.
18 And they shall come thither, and they shall take away all the detestable things thereof and all the abominations thereof from thence.
19 And I will give them one heart, and I will put a new spirit within you; and I will take the stony heart out of their flesh, and will give them a heart of flesh;
20 that they may walk in my statutes, and keep mine ordinances, and do them: and they shall be my people, and I will be their God.
21 But as for them whose heart walketh after the heart of their detestable things and their abominations, I will bring their way upon their own heads, saith the Lord Jehovah.
22 Then did the cherubim lift up their wings, and the wheels were beside them; and the glory of the God of Israel was over them above.
23 And the glory of Jehovah went up from the midst of the city, and stood upon the mountain which is on the east side of the city.
24 And the Spirit lifted me up, and brought me in the vision by the Spirit of God into Chaldea, to them of the captivity. So the vision that I had seen went up from me.
25 Then I spake unto them of the captivity all the things that Jehovah had showed me.

Chapter 12

1 The word of Jehovah also came unto me, saying,
2 Son of man, thou dwellest in the midst of the rebellious house, that have eyes to see, and see not, that have ears to hear, and hear not; for they are a rebellious house.
3 Therefore, thou son of man, prepare thee stuff for removing, and remove by day in their sight; and thou shalt remove from thy place to another place in their sight: it may be they will consider, though they are a rebellious house.
4 And thou shalt bring forth thy stuff by day in their sight, as stuff for removing; and thou shalt go forth thyself at even in their sight, as when men go forth into exile.
5 Dig thou through the wall in their sight, and carry out thereby.
6 In their sight shalt thou bear it upon thy shoulder, and carry it forth in the dark; thou shalt cover thy face, that thou see not the land: for I have set thee for a sign unto the house of Israel.
7 And I did so as I was commanded: I brought forth my stuff by day, as stuff for removing, and in the even I digged through the wall with my hand; I brought it forth in the dark, and bare it upon my shoulder in their sight.
8 And in the morning came the word of Jehovah unto me, saying,
9 Son of man, hath not the house of Israel, the rebellious house, said unto thee, What doest thou?
10 Say thou unto them, Thus saith the Lord Jehovah: This burden [concerneth] the prince in Jerusalem, and all the house of Israel among whom they are.
11 Say, I am your sign: like as I have done, so shall it be done unto them; they shall go into exile, into captivity.
12 And the prince that is among them shall bear upon his shoulder in the dark, and shall go forth: they shall dig through the wall to carry out thereby: he shall cover his face, because he shall not see the land with his eyes.
13 My net also will I spread upon him, and he shall be taken in my snare; and I will bring him to Babylon to the land of the Chaldeans; yet shall he not see it, though he shall die there.
14 And I will scatter toward every wind all that are round about him to help him, and all his bands; and I will draw out the sword after them.
15 And they shall know that I am Jehovah, when I shall disperse them among the nations, and scatter them through the countries.
16 But I will leave a few men of them from the sword, from the famine, and from the pestilence; that they may declare all their abominations among the nations whither they come; and they shall know that I am Jehovah.
17 Moreover the word of Jehovah came to me, saying,

18 Son of man, eat thy bread with quaking, and drink thy water with trembling and with fearfulness;
19 and say unto the people of the land, Thus saith the Lord Jehovah concerning the inhabitants of Jerusalem, and the land of Israel: They shall eat their bread with fearfulness, and drink their water in dismay, that her land may be desolate, [and despoiled] of all that is therein, because of the violence of all them that dwell therein.
20 And the cities that are inhabited shall be laid waste, and the land shall be a desolation; and ye shall know that I am Jehovah.
21 And the word of Jehovah came unto me, saying,
22 Son of man, what is this proverb that ye have in the land of Israel, saying, The days are prolonged, and every vision faileth?
23 Tell them therefore, Thus saith the Lord Jehovah: I will make this proverb to cease, and they shall no more use it as a proverb in Israel; but say unto them, The days are at hand, and the fulfilment of every vision.
24 For there shall be no more any false vision nor flattering divination within the house of Israel.
25 For I am Jehovah; I will speak, and the word that I shall speak shall be performed; it shall be no more deferred: for in your days, O rebellious house, will I speak the word, and will perform it, saith the Lord Jehovah.
26 Again the word of Jehovah came to me, saying,
27 Son of man, behold, they of the house of Israel say, The vision that he seeth is for many day to come, and he prophesieth of times that are far off.
28 Therefore say unto them, Thus saith the Lord Jehovah: There shall none of my words be deferred any more, but the word which I shall speak shall be performed, saith the Lord Jehovah.

Chapter 13

1 And the word of Jehovah came unto me, saying,
2 Son of man, prophesy against the prophets of Israel that prophesy, and say thou unto them that prophesy out of their own heart, Hear ye the word of Jehovah:
3 Thus saith the Lord Jehovah, Woe unto the foolish prophets, that follow their own spirit, and have seen nothing!
4 O Israel, thy prophets have been like foxes in the waste places.
5 Ye have not gone up into the gaps, neither built up the wall for the house of Israel, to stand in the battle in the day of Jehovah.
6 They have seen falsehood and lying divination, that say, Jehovah saith; but Jehovah hath not sent them: and they have made men to hope that the word would be confirmed.
7 Have ye not seen a false vision, and have ye not spoken a lying divination, in that ye say, Jehovah saith; albeit I have not spoken?
8 Therefore thus saith the Lord Jehovah: Because ye have spoken falsehood, and seen lies, therefore, behold, I am against you, saith the Lord Jehovah.
9 And my hand shall be against the prophets that see false visions, and that divine lies: they shall not be in the council of my people, neither shall they be written in the writing of the house of Israel, neither shall they enter into the land of Israel; and ye shall know that I am the Lord Jehovah.
10 Because, even because they have seduced my people, saying, Peace; and there is no peace; and when one buildeth up a wall, behold, they daub it with untempered [mortar]:
11 say unto them that daub it with untempered [mortar], that it shall fall: there shall be an overflowing shower; and ye, O great hailstones, shall fall; and a stormy wind shall rend it.
12 Lo, when the wall is fallen, shall it not be said unto you, Where is the daubing wherewith ye have daubed it?
13 Therefore thus saith the Lord Jehovah: I will even rend it with a stormy wind in my wrath; and there shall be an overflowing shower in mine anger, and great hailstones in wrath to consume it.
14 So will I break down the wall that ye have daubed with untempered [mortar], and bring it down to the ground, so that the foundation thereof shall be uncovered; and it shall fall, and ye shall be consumed in the midst thereof: and ye shall know that I am Jehovah.
15 Thus will I accomplish my wrath upon the wall, and upon them that have daubed it with untempered [mortar]; and I will say unto you, The wall is no more, neither they that daubed it;
16 [to wit], the prophets of Israel that prophesy concerning Jerusalem, and that see visions of peace for her, and there is no peace, saith the Lord Jehovah.
17 And thou, son of man, set thy face against the daughters of thy people, that prophesy out of their own heart; and prophesy thou against them,

18 and say, Thus saith the Lord Jehovah: Woe to the women that sew pillows upon all elbows, and make
kerchiefs for the head of [persons of] every stature to hunt souls! Will ye hunt the souls of my people,
and save souls alive for yourselves?
19 And ye have profaned me among my people for handfuls of barley and for pieces of bread, to slay
the souls that should not die, and to save the souls alive that should not live, by your lying to my people
that hearken unto lies.
20 Wherefore thus saith the Lord Jehovah: Behold, I am against your pillows, wherewith ye there hunt
the souls to make [them] fly, and I will tear them from your arms; and I will let the souls go, even the
souls that ye hunt to make [them] fly.
21 Your kerchiefs also will I tear, and deliver my people out of your hand, and they shall be no more in
your hand to be hunted; and ye shall know that I am Jehovah.
22 Because with lies ye have grieved the heart of the righteous, whom I have not made sad; and
strengthened the hands of the wicked, that he should not return from his wicked way, and be saved
alive:
23 Therefore ye shall no more see false visions, nor divine divinations: and I will deliver my people out
of your hand; and ye shall know that I am Jehovah.

Chapter 14

1 Then came certain of the elders of Israel unto me, and sat before me.
2 And the word of Jehovah came unto me, saying,
3 Son of man, these men have taken their idols into their heart, and put the stumblingblock of their
iniquity before their face: should I be inquired of at all by them?
4 Therefore speak unto them, and say unto them, Thus saith the Lord Jehovah: Every man of the house
of Israel that taketh his idols into his heart, and putteth the stumblingblock of his iniquity before his
face, and cometh to the prophet; I Jehovah will answer him therein according to the multitude of his
idols;
5 that I may take the house of Israel in their own heart, because they are all estranged from me through
their idols.
6 Therefore say unto the house of Israel, Thus saith the Lord Jehovah: Return ye, and turn yourselves
from your idols; and turn away your faces from all your abominations.
7 For every one of the house of Israel, or of the strangers that sojourn in Israel, that separateth himself
from me, and taketh his idols into his heart, and putteth the stumblingblock of his iniquity before his
face, and cometh to the prophet to inquire for himself of me; I Jehovah will answer him by myself:
8 and I will set my face against that man, and will make him an astonishment, for a sign and a proverb,
and I will cut him off from the midst of my people; and ye shall know that I am Jehovah.
9 And if the prophet be deceived and speak a word, I, Jehovah, have deceived that prophet, and I will
stretch out my hand upon him, and will destroy him from the midst of my people Israel.
10 And they shall bear their iniquity: the iniquity of the prophet shall be even as the iniquity of him that
seeketh [unto him];
11 that the house of Israel may go no more astray from me, neither defile themselves any more with all
their transgressions; but that they may be my people, and I may be their God, saith the Lord Jehovah.
12 And the word of Jehovah came unto me, saying,
13 Son of man, when a land sinneth against me by committing a trespass, and I stretch out my hand
upon it, and break the staff of the bread thereof, and send famine upon it, and cut off from it man and
beast;
14 though these three men, Noah, Daniel, and Job, were in it, they should deliver but their own souls by
their righteousness, saith the Lord Jehovah.
15 If I cause evil beasts to pass through the land, and they ravage it, and it be made desolate, so that no
man may pass through because of the beasts;
16 though these three men were in it, as I live, saith the Lord Jehovah, they should deliver neither sons
nor daughters; they only should be delivered, but the land should be desolate.
17 Or if I bring a sword upon that land, and say, Sword, go through the land; so that I cut off from it
man and beast;
18 though these three men were in it, as I live, saith the Lord Jehovah, they should deliver neither sons
nor daughters, but they only should be delivered themselves.
19 Or if I send a pestilence into that land, and pour out my wrath upon it in blood, to cut off from it
man and beast;
20 though Noah, Daniel, and Job, were in it, as I live, saith the Lord Jehovah, they should deliver neither

son nor daughter; they should but deliver their own souls by their righteousness.
21 For thus saith the Lord Jehovah: How much more when I send my four sore judgments upon Jerusalem, the sword, and the famine, and the evil beasts, and the pestilence, to cut off from it man and beast!
22 Yet, behold, therein shall be left a remnant that shall be carried forth, both sons and daughters: behold, they shall come forth unto you, and ye shall see their way and their doings; and ye shall be comforted concerning the evil that I have brought upon Jerusalem, even concerning all that I have brought upon it.
23 And they shall comfort you, when ye see their way and their doings; and ye shall know that I have not done without cause all that I have done in it, saith the Lord Jehovah.

Chapter 15

1 And the word of Jehovah came unto me, saying,
2 Son of man, what is the vine-tree more than any tree, the vine-branch which is among the trees of the forest?
3 Shall wood be taken thereof to make any work? or will men take a pin of it to hang any vessel thereon?
4 Behold, it is cast into the fire for fuel; the fire hath devoured both the ends of it, and the midst of it is burned: is it profitable for any work?
5 Behold, when it was whole, it was meet for no work: how much less, when the fire hath devoured it, and it is burned, shall it yet be meet for any work!
6 Therefore thus saith the Lord Jehovah: As the vine-tree among the trees of the forest, which I have given to the fire for fuel, so will I give the inhabitants of Jerusalem.
7 And I will set my face against them; they shall go forth from the fire, but the fire shall devour them; and ye shall know that I am Jehovah, when I set my face against them.
8 And I will make the land desolate, because they have committed a trespass, saith the Lord Jehovah.

Chapter 16

1 Again the word of Jehovah came unto me, saying,
2 Son of man, cause Jerusalem to know her abominations;
3 and say, Thus saith the Lord Jehovah unto Jerusalem: Thy birth and thy nativity is of the land of the Canaanite; the Amorite was thy father, and thy mother was a Hittite.
4 And as for thy nativity, in the day thou wast born thy navel was not cut, neither wast thou washed in water to cleanse thee; thou wast not salted at all, nor swaddled at all.
5 No eye pitied thee, to do any of these things unto thee, to have compassion upon thee; but thou wast cast out in the open field, for that thy person was abhorred, in the day that thou wast born.
6 And when I passed by thee, and saw thee weltering in thy blood, I said unto thee, [Though thou art] in thy blood, live; yea, I said unto thee, [Though thou art] in thy blood, live.
7 I caused thee to multiply as that which groweth in the field, and thou didst increase and wax great, and thou attainedst to excellent ornament; thy breasts were fashioned, and thy hair was grown; yet thou wast naked and bare.
8 Now when I passed by thee, and looked upon thee, behold, thy time was the time of love; and I spread my skirt over thee, and covered thy nakedness: yea, I sware unto thee, and entered into a covenant with thee, saith the Lord Jehovah, and thou becamest mine.
9 Then washed I thee with water; yea, I thoroughly washed away thy blood from thee, and I anointed thee with oil.
10 I clothed thee also with broidered work, and shod thee with sealskin, and I girded thee about with fine linen, and covered thee with silk.
11 And I decked thee with ornaments, and I put bracelets upon thy hands, and a chain on thy neck.
12 And I put a ring upon thy nose, and ear-rings in thine ears, and a beautiful crown upon thy head.
13 Thus wast thou decked with gold and silver; and thy raiment was of fine linen, and silk, and broidered work; thou didst eat fine flour, and honey, and oil; and thou wast exceeding beautiful, and thou didst prosper unto royal estate.
14 And thy renown went forth among the nations for thy beauty; for it was perfect, through my majesty which I had put upon thee, saith the Lord Jehovah.
15 But thou didst trust in thy beauty, and playedst the harlot because of thy renown, and pouredst out thy whoredoms on every one that passed by; his it was.
16 And thou didst take of thy garments, and madest for thee high places decked with divers colors, and

playedst the harlot upon them: [the like things] shall not come, neither shall it be [so].
17 Thou didst also take thy fair jewels of my gold and of my silver, which I had given thee, and madest for thee images of men, and didst play the harlot with them;
18 and thou tookest thy broidered garments, and coveredst them, and didst set mine oil and mine incense before them.
19 My bread also which I gave thee, fine flour, and oil, and honey, wherewith I fed thee, thou didst even set it before them for a sweet savor; and [thus] it was, saith the Lord Jehovah.
20 Moreover thou hast taken thy sons and thy daughters, whom thou hast borne unto me, and these hast thou sacrificed unto them to be devoured. Were thy whoredoms a small matter,
21 that thou hast slain my children, and delivered them up, in causing them to pass through [the fire] unto them?
22 And in all thine abominations and thy whoredoms thou hast not remembered the days of thy youth, when thou wast naked and bare, and wast weltering in thy blood.
23 And it is come to pass after all thy wickedness, (woe, woe unto thee! saith the Lord Jehovah,)
24 that thou hast built unto thee a vaulted place, and hast made thee a lofty place in every street.
25 Thou hast built thy lofty place at the head of every way, and hast made thy beauty an abomination, and hast opened thy feet to every one that passed by, and multiplied thy whoredom.
26 Thou hast also committed fornication with the Egyptians, thy neighbors, great of flesh; and hast multiplied thy whoredom, to provoke me to anger.
27 Behold therefore, I have stretched out my hand over thee, and have diminished thine ordinary [food], and delivered thee unto the will of them that hate thee, the daughters of the Philistines, that are ashamed of thy lewd way.
28 Thou hast played the harlot also with the Assyrians, because thou wast insatiable; yea, thou hast played the harlot with them, and yet thou wast not satisfied.
29 Thou hast moreover multiplied thy whoredom unto the land of traffic, unto Chaldea; and yet thou wast not satisfied herewith.
30 How weak is thy heart, saith the Lord Jehovah, seeing thou doest all these things, the work of an impudent harlot;
31 in that thou buildest thy vaulted place at the head of every way, and makest thy lofty place in every street, and hast not been as a harlot, in that thou scornest hire.
32 A wife that committeth adultery! that taketh strangers instead of her husband!
33 They give gifts to all harlots; but thou givest thy gifts to all thy lovers, and bribest them, that they may come unto thee on every side for thy whoredoms.
34 And thou art different from [other] women in thy whoredoms, in that none followeth thee to play the harlot; and whereas thou givest hire, and no hire is given unto thee, therefore thou art different.
35 Wherefore, O harlot, hear the word of Jehovah:
36 Thus saith the Lord Jehovah, Because thy filthiness was poured out, and thy nakedness uncovered through thy whoredoms with thy lovers; and because of all the idols of thy abominations, and for the blood of thy children, that thou didst give unto them;
37 therefore behold, I will gather all thy lovers, with whom thou hast taken pleasure, and all them that thou hast loved, with all them that thou hast hated; I will even gather them against thee on every side, and will uncover thy nakedness unto them, that they may see all thy nakedness.
38 And I will judge thee, as women that break wedlock and shed blood are judged; and I will bring upon thee the blood of wrath and jealousy.
39 I will also give thee into their hand, and they shall throw down thy vaulted place, and break down thy lofty places; and they shall strip thee of thy clothes, and take thy fair jewels; and they shall leave thee naked and bare.
40 They shall also bring up a company against thee, and they shall stone thee with stones, and thrust thee through with their swords.
41 And they shall burn thy houses with fire, and execute judgments upon thee in the sight of many women; and I will cause thee to cease from playing the harlot, and thou shalt also give no hire any more.
42 So will I cause my wrath toward thee to rest, and my jealousy shall depart from thee, and I will be quiet, and will be no more angry.
43 Because thou hast not remembered the days of thy youth, but hast raged against me in all these things; therefore, behold, I also will bring thy way upon thy head, saith the Lord Jehovah: and thou shalt not commit this lewdness with all thine abominations.
44 Behold, every one that useth proverbs shall use [this] proverb against thee, saying, As is the mother, so is her daughter.
45 Thou art the daughter of thy mother, that loatheth her husband and her children; and thou art the

sister of thy sisters, who loathed their husbands and their children: your mother was a Hittite, and your father an Amorite.
46 And thine elder sister is Samaria, that dwelleth at thy left hand, she and her daughters; and thy younger sister, that dwelleth at thy right hand, is Sodom and her daughters.
47 Yet hast thou not walked in their ways, nor done after their abominations; but, as [if that were] a very little [thing], thou wast more corrupt than they in all thy ways.
48 As I live, saith the Lord Jehovah, Sodom thy sister hath not done, she nor her daughters, as thou hast done, thou and thy daughters.
49 Behold, this was the iniquity of thy sister Sodom: pride, fulness of bread, and prosperous ease was in her and in her daughters; neither did she strengthen the hand of the poor and needy.
50 And they were haughty, and committed abomination before me: therefore I took them away as I saw [good].
51 Neither hath Samaria committed half of thy sins; but thou hast multiplied thine abominations more than they, and hast justified thy sisters by all thine abominations which thou hast done.
52 Thou also, bear thou thine own shame, in that thou hast given judgment for thy sisters; through thy sins that thou hast committed more abominable than they, they are more righteous that thou: yea, be thou also confounded, and bear thy shame, in that thou hast justified thy sisters.
53 And I will turn again their captivity, the captivity of Sodom and her daughters, and the captivity of Samaria and her daughters, and the captivity of thy captives in the midst of them;
54 that thou mayest bear thine own shame, and mayest be ashamed because of all that thou hast done, in that thou art a comfort unto them.
55 And thy sisters, Sodom and her daughters, shall return to their former estate; and Samaria and her daughters shall return to their former estate; and thou and thy daughters shall return to your former estate.
56 For thy sister Sodom was not mentioned by thy mouth in the day of thy pride,
57 before thy wickedness was uncovered, as at the time of the reproach of the daughters of Syria, and of all that are round about her, the daughters of the Philistines, that do despite unto thee round about.
58 Thou hast borne thy lewdness and thine abominations, saith Jehovah.
59 For thus saith the Lord Jehovah: I will also deal with thee as thou hast done, who hast despised the oath in breaking the covenant.
60 Nevertheless I will remember my covenant with thee in the days of thy youth, and I will establish unto thee an everlasting covenant.
61 Then shalt thou remember thy ways, and be ashamed, when thou shalt receive thy sisters, thine elder [sisters] and thy younger; and I will give them unto thee for daughters, but not by thy covenant.
62 And I will establish my covenant with thee; and thou shalt know that I am Jehovah;
63 that thou mayest remember, and be confounded, and never open thy mouth any more, because of thy shame, when I have forgiven thee all that thou hast done, saith the Lord Jehovah.

Chapter 17

1 And the word of Jehovah came unto me, saying,
2 Son of man, put forth a riddle, and speak a parable unto the house of Israel;
3 and say, Thus saith the Lord Jehovah: A great eagle with great wings and long pinions, full of feathers, which had divers colors, came unto Lebanon, and took the top of the cedar:
4 he cropped off the topmost of the young twigs thereof, and carried it unto a land of traffic; he set it in a city of merchants.
5 He took also of the seed of the land, and planted it in a fruitful soil; he placed it beside many waters; he set it as a willow-tree.
6 And it grew, and became a spreading vine of low stature, whose branches turned toward him, and the roots thereof were under him: so it became a vine, and brought forth branches, and shot forth sprigs.
7 There was also another great eagle with great wings and many feathers: and, behold, this vine did bend its roots toward him, and shot forth its branches toward him, from the beds of its plantation, that he might water it.
8 It was planted in a good soil by many waters, that it might bring forth branches, and that it might bear fruit, that it might be a goodly vine.
9 Say thou, Thus saith the Lord Jehovah: Shall it prosper? shall he not pull up the roots thereof, and cut off the fruit thereof, that it may wither; that all its fresh springing leaves may wither? and not by a strong arm or much people can it be raised from the roots thereof.
10 Yea, behold, being planted, shall it prosper? shall it not utterly wither, when the east wind toucheth

it? it shall wither in the beds where it grew.
11 Moreover the word of Jehovah came unto me, saying,
12 Say now to the rebellious house, Know ye not what these things mean? tell them, Behold, the king of Babylon came to Jerusalem, and took the king thereof, and the princes thereof, and brought them to him to Babylon:
13 and he took of the seed royal, and made a covenant with him; he also brought him under an oath, and took away the mighty of the land;
14 that the kingdom might be base, that it might not lift itself up, but that by keeping his covenant it might stand.
15 But he rebelled against him in sending his ambassadors into Egypt, that they might give him horses and much people. Shall he prosper? shall he escape that doeth such things? shall he break the covenant, and yet escape?
16 As I live, saith the Lord Jehovah, surely in the place where the king dwelleth that made him king, whose oath he despised, and whose covenant he brake, even with him in the midst of Babylon he shall die.
17 Neither shall Pharaoh with his mighty army and great company help him in the war, when they cast up mounds and build forts, to cut off many persons.
18 For he hath despised the oath by breaking the covenant; and behold, he had given his hand, and yet hath done all these things; he shall not escape.
19 Therefore thus saith the Lord Jehovah: As I live, surely mine oath that he hath despised, and my covenant that he hath broken, I will even bring it upon his own head.
20 And I will spread my net upon him, and he shall be taken in my snare, and I will bring him to Babylon, and will enter into judgment with him there for his trespass that he hath trespassed against me.
21 And all his fugitives in all his bands shall fall by the sword, and they that remain shall be scattered toward every wind: and ye shall know that I, Jehovah, have spoken it.
22 Thus saith the Lord Jehovah: I will also take of the lofty top of the cedar, and will set it; I will crop off from the topmost of its young twigs a tender one, and I will plant it upon a high and lofty mountain:
23 in the mountain of the height of Israel will I plant it; and it shall bring forth boughs, and bear fruit, and be a goodly cedar: and under it shall dwell all birds of every wing; in the shade of the branches thereof shall they dwell.
24 And all the trees of the field shall know that I, Jehovah, have brought down the high tree, have exalted the low tree, have dried up the green tree, and have made the dry tree to flourish; I, Jehovah, have spoken and have done it.

Chapter 18

1 The word of Jehovah came unto me again, saying,
2 What mean ye, that ye use this proverb concerning the land of Israel, saying, The fathers have eaten sour grapes, and the children's teeth are set on edge?
3 As I live, saith the Lord Jehovah, ye shall not have [occasion] any more to use this proverb in Israel.
4 Behold, all souls are mine; as the soul of the father, so also the soul of the son is mine: the soul that sinneth, it shall die.
5 But if a man be just, and do that which is lawful and right,
6 and hath not eaten upon the mountains, neither hath lifted up his eyes to the idols of the house of Israel, neither hath defiled his neighbor's wife, neither hath come near to a woman in her impurity,
7 and hath not wronged any, but hath restored to the debtor his pledge, hath taken nought by robbery, hath given his bread to the hungry, and hath covered the naked with a garment;
8 he that hath not given forth upon interest, neither hath taken any increase, that hath withdrawn his hand from iniquity, hath executed true justice between man and man,
9 hath walked in my statutes, and hath kept mine ordinances, to deal truly; he is just, he shall surely live, saith the Lord Jehovah.
10 If he beget a son that is a robber, a shedder of blood, and that doeth any one of these things,
11 and that doeth not any of those [duties], but even hath eaten upon the mountains, and defiled his neighbor's wife,
12 hath wronged the poor and needy, hath taken by robbery, hath not restored the pledge, and hath lifted up his eyes to the idols, hath committed abomination,
13 hath given forth upon interest, and hath taken increase; shall he then live? he shall not live: he hath done all these abominations; he shall surely die; his blood shall be upon him.
14 Now, lo, if he beget a son, that seeth all his father's sins, which he hath done, and feareth, and doeth

not such like;
15 that hath not eaten upon the mountains, neither hath lifted up his eyes to the idols of the house of
Israel, hath not defiled his neighbor's wife,
16 neither hath wronged any, hath not taken aught to pledge, neither hath taken by robbery, but hath
given his bread to the hungry, and hath covered the naked with a garment;
17 that hath withdrawn his hand from the poor, that hath not received interest nor increase, hath
executed mine ordinances, hath walked in my statutes; he shall not die for the iniquity of his father, he
shall surely live.
18 As for his father, because he cruelly oppressed, robbed his brother, and did that which is not good
among his people, behold, he shall die in his iniquity.
19 Yet say ye, Wherefore doth not the son bear the iniquity of the father? when the son hath done that
which is lawful and right, and hath kept all my statutes, and hath done them, he shall surely live.
20 The soul that sinneth, it shall die: the son shall not bear the iniquity of the father, neither shall the
father bear the iniquity of the son; the righteousness of the righteous shall be upon him, and the
wickedness of the wicked shall be upon him.
21 But if the wicked turn from all his sins that he hath committed, and keep all my statutes, and do that
which is lawful and right, he shall surely live, he shall not die.
22 None of his transgressions that he hath committed shall be remembered against him: in his
righteousness that he hath done he shall live.
23 Have I any pleasure in the death of the wicked? saith the Lord Jehovah; and not rather that he should
return from his way, and live?
24 But when the righteous turneth away from his righteousness, and committeth iniquity, and doeth
according to all the abominations that the wicked man doeth, shall he live? None of his righteous deeds
that he hath done shall be remembered: in his trespass that he hath trespassed, and in his sin that he
hath sinned, in them shall he die.
25 Yet ye say, The way of the Lord is not equal. Hear now, O house of Israel: Is not my way equal? are
not your ways unequal?
26 When the righteous man turneth away from his righteousness, and committeth iniquity, and dieth
therein; in his iniquity that he hath done shall he die.
27 Again, when the wicked man turneth away from his wickedness that he hath committed, and doeth
that which is lawful and right, he shall save his soul alive.
28 Because he considereth, and turneth away from all his transgressions that he hath committed, he shall
surely live, he shall not die.
29 Yet saith the house of Israel, The way of the Lord is not equal. O house of Israel, are not my ways
equal? are not your ways unequal?
30 Therefore I will judge you, O house of Israel, every one according to his ways, saith the Lord
Jehovah. Return ye, and turn yourselves from all your transgressions; so iniquity shall not be your ruin.
31 Cast away from you all your transgressions, wherein ye have transgressed; and make you a new heart
and a new spirit: for why will ye die, O house of Israel?
32 For I have no pleasure in the death of him that dieth, saith the Lord Jehovah: wherefore turn
yourselves, and live.

Chapter 19

1 Moreover, take thou up a lamentation for the princes of Israel,
2 and say, What was thy mother? A lioness: she couched among lions, in the midst of the young lions
she nourished her whelps.
3 And she brought up one of her whelps: he became a young lion, and he learned to catch the prey; he
devoured men.
4 The nations also heard of him; he was taken in their pit; and they brought him with hooks unto the
land of Egypt.
5 Now when she saw that she had waited, and her hope was lost, then she took another of her whelps,
and made him a young lion.
6 And he went up and down among the lions; he became a young lion, and he learned to catch the prey;
he devoured men.
7 And he knew their palaces, and laid waste their cities; and the land was desolate, and the fulness
thereof, because of the noise of his roaring.
8 Then the nations set against him on every side from the provinces; and they spread their net over him;
he was taken in their pit.

9 And they put him in a cage with hooks, and brought him to the king of Babylon; they brought him
into strongholds, that his voice should no more be heard upon the mountains of Israel.
10 Thy mother was like a vine, in thy blood, planted by the waters: it was fruitful and full of branches by
reason of many waters.
11 And it had strong rods for the sceptres of them that bare rule, and their stature was exalted among
the thick boughs, and they were seen in their height with the multitude of their branches.
12 But it was plucked up in fury, it was cast down to the ground, and the east wind dried up its fruit: its
strong rods were broken off and withered; the fire consumed them.
13 And now it is planted in the wilderness, in a dry and thirsty land.
14 And fire is gone out of the rods of its branches, it hath devoured its fruit, so that there is in it no
strong rod to be a sceptre to rule. This is a lamentation, and shall be for a lamentation.

Chapter 20

1 And it came to pass in the seventh year, in the fifth [month], the tenth [day] of the month, that certain
of the elders of Israel came to inquire of Jehovah, and sat before me.
2 And the word of Jehovah came unto me, saying,
3 Son of man, speak unto the elders of Israel, and say unto them, Thus saith the Lord Jehovah: Is it to
inquire of me that ye are come? As I live, saith the Lord Jehovah, I will not be inquired of by you.
4 Wilt thou judge them, son of man, wilt thou judge them? Cause them to know the abominations of
their fathers;
5 and say unto them, Thus saith the Lord Jehovah: In the day when I chose Israel, and sware unto the
seed of the house of Jacob, and made myself known unto them in the land of Egypt, when I sware unto
them, saying, I am Jehovah your God;
6 in that day I sware unto them, to bring them forth out of the land of Egypt into a land that I had
searched out for them, flowing with milk and honey, which is the glory of all lands.
7 And I said unto them, Cast ye away every man the abominations of his eyes, and defile not yourselves
with the idols of Egypt; I am Jehovah your God.
8 But they rebelled against me, and would not hearken unto me; they did not every man cast away the
abominations of their eyes, neither did they forsake the idols of Egypt. Then I said I would pour out my
wrath upon them, to accomplish my anger against them in the midst of the land of Egypt.
9 But I wrought for my name's sake, that it should not be profaned in the sight of the nations, among
which they were, in whose sight I made myself known unto them, in bringing them forth out of the land
of Egypt.
10 So I caused them to go forth out of the land of Egypt, and brought them into the wilderness.
11 And I gave them my statutes, and showed them mine ordinances, which if a man do, he shall live in
them.
12 Moreover also I gave them my sabbaths, to be a sign between me and them, that they might know
that I am Jehovah that sanctifieth them.
13 But the house of Israel rebelled against me in the wilderness: they walked not in my statutes, and they
rejected mine ordinances, which if a man keep, he shall live in them; and my sabbaths they greatly
profaned. Then I said I would pour out my wrath upon them in the wilderness, to consume them.
14 But I wrought for my name's sake, that it should not be profaned in the sight of the nations, in
whose sight I brought them out.
15 Moreover also I sware unto them in the wilderness, that I would not bring them into the land which I
had given them, flowing with milk and honey, which is the glory of all lands;
16 because they rejected mine ordinances, and walked not in my statutes, and profaned my sabbaths: for
their heart went after their idols.
17 Nevertheless mine eye spared them, and I destroyed them not, neither did I make a full end of them
in the wilderness.
18 And I said unto their children in the wilderness, Walk ye not in the statutes of your fathers, neither
observe their ordinances, nor defile yourselves with their idols.
19 I am Jehovah your God: walk in my statutes, and keep mine ordinances, and do them;
20 and hallow my sabbaths; and they shall be a sign between me and you, that ye may know that I am
Jehovah your God.
21 But the children rebelled against me; they walked not in my statutes, neither kept mine ordinances to
do them, which if a man do, he shall live in them; they profaned my sabbaths. Then I said I would pour
out my wrath upon them, to accomplish my anger against them in the wilderness.
22 Nevertheless I withdrew my hand, and wrought for my name's sake, that it should not be profaned in

the sight of the nations, in whose sight I brought them forth.
23 Moreover I sware unto them in the wilderness, that I would scatter them among the nations, and disperse them through the countries;
24 because they had not executed mine ordinances, but had rejected my statutes, and had profaned my sabbaths, and their eyes were after their fathers' idols.
25 Moreover also I gave them statutes that were not good, and ordinances wherein they should not live;
26 and I polluted them in their own gifts, in that they caused to pass through [the fire] all that openeth the womb, that I might make them desolate, to the end that they might know that I am Jehovah.
27 Therefore, son of man, speak unto the house of Israel, and say unto them, Thus saith the Lord Jehovah: In this moreover have your fathers blasphemed me, in that they have committed a trespass against me.
28 For when I had brought them into the land, which I sware to give unto them, then they saw every high hill, and every thick tree, and they offered there their sacrifices, and there they presented the provocation of their offering; there also they made their sweet savor, and they poured out there their drink-offerings.
29 Then I said unto them, What meaneth the high place whereunto ye go? So the name thereof is called Bamah unto this day.
30 Wherefore say unto the house of Israel, Thus saith the Lord Jehovah: Do ye pollute yourselves after the manner of your fathers? and play ye the harlot after their abominations?
31 and when ye offer your gifts, when ye make your sons to pass through the fire, do ye pollute yourselves with all your idols unto this day? and shall I be inquired of by you, O house of Israel? As I live, saith the Lord Jehovah, I will not be inquired of by you;
32 and that which cometh into your mind shall not be at all, in that ye say, We will be as the nations, as the families of the countries, to serve wood and stone.
33 As I live, saith the Lord Jehovah, surely with a mighty hand, and with an outstretched arm, and with wrath poured out, will I be king over you:
34 and I will bring you out from the peoples, and will gather you out of the countries wherein ye are scattered, with a mighty hand, and with an outstretched arm, and with wrath poured out;
35 and I will bring you into the wilderness of the peoples, and there will I enter into judgment with you face to face.
36 Like as I entered into judgment with your fathers in the wilderness of the land of Egypt, so will I enter into judgment with you, saith the Lord Jehovah.
37 And I will cause you to pass under the rod, and I will bring you into the bond of the covenant;
38 and I will purge out from among you the rebels, and them that transgress against me; I will bring them forth out of the land where they sojourn, but they shall not enter into the land of Israel: and ye shall know that I am Jehovah.
39 As for you, O house of Israel, thus saith the Lord Jehovah: Go ye, serve every one his idols, and hereafter also, if ye will not hearken unto me; but my holy name shall ye no more profane with your gifts, and with your idols.
40 For in my holy mountain, in the mountain of the height of Israel, saith the Lord Jehovah, there shall all the house of Israel, all of them, serve me in the land: there will I accept them, and there will I require your offerings, and the first-fruits of your oblations, with all your holy things.
41 As a sweet savor will I accept you, when I bring you out from the peoples, and gather you out of the countries wherein ye have been scattered; and I will be sanctified in you in the sight of the nations.
42 And ye shall know that I am Jehovah, when I shall bring you into the land of Israel, into the country which I sware to give unto your fathers.
43 And there shall ye remember your ways, and all your doings, wherein ye have polluted yourselves; and ye shall loathe yourselves in your own sight for all your evils that ye have committed.
44 And ye shall know that I am Jehovah, when I have dealt with you for my name's sake, not according to your evil ways, nor according to your corrupt doings, O ye house of Israel, saith the Lord Jehovah.
45 And the word of Jehovah came unto me, saying,
46 Son of man, set thy face toward the south, and drop [thy word] toward the south, and prophesy against the forest of the field in the South;
47 and say to the forest of the South, Hear the word of Jehovah: Thus saith the Lord Jehovah, Behold, I will kindle a fire in thee, and it shall devour every green tree in thee, and every dry tree: the flaming flame shall not be quenched, and all faces from the south to the north shall be burnt thereby.
48 And all flesh shall see that I, Jehovah, have kindled it; it shall not be quenched.
49 Then said I, Ah Lord Jehovah! they say of me, Is he not a speaker of parables?

Chapter 21

1 And the word of Jehovah came unto me, saying,
2 Son of man, set thy face toward Jerusalem, and drop [thy word] toward the sanctuaries, and prophesy against the land of Israel;
3 and say to the land of Israel, Thus saith Jehovah: Behold, I am against thee, and will draw forth my sword out of its sheath, and will cut off from thee the righteous and the wicked.
4 Seeing then that I will cut off from thee the righteous and the wicked, therefore shall my sword go forth out of its sheath against all flesh from the south to the north:
5 and all flesh shall know that I, Jehovah, have drawn forth my sword out of its sheath; it shall not return any more.
6 Sigh therefore, thou son of man; with the breaking of thy loins and with bitterness shalt thou sigh before their eyes.
7 And it shall be, when they say unto thee, Wherefore sighest thou? that thou shalt say, Because of the tidings, for it cometh; and every heart shall melt, and all hands shall be feeble, and every spirit shall faint, and all knees shall be weak as water: behold, it cometh, and it shall be done, saith the Lord Jehovah.
8 And the word of Jehovah came unto me, saying,
9 Son of man, prophesy, and say, Thus saith Jehovah: Say, A sword, a sword, it is sharpened, and also furbished;
10 it is sharpened that it may make a slaughter; it is furbished that it may be as lightning: shall we then make mirth? the rod of my son, it contemneth every tree.
11 And it is given to be furbished, that it may be handled: the sword, it is sharpened, yea, it is furbished, to give it into the hand of the slayer.
12 Cry and wail, son of man; for it is upon my people, it is upon all the princes of Israel: they are delivered over to the sword with my people; smite therefore upon thy thigh.
13 For there is a trial; and what if even the rod that contemneth shall be no more? saith the Lord Jehovah.
14 Thou therefore, son of man, prophesy, and smite thy hands together; and let the sword be doubled the third time, the sword of the deadly wounded: it is the sword of the great one that is deadly wounded, which entereth into their chambers.
15 I have set the threatening sword against all their gates, that their heart may melt, and their stumblings be multiplied: ah! it is made as lightning, it is pointed for slaughter.
16 Gather thee together, go to the right, set thyself in array, go to the left, whithersoever thy face is set.
17 I will also smite my hands together, and I will cause my wrath to rest: I, Jehovah, have spoken it.
18 The word of Jehovah came unto me again, saying,
19 Also, thou son of man, appoint thee two ways, that the sword of the king of Babylon may come; they twain shall come forth out of one land: and mark out a place, mark it out at the head of the way to the city.
20 Thou shalt appoint a way for the sword to come to Rabbah of the children of Ammon, and to Judah in Jerusalem the fortified.
21 For the king of Babylon stood at the parting of the way, at the head of the two ways, to use divination: he shook the arrows to and fro, he consulted the teraphim, he looked in the liver.
22 In his right hand was the divination [for] Jerusalem, to set battering rams, to open the mouth in the slaughter, to lift up the voice with shouting, to set battering rams against the gates, to cast up mounds, to build forts.
23 And it shall be unto them as a false divination in their sight, who have sworn oaths unto them; but he bringeth iniquity to remembrance, that they may be taken.
24 Therefore thus saith the Lord Jehovah: Because ye have made your iniquity to be remembered, in that your transgressions are uncovered, so that in all your doings your sins do appear; because that ye are come to remembrance, ye shall be taken with the hand.
25 And thou, O deadly wounded wicked one, the prince of Israel, whose day is come, in the time of the iniquity of the end,
26 thus saith the Lord Jehovah: Remove the mitre, and take off the crown; this [shall be] no more the same; exalt that which is low, and abase that which is high.
27 I will overturn, overturn, overturn it: this also shall be no more, until he come whose right it is; and I will give it [him].
28 And thou, son of man, prophesy, and say, Thus saith the Lord Jehovah concerning the children of Ammon, and concerning their reproach; and say thou, A sword, a sword is drawn, for the slaughter it is furbished, to cause it to devour, that it may be as lightning;

29 while they see for thee false visions, while they divine lies unto thee, to lay thee upon the necks of the wicked that are deadly wounded, whose day is come in the time of the iniquity of the end.
30 Cause it to return into its sheath. In the place where thou wast created, in the land of thy birth, will I judge thee.
31 And I will pour out mine indignation upon thee; I will blow upon thee with the fire of my wrath; and I will deliver thee into the hand of brutish men, skilful to destroy.
32 Thou shalt be for fuel to the fire; thy blood shall be in the midst of the land; thou shalt be no more remembered: for I, Jehovah, have spoken it.

Chapter 22

1 Moreover the word of Jehovah came unto me, saying,
2 And thou, son of man, wilt thou judge, wilt thou judge the bloody city? then cause her to know all her abominations.
3 And thou shalt say, Thus saith the Lord Jehovah: A city that sheddeth blood in the midst of her, that her time may come, and that maketh idols against herself to defile her!
4 Thou art become guilty in thy blood that thou hast shed, and art defiled in thine idols which thou hast made; and thou hast caused thy days to draw near, and art come even unto thy years: therefore have I made thee a reproach unto the nations, and a mocking to all the countries.
5 Those that are near, and those that are far from thee, shall mock thee, thou infamous one [and] full of tumult.
6 Behold, the princes of Israel, every one according to his power, have been in thee to shed blood.
7 In thee have they set light by father and mother; in the midst of thee have they dealt by oppression with the sojourner; in thee have they wronged the fatherless and the widow.
8 Thou hast despised my holy things, and hast profaned my sabbaths.
9 Slanderous men have been in thee to shed blood; and in thee they have eaten upon the mountains: in the midst of thee they have committed lewdness.
10 In thee have they uncovered their fathers' nakedness; in thee have they humbled her that was unclean in her impurity.
11 And one hath committed abomination with his neighbor's wife; and another hath lewdly defiled his daughter-in-law; and another in thee hath humbled his sister, his father's daughter.
12 In thee have they taken bribes to shed blood; thou hast taken interest and increase, and thou hast greedily gained of thy neighbors by oppression, and hast forgotten me, saith the Lord Jehovah.
13 Behold, therefore, I have smitten my hand at thy dishonest gain which thou hast made, and at thy blood which hath been in the midst of thee.
14 Can thy heart endure, or can thy hands be strong, in the days that I shall deal with thee? I, Jehovah, have spoken it, and will do it.
15 And I will scatter thee among the nations, and disperse thee through the countries; and I will consume thy filthiness out of thee.
16 And thou shalt be profaned in thyself, in the sight of the nations; and thou shalt know that I am Jehovah.
17 And the word of Jehovah came unto me, saying,
18 Son of man, the house of Israel is become dross unto me: all of them are brass and tin and iron and lead, in the midst of the furnace; they are the dross of silver.
19 Therefore thus saith the Lord Jehovah: Because ye are all become dross, therefore, behold, I will gather you into the midst of Jerusalem.
20 As they gather silver and brass and iron and lead and tin into the midst of the furnace, to blow the fire upon it, to melt it; so will I gather you in mine anger and in my wrath, and I will lay you there, and melt you.
21 Yea, I will gather you, and blow upon you with the fire of my wrath, and ye shall be melted in the midst thereof.
22 As silver is melted in the midst of the furnace, so shall ye be melted in the midst thereof; and ye shall know that I, Jehovah, have poured out my wrath upon you.
23 And the word of Jehovah came unto me, saying,
24 Son of man, say unto her, Thou art a land that is not cleansed, nor rained upon in the day of indignation.
25 There is a conspiracy of her prophets in the midst thereof, like a roaring lion ravening the prey: they have devoured souls; they take treasure and precious things; they have made her widows many in the midst thereof.

26 Her priests have done violence to my law, and have profaned my holy things: they have made no
distinction between the holy and the common, neither have they caused men to discern between the
unclean and the clean, and have hid their eyes from my sabbaths, and I am profaned among them.
27 Her princes in the midst thereof are like wolves ravening the prey, to shed blood, [and] to destroy
souls, that they may get dishonest gain.
28 And her prophets have daubed for them with untempered [mortar], seeing false visions, and divining
lies unto them, saying, Thus saith the Lord Jehovah, when Jehovah hath not spoken.
29 The people of the land have used oppression, and exercised robbery; yea, they have vexed the poor
and needy, and have oppressed the sojourner wrongfully.
30 And I sought for a man among them, that should build up the wall, and stand in the gap before me
for the land, that I should not destroy it; but I found none.
31 Therefore have I poured out mine indignation upon them; I have consumed them with the fire of my
wrath: their own way have I brought upon their heads, saith the Lord Jehovah.

Chapter 23

1 The word of Jehovah came again unto me, saying,
2 Son of man, there were two women, the daughters of one mother:
3 and they played the harlot in Egypt; they played the harlot in their youth; there were their breasts
pressed, and there was handled the bosom of their virginity.
4 And the names of them were Oholah the elder, and Oholibah her sister: and they became mine, and
they bare sons and daughters. And as for their names, Samaria is Oholah, and Jerusalem Oholibah.
5 And Oholah played the harlot when she was mine; and she doted on her lovers, on the Assyrians [her]
neighbors,
6 who were clothed with blue, governors and rulers, all of them desirable young men, horsemen riding
upon horses.
7 And she bestowed her whoredoms upon them, the choicest men of Assyria all of them; and on
whomsoever she doted, with all their idols she defiled herself.
8 Neither hath she left her whoredoms since [the days of] Egypt; for in her youth they lay with her, and
they handled the bosom of her virginity; and they poured out their whoredom upon her.
9 Wherefore I delivered her into the hand of her lovers, into the hand of the Assyrians, upon whom she
doted.
10 These uncovered her nakedness; they took her sons and her daughters; and her they slew with the
sword: and she became a byword among women; for they executed judgments upon her.
11 And her sister Oholibah saw this, yet was she more corrupt in her doting than she, and in her
whoredoms which were more than the whoredoms of her sister.
12 She doted upon the Assyrians, governors and rulers, [her] neighbors, clothed most gorgeously,
horsemen riding upon horses, all of them desirable young men.
13 And I saw that she was defiled; they both took one way.
14 And she increased her whoredoms; for she saw men portrayed upon the wall, the images of the
Chaldeans portrayed with vermilion,
15 girded with girdles upon their loins, with flowing turbans upon their heads, all of them princes to
look upon, after the likeness of the Babylonians in Chaldea, the land of their nativity.
16 And as soon as she saw them she doted upon them, and sent messengers unto them into Chaldea.
17 And the Babylonians came to her into the bed of love, and they defiled her with their whoredom, and
she was polluted with them, and her soul was alienated from them.
18 So she uncovered her whoredoms, and uncovered her nakedness: then my soul was alienated from
her, like as my soul was alienated from her sister.
19 Yet she multiplied her whoredoms, remembering the days of her youth, wherein she had played the
harlot in the land of Egypt.
20 And she doted upon their paramours, whose flesh is as the flesh of asses, and whose issue is like the
issue of horses.
21 Thus thou calledst to remembrance the lewdness of thy youth, in the handling of thy bosom by the
Egyptians for the breasts of thy youth.
22 Therefore, O Oholibah, thus saith the Lord Jehovah: Behold, I will raise up thy lovers against thee,
from whom thy soul is alienated, and I will bring them against thee on every side:
23 the Babylonians and all the Chaldeans, Pekod and Shoa and Koa, [and] all the Assyrians with them;
desirable young men, governors and rulers all of them, princes and men of renown, all of them riding
upon horses.

24 And they shall come against thee with weapons, chariots, and wagons, and with a company of peoples; they shall set themselves against thee with buckler and shield and helmet round about; and I will commit the judgment unto them, and they shall judge thee according to their judgments.
25 And I will set my jealousy against thee, and they shall deal with thee in fury; they shall take away thy nose and thine ears; and thy residue shall fall by the sword: they shall take thy sons and thy daughters; and thy residue shall be devoured by the fire.
26 They shall also strip thee of thy clothes, and take away thy fair jewels.
27 Thus will I make thy lewdness to cease from thee, and thy whoredom [brought] from the land of Egypt; so that thou shalt not lift up thine eyes unto them, nor remember Egypt any more.
28 For thus saith the Lord Jehovah: Behold, I will deliver thee into the hand of them whom thou hatest, into the hand of them from whom thy soul is alienated;
29 and they shall deal with thee in hatred, and shall take away all thy labor, and shall leave thee naked and bare; and the nakedness of thy whoredoms shall be uncovered, both thy lewdness and thy whoredoms.
30 These things shall be done unto thee, for that thou hast played the harlot after the nations, and because thou art polluted with their idols.
31 Thou hast walked in the way of thy sister; therefore will I give her cup into thy hand.
32 Thus saith the Lord Jehovah: Thou shalt drink of thy sister's cup, which is deep and large; thou shalt be laughed to scorn and had in derision; it containeth much.
33 Thou shalt be filled with drunkenness and sorrow, with the cup of astonishment and desolation, with the cup of thy sister Samaria.
34 Thou shalt even drink it and drain it out, and thou shalt gnaw the sherds thereof, and shalt tear thy breasts; for I have spoken it, saith the Lord Jehovah.
35 Therefore thus saith the Lord Jehovah: Because thou hast forgotten me, and cast me behind thy back, therefore bear thou also thy lewdness and thy whoredoms.
36 Jehovah said moreover unto me: Son of man, wilt thou judge Oholah and Oholibah? then declare unto them their abominations.
37 For they have committed adultery, and blood is in their hands; and with their idols have they committed adultery; and they have also caused their sons, whom they bare unto me, to pass through [the fire] unto them to be devoured.
38 Moreover this they have done unto me: they have defiled my sanctuary in the same day, and have profaned my sabbaths.
39 For when they had slain their children to their idols, then they came the same day into my sanctuary to profane it; and, lo, thus have they done in the midst of my house.
40 And furthermore ye have sent for men that come from far, unto whom a messenger was sent, and, lo, they came; for whom thou didst wash thyself, paint thine eyes, and deck thyself with ornaments,
41 and sit upon a stately bed, with a table prepared before it, whereupon thou didst set mine incense and mine oil.
42 And the voice of a multitude being at ease was with her: and with men of the common sort were brought drunkards from the wilderness; and they put bracelets upon the hands of them [twain], and beautiful crowns upon their heads.
43 Then said I of her that was old in adulteries, Now will they play the harlot with her, and she [with them].
44 And they went in unto her, as they go in unto a harlot: so went they in unto Oholah and unto Oholibah, the lewd women.
45 And righteous men, they shall judge them with the judgment of adulteresses, and with the judgment of women that shed blood; because they are adulteresses, and blood is in their hands.
46 For thus saith the Lord Jehovah: I will bring up a company against them, and will give them to be tossed to and fro and robbed.
47 And the company shall stone them with stones, and despatch them with their swords; they shall slay their sons and their daughters, and burn up their houses with fire.
48 Thus will I cause lewdness to cease out of the land, that all women may be taught not to do after your lewdness.
49 And they shall recompense your lewdness upon you, and ye shall bear the sins of your idols; and ye shall know that I am the Lord Jehovah.

Chapter 24

1 Again, in the ninth year, in the tenth month, in the tenth [day] of the month, the word of Jehovah

came unto me, saying,
2 Son of man, write thee the name of the day, [even] of this selfsame day: the king of Babylon drew
close unto Jerusalem this selfsame day.
3 And utter a parable unto the rebellious house, and say unto them, Thus saith the Lord Jehovah, Set on
the caldron, set it on, and also pour water into it:
4 gather the pieces thereof into it, even every good piece, the thigh, and the shoulder; fill it with the
choice bones.
5 Take the choice of the flock, and also a pile [of wood] for the bones under [the caldron]; make it boil
well; yea, let the bones thereof be boiled in the midst of it.
6 Wherefore thus saith the Lord Jehovah: Woe to the bloody city, to the caldron whose rust is therein,
and whose rust is not gone out of it! take out of it piece after piece; No lot is fallen upon it.
7 For her blood is in the midst of her; she set it upon the bare rock; she poured it not upon the ground,
to cover it with dust.
8 That it may cause wrath to come up to take vengeance, I have set her blood upon the bare rock, that it
should not be covered.
9 Therefore thus saith the Lord Jehovah: Woe to the bloody city! I also will make the pile great.
10 Heap on the wood, make the fire hot, boil well the flesh, and make thick the broth, and let the bones
be burned.
11 Then set it empty upon the coals thereof, that it may be hot, and the brass thereof may burn, and that
the filthiness of it may be molten in it, that the rust of it may be consumed.
12 She hath wearied [herself] with toil; yet her great rust goeth not forth out of her; her rust [goeth not
forth] by fire.
13 In thy filthiness is lewdness: because I have cleansed thee and thou wast not cleansed, thou shalt not
be cleansed from thy filthiness any more, till I have caused my wrath toward thee to rest.
14 I, Jehovah, have spoken it: it shall come to pass, and I will do it: I will not go back, neither will I
spare, neither will I repent; according to thy ways, and according to thy doings, shall they judge thee,
saith the Lord Jehovah.
15 Also the word of Jehovah came unto me, saying,
16 Son of man, behold, I take away from thee the desire of thine eyes with a stroke: yet thou shalt
neither mourn nor weep, neither shall thy tears run down.
17 Sigh, but not aloud, make no mourning for the dead; bind thy headtire upon thee, and put thy shoes
upon thy feet, and cover not thy lips, and eat not the bread of men.
18 So I spake unto the people in the morning; and at even my wife died; and I did in the morning as I
was commanded.
19 And the people said unto me, Wilt thou not tell us what these things are to us, that thou doest so?
20 Then I said unto them, The word of Jehovah came unto me, saying,
21 Speak unto the house of Israel, Thus saith the Lord Jehovah: Behold, I will profane my sanctuary, the
pride of your power, the desire of your eyes, and that which your soul pitieth; and your sons and your
daughters whom ye have left behind shall fall by the sword.
22 And ye shall do as I have done: ye shall not cover your lips, nor eat the bread of men.
23 And your tires shall be upon your heads, and your shoes upon your feet: ye shall not mourn nor
weep; but ye shall pine away in your iniquities, and moan one toward another.
24 Thus shall Ezekiel be unto you a sign; according to all that he hath done shall ye do: when this
cometh, then shall ye know that I am the Lord Jehovah.
25 And thou, son of man, shall it not be in the day when I take from them their strength, the joy of their
glory, the desire of their eyes, and that whereupon they set their heart, their sons and their daughters,
26 that in that day he that escapeth shall come unto thee, to cause thee to hear it with thine ears?
27 In that day shall thy mouth be opened to him that is escaped, and thou shalt speak, and be no more
dumb: so shalt thou be a sign unto them; and they shall know that I am Jehovah.

Chapter 25

1 And the word of Jehovah came unto me, saying,
2 Son of man, set thy face toward the children of Ammon, and prophesy against them:
3 and say unto the children of Ammon, Hear the word of the Lord Jehovah: Thus saith the Lord
Jehovah, Because thou saidst, Aha, against my sanctuary, when it was profaned; and against the land of
Israel, when it was made desolate; and against the house of Judah, when they went into captivity:
4 therefore, behold, I will deliver thee to the children of the east for a possession, and they shall set their
encampments in thee, and make their dwellings in thee; they shall eat thy fruit, and they shall drink thy

milk.
5 And I will make Rabbah a stable for camels, and the children of Ammon a couching-place for flocks: and ye shall know that I am Jehovah.
6 For thus saith the Lord Jehovah: Because thou hast clapped thy hands, and stamped with the feet, and rejoiced with all the despite of thy soul against the land of Israel;
7 therefore, behold, I have stretched out my hand upon thee, and will deliver thee for a spoil to the nations; and I will cut thee off from the peoples, and I will cause thee to perish out of the countries: I will destroy thee; and thou shalt know that I am Jehovah.
8 Thus saith the Lord Jehovah: Because that Moab and Seir do say, Behold, the house of Judah is like unto all the nations;
9 therefore, behold, I will open the side of Moab from the cities, from his cities which are on his frontiers, the glory of the country, Beth-jeshimoth, Baal-meon, and Kiriathaim,
10 unto the children of the east, [to go] against the children of Ammon; and I will give them for a possession, that the children of Ammon may not be remembered among the nations.
11 and I will execute judgments upon Moab; and they shall know that I am Jehovah.
12 Thus saith the Lord Jehovah: Because that Edom hath dealt against the house of Judah by taking vengeance, and hath greatly offended, and revenged himself upon them;
13 therefore thus saith the Lord Jehovah, I will stretch out my hand upon Edom, and will cut off man and beast from it; and I will make it desolate from Teman; even unto Dedan shall they fall by the sword.
14 And I will lay my vengeance upon Edom by the hand of my people Israel; and they shall do in Edom according to mine anger and according to my wrath; and they shall know my vengeance, saith the Lord Jehovah.
15 Thus saith the Lord Jehovah: Because the Philistines have dealt by revenge, and have taken vengeance with despite of soul to destroy with perpetual enmity;
16 therefore thus saith the Lord Jehovah, Behold, I will stretch out my hand upon the Philistines, and I will cut off the Cherethites, and destroy the remnant of the sea coast.
17 And I will execute great vengeance upon them with wrathful rebukes; and they shall know that I am Jehovah, when I shall lay my vengeance upon them.

Chapter 26

1 And it came to pass in the eleventh year, in the first [day] of the month, that the word of Jehovah came unto me, saying,
2 Son of man, because that Tyre hath said against Jerusalem, Aha, she is broken [that was] the gate of the peoples; she is turned unto me; I shall be replenished, now that she is laid waste:
3 therefore thus saith the Lord Jehovah, Behold, I am against thee, O Tyre, and will cause many nations to come up against thee, as the sea causeth its waves to come up.
4 And they shall destroy the walls of Tyre, and break down her towers: I will also scrape her dust from her, and make her a bare rock.
5 She shall be a place for the spreading of nets in the midst of the sea; for I have spoken it, saith the Lord Jehovah; and she shall become a spoil to the nations.
6 And her daughters that are in the field shall be slain with the sword: and they shall know that I am Jehovah.
7 For thus saith the Lord Jehovah: Behold, I will bring upon Tyre Nebuchadrezzar king of Babylon, king of kings, from the north, with horses, and with chariots, and with horsemen, and a company, and much people.
8 He shall slay with the sword thy daughters in the field; and he shall make forts against thee, and cast up a mound against thee, and raise up the buckler against thee.
9 And he shall set his battering engines against thy walls, and with his axes he shall break down thy towers.
10 By reason of the abundance of his horses their dust shall cover thee: thy walls shall shake at the noise of the horsemen, and of the wagons, and of the chariots, when he shall enter into thy gates, as men enter into a city wherein is made a breach.
11 With the hoofs of his horses shall he tread down all thy streets; he shall slay thy people with the sword; and the pillars of thy strength shall go down to the ground.
12 And they shall make a spoil of thy riches, and make a prey of thy merchandise; and they shall break down thy walls, and destroy thy pleasant houses; and they shall lay thy stones and thy timber and thy dust in the midst of the waters.
13 And I will cause the noise of thy songs to cease; and the sound of thy harps shall be no more heard.

14 And I will make thee a bare rock; thou shalt be a place for the spreading of nets; thou shalt be built no more: for I Jehovah have spoken it, saith the Lord Jehovah.
15 Thus saith the Lord Jehovah to Tyre: shall not the isles shake at the sound of thy fall, when the wounded groan, when the slaughter is made in the midst of thee?
16 Then all the princes of the sea shall come down from their thrones, and lay aside their robes, and strip off their broidered garments: they shall clothe themselves with trembling; they shall sit upon the ground, and shall tremble every moment, and be astonished at thee.
17 And they shall take up a lamentation over thee, and say to thee, How art thou destroyed, that wast inhabited by seafaring men, the renowned city, that was strong in the sea, she and her inhabitants, that caused their terror to be on all that dwelt there!
18 Now shall the isles tremble in the day of thy fall; yea, the isles that are in the sea shall be dismayed at thy departure.
19 For thus saith the Lord Jehovah: When I shall make thee a desolate city, like the cities that are not inhabited; when I shall bring up the deep upon thee, and the great waters shall cover thee;
20 then will I bring thee down with them that descend into the pit, to the people of old time, and will make thee to dwell in the nether parts of the earth, in the places that are desolate of old, with them that go down to the pit, that thou be not inhabited; and I will set glory in the land of the living:
21 I will make thee a terror, and thou shalt no more have any being; though thou be sought for, yet shalt thou never be found again, saith the Lord Jehovah.

Chapter 27

1 The word of Jehovah came again unto me, saying,
2 And thou, son of man, take up a lamentation over Tyre;
3 and say unto Tyre, O thou that dwellest at the entry of the sea, that art the merchant of the peoples unto many isles, thus saith the Lord Jehovah: Thou, O Tyre, hast said, I am perfect in beauty.
4 Thy borders are in the heart of the seas; thy builders have perfected thy beauty.
5 They have made all thy planks of fir-trees from Senir; they have taken a cedar from Lebanon to make a mast for thee.
6 Of the oaks of Bashan have they made thine oars; they have made thy benches of ivory inlaid in boxwood, from the isles of Kittim.
7 Of fine linen with broidered work from Egypt was thy sail, that it might be to thee for an ensign; blue and purple from the isles of Elishah was thine awning.
8 The inhabitants of Sidon and Arvad were thy rowers: thy wise men, O Tyre, were in thee, they were thy pilots.
9 The old men of Gebal and the wise men thereof were in thee thy calkers: all the ships of the sea with their mariners were in thee to deal in thy merchandise.
10 Persia and Lud and Put were in thine army, thy men of war: they hanged the shield and helmet in thee; they set forth thy comeliness.
11 The men of Arvad with thine army were upon thy walls round about, and valorous men were in thy towers; they hanged their shields upon thy walls round about; they have perfected thy beauty.
12 Tarshish was thy merchant by reason of the multitude of all kinds of riches; with silver, iron, tin, and lead, they traded for thy wares.
13 Javan, Tubal, and Meshech, they were thy traffickers; they traded the persons of men and vessels of brass for thy merchandise.
14 They of the house of Togarmah traded for thy wares with horses and war-horses and mules.
15 The men of Dedan were thy traffickers; many isles were the mart of thy hand: they brought thee in exchange horns of ivory and ebony.
16 Syria was thy merchant by reason of the multitude of thy handiworks: they traded for thy wares with emeralds, purple, and broidered work, and fine linen, and coral, and rubies.
17 Judah, and the land of Israel, they were thy traffickers: they traded for thy merchandise wheat of Minnith, and pannag, and honey, and oil, and balm.
18 Damascus was thy merchant for the multitude of thy handiworks, by reason of the multitude of all kinds of riches, with the wine of Helbon, and white wool.
19 Vedan and Javan traded with yarn for thy wares: bright iron, cassia, and calamus, were among thy merchandise.
20 Dedan was thy trafficker in precious cloths for riding.
21 Arabia, and all the princes of Kedar, they were the merchants of thy hand; in lambs, and rams, and goats, in these were they thy merchants.

22 The traffickers of Sheba and Raamah, they were thy traffickers; they traded for thy wares with the chief of all spices, and with all precious stones, and gold.
23 Haran and Canneh and Eden, the traffickers of Sheba, Asshur [and] Chilmad, were thy traffickers.
24 These were thy traffickers in choice wares, in wrappings of blue and broidered work, and in chests of rich apparel, bound with cords and made of cedar, among thy merchandise.
25 The ships of Tarshish were thy caravans for thy merchandise: and thou wast replenished, and made very glorious in the heart of the seas.
26 Thy rowers have brought thee into great waters: the east wind hath broken thee in the heart of the seas.
27 Thy riches, and thy wares, thy merchandise, thy mariners, and thy pilots, thy calkers, and the dealers in thy merchandise, and all thy men of war, that are in thee, with all thy company which is in the midst of thee, shall fall into the heart of the seas in the day of thy ruin.
28 At the sound of the cry of thy pilots the suburbs shall shake.
29 And all that handled the oar, the mariners, [and] all the pilots of the sea, shall come down from their ships; they shall stand upon the land,
30 and shall cause their voice to be heard over thee, and shall cry bitterly, and shall cast up dust upon their heads, they shall wallow themselves in the ashes:
31 and they shall make themselves bald for thee, and gird them with sackcloth, and they shall weep for thee in bitterness of soul with bitter mourning.
32 And in their wailing they shall take up a lamentation for thee, and lament over thee, [saying], Who is there like Tyre, like her that is brought to silence in the midst of the sea?
33 When thy wares went forth out of the seas, thou filledst many peoples; thou didst enrich the kings of the earth with the multitude of thy riches and of thy merchandise.
34 In the time that thou wast broken by the seas in the depths of the waters, thy merchandise and all thy company did fall in the midst of thee.
35 All the inhabitants of the isles are astonished at thee, and their kings are horribly afraid; they are troubled in their countenance.
36 The merchants among the peoples hiss at thee; thou art become a terror, and thou shalt nevermore have any being.

Chapter 28

1 The word of Jehovah came again unto me, saying,
2 Son of man, say unto the prince of Tyre, Thus saith the Lord Jehovah: Because thy heart is lifted up, and thou hast said, I am a god, I sit in the seat of God, in the midst of the seas; yet thou art man, and not God, though thou didst set thy heart as the heart of God;-
3 behold, thou art wiser than Daniel; there is no secret that is hidden from thee;
4 by thy wisdom and by thine understanding thou hast gotten thee riches, and hast gotten gold and silver into thy treasures;
5 by thy great wisdom [and] by thy traffic hast thou increased thy riches, and thy heart is lifted up because of thy riches;-
6 therefore thus saith the Lord Jehovah: Because thou hast set thy heart as the heart of God,
7 therefore, behold, I will bring strangers upon thee, the terrible of the nations; and they shall draw their swords against the beauty of thy wisdom, and they shall defile thy brightness.
8 They shall bring thee down to the pit; and thou shalt die the death of them that are slain, in the heart of the seas.
9 Wilt thou yet say before him that slayeth thee, I am God? but thou art man, and not God, in the hand of him that woundeth thee.
10 Thou shalt die the death of the uncircumcised by the hand of strangers: for I have spoken it, saith the Lord Jehovah.
11 Moreover the word of Jehovah came unto me, saying,
12 Son of man, take up a lamentation over the king of Tyre, and say unto him, Thus saith the Lord Jehovah: Thou sealest up the sum, full of wisdom, and perfect in beauty.
13 Thou wast in Eden, the garden of God; every precious stone was thy covering, the sardius, the topaz, and the diamond, the beryl, the onyx, and the jasper, the sapphire, the emerald, and the carbuncle, and gold: the workmanship of thy tabrets and of thy pipes was in thee; in the day that thou wast created they were prepared.
14 Thou wast the anointed cherub that covereth: and I set thee, [so that] thou wast upon the holy mountain of God; thou hast walked up and down in the midst of the stones of fire.

15 Thou wast perfect in thy ways from the day that thou wast created, till unrighteousness was found in thee.
16 By the abundance of thy traffic they filled the midst of thee with violence, and thou hast sinned: therefore have I cast thee as profane out of the mountain of God; and I have destroyed thee, O covering cherub, from the midst of the stones of fire.
17 Thy heart was lifted up because of thy beauty; thou hast corrupted thy wisdom by reason of thy brightness: I have cast thee to the ground; I have laid thee before kings, that they may behold thee.
18 By the multitude of thine iniquities, in the unrighteousness of thy traffic, thou hast profaned thy sanctuaries; therefore have I brought forth a fire from the midst of thee; it hath devoured thee, and I have turned thee to ashes upon the earth in the sight of all them that behold thee.
19 All they that know thee among the peoples shall be astonished at thee: thou art become a terror, and thou shalt nevermore have any being.
20 And the word of Jehovah came unto me, saying,
21 Son of man, set thy face toward Sidon, and prophesy against it,
22 and say, Thus saith the Lord Jehovah: Behold, I am against thee, O Sidon; and I will be glorified in the midst of thee; and they shall know that I am Jehovah, when I shall have executed judgments in her, and shall be sanctified in her.
23 For I will send pestilence into her, and blood into her streets; and the wounded shall fall in the midst of her, with the sword upon her on every side; and they shall know that I am Jehovah.
24 And there shall be no more a pricking brier unto the house of Israel, nor a hurting thorn of any that are round about them, that did despite unto them; and they shall know that I am the Lord Jehovah.
25 Thus saith the Lord Jehovah: When I shall have gathered the house of Israel from the peoples among whom they are scattered, and shall be sanctified in them in the sight of the nations, then shall they dwell in their own land which I gave to my servant Jacob.
26 And they shall dwell securely therein; yea, they shall build houses, and plant vineyards, and shall dwell securely, when I have executed judgments upon all those that do them despite round about them; and they shall know that I am Jehovah their God.

Chapter 29

1 In the tenth year, in the tenth [month], in the twelfth [day] of the month, the word of Jehovah came unto me, saying,
2 Son of man, set thy face against Pharaoh king of Egypt, and prophesy against him, and against all Egypt;
3 speak, and say, Thus saith the Lord Jehovah: Behold, I am against thee, Pharaoh king of Egypt, the great monster that lieth in the midst of his rivers, that hath said, My river is mine own, and I have made it for myself.
4 And I will put hooks in thy jaws, and I will cause the fish of thy rivers to stick unto thy scales; and I will bring thee up out of the midst of thy rivers, with all the fish of thy rivers which stick unto thy scales.
5 And I will cast thee forth into the wilderness, thee and all the fish of thy rivers: thou shalt fall upon the open field; thou shalt not be brought together, nor gathered; I have given thee for food to the beasts of the earth and to the birds of the heavens.
6 And all the inhabitants of Egypt shall know that I am Jehovah, because they have been a staff of reed to the house of Israel.
7 When they took hold of thee by thy hand, thou didst break, and didst rend all their shoulders; and when they leaned upon thee, thou brakest, and madest all their loins to be at a stand.
8 Therefore thus saith the Lord Jehovah: Behold, I will bring a sword upon thee, and will cut off from thee man and beast.
9 And the land of Egypt shall be a desolation and a waste; and they shall know that I am Jehovah. Because he hath said, The river is mine, and I have made it;
10 therefore, behold, I am against thee, and against thy rivers, and I will make the land of Egypt an utter waste and desolation, from the tower of Seveneh even unto the border of Ethiopia.
11 No foot of man shall pass through it, nor foot of beast shall pass through it, neither shall it be inhabited forty years.
12 And I will make the land of Egypt a desolation in the midst of the countries that are desolate; and her cities among the cities that are laid waste shall be a desolation forty years; and I will scatter the Egyptians among the nations, and will disperse them through the countries.
13 For thus saith the Lord Jehovah: At the end of forty years will I gather the Egyptians from the peoples whither they were scattered;

14 and I will bring back the captivity of Egypt, and will cause them to return into the land of Pathros, into the land of their birth; and they shall be there a base kingdom.
15 It shall be the basest of the kingdoms; neither shall it any more lift itself up above the nations: and I will diminish them, that they shall no more rule over the nations.
16 And it shall be no more the confidence of the house of Israel, bringing iniquity to remembrance, when they turn to look after them: and they shall know that I am the Lord Jehovah.
17 And it came to pass in the seven and twentieth year, in the first [month], in the first [day] of the month, the word of Jehovah came unto me, saying,
18 Son of man, Nebuchadrezzar king of Babylon caused his army to serve a great service against Tyre: every head was made bald, and every shoulder was worn; yet had he no wages, nor his army, from Tyre, for the service that he had served against it.
19 Therefore thus saith the Lord Jehovah: Behold, I will give the land of Egypt unto Nebuchadrezzar king of Babylon; and he shall carry off her multitude, and take her spoil, and take her prey; and it shall be the wages for his army.
20 I have given him the land of Egypt as his recompense for which he served, because they wrought for me, saith the Lord Jehovah.
21 In that day will I cause a horn to bud forth unto the house of Israel, and I will give thee the opening of the mouth in the midst of them; and they shall know that I am Jehovah.

Chapter 30

1 The word of Jehovah came again unto me, saying,
2 Son of man, prophesy, and say, Thus saith the Lord Jehovah: Wail ye, Alas for the day!
3 For the day is near, even the day of Jehovah is near; it shall be a day of clouds, a time of the nations.
4 And a sword shall come upon Egypt, and anguish shall be in Ethiopia, when the slain shall fall in Egypt; and they shall take away her multitude, and her foundations shall be broken down.
5 Ethiopia, and Put, and Lud, and all the mingled people, and Cub, and the children of the land that is in league, shall fall with them by the sword.
6 Thus saith Jehovah: They also that uphold Egypt shall fall; and the pride of her power shall come down: from the tower of Seveneh shall they fall in it by the sword, saith the Lord Jehovah.
7 And they shall be desolate in the midst of the countries that are desolate; and her cities shall be in the midst of the cities that are wasted.
8 And they shall know at I am Jehovah, when I have set a fire in Egypt, and all her helpers are destroyed.
9 In that day shall messengers go forth from before me in ships to make the careless Ethiopians afraid; and there shall be anguish upon them, as in the day of Egypt; for, lo, it cometh.
10 Thus saith the Lord Jehovah: I will also make the multitude of Egypt to cease, by the hand of Nebuchadrezzar king of Babylon.
11 He and his people with him, the terrible of the nations, shall be brought in to destroy the land; and they shall draw their swords against Egypt, and fill the land with the slain.
12 And I will make the rivers dry, and will sell the land into the hand of evil men; and I will make the land desolate, and all that is therein, by the hand of strangers: I, Jehovah, have spoken it.
13 Thus saith the Lord Jehovah: I will also destroy the idols, and I will cause the images to cease from Memphis; and there shall be no more a prince from the land of Egypt: and I will put a fear in the land of Egypt.
14 And I will make Pathros desolate, and will set a fire in Zoan, and will execute judgments upon No.
15 And I will pour my wrath upon Sin, the stronghold of Egypt; and I will cut off the multitude of No.
16 And I will set a fire in Egypt: Sin shall be in great anguish, and No shall be broken up; and Memphis [shall have] adversaries in the day-time.
17 The young men of Aven and of Pibeseth shall fall by the sword; and these [cities] shall go into captivity.
18 At Tehaphnehes also the day shall withdraw itself, when I shall break there the yokes of Egypt, and the pride of her power shall cease in her: as for her, a cloud shall cover her, and her daughters shall go into captivity.
19 Thus will I execute judgments upon Egypt; and they shall know that I am Jehovah.
20 And it came to pass in the eleventh year, in the first [month], in the seventh [day] of the month, that the word of Jehovah came unto me, saying,
21 Son of man, I have broken the arm of Pharaoh king of Egypt; and, lo, it hath not been bound up, to apply [healing] medicines, to put a bandage to bind it, that it be strong to hold the sword.

22 Therefore thus saith the Lord Jehovah: Behold, I am against Pharaoh king of Egypt, and will break
his arms, the strong [arm], and that which was broken; and I will cause the sword to fall out of his hand.
23 And I will scatter the Egyptians among the nations, and will disperse them through the countries.
24 And I will strengthen the arms of the king of Babylon, and put my sword in his hand: but I will break
the arms of Pharaoh, and he shall groan before him with the groanings of a deadly wounded man.
25 And I will hold up the arms of the king of Babylon; and the arms of Pharaoh shall fall down; and
they shall know that I am Jehovah, when I shall put my sword into the hand of the king of Babylon, and
he shall stretch it out upon the land of Egypt.
26 And I will scatter the Egyptians among the nations, and disperse them through the countries; and
they shall know that I am Jehovah.

Chapter 31

1 And it came to pass in the eleventh year, in the third [month], in the first [day] of the month, that the
word of Jehovah came unto me, saying,
2 Son of man, say unto Pharaoh king of Egypt, and to his multitude: Whom art thou like in thy
greatness?
3 Behold, the Assyrian was a cedar in Lebanon with fair branches, and with a forest-like shade, and of
high stature; and its top was among the thick boughs.
4 The waters nourished it, the deep made it to grow: the rivers thereof ran round about its plantation;
and it sent out its channels unto all the trees of the field.
5 Therefore its stature was exalted above all the trees of the field; and its boughs were multiplied, and its
branches became long by reason of many waters, when it shot [them] forth.
6 All the birds of the heavens made their nests in its boughs; and under its branches did all the beasts of
the field bring forth their young; and under its shadow dwelt all great nations.
7 Thus was it fair in its greatness, in the length of its branches; for its root was by many waters.
8 The cedars in the garden of God could not hide it; the fir-trees were not like its boughs, and the plane-
trees were not as its branches; nor was any tree in the garden of God like unto it in its beauty.
9 I made it fair by the multitude of its branches, so that all the trees of Eden, that were in the garden of
God, envied it.
10 Therefore thus said the Lord Jehovah: Because thou art exalted in stature, and he hath set his top
among the thick boughs, and his heart is lifted up in his height;
11 I will even deliver him into the hand of the mighty one of the nations; he shall surely deal with him; I
have driven him out for his wickedness.
12 And strangers, the terrible of the nations, have cut him off, and have left him: upon the mountains
and in all the valleys his branches are fallen, and his boughs are broken by all the watercourses of the
land; and all the peoples of the earth are gone down from his shadow, and have left him.
13 Upon his ruin all the birds of the heavens shall dwell, and all the beasts of the field shall be upon his
branches;
14 to the end that none of all the trees by the waters exalt themselves in their stature, neither set their
top among the thick boughs, nor that their mighty ones stand up on their height, [even] all that drink
water: for they are all delivered unto death, to the nether parts of the earth, in the midst of the children
of men, with them that go down to the pit.
15 Thus saith the Lord Jehovah: In the day when he went down to Sheol I caused a mourning: I covered
the deep for him, and I restrained the rivers thereof; and the great waters were stayed; and I caused
Lebanon to mourn for him, and all the trees of the field fainted for him.
16 I made the nations to shake at the sound of his fall, when I cast him down to Sheol with them that
descend into the pit; and all the trees of Eden, the choice and best of Lebanon, all that drink water, were
comforted in the nether parts of the earth.
17 They also went down into Sheol with him unto them that are slain by the sword; yea, they that were
his arm, [that] dwelt under his shadow in the midst of the nations.
18 To whom art thou thus like in glory and in greatness among the trees of Eden? yet shalt thou be
brought down with the trees of Eden unto the nether parts of the earth: thou shalt lie in the midst of the
uncircumcised, with them that are slain by the sword. This is Pharaoh and all his multitude, saith the
Lord Jehovah.
Chapter 32

1 And it came to pass in the twelfth year, in the twelfth month, in the first [day] of the month, that the
word of Jehovah came unto me, saying,

2 Son of man, take up a lamentation over Pharaoh king of Egypt, and say unto him, Thou wast likened unto a young lion of the nations: yet art thou as a monster in the seas; and thou didst break forth with thy rivers, and troubledst the waters with thy feet, and fouledst their rivers.
3 Thus saith the Lord Jehovah: I will spread out my net upon thee with a company of many peoples; and they shall bring thee up in my net.
4 And I will leave thee upon the land, I will cast thee forth upon the open field, and will cause all the birds of the heavens to settle upon thee, and I will satisfy the beasts of the whole earth with thee.
5 And I will lay thy flesh upon the mountains, and fill the valleys with thy height.
6 I will also water with thy blood the land wherein thou swimmest, even to the mountains; and the watercourses shall be full of thee.
7 And when I shall extinguish thee, I will cover the heavens, and make the stars thereof dark; I will cover the sun with a cloud, and the moon shall not give its light.
8 All the bright lights of heaven will I make dark over thee, and set darkness upon thy land, saith the Lord Jehovah.
9 I will also vex the hearts of many peoples, when I shall bring thy destruction among the nations, into the countries which thou hast not known.
10 Yea, I will make many peoples amazed at thee, and their kings shall be horribly afraid for thee, when I shall brandish my sword before them; and they shall tremble at every moment, every man for his own life, in the day of thy fall.
11 For thus saith the Lord Jehovah: The sword of the king of Babylon shall come upon thee.
12 By the swords of the mighty will I cause thy multitude to fall; the terrible of the nations are they all: and they shall bring to nought the pride of Egypt, and all the multitude thereof shall be destroyed.
13 I will destroy also all the beasts thereof from beside many waters; neither shall the foot of man trouble them any more, nor the hoofs of beasts trouble them.
14 Then will I make their waters clear, and cause their rivers to run like oil, saith the Lord Jehovah.
15 When I shall make the land of Egypt desolate and waste, a land destitute of that whereof it was full, when I shall smite all them that dwell therein, then shall they know that I am Jehovah.
16 This is the lamentation wherewith they shall lament; the daughters of the nations shall lament therewith; over Egypt, and over all her multitude, shall they lament therewith, saith the Lord Jehovah.
17 It came to pass also in the twelfth year, in the fifteenth [day] of the month, that the word of Jehovah came unto me, saying,
18 Son of man, wail for the multitude of Egypt, and cast them down, even her, and the daughters of the famous nations, unto the nether parts of the earth, with them that go down into the pit.
19 Whom dost thou pass in beauty? go down, and be thou laid with the uncircumcised.
20 They shall fall in the midst of them that are slain by the sword: she is delivered to the sword; draw her away and all her multitudes.
21 The strong among the mighty shall speak to him out of the midst of Sheol with them that help him: they are gone down, they lie still, even the uncircumcised, slain by the sword.
22 Asshur is there and all her company; her graves are round about her; all of them slain, fallen by the sword;
23 whose graves are set in the uttermost parts of the pit, and her company is round about her grave; all of them slain, fallen by the sword, who caused terror in the land of the living.
24 There is Elam and all her multitude round about her grave; all of them slain, fallen by the sword, who are gone down uncircumcised into the nether parts of the earth, who caused their terror in the land of the living, and have borne their shame with them that go down to the pit.
25 They have set her a bed in the midst of the slain with all her multitude; her graves are round about her; all of them uncircumcised, slain by the sword; for their terror was caused in the land of the living, and they have borne their shame with them that go down to the pit: he is put in the midst of them that are slain.
26 There is Meshech, Tubal, and all their multitude; their graves are round about them; all of them uncircumcised, slain by the sword; for they caused their terror in the land of the living.
27 And they shall not lie with the mighty that are fallen of the uncircumcised, that are gone down to Sheol with their weapons of war, and have laid their swords under their heads, and their iniquities are upon their bones; for [they were] the terror of the mighty in the land of the living.
28 But thou shalt be broken in the midst of the uncircumcised, and shalt lie with them that are slain by the sword.
29 There is Edom, her kings and all her princes, who in their might are laid with them that are slain by the sword: they shall lie with the uncircumcised, and with them that go down to the pit.
30 There are the princes of the north, all of them, and all the Sidonians, who are gone down with the

slain; in the terror which they caused by their might they are put to shame; and they lie uncircumcised
with them that are slain by the sword, and bear their shame with them that go down to the pit.
31 Pharaoh shall see them, and shall be comforted over all his multitude, even Pharaoh and all his army,
slain by the sword, saith the Lord Jehovah.
32 For I have put his terror in the land of the living; and he shall be laid in the midst of the
uncircumcised, with them that are slain by the sword, even Pharaoh and all his multitude, saith the Lord
Jehovah.

Chapter 33

1 And the word of Jehovah came unto me, saying,
2 Son of man, speak to the children of thy people, and say unto them, When I bring the sword upon a
land, and the people of the land take a man from among them, and set him for their watchman;
3 if, when he seeth the sword come upon the land, he blow the trumpet, and warn the people;
4 then whosoever heareth the sound of the trumpet, and taketh not warning, if the sword come, and
take him away, his blood shall be upon his own head.
5 He heard the sound of the trumpet, and took not warning; his blood shall be upon him; whereas if he
had taken warning, he would have delivered his soul.
6 But if the watchman see the sword come, and blow not the trumpet, and the people be not warned,
and the sword come, and take any person from among them; he is taken away in his iniquity, but his
blood will I require at the watchman's hand.
7 So thou, son of man, I have set thee a watchman unto the house of Israel; therefore hear the word at
my mouth, and give them warning from me.
8 When I say unto the wicked, O wicked man, thou shalt surely die, and thou dost not speak to warn the
wicked from his way; that wicked man shall die in his iniquity, but his blood will I require at thy hand.
9 Nevertheless, if thou warn the wicked of his way to turn from it, and he turn not from his way; he
shall die in his iniquity, but thou hast delivered thy soul.
10 And thou, son of man, say unto the house of Israel: Thus ye speak, saying, Our transgressions and
our sins are upon us, and we pine away in them; how then can we live?
11 Say unto them, As I live, saith the Lord Jehovah, I have no pleasure in the death of the wicked; but
that the wicked turn from his way and live: turn ye, turn ye from your evil ways; for why will ye die, O
house of Israel?
12 And thou, son of man, say unto the children of thy people, The righteousness of the righteous shall
not deliver him in the day of his transgression; and as for the wickedness of the wicked, he shall not fall
thereby in the day that he turneth from his wickedness; neither shall he that is righteous be able to live
thereby in the day that he sinneth.
13 When I say to the righteous, that he shall surely live; if he trust to his righteousness, and commit
iniquity, none of his righteous deeds shall be remembered; but in his iniquity that he hath committed,
therein shall he die.
14 Again, when I say unto the wicked, Thou shalt surely die; if he turn from his sin, and do that which is
lawful and right;
15 if the wicked restore the pledge, give again that which he had taken by robbery, walk in the statutes
of life, committing no iniquity; he shall surely live, he shall not die.
16 None of his sins that he hath committed shall be remembered against him: he hath done that which
is lawful and right; he shall surely live.
17 Yet the children of thy people say, The way of the Lord is not equal: but as for them, their way is not
equal.
18 When the righteous turneth from his righteousness, and committeth iniquity, he shall even die
therein.
19 And when the wicked turneth from his wickedness, and doeth that which is lawful and right, he shall
live thereby.
20 Yet ye say, The way of the Lord is not equal. O house of Israel, I will judge you every one after his
ways.
21 And it came to pass in the twelfth year of our captivity, in the tenth [month], in the fifth [day] of the
month, that one that had escaped out of Jerusalem came unto me, saying, The city is smitten.
22 Now the hand of Jehovah had been upon me in the evening, before he that was escaped came; and
he had opened my mouth, until he came to me in the morning; and my mouth was opened, and I was
no more dumb.
23 And the word of Jehovah came unto me, saying,

24 Son of man, they that inhabit those waste places in the land of Israel speak, saying, Abraham was
one, and he inherited the land: but we are many; the land is given us for inheritance.
25 Wherefore say unto them, Thus saith the Lord Jehovah: Ye eat with the blood, and lift up your eyes
unto your idols, and shed blood: and shall ye possess the land?
26 Ye stand upon your sword, ye work abomination, and ye defile every one his neighbor's wife: and
shall ye possess the land?
27 Thus shalt thou say unto them, Thus saith the Lord Jehovah: As I live, surely they that are in the
waste places shall fall by the sword; and him that is in the open field will I give to the beasts to be
devoured; and they that are in the strongholds and in the caves shall die of the pestilence.
28 And I will make the land a desolation and an astonishment; and the pride of her power shall cease;
and the mountains of Israel shall be desolate, so that none shall pass through.
29 Then shall they know that I am Jehovah, when I have made the land a desolation and an
astonishment, because of all their abominations which they have committed.
30 And as for thee, son of man, the children of thy people talk of thee by the walls and in the doors of
the houses, and speak one to another, every one to his brother, saying, Come, I pray you, and hear what
is the word that cometh forth from Jehovah.
31 And they come unto thee as the people cometh, and they sit before thee as my people, and they hear
thy words, but do them not; for with their mouth they show much love, but their heart goeth after their
gain.
32 And, lo, thou art unto them as a very lovely song of one that hath a pleasant voice, and can play well
on an instrument; for they hear thy words, but they do them not.
33 And when this cometh to pass, (behold, it cometh,) then shall they know that a prophet hath been
among them.

Chapter 34

1 And the word of Jehovah came unto me, saying,
2 Son of man, prophesy against the shepherds of Israel, prophesy, and say unto them, even to the
shepherds, Thus saith the Lord Jehovah: Woe unto the shepherds of Israel that do feed themselves!
should not the shepherds feed the sheep?
3 Ye eat the fat, and ye clothe you with the wool, ye kill the fatlings; but ye feed not the sheep.
4 The diseased have ye not strengthened, neither have ye healed that which was sick, neither have ye
bound up that which was broken, neither have ye brought back that which was driven away, neither
have ye sought that which was lost; but with force and with rigor have ye ruled over them.
5 And they were scattered, because there was no shepherd; and they became food to all the beasts of the
field, and were scattered.
6 My sheep wandered through all the mountains, and upon every high hill: yea, my sheep were scattered
upon all the face of the earth; and there was none that did search or seek [after them].
7 Therefore, ye shepherds, hear the word of Jehovah:
8 As I live, saith the Lord Jehovah, surely forasmuch as my sheep became a prey, and my sheep became
food to all the beasts of the field, because there was no shepherd, neither did my shepherds search for
my sheep, but the shepherds fed themselves, and fed not my sheep;
9 therefore, ye shepherds, hear the word of Jehovah:
10 Thus saith the Lord Jehovah: Behold, I am against the shepherds; and I will require my sheep at their
hand, and cause them to cease from feeding the sheep; neither shall the shepherds feed themselves any
more; and I will deliver my sheep from their mouth, that they may not be food for them.
11 For thus saith the Lord Jehovah: Behold, I myself, even I, will search for my sheep, and will seek
them out.
12 As a shepherd seeketh out his flock in the day that he is among his sheep that are scattered abroad,
so will I seek out my sheep; and I will deliver them out of all places whither they have been scattered in
the cloudy and dark day.
13 And I will bring them out from the peoples, and gather them from the countries, and will bring them
into their own land; and I will feed them upon the mountains of Israel, by the watercourses, and in all
the inhabited places of the country.
14 I will feed them with good pasture; and upon the mountains of the height of Israel shall their fold be:
there shall they lie down in a good fold; and on fat pasture shall they feed upon the mountains of Israel.
15 I myself will be the shepherd of my sheep, and I will cause them to lie down, saith the Lord Jehovah.
16 I will seek that which was lost, and will bring back that which was driven away, and will bind up that
which was broken, and will strengthen that which was sick: but the fat and the strong I will destroy; I

will feed them in justice.
17 And as for you, O my flock, thus saith the Lord Jehovah: Behold, I judge between sheep and sheep, the rams and the he-goats.
18 Seemeth it a small thing unto you to have fed upon the good pasture, but ye must tread down with your feet the residue of your pasture? and to have drunk of the clear waters, but ye must foul the residue with your feet?
19 And as for my sheep, they eat that which ye have trodden with your feet, and they drink that which ye have fouled with your feet.
20 Therefore thus saith the Lord Jehovah unto them: Behold, I, even I, will judge between the fat sheep and the lean sheep.
21 Because ye thrust with side and with shoulder, and push all the diseased with your horns, till ye have scattered them abroad;
22 therefore will I save my flock, and they shall no more be a prey; and I will judge between sheep and sheep.
23 And I will set up one shepherd over them, and he shall feed them, even my servant David; he shall feed them, and he shall be their shepherd.
24 And I, Jehovah, will be their God, and my servant David prince among them; I, Jehovah, have spoken it.
25 And I will make with them a covenant of peace, and will cause evil beasts to cease out of the land; and they shall dwell securely in the wilderness, and sleep in the woods.
26 And I will make them and the places round about my hill a blessing; and I will cause the shower to come down in its season; there shall be showers of blessing.
27 And the tree of the field shall yield its fruit, and the earth shall yield its increase, and they shall be secure in their land; and they shall know that I am Jehovah, when I have broken the bars of their yoke, and have delivered them out of the hand of those that made bondmen of them.
28 And they shall no more be a prey to the nations, neither shall the beasts of the earth devour them; but they shall dwell securely, and none shall make them afraid.
29 And I will raise up unto them a plantation for renown, and they shall be no more consumed with famine in the land, neither bear the shame of the nations any more.
30 And they shall know that I, Jehovah, their God am with them, and that they, the house of Israel, are my people, saith the Lord Jehovah.
31 And ye my sheep, the sheep of my pasture, are men, and I am your God, saith the Lord Jehovah.

Chapter 35

1 Moreover the word of Jehovah came unto me, saying,
2 Son of man, set thy face against mount Seir, and prophesy against it,
3 and say unto it, Thus saith the Lord Jehovah: Behold, I am against thee, O mount Seir, and I will stretch out my hand against thee, and I will make thee a desolation and an astonishment.
4 I will lay thy cities waste, and thou shalt be desolate; and thou shalt know that I am Jehovah.
5 Because thou hast had a perpetual enmity, and hast given over the children of Israel to the power of the sword in the time of their calamity, in the time of the iniquity of the end;
6 therefore, as I live, saith the Lord Jehovah, I will prepare thee unto blood, and blood shall pursue thee: since thou hast not hated blood, therefore blood shall pursue thee.
7 Thus will I make mount Seir an astonishment and a desolation; and I will cut off from it him that passeth through and him that returneth.
8 And I will fill its mountains with its slain: in thy hills and in thy valleys and in all thy watercourses shall they fall that are slain with the sword.
9 I will make thee a perpetual desolation, and thy cities shall not be inhabited; and ye shall know that I am Jehovah.
10 Because thou hast said, These two nations and these two countries shall be mine, and we will possess it; whereas Jehovah was there:
11 therefore, as I live, saith the Lord Jehovah, I will do according to thine anger, and according to thine envy which thou hast showed out of thy hatred against them; and I will make myself known among them, when I shall judge thee.
12 And thou shalt know that I, Jehovah, have heard all thy revilings which thou hast spoken against the mountains of Israel, saying, They are laid desolate, they are given us to devour.
13 And ye have magnified yourselves against me with your mouth, and have multiplied your words against me: I have heard it.

14 Thus saith the Lord Jehovah: When the whole earth rejoiceth, I will make thee desolate.
15 As thou didst rejoice over the inheritance of the house of Israel, because it was desolate, so will I do unto thee: thou shalt be desolate, O mount Seir, and all Edom, even all of it; and they shall know that I am Jehovah.

Chapter 36

1 And thou, son of man, prophesy unto the mountains of Israel, and say, Ye mountains of Israel, hear the word of Jehovah.
2 Thus saith the Lord Jehovah: Because the enemy hath said against you, Aha! and, The ancient high places are ours in possession;
3 therefore prophesy, and say, Thus saith the Lord Jehovah: Because, even because they have made you desolate, and swallowed you up on every side, that ye might be a possession unto the residue of the nations, and ye are taken up in the lips of talkers, and the evil report of the people;
4 therefore, ye mountains of Israel, hear the word of the Lord Jehovah: Thus saith the Lord Jehovah to the mountains and to the hills, to the watercourses and to the valleys, to the desolate wastes and to the cities that are forsaken, which are become a prey and derision to the residue of the nations that are round about;
5 therefore thus saith the Lord Jehovah: Surely in the fire of my jealousy have I spoken against the residue of the nations, and against all Edom, that have appointed my land unto themselves for a possession with the joy of all their heart, with despite of soul, to cast it out for a prey.
6 Therefore prophesy concerning the land of Israel, and say unto the mountains and to the hills, to the watercourses and to the valleys, Thus saith the Lord Jehovah: Behold, I have spoken in my jealousy and in my wrath, because ye have borne the shame of the nations:
7 therefore thus saith the Lord Jehovah: I have sworn, [saying], Surely the nations that are round about you, they shall bear their shame.
8 But ye, O mountains of Israel, ye shall shoot forth your branches, and yield your fruit to my people Israel; for they are at hand to come.
9 For, behold, I am for you, and I will turn into you, and ye shall be tilled and sown;
10 and I will multiply men upon you, all the house of Israel, even all of it; and the cities shall be inhabited, and the waste places shall be builded;
11 and I will multiply upon you man and beast; and they shall increase and be fruitful; and I will cause you to be inhabited after your former estate, and will do better [unto you] than at your beginnings: and ye shall know that I am Jehovah.
12 Yea, I will cause men to walk upon you, even my people Israel; and they shall possess thee, and thou shalt be their inheritance, and thou shalt no more henceforth bereave them of children.
13 Thus saith the Lord Jehovah: Because they say unto you, Thou [land] art a devourer of men, and hast been a bereaver of thy nation;
14 therefore thou shalt devour men no more, neither bereave thy nation any more, saith the Lord Jehovah;
15 neither will I let thee hear any more the shame of the nations, neither shalt thou bear the reproach of the peoples any more, neither shalt thou cause thy nation to stumble any more, saith the Lord Jehovah.
16 Moreover the word of Jehovah came unto me, saying,
17 Son of man, when the house of Israel dwelt in their own land, they defiled it by their way and by their doings: their way before me was as the uncleanness of a woman in her impurity.
18 Wherefore I poured out my wrath upon them for the blood which they had poured out upon the land, and because they had defiled it with their idols;
19 and I scattered them among the nations, and they were dispersed through the countries: according to their way and according to their doings I judged them.
20 And when they came unto the nations, whither they went, they profaned my holy name; in that men said of them, These are the people of Jehovah, and are gone forth out of his land.
21 But I had regard for my holy name, which the house of Israel had profaned among the nations, whither they went.
22 Therefore say unto the house of Israel, Thus saith the Lord Jehovah: I do not [this] for your sake, O house of Israel, but for my holy name, which ye have profaned among the nations, whither ye went.
23 And I will sanctify my great name, which hath been profaned among the nations, which ye have profaned in the midst of them; and the nations shall know that I am Jehovah, saith the Lord Jehovah, when I shall be sanctified in you before their eyes.
24 For I will take you from among the nations, and gather you out of all the countries, and will bring

you into your own land.
25 And I will sprinkle clean water upon you, and ye shall be clean: from all your filthiness, and from all your idols, will I cleanse you.
26 A new heart also will I give you, and a new spirit will I put within you; and I will take away the stony heart out of your flesh, and I will give you a heart of flesh.
27 And I will put my Spirit within you, and cause you to walk in my statutes, and ye shall keep mine ordinances, and do them.
28 And ye shall dwell in the land that I gave to your fathers; and ye shall be my people, and I will be your God.
29 And I will save you from all your uncleannesses: and I will call for the grain, and will multiply it, and lay no famine upon you.
30 And I will multiply the fruit of the tree, and the increase of the field, that ye may receive no more the reproach of famine among the nations.
31 Then shall ye remember your evil ways, and your doings that were not good; and ye shall loathe yourselves in your own sight for your iniquities and for your abominations.
32 Nor for your sake do I [this], saith the Lord Jehovah, be it known unto you: be ashamed and confounded for your ways, O house of Israel.
33 Thus saith the Lord Jehovah: In the day that I cleanse you from all your iniquities, I will cause the cities to be inhabited, and the waste places shall be builded.
34 And the land that was desolate shall be tilled, whereas it was a desolation in the sight of all that passed by.
35 And they shall say, This land that was desolate is become like the garden of Eden; and the waste and desolate and ruined cities are fortified and inhabited.
36 Then the nations that are left round about you shall know that I, Jehovah, have builded the ruined places, and planted that which was desolate: I, Jehovah, have spoken it, and I will do it.
37 Thus saith the Lord Jehovah: For this, moreover, will I be inquired of by the house of Israel, to do it for them: I will increase them with men like a flock.
38 As the flock for sacrifice, as the flock of Jerusalem in her appointed feasts, so shall the waste cities be filled with flocks of men; and they shall know that I am Jehovah.

Chapter 37

1 The hand of Jehovah was upon me, and he brought me out in the Spirit of Jehovah, and set me down in the midst of the valley; and it was full of bones.
2 And he caused me to pass by them round about: and, behold, there were very many in the open valley; and, lo, they were very dry.
3 And he said unto me, Son of man, can these bones live? And I answered, O Lord Jehovah, thou knowest.
4 Again he said unto me, Prophesy over these bones, and say unto them, O ye dry bones, hear the word of Jehovah.
5 Thus saith the Lord Jehovah unto these bones: Behold, I will cause breath to enter into you, and ye shall live.
6 And I will lay sinews upon you, and will bring up flesh upon you, and cover you with skin, and put breath in you, and ye shall live; and ye shall know that I am Jehovah.
7 So I prophesied as I was commanded: and as I prophesied, there was a noise, and, behold, an earthquake; and the bones came together, bone to its bone.
8 And I beheld, and, lo, there were sinews upon them, and flesh came up, and skin covered them above; but there was no breath in them.
9 Then said he unto me, Prophesy unto the wind, prophesy, son of man, and say to the wind, Thus saith the Lord Jehovah: Come from the four winds, O breath, and breathe upon these slain, that they may live.
10 So I prophesied as he commanded me, and the breath came into them, and they lived, and stood up upon their feet, an exceeding great army.
11 Then he said unto me, Son of man, these bones are the whole house of Israel: behold, they say, Our bones are dried up, and our hope is lost; we are clean cut off.
12 Therefore prophesy, and say unto them, Thus saith the Lord Jehovah: Behold, I will open your graves, and cause you to come up out of your graves, O my people; and I will bring you into the land of Israel.
13 And ye shall know that I am Jehovah, when I have opened your graves, and caused you to come up

out of your graves, O my people.
14 And I will put my Spirit in you, and ye shall live, and I will place you in your own land: and ye shall know that I, Jehovah, have spoken it and performed it, saith Jehovah.
15 The word of Jehovah came again unto me, saying,
16 And thou, son of man, take thee one stick, and write upon it, For Judah, and for the children of Israel his companions: then take another stick, and write upon it, For Joseph, the stick of Ephraim, and [for] all the house of Israel his companions:
17 and join them for thee one to another into one stick, that they may become one in thy hand.
18 And when the children of thy people shall speak unto thee, saying, Wilt thou not show us what thou meanest by these?
19 say unto them, Thus saith the Lord Jehovah: Behold, I will take the stick of Joseph, which is in the hand of Ephraim, and the tribes of Israel his companions; and I will put them with it, [even] with the stick of Judah, and make them one stick, and they shall be one in my hand.
20 And the sticks whereon thou writest shall be in thy hand before their eyes.
21 And say unto them, Thus saith the Lord Jehovah: Behold, I will take the children of Israel from among the nations, whither they are gone, and will gather them on every side, and bring them into their own land:
22 and I will make them one nation in the land, upon the mountains of Israel; and one king shall be king to them all; and they shall be no more two nations, neither shall they be divided into two kingdoms any more at all;
23 neither shall they defile themselves any more with their idols, nor with their detestable things, nor with any of their transgressions; but I will save them out of all their dwelling-places, wherein they have sinned, and will cleanse them: so shall they be my people, and I will be their God.
24 And my servant David shall be king over them; and they all shall have one shepherd: they shall also walk in mine ordinances, and observe my statutes, and do them.
25 And they shall dwell in the land that I have given unto Jacob my servant, wherein your fathers dwelt; and they shall dwell therein, they, and their children, and their children's children, for ever: and David my servant shall be their prince for ever.
26 Moreover I will make a covenant of peace with them; it shall be an everlasting covenant with them; and I will place them, and multiply them, and will set my sanctuary in the midst of them for evermore.
27 My tabernacle also shall be with them; and I will be their God, and they shall be my people.
28 And the nations shall know that I am Jehovah that sanctifieth Israel, when my sanctuary shall be in the midst of them for evermore.

Chapter 38

1 And the word of Jehovah came unto me, saying,
2 Son of man, set thy face toward Gog, of the land of Magog, the prince of Rosh, Meshech, and Tubal, and prophesy against him,
3 and say, Thus saith the Lord Jehovah: Behold, I am against thee, O Gog, prince of Rosh, Meshech, and Tubal:
4 and I will turn thee about, and put hooks into thy jaws, and I will bring thee forth, and all thine army, horses and horsemen, all of them clothed in full armor, a great company with buckler and shield, all of them handling swords;
5 Persia, Cush, and Put with them, all of them with shield and helmet;
6 Gomer, and all his hordes; the house of Togarmah in the uttermost parts of the north, and all his hordes; even many peoples with thee.
7 Be thou prepared, yea, prepare thyself, thou, and all thy companies that are assembled unto thee, and be thou a guard unto them.
8 After many days thou shalt be visited: in the latter years thou shalt come into the land that is brought back from the sword, that is gathered out of many peoples, upon the mountains of Israel, which have been a continual waste; but it is brought forth out of the peoples, and they shall dwell securely, all of them.
9 And thou shalt ascend, thou shalt come like a storm, thou shalt be like a cloud to cover the land, thou, and all thy hordes, and many peoples with thee.
10 Thus saith the Lord Jehovah: It shall come to pass in that day, that things shall come into thy mind, and thou shalt devise an evil device:
11 and thou shalt say, I will go up to the land of unwalled villages; I will go to them that are at rest, that dwell securely, all of them dwelling without walls, and having neither bars nor gates;

12 to take the spoil and to take the prey; to turn thy hand against the waste places that are [now] inhabited, and against the people that are gathered out of the nations, that have gotten cattle and goods, that dwell in the middle of the earth.
13 Sheba, and Dedan, and the merchants of Tarshish, with all the young lions thereof, shall say unto thee, Art thou come to take the spoil? hast thou assembled thy company to take the prey? to carry away silver and gold, to take away cattle and goods, to take great spoil?
14 Therefore, son of man, prophesy, and say unto Gog, Thus saith the Lord Jehovah: In that day when my people Israel dwelleth securely, shalt thou not know it?
15 And thou shalt come from thy place out of the uttermost parts of the north, thou, and many peoples with thee, all of them riding upon horses, a great company and a mighty army;
16 and thou shalt come up against my people Israel, as a cloud to cover the land: it shall come to pass in the latter days, that I will bring thee against my land, that the nations may know me, when I shall be sanctified in thee, O Gog, before their eyes.
17 Thus saith the Lord Jehovah: Art thou he of whom I spake in old time by my servants the prophets of Israel, that prophesied in those days for [many] years that I would bring thee against them?
18 And it shall come to pass in that day, when Gog shall come against the land of Israel, saith the Lord Jehovah, that my wrath shall come up into my nostrils.
19 For in my jealousy and in the fire of my wrath have I spoken, Surely in that day there shall be a great shaking in the land of Israel;
20 so that the fishes of the sea, and the birds of the heavens, and the beasts of the field, and all creeping things that creep upon the earth, and all the men that are upon the face of the earth, shall shake at my presence, and the mountains shall be thrown down, and the steep places shall fall, and every wall shall fall to the ground.
21 And I will call for a sword against him unto all my mountains, saith the Lord Jehovah: every man's sword shall be against his brother.
22 And with pestilence and with blood will I enter into judgment with him; and I will rain upon him, and upon his hordes, and upon the many peoples that are with him, an overflowing shower, and great hailstones, fire, and brimstone.
23 And I will magnify myself, and sanctify myself, and I will make myself known in the eyes of many nations; and they shall know that I am Jehovah.

Chapter 39

1 And thou, son of man, prophesy against Gog, and say, Thus saith the Lord Jehovah: Behold, I am against thee, O Gog, prince of Rosh, Meshech, and Tubal:
2 and I will turn thee about, and will lead thee on, and will cause thee to come up from the uttermost parts of the north; and I will bring thee upon the mountains of Israel;
3 and I will smite thy bow out of thy left hand, and will cause thine arrows to fall out of thy right hand.
4 Thou shalt fall upon the mountains of Israel, thou, and all thy hordes, and the peoples that are with thee: I will give thee unto the ravenous birds of every sort, and to the beasts of the field to be devoured.
5 Thou shalt fall upon the open field; for I have spoken it, saith the Lord Jehovah.
6 And I will send a fire on Magog, and on them that dwell securely in the isles; and they shall know that I am Jehovah.
7 And my holy name will I make known in the midst of my people Israel; neither will I suffer my holy name to be profaned any more: and the nations shall know that I am Jehovah, the Holy One in Israel.
8 Behold, it cometh, and it shall be done, saith the Lord Jehovah; this is the day whereof I have spoken.
9 And they that dwell in the cities of Israel shall go forth, and shall make fires of the weapons and burn them, both the shields and the bucklers, the bows and the arrows, and the handstaves, and the spears, and they shall make fires of them seven years;
10 so that they shall take no wood out of the field, neither cut down any out of the forests; for they shall make fires of the weapons; and they shall plunder those that plundered them, and rob those that robbed them, saith the Lord Jehovah.
11 And it shall come to pass in that day, that I will give unto Gog a place for burial in Israel, the valley of them that pass through on the east of the sea; and it shall stop them that pass through: and there shall they bury Gog and all his multitude; and they shall call it The valley of Hamon-gog.
12 And seven months shall the house of Israel be burying them, that they may cleanse the land.
13 Yea, all the people of the land shall bury them; and it shall be to them a renown in the day that I shall be glorified, saith the Lord Jehovah.
14 And they shall set apart men of continual employment, that shall pass through the land, and, with

them that pass through, those that bury them that remain upon the face of the land, to cleanse it: after the end of seven months shall they search.
15 And they that pass through the land shall pass through; and when any seeth a man's bone, then shall he set up a sign by it, till the buriers have buried it in the valley of Hamon-gog.
16 And Hamonah shall also be the name of a city. Thus shall they cleanse the land.
17 And thou, son of man, thus saith the Lord Jehovah: Speak unto the birds of every sort, and to every beast of the field, Assemble yourselves, and come; gather yourselves on every side to my sacrifice that I do sacrifice for you, even a great sacrifice upon the mountains of Israel, that ye may eat flesh and drink blood.
18 Ye shall eat the flesh of the mighty, and drink the blood of the princes of the earth, of rams, of lambs, and of goats, of bullocks, all of them fatlings of Bashan.
19 And ye shall eat fat till ye be full, and drink blood till ye be drunken, of my sacrifice which I have sacrificed for you.
20 And ye shall be filled at my table with horses and chariots, with mighty men, and with all men of war, saith the Lord Jehovah.
21 And I will set my glory among the nations; and all the nations shall see my judgment that I have executed, and my hand that I have laid upon them.
22 So the house of Israel shall know that I am Jehovah their God, from that day and forward.
23 And the nations shall know that the house of Israel went into captivity for their iniquity; because they trespassed against me, and I hid my face from them: so I gave them into the hand of their adversaries, and they fell all of them by the sword.
24 According to their uncleanness and according to their transgressions did I unto them; and I hid my face from them.
25 Therefore thus saith the Lord Jehovah: Now will I bring back the captivity of Jacob, and have mercy upon the whole house of Israel; and I will be jealous for my holy name.
26 And they shall bear their shame, and all their trespasses whereby they have trespassed against me, when they shall dwell securely in their land, and none shall make them afraid;
27 when I have brought them back from the peoples, and gathered them out of their enemies' lands, and am sanctified in them in the sight of many nations.
28 And they shall know that I am Jehovah their God, in that I caused them to go into captivity among the nations, and have gathered them unto their own land; and I will leave none of them any more there;
29 neither will I hide my face any more from them; for I have poured out my Spirit upon the house of Israel, saith the Lord Jehovah.

Chapter 40

1 In the five and twentieth year of our captivity, in the beginning of the year, in the tenth [day] of the month, in the fourteenth year after that the city was smitten, in the selfsame day, the hand of Jehovah was upon me, and he brought me thither.
2 In the visions of God brought he me into the land of Israel, and set me down upon a very high mountain, whereon was as it were the frame of a city on the south.
3 And he brought me thither; and, behold, there was a man, whose appearance was like the appearance of brass, with a line of flax in his hand, and a measuring reed; and he stood in the gate.
4 And the man said unto me, Son of man, behold with thine eyes, and hear with thine ears, and set thy heart upon all that I shall show thee; for, to the intent that I may show them unto thee, art thou brought hither: declare all that thou seest to the house of Israel.
5 And, behold, a wall on the outside of the house round about, and in the man's hand a measuring reed six cubits long, of a cubit and a handbreadth each: so he measured the thickness of the building, one reed; and the height, one reed.
6 Then came he unto the gate which looketh toward the east, and went up the steps thereof: and he measured the threshold of the gate, one reed broad; and the other threshold, one reed broad.
7 And every lodge was one reed long, and one reed broad; and [the space] between the lodges was five cubits; and the threshold of the gate by the porch of the gate toward the house was one reed.
8 He measured also the porch of the gate toward the house, one reed.
9 Then measured he the porch of the gate, eight cubits; and the posts thereof, two cubits; and the porch of the gate was toward the house.
10 And the lodges of the gate eastward were three on this side, and three on that side; they three were of one measure: and the posts had one measure on this side and on that side.
11 And he measured the breadth of the opening of the gate, ten cubits; and the length of the gate,

thirteen cubits;
12 and a border before the lodges, one cubit [on this side], and a border, one cubit on that side; and the lodges, six cubits on this side, and six cubits on that side.
13 And he measured the gate from the roof of the one lodge to the roof of the other, a breadth of five and twenty cubits; door against door.
14 He made also posts, threescore cubits; and the court [reached] unto the posts, round about the gate.
15 And [from] the forefront of the gate at the entrance unto the forefront of the inner porch of the gate were fifty cubits.
16 And there were closed windows to the lodges, and to their posts within the gate round about, and likewise to the arches; and windows were round about inward; and upon [each] post were palm-trees.
17 Then brought he me into the outer court; and, lo, there were chambers and a pavement, made for the court round about: thirty chambers were upon the pavement.
18 And the pavement was by the side of the gates, answerable unto the length of the gates, even the lower pavement.
19 Then he measured the breadth from the forefront of the lower gate unto the forefront of the inner court without, a hundred cubits, [both] on the east and on the north.
20 And the gate of the outer court whose prospect is toward the north, he measured the length thereof and the breadth thereof.
21 And the lodges thereof were three on this side and three on that side; and the posts thereof and the arches thereof were after the measure of the first gate: the length thereof was fifty cubits, and the breadth five and twenty cubits.
22 And the windows thereof, and the arches thereof, and the palm-trees thereof, were after the measure of the gate whose prospect is toward the east; and they went up unto it by seven steps; and the arches thereof were before them.
23 And there was a gate to the inner court over against the [other] gate, [both] on the north and on the east; and he measured from gate to gate a hundred cubits.
24 And he led me toward the south; and, behold, a gate toward the south: and he measured the posts thereof and the arches thereof according to these measures.
25 And there were windows in it and in the arches thereof round about, like those windows: the length was fifty cubits, and the breadth five and twenty cubits.
26 And there were seven steps to go up to it, and the arches thereof were before them; and it had palm-trees, one on this side, and another on that side, upon the posts thereof.
27 And there was a gate to the inner court toward the south: and he measured from gate to gate toward the south a hundred cubits.
28 Then he brought me to the inner court by the south gate: and he measured the south gate according to these measures;
29 and the lodges thereof, and the posts thereof, and the arches thereof, according to these measures: and there were windows in it and in the arches thereof round about; it was fifty cubits long, and five and twenty cubits broad.
30 And there were arches round about, five and twenty cubits long, and five cubits broad.
31 And the arches thereof were toward the outer court; and palm-trees were upon the posts thereof: and the ascent to it had eight steps.
32 And he brought me into the inner court toward the east: and he measured the gate according to these measures;
33 and the lodges thereof, and the posts thereof, and the arches thereof, according to these measures: and there were windows therein and in the arches thereof round about; it was fifty cubits long, and five and twenty cubits broad.
34 And the arches thereof were toward the outer court; and palm-trees were upon the posts thereof, on this side, and on that side: and the ascent to it had eight steps.
35 And he brought me to the north gate: and he measured [it] according to these measures;
36 the lodges thereof, the posts thereof, and the arches thereof: and there were windows therein round about; the length was fifty cubits, and the breadth five and twenty cubits.
37 And the posts thereof were toward the outer court; and palm-trees were upon the posts thereof, on this side, and on that side: and the ascent to it had eight steps.
38 And a chamber with the door thereof was by the posts at the gates; there they washed the burnt-offering.
39 And in the porch of the gate were two tables on this side, and two tables on that side, to slay thereon the burnt-offering and the sin-offering and the trespass-offering.
40 And on the [one] side without, as one goeth up to the entry of the gate toward the north, were two

tables; and on the other side, which belonged to the porch of the gate, were two tables.
41 Four tables were on this side, and four tables on that side, by the side of the gate; eight tables, whereupon they slew [the sacrifices].
42 And there were four tables for the burnt-offering, of hewn stone, a cubit and a half long, and a cubit and a half broad, and one cubit high; whereupon they laid the instruments wherewith they slew the burnt-offering and the sacrifice.
43 And the hooks, a handbreadth long, were fastened within round about: and upon the tables was the flesh of the oblation.
44 And without the inner gate were chambers for the singers in the inner court, which was at the side of the north gate; and their prospect was toward the south; one at the side of the east gate having the prospect toward the north.
45 And he said unto me, This chamber, whose prospect is toward the south, is for the priests, the keepers of the charge of the house;
46 and the chamber whose prospect is toward the north is for the priests, the keepers of the charge of the altar: these are the sons of Zadok, who from among the sons of Levi come near to Jehovah to minister unto him.
47 And he measured the court, a hundred cubits long, and a hundred cubits broad, foursquare; and the altar was before the house.
48 Then he brought me to the porch of the house, and measured each post of the porch, five cubits on this side, and five cubits on that side: and the breadth of the gate was three cubits on this side, and three cubits on that side.
49 The length of the porch was twenty cubits, and the breadth eleven cubits; even by the steps whereby they went up to it: and there were pillars by the posts, one on this side, and another on that side.

Chapter 41

1 And he brought me to the temple, and measured the posts, six cubits broad on the one side, and six cubits broad on the other side, which was the breadth of the tabernacle.
2 And the breadth of the entrance was ten cubits; and the sides of the entrance were five cubits on the one side, and five cubits on the other side: and he measured the length thereof, forty cubits, and the breadth, twenty cubits.
3 Then went he inward, and measured each post of the entrance, two cubits; and the entrance, six cubits; and the breadth of the entrance, seven cubits.
4 And he measured the length thereof, twenty cubits, and the breadth, twenty cubits, before the temple: and he said unto me, This is the most holy place.
5 Then he measured the wall of the house, six cubits; and the breadth of every side-chamber, four cubits, round about the house on every side.
6 And the side-chambers were in three stories, one over another, and thirty in order; and they entered into the wall which belonged to the house for the side-chambers round about, that they might have hold [therein], and not have hold in the wall of the house.
7 And the side-chambers were broader as they encompassed [the house] higher and higher; for the encompassing of the house went higher and higher round about the house: therefore the breadth of the house [continued] upward; and so one went up [from] the lowest [chamber] to the highest by the middle [chamber].
8 I saw also that the house had a raised basement round about: the foundations of the side-chambers were a full reed of six great cubits.
9 The thickness of the wall, which was for the side-chambers, on the outside, was five cubits: and that which was left was the place of the side-chambers that belonged to the house.
10 And between the chambers was a breadth of twenty cubits round about the house on every side.
11 And the doors of the side-chambers were toward [the place] that was left, one door toward the north, and another door toward the south: and the breadth of the place that was left was five cubits round about.
12 And the building that was before the separate place at the side toward the west was seventy cubits broad; and the wall of the building was five cubits thick round about, and the length thereof ninety cubits.
13 So he measured the house, a hundred cubits long; and the separate place, and the building, with the walls thereof, a hundred cubits long;
14 also the breadth of the face of the house, and of the separate place toward the east, a hundred cubits.
15 And he measured the length of the building before the separate place which was at the back thereof,

and the galleries thereof on the one side and on the other side, a hundred cubits; and the inner temple, and the porches of the court;
16 the thresholds, and the closed windows, and the galleries round about on their three stories, over against the threshold, ceiled with wood round about, and [from] the ground up to the windows, (now the windows were covered),
17 to [the space] above the door, even unto the inner house, and without, and by all the wall round about within and without, by measure.
18 And it was made with cherubim and palm-trees; and a palm-tree was between cherub and cherub, and every cherub had two faces;
19 so that there was the face of a man toward the palm-tree on the one side, and the face of a young lion toward the palm-tree on the other side. [thus was it] made through all the house round about:
20 from the ground unto above the door were cherubim and palm-trees made: thus was the wall of the temple.
21 As for the temple, the door-posts were squared; and as for the face of the sanctuary, the appearance [thereof] was as the appearance [of the temple].
22 The altar was of wood, three cubits high, and the length thereof two cubits; and the corners thereof, and the length thereof, and the walls thereof, were of wood: and he said unto me, This is the table that is before Jehovah.
23 And the temple and the sanctuary had two doors.
24 And the doors had two leaves [apiece], two turning leaves: two [leaves] for the one door, and two leaves for the other.
25 And there were made on them, on the doors of the temple, cherubim and palm-trees, like as were made upon the walls; and there was a threshold of wood upon the face of the porch without.
26 And there were closed windows and palm-trees on the one side and on the other side, on the sides of the porch: thus were the side-chambers of the house, and the thresholds.

Chapter 42

1 Then he brought me forth into the outer court, the way toward the north: and he brought me into the chamber that was over against the separate place, and which was over against the building toward the north.
2 Before the length of a hundred cubits was the north door, and the breadth was fifty cubits.
3 Over against the twenty [cubits] which belonged to the inner court, and over against the pavement which belonged to the outer court, was gallery against gallery in the third story.
4 And before the chambers was a walk of ten cubits' breadth inward, a way of one cubit; and their doors were toward the north.
5 Now the upper chambers were shorter; for the galleries took away from these, more than from the lower and the middlemost, in the building.
6 For they were in three stories, and they had not pillars as the pillars of the courts: therefore [the uppermost] was straitened more than the lowest and the middlemost from the ground.
7 And the wall that was without by the side of the chambers, toward the outer court before the chambers, the length thereof was fifty cubits.
8 For the length of the chambers that were in the outer court was fifty cubits: and, lo, before the temple were a hundred cubits.
9 And from under these chambers was the entry on the east side, as one goeth into them from the outer court.
10 In the thickness of the wall of the court toward the east, before the separate place, and before the building, there were chambers.
11 And the way before them was like the appearance of [the way of] the chambers which were toward the north; according to their length so was their breadth: and all their egresses were both according to their fashions, and according to their doors.
12 And according to the doors of the chambers that were toward the south was a door at the head of the way, even the way directly before the wall toward the east, as one entereth into them.
13 Then said he unto me, The north chambers and the south chambers, which are before the separate place, they are the holy chambers, where the priests that are near unto Jehovah shall eat the most holy things: there shall they lay the most holy things, and the meal-offering, and the sin-offering, and the trespass-offering; for the place is holy.
14 When the priests enter in, then shall they not go out of the holy place into the outer court, but there they shall lay their garments wherein they minister; for they are holy: and they shall put on other

garments, and shall approach to that which pertaineth to the people.
15 Now when he had made an end of measuring the inner house, he brought me forth by the way of the gate whose prospect is toward the east, and measured it round about.
16 He measured on the east side with the measuring reed five hundred reeds, with the measuring reed round about.
17 He measured on the north side five hundred reeds with the measuring reed round about.
18 He measured on the south side five hundred reeds with the measuring reed.
19 He turned about to the west side, and measured five hundred reeds with the measuring reed.
20 He measured it on the four sides: it had a wall round about, the length five hundred, and the breadth five hundred, to make a separation between that which was holy and that which was common.

Chapter 43

1 Afterward he brought me to the gate, even the gate that looketh toward the east.
2 And, behold, the glory of the God of Israel came from the way of the east: and his voice was like the sound of many waters; and the earth shined with his glory.
3 And it was according to the appearance of the vision which I saw, even according to the vision that I saw when I came to destroy the city; and the visions were like the vision that I saw by the river Chebar; and I fell upon my face.
4 And the glory of Jehovah came into the house by the way of the gate whose prospect is toward the east.
5 And the Spirit took me up, and brought me into the inner court; and, behold, the glory of Jehovah filled the house.
6 And I heard one speaking unto me out of the house; and a man stood by me.
7 And he said unto me, Son of man, [this is] the place of my throne, and the place of the soles of my feet, where I will dwell in the midst of the children of Israel for ever. And the house of Israel shall no more defile my holy name, neither they, nor their kings, by their whoredom, and by the dead bodies of their kings [in] their high places;
8 in their setting of their threshold by my threshold, and their door-post beside my door-post, and there was [but] the wall between me and them; and they have defiled my holy name by their abominations which they have committed: wherefore I have consumed them in mine anger.
9 Now let them put away their whoredom, and the dead bodies of their kings, far from me; and I will dwell in the midst of them for ever.
10 Thou, son of man, show the house to the house of Israel, that they may be ashamed of their iniquities; and let them measure the pattern.
11 And if they be ashamed of all that they have done, make known unto them the form of the house, and the fashion thereof, and the egresses thereof, and the entrances thereof, and all the forms thereof, and all the ordinances thereof, and all the forms thereof, and all the laws thereof; and write it in their sight; that they may keep the whole form thereof, and all the ordinances thereof, and do them.
12 This is the law of the house: upon the top of the mountain the whole limit thereof round about shall be most holy. Behold, this is the law of the house.
13 And these are the measures of the altar by cubits (the cubit is a cubit and a handbreadth): the bottom shall be a cubit, and the breadth a cubit, and the border thereof by the edge thereof round about a span; and this shall be the base of the altar.
14 And from the bottom upon the ground to the lower ledge shall be two cubits, and the breadth one cubit; and from the lesser ledge to the greater ledge shall be four cubits, and the breadth a cubit.
15 And the upper altar shall be four cubits; and from the altar hearth and upward there shall be four horns.
16 And the altar hearth shall be twelve [cubits] long by twelve broad, square in the four sides thereof.
17 And the ledge shall be fourteen [cubits] long by fourteen broad in the four sides thereof; and the border about it shall be half a cubit; and the bottom thereof shall be a cubit round about; and the steps thereof shall look toward the east.
18 And he said unto me, Son of man, thus saith the Lord Jehovah: These are the ordinances of the altar in the day when they shall make it, to offer burnt-offerings thereon, and to sprinkle blood thereon.
19 Thou shalt give to the priests the Levites that are of the seed of Zadok, who are near unto me, to minister unto me, saith the Lord Jehovah, a young bullock for a sin-offering.
20 And thou shalt take of the blood thereof, and put it on the four horns of it, and on the four corners of the ledge, and upon the border round about: thus shalt thou cleanse it and make atonement for it.
21 Thou shalt also take the bullock of the sin-offering, and it shall be burnt in the appointed place of the

house, without the sanctuary.
22 And on the second day thou shalt offer a he-goat without blemish for a sin-offering; and they shall cleanse the altar, as they did cleanse it with the bullock.
23 When thou hast made an end of cleansing it, thou shalt offer a young bullock without blemish, and a ram out of the flock without blemish.
24 And thou shalt bring them near before Jehovah, and the priests shall cast salt upon them, and they shall offer them up for a burnt-offering unto Jehovah.
25 Seven days shalt thou prepare every day a goat for a sin-offering: they shall also prepare a young bullock, and a ram out of the flock, without blemish.
26 Seven days shall they make atonement for the altar and purify it; so shall they consecrate it.
27 And when they have accomplished the days, it shall be that upon the eighth day, and forward, the priests shall make your burnt-offerings upon the altar, and your peace-offerings; and I will accept you, saith the Lord Jehovah.

Chapter 44

1 Then he brought me back by the way of the outer gate of the sanctuary, which looketh toward the east; and it was shut.
2 And Jehovah said unto me, This gate shall be shut; it shall not be opened, neither shall any man enter in by it; for Jehovah, the God of Israel, hath entered in by it; therefore it shall be shut.
3 As for the prince, he shall sit therein as prince to eat bread before Jehovah; he shall enter by the way of the porch of the gate, and shall go out by the way of the same.
4 Then he brought me by the way of the north gate before the house; and I looked, and, behold, the glory of Jehovah filled the house of Jehovah: and I fell upon my face.
5 And Jehovah said unto me, Son of man, mark well, and behold with thine eyes, and hear with thine ears all that I say unto thee concerning all the ordinances of the house of Jehovah, and all the laws thereof; and mark well the entrance of the house, with every egress of the sanctuary.
6 And thou shalt say to the rebellious, even to the house of Israel, Thus saith the Lord Jehovah: O ye house of Israel, let it suffice you of all your abominations,
7 in that ye have brought in foreigners, uncircumcised in heart and uncircumcised in flesh, to be in my sanctuary, to profane it, even my house, when ye offer my bread, the fat and the blood, and they have broken my covenant, [to add] unto all your abominations.
8 And ye have not kept the charge of my holy things; but ye have set keepers of my charge in my sanctuary for yourselves.
9 Thus saith the Lord Jehovah, No foreigner, uncircumcised in heart and uncircumcised in flesh, shall enter into my sanctuary, of any foreigners that are among the children of Israel.
10 But the Levites that went far from me, when Israel went astray, that went astray from me after their idols, they shall bear their iniquity.
11 Yet they shall be ministers in my sanctuary, having oversight at the gates of the house, and ministering in the house: they shall slay the burnt-offering and the sacrifice for the people, and they shall stand before them to minister unto them.
12 Because they ministered unto them before their idols, and became a stumblingblock of iniquity unto the house of Israel; therefore have I lifted up my hand against them, saith the Lord Jehovah, and they shall bear their iniquity.
13 And they shall not come near unto me, to execute the office of priest unto me, nor to come near to any of my holy things, unto the things that are most holy; but they shall bear their shame, and their abominations which they have committed.
14 Yet will I make them keepers of the charge of the house, for all the service thereof, and for all that shall be done therein.
15 But the priests the Levites, the sons of Zadok, that kept the charge of my sanctuary when the children of Israel went astray from me, they shall come near to me to minister unto me; and they shall stand before me to offer unto me the fat and the blood, saith the Lord Jehovah:
16 they shall enter into my sanctuary, and they shall come near to my table, to minister unto me, and they shall keep my charge.
17 And it shall be that, when they enter in at the gates of the inner court, they shall be clothed with linen garments; and no wool shall come upon them, while they minister in the gates of the inner court, and within.
18 They shall have linen tires upon their heads, and shall have linen breeches upon their loins; they shall not gird themselves with [anything that causeth] sweat.

19 And when they go forth into the outer court, even into the outer court to the people, they shall put off their garments wherein they minister, and lay them in the holy chambers; and they shall put on other garments, that they sanctify not the people with their garments.
20 Neither shall they shave their heads, nor suffer their locks to grow long; they shall only cut off the hair of their heads.
21 Neither shall any of the priests drink wine, when they enter into the inner court.
22 Neither shall they take for their wives a widow, nor her that is put away; but they shall take virgins of the seed of the house of Israel, or a widow that is the widow of a priest.
23 And they shall teach my people the difference between the holy and the common, and cause them to discern between the unclean and the clean.
24 And in a controversy they shall stand to judge; according to mine ordinances shall they judge it: and they shall keep my laws and my statutes in all my appointed feasts; and they shall hallow my sabbaths.
25 And they shall go in to no dead person to defile themselves; but for father, or for mother, or for son, or for daughter, for brother, or for sister that hath had no husband, they may defile themselves.
26 And after he is cleansed, they shall reckon unto him seven days.
27 And in the day that he goeth into the sanctuary, into the inner court, to minister in the sanctuary, he shall offer his sin-offering, saith the Lord Jehovah.
28 And they shall have an inheritance: I am their inheritance; and ye shall give them no possession in Israel; I am their possession.
29 They shall eat the meal-offering, and the sin-offering, and the trespass-offering; and every devoted thing in Israel shall be theirs.
30 And the first of all the first-fruits of every thing, and every oblation of everything, of all your oblations, shall be for the priest: ye shall also give unto the priests the first of your dough, to cause a blessing to rest on thy house.
31 The priests shall not eat of anything that dieth of itself, or is torn, whether it be bird or beast.

Chapter 45

1 Moreover, when ye shall divide by lot the land for inheritance, ye shall offer an oblation unto Jehovah, a holy portion of the land; the length shall be the length of five and twenty thousand [reeds], and the breadth shall be ten thousand: it shall be holy in all the border thereof round about.
2 Of this there shall be for the holy place five hundred [in length] by five hundred [in breadth], square round about; and fifty cubits for the suburbs thereof round about.
3 And of this measure shalt thou measure a length of five and twenty thousand, and a breadth of ten thousand: and in it shall be the sanctuary, which is most holy.
4 It is a holy portion of the land; it shall be for the priests, the ministers of the sanctuary, that come near to minister unto Jehovah; and it shall be a place for their houses, and a holy place for the sanctuary.
5 And five and twenty thousand in length, and ten thousand in breadth, shall be unto the Levites, the ministers of the house, for a possession unto themselves, [for] twenty chambers.
6 And ye shall appoint the possession of the city five thousand broad, and five and twenty thousand long, side by side with the oblation of the holy portion: it shall be for the whole house of Israel.
7 And [whatsoever is] for the prince [shall be] on the one side and on the other side of the holy oblation and of the possession of the city, in front of the holy oblation and in front of the possession of the city, on the west side westward, and on the east side eastward; and in length answerable unto one of the portions, from the west border unto the east border.
8 In the land it shall be to him for a possession in Israel: and my princes shall no more oppress my people; but they shall give the land to the house of Israel according to their tribes.
9 Thus saith the Lord Jehovah: Let it suffice you, O princes of Israel: remove violence and spoil, and execute justice and righteousness; take away your exactions from my people, saith the Lord Jehovah.
10 Ye shall have just balances, and a just ephah, and a just bath.
11 The ephah and the bath shall be of one measure, that the bath may contain the tenth part of a homer, and the ephah the tenth part of a homer: the measure thereof shall be after the homer.
12 And the shekel shall be twenty gerahs; twenty shekels, five and twenty shekels, fifteen shekels, shall be your maneh.
13 This is the oblation that ye shall offer: the sixth part of an ephah from a homer of wheat; and ye shall give the sixth part of an ephah from a homer of barley;
14 and the set portion of oil, of the bath of oil, the tenth part of a bath out of the cor, [which is] ten baths, even a homer; (for ten baths are a homer;)
15 and one lamb of the flock, out of two hundred, from the well-watered pastures of Israel; -for a meal-

offering, and for a burnt-offering, and for peace-offerings, to make atonement for them, saith the Lord Jehovah.
16 All the people of the land shall give unto this oblation for the prince in Israel.
17 And it shall be the prince's part to give the burnt-offerings, and the meal-offerings, and the drink-offerings, in the feasts, and on the new moons, and on the sabbaths, in all the appointed feasts of the house of Israel: he shall prepare the sin-offering, and the meal-offering, and the burnt-offering, and the peace-offerings, to make atonement for the house of Israel.
18 Thus saith the Lord Jehovah: In the first [month], in the first [day] of the month, thou shalt take a young bullock without blemish; and thou shalt cleanse the sanctuary.
19 And the priest shall take of the blood of the sin-offering, and put it upon the door-posts of the house, and upon the four corners of the ledge of the altar, and upon the posts of the gate of the inner court.
20 And so thou shalt do on the seventh [day] of the month for every one that erreth, and for him that is simple: so shall ye make atonement for the house.
21 In the first [month], in the fourteenth day of the month, ye shall have the passover, a feast of seven days; unleavened bread shall be eaten.
22 And upon that day shall the prince prepare for himself and for all the people of the land a bullock for a sin-offering.
23 And the seven days of the feast he shall prepare a burnt-offering to Jehovah, seven bullocks and seven rams without blemish daily the seven days; and a he-goat daily for a sin-offering.
24 And he shall prepare a meal-offering, an ephah for a bullock, and an ephah for a ram, and a hin of oil to an ephah.
25 In the seventh [month], in the fifteenth day of the month, in the feast, shall he do the like the seven days; according to the sin-offering, according to the burnt-offering, and according to the meal-offering, and according to the oil.

Chapter 46

1 Thus saith the Lord Jehovah: The gate of the inner court that looketh toward the east shall be shut the six working days; but on the sabbath day it shall be opened, and on the day of the new moon it shall be opened.
2 And the prince shall enter by the way of the porch of the gate without, and shall stand by the post of the gate; and the priests shall prepare his burnt-offering and his peace-offerings, and he shall worship at the threshold of the gate: then he shall go forth; but the gate shall not be shut until the evening.
3 And the people of the land shall worship at the door of that gate before Jehovah on the sabbaths and on the new moons.
4 And the burnt-offering that the prince shall offer unto Jehovah shall be on the sabbath day six lambs without blemish and a ram without blemish;
5 and the meal-offering shall be an ephah for the ram, and the meal-offering for the lambs as he is able to give, and a hin of oil to an ephah.
6 And on the day of the new moon it shall be a young bullock without blemish, and six lambs, and a ram; they shall be without blemish:
7 and he shall prepare a meal-offering, an ephah for the bullock, and an ephah for the ram, and for the lambs according as he is able, and a hin of oil to an ephah.
8 And when the prince shall enter, he shall go in by the way of the porch of the gate, and he shall go forth by the way thereof.
9 But when the people of the land shall come before Jehovah in the appointed feasts, he that entereth by the way of the north gate to worship shall go forth by the way of the south gate; and he that entereth by the way of the south gate shall go forth by the way of the north gate: he shall not return by the way of the gate whereby he came in, but shall go forth straight before him.
10 And the prince, when they go in, shall go in in the midst of them; and when they go forth, they shall go forth [together].
11 And in the feasts and in the solemnities the meal-offering shall be an ephah for a bullock, and an ephah for a ram, and for the lambs as he is able to give, and a hin of oil to an ephah.
12 And when the prince shall prepare a freewill-offering, a burnt-offering or peace-offerings as a freewill-offering unto Jehovah, one shall open for him the gate that looketh toward the east; and he shall prepare his burnt-offering and his peace-offerings, as he doth on the sabbath day: then he shall go forth; and after his going forth one shall shut the gate.
13 And thou shalt prepare a lamb a year old without blemish for a burnt-offering unto Jehovah daily:

morning by morning shalt thou prepare it.
14 And thou shalt prepare a meal-offering with it morning by morning, the sixth part of an ephah, and the third part of a hin of oil, to moisten the fine flour; a meal-offering unto Jehovah continually by a perpetual ordinance.
15 Thus shall they prepare the lamb, and the meal-offering, and the oil, morning by morning, for a continual burnt-offering.
16 Thus saith the Lord Jehovah: If the prince give a gift unto any of his sons, it is his inheritance, it shall belong to his sons; it is their possession by inheritance.
17 But if he give of his inheritance a gift to one of his servants, it shall be his to the year of liberty; then it shall return to the prince; but as for his inheritance, it shall be for his sons.
18 Moreover the prince shall not take of the people's inheritance, to thrust them out of their possession; he shall give inheritance to his sons out of his own possession, that my people be not scattered every man from his possession.
19 Then he brought me through the entry, which was at the side of the gate, into the holy chambers for the priests, which looked toward the north: and, behold, there was a place on the hinder part westward.
20 And he said unto me, This is the place where the priests shall boil the trespass-offering and the sin-offering, [and] where they shall bake the meal-offering; that they bring them not forth into the outer court, to sanctify the people.
21 Then he brought me forth into the outer court, and caused me to pass by the four corners of the court; and, behold, in every corner of the court there was a court.
22 In the four corners of the court there were courts inclosed, forty [cubits] long and thirty broad: these four in the corners were of one measure.
23 And there was a wall round about in them, round about the four, and boiling-places were made under the walls round about.
24 Then said he unto me, These are the boiling-houses, where the ministers of the house shall boil the sacrifice of the people.

Chapter 47

1 And he brought me back unto the door of the house; and, behold, waters issued out from under the threshold of the house eastward; (for the forefront of the house was toward the east;) and the waters came down from under, from the right side of the house, on the south of the altar.
2 Then he brought me out by the way of the gate northward, and led me round by the way without unto the outer gate, by the way of [the gate] that looketh toward the east; and, behold, there ran out waters on the right side.
3 When the man went forth eastward with the line in his hand, he measured a thousand cubits, and he caused me to pass through the waters, waters that were to the ankles.
4 Again he measured a thousand, and caused me to pass through the waters, waters that were to the knees. Again he measured a thousand, and caused me to pass through [the waters], waters that were to the loins.
5 Afterward he measured a thousand; [and it was] a river that I could not pass through; for the waters were risen, waters to swim in, a river that could not be passed through.
6 And he said unto me, Son of man, hast thou seen [this]? Then he brought me, and caused me to return to the bank of the river.
7 Now when I had returned, behold, upon the bank of the river were very many trees on the one side and on the other.
8 Then said he unto me, These waters issue forth toward the eastern region, and shall go down into the Arabah; and they shall go toward the sea; into the sea [shall the waters go] which were made to issue forth; and the waters shall be healed.
9 And it shall come to pass, that every living creature which swarmeth, in every place whither the rivers come, shall live; and there shall be a very great multitude of fish; for these waters are come thither, and [the waters of the sea] shall be healed, and everything shall live whithersoever the river cometh.
10 And it shall come to pass, that fishers shall stand by it: from En-gedi even unto En-eglaim shall be a place for the spreading of nets; their fish shall be after their kinds, as the fish of the great sea, exceeding many.
11 But the miry places thereof, and the marshes thereof, shall not be healed; they shall be given up to salt.
12 And by the river upon the bank thereof, on this side and on that side, shall grow every tree for food, whose leaf shall not whither, neither shall the fruit thereof fail: it shall bring forth new fruit every month,

because the waters thereof issue out of the sanctuary; and the fruit thereof shall be for food, and the leaf thereof for healing.
13 Thus saith the Lord Jehovah: This shall be the border, whereby ye shall divide the land for inheritance according to the twelve tribes of Israel: Joseph [shall have two] portions.
14 And ye shall inherit it, one as well as another; for I sware to give it unto your fathers: and this land shall fall unto you for inheritance.
15 And this shall be the border of the land: On the north side, from the great sea, by the way of Hethlon, unto the entrance of Zedad;
16 Hamath, Berothah, Sibraim, which is between the border of Damascus and the border of Hamath; Hazer-hatticon, which is by the border of Hauran.
17 And the border from the sea, shall be Hazar-enon at the border of Damascus; and on the north northward is the border of Hamath. This is the north side.
18 And the east side, between Hauran and Damascus and Gilead, and the land of Israel, shall be the Jordan; from the [north] border unto the east sea shall ye measure. This is the east side.
19 And the south side southward shall be from Tamar as far as the waters of Meriboth-kadesh, to the brook [of Egypt], unto the great sea. This is the south side southward.
20 And the west side shall be the great sea, from the [south] border as far as over against the entrance of Hamath. This is the west side.
21 So shall ye divide this land unto you according to the tribes of Israel.
22 And it shall come to pass, that ye shall divide it by lot for an inheritance unto you and to the strangers that sojourn among you, who shall beget children among you; and they shall be unto you as the home-born among the children of Israel; they shall have inheritance with you among the tribes of Israel.
23 And it shall come to pass, that in what tribe the stranger sojourneth, there shall ye give him his inheritance, saith the Lord Jehovah.

Chapter 48

1 Now these are the names of the tribes: From the north end, beside the way of Hethlon to the entrance of Hamath, Hazar-enan at the border of Damascus, northward beside Hamath, (and they shall have their sides east [and] west,) Dan, one [portion].
2 And by the border of Dan, from the east side unto the west side, Asher, one [portion].
3 And by the border of Asher, from the east side even unto the west side, Naphtali, one [portion].
4 And by the border of Naphtali, from the east side unto the west side, Manasseh, one [portion].
5 And by the border of Manasseh, from the east side unto the west side, Ephraim, one [portion].
6 And by the border of Ephraim, from the east side even unto the west side, Reuben, one [portion].
7 And by the border of Reuben, from the east side unto the west side, Judah, one [portion].
8 And by the border of Judah, from the east side unto the west side, shall be the oblation which ye shall offer, five and twenty thousand [reeds] in breadth, and in length as one of the portions, from the east side unto the west side: and the sanctuary shall be in the midst of it.
9 The oblation that ye shall offer unto Jehovah shall be five and twenty thousand [reeds] in length, and ten thousand in breadth.
10 And for these, even for the priests, shall be the holy oblation: toward the north five and twenty thousand [in length], and toward the west ten thousand in breadth, and toward the east ten thousand in breadth, and toward the south five and twenty thousand in length: and the sanctuary of Jehovah shall be in the midst thereof.
11 [It shall be] for the priests that are sanctified of the sons of Zadok, that have kept my charge, that went not astray when the children of Israel went astray, as the Levites went astray.
12 And it shall be unto them an oblation from the oblation of the land, a thing most holy, by the border of the Levites.
13 And answerable unto the border of the priests, the Levites shall have five and twenty thousand in length, and ten thousand in breadth: all the length shall be five and twenty thousand, and the breadth ten thousand.
14 And they shall sell none of it, nor exchange it, nor shall the first-fruits of the land be alienated; for it is holy unto Jehovah.
15 And the five thousand that are left in the breadth, in front of the five and twenty thousand, shall be for common use, for the city, for dwelling and for suburbs; and the city shall be in the midst thereof.
16 And these shall be the measures thereof: the north side four thousand and five hundred, and the south side four thousand and five hundred, and on the east side four thousand and five hundred, and

the west side four thousand and five hundred.
17 And the city shall have suburbs: toward the north two hundred and fifty, and toward the south two hundred and fifty, and toward the east two hundred and fifty, and toward the west two hundred and fifty.
18 And the residue in the length, answerable unto the holy oblation, shall be ten thousand eastward, and ten thousand westward; and it shall be answerable unto the holy oblation; and the increase thereof shall be for food unto them that labor in the city.
19 And they that labor in the city, out of all the tribes of Israel, shall till it.
20 All the oblation shall be five and twenty thousand by five and twenty thousand: ye shall offer the holy oblation four-square, with the possession of the city.
21 And the residue shall be for the prince, on the one side and on the other of the holy oblation and of the possession of the city; in front of the five and twenty thousand of the oblation toward the east border, and westward in front of the five and twenty thousand toward the west border, answerable unto the portions, it shall be for the prince: and the holy oblation and the sanctuary of the house shall be in the midst thereof.
22 Moreover from the possession of the Levites, and from the possession of the city, being in the midst of that which is the prince's, between the border of Judah and the border of Benjamin, it shall be for the prince.
23 And as for the rest of the tribes: from the east side unto the west side, Benjamin, one [portion].
24 And by the border of Benjamin, from the east side unto the west side, Simeon, one [portion].
25 And by the border of Simeon, from the east side unto the west side, Issachar, one [portion].
26 And by the border of Issachar, from the east side unto the west side, Zebulun, one [portion].
27 And by the border of Zebulun, from the east side unto the west side, Gad, one [portion].
28 And by the border of Gad, at the south side southward, the border shall be even from Tamar unto the waters of Meribath-kadesh, to the brook [of Egypt], unto the great sea.
29 This is the land which ye shall divide by lot unto the tribes of Israel for inheritance, and these are their several portions, saith the Lord Jehovah.
30 And these are the egresses of the city: On the north side four thousand and five hundred [reeds] by measure;
31 and the gates of the city shall be after the names of the tribes of Israel, three gates northward: the gate of Reuben, one; the gate of Judah, one; the gate of Levi, one.
32 And at the east side four thousand and five hundred [reeds], and three gates: even the gate of Joseph, one; the gate of Benjamin, one; the gate of Dan, one.
33 And at the south side four thousand and five hundred [reeds] by measure, and three gates: the gate of Simeon, one; the gate of Issachar, one; the gate of Zebulun, one.
34 At the west side four thousand and five hundred [reeds], with their three gates: the gate of Gad, one; the gate of Asher, one; the gate of Naphtali, one
35 It shall be eighteen thousand [reeds] round about: and the name of the city from that day shall be, Jehovah is there.

EZEKIEL

BIBLE IN BASIC ENGLISH

1

1 Now it came about in the thirtieth year, in the fourth month, on the fifth day of the month, while I
was by the river Chebar among those who had been made prisoners, that the heavens were made open
and I saw visions of God. 2 On the fifth day of the month, in the fifth year after King Jehoiachin had
been made a prisoner, 3 The word of the Lord came to me, Ezekiel the priest, the son of Buzi, in the
land of the Chaldaeans by the river Chebar; and the hand of the Lord was on me there. 4 And, looking,
I saw a storm-wind coming out of the north, a great cloud with flames of fire coming after one another,
and a bright light shining round about it and in the heart of it was something coloured like electrum. 5
And in the heart of it were the forms of four living beings. And this was what they were like; they had
the form of a man. 6 And every one had four faces, and every one of them had four wings. 7 And their
feet were straight feet; and the under sides of their feet were like the feet of oxen; and they were shining
like polished brass. 8 And they had the hands of a man under their wings; the four of them had faces on
their four sides. 9 They went without turning, every one went straight forward. 10 As for the form of
their faces, they had the face of a man, and the four of them had the face of a lion on the right side, and
the four of them had the face of an ox on the left side, and the four of them had the face of an eagle. 11
And their wings were separate at the top; two of the wings of every one were joined one to another, and
two were covering their bodies. 12 Every one of them went straight forward; wherever the spirit was to
go they went; they went on without turning. 13 And between the living beings it was like burning coals
of fire, as if flames were going one after the other between the living beings; and the fire was bright, and
out of the fire went thunder-flames. 14 And the living beings went out and came back as quickly as a
thunder-flame. 15 Now while I was looking at the four living beings, I saw one wheel on the earth, by
the side of the living beings, for the four of them. 16 The form of the wheels and their work was like a
beryl; the four of them had the same form and design, and they were like a wheel inside a wheel. 17 The
four of them went straight forward without turning to one side. 18 And I saw that they had edges, and
their edges, even of the four, were full of eyes round about. 19 And when the living beings went on, the
wheels went by their side; and when the living beings were lifted up from the earth, the wheels were
lifted up. 20 Wherever the spirit was to go they went; and the wheels were lifted up by their side: for the
spirit of the living beings was in the wheels. 21 When these went on, the others went; and when these
came to rest, the others came to rest; and when these were lifted up from the earth, the wheels were
lifted up by their side: for the spirit of the living beings was in the wheels. 22 And over the heads of the
living beings there was the form of an arch, looking like ice, stretched out over their heads on high. 23
Under the arch their wings were straight, one stretched out to another: every one had two wings
covering their bodies on this side and two covering their bodies on that side. 24 And when they went,
the sound of their wings was like the sound of great waters to my ears, like the voice of the Ruler of all,
a sound like the rushing of an army: when they came to rest they let down their wings. 25 And there was
a voice from the top of the arch which was over their heads: when they came to rest they let down their
wings. 26 And on the top of the arch which was over their heads was the form of a king's seat, like a
sapphire stone; and on the form of the seat was the form of a man seated on it on high. 27 And I saw it
coloured like electrum, with the look of fire in it and round it, going up from what seemed to be the
middle of his body; and going down from what seemed to be the middle of his body I saw what was like
fire, and there was a bright light shining round him. 28 Like the bow in the cloud on a day of rain, so
was the light shining round him. And this is what the glory of the Lord was like. And when I saw it I
went down on my face, and the voice of one talking came to my ears.

2

1 And he said to me, Son of man, get up on your feet, so that I may say words to you. 2 And at his
words the spirit came into me and put me on my feet; and his voice came to my ears. 3 And he said to
me, Son of man, I am sending you to the children of Israel, to an uncontrolled nation which has gone
against me: they and their fathers have been sinners against me even to this very day. 4 And the children
are hard and stiff-hearted; I am sending you to them: and you are to say to them, These are the words of
the Lord. 5 And they, if they give ear to you or if they do not give ear (for they are an uncontrolled
people), will see that there has been a prophet among them. 6 And you, son of man, have no fear of
them or of their words, even if sharp thorns are round you and you are living among scorpions: have no
fear of their words and do not be overcome by their looks, for they are an uncontrolled people. 7 And
you are to give them my words, if they give ear to you or if they do not: for they are uncontrolled. 8 But
you, son of man, give ear to what I say to you, and do not be uncontrolled like that uncontrolled people:
let your mouth be open and take what I give you. 9 And looking, I saw a hand stretched out to me, and
I saw the roll of a book in it; 10 And he put it open before me, and it had writing on the front and on
the back; words of grief and sorrow and trouble were recorded in it.

3

1 And he said to me, Son of man, take this roll for your food, and go and say my words to the children
of Israel. 2 And, on my opening my mouth, he made me take the roll as food. 3 And he said to me, Son
of man, let your stomach make a meal of it and let your inside be full of this roll which I am giving you.
Then I took it, and it was sweet as honey in my mouth. 4 And he said to me, Son of man, go now to the
children of Israel, and say my words to them. 5 For you are not sent to a people whose talk is strange
and whose language is hard, but to the children of Israel; 6 Not to a number of peoples whose talk is
strange and whose language is hard and whose words are not clear to you. Truly, if I sent you to them
they would give ear to you. 7 But the children of Israel will not give ear to you; for they have no mind to
give ear to me: for all the children of Israel have a hard brow and a stiff heart. 8 See, I have made your
face hard against their faces, and your brow hard against their brows. 9 Like a diamond harder than rock
I have made your brow: have no fear of them and do not be overcome by their looks, for they are an
uncontrolled people. 10 Then he said to me, Son of man, take into your heart all my words which I am
about to say to you, and let your ears be open to them. 11 And go now to those who have been taken
away as prisoners, to the children of your people, and say to them, This is what the Lord has said; if they
give ear or if they do not. 12 Then I was lifted up by the wind, and at my back the sound of a great
rushing came to my ears when the glory of the Lord was lifted up from his place. 13 And there was the
sound of the wings of the living beings touching one another, and the sound of the wheels at their side,
the sound of a great rushing. 14 And the wind, lifting me up, took me away: and I went in the heat of
my spirit, and the hand of the Lord was strong on me. 15 Then I came to those who had been taken
away as prisoners, who were at Telabib by the river Chebar, and I was seated among them full of
wonder for seven days. 16 And at the end of seven days, the word of the Lord came to me, saying, 17
Son of man, I have made you a watchman for the children of Israel: so give ear to the word of my
mouth, and give them word from me of their danger. 18 When I say to the evil-doer, Death will
certainly be your fate; and you give him no word of it and say nothing to make clear to the evil-doer the
danger of his evil way, so that he may be safe; that same evil man will come to death in his evil-doing;
but I will make you responsible for his blood. 19 But if you give the evil-doer word of his danger, and he
is not turned from his sin or from his evil way, death will overtake him in his evil-doing; but your life
will be safe. 20 Again, when an upright man, turning away from his righteousness, does evil, and I put a
cause of falling in his way, death will overtake him: because you have given him no word of his danger,
death will overtake him in his evil-doing, and there will be no memory of the upright acts which he has
done; but I will make you responsible for his blood. 21 But if you say to the upright man that he is not
to do evil, he will certainly keep his life because he took note of your word; and your life will be safe. 22
And the hand of the Lord was on me there; and he said, Get up and go out into the valley and there I
will have talk with you. 23 Then I got up and went out into the valley; and I saw the glory of the Lord
resting there as I had seen it by the river Chebar; and I went down on my face. 24 Then the spirit came
into me and put me on my feet; and he had talk with me and said to me, Go and keep yourself shut up
inside your house. 25 But see, O son of man, I will put bands on you, prisoning you in them, and you
will not go out among them: 26 And I will make your tongue fixed to the roof of your mouth, so that
you have no voice and may not make protests to them: for they are an uncontrolled people. 27 But
when I have talk with you I will make your mouth open, and you are to say to them, This is what the

Lord has said: Let the hearer give ear; and as for him who will not, let him keep his ears shut: for they are an uncontrolled people.

4

1 And you, son of man, take a back and put it before you and on it make a picture of a town, even Jerusalem. 2 And make an attack on it, shutting it in, building strong places against it, and making high an earthwork against it; and put up tents against it, placing engines all round it for smashing down its walls. 3 And take a flat iron plate, and put it for a wall of iron between you and the town: and let your face be turned to it, and it will be shut in and you will make an attack on it. This will be a sign to the children of Israel. 4 Then, stretching yourself out on your left side, take the sin of the children of Israel on yourself: for as long as you are stretched out, so long will the sin of the children of Israel be on you. 5 For I have had the years of their sin measured for you by a number of days, even three hundred and ninety days: and you will take on yourself the sin of the children of Israel. 6 And when these days are ended, turning on your right side, you are to take on yourself the sin of the children of Judah: forty days, a day for a year, I have had it fixed for you. 7 And let your face be turned to where Jerusalem is shut in, with your arm uncovered, and be a prophet against it. 8 And see, I will put bands on you; and you will be stretched out without turning from one side to the other till the days of your attack are ended. 9 And take for yourself wheat and barley and different sorts of grain, and put them in one vessel and make bread for yourself from them; all the days when you are stretched on your side it will be your food. 10 And you are to take your food by weight, twenty shekels a day: you are to take it at regular times. 11 And you are to take water by measure, the sixth part of a hin: you are to take it at regular times. 12 And let your food be barley cakes, cooking it before their eyes with the waste which comes out of a man. 13 And the Lord said, Even so the children of Israel will have unclean bread for their food among the nations where I am driving them. 14Then I said, Ah, Lord! see, my soul has never been unclean, and I have never taken as my food anything which has come to a natural death or has been broken by beasts, from the time when I was young even till now; no disgusting flesh has ever come into my mouth. 15 Then he said to me, See, I have given you cow's waste in place of man's waste, and you will make your bread ready on it. 16 And he said to me, Son of man, see, I will take away from Jerusalem her necessary bread: they will take their bread by weight and with care, measuring out their drinking-water with fear and wonder: 17 So that they may be in need of bread and water and be wondering at one another, wasting away in their sin.

5

1 And you, son of man, take a sharp sword, using it like a haircutter's blade, and making it go over your head and the hair of your chin: and take scales for separating the hair by weight. 2 You are to have a third part burned with fire inside the town, when the days of the attack are ended; and a third part you are to take and give blows with the sword round about it; and give a third part for the wind to take away, and let loose a sword after them. 3 And take from them a small number of hairs, folding them in your skirts. 4 And again take some of these and put them in the fire, burning them up in the fire; and say to all the children of Israel, 5 This is what the Lord has said: This is Jerusalem: I have put her among the nations, and countries are round her on every side; 6 And she has gone against my orders by doing evil more than the nations, and against my rules more than the countries round her: for they have given up my orders, and as for my rules, they have not gone in the way of them. 7 For this cause the Lord has said: Because you have been more uncontrolled than the nations round about you, and have not been guided by my rules or kept my orders, but have kept the orders of the nations round about you; 8 For this cause the Lord has said: See, I, even I, am against you; and I will be judging among you before the eyes of the nations. 9 And I will do in you what I have not done and will not do again, because of all your disgusting ways. 10 For this cause fathers will take their sons for food among you, and sons will make a meal of their fathers; and I will be judge among you, and all the rest of you I will send away to every wind. 11 For this cause, by my life, says the Lord, because you have made my holy place unclean with all your hated things and all your disgusting ways, you will become disgusting to me; my eye will have no mercy and I will have no pity. 12 A third of you will come to death from disease, wasting away among you through need of food; a third will be put to the sword round about you; and a third I will send away to every wind, letting loose a sword after them. 13 So my wrath will be complete and my passion will come to rest on them; and they will be certain that I the Lord have given the word of decision, when my wrath against them is complete. 14 And I will make you a waste and a name of shame among the nations round about you, in the eyes of everyone who goes by. 15 And you will be a

name of shame and a cause of bitter words, an example and a wonder to the nations round about you, when I give effect to my judging among you in wrath and in passion and in burning protests: I the Lord have said it: 16 When I send on you the evil arrows of disease, causing destruction, which I will send to put an end to you; and, further, I will take away your necessary food. 17 And I will send on you need of food and evil beasts, and they will be a cause of loss to you; and disease and violent death will go through you; and I will send the sword on you: I the Lord have said it.

6

1 And the word of the Lord came to me, saying, 2 Son of man, let your face be turned to the mountains of Israel, and be a prophet to them, and say, 3 You mountains of Israel, give ear to the words of the Lord: this is what the Lord has said to the mountains and the hills, to the waterways and the valleys: See, I, even I, am sending on you a sword for the destruction of your high places. 4 And your altars will be made waste, and your sun-images will be broken: and I will have your dead men placed before your images. 5 And I will put the dead bodies of the children of Israel in front of their images, sending your bones in all directions about your altars. 6 In all your living-places the towns will become broken walls, and the high places made waste; so that your altars may be broken down and made waste, and your images broken and ended, and so that your sun-images may be cut down and your works rubbed out. 7 And the dead will be falling down among you, and you will be certain that I am the Lord. 8 But still, I will keep a small band safe from the sword among the nations, when you are sent wandering among the countries. 9 And those of you who are kept safe will have me in mind among the nations where they have been taken away as prisoners, how I sent punishment on their hearts which were untrue to me, and on their eyes which were turned to their false gods: and they will be full of hate for themselves because of the evil things which they have done in all their disgusting ways. 10 And they will be certain that I am the Lord: not for nothing did I say that I would do this evil to them. 11 This is what the Lord has said: Give blows with your hand, stamping with your foot, and say, O sorrow! because of all the evil and disgusting ways of the children of Israel: for death will overtake them by the sword and through need of food and by disease. 12 He who is far away will come to his death by disease; he who is near will be put to the sword; he who is shut up will come to his death through need of food; and I will give full effect to my passion against them. 13 And you will be certain that I am the Lord, when their dead men are stretched among their images round about their altars on every high hill, on all the tops of the mountains, and under every branching tree, and under every thick oak-tree, the places where they made sweet smells to all their images. 14 And my hand will be stretched out against them, making the land waste and unpeopled, from the waste land to Riblah, through all their living-places: and they will be certain that I am the Lord.

7

1 And the word of the Lord came to me, saying, 2 And you, son of man, say, This is what the Lord has said to the land of Israel: An end has come, the end has come on the four quarters of the land. 3 Now the end has come on you, and I will send my wrath on you, judging you for your ways, I will send punishment on you for all your disgusting acts. 4 My eye will not have mercy on you, and I will have no pity: but I will send the punishment of your ways on you, and your disgusting works will be among you: and you will be certain that I am the Lord. 5 This is what the Lord has said: An evil, even one evil; see, it is coming. 6 An end has come, the end has come; see, it is coming on you. 7 The crowning time has come on you, O people of the land: the time has come, the day is near; the day will not be slow in coming, it will not keep back. 8 Now, in a little time, I will let loose my passion on you, and give full effect to my wrath against you, judging you for your ways, and sending punishment on you for all your disgusting works. 9 My eye will not have mercy, and I will have no pity: I will send on you the punishment of your ways, and your disgusting works will be among you; and you will see that I am the Lord who gives punishment. 10 See, the day; see, it is coming: the crowning time has gone out; the twisted way is flowering, pride has put out buds. 11 Violent behaviour has been lifted up into a rod of evil; it will not be slow in coming, it will not keep back. 12The time has come, the day is near: let not him who gives a price for goods be glad, or him who gets the price have sorrow: 13 For the trader will not go back to the things for which he had his price, even while he is still living: 14 And he who has given a price for goods will not get them, for my wrath is on all of them. 15 Outside is the sword, and inside disease and need of food: he who is in the open country will be put to the sword; he who is in the town will come to his end through need of food and disease. 16 And those of them who get away safely will go and be in the secret places like the doves of the valleys, all of them will come to death, every one

in his sin. 17 All hands will be feeble and all knees without strength, like water. 18 And they will put haircloth round them, and deep fear will be covering them; and shame will be on all faces, and the hair gone from all their heads. 19 They will put out their silver into the streets, and their gold will be as an unclean thing; their silver and their gold will not be able to keep them safe in the day of the wrath of the Lord; they will not get their desire or have food for their need: because it has been the cause of their falling into sin. 20 As for their beautiful ornament, they had put it on high, and had made the images of their disgusting and hated things in it: for this cause I have made it an unclean thing to them. 21 And I will give it into the hands of men from strange lands who will take it by force, and to the evil-doers of the earth to have for themselves; and they will make it unholy. 22 And my face will be turned away from them, and they will make my secret place unholy: violent men will go into it and make it unholy. 23 Make the chain: for the land is full of crimes of blood, and the town is full of violent acts. 24 For this reason I will send the worst of the nations and they will take their houses for themselves: I will make the pride of their strength come to an end; and their holy places will be made unclean. 25 Shaking fear is coming; and they will be looking for peace, and there will be no peace. 26 Destruction will come on destruction, and one story after another; and the vision of the prophet will be shamed, and knowledge of the law will come to an end among the priests, and wisdom among the old. 27 The king will give himself up to sorrow, and the ruler will be clothed with wonder, and the hands of the people of the land will be troubled: I will give them punishment for their ways, judging them as it is right for them to be judged; and they will be certain that I am the Lord.

8

1 Now in the sixth year, in the sixth month, on the fifth day of the month, when I was in my house and the responsible men of Judah were seated before me, the hand of the Lord came on me there. 2 And looking, I saw a form like fire; from the middle of his body and down there was fire: and up from the middle of his body a sort of shining, like electrum. 3 And he put out the form of a hand and took me by the hair of my head; and the wind, lifting me up between the earth and the heaven, took me in the visions of God to Jerusalem, to the way into the inner door facing to the north; where was the seat of the image of envy. 4 And I saw the glory of the Lord there, as in the vision which I saw in the valley. 5 Then he said to me, Son of man, now let your eyes be lifted up in the direction of the north; and on looking in the direction of the north, to the north of the doorway of the altar, I saw this image of envy by the way in. 6 And he said to me, Son of man, do you see what they are doing? even the very disgusting things which the children of Israel are doing here, causing me to go far away from my holy place? but you will see other most disgusting things. 7 And he took me to the door of the open place; and looking, I saw a hole in the wall. 8 And he said to me, Son of man, make a hole in the wall: and after making a hole in the wall I saw a door. 9 And he said to me, Go in and see the evil and disgusting things which they are doing here. 10 So I went in and saw; and there every sort of living thing which goes flat on the earth, and unclean beasts, and all the images of the children of Israel, were pictured round about on the wall. 11 And before them seventy of the responsible men of the children of Israel had taken their places, every man with a vessel for burning perfumes in his hand, and in the middle of them was Jaazaniah, the son of Shaphan; and a cloud of smoke went up from the burning perfume. 12 And he said to me, Son of man, have you seen what the responsible men of the children of Israel do in the dark, every man in his room of pictured images? for they say, The Lord does not see us; the Lord has gone away from the land. 13 Then he said to me, You will see even more disgusting things which they do. 14 Then he took me to the door of the way into the Lord's house looking to the north; and there women were seated weeping for Tammuz. 15 Then he said to me, Have you seen this, O son of man? you will see even more disgusting things than these. 16 And he took me into the inner square of the Lord's house, and at the door of the Temple of the Lord, between the covered way and the altar, there were about twenty-five men with their backs turned to the Temple of the Lord and their faces turned to the east; and they were worshipping the sun, turning to the east. 17 Then he said to me, Have you seen this, O son of man? is it a small thing to the children of Judah that they do the disgusting things which they are doing here? for they have made the land full of violent behaviour, making me angry again and again: and see, they put the branch to my nose. 18 For this reason I will let loose my wrath: my eye will not have mercy, and I will have no pity.

9

1 Then crying out in my hearing in a loud voice, he said, Let the overseers of the town come near, every man armed. 2 And six men came from the way of the higher doorway looking to the north, every man

with his axe in his hand: and one man among them was clothed in linen, with a writer's inkpot at his
side. And they went in and took their places by the brass altar. 3 And the glory of the God of Israel had
gone up from the winged ones on which it was resting, to the doorstep of the house. And crying out to
the man clothed in linen who had the writer's inkpot at his side, 4 The Lord said to him, Go through the
town, through the middle of Jerusalem, and put a mark on the brows of the men who are sorrowing and
crying for all the disgusting things which are done in it. 5 And to these he said in my hearing, Go
through the town after him using your axes: do not let your eyes have mercy, and have no pity: 6 Give
up to destruction old men and young men and virgins, little children and women: but do not come near
any man who has the mark on him: and make a start at my holy place. So they made a start with the old
men who were before the house. 7 And he said to them, Make the house unclean, make the open places
full of dead: go forward and send destruction on the town. 8 Now while they were doing so, and I was
untouched, I went down on my face, and crying out, I said, Ah, Lord! will you give all the rest of Israel
to destruction in letting loose your wrath on Jerusalem? 9 Then he said to me, The sin of the children of
Israel and Judah is very, very great, and the land is full of blood and the town full of evil ways: for they
say, The Lord has gone away from the land, and the Lord does not see. 10 And as for me, my eye will
not have mercy, and I will have no pity, but I will send the punishment of their ways on their heads. 11
Then the man clothed in linen, who had the inkpot at his side, came back and said, I have done what
you gave me orders to do.

10

1 Then looking, I saw that on the arch which was over the head of the winged ones there was seen over
them what seemed like a sapphire stone, having the form of a king's seat. 2 And he said to the man
clothed in linen, Go in between the wheels, under the winged ones, and get your two hands full of
burning coals from between the winged ones and send them in a shower over the town. And he went in
before my eyes. 3 Now the winged ones were stationed on the right side of the house when the man
went in; and the inner square was full of the cloud. 4 And the glory of the Lord went up from the
winged ones and came to rest over the doorstep of the house; and the house was full of the cloud and
the open square was full of the shining of the Lord's glory. 5 And the sound of the wings of the winged
ones was clear even in the outer square, like the voice of the Ruler of all. 6 And when he gave orders to
the man clothed in linen, saying, Take fire from between the wheels, from between the winged ones,
then he went in and took his place at the side of a wheel. 7 And stretching out his hand to the fire which
was between the winged ones, he took some of it and went out. 8 And I saw the form of a man's hands
among the winged ones under their wings. 9 And looking, I saw four wheels by the side of the winged
ones, one wheel by the side of a winged one and another wheel by the side of another: and the wheels
were like the colour of a beryl stone to the eye. 10 In form the four of them were all the same, they
seemed like a wheel inside a wheel. 11 When they were moving, they went on their four sides without
turning; they went after the head in the direction in which it was looking; they went without turning. 12
And the edges of the four wheels were full of eyes round about. 13 As for the wheels, they were named
in my hearing, the circling wheels.14 And every one had four faces: the first face was the face of a
winged one, and the second was the face of a man, and the third the face of a lion, and the fourth the
face of an eagle. 15 And the winged ones went up on high: this is the living being which I saw by the
river Chebar. 16 And when the winged ones went, the wheels went by their side: and when their wings
were lifted to take them up from the earth, the wheels were not turned from their side. 17 When they
were at rest in their place, these were at rest; when they were lifted up, these went up with them: for the
spirit of life was in them. 18 Then the glory of the Lord went out from the doorstep of the house, and
came to rest over the winged ones. 19 And the winged ones, lifting up their wings, went up from the
earth before my eyes, with the wheels by their side: and they came to rest at the east doorway of the
Lord's house; and the glory of the God of Israel was over them on high. 20 This is the living being
which I saw under the God of Israel by the river Chebar; and it was clear to me that they were the
winged ones. 21 Every one had four faces and every one had four wings; and hands like a man's hands
were under their wings. 22 As for the form of their faces, they were the faces whose form I saw by the
river Chebar; when they went, every one of them went straight forward.

11

1 And the wind, lifting me up, took me to the east doorway of the Lord's house, looking to the east: and
at the door I saw twenty-five men; and among them I saw Jaazaniah, the son of Azzur, and Pelatiah, the
son of Benaiah, rulers of the people. 2 Then he said to me, Son of man, these are the men who are

designing evil, who are teaching evil ways in this town: 3 Who say, This is not the time for building houses: this town is the cooking-pot and we are the flesh. 4 For this cause be a prophet against them, be a prophet, O son of man. 5 And the spirit of the Lord came on me, and he said to me, Say, These are the words of the Lord: This is what you have said, O children of Israel; what comes into your mind is clear to me. 6 You have made great the number of your dead in this town, you have made its streets full of dead men. 7 For this reason the Lord has said: Your dead whom you have put down in its streets, they are the flesh, and this town is the cooking-pot: but I will make you come out from inside it. 8 You have been fearing the sword, and I will send the sword on you, says the Lord. 9 I will make you come out from inside the town and will give you up into the hands of men from other lands, and will be judge among you. 10 You will come to your death by the sword; and I will be your judge in the land of Israel; and you will be certain that I am the Lord. 11 This town will not be your cooking-pot, and you will not be the flesh inside it; I will be your judge at the limit of the land of Israel; 12 And you will be certain that I am the Lord: for you have not been guided by my rules or given effect to my orders, but you have been living by the orders of the nations round about you. 13 Now while I was saying these things, death came to Pelatiah, the son of Benaiah. Then falling down on my face and crying out with a loud voice, I said, Ah, Lord! will you put an end to all the rest of Israel? 14 And the word of the Lord came to me, saying, 15 Son of man, your countrymen, your relations, and all the children of Israel, all of them, are those to whom the people of Jerusalem have said, Go far from the Lord; this land is given to us for a heritage: 16 For this reason say, This is what the Lord has said: Though I have had them moved far off among the nations, and though I have sent them wandering among the countries, still I have been a safe place for them for a little time in the countries where they have come. 17 Then say, This is what the Lord has said: I will get you together from the peoples, and make you come out of the countries where you have been sent in flight, and I will give you the land of Israel. 18 And they will come there, and take away all the hated and disgusting things from it. 19 And I will give them a new heart, and I will put a new spirit in them; and I will take the heart of stone out of their flesh and give them a heart of flesh: 20 So that they may be guided by my rules and keep my orders and do them: and they will be to me a people, and I will be to them a God. 21 But as for those whose heart goes after their hated and disgusting things, I will send on their heads the punishment of their ways, says the Lord. 22 Then the wings of the winged ones were lifted up, and the wheels were by their side; and the glory of the God of Israel was over them on high. 23 And the glory of the Lord went up from inside the town, and came to rest on the mountain on the east side of the town. 24 And the wind, lifting me up, took me in the visions of God into Chaldaea, to those who had been taken away as prisoners. So the vision which I had seen went away from me. 25 Then I gave an account to those who had been taken prisoners of all the things which the Lord had made me see.

12

1 And the word of the Lord came to me, saying, 2 Son of man, you are living among an uncontrolled people, who have eyes to see but see not, and ears for hearing but they do not give ear; for they are an uncontrolled people. 3 And you, O son of man, by day, before their eyes, get ready the vessels of one who is taken away, and go away from your place to another place before their eyes: it may be that they will see, though they are an uncontrolled people. 4 By day, before their eyes, take out your vessels like those of one who is taken away: and go out in the evening before their eyes, like those who are taken away as prisoners. 5 Make a hole in the wall, before their eyes, and go out through it. 6 And before their eyes, take your goods on your back and go out in the dark; go with your face covered: for I have made you a sign to the children of Israel. 7 And I did as I was ordered: I took out my vessels by day, like those of one who is taken away, and in the evening I made a hole through the wall with a tent-pin; and in the dark I went out, taking my things on my back before their eyes. 8 And in the morning the word of the Lord came to me, saying, 9 Son of man, has not Israel, the uncontrolled people, said to you, What are you doing? 10 You are to say to them, This is what the Lord has said: This word has to do with the ruler in Jerusalem and all the children of Israel in it. 11 Say, I am your sign: as I have done, so will it be done to them: they will go away as prisoners. 12 And the ruler who is among them will take his goods on his back in the dark and go out: he will make a hole in the wall through which to go out: he will have his face covered so that he may not be seen. 13 And my net will be stretched out on him, and he will be taken in my cords: and I will take him to Babylon to the land of the Chaldaeans; but he will not see it, and there death will come to him. 14 And all his helpers round about him and all his armies I will send in flight to every wind; and I will let loose a sword after them. 15 And they will be certain that I am the Lord, when I send them in flight among the nations, driving them out through the countries. 16 But a small number of them I will keep from the sword, from the need of food, and from disease, so that they

may make clear all their disgusting ways among the nations where they come; and they will be certain that I am the Lord. 17 Then the word of the Lord came to me, saying, 18 Son of man, take your food with shaking fear, and your water with trouble and care; 19 And say to the people of the land, This is what the Lord has said about the people of Jerusalem and the land of Israel: They will take their food with care and their drink with wonder, so that all the wealth of their land may be taken from it because of the violent ways of the people living in it. 20 And the peopled towns will be made waste, and the land will become a wonder; and you will be certain that I am the Lord. 21 And the word of the Lord came to me, saying, 22 Son of man, what is this saying which you have about the land of Israel, The time is long and every vision comes to nothing? 23 For this cause say to them, This is what the Lord has said: I have made this saying come to an end, and it will no longer be used as a common saying in Israel; but say to them, The days are near, and the effect of every vision. 24 For there will be no more false visions or smooth use of secret arts in Israel. 25 For I am the Lord; I will say the word and what I say I will do; it will not be put off: for in your days, O uncontrolled people, I will say the word and do it, says the Lord. 26 Again the word of the Lord came to me, saying, 27 Son of man, see, the children of Israel say, The vision which he sees is for the days which are a long way off, and his words are of times still far away. 28 Say to them then, This is what the Lord has said: Not one of my words will be put off any longer, but what I say I will do, says the Lord.

13

1 And the word of the Lord came to me, saying, 2 Son of man, be a prophet against the prophets of Israel, and say to those prophets whose words are the invention of their hearts, Give ear to the word of the Lord; 3 This is what the Lord has said: A curse on the foolish prophets who go after the spirit which is in them and have seen nothing! 4 O Israel, your prophets have been like jackals in the waste places. 5 You have not gone up into the broken places or made up the wall for the children of Israel to take your place in the fight in the day of the Lord. 6 They have seen visions without substance and made use of secret arts, who say, The Lord has said; and the Lord has not sent them: hoping that the word would have effect. 7 Have you not seen a vision without substance and have you not falsely made use of secret arts, when you say, The Lord has said; though I have said nothing? 8 So this is what the Lord has said: Because your words are without substance and your visions are false, see, I am against you, says the Lord. 9 And my hand will be against the prophets who see visions without substance and who make false use of secret arts: they will not be in the secret of my people, and they will not be recorded in the list of the children of Israel, and they will not come into the land of Israel; and it will be clear to you that I am the Lord. 10 Because, even because they have been guiding my people into error, saying, Peace; when there is no peace; and in the building of a division wall they put whitewash on it: 11 Say to those who put whitewash on it, There will be an overflowing shower; and you, O ice-drops, will come raining down; and it will be broken in two by the storm-wind. 12 And when the wall has come down, will they not say to you, Where is the whitewash which you put on it? 13 For this reason, the Lord has said: I will have it broken in two by a storm-wind in my passion; and there will be an overflowing shower in my wrath, and you, O ice-drops, will come raining angrily down. 14 So I will let the wall, which you were covering with whitewash, be broken down; I will have it levelled to the earth so that its base is uncovered: it will come down, and destruction will come on you with it; and it will be clear to you that I am the Lord. 15 So I will let loose my passion on the wall in full measure, and on those who put whitewash on it; and I will say to you, Where is the wall, and where are those who put whitewash on it? 16 Even the prophets of Israel who say words to Jerusalem, who see visions of peace for her when there is no peace, says the Lord. 17 And you, son of man, let your face be turned against the daughters of your people, who are acting the part of prophets at their pleasure; be a prophet against them, and say, 18 This is what the Lord has said: A curse is on the women who are stitching bands on all arms and putting veils on the heads of those of every size, so that they may go after souls! Will you go after the souls of my people and keep yourselves safe from death? 19 And you have put me to shame among my people for a little barley and some bits of bread, sending death on souls for whom there is no cause of death, and keeping those souls living who have no right to life, by the false words you say to my people who give ear to what is false. 20 For this cause the Lord has said: See, I am against your bands with which you go after souls, and I will violently take them off their arms; and I will let loose the souls, even the souls whom you go after freely. 21 And I will have your veils violently parted in two, and will make my people free from your hands, and they will no longer be in your power for you to go after them; and you will be certain that I am the Lord. 22 Because with your false words you have given pain to the heart of the upright man when I had not made him sad; in order to make strong the hands of the evil-doer so that he may not be turned from his evil way and get life: 23 For this cause you will see no more foolish visions

or make false use of secret arts: and I will make my people free from your power; and you will be certain
that I am the Lord.

14

1 Then certain of the responsible men of Israel came to me and took their seats before me. 2 And the
word of the Lord came to me, saying, 3 Son of man, these men have taken their false gods into their
hearts and put before their faces the sin which is the cause of their fall: am I to give ear when they come
to me for directions? 4 For this cause say to them, These are the words of the Lord: Every man of Israel
who has taken his false god into his heart, and put before his face the sin which is the cause of his fall,
and comes to the prophet; I the Lord will give him an answer by myself in agreement with the number
of his false gods; 5 So as to take the children of Israel in the thoughts of their hearts, because they have
become strange to me through their false gods. 6 For this cause say to the children of Israel, These are
the words of the Lord: Come back and give up your false gods and let your faces be turned from your
disgusting things. 7 When any one of the men of Israel, or of those from other lands who are living in
Israel, who has become strange to me, and takes his false gods into his heart, and puts before his face
the sin which is the cause of his fall, comes to the prophet to get directions from me; I the Lord will give
him an answer by myself: 8 And my face will be turned against that man, and I will make him a sign and
a common saying, cutting him off from among my people; and you will be certain that I am the Lord. 9
And if the prophet, tricked by deceit, says anything, it is I the Lord by whom he has been tricked, and I
will put out my hand against him, and he will be cut off from among my people Israel. 10 And the
punishment of their sin will be on them: the sin of the prophet will be the same as the sin of him who
goes to him for directions; 11 So that the children of Israel may no longer go wandering away from me,
or make themselves unclean with all their wrongdoing; but they will be my people, and I will be their
God, says the Lord. 12 And the word of the Lord came to me, saying, 13 Son of man, when a land,
sinning against me, does wrong, and my hand is stretched out against it, and the support of its bread is
broken, and I make it short of food, cutting off man and beast from it: 14 Even if these three men,
Noah, Daniel, and Job, were in it, only themselves would they keep safe by their righteousness, says the
Lord. 15 Or if I send evil beasts through the land causing destruction and making it waste, so that no
man may go through because of the beasts: 16 Even if these three men were in it, by my life, says the
Lord, they would not keep safe their sons or daughters, but only themselves, and the land would be
made waste. 17 Or if I send a sword against that land, and say, Sword, go through the land, cutting off
from it man and beast:18 Even if these three men were in it, by my life, says the Lord, they would not
keep safe their sons or daughters, but only themselves. 19 Or if I send disease into that land, letting
loose my wrath on it in blood, cutting off from it man and beast: 20 Even if Noah, Daniel, and Job were
in it, by my life, says the Lord, they would not keep son or daughter safe; only themselves would they
keep safe through their righteousness. 21 For this is what the Lord has said: How much more when I
send my four bitter punishments on Jerusalem, the sword and need of food and evil beasts and disease,
cutting off from it man and beast? 22 But truly, there will still be a small band who will be safe, even
sons and daughters: and they will come out to you, and you will see their ways and their doings: and you
will be comforted about the evil which I have sent on Jerusalem, even about everything I have sent on
it. 23 They will give you comfort when you see their ways and their doings: and you will be certain that
not for nothing have I done all the things I have done in it, says the Lord.

15

1 And the word of the Lord came to me, saying, 2 Son of man, what is the vine-tree more than any
branching tree which is among the trees of the woods? 3 Will its wood be used for any work? do men
make of it a pin for hanging any vessel on? 4 See, it is put into the fire for burning: the fire has made a
meal of its two ends and the middle part of it is burned; is it good for any work? 5 Truly, before it was
cut down, it was not used for any purpose: how much less, when the fire has made a meal of it and it is
burned, will it be made into anything? 6 For this cause the Lord has said: Like the vine-tree among the
trees of the woods which I have given to the fire for burning, so will I give the people of Jerusalem. 7
And my face will be turned against them; and though they have come out of the fire they will be burned
up by it; and it will be clear to you that I am the Lord when my face is turned against them. 8 And I will
make the land a waste because they have done evil, says the Lord.

16

1 And the word of the Lord came to me, saying, 2 Son of man, make clear to Jerusalem her disgusting ways, 3 And say, This is what the Lord has said to Jerusalem: Your start and your birth was from the land of the Canaanite; an Amorite was your father and your mother was a Hittite. 4 As for your birth, on the day of your birth your cord was not cut and you were not washed in water to make you clean; you were not salted or folded in linen bands. 5 No eye had pity on you to do any of these things to you or to be kind to you; but you were put out into the open country, because your life was hated at the time of your birth. 6 And when I went past you and saw you stretched out in your blood, I said to you, Though you are stretched out in your blood, have life; 7 And be increased in number like the buds of the field; and you were increased and became great, and you came to the time of love: your breasts were formed and your hair was long; but you were uncovered and without clothing. 8 Now when I went past you, looking at you, I saw that your time was the time of love; and I put my skirts over you, covering your unclothed body: and I gave you my oath and made an agreement with you, says the Lord, and you became mine. 9 Then I had you washed with water, washing away all your blood and rubbing you with oil. 10 And I had you clothed with needlework, and put leather shoes on your feet, folding fair linen about you and covering you with silk. 11 And I made you fair with ornaments and put jewels on your hands and a chain on your neck. 12 And I put a ring in your nose and ear-rings in your ears and a beautiful crown on your head. 13 So you were made beautiful with gold and silver; and your clothing was of the best linen and silk and needlework; your food was the best meal and honey and oil: and you were very beautiful. 14 You were so beautiful that the story of you went out into all nations; you were completely beautiful because of my glory which I had put on you, says the Lord. 15 But you put your faith in the fact that you were beautiful, acting like a loose woman because you were widely talked of, and offering your cheap love to everyone who went by, whoever it might be. 16 And you took your robes and made high places for yourself ornamented with every colour, acting like a loose woman on them, without shame or fear. 17 And you took the fair jewels, my silver and gold which I had given to you, and made for yourself male images, acting like a loose woman with them; 18 And you took your robes of needlework for their clothing, and put my oil and my perfume before them. 19 And my bread which I gave you, the best meal and oil and honey which I gave you for your food, you put it before them for a sweet smell, says the Lord. 20 And you took your sons and your daughters whom I had by you, offering even these to them to be their food. Was your loose behaviour so small a thing, 21 That you put my children to death and gave them up to go through the fire to them? 22 And in all your disgusting and false behaviour you had no memory of your early days, when you were uncovered and without clothing, stretched out in your blood. 23 And it came about, after all your evil-doing, says the Lord, 24 That you made for yourself an arched room in every open place. 25 You put up your high places at the top of every street, and made the grace of your form a disgusting thing, opening your feet to everyone who went by, increasing your loose ways. 26 And you went with the Egyptians, your neighbours, great of flesh; increasing your loose ways, moving me to wrath. 27 Now, then, my hand is stretched out against you, cutting down your fixed amount, and I have given you up to the desire of your haters, the daughters of the Philistines who are shamed by your loose ways. 28 And you went with the Assyrians, because of your desire which was without measure; you were acting like a loose woman with them, and still you had not enough. 29 And you went on in your loose ways, even as far as the land of Chaldaea, and still you had not enough. 30 How feeble is your heart, says the Lord, seeing that you do all these things, the work of a loose and overruling woman; 31 For you have made your arched room at the top of every street, and your high place in every open place; though you were not like a loose woman in getting together your payment. 32 The untrue wife who takes strange lovers in place of her husband! 33 They give payment to all loose women: but you give rewards to your lovers, offering them payment so that they may come to you on every side for your cheap love. 34 And in your loose behaviour you are different from other women, for no one goes after you to make love to you: and because you give payment and no payment is given to you, in this you are different from them. 35 For this cause, O loose woman, give ear to the voice of the Lord: 36 This is what the Lord has said: Because your unclean behaviour was let loose and your body uncovered in your loose ways with your lovers and with your disgusting images, and for the blood of your children which you gave to them; 37 For this cause I will get together all your lovers with whom you have taken your pleasure, and all those to whom you have given your love, with all those who were hated by you; I will even make them come together against you on every side, and I will have you uncovered before them so that they may see your shame. 38 And you will be judged by me as women are judged who have been untrue to their husbands and have taken life; and I will let loose against you passion and bitter feeling. 39 I will give you into their hands, and your arched room will be overturned and your high places broken down; they will take your clothing off you and take away your fair jewels: and when they have done, you will be uncovered and shamed. 40 And they will get together a meeting against you, stoning you with stones and wounding you with their

swords. 41 And they will have you burned with fire, sending punishments on you before the eyes of great numbers of women; and I will put an end to your loose ways, and you will no longer give payment. 42 And the heat of my wrath against you will have an end, and my bitter feeling will be turned away from you, and I will be quiet and will be angry no longer.43 Because you have not kept in mind the days when you were young, but have been troubling me with all these things; for this reason I will make the punishment of your ways come on your head, says the Lord, because you have done this evil thing in addition to all your disgusting acts. 44 See, in every common saying about you it will be said, As the mother is, so is her daughter. 45 You are the daughter of your mother whose soul is turned in disgust from her husband and her children; and you are the sister of your sisters who were turned in disgust from their husbands and their children: your mother was a Hittite and your father an Amorite. 46 Your older sister is Samaria, living at your left hand, she and her daughters: and your younger sister, living at your right hand, is Sodom and her daughters. 47 Still you have not gone in their ways or done the disgusting things which they have done; but, as if that was only a little thing, you have gone deeper in evil than they in all your ways. 48 By my life, says the Lord, Sodom your sister never did, she or her daughters, what you and your daughters have done. 49 Truly, this was the sin of your sister Sodom: pride, a full measure of food, and the comforts of wealth in peace, were seen in her and her daughters, and she gave no help to the poor or to those in need. 50 They were full of pride and did what was disgusting to me: and so I took them away as you have seen. 51 And Samaria has not done half your sins; but you have made the number of your disgusting acts greater than theirs, making your sisters seem more upright than you by all the disgusting things which you have done. 52And you yourself will be put to shame, in that you have given the decision for your sisters; through your sins, which are more disgusting than theirs, they are more upright than you: truly, you will be shamed and made low, for you have made your sisters seem upright. 53 And I will let their fate be changed, the fate of Sodom and her daughters, and the fate of Samaria and her daughters, and your fate with theirs. 54 So that you will be shamed and made low because of all you have done, when I have mercy on you. 55 And your sisters, Sodom and her daughters, will go back to their first condition, and Samaria and her daughters will go back to their first condition, and you and your daughters will go back to your first condition. 56 Was not your sister Sodom an oath in your mouth in the day of your pride, 57 Before your shame was uncovered? Now you have become like her a word of shame to the daughters of Edom and all who are round about you, the daughters of the Philistines who put shame on you round about. 58 The reward of your evil designs and your disgusting ways has come on you, says the Lord. 59 For this is what the Lord has said: I will do to you as you have done, you who, putting the oath on one side, have let the agreement be broken. 60 But still I will keep in mind the agreement made with you in the days when you were young, and I will make with you an eternal agreement. 61 Then at the memory of your ways you will be overcome with shame, when I take your sisters, the older and the younger, and give them to you for daughters, but not by your agreement. 62 And I will make my agreement with you; and you will be certain that I am the Lord: 63 So that, at the memory of these things, you may be at a loss, never opening your mouth because of your shame; when you have my forgiveness for all you have done, says the Lord.

17

1 And the word of the Lord came to me, saying, 2 Son of man, give out a dark saying, and make a comparison for the children of Israel, 3 And say, This is what the Lord has said: A great eagle with great wings, full of long feathers of different colours, came to Lebanon, and took the top of the cedar: 4 Biting off the highest of its young branches, he took it to the land of Canaan, and put it in a town of traders. 5And he took some of the seed of the land, planting it in fertile earth, placing it by great waters; he put it in like a willow-tree. 6 And its growth went on and it became a vine, low and widely stretching, whose branches were turned to him and its roots were under him: so it became a vine, putting out branches and young leaves. 7 And there was another eagle with great wings and thick feathers: and now this vine, pushing out its roots to him, sent out its branches in his direction from the bed where it was planted, so that he might give it water. 8 He had it planted in a good field by great waters so that it might put out branches and have fruit and be a strong vine. 9 Say, This is what the Lord has said: Will it do well? will he not have its roots pulled up and its branches cut off, so that all its young leaves may become dry and it may be pulled up by its roots? 10 And if it is planted will it do well? will it not become quite dry at the touch of the east wind, drying up in the bed where it was planted? 11 Then the word of the Lord came to me, saying, 12 Say now to this uncontrolled people, Are these things not clear to you? Say to them, See, the king of Babylon came to Jerusalem and took its king and its rulers away with him to Babylon; 13 And he took one of the sons of the king and made an agreement with him; and he put

him under an oath, and took away the great men of the land: 14 So that the kingdom might be made low
with no power of lifting itself up, but might keep his agreement to be his servants. 15 But he went
against his authority in sending representatives to Egypt to get from them horses and a great army. Will
he do well? will he be safe who does such things? if the agreement is broken will he be safe? 16 By my
life, says the Lord, truly in the place of the king who made him king, whose oath he put on one side and
let his agreement with him be broken, even in Babylon he will come to his death. 17 And Pharaoh with
his strong army and great forces will be no help to him in the war, when they put up earthworks and
make strong walls for the cutting off of lives: 18 For he put his oath on one side in letting the agreement
be broken; and though he had given his hand to it, he did all these things; he will not get away safe. 19
And so the Lord has said, By my life, truly, for my oath which he put on one side, and my agreement
which has been broken, I will send punishment on his head. 20 My net will be stretched out over him,
and he will be taken in my cords, and I will send him to Babylon, and there I will be his judge for the
wrong which he has done against me. 21 All his best fighting-men will be put to the sword, and the rest
will be sent away to every wind: and you will be certain that I the Lord have said it. 22 This is what the
Lord has said: Further, I will take the highest top of the cedar and put it in the earth; cutting off from
the highest of his young branches a soft one, I will have it planted on a high and great mountain; 23 It
will be planted on the high mountain of Israel: it will put out branches and have fruit and be a fair cedar:
under it all birds of every sort will make their living-place, resting in the shade of its branches. 24 And it
will be clear to all the trees of the field that I the Lord have made low the high tree and made high the
low tree, drying up the green tree and making the dry tree full of growth; I the Lord have said it and
have done it.

18

1 The word of the Lord came to me again, saying, 2 Why do you make use of this saying about the land
of Israel, The fathers have been tasting bitter grapes and the children's teeth are on edge? 3 By my life,
says the Lord, you will no longer have this saying in Israel. 4 See, all souls are mine; as the soul of the
father, so the soul of the son is mine: death will be the fate of the sinner's soul. 5 But if a man is upright,
living rightly and doing righteousness, 6 And has not taken flesh with the blood for food, or given
worship to the images of the children of Israel; if he has not had connection with his neighbour's wife,
or come near to a woman at the time when she is unclean; 7 And has done no wrong to any, but has
given back to the debtor what is his, and has taken no one's goods by force, and has given food to him
who was in need of it, and clothing to him who was without it; 8 And has not given his money out at
interest or taken great profits, and, turning his hand from evil-doing, has kept faith between man and
man, 9 And has been guided by my rules and has kept my laws and done them: he is upright, life will
certainly be his, says the Lord. 10 If he has a son who is a thief, a taker of life, who does any of these
things, 11 Who has taken flesh with the blood as food, and has had connection with his neighbour's
wife, 12 Has done wrong to the poor and to him who is in need, and taken property by force, and has
not given back to one in his debt what is his, and has given worship to images and has done disgusting
things, 13 And has given out his money at interest and taken great profits: he will certainly not go on
living: he has done all these disgusting things: death will certainly be his fate; his blood will be on him.
14 Now if he has a son who sees all his father's sins which he has done, and in fear does not do the
same: 15 Who has not taken the flesh with the blood for food, or given worship to the images of the
children of Israel, and has not had connection with his neighbour's wife, 16 Or done wrong to any, or
taken anything from one in his debt, or taken goods by force, but has given food to him who was in
need of it, and clothing to him who was without it;17 Who has kept his hand from evil-doing and has
not taken interest or great profits, who has done my orders and been guided by my rules: he will
certainly not be put to death for the evil-doing of his father; life will certainly be his. 18 As for his father,
because he was cruel, took goods by force, and did what is not good among his people, truly, death will
overtake him in his evil-doing. 19 But you say, Why does not the son undergo punishment for the evil-
doing of the father? When the son has done what is ordered and right, and has kept my rules and done
them, life will certainly be his. 20 The soul which does sin will be put to death: the son will not be made
responsible for the evil-doing of the father, or the father for the evil-doing of the son; the righteousness
of the upright will be on himself, and the evil-doing of the evil-doer on himself. 21 But if the evil-doer,
turning away from all the sins which he has done, keeps my rules and does what is ordered and right, life
will certainly be his; death will not be his fate. 22 Not one of the sins which he has done will be kept in
memory against him: in the righteousness which he has done he will have life. 23 Have I any pleasure in
the death of the evil-doer? says the Lord: am I not pleased if he is turned from his way so that he may
have life? 24 But when the upright man, turning away from his righteousness, does evil, like all the

disgusting things which the evil man does, will he have life? Not one of his upright acts will be kept in memory: in the wrong which he has done and in his sin death will overtake him. 25 But you say, The way of the Lord is not equal. Give ear, now, O children of Israel; is my way not equal? are not your ways unequal? 26 When the upright man, turning away from his righteousness, does evil, death will overtake him; in the evil which he has done death will overtake him.27 Again, when the evil-doer, turning away from the evil he has done, does what is ordered and right, he will have life for his soul. 28 Because he had fear and was turned away from all the wrong which he had done, life will certainly be his, death will not be his fate. 29 But still the children of Israel say, The way of the Lord is not equal. O children of Israel, are my ways not equal? are not your ways unequal? 30 For this cause I will be your judge, O children of Israel, judging every man by his ways, says the Lord. Come back and be turned from all your sins; so that they may not be the cause of your falling into evil. 31 Put away all your evil-doing in which you have done sin; and make for yourselves a new heart and a new spirit: why are you desiring death, O children of Israel? 32 For I have no pleasure in the death of him on whom death comes, says the Lord: be turned back then, and have life.

19

1 Take up now a song of grief for the ruler of Israel, and say, 2 What was your mother? Like a she-lion among lions, stretched out among the young lions she gave food to her little ones. 3 And one of her little ones came to growth under her care, and became a young lion, learning to go after beasts for his food; and he took men for his meat. 4 And the nations had news of him; he was taken in the hole they had made: and, pulling him with hooks, they took him into the land of Egypt. 5 Now when she saw that her hope was made foolish and gone, she took another of her little ones and made him into a young lion. 6 And he went up and down among the lions and became a young lion, learning to go after beasts for his food; and he took men for his meat. 7 And he sent destruction on their widows and made waste their towns; and the land and everything in it became waste because of the loud sound of his voice. 8 Then the nations came against him from the kingdoms round about: their net was stretched over him and he was taken in the hole they had made. 9 They made him a prisoner with hooks, and took him to the king of Babylon; they put him in the strong place so that his voice might be sounding no longer on the mountains of Israel. 10 Your mother was in comparison like a vine, planted by the waters: she was fertile and full of branches because of the great waters. 11 And she had a strong rod for a rod of authority for the rulers, and it became tall among the clouds and it was seen lifted up among the number of its branches. 12 But she was uprooted in burning wrath, and made low on the earth; the east wind came, drying her up, and her branches were broken off; her strong rod became dry, the fire made a meal of it. 13 And now she is planted in the waste land, in a dry and unwatered country. 14 And fire has gone out from her rod, causing the destruction of her branches, so that there is no strong rod in her to be the ruler's rod of authority. This is a song of grief, and it was for a song of grief.

20

1 Now it came about in the seventh year, in the fifth month, on the tenth day of the month, that certain of the responsible men of Israel came to get directions from the Lord and were seated before me. 2 Then the word of the Lord came to me, saying, 3 Son of man, say to the responsible men of Israel, This is what the Lord has said: Have you come to get directions from me? By my life, says the Lord, you will get no directions from me. 4 Will you be their judge, O son of man, will you be their judge? make clear to them the disgusting ways of their fathers, 5 And say to them, This is what the Lord has said: In the day when I took Israel for myself, when I made an oath to the seed of the family of Jacob, and I gave them knowledge of myself in the land of Egypt, saying to them with an oath, I am the Lord your God; 6 In that day I gave my oath to take them out of the land of Egypt into a land which I had been searching out for them, a land flowing with milk and honey, the glory of all lands: 7 And I said to them, Let every man among you put away the disgusting things to which his eyes are turned, and do not make yourselves unclean with the images of Egypt; I am the Lord your God. 8 But they would not be controlled by me, and did not give ear to me; they did not put away the disgusting things to which their eyes were turned, or give up the images of Egypt: then I said I would let loose my passion on them to give full effect to my wrath against them in the land of Egypt. 9 And I was acting for the honour of my name, so that it might not be made unclean before the eyes of the nations among whom they were, and before whose eyes I gave them knowledge of myself, by taking them out of the land of Egypt. 10 So I made them go out of the land of Egypt and took them into the waste land. 11 And I gave them my rules and made clear to them my orders, which, if a man keeps them, will be life to him. 12 And further, I gave them my

Sabbaths, to be a sign between me and them, so that it might be clear that I, who make them holy, am
the Lord. 13 But the children of Israel would not be controlled by me in the waste land: they were not
guided by my rules, and they were turned away from my orders, which, if a man does them, will be life
to him; and they had no respect for my Sabbaths: then I said that I would let loose my passion on them
in the waste land, and put an end to them. 14 And I was acting for the honour of my name, so that it
might not be made unclean in the eyes of the nations, before whose eyes I had taken them out. 15 And
further, I gave my oath to them in the waste land, that I would not take them into the land which I had
given them, a land flowing with milk and honey, the glory of all lands; 16 Because they were turned away
from my orders, and were not guided by my rules, and had no respect for my Sabbaths: for their hearts
went after their images. 17 But still my eye had pity on them and I kept them from destruction and did
not put an end to them completely in the waste land. 18 And I said to their children in the waste land,
Do not be guided by the rules of your fathers or keep their orders or make yourselves unclean with their
images: 19 I am the Lord your God; be guided by my rules and keep my orders and do them: 20 And
keep my Sabbaths holy; and they will be a sign between me and you so that it may be clear to you that I
am the Lord your God. 21 But the children would not be controlled by me; they were not guided by my
rules, and they did not keep and do my orders, which, if a man does them, will be life to him; and they
had no respect for my Sabbaths: then I said I would let loose my passion on them to give full effect to
my wrath against them in the waste land. 22 And I was acting for the honour of my name, so that it
might not be made unclean in the eyes of the nations, before whose eyes I had taken them out. 23
Further, I gave my oath to them in the waste land that I would send them wandering among the nations,
driving them out among the countries; 24 Because they had not done my orders, but had been turned
away from my rules, and had not given respect to my Sabbaths, and their eyes were turned to the images
of their fathers. 25 And further, I gave them rules which were not good and orders in which there was
no life for them; 26 I made them unclean in the offerings they gave, causing them to make every first
child go through the fire, so that I might put an end to them. 27 For this cause, son of man, say to the
children of Israel, This is what the Lord has said: In this your fathers have further put shame on my
name by doing wrong against me. 28 For when I had taken them into the land which I made an oath to
give to them, then they saw every high hill and every branching tree and made their offerings there,
moving me to wrath by their offerings; and there the sweet smell of their offerings went up and their
drink offerings were drained out. 29 Then I said to them, What is this high place where you go to no
purpose? And it is named Bamah to this day. 30 For this cause say to the children of Israel, This is what
the Lord has said: Are you making yourselves unclean as your fathers did? are you being untrue to me by
going after their disgusting works? 31 And when you give your offerings, causing your sons to go
through the fire, you make yourselves unclean with all your images to this day; and will you come to me
for directions, O children of Israel? By my life, says the Lord, you will get no direction from me. 32 And
that which comes into your minds will never take place; when you say, We will be like the nations, like
the families of the countries, servants of wood and stone; 33 By my life, says the Lord, truly, with a
strong hand and with an outstretched arm and with burning wrath let loose, I will be King over you: 34
And I will take you out from the peoples and get you together out of the countries where you are
wandering, with a strong hand and with an outstretched arm and with burning wrath let loose: 35 And I
will take you into the waste land of the peoples, and there I will take up the cause with you face to
face.36 As I took up the cause with your fathers in the waste land of the land of Egypt, so will I take up
the cause with you says the Lord. 37 And I will make you go under the rod and will make you small in
number: 38 Clearing out from among you all those who are uncontrolled and who are sinning against
me; I will take them out of the land where they are living, but they will not come into the land of Israel:
and you will be certain that I am the Lord. 39 As for you, O children of Israel, the Lord has said: Let
every man completely put away his images and give ear to me: and let my holy name no longer be
shamed by your offerings and your images. 40 For in my holy mountain, in the high mountain of Israel,
says the Lord, there all the children of Israel, all of them, will be my servants in the land; there I will take
pleasure in them, and there I will be worshipped with your offerings and the first-fruits of the things you
give, and with all your holy things. 41 I will take pleasure in you as in a sweet smell, when I take you out
from the peoples and get you together from the countries where you have been sent in flight; and I will
make myself holy in you before the eyes of the nations. 42 And you will be certain that I am the Lord,
when I take you into the land of Israel, into the country which I made an oath to give to your fathers. 43
And there, at the memory of your ways and of all the things you did to make yourselves unclean, you
will have bitter hate for yourselves because of all the evil things you have done. 44 And you will be
certain that I am the Lord, when I take you in hand for the honour of my name, and not for your evil
ways or your unclean doings, O children of Israel, says the Lord. 45 Then the word of the Lord came to
me, saying, 46 Son of man, let your face be turned to the south, let your words be dropped to the south,

and be a prophet against the woodland of the South; 47 And say to the woodland of the South, Give ear
to the words of the Lord: this is what the Lord has said: See, I will have a fire lighted in you, for the
destruction of every green tree in you and every dry tree: the flaming flame will not be put out, and all
faces from the south to the north will be burned by it. 48 And all flesh will see that I the Lord have had
it lighted: it will not be put out. 49 Then I said, Ah, Lord! they say of me, Is he not a maker of stories?

21

1 And the word of the Lord came to me, saying, 2 Son of man, let your face be turned to Jerusalem, let
your words be dropped in the direction of her holy place, and be a prophet against the land of Israel; 3
And say to the land of Israel, These are the words of the Lord: See, I am against you, and I will take my
sword out of its cover, cutting off from you the upright and the evil. 4 Because I am going to have the
upright and the evil cut off from you, for this cause my sword will go out from its cover against all flesh
from the south to the north: 5 And all flesh will see that I the Lord have taken my sword out of its
cover: and it will never go back. 6 Make sounds of grief, son of man; with body bent and a bitter heart
make sounds of grief before their eyes. 7 And when they say to you, Why are you making sounds of
grief? then say, Because of the news, for it is coming: and every heart will become soft, and all hands will
be feeble, and every spirit will be burning low, and all knees will be turned to water: see, it is coming and
it will be done, says the Lord. 8 And the word of the Lord came to me, saying, 9 Son of man, say as a
prophet, These are the words of the Lord: Say, A sword, a sword which has been made sharp and
polished: 10 It has been made sharp to give death; it is polished so that it may be like a thunder-flame: ...
11 And I have given it to the polisher so that it may be taken in the hand: he has made the sword sharp,
he has had it polished, to put it into the hand of him who gives death. 12 Give loud cries and make
sounds of grief, O son of man: for it has come on my people, it has come on all the rulers of Israel: fear
of the sword has come on my people: for this cause give signs of grief. 13 ... 14 So then, son of man, be
a prophet, and put your hands together with a loud sound, and give two blows with the sword, and even
three; it is the sword of those who are wounded, even the sword of the wounded; the great sword which
goes round about them. 15 In order that hearts may become soft, and the number of those who are
falling may be increased, I have sent death by the sword against all their doors: you are made like a
flame, you are polished for death. 16 Be pointed to the right, to the left, wherever your edge is ordered.
17 And I will put my hands together with a loud sound, and I will let my wrath have rest: I the Lord
have said it. 18 And the word of the Lord came to me again, saying, 19 And you, son of man, have two
ways marked out, so that the sword of the king of Babylon may come; let the two of them come out of
one land: and let there be a pillar at the top of the road: 20 Put a pillar at the top of the road for the
sword to come to Rabbah in the land of the children of Ammon, and to Judah and to Jerusalem in the
middle of her. 21 For the king of Babylon took his place at the parting of the ways, at the top of the two
roads, to make use of secret arts: shaking the arrows this way and that, he put questions to the images of
his gods, he took note of the inner parts of dead beasts. 22 At his right hand was the fate of Jerusalem,
to give orders for destruction, to send up the war-cry, to put engines of war against the doors, lifting up
earthworks, building walls. 23 And this answer given by secret arts will seem false to those who have
given their oaths and have let them be broken: but he will keep the memory of evil-doing so that they
may be taken. 24 For this cause the Lord has said: Because you have made your evil-doing come to
mind by the uncovering of your wrongdoing, causing your sins to be seen in all your evil-doings;
because you have come to mind, you will be taken in them. 25 And you, O evil one, wounded to death,
O ruler of Israel, whose day has come in the time of the last punishment; 26 This is what the Lord has
said: Take away the holy head-dress, take off the crown: this will not be again: let that which is low be
lifted up, and that which is high be made low. 27 I will let it be overturned, overturned, overturned: this
will not be again till he comes whose right it is; and I will give it to him. 28 And you, son of man, say as
a prophet, This is what the Lord has said about the children of Ammon and about their shame: Say, A
sword, even a sword let loose, polished for death, to make it shining so that it may be like a flame: 29
Your vision is to no purpose, your use of secret arts gives a false answer, to put it on the necks of evil-
doers who are wounded to death, whose day has come, in the time of the last punishment. 30 Go back
into your cover. In the place where you were made, in the land from which you were taken, I will be
your judge. 31 And I will let loose my burning passion on you, breathing out on you the fire of my
wrath: and I will give you up into the hands of men like beasts, trained to destruction. 32 You will be
food for the fire; your blood will be drained out in the land; there will be no more memory of you: for I
the Lord have said it.

22

1 And the word of the Lord came to me, saying, 2 And you, son of man, will you be a judge, will you be
a judge of the town of blood? then make clear to her all her disgusting ways. 3 And you are to say, This
is what the Lord has said: A town causing blood to be drained out in her streets so that her time may
come, and making images in her to make her unclean! 4 You are responsible for the blood drained out
by you, and you are unclean through the images which you have made; and you have made your day
come near, and the time of your judging has come; for this cause I have made you a name of shame to
the nations and a cause of laughing to all countries. 5 Those who are near and those who are far from
you will make sport of you; your name is unclean, you are full of sounds of fear. 6 See, the rulers of
Israel, every one in his family, have been causing death in you. 7 In you they have had no respect for
father and mother; in you they have been cruel to the man from a strange land; in you they have done
wrong to the child without a father and to the widow. 8 You have made little of my holy things, and
have made my Sabbaths unclean. 9 In you there are men who say evil of others, causing death; in you
they have taken the flesh with the blood for food; in your streets they have put evil designs into effect.
10 In you they have let the shame of their fathers be seen; in you they have done wrong to a woman at
the time when she was unclean. 11 And in you one man has done what was disgusting with his
neighbour's wife; and another has made his daughter-in-law unclean; and another has done wrong to his
sister, his father's daughter.12 In you they have taken rewards as the price of blood; you have taken
interest and great profits, and you have taken away your neighbours' goods by force, and have not kept
me in mind, says the Lord. 13 See, then, I have made my hands come together in wrath against your
taking of goods by force and against the blood which has been flowing in you. 14 Will your heart be
high or your hands strong in the days when I take you in hand? I the Lord have said it and will do it. 15
And I will send you in flight among the nations and wandering among the countries; and I will
completely take away out of you everything which is unclean. 16 And you will be made low before the
eyes of the nations; and it will be clear to you that I am the Lord. 17 And the word of the Lord came to
me, saying, 18 Son of man, the children of Israel have become like the poorest sort of waste metal to
me: they are all silver and brass and tin and iron and lead mixed with waste. 19 For this cause the Lord
has said: Because you have all become waste metal, see, I will get you together inside Jerusalem. 20 As
they put silver and brass and iron and lead and tin together inside the oven, heating up the fire on it to
make it soft; so will I get you together in my wrath and in my passion, and, heating the fire with my
breath, will make you soft. 21 Yes, I will take you, breathing on you the fire of my wrath, and you will
become soft in it. 22 As silver becomes soft in the oven, so you will become soft in it; and you will be
certain that I the Lord have let loose my passion on you. 23 And the word of the Lord came to me,
saying, 24 Son of man, say to her, You are a land on which no rain or thunderstorm has come in the day
of wrath. 25 Her rulers in her are like a loud-voiced lion violently taking his food; they have made a meal
of souls; they have taken wealth and valued property; they have made great the number of widows in
her. 26 Her priests have been acting violently against my law; they have made my holy things unclean:
they have made no division between what is holy and what is common, and they have not made it clear
that the unclean is different from the clean, and their eyes have been shut to my Sabbaths, and I am not
honoured among them. 27 Her rulers in her are like wolves violently taking their food; putting men to
death and causing the destruction of souls, so that they may get their profit. 28 And her prophets have
been using whitewash, seeing foolish visions and making false use of secret arts, saying, This is what the
Lord has said, when the Lord has said nothing. 29 The people of the land have been acting cruelly,
taking men's goods by force; they have been hard on the poor and those in need, and have done wrong
to the man from a strange land. 30 And I was looking for a man among them who would make up the
wall and take his station in the broken place before me for the land, so that I might not send destruction
on it: but there was no one. 31 And I let loose my passion on them, and have put an end to them in the
fire of my wrath: I have made the punishment of their ways come on their heads, says the Lord.

23

1 The word of the Lord came to me again, saying, 2 Son of man, there were two women, daughters of
one mother: 3 They were acting like loose women in Egypt; when they were young their behaviour was
loose: there their breasts were crushed, even the points of their young breasts were crushed. 4 Their
names were Oholah, the older, and Oholibah, her sister: and they became mine, and gave birth to sons
and daughters. As for their names, Samaria is Oholah, and Jerusalem, Oholibah 5 And Oholah was
untrue to me when she was mine; she was full of desire for her lovers, even for the Assyrians, her
neighbours, 6 Who were clothed in blue, captains and rulers, all of them young men to be desired,
horsemen seated on horses. 7 And she gave her unclean love to them, all of them the noblest men of

Assyria: and she made herself unclean with the images of all who were desired by her. 8 And she has not given up her loose ways from the time when she was in Egypt; for when she was young they were her lovers, and by them her young breasts were crushed, and they let loose on her their unclean desire. 9 For this cause I gave her up into the hands of her lovers, into the hands of the Assyrians on whom her desire was fixed. 10 By these her shame was uncovered: they took her sons and daughters and put her to death with the sword: and she became a cause of wonder to women; for they gave her the punishment which was right. 11 And her sister Oholibah saw this, but her desire was even more unmeasured, and her loose behaviour was worse than that of her sister. 12 She was full of desire for the Assyrians, captains and rulers, her neighbours, clothed in blue, horsemen going on horses, all of them young men to be desired. 13 And I saw that she had become unclean; the two of them went the same way. 14 And her loose behaviour became worse; for she saw men pictured on a wall, pictures of the Chaldaeans painted in bright red 15 With bands round their bodies and with head-dresses hanging round their heads, all of them looking like rulers, like the Babylonians, the land of whose birth is Chaldaea. 16 And when she saw them she was full of desire for them, and sent servants to them in Chaldaea. 17 And the Babylonians came to her, into the bed of love, and made her unclean with their loose desire, and she became unclean with them, and her soul was turned from them. 18 So her loose behaviour was clearly seen and her shame uncovered: then my soul was turned from her as it had been turned from her sister. 19 But still she went on the more with her loose behaviour, keeping in mind the early days when she had been a loose woman in the land of Egypt 20 And she was full of desire for her lovers, whose flesh is like the flesh of asses and whose seed is like the seed of horses. 21 And she made the memory of the loose ways of her early years come back to mind, when her young breasts were crushed by the Egyptians 22 For this cause, O Oholibah, this is what the Lord has said: See, I will make your lovers come up against you, even those from whom your soul is turned away in disgust; and I will make them come up against you on every side; 23 The Babylonians and all the Chaldaeans, Pekod and Shoa and Koa, and all the Assyrians with them: young men to be desired, captains and rulers all of them, and chiefs, her neighbours, all of them on horseback. 24 And they will come against you from the north on horseback, with war-carriages and a great band of peoples; they will put themselves in order against you with breastplate and body-cover and metal head-dress round about you: and I will make them your judges, and they will give their decision against you as seems right to them. 25 And my bitter feeling will be working against you, and they will take you in hand with passion; they will take away your nose and your ears, and the rest of you will be put to the sword: they will take your sons and daughters, and the rest of you will be burned up in the fire. 26 And they will take all your clothing off you and take away your ornaments. 27 So I will put an end to your evil ways and your loose behaviour which came from the land of Egypt: and your eyes will never be lifted up to them again, and you will have no more memory of Egypt. 28 For this is what the Lord has said: See, I will give you up into the hands of those who are hated by you, into the hands of those from whom your soul is turned away in disgust: 29 And they will take you in hand with hate, and take away all the fruit of your work, and let you be unveiled and without clothing: and the shame of your loose behaviour will be uncovered, your evil designs and your loose ways. 30 They will do these things to you because you have been untrue to me, and have gone after the nations, and have become unclean with their images. 31 You have gone in the way of your sister; and I will give her cup into your hand. 32 This is what the Lord has said: You will take a drink from your sister's cup, which is deep and wide: you will be laughed at and looked down on, more than you are able to undergo. 33 You will be broken and full of sorrow, with the cup of wonder and destruction, with the cup of your sister Samaria. 34 And after drinking it and draining it out, you will take the last drops of it to the end, pulling off your breasts: for I have said it, says the Lord. 35 So this is what the Lord has said: Because you have not kept me in your memory, and because your back has been turned to me, you will even undergo the punishment of your evil designs and your loose ways. 36 Then the Lord said to me: Son of man, will you be the judge of Oholibah? then make clear to her the disgusting things she has done 37 For she has been false to me, and blood is on her hands, and with her images she has been untrue; and more than this, she made her sons, whom she had by me, go through the fire to them to be burned up. 38 Further, this is what she has done to me: she has made my holy place unclean and has made my Sabbaths unclean 39 For when she had made an offering of her children to her images, she came into my holy place to make it unclean; see, this is what she has done inside my house. 40 And she even sent for men to come from far away, to whom a servant was sent, and they came: for whom she was washing her body and painting her eyes and making herself fair with ornaments. 41 And she took her seat on a great bed, with a table put ready before it on which she put my perfume and my oil. 42 ... and they put jewels on her hands and beautiful crowns on her head. 43 Then I said ... now she will go on with her loose ways. 44 And they went in to her, as men go to a loose woman: so they went in to Oholibah, the loose woman. 45 And upright men will be her judges, judging her as false wives and women who take lives are judged; because she has been untrue to me and blood is on her hands. 46 For this is what the Lord has said: I will make a great meeting of the people come together against her, and will send on her shaking fear and take everything from her. 47 And the meeting, after stoning her with stones, will put an end to her with their swords; they will put her sons and daughters to death and have her house burned up with fire. 48 And I will put an end to evil in all the land, teaching all women not to do as you have done. 49 And I will send on you the punishment of your evil ways, and you will be rewarded for your sins with your images: and you will be certain that I am the Lord.

24

1 And the word of the Lord came to me in the ninth year, in the tenth month, on the tenth day of the month, saying, 2 Son of man, put down in writing this very day: The king of Babylon let loose the weight of his attack against Jerusalem on this very day. 3 And make a comparison for this uncontrolled people, and say to them, This is what the Lord has said: Put on the cooking-pot, put it on the fire and put water in it: 4 And get the bits together, the fat tail, every good part, the leg and the top part of it: make it full of the best bones. 5 Take the best of the flock, put much wood under it: see that its bits are boiling well; let the bones be cooked inside it. 6 For this is what the Lord has said: A curse is on the town of blood, the cooking-pot which is unclean inside, which has never been made clean! take out its bits; its fate is still to come on it. 7 For her blood is in her; she has put it on the open rock not draining it on to the earth so that it might be covered with dust; 8 In order that it might make wrath come up to give punishment, she has put her blood on the open rock, so that it may not be covered. 9 For this cause the Lord has said: A curse is on the town of blood! and I will make great the burning mass. 10 Put on much wood, heating up the fire, boiling the flesh well, and making the soup thick, and let the bones be burned. 11 And I will put her on the coals so that she may be heated and her brass burned, so that what is unclean in her may become soft and her waste be completely taken away. 12 I have made myself tired to no purpose: still all the waste which is in her has not come out, it has an evil smell. 13 As for your unclean purpose: because I have been attempting to make you clean, but you have not been made clean from it, you will not be made clean till I have let loose my passion on you in full measure. 14 I the Lord have said the word and I will do it; I will not go back or have mercy, and my purpose will not be changed; in the measure of your ways and of your evil doings you will be judged, says the Lord. 15 And the word of the Lord came to me, saying, 16 Son of man, see, I am taking away the desire of your eyes by disease: but let there be no sorrow or weeping or drops running from your eyes. 17 Let there be no sound of sorrow; make no weeping for your dead, put on your head-dress and your shoes on your feet, let not your lips be covered, and do not take the food of those in grief. 18 So in the morning I was teaching the people and in the evening death took my wife; and in the morning I did what I had been ordered to do. 19 And the people said to me, Will you not make clear to us the sense of these things; is it for us you do them? 20 Then I said to them, The word of the Lord came to me, saying, 21 Say to the people of Israel, The Lord has said, See, I will make my holy place unclean, the pride of your strength, the pleasure of your eyes, and the desire of your soul; and your sons and daughters, who did not come with you here, will be put to the sword. 22 And you will do as I have done, not covering your lips or taking the food of those in grief. 23 And your head-dresses will be on your heads and your shoes on your feet: there will be no sorrow or weeping; but you will be wasting away in the punishment of your evil-doing, and you will be looking at one another in wonder. 24 And Ezekiel will be a sign to you; everything he has done you will do: when this takes place, you will be certain that I am the Lord. 25 And as for you, son of man, your mouth will be shut in the day when I take from them their strength, the joy of their glory, the desire of their eyes, and that on which their hearts are fixed, and their sons and daughters. 26 In that day, one who has got away safe will come to you to give you news of it. 27 In that day your mouth will be open to him who has got away safe, and you will say words to him and your lips will no longer be shut: so you will be a sign to them and they will be certain that I am the Lord.

25

1 And the word of the Lord came to me, saying, 2 Son of man, let your face be turned to the children of Ammon, and be a prophet against them: 3 And say to the children of Ammon, Give ear to the word of the Lord; this is what the Lord has said: Because you said, Aha! against my holy place when it was made unclean, and against the land of Israel when it was made waste, and against the people of Judah when they were taken away as prisoners; 4 For this cause I will give you up to the children of the east for their heritage, and they will put their tent-circles in you and make their houses in you; they will take your fruit for their food and your milk for their drink. 5 And I will make Rabbah a place for housing camels, and

the children of Ammon a resting-place for flocks: and you will be certain that I am the Lord. 6 For the
Lord has said, Because you have made sounds of joy with your hands, stamping your feet, and have
been glad, putting shame with all your soul on the land of Israel; 7 For this cause my hand has been
stretched out against you, and I will give up your goods to be taken by the nations; I will have you cut
off from the peoples and will put an end to you among the countries: I will give you up to destruction;
and you will be certain that I am the Lord. 8 This is what the Lord has said: Because Moab and Seir are
saying, See, the people of Judah are like all the nations; 9 For this cause, I will let the side of Moab be
uncovered, and his towns on every side, the glory of the land, Beth-jeshimoth, Baal-meon and as far as
Kiriathaim. 10 To the children of the east I have given her for a heritage, as well as the children of
Ammon, so that there may be no memory of her among the nations: 11 And I will be the judge of
Moab; and they will see that I am the Lord. 12 This is what the Lord has said: Because Edom has taken
his payment from the people of Judah, and has done great wrong in taking payment from them; 13 The
Lord has said, My hand will be stretched out against Edom, cutting off from it man and beast: and I will
make it waste, from Teman even as far as Dedan they will be put to the sword. 14 I will take payment
from Edom because of my people Israel; and I will take Edom in hand in my wrath and in my passion:
and they will have experience of my reward, says the Lord. 15 This is what the Lord has said: Because
the Philistines have taken payment, with the purpose of causing shame and destruction with unending
hate; 16 The Lord has said, See, my hand will be stretched out against the Philistines, cutting off the
Cherethites and sending destruction on the rest of the sea-land. 17 And I will take great payment from
them with acts of wrath; and they will be certain that I am the Lord when I send my punishment on
them.

26

1 Now in the eleventh year, on the first day of the month, the word of the Lord came to me, saying, 2
Son of man, because Tyre has said against Jerusalem, Aha, she who was the doorway of the peoples is
broken; she is turned over to them; she who was full is made waste; 3 For this cause the Lord has said,
See, I am against you, O Tyre, and will send up a number of nations against you as the sea sends up its
waves. 4 And they will give the walls of Tyre to destruction and have its towers broken: and I will take
even her dust away from her, and make her an uncovered rock 5 She will be a place for the stretching
out of nets in the middle of the sea; for I have said it, says the Lord: and her goods will be given over to
the nations. 6 And her daughters in the open country will be put to the sword: and they will be certain
that I am the Lord. 7 For this is what the Lord has said: See, I will send up from the north
Nebuchadrezzar, king of Babylon, king of kings, against Tyre, with horses and war-carriages and with an
army and great numbers of people. 8 He will put to the sword your daughters in the open country: he
will make strong walls against you and put up an earthwork against you, arming himself for war against
you. 9 He will put up his engines of war against your walls, and your towers will be broken down by his
axes. 10 Because of the number of his horses you will be covered with their dust: your walls will be
shaking at the noise of the horsemen and of the wheels and of the war-carriages, when he comes
through your doorways, as into a town which has been broken open. 11 Your streets will be stamped
down by the feet of his horses: he will put your people to the sword, and will send down the pillars of
your strength to the earth. 12 They will take by force all your wealth and go off with the goods with
which you do trade: they will have your walls broken down and all the houses of your desire given up to
destruction: they will put your stones and your wood and your dust deep in the water. 13 I will put an
end to the noise of your songs, and the sound of your instruments of music will be gone for ever. 14 I
will make you an uncovered rock: you will be a place for the stretching out of nets; there will be no
building you up again: for I the Lord have said it, says the Lord. 15 This is what the Lord has said to
Tyre: Will not the sea-lands be shaking at the sound of your fall, when the wounded give cries of pain,
when men are put to the sword in you? 16 Then all the rulers of the sea will come down from their high
seats, and put away their robes and take off their clothing of needlework: they will put on the clothing of
grief, they will take their seats on the earth, shaking with fear every minute and overcome with wonder
at you. 17 And they will send up a song of grief for you, and say to you, What destruction has come on
you, how are you cut off from the sea, the noted town, which was strong in the sea, she and her people,
causing the fear of them to come on all the dry land! 18 Now the sea-lands will be shaking in the day of
your fall; and all the ships on the sea will be overcome with fear at your going. 19 For this is what the
Lord has said: I will make you a waste town, like the towns which are unpeopled; when I make the deep
come upon you, covering you with great waters. 20 Then I will make you go down with those who go
down into the underworld, to the people of the past, causing your living-place to be in the deepest parts
of the earth, in places long unpeopled, with those who go down into the deep, so that there will be no

one living in you; and you will have no glory in the land of the living. 21 I will make you a thing of fear,
and you will come to an end: even if you are looked for, you will not be seen again for ever, says the
Lord.

27

1 The word of the Lord came to me again, saying, 2 And you, son of man, make a song of grief for
Tyre; 3 And say to Tyre, O you who are seated at the doorway of the sea, trading for the peoples with
the great sea-lands, these are the words of the Lord: You, O Tyre, have said, I am a ship completely
beautiful. 4 Your builders have made your outlines in the heart of the seas, they have made you
completely beautiful.5 They have made all your boards of fir-trees from Senir: they have taken cedars
from Lebanon to make the supports for your sails. 6 Of oak-trees from Bashan they have made your
driving blades; they have made your floors of ivory and boxwood from the sea-lands of Kittim. 7 The
best linen with needlework from Egypt was your sail, stretched out to be a flag for you; blue and purple
from the sea-lands of Elishah gave you shade. 8 The people of Zidon and Arvad were your boatmen;
the wise men of Zemer were in you; they were guiding your ships; 9 The responsible men of Gebal and
its wise men were in you, making your boards watertight: all the ships of the sea with their seamen were
in you trading in your goods. 10 Cush and Lud and Put were in your army, your men of war, hanging up
their body-covers and head-dresses of war in you: they gave you your glory. 11 The men of Arvad in
your army were on your walls, and were watchmen in your towers, hanging up their arms on your walls
round about; they made you completely beautiful. 12 Tarshish did business with you because of the
great amount of your wealth; they gave silver, iron, tin, and lead for your goods. 13 Javan, Tubal, and
Meshech were your traders; they gave living men and brass vessels for your goods. 14 The people of
Togarmah gave horses and war-horses and transport beasts for your goods. 15 The men of Rodan were
your traders: a great number of sea-lands did business with you: they gave you horns of ivory and ebony
as an offering. 16 Edom did business with you because of the great number of things which you made;
they gave emeralds, purple, and needlework, and the best linen and coral and rubies for your goods. 17
Judah and the land of Israel were your traders; they gave grain of Minnith and sweet cakes and honey
and oil and perfume for your goods. 18 Damascus did business with you because of the great amount of
your wealth, with wine of Helbon and white wool. 19 ... for your goods: they gave polished iron and
spices for your goods. 20Dedan did trade with you in cloths for the backs of horses. 21 Arabia and all
the rulers of Kedar did business with you; in lambs and sheep and goats, in these they did business with
you. 22 The traders of Sheba and Raamah did trade with you; they gave the best of all sorts of spices
and all sorts of stones of great price and gold for your goods. 23 Haran and Canneh and Eden, the
traders of Asshur and all the Medes: 24 These were your traders in beautiful robes, in rolls of blue and
needlework, and in chests of coloured cloth, corded with cords and made of cedar-wood, in them they
did trade with you. 25 Tarshish ships did business for you in your goods: and you were made full, and
great was your glory in the heart of the seas. 26 Your boatmen have taken you into great waters: you
have been broken by the east wind in the heart of the seas. 27 Your wealth and your goods, the things in
which you do trade, your seamen and those guiding your ships, those who make your boards watertight,
and those who do business with your goods, and all your men of war who are in you, with all who have
come together in you, will go down into the heart of the seas in the day of your downfall. 28 At the
sound of the cry of your ships' guides, the boards of the ship will be shaking. 29 And all the boatmen,
the seamen and those who are expert at guiding a ship through the sea, will come down from their ships
and take their places on the land; 30 And their voices will be sounding over you, and crying bitterly they
will put dust on their heads, rolling themselves in the dust: 31 And they will have the hair of their heads
cut off because of you, and will put haircloth on their bodies, weeping for you with bitter grief in their
souls, even with bitter sorrow. 32 And in their weeping they will make a song of grief for you, sorrowing
over you and saying, Who is like Tyre, who has come to an end in the deep sea? 33 When your goods
went out over the seas, you made numbers of peoples full; the wealth of the kings of the earth was
increased with your great wealth and all your goods. 34 Now that you are broken by the seas in the deep
waters, your goods and all your people will go down with you. 35 All the people of the sea-lands are
overcome with wonder at you, and their kings are full of fear, their faces are troubled. 36 Those who do
business among the peoples make sounds of surprise at you; you have become a thing of fear, you have
come to an end for ever.

28

1 The word of the Lord came to me again, saying, 2 Son of man, say to the ruler of Tyre, This is what

the Lord has said: Because your heart has been lifted up, and you have said, I am a god, I am seated on the seat of God in the heart of the seas; but you are man and not God, though you have made your heart as the heart of God: 3 See, you are wiser than Daniel; there is no secret which is deeper than your knowledge: 4 By your wisdom and deep knowledge you have got power for yourself, and put silver and gold in your store-houses: 5 By your great wisdom and by your trade your power is increased, and your heart is lifted up because of your power: 6 For this cause the Lord has said: Because you have made your heart as the heart of God, 7 See, I am sending against you strange men, feared among the nations: they will let loose their swords against your bright wisdom, they will make your glory a common thing. 8They will send you down to the underworld, and your death will be the death of those who are put to the sword in the heart of the seas. 9 Will you say, in the face of those who are taking your life, I am God? but you are man and not God in the hands of those who are wounding you. 10 Your death will be the death of those who are without circumcision, by the hands of men from strange lands: for I have said it, says the Lord. 11 Then the word of the Lord came to me, saying, 12 Son of man, make a song of grief for the king of Tyre, and say to him, This is what the Lord has said: You are all-wise and completely beautiful; 13 You were in Eden, the garden of God; every stone of great price was your clothing, the sardius, the topaz, and the diamond, the beryl, the onyx, and the jasper, the emerald and the carbuncle: your store-houses were full of gold, and things of great price were in you; in the day when you were made they were got ready. 14 I gave you your place with the winged one; I put you on the mountain of God; you went up and down among the stones of fire. 15 There has been no evil in your ways from the day when you were made, till sin was seen in you. 16 Through all your trading you have become full of violent ways, and have done evil: so I sent you out shamed from the mountain of God; the winged one put an end to you from among the stones of fire. 17 Your heart was lifted up because you were beautiful, you made your wisdom evil through your sin: I have sent you down, even to the earth; I have made you low before kings, so that they may see you. 18 By all your sin, even by your evil trading, you have made your holy places unclean; so I will make a fire come out from you, it will make a meal of you, and I will make you as dust on the earth before the eyes of all who see you. 19 All who have knowledge of you among the peoples will be overcome with wonder at you: you have become a thing of fear, and you will never be seen again. 20 And the word of the Lord came to me, saying, 21 Son of man, let your face be turned to Zidon, and be a prophet against it, and say, 22 These are the words of the Lord: See, I am against you, O Zidon; and I will get glory for myself in you: and they will be certain that I am the Lord, when I send my punishments on her, and I will be seen to be holy in her. 23 And I will send on her disease and blood in her streets; and the wounded will be falling in the middle of her, and the sword will be against her on every side; and they will be certain that I am the Lord. 24 And there will no longer be a plant with sharp points wounding the children of Israel, or a thorn troubling them among any who are round about them, who put shame on them; and they will be certain that I am the Lord. 25 This is what the Lord has said: When I have got together the children of Israel from the peoples among whom they are wandering, and have been made holy among them before the eyes of the nations, then they will have rest in the land which is theirs, which I gave to my servant Jacob 26 And they will be safe there, building houses and planting vine-gardens and living without fear; when I have sent my punishments on all those who put shame on them round about them; and they will be certain that I am the Lord their God.

29

1 In the tenth year, in the tenth month, on the twelfth day of the month, the word of the Lord came to me, saying, 2 Son of man, let your face be turned against Pharaoh, king of Egypt, and be a prophet against him and against all Egypt: 3 Say to them, These are the words of the Lord: See, I am against you, Pharaoh, king of Egypt, the great river-beast stretched out among his Nile streams, who has said, The Nile is mine, and I have made it for myself. 4 And I will put hooks in your mouth, and the fish of your streams will be hanging from your skin; and I will make you come up out of your streams, with all the fish of your streams hanging from your skin. 5 And I will let you be in the waste land, you and all the fish of your streams: you will go down on the face of the land; you will not be taken up or put to rest in the earth; I have given you for food to the beasts of the field and the birds of the heaven. 6 And it will be clear to all the people of Egypt that I am the Lord, because you have been a false support to the children of Israel. 7 When they took a grip of you in their hands, you were crushed so that their arms were broken: and when they put their weight on you for support, you were broken and all their muscles gave way. 8 For this cause the Lord has said: See, I am sending a sword on you, cutting off from you man and beast. 9 And the land of Egypt will be an unpeopled waste; and they will be certain that I am the Lord: because he has said, The Nile is mine, and I made it. 10 See, then, I am against you and against

your streams, and I will make the land of Egypt an unpeopled waste, from Migdol to Syene, even as far as the edge of Ethiopia. 11 No foot of man will go through it and no foot of beast, and it will be unpeopled for forty years. 12 I will make the land of Egypt a waste among the countries which are made waste, and her towns will be unpeopled among the towns which have been made waste, for forty years: and I will send the Egyptians in flight among the nations and wandering through the countries. 13 For this is what the Lord has said: At the end of forty years I will get the Egyptians together from the peoples where they have gone in flight: 14 I will let the fate of Egypt be changed, and will make them come back into the land of Pathros, into the land from which they came; and there they will be an unimportant kingdom. 15 It will be the lowest of the kingdoms, and never again will it be lifted up over the nations: I will make them small, so that they may not have rule over the nations. 16 And Egypt will no longer be the hope of the children of Israel, causing sin to come to mind when their eyes are turned to them: and they will be certain that I am the Lord. 17 Now in the twenty-seventh year, in the first month, on the first day of the month, the word of the Lord came to me, saying, 18 Son of man, Nebuchadrezzar, king of Babylon, made his army do hard work against Tyre, and the hair came off every head and every arm was rubbed smooth: but he and his army got no payment out of Tyre for the hard work which he had done against it. 19 For this cause the Lord has said: See, I am giving the land of Egypt to Nebuchadrezzar, king of Babylon: he will take away her wealth, and take her goods by force and everything which is there; and this will be the payment for his army. 20 I have given him the land of Egypt as the reward for his hard work, because they were working for me, says the Lord. 21 In that day I will make a horn put out buds for the children of Israel, and I will let your words come freely among them, and they will be certain that I am the Lord.

30

1 The word of the Lord came to me again, saying, 2 Son of man, be a prophet, and say, These are the words of the Lord: Give a cry, Aha, for the day! 3 For the day is near, the day of the Lord is near, a day of cloud; it will be the time of the nations. 4 And a sword will come on Egypt, and cruel pain will be in Ethiopia, when they are falling by the sword in Egypt; and they will take away her wealth and her bases will be broken down. 5 Ethiopia and Put and Lud and all the mixed people and Libya and the children of the land of the Cherethites will all be put to death with them by the sword. 6 This is what the Lord has said: The supporters of Egypt will have a fall, and the pride of her power will come down: from Migdol to Syene they will be put to the sword in it, says the Lord. 7 And she will be made waste among the countries which have been made waste, and her towns will be among the towns which are unpeopled. 8 And they will be certain that I am the Lord, when I have put a fire in Egypt and all her helpers are broken. 9 In that day men will go out quickly to take the news, causing fear in untroubled Ethiopia; and bitter pain will come on them as in the day of Egypt; for see, it is coming. 10 This is what the Lord has said: I will put an end to great numbers of the people of Egypt by the hand of Nebuchadrezzar, king of Babylon. 11 He and the people with him, causing fear among the nations, will be sent for the destruction of the land; their swords will be let loose against Egypt and the land will be full of dead. 12 And I will make the Nile streams dry, and will give the land into the hands of evil men, causing the land and everything in it to be wasted by the hands of men from a strange country: I the Lord have said it. 13 This is what the Lord has said: In addition to this, I will give up the images to destruction and put an end to the false gods in Noph; never again will there be a ruler in the land of Egypt: and I will put a fear in the land of Egypt. 14 And I will make Pathros a waste, and put a fire in Zoan, and send my punishments on No. 15 I will let loose my wrath on Sin, the strong place of Egypt, cutting off the mass of the people of No. 16 And I will put a fire in Egypt; Syene will be twisting in pain, and No will be broken into, as by the onrush of waters. 17 The young men of On and Pi-beseth will be put to the sword: and these towns will be taken away prisoners. 18 And at Tehaphnehes the day will become dark, when the yoke of Egypt is broken there, and the pride of her power comes to an end: as for her, she will be covered with a cloud, and her daughters will be taken away prisoners. 19 And I will send my punishments on Egypt: and they will be certain that I am the Lord. 20 Now in the eleventh year, in the first month, on the seventh day of the month, the word of the Lord came to me, saying, 21 Son of man, the arm of Pharaoh, king of Egypt, has been broken by me, and no band has been put round it to make it well, no band has been twisted round it to make it strong for gripping the sword. 22 For this cause the Lord has said: See, I am against Pharaoh, king of Egypt, and by me his strong arm will be broken; and I will make the sword go out of his hand. 23 And I will send the Egyptians in flight among the nations and wandering through the countries. 24 And I will make the arms of the king of Babylon strong, and will put my sword in his hand: but Pharaoh's arms will be broken, and he will give cries of pain before him like the cries of a man wounded to death. 25 And I will make the arms of the

king of Babylon strong, and the arms of Pharaoh will be hanging down; and they will be certain that I
am the Lord, when I put my sword into the hand of the king of Babylon and it is stretched out against
the land of Egypt. 26 And I will send the Egyptians in flight among the nations and wandering through
the countries; and they will be certain that I am the Lord.

31

1 Now in the eleventh year, in the third month, on the first day of the month, the word of the Lord
came to me, saying, 2 Son of man, say to Pharaoh, king of Egypt, and to his people; Whom are you like
in your great power? 3 See, a pine-tree with beautiful branches and thick growth, giving shade and very
tall; and its top was among the clouds. 4 It got strength from the waters and the deep made it tall: its
streams went round about its planted land and it sent out its waterways to all the trees of the field. 5 In
this way it became taller than all the trees of the field; and its branches were increased and its arms
became long because of the great waters. 6 In its branches all the birds of heaven came to rest, and
under its arms all the beasts of the field gave birth to their young, and great nations were living in its
shade. 7 So it was beautiful, being so tall and its branches so long, for its root was by great waters. 8 No
cedars were equal to it in the garden of God; the fir-trees were not like its branches, and plane-trees
were as nothing in comparison with its arms; no tree in the garden of God was so beautiful. 9 I made it
beautiful with its mass of branches: so that all the trees in the garden of God were full of envy of it. 10
For this cause the Lord has said: Because he is tall, and has put his top among the clouds, and his heart
is full of pride because he is so high, 11 I have given him up into the hands of a strong one of the
nations; he will certainly give him the reward of his sin, driving him out. 12 And men from strange
lands, who are to be feared among the nations, after cutting him off, have let him be: on the mountains
and in all the valleys his branches have come down; his arms are broken by all the waterways of the land;
all the peoples of the earth have gone from his shade, and have let him be. 13 All the birds of heaven
have come to rest on his broken stem where it is stretched on the earth, and all the beasts of the field
will be on his branches: 14 In order that no trees by the waters may be lifted up in their growth, putting
their tops among the clouds; and that no trees which are watered may take their place on high: for they
are all given up to death, to the lowest parts of the earth among the children of men, with those who go
down to the underworld. 15 This is what the Lord has said: The day when he goes down to the
underworld, I will make the deep full of grief for him; I will keep back her streams and the great waters
will be stopped: I will make Lebanon dark for him, and all the trees of the field will be feeble because of
him. 16 I will send shaking on the nations at the sound of his fall, when I send him down to the
underworld with those who go down into the deep: and on earth they will be comforting themselves, all
the trees of Eden, the best of Lebanon, even all the watered ones. 17 And they will go down with him to
the underworld, to those who have been put to the sword; even those who were his helpers, living under
his shade among the nations 18 Whom then are you like? for you will be sent down with the trees of
Eden into the lowest parts of the earth: there you will be stretched out among those without
circumcision, with those who were put to the sword. This is Pharaoh and all his people, says the Lord.

32

1 And it came about in the twelfth year, in the twelfth month, on the first day of the month, that the
word of the Lord came to me, saying, 2 Son of man, make a song of grief for Pharaoh, king of Egypt,
and say to him, Young lion of the nations, destruction has come on you; and you were like a sea-beast in
the seas, sending out bursts of water, troubling the waters with your feet, making their streams dirty. 3
This is what the Lord has said: My net will be stretched out over you, and I will take you up in my
fishing-net. 4 And I will let you be stretched on the land; I will send you out violently into the open
field; I will let all the birds of heaven come to rest on you and will make the beasts of all the earth full of
you. 5 And I will put your flesh on the mountains, and make the valleys full of your blood. 6 And the
land will be watered with your blood, and the waterways will be full of you. 7 And when I put out your
life, the heaven will be covered and its stars made dark; I will let the sun be covered with a cloud and the
moon will not give her light. 8 All the bright lights of heaven I will make dark over you, and put dark
night on your land, says the Lord. 9 And the hearts of numbers of peoples will be troubled, when I send
your prisoners among the nations, into a country which is strange to you. 10 And I will make a number
of peoples overcome with wonder at you, and their kings will be full of fear because of you, when my
sword is waved before them: they will be shaking every minute, every man fearing for his life, in the day
of your fall. 11 For this is what the Lord has said: The sword of the king of Babylon will come on you.
12 I will let the swords of the strong be the cause of the fall of your people; all of them men to be feared

among the nations: and they will make waste the pride of Egypt, and all its people will come to destruction. 13 And I will put an end to all her beasts which are by the great waters, and they will never again be troubled by the foot of man or by the feet of beasts. 14 Then I will make their waters clear and their rivers will be flowing like oil, says the Lord. 15 When I make Egypt an unpeopled waste, cutting off from the land all the things in it; when I send punishment on all those living in it, then it will be clear to them that I am the Lord. 16 It is a song of grief, and people will give voice to it, the daughters of the nations will give voice to it, even for Egypt and all her people, says the Lord. 17 And in the twelfth year, on the fifteenth day of the month, the word of the Lord came to me, saying, 18 Son of man, let your voice be loud in sorrow for the people of Egypt and send them down, even you and the daughters of the nations; I will send them down into the lowest parts of the earth, with those who go down into the underworld. 19 Are you more beautiful than any? go down, and take your rest among those without circumcision, 20 Among those who have been put to the sword: they will give a resting-place with them to all their people. 21 The strong among the great ones will say to him from the underworld, Are you more beautiful than any? go down, you and your helpers, and take your rest among those without circumcision, and those who have been put to the sword. 22 There is Asshur and all her army, round about her last resting-place: all of them put to death by the sword: 23 Whose resting-places are in the inmost parts of the underworld, who were a cause of fear in the land of the living. 24 There is Elam and all her people, round about her last resting-place: all of them put to death by the sword, who have gone down without circumcision into the lowest parts of the earth, who were a cause of fear in the land of the living, and are put to shame with those who go down to the underworld: 25 They have made a bed for her among the dead, and all her people are round about her resting-place: all of them without circumcision, put to death with the sword; for they were a cause of fear in the land of the living, and are put to shame with those who go down to the underworld: they have been given a place among those who have been put to the sword. 26 There is Meshech, Tubal, and all her people, round about her last resting-place: all of them without circumcision, put to death by the sword; for they were a cause of fear in the land of the living. 27 And they have been put to rest with the fighting men who came to their end in days long past, who went down to the underworld with their instruments of war, placing their swords under their heads, and their body-covers are over their bones; for their strength was a cause of fear in the land of the living. 28 But you will have your bed among those without circumcision, and will be put to rest with those who have been put to death with the sword. 29 There is Edom, her kings and all her princes, who have been given a resting-place with those who were put to the sword: they will be resting among those without circumcision, even with those who go down to the underworld. 30 There are the chiefs of the north, all of them, and all the Zidonians, who have gone down with those who have been put to the sword: they are shamed on account of all the fear caused by their strength; they are resting there without circumcision, among those who have been put to the sword, and are put to shame with those who go down to the underworld. 31 Pharaoh will see them and be comforted on account of all his people: even Pharaoh and all his army, put to death by the sword, says the Lord. 32 For he put his fear in the land of the living: and he will be put to rest among those without circumcision, with those who have been put to death with the sword, even Pharaoh and all his people, says the Lord.

33

1 And the word of the Lord came to me, saying, 2 Son of man, give a word to the children of your people, and say to them, When I make the sword come on a land, if the people of the land take a man from among their number and make him their watchman: 3 If, when he sees the sword coming on the land, by sounding the horn he gives the people news of their danger; 4 Then anyone who, hearing the sound of the horn, does not take note of it, will himself be responsible for his death, if the sword comes and takes him away. 5 On hearing the sound of the horn, he did not take note; his blood will be on him; for if he had taken note his life would have been safe. 6 But if the watchman sees the sword coming, and does not give a note on the horn, and the people have no word of the danger, and the sword comes and takes any person from among them; he will be taken away in his sin, but I will make the watchman responsible for his blood. 7 So you, son of man, I have made you a watchman for the children of Israel; and you are to give ear to the word of my mouth and give them news from me of their danger. 8 When I say to the evil-doer, Death will certainly overtake you; and you say nothing to make clear to the evil-doer the danger of his way; death will overtake that evil man in his evil-doing, but I will make you responsible for his blood. 9 But if you make clear to the evil-doer the danger of his way for the purpose of turning him from it, and he is not turned from his way, death will overtake him in his evil-doing, but your life will be safe. 10 And you, son of man, say to the children of Israel, You say, Our wrongdoing and our sins are on us and we are wasting away in them; how then may we have life? 11 Say to them, By

my life, says the Lord, I have no pleasure in the death of the evil-doer; it is more pleasing to me if he is
turned from his way and has life: be turned, be turned from your evil ways; why are you looking for
death, O children of Israel? 12 And you, son of man, say to the children of your people, The
righteousness of the upright man will not make him safe in the day when he does wrong; and the evil-
doing of the evil man will not be the cause of his fall in the day when he is turned from his evil-doing;
and the upright man will not have life because of his righteousness in the day when he does evil. 13
When I say to the upright that life will certainly be his; if he puts his faith in his righteousness and does
evil, not one of his upright acts will be kept in memory; but in the evil he has done, death will overtake
him. 14 And when I say to the evil-doer, Death will certainly be your fate; if he is turned from his sin
and does what is ordered and right; 15 If the evil-doer lets one who is in his debt have back what is his,
and gives back what he had taken by force, and is guided by the rules of life, doing no evil; life will
certainly be his, death will not overtake him. 16 Not one of the sins which he has done will be kept in
mind against him: he has done what is ordered and right, life will certainly be his. 17 But the children of
your people say, The way of the Lord is not equal: when it is they whose way is not equal. 18 When the
upright man, turning away from his righteousness, does evil, death will overtake him in it. 19 And when
the evil man, turning away from his evil-doing, does what is ordered and right, he will get life by it. 20
And still you say, The way of the Lord is not equal. O children of Israel, I will be your judge, giving to
everyone the reward of his ways. 21 Now in the twelfth year after we had been taken away prisoners, in
the tenth month, on the fifth day of the month, one who had got away in flight from Jerusalem came to
me, saying, The town has been taken. 22 Now the hand of the Lord had been on me in the evening,
before the man who had got away came to me; and he made my mouth open, ready for his coming to
me in the morning; and my mouth was open and I was no longer without voice. 23 And the word of the
Lord came to me, saying, 24 Son of man, those who are living in these waste places in the land of Israel
say, Abraham was but one, and he had land for his heritage: but we are a great number; the land is given
to us for our heritage. 25 For this cause say to them, This is what the Lord has said: You take your meat
with the blood, your eyes are lifted up to your images, and you are takers of life: are you to have the land
for your heritage? 26 You put your faith in your swords, you do disgusting things, everyone takes his
neighbour's wife: are you to have the land for your heritage? 27 This is what you are to say to them: The
Lord has said, By my life, truly, those who are in the waste places will be put to the sword, and him who
is in the open field I will give to the beasts for their food, and those who are in the strong places and in
holes in the rocks will come to their death by disease. 28 And I will make the land a waste and a cause of
wonder, and the pride of her strength will come to an end; and the mountains of Israel will be made
waste so that no one will go through. 29 Then they will be certain that I am the Lord, when I have made
the land a waste and a cause of wonder, because of all the disgusting things which they have done, 30
And as for you, son of man, the children of your people are talking together about you by the walls and
in the doorways of the houses, saying to one another, Come now, give ear to the word which comes
from the Lord. 31 And they come to you as my people come, and are seated before you as my people,
hearing your words but doing them not: for deceit is in their mouth and their heart goes after profit for
themselves. 32 And truly you are to them like a love song by one who has a very pleasing voice and is an
expert player on an instrument: for they give ear to your words but do them not. 33 And when this
comes about (see, it is coming), then it will be clear to them that a prophet has been among them.

34

1 And the word of the Lord came to me, saying, 2 Son of man, be a prophet against the keepers of the
flock of Israel, and say to them, O keepers of the sheep! this is the word of the Lord: A curse is on the
keepers of the flock of Israel who take the food for themselves! is it not right for the keepers to give the
food to the sheep? 3 You take the milk and are clothed with the wool, you put the fat beasts to death,
but you give the sheep no food. 4 You have not made the diseased ones strong or made well that which
was ill; you have not put bands on the broken or got back that which had been sent away or made
search for the wandering ones; and the strong you have been ruling cruelly. 5 And they were wandering
in every direction because there was no keeper: and they became food for all the beasts of the field. 6
And my sheep went out of the way, wandering through all the mountains and on every high hill: my
sheep went here and there over all the face of the earth; and no one was troubled about them or went in
search of them. 7 For this cause, O keepers of the flock, give ear to the word of the Lord: 8 By my life,
says the Lord, truly, because my sheep have been taken away, and my sheep became food for all the
beasts of the field, because there was no keeper, and my keepers did not go in search of the sheep, but
the keepers took food for themselves and gave my sheep no food; 9 For this reason, O you keepers of
the flock, give ear to the word of the Lord; 10 This is what the Lord has said: See I am against the

keepers of the flock, and I will make search and see what they have done with my sheep, and will let
them be keepers of my sheep no longer; and the keepers will no longer get food for themselves; I will
take my sheep out of their mouths so that they may not be food for them. 11 For this is what the Lord
has said: Truly, I, even I, will go searching and looking for my sheep. 12 As the keeper goes looking for
his flock when he is among his wandering sheep, so I will go looking for my sheep, and will get them
safely out of all the places where they have been sent wandering in the day of clouds and black night. 13
And I will take them out from among the peoples, and get them together from the countries, and will
take them into their land; and I will give them food on the mountains of Israel by the water-streams and
wherever men are living in the country. 14 I will give them good grass-land for their food, and their safe
place will be the mountains of the high place of Israel: there they will take their rest in a good place, and
on fat grass-land they will take their food on the mountains of Israel. 15 I myself will give food to my
flock, and I will give them rest, says the Lord. 16 I will go in search of that which had gone wandering
from the way, and will get back that which had been sent in flight, and will put bands on that which was
broken, and give strength to that which was ill: but the fat and the strong I will give up to destruction; I
will give them for their food the punishment which is theirs by right. 17 And as for you, O my flock,
says the Lord, truly, I will be judge between sheep and sheep, the he-sheep and the he-goats. 18 Does it
seem a small thing to you to have taken your food on good grass-land while the rest of your grass-land is
stamped down under your feet? and that after drinking from clear waters you make the rest of the
waters dirty with your feet? 19 And as for my sheep, their food is the grass which has been stamped on
by your feet, and their drink the water which has been made dirty by your feet. 20 For this reason the
Lord has said to them, Truly, I, even I, will be judge between the fat sheep and the thin sheep. 21
Because you have been pushing with side and leg, pushing the diseased with your horns till they were
sent away in every direction; 22 I will make my flock safe, and they will no longer be taken away, and I
will be judge between sheep and sheep. 23 And I will put over them one keeper, and he will give them
food, even my servant David; he will give them food and be their keeper. 24 And I the Lord will be their
God and my servant David their ruler; I the Lord have said it. 25 And I will make with them an
agreement of peace, and will put an end to evil beasts through all the land: and they will be living safely
in the waste land, sleeping in the woods. 26 And I will give the rain at the right time, and I will make the
shower come down at the right time; there will be showers of blessing. 27 And the tree of the field will
give its fruit and the earth will give its increase, and they will be safe in their land; and they will be certain
that I am the Lord, when I have had their yoke broken and have given them salvation from the hands of
those who made them servants. 28 And their goods will no longer be taken by the nations, and they will
not again be food for the beasts of the earth; but they will be living safely and no one will be a cause of
fear to them. 29 And I will give them planting-places of peace, and they will no longer be wasted from
need of food or put to shame by the nations. 30 And they will be certain that I the Lord their God am
with them, and that they, the children of Israel, are my people, says the Lord. 31 And you are my sheep,
the sheep of my grass-lands, and I am your God, says the Lord.

35

1 Then the word of the Lord came to me, saying, 2 Son of man, let your face be turned to Mount Seir,
and be a prophet against it, 3 And say to it, This is what the Lord has said: See, I am against you, O
Mount Seir, and my hand will be stretched out against you, and I will make you a waste and a cause for
wonder. 4 I will make your towns unpeopled and you will be a waste; and you will be certain that I am
the Lord. 5 Because yours has been a hate without end, and you have given up the children of Israel to
the power of the sword in the time of their trouble, in the time of the punishment of the end: 6 For this
cause, by my life, says the Lord, because you have been sinning through blood, blood will come after
you. 7 And I will make Mount Seir a cause for wonder and a waste, cutting off from it all comings and
goings. 8 I will make his mountains full of those who have been put to death; in your valleys and in all
your water-streams men will be falling by the sword. 9 I will make you waste for ever, and your towns
will be unpeopled: and you will be certain that I am the Lord. 10 Because you have said, The two
nations and the two countries are to be mine, and we will take them for our heritage; though the Lord
was there: 11 For this cause, by my life, says the Lord, I will do to you as you have done in your wrath
and in your envy, which you have made clear in your hate for them; and I will make clear to you who I
am when you are judged by me. 12 And you will see that I the Lord have had knowledge of all the bitter
things which you have said against the mountains of Israel, saying, They have been made waste, they are
given to us to take for our heritage. 13 And you have made yourselves great against me with your
mouths, increasing your words against me; and it has come to my ears. 14 This is what the Lord has
said: Because you were glad over my land when it was a waste, so will I do to you: 15 You will become a

waste, O Mount Seir, and all Edom, even all of it: and you will be certain that I am the Lord.

36

1 And you, son of man, be a prophet about the mountains of Israel, and say, You mountains of Israel,
give ear to the word of the Lord: 2 This is what the Lord has said: Because your hater has said against
you, Aha! and, The old waste places are our heritage, we have taken them: 3 For this cause be a prophet,
and say, This is what the Lord has said: Because, even because they have been glad over you and put you
to shame on every side, because you have become a heritage for the rest of the nations, and you are
taken up on the lips of talkers and in the evil talk of the people: 4 For this reason, you mountains of
Israel, give ear to the word of the Lord; this is what the Lord has said to the mountains and to the hills,
to the streams and to the valleys, to the unpeopled wastes and to the towns where no one is living, from
which the goods have been taken and which have been put to shame by the rest of the nations who are
round about: 5 For this cause the Lord has said: Truly, in the heat of my bitter feeling I have said things
against the rest of the nations and against all Edom, who have taken my land as a heritage for
themselves with the joy of all their heart, and with bitter envy of soul have made attacks on it: 6 For this
cause be a prophet about the land of Israel, and say to the mountains and to the hills, to the streams and
to the valleys, This is what the Lord has said: Truly, in my bitter feeling and in my wrath I have said
these things, because you have undergone the shame of the nations: 7 For this cause the Lord has said,
See, I have taken an oath that the nations which are round about you are themselves to undergo the
shame which they have put on you. 8 But you, O mountains of Israel, will put out your branches and
give your fruit to my people Israel; for they are ready to come. 9 For truly I am for you, and I will be
turned to you, and you will be ploughed and planted: 10 And I will let your numbers be increased, all the
children of Israel, even all of them: and the towns will be peopled and the waste places will have
buildings; 11 Man and beast will be increased in you, and they will have offspring and be fertile: I will
make you thickly peopled as you were before, and will do more for you than at the first: and you will be
certain that I am the Lord. 12 Yes, I will have you walked on by the feet of men, even my people Israel;
they will have you for a heritage and you will be theirs, and never again will you take their children from
them. 13 This is what the Lord has said: Because they say to you, You, O land, are the destruction of
men, causing loss of children to your nation; 14 For this reason you will no longer take the lives of men
and will never again be the cause of loss of children to your nation, says the Lord. 15 And I will not let
the shaming of the nations come to your ears, and no longer will you be looked down on by the peoples,
says the Lord. 16 Then the word of the Lord came to me, saying, 17 Son of man, when the children of
Israel were living in their land, they made it unclean by their way and their acts: their way before me was
as when a woman is unclean at the time when she is kept separate. 18 So I let loose my wrath on them
because of those whom they had violently put to death in the land, and because they had made it
unclean with their images: 19 And I sent them in flight among the nations and wandering through the
countries: I was their judge, rewarding them for their way and their acts. 20 And when they came among
the nations, wherever they went, they made my holy name unclean, when it was said of them, These are
the people of the Lord who have gone out from his land. 21 But I had pity for my holy name which the
children of Israel had made unclean wherever they went. 22 For this cause say to the children of Israel,
This is what the Lord has said: I am doing this, not because of you, O children of Israel, but because of
my holy name, which you have made unclean among the nations wherever you went. 23And I will make
holy my great name which has been made unclean among the nations, which you have made unclean
among them; and it will be clear to the nations that I am the Lord, says the Lord, when I make myself
holy in you before their eyes. 24 For I will take you out from among the nations, and get you together
from all the countries, and take you into your land. 25 And I will put clean water on you so that you may
be clean: from all your unclean ways and from all your images I will make you clean. 26 And I will give
you a new heart and put a new spirit in you: I will take away the heart of stone from your flesh, and give
you a heart of flesh. 27 And I will put my spirit in you, causing you to be guided by my rules, and you
will keep my orders and do them. 28 So that you may go on living in the land which I gave to your
fathers; and you will be to me a people, and I will be to you a God. 29 And I will make you free from all
your unclean ways: and at my voice the grain will come up and be increased, and I will not let you be
short of food. 30 And I will make the tree give more fruit and the field fuller produce, and no longer will
you be shamed among the nations for need of food. 31 And at the memory of your evil ways and your
wrongdoings, you will have bitter hate for yourselves because of your evil-doings and your disgusting
ways, O children of Israel. 32 Not because of you am I doing it, says the Lord; let it be clear to you, and
be shamed and made low because of your ways, O children of Israel. 33 This is what the Lord has said:
In the day when I make you clean from all your evil-doings I will let the towns be peopled and there will

be building on the waste places. 34 And the land which was waste will be farmed, in place of being a
waste in the eyes of everyone who went by. 35 And they will say, This land which was waste has become
like the garden of Eden; and the towns which were unpeopled and wasted and pulled down are walled
and peopled. 36 Then the rest of the nations round about you will be certain that I the Lord am the
builder of the places which were pulled down and the planter of that which was waste: I the Lord have
said it, and I will do it. 37 This is what the Lord has said: The children of Israel will again make prayer to
me for this, that I may do it for them; I will make them increased with men like a flock. 38 Like sheep
for the offerings, like the sheep of Jerusalem at her fixed feasts, so the unpeopled towns will be made
full of men: and they will be certain that I am the Lord.

37

1 The hand of the Lord had been on me, and he took me out in the spirit of the Lord and put me down
in the middle of the valley; and it was full of bones; 2 And he made me go past them round about: and I
saw that there was a very great number of them on the face of the wide valley, and they were very dry. 3
And he said to me, Son of man, is it possible for these bones to come to life? And I made answer, and
said, It is for you to say, O Lord. 4 And again he said to me, Be a prophet to these bones, and say to
them, O you dry bones, give ear to the word of the Lord. 5 This is what the Lord has said to these
bones: See, I will make breath come into you so that you may come to life; 6 And I will put muscles on
you and make flesh come on you, and put skin over you, and breath into you, so that you may have life;
and you will be certain that I am the Lord. 7 So I gave the word as I was ordered: and at my words there
was a shaking of the earth, and the bones came together, bone to bone. 8 And looking I saw that there
were muscles on them and flesh came up, and they were covered with skin: but there was no breath in
them. 9 And he said to me, Be a prophet to the wind, be a prophet, son of man, and say to the wind,
The Lord has said: Come from the four winds, O wind, breathing on these dead so that they may come
to life. 10 And I gave the word at his orders, and breath came into them, and they came to life and got
up on their feet, a very great army. 11 Then he said to me, Son of man, these bones are all the children
of Israel: and see, they are saying, Our bones have become dry our hope is gone, we are cut off
completely. 12 For this cause be a prophet to them, and say, This is what the Lord has said: See, I am
opening the resting-places of your dead, and I will make you come up out of your resting-places, O my
people; and I will take you into the land of Israel. 13 And you will be certain that I am the Lord by my
opening the resting-places of your dead and making you come up out of your resting-places, O my
people. 14 And I will put my spirit in you, so that you may come to life, and I will give you a rest in your
land: and you will be certain that I the Lord have said it and have done it, says the Lord. 15 And the
word of the Lord came to me, saying, 16 And you, son of man, take one stick, writing on it, For Judah
and for the children of Israel who are in his company: then take another stick, writing on it, For Joseph,
the stick of Ephraim, and all the children of Israel who are in his company: 17 Then, joining them one
to another, make them one stick, so that they may be one in your hand. 18 And when the children of
your people say to you, Will you not make clear to us what these things have to do with us? 19 Then say
to them, This is what the Lord has said: See, I am taking the stick of Joseph, which is in the hand of
Ephraim, and the tribes of Israel who are in his company; and I will put it on the stick of Judah and
make them one stick, and they will be one in my hand.20 And the sticks with your writing on them will
be in your hand before their eyes. 21 And say to them, These are the words of the Lord: See, I am taking
the children of Israel from among the nations where they have gone, and will get them together on
every side, and take them into their land: 22 And I will make them one nation in the land, on the
mountains of Israel; and one king will be king over them all: and they will no longer be two nations, and
will no longer be parted into two kingdoms: 23 And they will no longer make themselves unclean with
their images or with their hated things or with any of their sins: but I will give them salvation from all
their turning away in which they have done evil, and will make them clean; and they will be to me a
people, and I will be to them a God. 24 And my servant David will be king over them; and they will all
have one keeper: and they will be guided by my orders and will keep my rules and do them. 25 And they
will be living in the land which I gave to Jacob, my servant, in which your fathers were living; and they
will go on living there, they and their children and their children's children, for ever: and David, my
servant, will be their ruler for ever. 26 And I will make an agreement of peace with them: it will be an
eternal agreement with them: and I will have mercy on them and make their numbers great, and will put
my holy place among them for ever. 27 And my House will be over them; and I will be to them a God,
and they will be to me a people. 28 And the nations will be certain that I who make Israel holy am the
Lord, when my holy place is among them for ever.

38

1 And the word of the Lord came to me, saying, 2 Son of man, let your face be turned against Gog, of
the land of Magog, the ruler of Rosh, Meshech, and Tubal, and be a prophet against him, 3 And say,
This is what the Lord has said: See, I am against you, O Gog, ruler of Rosh, Meshech, and Tubal: 4 And
turning you round, I will put hooks in your mouth and make you come out with all your army, horses
and horsemen, all of them in full war-dress, a great force with breastplate and body-cover, all of them
armed with swords: 5 Persia, Cush, and Put with them; all of them with body-cover and metal head-
dress: 6Gomer and all her forces; the people of Togarmah in the inmost parts of the north, with all his
forces: a great number of peoples with you. 7 Be ready, make yourself ready, you and all the forces who
are with you, and be ready for my orders. 8 After a long time you will get your orders: in the last years
you will come into the land which has been given back from the sword, which has been got together out
of a great number of peoples, on the mountains of Israel which have ever been a waste: but it has been
taken out from the peoples and they will be living, all of them, without fear of danger. 9 And you will go
up, you will come like a storm, you will be like a cloud covering the land, you and all your forces, and a
great number of peoples with you. 10 This is what the Lord has said: In that day it will come about that
things will come into your mind, and you will have thoughts of an evil design: 11 And you will say, I will
go up to the land of small unwalled towns; I will go to those who are quiet, living, all of them, without
fear of danger, without walls or locks or doors: 12 To take their property by force and go off with their
goods; turning your hand against the waste places which now are peopled, and against the people who
have been got together out of the nations, who have got cattle and goods for themselves, who are living
in the middle of the earth. 13Sheba, and Dedan and her traders, Tarshish with all her traders, will say to
you, Have you come to take our goods? have you got your armies together to take away our property by
force? to take away silver and gold, cattle and goods, to go off with great wealth? 14 For this cause, son
of man, be a prophet and say to Gog, These are the words of the Lord: In that day, when my people
Israel are living without fear of danger, will you not be moved against them? 15 And you will come from
your place in the inmost parts of the north, you and a great number of peoples with you, all of them on
horseback, a great force and a strong army: 16 And you will come up against my people Israel, like a
cloud covering the land; and it will come about, in the last days, that I will make you come against my
land, so that the nations may have knowledge of me when I make myself holy in you, O Gog, before
their eyes. 17 This is what the Lord has said: You are he of whom I gave them word in earlier times by
my servants, the prophets of Israel, who in those days went on saying, year after year, that I would make
you come up against them. 18 And it will come about in that day, when Gog comes up against the land
of Israel, says the Lord, that my wrath will come up, and my passion and my bitter feeling. 19 For in the
fire of my wrath I have said, Truly, in that day there will be a great shaking in the land of Israel; 20 So
that the fish of the sea and the birds of heaven and the beasts of the field and everything moving on the
earth, and all the men who are on the face of the earth, will be shaking before me, and the mountains
will be overturned and the high places will come down, and every wall will come falling down to the
earth. 21 And I will send to all my mountains for a sword against him, says the Lord: every man's sword
will be against his brother. 22 And I will take up my cause against him with disease and with blood; and
I will send down on him and on his forces and on the peoples who are with him, an overflowing shower
and great ice-drops, fire, and burning. 23 And I will make my name great and make myself holy, and I
will make myself clear to a number of nations; and they will be certain that I am the Lord.

39

1 And you, son of man, be a prophet against Gog, and say, These are the words of the Lord: See, I am
against you, O Gog, ruler of Rosh, Meshech, and Tubal: 2 And turning you round, I will be your guide,
and make you come up from the inmost parts of the north; I will make you come on to the mountains
of Israel:3 And with a blow I will send your bow out of your left hand and your arrows falling from your
right hand. 4 On the mountains of Israel you will come down, you and all your forces and the peoples
who are with you: I will give you to cruel birds of every sort and to the beasts of the field to be their
food. 5 You will come down in the open field: for I have said it, says the Lord. 6 And I will send a fire
on Magog, and on those who are living in the sea-lands without fear: and they will be certain that I am
the Lord. 7 And I will make clear my holy name among my people Israel; I will no longer let my holy
name be made unclean: and the nations will be certain that I am the Lord, the Holy One in Israel. 8 See,
it is coming and it will be done, says the Lord; this is the day of which I have given word. 9 And those
who are living in the towns of Israel will go out and make fires of the instruments of war, burning the
body-covers and the breastplates, the bows and the arrows and the sticks and the spears, and for seven

years they will make fires of them: 10And they will take no wood out of the field or have any cut down in the woods; for they will make their fires of the instruments of war: and they will take by force the property of those who took their property, and go off with the goods of those who took their goods, says the Lord. 11 And it will come about in those days, that I will give to Gog a last resting-place there in Israel, in the valley of Abarim on the east of the sea: and those who go through will be stopped: and there Gog and all his people will be put to rest, and the place will be named, The valley of Hamon-gog. 12 And the children of Israel will be seven months putting them in the earth, so as to make the land clean. 13 And all the people of the land will put them in the earth; and it will be to their honour in the day when I let my glory be seen, says the Lord. 14 And they will put on one side men to do no other work but to go through the land and put in the earth the rest of those who are still on the face of the land, to make it clean: after seven months are ended they are to make a search. 15And while they go through the land, if anyone sees a man's bone, he is to put up a sign by the place till those who are doing the work have put it in the earth in the valley of Hamon-gog. 16 And there they will put all the army of Gog in the earth. So they will make the land clean. 17 And you, son of man, this is what the Lord has said: Say to the birds of every sort and to all the beasts of the field, Get together and come; come together on every side to the offering which I am putting to death for you, a great offering on the mountains of Israel, so that you may have flesh for your food and blood for your drink. 18 The flesh of the men of war will be your food, and your drink the blood of the princes of the earth, of sheep and lambs, of he-goats, of oxen, all of them fat beasts of Bashan. 19 You will go on feasting on the fat till you are full, and drinking the blood till you are overcome with it, of my offering which I have put to death for you. 20 At my table you will have food in full measure, horses and war-carriages, great men and all the men of war, says the Lord. 21 And I will put my glory among the nations, and all the nations will see my punishments which I have put into effect, and my hand which I have put on them. 22 So the children of Israel will be certain that I am the Lord their God, from that day and for the future. 23 And it will be clear to the nations that the children of Israel were taken away prisoners for their evil-doing; because they did wrong against me, and my face was covered from them: so I gave them up into the hands of their attackers, and they all came to their end by the sword. 24 In the measure of their unclean ways and their sins, so I did to them; and I kept my face covered from them. 25 For this cause the Lord has said, Now I will let the fate of Jacob be changed, and I will have mercy on all the children of Israel, and will take care of the honour of my holy name. 26 And they will be conscious of their shame and of all the wrong which they have done against me, when they are living in their land with no sense of danger and with no one to be a cause of fear to them; 27 When I have taken them back from among the peoples and got them together out of the lands of their haters, and have made myself holy in them before the eyes of a great number of nations.28 And they will be certain that I am the Lord their God, because I sent them away as prisoners among the nations, and have taken them together back to their land; and I have not let one of them be there any longer. 29 And my face will no longer be covered from them: for I have sent the out-flowing of my spirit on the children of Israel, says the Lord.

40

1 In the twenty-fifth year after we had been taken away prisoners, in the first month of the year, on the tenth day of the month, in the fourteenth year after the town was taken, on the very same day, the hand of the Lord was on me, and he took me there. 2 In the visions of God he took me into the land of Israel, and put me down on a very high mountain, on which there was, as it seemed, a building like a town opposite me. 3 He took me there, and I saw a man, looking like brass, with a linen cord in his hand and a measuring rod: and he was stationed in the doorway. 4 And the man said to me, Son of man, see with your eyes and give hearing with your ears, and take to heart everything I am going to let you see; for in order that I might let you see them, you have come here: and give an account of all you see to the children of Israel. 5 And there was a wall on the outside of the house all round, and in the man's hand there was a measuring rod six cubits long by a cubit and a hand's measure: so he took the measure of the building from side to side, one rod; and from base to top, one rod. 6 Then he came to the doorway looking to the east, and went up by its steps; and he took the measure of the doorstep, one rod wide. 7 And the watchmen's rooms were one rod long and one rod wide; and the space between the rooms was five cubits; the doorstep of the doorway, by the covered way of the doorway inside, was one rod. 8 And he took the measure of the covered way of the doorway inside, 9 Eight cubits; and its uprights, two cubits; the covered way of the doorway was inside. 10 And the rooms of the doorway on the east were three on this side and three on that; all three were of the same size; and the uprights on this side and on that were of the same size. 11 And he took the measure of the opening of the doorway, ten cubits wide; and the way down the doorway was thirteen cubits; 12 And the space in front of the

rooms, a cubit on this side and a cubit on that side; and the rooms six cubits on this side and six cubits
on that. 13 And he took the measure of the doorway from the back of one room to the back of the
other, twenty-five cubits across, from door to door. 14 And he took the measure of the covered way,
twenty cubits; and opening from the covered way of the doorway was the open square round about. 15
And from before the opening of the doorway to before the inner covered way of the doorway was fifty
cubits. 16 And the rooms and their uprights had sloping windows inside the doorway all round, and in
the same way the covered way had windows all round on the inside: and on every upright there were
palm-trees. 17 Then he took me into the outer square, and there were rooms and a stone floor made for
the open square all round: there were thirty rooms on the stone floor. 18 And the stone floor was by the
side of the doorways, and was as wide as the doorways were long, even the lower floor. 19 Then he took
the measure of the square across, from before the lower doorway inside to before the inner doorway
outside, one hundred cubits. And he took me in the direction of the north, 20 And there was a doorway
to the outer square, looking to the north; and he took the measure of it to see how wide and how long it
was. 21 And it had three rooms on this side of it and three on that; its uprights and its covered ways
were the same size as those of the first doorway: it was fifty cubits long and twenty-five cubits wide. 22
And its windows, and the windows of its covered ways, and its palm-trees, were the same as those of the
doorway looking to the east; and there were seven steps up to it; and the covered way went inside. 23
And there was a doorway to the inner square opposite the doorway on the north, like the doorway on
the east; and he took the measure from doorway to doorway, a hundred cubits. 24 And he took me to
the south, and I saw a doorway looking to the south: and he took the measure of its rooms and its
uprights and its covered ways by these measures. 25 And there were windows in it and in the covered
way all round, like the other windows: it was fifty cubits long and twenty-five cubits wide. 26 And there
were seven steps up to it, and its covered way went inside: and it had palm-trees, one on this side and
one on that, on its uprights. 27 And there was a doorway to the inner square looking to the south: he
took the measure from doorway to doorway to the south, a hundred cubits. 28 Then he took me to the
inner square by the south doorway: and he took the measure of the south doorway by these measures;
29 And the rooms in it and the uprights and the covered ways, by these measures: 30 And there were
windows in it and in the covered way all round: it was fifty cubits long and twenty-five cubits wide. 31
The covered way was on the side nearest the outer square; and there were palm-trees on the uprights:
and there were eight steps going up to it. 32 And he took me into the inner square facing the east: and
he took the measure of the doorway by these measures; 33 And of the rooms in it and its uprights and
its covered ways, by these measures: and there were windows in it and in the covered way round about:
it was fifty cubits long and twenty-five cubits wide.34 And the covered way was on the side nearest the
outer square; there were palm-trees on the uprights, on this side and on that: and there were eight steps
going up to it. 35 And he took me to the north doorway: and he took the measure of it by these
measures; 36 Its rooms, its uprights, and its covered way had the same measures, and its covered way
had windows all round: it was fifty cubits long and twenty-five cubits wide. 37 Its uprights were on the
side nearest to the outer square; there were palm-trees on the uprights, on this side and on that: and
there were eight steps going up to it. 38 And there was a room with a door in the covered way of the
doorway, where the burned offering was washed.39 And in the covered way of the doorway there were
two tables on this side and two tables on that side, on which the burned offering and the sin-offering
and the offering for error were put to death: 40 On the outer side, to the north, as one goes up to the
opening of the doorway, were two tables. 41 There were four tables on one side and four tables on the
other, by the side of the doorway; eight tables, on which they put to death the beasts for the offerings.
42 And there were four tables for the burned offering, made of cut stone, one and a half cubits long,
one and a half cubits wide and a cubit high, where the instruments were placed which were used for
putting to death the burned offering and the beasts for the offerings. 43 And they had edges all round as
wide as a man's hand: and on the tables was the flesh of the offerings. 44 And he took me into the inner
square, and there were two rooms in the inner square, one at the side of the north doorway, facing
south; and one at the side of the south doorway, facing north.45 And he said to me, This room, facing
south, is for the priests who have the care of the house. 46 And the room facing north is for the priests
who have the care of the altar: these are the sons of Zadok, who, from among the sons of Levi, come
near to the Lord to do the work of his house. 47 And he took the measure of the open square, a
hundred cubits long and a hundred cubits wide, being square; and the altar was in front of the house. 48
Then he took me to the covered way before the house, and took the measure of its uprights, five cubits
on one side and five cubits on the other: and the doorway was fourteen cubits wide; and the side-walls
of the doorway were three cubits on one side and three cubits on the other. 49 The covered way was
twenty cubits long and twelve cubits wide, and they went up to it by ten steps; and there were pillars by
the uprights, one on one side and one on the other.

41

1 And he took me to the Temple, and took the measure of the uprights, six cubits wide on one side and six cubits wide on the other. 2 And the door-opening was ten cubits wide; and the side walls of the door-opening were five cubits on one side and five cubits on the other: and it was forty cubits long and twenty cubits wide. 3 And he went inside and took the measure of the uprights of the door-opening, two cubits: and the door-opening, six cubits; and the side-walls of the door-opening were seven cubits on one side and seven cubits on the other. 4 And by his measure it was twenty cubits long and twenty cubits wide in front of the Temple: and he said to me, This is the most holy place. 5 Then he took the measure of the wall of the house, which was six cubits; and of the side-rooms round the house, which were four cubits wide. 6 And the side-rooms, room over room, were three times thirty; there were inlets in the wall of the house for the side-rooms round about, for supports in the wall of the house. 7 The side-rooms became wider as they went higher up the house, by the amount of the space let into the wall up round about the house, because of the inlets in the house; and one went up from the lowest floor by steps to the middle, and from the middle to the upper floor. 8 And I saw that the house had a stone floor all round; the bases of the side-rooms were a full rod of six great cubits high. 9 The wall supporting the side-rooms on the outside was five cubits thick: and there was a free space of five cubits between the side-rooms of the house. 10 And between the rooms was a space twenty cubits wide all round the house. 11 And the free space had doors opening from the side-rooms, one door on the north and one door on the south: and the free space was five cubits wide all round. 12 And the building which was in front of the separate place at the side to the west was seventy cubits wide; the wall of the building was five cubits thick all round and ninety cubits long. 13 And he took the measure of the house; it was a hundred cubits long; and the separate place and the building with its walls was a hundred cubits long; 14 And the east front of the house and of the separate place was a hundred cubits wide. 15 And he took the measure of the building in front of the separate place which was at the back of it, and the pillared walks on one side and on the other side; they were a hundred cubits long; and the Temple and the inner part and its outer covered way were covered in; 16 And the sloping windows and the covered ways round all three of them were of shakiph-wood all round from the level of the earth up to the windows; 17 And there was a roof over the doorway and as far as the inner house, and to the outside and on the wall all round, inside and outside.18 And it had pictured forms of winged beings and palm-trees; a palm-tree between two winged ones, and every winged one had two faces; 19 So that there was the face of a man turned to the palm-tree on one side, and the face of a young lion on the other side: so it was made all round the house. 20 From earth level up to the windows there were winged ones and palm-trees pictured on the wall. 21 ... 22 The altar was made of wood, and was three cubits high and two cubits long; it had angles, and its base and sides were of wood; and he said to me, This is the table which is before the Lord. 23 The Temple had two doors. 24 And the holy place had two doors, and the doors had two turning leaves, two for one and two for the other. 25 And on them were pictured winged ones and palm-trees, as on the walls; and a ... of wood was on the front of the covered way outside. 26 And there were sloping windows and palm-trees on one side and on the other, on the sides of the covered way: and the side-rooms of the house and the ...

42

1 And he took me out into the inner square in the direction of the north: and he took me into the rooms which were opposite the separate place and opposite the building to the north. 2 On the north side it was a hundred cubits long and fifty cubits wide, 3 Opposite the space of twenty cubits which was part of the inner square, and opposite the stone floor of the outer square. There were covered ways facing one another on the third floor. 4 And in front of the rooms was a walk, ten cubits wide and a hundred cubits long; and their doors were facing north. 5 And the higher rooms were shorter: for the covered ways took up more space from these than from the lower and middle rooms. 6 For they were on three floors, and they had no pillars like the pillars of the outer square; so the highest was narrower than the lowest and middle floors from the earth level. 7 And the wall which went outside by the side of the rooms, in the direction of the outer square in front of the rooms, was fifty cubits long. 8 For the rooms in the outer square were fifty cubits long: and in front of the Temple was a space of a hundred cubits. 9 And under these rooms was the way in from the east side, as one goes into them from the outer square at the head of the outer wall. 10 (And he took me) to the south, and in front of the separate place and in front of the building there were rooms. 11 And there was a walk in front of them like that by the rooms on the north; they were equally long and wide; and the ways out of them were the same in design and had

the same sort of doors. 12 And under the rooms on the south was a door at the head of the outer wall in the direction of the east as one goes in. 13 And he said to me, The north rooms and the south rooms in front of the separate place are the holy rooms, where the priests who come near the Lord take the most holy things for their food: there the most holy things are placed, with the meal offering and the sin-offering and the offering for error; for the place is holy. 14 When the priests go in, they may not go out of the holy place into the outer square, and there they are to put the robes in which they do the work of the Lord's house, for they are holy: and they have to put on other clothing before they come near that which has to do with the people. 15 And when he had come to the end of measuring the inner house, he took me out to the doorway looking to the east, and took its measure all round. 16 He went round and took the measure of it on the east side with the measuring rod, five hundred, measured with the rod all round. 17And he went round and took the measure of it on the north side with the measuring rod, five hundred, measured with the rod all round. 18 And he went round and took the measure of it on the south side with the measuring rod, five hundred, measured with the rod all round. 19 And he went round and took the measure of it on the west side with the measuring rod, five hundred, measured with the rod all round. 20He took its measure on the four sides: and it had a wall all round, five hundred long and five hundred wide, separating what was holy from what was common.

43

1 And he took me to the doorway looking to the east: 2 And there was the glory of the God of Israel coming from the way of the east: and his voice was like the sound of great waters, and the earth was shining with his glory. 3 And the vision which I saw was like the vision I had seen when he came for the destruction of the town: and like the vision which I saw by the river Chebar; and I went down on my face.4 And the glory of the Lord came into the house by the way of the doorway looking to the east. 5 And the spirit, lifting me up, took me into the inner square; and I saw that the house was full of the glory of the Lord. 6 And the voice of one talking to me came to my ears from inside the house; and the man was by my side. 7 And he said to me, Son of man, this is the place where the seat of my power is and the resting-place of my feet, where I will be among the children of Israel for ever: and no longer will the people of Israel make my holy name unclean, they or their kings, by their loose ways and by the dead bodies of their kings; 8 By putting their doorstep by my doorstep, and the pillar of their door by the pillar of my door, with only a wall between me and them; and they have made my holy name unclean by the disgusting things which they have done: so in my wrath I sent destruction on them. 9 Now let them put their loose ways and the dead bodies of their kings far from me, and I will be among them for ever. 10 You, son of man, give the children of Israel an account of this house, so that they may be shamed because of their evil-doing: and let them see the vision of it and its image. 11 And they will be shamed by what they have done; so give them the knowledge of the form of the house and its structure, and the ways out of it and into it, and all its laws and its rules, writing it down for them: so that they may keep all its laws and do them. 12 This is the law of the house: On the top of the mountain all the space round it on every side will be most holy. See, this is the law of the house. 13 And these are the measures of the altar in cubits: (the cubit being a cubit and a hand's measure;) its hollow base is a cubit high and a cubit wide, and it has an overhanging edge as wide as a hand-stretch all round it: 14 And from the base on the earth level to the lower shelf, the altar is two cubits high and a cubit wide; and from the smaller shelf to the greater shelf it is four cubits high and a cubit wide. 15 And the fireplace is four cubits high: and coming up from the fireplace are the horns, a cubit high. 16 And the fireplace is twelve cubits long and twelve cubits wide, square on its four sides. 17 And the shelf is fourteen cubits long and fourteen cubits wide, on its four sides; the edge round it is half a cubit; the base of it is a cubit all round, and its steps are facing the east.18 And he said to me, Son of man, the Lord God has said, These are the rules for the altar, when they make it, for the offering of burned offerings on it and the draining out of the blood. 19 You are to give to the priests, the Levites of the seed of Zadok, who come near to me, says the Lord God, to do my work, a young ox for a sin-offering. 20 You are to take some of its blood and put it on the four horns and on the four angles of the shelf and on the edge all round: and you are to make it clean and free from sin. 21 And you are to take the ox of the sin-offering, and have it burned in the special place ordered for it in the house, outside the holy place. 22 And on the second day you are to have a he-goat without any mark on it offered for a sin-offering; and they are to make the altar clean as they did with the young ox. 23 And after you have made it clean, let a young ox without a mark be offered, and a male sheep from the flock without a mark. 24 And you are to take them before the Lord, and the priests will put salt on them, offering them up for a burned offering to the Lord. 25 Every day for seven days you are to give a goat for a sin-offering: and let them give in addition a young ox and a male sheep from the flock without any mark on them. 26 For seven days they are to make offerings to

take away sin from the altar and to make it clean; so they are to make it holy. 27 And when these days have come to an end, then on the eighth day and after, the priests will make your burned offerings on the altar and your peace-offerings; and I will take pleasure in you, says the Lord.

44

1 And he took me back to the outer doorway of the holy place, looking to the east; and it was shut. 2 And the Lord said to me, This doorway is to be shut, it is not to be open, and no man is to go in by it, because the Lord, the God of Israel, has gone in by it; and it is to be shut. 3 But the ruler will be seated there to take his food before the Lord; he will go in by the covered way to the door, and will come out by the same way. 4 And he took me to the north doorway in front of the house; and, looking, I saw that the house of the Lord was full of the glory of the Lord; and I went down on my face. 5 And the Lord said to me, Son of man, take to heart, and let your eyes see and your ears be open to everything I say to you about all the rules of the house of the Lord and all its laws; and take note of the ways into the house and all the ways out of the holy place. 6 And say to the uncontrolled children of Israel, This is what the Lord has said: O you children of Israel, let it be enough for you, among the disgusting things which you have done, 7 To have let men from strange lands, without circumcision of heart or flesh, come into my holy place, making my house unclean; and to have made the offering of my food, even the fat and the blood; and in addition to all your disgusting ways, you have let my agreement be broken. 8 And you have not taken care of my holy things; but you have put them as keepers to take care of my work in my holy place. 9 For this cause the Lord has said, No man from a strange land, without circumcision of heart and flesh, of all those who are living among the children of Israel, is to come into my holy place. 10 But as for the Levites, who went far from me, when Israel went out of the right way, turning away from me to go after their images; their punishment will come on them. 11 But they may be caretakers in my holy place, and overseers at the doors of the house, doing the work of the house: they will put to death the burned offering and the beasts offered for the people, and they will take their place before them as their servants. 12 Because they did this work for them before their images, and became a cause of sin to the children of Israel; for this cause my hand has been lifted up against them, says the Lord, and their punishment will be on them. 13 And they will not come near me to do the work of priests to me, or come near any of my holy things, or the things which are most holy: but their shame will be on them, and the punishment for the disgusting things which they have done. 14 But I will make them responsible for the care of the house and all its work and everything which is done in it. 15 But as for the priests, the sons of Zadok, who took care of my holy place when the children of Israel were turned away from me, they are to come near me to do my work, they will take their places before me, offering to me the fat and the blood, says the Lord; 16 They are to come into my holy place and they are to come near to my table, to do my work and have the care of my house. 17 And when they come in by the doorways of the inner square, they are to be clothed in linen robes; there is to be no wool on them while they are doing my work in the doorway of the inner square and inside the house. 18 They are to have linen head-dresses on their heads and linen trousers on their legs, and they are to have nothing round them to make their skin wet with heat. 19 And when they go out into the outer square to the people, they are to take off the robes in which they do the work of priests, and put them away in the holy rooms, and put on other clothing, so that the people may not be made holy by their robes. 20 They are not to have all the hair cut off their heads, and they are not to let their hair get long, but they are to have the ends of their hair cut. 21 The priests are not to take wine when they go into the inner square. 22 And they are not to take as wives any widow or woman whose husband has put her away: but they may take virgins of the seed of Israel, or a widow who is the widow of a priest. 23 And they are to make clear to my people the division between what is holy and what is common, and to give them the knowledge of what is clean and what is unclean. 24 In any cause, they are to be in the position of judges, judging in harmony with my decisions: they are to keep my laws and my rules in all my fixed feasts; and they are to keep my Sabbaths holy. 25 They are not to come near any dead person so as to become unclean: but for a father or mother or son or daughter or brother or for a sister who has no husband, they may make themselves unclean. 26 And after he has been made clean, seven days are to be numbered for him. 27 And on the day when he goes into the inner square, to do the work of the holy place, he is to make his sin-offering, says the Lord. 28 And they are to have no heritage; I am their heritage: you are to give them no property in Israel; I am their property. 29 Their food is to be the meal offering and the sin-offering and the offering for error; and everything given specially to the Lord in Israel will be theirs. 30 And the best of all the first-fruits of everything, and every offering which is lifted up of all your offerings, will be for the priests: and you are to give the priest the first of your bread-making, so causing a blessing to come on your house. 31 The priests may not take for food any bird or beast which has come to a natural

death or whose death has been caused by another animal.

45

1 And when you are making a distribution of the land, by the decision of the Lord, for your heritage,
you are to make an offering to the Lord of a part of the land as holy: it is to be twenty-five thousand
long and twenty thousand wide: all the land inside these limits is to be holy. 2 Of this, a square five
hundred long and five hundred wide is to be for the holy place, with a space of fifty cubits all round it. 3
And of this measure, let a space be measured, twenty-five thousand long and ten thousand wide: in it
there will be the holy place, even the most holy. 4 This holy part of the land is to be for the priests, the
servants of the holy place, who come near to the Lord to do his work; it is to be a place for their houses
and for grass-land and for cattle. 5 A space of land twenty-five thousand long and ten thousand wide is
to be for the Levites, the servants of the house, a property for themselves, for towns for their living-
places. 6 And as the property for the town you are to have a part five thousand wide and twenty-five
thousand long, by the side of the offering of the holy part of the land: this is to be for all the children of
Israel. 7 And for the ruler there is to be a part on one side and on the other side of the holy offering and
of the property of the town, in front of the holy offering and in front of the property of the town on the
west of it and on the east: measured in the same line as one of the parts of the land, from its limit on the
west to its limit on the east of the land. 8 And this will be his heritage in Israel: and my rulers will no
longer be cruel masters to my people; but they will give the land as a heritage to the children of Israel by
their tribes. 9 This is what the Lord has said: Let this be enough for you, O rulers of Israel: let there be
an end of violent behaviour and wasting; do what is right, judging uprightly; let there be no more driving
out of my people, says the Lord. 10 Have true scales and a true ephah and a true bath. 11 The ephah and
the bath are to be of the same measure, so that the bath is equal to a tenth of a homer, and the ephah to
a tenth of a homer: the unit of measure is to be a homer. 12 And the shekel is to be twenty gerahs: five
shekels are five, and ten shekels are ten, and your maneh is to be fifty shekels 13 This is the offering you
are to give: a sixth of an ephah out of a homer of wheat, and a sixth of an ephah out of a homer of
barley; 14 And the fixed measure of oil is to be a tenth of a bath from the cor, for ten baths make up the
cor; 15 And one lamb from the flock out of every two hundred, from all the families of Israel, for a meal
offering and for a burned offering and for peace-offerings, to take away their sin, says the Lord. 16 All
the people are to give this offering to the ruler. 17 And the ruler will be responsible for the burned
offering and the meal offering and the drink offering, at the feasts and the new moons and the Sabbaths,
at all the fixed feasts of the children of Israel: he will give the sin-offering and meal offering and burned
offering and the peace-offerings, to take away the sin of the children of Israel. 18 This is what the Lord
has said: In the first month, on the first day of the month, you are to take a young ox without any mark
on him, and you are to make the holy place clean. 19 And the priest is to take some of the blood of the
sin-offering and put it on the uprights at the sides of the doors of the house, and on the four angles of
the shelf of the altar, and on the sides of the doorway of the inner square. 20 And this you are to do on
the seventh day of the month for everyone who is in error and for the feeble-minded: you are to make
the house free from sin. 21 In the first month, on the fourteenth day of the month, you are to have the
Passover, a feast of seven days; unleavened bread is to be your food. 22 And on that day the ruler is to
give for himself and for all the people of the land an ox for a sin-offering. 23 And on the seven days of
the feast he is to give a burned offering to the Lord, seven oxen and seven sheep without any mark on
them, every day for seven days; and a he-goat every day for a sin-offering. 24 And he is to give a meal
offering, an ephah for every ox and an ephah for every sheep and a hin of oil to every ephah. 25 In the
seventh month, on the fifteenth day of the month, at the feast, he is to give the same for seven days; the
sin-offering, the burned offering, the meal offering, and the oil as before.

46

1 This is what the Lord has said: The doorway of the inner square looking to the east is to be shut on
the six working days; but on the Sabbath it is to be open, and at the time of the new moon it is to be
open. 2And the ruler is to go in through the covered way of the outer doorway outside, and take his
place by the pillar of the doorway, and the priests will make his burned offering and his peace-offerings
and he will give worship at the doorstep of the doorway; then he will go out, and the door will not be
shut till the evening. 3And the people of the land are to give worship at the door of that doorway before
the Lord on the Sabbaths and at the new moons. 4 And the burned offering offered to the Lord by the
ruler on the Sabbath day is to be six lambs without a mark on them and a male sheep without a mark; 5
And the meal offering is to be an ephah for the sheep, and for the lambs whatever he is able to give, and

a hin of oil to an ephah. 6 And at the time of the new moon it is to be a young ox of the herd without a
mark on him, and six lambs and a male sheep, all without a mark: 7 And he is to give a meal offering, an
ephah for the ox and an ephah for the sheep, and for the lambs whatever he is able to give, and a hin of
oil to an ephah. 8 And when the ruler comes in, he is to go in through the covered way of the doorway,
and he is to go out by the same way. 9 But when the people of the land come before the Lord at the
fixed feasts, he who comes in by the north doorway to give worship is to go out by the south doorway;
and he who comes in by the south doorway is to go out by the north doorway: he is not to come back
by the doorway through which he went in, but is to go straight before him. 10 And the ruler, when they
come in, is to come among them, and is to go out when they go out. 11 At the feasts and the fixed
meetings the meal offerings are to be an ephah for an ox, and an ephah for a male sheep, and for the
lambs whatever he is able to give, and a hin of oil to an ephah. 12 And when the ruler makes a free
offering, a burned offering or a peace-offering freely given to the Lord, the doorway looking to the east
is to be made open for him, and he is to make his burned offering and his peace-offerings as he does on
the Sabbath day: and he will go out; and the door will be shut after he has gone out. 13 And you are to
give a lamb a year old without any mark on it for a burned offering to the Lord every day: morning by
morning you are to give it. 14 And you are to give, morning by morning, a meal offering with it, a sixth
of an ephah and a third of a hin of oil dropped on the best meal; a meal offering offered to the Lord at
all times by an eternal order. 15 And they are to give the lamb and the meal offering and the oil,
morning by morning, for a burned offering at all times. 16 This is what the Lord has said: If the ruler
gives a property to any of his sons, it is his heritage and will be the property of his sons; it is theirs for
their heritage. 17 And if he gives a part of his heritage to one of his servants, it will be his till the year of
making free, and then it will go back to the ruler; for it is his sons' heritage, and is to be theirs. 18 And
the ruler is not to take the heritage of any of the people, driving them out of their property; he is to give
a heritage to his sons out of the property which is his: so that my people may not be sent away from
their property. 19 And he took me through by the way in at the side of the doorway into the holy rooms
which are the priests', looking to the north: and I saw a place at the side of them to the west. 20 And he
said to me, This is the place where the offering for error and the sin-offering are to be cooked in water
by the priests, and where the meal offering is to be cooked in the oven; so that they may not be taken
out into the outer square to make the people holy. 21 And he took me out into the outer square and
made me go by the four angles of the square; and I saw that in every angle of the open square there was
a space shut in. 22 In the four angles there were spaces walled in, forty cubits long and thirty wide; the
four were of the same size. 23 And there was a line of wall all round inside them, round all four, and
boiling-places were made under it all round about. 24 And he said to me, These are the boiling-rooms,
where the offering of the people is cooked by the servants of the house.

47

1 And he took me back to the door of the house; and I saw that waters were flowing out from under the
doorstep of the house on the east, for the house was facing east: and the waters came down from under,
from the right side of the house, on the south side of the altar. 2 And he took me out by the north
doorway, and made me go round to the outside of the doorway looking to the east; and I saw waters
running slowly out on the south side. 3 And the man went out to the east with the line in his hand, and
after measuring a thousand cubits, he made me go through the waters, which came over my feet. 4 And
again, measuring a thousand cubits, he made me go through the waters which came up to my knees.
Again, measuring a thousand, he made me go through the waters up to the middle of my body. 5 Again,
after his measuring a thousand, it became a river which it was not possible to go through: for the waters
had become deep enough for swimming, a river it was not possible to go through. 6 And he said to me,
Son of man, have you seen this? Then he took me to the river's edge. 7 And he took me back, and I saw
at the edge of the river a very great number of trees on this side and on that. 8 And he said to me, These
waters are flowing out to the east part of the land and down into the Arabah; and they will go to the sea,
and the waters will be made sweet. 9 And it will come about that every living and moving thing,
wherever their streams come, will have life; and there will be very much fish because these waters have
come there and have been made sweet: and everything wherever the river comes will have life. 10 And
fishermen will take up their places by it: from En-gedi as far as En-eglaim will be a place for the
stretching out of nets; the fish will be of every sort, like the fish of the Great Sea, a very great number.
11 The wet places and the pools will not be made sweet; they will be given up to salt. 12 And by the
edge of the river, on this side and on that, will come up every tree used for food, whose leaves will ever
be green and its fruit will not come to an end: it will have new fruit every month, because its waters
come out from the holy place: the fruit will be for food and the leaf will make well those who are ill. 13

This is what the Lord has said: These are the limits by which you will take up your heritage in the land
among the twelve tribes of Israel: Joseph is to have two parts. 14 And you are to make an equal division
of it; as I gave my oath to your fathers to give it to you: for this land is to be your heritage. 15 And this
is to be the limit of the land: on the north side, from the Great Sea, in the direction of Hethlon, as far as
the way into Hamath; 16 To Zedad, Berothah, Sibraim, which is between the limit of Damascus and the
limit of Hazar-hatticon, which is on the limit of Hauran. 17 And this is the limit from the sea in the
direction of Hazar-enon; and the limit of Damascus is to the north, and on the north is the limit of
Hamath. This is the north side. 18 And the east side will be from Hazar-enon, which is between Hauran
and Damascus; and between Gilead and the land of Israel the Jordan will be the limit, to the east sea, to
Tamar. This is the east side. 19 And the south side to the south will be from Tamar as far as the waters
of Meribath-kadesh, to the stream of Egypt, to the Great Sea. This is the south side, on the south. 20
And the west side will be the Great Sea, from the limit on the south to a point opposite the way into
Hamath. This is the west side. 21 You will make a division of the land among you, tribe by tribe. 22 And
you are to make a distribution of it, by the decision of the Lord, for a heritage to you and to the men
from other lands who are living among you and who have children in your land: they will be the same to
you as if they were Israelites by birth, they will have their heritage with you among the tribes of Israel. 23
In whatever tribe the man from a strange land is living, there you are to give him his heritage, says the
Lord.

48

1 Now these are the names of the tribes: from the north end, from the west on the way of Hethlon to
the way into Hamath, in the direction of Hazar-enon, with the limit of Damascus to the north, by
Hamath; and on the limit from the east side to the west side: Dan, one part. 2 And on the limit of Dan,
from the east side to the west side: Asher, one part. 3 And on the limit of Asher, from the east side to
the west side: Naphtali, one part. 4 And on the limit of Naphtali, from the east side to the west side:
Manasseh, one part.5 And on the limit of Manasseh, from the east side to the west side: Ephraim, one
part. 6 And on the limit of Ephraim, from the east side to the west side: Reuben, one part. 7 And on the
limit of Reuben, from the east side to the west side: Judah, one part. 8 And on the limit of Judah, from
the east side to the west side, will be the offering which you are to make, twenty-five thousand wide, and
as long as one of the parts, from the east side to the west side: and the holy place will be in the middle of
it. 9 The offering you will give to the Lord is to be twenty-five thousand long and twenty-five thousand
wide. 10 And for these, that is the priests, the holy offering is to be twenty-five thousand long to the
north, ten thousand wide to the west, ten thousand wide to the east and twenty-five thousand long to
the south; and the holy place of the Lord will be in the middle of it. 11 For the priests who have been
made holy, those of the sons of Zadok who kept the orders I gave them, who did not go out of the right
way when the children of Israel went from the way, as the Levites did, 12 Even for them will be the
offering from the offering of the land, a thing most holy, on the limit of the land given to the Levites. 13
And the Levites are to have a part of the land equal to the limit of the priests', twenty-five thousand long
and ten thousand wide, all of it together to be twenty-five thousand long and twenty thousand wide. 14
And they are not to let any of it go for a price, or give it in exchange; and the part of the land given to
the Lord is not to go into other hands: for it is holy to the Lord. 15 And the other five thousand,
measured from side to side, in front of the twenty-five thousand, is to be for common use, for the town,
for living in and for a free space: and the town will be in the middle of it. 16 And these will be its
measures: the north side, four thousand five hundred, and the south side, four thousand five hundred,
and on the east side, four thousand five hundred, and on the west side, four thousand five hundred. 17
And the town will have a free space on the north of two hundred and fifty, on the south of two hundred
and fifty, on the east of two hundred and fifty, and on the west of two hundred and fifty. 18 And the
rest, in measure as long as the holy offering, will be ten thousand to the east and ten thousand to the
west: and its produce will be for food for the workers of the town. 19 It will be farmed by workers of
the town from all the tribes of Israel. 20 The size of the offering all together is to be twenty-five
thousand by twenty-five thousand: you are to make the holy offering a square, together with the
property of the town. 21 And the rest is to be for the prince, on this side and on that side of the holy
offering and of the property of the town, in front of the twenty-five thousand to the east, as far as the
east limit, and to the west, in front of the twenty-five thousand, as far as the west limit, and of the same
measure as those parts; it will be the property of the prince: and the holy offering and holy place of the
house will be in the middle of it. 22 And the property of the Levites and the property of the town will be
in the middle of the prince's property; between the limit of Judah's part and the limit of Benjamin's part
will be for the prince. 23 And as for the rest of the tribes: from the east side to the west side: Benjamin,

one part.24 And on the limit of Benjamin, from the east side to the west side: Simeon, one part. 25 And
on the limit of Simeon, from the east side to the west side: Issachar, one part. 26 And on the limit of
Issachar, from the east side to the west side: Zebulun, one part. 27 And on the limit of Zebulun, from
the east side to the west side: Gad one part. 28 And on the limit of Gad, on the south side and to the
south of it, the limit will be from Tamar to the waters of Meribath-kadesh, to the stream, to the Great
Sea. 29 This is the land of which distribution is to be made by the decision of the Lord, among the tribes
of Israel for their heritage, and these are their heritages, says the Lord. 30 And these are the outskirts of
the town: on the north side, four thousand five hundred by measure; 31 And the doors of the town are
to be named by the names of the tribes of Israel; three doors on the north, one for Reuben, one for
Judah, one for Levi; 32And at the east side, four thousand five hundred by measure, and three doors,
one for Joseph, one for Benjamin, one for Dan; 33 And at the south side, four thousand five hundred
by measure, and three doors, one for Simeon, one for Issachar, one for Zebulun; 34 At the west side,
four thousand five hundred by measure, with their three doors, one for Gad, one for Asher, one for
Naphtali. 35 It is to be eighteen thousand all round: and the name of the town from that day will be,
The Lord is there.

EZEKIEL

THE WEBSTER BIBLE

1

1:1 Now it came to pass in the thirtieth year, in the fourth month, in the fifth day of the month, as I was among the captives by the river of Kebar, that the heavens were opened, and I saw visions of God.
1:2 In the fifth day of the month, which was the fifth year of king Jehoiachin's captivity,
1:3 The word of the LORD came expressly to Ezekiel the priest, the son of Buzi, in the land of the Chaldeans by the river Kebar; and the hand of the LORD was there upon him.
1:4 And I looked, and behold, a whirlwind came out of the north, a great cloud, and a fire infolding itself, and a brightness was about it, and from the midst of it as the color of amber, from the midst of the fire.
1:5 Also from the midst of it came the likeness of four living creatures. And this was their appearance; they had the likeness of a man.
1:6 And every one had four faces, and every one had four wings.
1:7 And their feet were straight feet; and the sole of their feet was like the sole of a calf's foot: and they sparkled like the color of burnished brass.
1:8 And they had the hands of a man under their wings on their four sides; and they four had their faces and their wings.
1:9 Their wings were joined one to another; they turned not when they went; they went every one straight forward.
1:10 As for the likeness of their faces, they four had the face of a man and the face of a lion, on the right side: and they four had the face of an ox on the left side; they four also had the face of an eagle.
1:11 Thus were their faces: and their wings were stretched upward; two wings of every one were joined one to another, and two covered their bodies.
1:12 And they went every one straight forward: whither the spirit was to go, they went; and they turned not when they went.
1:13 As for the likeness of the living creatures, their appearance was like burning coals of fire, and like the appearance of lamps: it went up and down among the living creatures; and the fire was bright, and out of the fire went forth lightning.
1:14 And the living creatures ran and returned as the appearance of a flash of lightning.
1:15 Now as I beheld the living creatures, behold one wheel upon the earth by the living creatures, with his four faces.
1:16 The appearance of the wheels and their work was like the color of a beryl: and they four had one likeness: and their appearance and their work was as it were a wheel in the middle of a wheel.
1:17 When they went, they went upon their four sides: and they returned not when they went.
1:18 As for their rings, they were so high that they were dreadful; and their rings were full of eyes around them four.
1:19 And when the living creatures went, the wheels went by them: and when the living creatures were lifted up from the earth, the wheels were lifted up.
1:20 Whithersoever the spirit was to go, they went, thither was their spirit to go; and the wheels were lifted up over against them: for the spirit of the living creature was in the wheels.
1:21 When those went, these went; and when those stood, these stood; and when those were lifted up from the earth, the wheels were lifted up over against them: for the spirit of the living creature was in the wheels.
1:22 And the likeness of the firmament upon the heads of the living creature was as the color of the terrible crystal, stretched forth over their heads above.
1:23 And under the firmament were their wings straight, the one towards the other: every one had two, which covered on this side, and every one had two, which covered on that side, their bodies.

1:24 And when they went, I heard the noise of their wings, like the noise of great waters, as the voice of the Almighty, the voice of speech, as the noise of a host: when they stood, they let down their wings.
1:25 And there was a voice from the firmament that was over their heads, when they stood, and had let down their wings.
1:26 And above the firmament that was over their heads was the likeness of a throne, as the appearance of a sapphire stone: and upon the likeness of the throne was the likeness as the appearance of a man above upon it.
1:27 And I saw as the color of amber, as the appearance of fire around within it, from the appearance of his loins even upward, and from the appearance of his loins even downward, I saw as it were the appearance of fire, and it had brightness on all sides.
1:28 As the appearance of the bow that is in the cloud in the day of rain, so was the appearance of the brightness around. This was the appearance of the likeness of the glory of the LORD. And when I saw it, I fell upon my face, and I heard a voice of one speaking.

2

2:1 And he said to me, Son of man, stand upon thy feet, and I will speak to thee.
2:2 And the spirit entered into me when he spoke to me, and set me upon my feet, that I heard him that spoke to me.
2:3 And he said to me, Son of man, I send thee to the children of Israel, to a rebellious nation that hath rebelled against me: they and their fathers have transgressed against me: even to this very day.
2:4 For they are impudent children and obstinate in heart. I send thee to them; and thou shalt say to them, Thus saith the Lord GOD.
2:5 And they, whether they will hear, or whether they will forbear, (for they are a rebellious house,) yet shall know that there hath been a prophet among them.
2:6 And thou, son of man, be not afraid of them, neither be afraid of their words, though briers and thorns are with thee, and thou dost dwell among scorpions: be not afraid of their words, nor be dismayed at their looks, though they are a rebellious house.
2:7 And thou shalt speak my words to them, whether they will hear, or whether they will forbear: for they are most rebellious.
2:8 But thou, son of man, hear what I say to thee; Be not thou rebellious like that rebellious house: open thy mouth, and eat that which I give thee.
2:9 And when I looked, behold, a hand was sent to me; and lo, a roll of a book was in it;
2:10 And he spread it before me: and it was written within and without: and there was written in it lamentations, and mourning, and woe.

3

3:1 Moreover he said to me, Son of man, eat what thou findest; eat this roll, and go, speak to the house of Israel.
3:2 So I opened my mouth, and he caused me to eat that roll.
3:3 And he said to me, Son of man, cause thy belly to eat, and fill thy bowels with this roll that I give thee. Then did I eat it; and it was in my mouth as honey for sweetness.
3:4 And he said to me, Son of man, depart, go to the house of Israel, and speak with my words to them.
3:5 For thou art not sent to a people of a strange speech and of a hard language, but to the house of Israel;
3:6 Not to many people of a strange speech and of a hard language, whose words thou canst not understand. Surely, had I sent thee to them, they would have hearkened to thee.
3:7 But the house of Israel will not hearken to thee; for they will not hearken to me: for all the house of Israel are impudent and hard-hearted.
3:8 Behold, I have made thy face strong against their faces, and thy forehead strong against their foreheads.
3:9 As an adamant harder than flint have I made thy forehead: fear them not, neither be dismayed at their looks, though they are a rebellious house.
3:10 Moreover he said to me, Son of man, all my words that I shall speak to thee receive in thy heart, and hear with thy ears.
3:11 And depart, go to them of the captivity, to the children of thy people, and speak to them, and tell

them, Thus saith the Lord GOD; whether they will hear, or whether they will forbear.
3:12 Then the spirit took me up, and I heard behind me a voice of a great rushing, saying, Blessed be the
glory of the LORD from his place.
3:13 I heard also the noise of the wings of the living creatures that touched one another, and the noise
of the wheels over against them, and the noise of a great rushing.
3:14 So the spirit lifted me up, and took me away, and I went in bitterness, in the heat of my spirit; but
the hand of the LORD was strong upon me.
3:15 Then I came to them of the captivity at Tel-abib, that dwelt by the river of Kebar, and I sat where
they sat, and remained there astonished among them seven days.
3:16 And it came to pass at the end of seven days, that the word of the LORD came to me, saying,
3:17 Son of man, I have made thee a watchman to the house of Israel: therefore hear the word at my
mouth, and give them warning from me.
3:18 When I say to the wicked, Thou shalt surely die; and thou givest him not warning, nor speakest to
warn the wicked from his wicked way, to save his life; the same wicked man shall die in his iniquity; but
his blood will I require at thy hand.
3:19 Yet if thou shalt warn the wicked, and he shall not turn from his wickedness, nor from his wicked
way, he shall die in his iniquity; but thou hast delivered thy soul.
3:20 Again, When a righteous man doth turn from his righteousness, and commit iniquity, and I lay a
stumbling-block before him, he shall die: because thou hast not given him warning, he shall die in his
sin, and his righteousness which he hath done shall not be remembered; but his blood will I require at
thy hand.
3:21 Nevertheless if thou shalt warn the righteous man, that the righteous sin not, and he doth not sin,
he shall surely live, because he is warned; also thou hast delivered thy soul.
3:22 And the hand of the LORD was there upon me; and he said to me, Arise, go forth into the plain,
and I will there talk with thee.
3:23 Then I arose, and went forth into the plain; and behold, the glory of the LORD stood there, as the
glory which I saw by the river of Kebar: and I fell on my face.
3:24 Then the spirit entered into me, and set me upon my feet, and spoke with me, and said to me, Go,
shut thyself within thy house.
3:25 But thou, O son of man, behold, they shall put bands upon thee, and shall bind thee with them,
and thou shalt not go out among them:
3:26 And I will make thy tongue cleave to the roof of thy mouth, that thou shalt be dumb, and shalt not
be to them a reprover: for they are a rebellious house.
3:27 But when I speak with thee, I will open thy mouth, and thou shalt say to them, Thus saith the Lord
GOD; He that heareth, let him hear; and he that forbeareth, let him forbear: for they are a rebellious
house.

4

4:1 Thou also, son of man, take thee a tile, and lay it before thee, and pourtray upon it the city, even
Jerusalem;
4:2 And lay siege against it, and build a fort against it, and cast a mount against it; set the camp also
against it, and set battering rams against it on every side.
4:3 Moreover take thou to thee an iron pan, and set it for a wall of iron between thee and the city: and
set thy face against it, and it shall be besieged, and thou shalt lay siege against it. This shall be a sign to
the house of Israel.
4:4 Lie thou also upon thy left side, and lay the iniquity of the house of Israel upon it: according to the
number of the days that thou shalt lie upon it thou shalt bear their iniquity.
4:5 For I have laid upon thee the years of their iniquity, according to the number of the days, three
hundred and ninety days: so shalt thou bear the iniquity of the house of Israel.
4:6 And when thou hast accomplished them, lie again on thy right side, and thou shalt bear the iniquity
of the house of Judah forty days: I have appointed thee each day for a year.
4:7 Therefore thou shalt set thy face towards the siege of Jerusalem, and thy arm shall be uncovered, and
thou shalt prophesy against it.
4:8 And behold, I will lay bands upon thee, and thou shalt not turn thee from one side to another, till
thou hast ended the days of thy siege.
4:9 Take thou also to thee wheat, and barley, and beans, and lentils, and millet, and fitches, and put them
in one vessel, and make thee bread thereof, according to the number of the days that thou shalt lie upon

thy side, three hundred and ninety days shalt thou eat of it.
4:10 And thy food which thou shalt eat shall be by weight, twenty shekels a day: from time to time shalt thou eat it.
4:11 Thou shalt drink also water by measure, the sixth part of a hin: from time to time shalt thou drink.
4:12 And thou shalt eat it as barley cakes, and thou shalt bake it with human excrement in their sight.
4:13 And the LORD said, Even thus shall the children of Israel eat their defiled bread among the Gentiles, whither I will drive them.
4:14 Then said I, Ah Lord GOD! behold, my soul hath not been polluted: for from my youth even till now have I not eaten of that which dieth of itself, or is torn in pieces; neither hath abominable flesh come into my mouth.
4:15 Then he said to me, Lo, I have given thee cow's dung for man's dung, and thou shalt prepare thy bread with them.
4:16 Moreover he said to me, Son of man, behold, I will break the staff of bread in Jerusalem: and they shall eat bread by weight, and with care; and they shall drink water by measure, and with astonishment.
4:17 That they may want bread and water, and be astonished one with another, and consume away for their iniquity.

5

5:1 And thou, son of man, take thee a sharp knife, take thee a barber's razor, and cause it to pass upon thy head and upon thy beard: then take to thee balances to weigh, and divide the hair.
5:2 Thou shalt burn with fire a third part in the midst of the city, when the days of the siege are fulfilled: and thou shalt take a third part, and smite about it with a knife: and a third part thou shalt scatter in the wind; and I will draw out a sword after them.
5:3 Thou shalt also take of them a few in number, and bind them in thy skirts.
5:4 Then take of them again, and cast them into the midst of the fire, and burn them in the fire: from which a fire shall come forth into all the house of Israel.
5:5 Thus saith the Lord GOD; This is Jerusalem: I have set it in the midst of the nations and countries that are around her.
5:6 And she hath changed my judgments into wickedness more than the nations, and my statutes more than the countries that are around her: for they have refused my judgments and my statutes, they have not walked in them.
5:7 Therefore thus saith the Lord GOD; Because ye multiplied more than the nations that are around you, and have not walked in my statutes, neither have kept my judgments, neither have done according to the judgments of the nations that are around you:
5:8 Therefore thus saith the Lord GOD; Behold, I, even I, am against thee, and will execute judgments in the midst of thee in the sight of the nations.
5:9 And I will do in thee that which I have not done, and the like to which I will not do any more, because of all thy abominations.
5:10 Therefore the fathers shall eat the sons in the midst of thee, and the sons shall eat their fathers; and I will execute judgments in thee, and the whole remnant of thee will I scatter into all the winds.
5:11 Wherefore, as I live, saith the Lord GOD; Surely, because thou hast defiled my sanctuary with all thy detestable things, and with all thy abominations, therefore I will also diminish thee; neither shall my eye spare, neither will I have any pity.
5:12 A third part of thee shall die with the pestilence, and with famine shall they be consumed in the midst of thee: and a third part shall fall by the sword around thee; and I will scatter a third part into all the winds, and I will draw out a sword after them.
5:13 Thus shall my anger be accomplished, and I will cause my fury to rest upon them, and I will be comforted: and they shall know that I the LORD have spoken it in my zeal, when I have accomplished my fury in them.
5:14 Moreover I will make thee waste, and a reproach among the nations that are around thee, in the sight of all that pass by.
5:15 So it shall be a reproach and a taunt, an instruction and an astonishment to the nations that are around thee, when I shall execute judgments in thee in anger and in fury and in furious rebukes. I the LORD have spoken it.
5:16 When I shall send upon them the evil arrows of famine, which shall be for their destruction, and which I will send to destroy you: and I will increase the famine upon you, and will break your staff of bread:

5:17 So will I send upon you famine and evil beasts, and they shall bereave thee; and pestilence and blood shall pass through thee; and I will bring the sword upon thee. I the LORD have spoken it.

6

6:1 And the word of the LORD came to me, saying,
6:2 Son of man, set thy face towards the mountains of Israel, and prophesy against them,
6:3 And say, Ye mountains of Israel, hear the word of the Lord GOD: Thus saith the Lord GOD to the mountains, and to the hills, to the rivers, and to the valleys; Behold, I, even I, will bring a sword upon you, and I will destroy your high places.
6:4 And your altars shall be desolate, and your images shall be broken: and I will cast down your slain men before your idols.
6:5 And I will lay the dead carcasses of the children of Israel before their idols; and I will scatter your bones about your altars.
6:6 In all your dwelling-places the cities shall be laid waste, and the high places shall be desolate; that your altars may be laid waste and made desolate, and your idols may be broken and cease, and your images may be cut down, and your works may be abolished.
6:7 And the slain shall fall in the midst of you, and ye shall know that I am the LORD.
6:8 Yet will I leave a remnant, that ye may have some that shall escape the sword among the nations, when ye shall be scattered through the countries.
6:9 And they that escape of you shall remember me among the nations whither they shall be carried captives, because I am broken with their apostate heart, which hath departed from me, and with their eyes which go astray after their idols: and they shall lothe themselves for the evils which they have committed in all their abominations.
6:10 And they shall know that I am the LORD, and that I have not said in vain that I would do this evil to them.
6:11 Thus saith the Lord GOD; Smite with thy hand, and stamp with thy foot, and say, Alas, for all the evil abominations of the house of Israel! for they shall fall by the sword, by the famine, and by the pestilence.
6:12 He that is far off shall die by the pestilence; and he that is near shall fall by the sword; and he that remaineth and is besieged shall die by the famine: thus will I accomplish my fury upon them.
6:13 Then shall ye know that I am the LORD, when their slain men shall be among their idols round about their altars, upon every high hill, on all the tops of the mountains, and under every green tree, and under every thick oak, the place where they offered sweet savor to all their idols.
6:14 So will I stretch out my hand upon them, and make the land desolate, even, more desolate than the wilderness towards Diblath, in all their habitations: and they shall know that I am the LORD.

7

7:1 Moreover the word of the LORD came to me, saying,
7:2 Also, thou son of man, thus saith the Lord GOD to the land of Israel; An end, the end is come upon the four corners of the land.
7:3 Now is the end come upon thee, and I will send my anger upon thee, and will judge thee according to thy ways, and will recompense upon thee all thy abominations.
7:4 And my eye shall not spare thee, neither will I have pity: but I will recompense thy ways upon thee, and thy abominations shall be in the midst of thee: and ye shall know that I am the LORD.
7:5 Thus saith the Lord GOD; An evil, an only evil, behold, is come.
7:6 An end is come, the end is come: it watcheth for thee; behold, it is come.
7:7 The morning is come upon thee, O thou that dwellest in the land: the time is come, the day of trouble is near, and not the sounding again of the mountains.
7:8 Now will I shortly pour out my fury upon thee, and accomplish my anger upon thee: and I will judge thee according to thy ways, and will recompense thee for all thy abominations.
7:9 And my eye shall not spare, neither will I have pity: I will recompense thee according to thy ways and thy abominations that are in the midst of thee; and ye shall know that I am the LORD that smiteth.
7:10 Behold the day, behold, it is come; the morning is gone forth; the rod hath blossomed, pride hath budded.
7:11 Violence hath risen into a rod of wickedness: none of them shall remain, nor of their multitude, nor

of any of theirs: neither shall there be wailing for them.
7:12 The time is come, the day draweth near: let not the buyer rejoice, nor the seller mourn: for wrath is upon all the multitude thereof.
7:13 For the seller shall not return to that which is sold, although they were yet alive: for the vision is concerning the whole multitude thereof, which shall not return; neither shall any strengthen himself in the iniquity of his life.
7:14 They have blown the trumpet, even to make all ready; but none goeth to the battle: for my wrath is upon all the multitude thereof:
7:15 The sword is without, and the pestilence and the famine within: he that is in the field shall die with the sword; and he that is in the city, famine and pestilence shall devour him.
7:16 But they that escape of them shall escape, and shall be on the mountains like doves of the valleys, all of them mourning, every one for his iniquity.
7:17 All hands shall be feeble, and all knees shall be weak as water.
7:18 They shall also gird themselves with sackcloth, and horror shall cover them; and shame shall be upon all faces, and baldness upon all their heads.
7:19 They shall cast their silver in the streets, and their gold shall be removed: their silver and their gold shall not be able to deliver them in the day of the wrath of the LORD: they shall not satisfy their souls, neither fill their bowels because it is the stumbling-block of their iniquity.
7:20 As for the beauty of his ornament, he set it in majesty: but they made the images of their abominations and of their detestable things therein: therefore have I set it far from them.
7:21 And I will give it into the hands of the strangers for a prey, and to the wicked of the earth for a spoil; and they shall pollute it.
7:22 My face will I turn also from them, and they shall pollute my secret place: for the robbers shall enter into it, and defile it.
7:23 Make a chain: for the land is full of bloody crimes, and the city is full of violence.
7:24 Wherefore I will bring the worst of the heathen, and they shall possess their houses: I will also make the pomp of the strong to cease, and their holy places shall be defiled.
7:25 Destruction cometh; and they shall seek peace, and there shall be none.
7:26 Mischief shall come upon mischief, and rumor shall be upon rumor; then shall they seek a vision of the prophet; but the law shall perish from the priest, and counsel from the elders.
7:27 The king shall mourn, and the prince shall be clothed with desolation, and the hands of the people of the land shall be troubled: I will do to them after their way, and according to their deserts will I judge them, and they shall know that I am the LORD.

8

8:1 And it came to pass in the sixth year, in the sixth month, in the fifth day of the month, as I sat in my house, and the elders of Judah sat before me, that the hand of the Lord GOD fell there upon me.
8:2 Then I beheld, and lo a likeness as the appearance of fire: from the appearance of his loins even downward, fire; and from his loins even upward, as the appearance of brightness, as the color of amber.
8:3 And he put forth the form of a hand, and took me by a lock of my head; and the spirit lifted me up between the earth and the heaven, and brought me in the visions of God to Jerusalem, to the door of the inner gate that looketh towards the north; where was the seat of the image of jealousy, which provoketh to jealousy.
8:4 And behold, the glory of the God of Israel was there, according to the vision that I saw in the plain.
8:5 Then said he to me, Son of man, lift up thy eyes now the way towards the north. So I lifted up my eyes the way towards the north, and behold northward at the gate of the altar this image of jealousy in the entry.
8:6 He said furthermore to me, Son of man, seest thou what they do? even the great abominations that the house of Israel committeth here, that I should withdraw from my sanctuary? but turn thee yet again, and thou shalt see greater abominations.
8:7 And he brought me to the door of the court; and when I looked, behold a hole in the wall.
8:8 Then said he to me, Son of man, dig now in the wall: and when I had digged in the wall, behold a door.
8:9 And he said to me, Go in, and behold the wicked abominations that they do here.
8:10 So I went in and saw; and behold every form of creeping animals, and abominable beasts, and all the idols of the house of Israel, portrayed around upon the wall.
8:11 And there stood before them seventy men of the elders of the house of Israel, and in the midst of

them stood Jaazaniah the son of Shaphan, with every man his censer in his hand; and a thick cloud of incense went up.
8:12 Then said he to me, Son of man, hast thou seen what the elders of the house of Israel do in the dark, every man in the chambers of his imagery? for they say, The LORD seeth us not; the LORD hath forsaken the earth.
8:13 He said also to me, Turn thee yet again, and thou shalt see greater abominations that they do.
8:14 Then he brought me to the door of the gate of the LORD'S house which was towards the north; and behold, there sat women weeping for Tammuz.
8:15 Then said he to me, Hast thou seen this, O son of man? turn thee yet again, and thou shalt see greater abominations than these.
8:16 And he brought me into the inner court of the LORD'S house, and behold, at the door of the temple of the LORD, between the porch and the altar, were about five and twenty men, with their backs towards the temple of the LORD, and their faces towards the east; and they worshiped the sun towards the east.
8:17 Then he said to me, Hast thou seen this, O son of man? Is it a light thing to the house of Judah that they commit the abominations which they commit here? for they have filled the land with violence, and have returned to provoke me to anger: and lo, they put the branch to their nose.
8:18 Therefore will I also deal in fury: my eye shall not spare, neither will I have pity: and though they cry in my ears with a loud voice, yet I will not hear them.

9

9:1 He cried also in my ears with a loud voice, saying, Cause them that have charge over the city to draw near, even every man with his destroying weapon in his hand.
9:2 And behold, six men came from the way of the higher gate, which lieth towards the north, and every man a slaughter-weapon in his hand; and one man among them was clothed with linen, with a writer's inkhorn by his side: and they went in and stood beside the brazen altar.
9:3 And the glory of the God of Israel had gone up from the cherub on which he was, to the threshhold of the house. And he called to the man clothed with linen, who had the writer's inkhorn by his side;
9:4 And the LORD said to him, Go through the midst of the city, through the midst of Jerusalem, and set a mark upon the foreheads of the men that sigh and that cry for all the abominations that are done in the midst of it.
9:5 And to the others he said in my hearing, Go ye after him through the city, and smite: let not your eye spare, neither have ye pity:
9:6 Slay utterly old and young, both maids, and little children, and women: but come not near any man upon whom is the mark; and begin at my sanctuary. Then they began at the elderly men who were before the house.
9:7 And he said to them, Defile the house, and fill the courts with the slain: go ye forth. And they went forth, and slew in the city.
9:8 And it came to pass, while they were slaying them, and I was left, that I fell upon my face, and cried, and said, Ah Lord GOD! wilt thou destroy all the residue of Israel in thy pouring out of thy fury upon Jerusalem?
9:9 Then said he to me, The iniquity of the house of Israel and Judah is exceeding great, and the land is full of blood, and the city full of perverseness: for they say, The LORD hath forsaken the earth, and the LORD seeth not.
9:10 And as for me also, my eye shall not spare, neither will I have pity, but I will recompense their way upon their head.
9:11 And behold, the man clothed with linen, who had the inkhorn by his side, reported the matter, saying, I have done as thou hast commanded me.

10

10:1 Then I looked, and behold, in the firmament that was above the head of the cherubim there appeared over them as it were a sapphire stone, as the appearance of the likeness of a throne.
10:2 And he spoke to the man clothed with linen, and said, Go in between the wheels, even under the cherub, and fill thy hand with coals of fire from between the cherubim, and scatter them over the city. And he entered in my sight.
10:3 Now the cherubim stood on the right side of the house, when the man went in; and the cloud filled

the inner court.
10:4 Then the glory of the LORD went up from the cherub, and stood over the threshhold of the house; and the house was filled with the cloud, and the court was full of the brightness of the LORD'S glory.
10:5 And the sound of the cherubim's wings was heard even to the outer court, as the voice of the Almighty God when he speaketh.
10:6 And it came to pass, that when he had commanded the man clothed with linen, saying, Take fire from between the wheels, from between the cherubim; then he went in, and stood beside the wheels.
10:7 And one cherub stretched forth his hand from between the cherubim, to the fire that was between the cherubim, and took of it, and put it into the hands of him that was clothed with linen: who took it, and went out.
10:8 And there appeared in the cherubim the form of a man's hand under their wings.
10:9 And when I looked, behold the four wheels by the cherubim, one wheel by one cherub, and another wheel by another cherub: and the appearance of the wheels was as the color of a beryl stone.
10:10 And as for their appearances, they four had one likeness, as if a wheel had been in the midst of a wheel.
10:11 When they went, they went upon their four sides; they turned not as they went, but to the place whither the head looked, they followed it; they turned not as they went.
10:12 And their whole body, and their backs, and their hands, and their wings, and the wheels, were full of eyes on every side, even the wheels that they four had.
10:13 As for the wheels, it was cried to them in my hearing, O wheel.
10:14 And every one had four faces: the first face was the face of a cherub, and the second face was the face of a man, and the third the face of a lion, and the fourth the face of an eagle.
10:15 And the cherubim were lifted up. This is the living creature that I saw by the river of Kebar.
10:16 And when the cherubim went, the wheels went by them: and when the cherubim lifted up their wings to mount up from the earth, the same wheels also turned not from beside them.
10:17 When they stood, these stood; and when they were lifted up, these lifted up themselves also: for the spirit of the living creature was in them.
10:18 Then the glory of the LORD departed from off the threshhold of the house, and stood over the cherubim.
10:19 And the cherubim lifted up their wings, and mounted up from the earth in my sight: when they went out, the wheels also were beside them, and every one stood at the door of the east-gate of the LORD'S house; and the glory of the God of Israel was over them above.
10:20 This is the living creature that I saw under the God of Israel by the river of Kebar; and I knew that they were the cherubim.
10:21 Every one had four faces each, and every one four wings; and the likeness of the hands of a man was under their wings.
10:22 And the likeness of their faces was the same faces which I saw by the river of Kebar, their appearances and themselves: they went every one straight forward.

11

11:1 Moreover the spirit lifted me up, and brought me to the east-gate of the LORD'S house, which looketh eastward: and behold, at the door of the gate five and twenty men; among whom I saw Jaazaniah the son of Azur, and Pelatiah the son of Benaiah, princes of the people.
11:2 Then said he to me, Son of man, these are the men that devise mischief, and give wicked counsel in this city:
11:3 Who say, It is not near; let us build houses: this city is the caldron, and we are the flesh.
11:4 Therefore prophesy against them, prophesy, O son of man.
11:5 And the spirit of the LORD fell upon me, and said to me, Speak; Thus saith the LORD; Thus have ye said, O house of Israel: for I know the things that come into your mind, every one of them.
11:6 Ye have multiplied your slain in this city, and ye have filled its streets with the slain.
11:7 Therefore thus saith the Lord GOD; Your slain whom ye have laid in the midst of it, they are the flesh, and this city is the caldron: but I will bring you forth out of the midst of it.
11:8 Ye have feared the sword; and I will bring a sword upon you, saith the Lord GOD.
11:9 And I will bring you out of the midst of it, and deliver you into the hands of strangers, and will execute judgments among you.
11:10 Ye shall fall by the sword; I will judge you in the border of Israel; and ye shall know that I am the LORD.

11:11 This city shall not be your caldron, neither shall ye be the flesh in the midst of it; but I will judge you in the border of Israel:
11:12 And ye shall know that I am the LORD: for ye have not walked in my statutes, neither executed my judgments, but have done after the manners of the heathen that are around you.
11:13 And it came to pass, when I prophesied, that Pelatiah the son of Benaiah died. Then I fell down upon my face, and cried with a loud voice, and said, Ah Lord GOD! wilt thou make a full end of the remnant of Israel?
11:14 Again the word of the LORD came to me, saying,
11:15 Son of man, thy brethren, even thy brethren, the men of thy kindred, and all the house of Israel wholly, are they to whom the inhabitants of Jerusalem have said, Retire far from the LORD: to us is this land given in possession.
11:16 Therefore say, Thus saith the Lord GOD; Although I have cast them far off among the heathen, and although I have scattered them among the countries, yet will I be to them as a little sanctuary in the countries where they shall come.
11:17 Therefore say, Thus saith the Lord GOD; I will even gather you from the people, and assemble you out of the countries where ye have been scattered, and I will give you the land of Israel.
11:18 And they shall come thither, and they shall take away from thence all its detestable things, and all its abominations.
11:19 And I will give them one heart, and I will put a new spirit within you; and I will take the stony heart out of their flesh, and will give them a heart of flesh:
11:20 That they may walk in my statutes, and keep my ordinances, and do them: and they shall be my people, and I will be their God.
11:21 But as for them whose heart walketh after the heart of their detestable things and their abominations, I will recompense their way upon their own heads, saith the Lord GOD.
11:22 Then the cherubim raised their wings, and the wheels beside them; and the glory of the God of Israel was over them above.
11:23 And the glory of the LORD went up from the midst of the city, and stood upon the mountain which is on the east side of the city.
11:24 Afterwards the spirit took me up, and brought me in vision by the Spirit of God into Chaldea, to them of the captivity. So the vision that I had seen went up from me.
11:25 Then I spoke to them of the captivity all the things that the LORD had shown me.

12

12:1 The word of the LORD also came to me, saying,
12:2 Son of man, thou dwellest in the midst of a rebellious house, who have eyes to see, and see not; they have ears to hear, and hear not: for they are a rebellious house.
12:3 Therefore, thou son of man, prepare thee stuff for removing, and remove by day in their sight; and thou shalt remove from thy place to another place in their sight; it may be they will consider, though they are a rebellious house.
12:4 Then shalt thou bring forth thy stuff by day in their sight, as stuff for removing: and thou shalt go forth at evening in their sight, as they that go forth into captivity.
12:5 Dig thou through the wall in their sight, and carry out thereby.
12:6 In their sight shalt thou bear it upon thy shoulders, and carry it forth in the twilight: thou shalt cover thy face, that thou mayest not see the ground: for I have set thee for a sign to the house of Israel.
12:7 And I did so as I was commanded: I brought forth my stuff by day, as stuff for captivity, and in the evening I digged through the wall with my hand; I brought it forth in the twilight, and I bore it upon my shoulder in their sight.
12:8 And in the morning came the word of the LORD to me, saying,
12:9 Son of man, hath not the house of Israel, the rebellious house, said to thee, What doest thou?
12:10 Say thou to them, Thus saith the Lord GOD, This burden concerneth the prince in Jerusalem, and all the house of Israel that are among them.
12:11 Say, I am your sign: as I have done, so shall it be done to them: they shall remove and go into captivity.
12:12 And the prince that is among them shall bear upon his shoulder in the twilight, and shall go forth: they shall dig through the wall to carry out thereby: he shall cover his face, that he may not see the ground with his eyes.
12:13 My net also will I spread upon him, and he shall be taken in my snare: and I will bring him to

Babylon to the land of the Chaldeans, yet shall he not see it, though he shall die there.
12:14 And I will scatter towards every wind all that are about him to help him, and all his bands; and I will draw out the sword after them.
12:15 And they shall know that I am the LORD, when I shall scatter them among the nations, and disperse them in the countries.
12:16 But I will leave a few men of them from the sword, from the famine, and from the pestilence; that they may declare all their abominations among the heathen whither they come; and they shall know that I am the LORD.
12:17 Moreover the word of the LORD came to me, saying,
12:18 Son of man, eat thy bread with quaking, and drink thy water with trembling and with solicitude.
12:19 And say to the people of the land, Thus saith the Lord GOD of the inhabitants of Jerusalem, and of the land of Israel; They shall eat their bread with solicitude, and drink their water with astonishment, that her land may be desolate from all that is therein, because of the violence of all them that dwell therein.
12:20 And the cities that are inhabited shall be laid waste, and the land shall be desolate; and ye shall know that I am the LORD.
12:21 And the word of the LORD came to me, saying,
12:22 Son of man, what is that proverb that ye have in the land of Israel, saying, The days are prolonged, and every vision faileth?
12:23 Tell them therefore, Thus saith the Lord GOD: I will make this proverb to cease, and they shall no more use it as a proverb in Israel; but say to them, The days are at hand, and the effect of every vision.
12:24 For there shall no more be any vain vision nor flattering divination within the house of Israel.
12:25 For I am the LORD: I will speak, and the word that I shall speak shall come to pass; it shall no more be prolonged: for in your days, O rebellious house, will I say the word, and will perform it, saith the Lord GOD.
12:26 Again the word of the LORD came to me, saying,
12:27 Son of man, behold, they of the house of Israel say, The vision that he seeth is for many days to come, and he prophesieth of the times that are distant.
12:28 Therefore say to them, Thus saith the Lord GOD; There shall none of my words be further deferred, but the word which I have spoken shall be done, saith the Lord GOD.

13

13:1 And the word of the LORD came to me, saying,
13:2 Son of man, prophesy against the prophets of Israel that prophesy, and say thou to them that prophesy out of their own hearts, Hear ye the word of the LORD;
13:3 Thus saith the Lord GOD; Woe to the foolish prophets, that follow their own spirit, and have seen nothing!
13:4 O Israel, thy prophets are like the foxes in the deserts.
13:5 Ye have not gone up into the gaps, neither made up the hedge for the house of Israel to stand in the battle in the day of the LORD.
13:6 They have seen vanity and lying divination, saying, The LORD saith: and the LORD hath not sent them: and they have made others to hope that they would confirm the word.
13:7 Have ye not seen a vain vision, and have ye not spoken a lying divination, whereas ye say, The LORD saith it, although I have not spoken?
13:8 Therefore thus saith the Lord GOD; Because ye have spoken vanity, and seen lies, therefore, behold, I am against you, saith the Lord GOD.
13:9 And my hand shall be upon the prophets that see vanity, and that divine lies: they shall not be in the assembly of my people, neither shall they be written in the writing of the house of Israel, neither shall they enter into the land of Israel; and ye shall know that I am the Lord GOD.
13:10 Because, even because they have seduced my people, saying, Peace; and there was no peace; and one built up a wall, and lo, others daubed it with untempered mortar:
13:11 Say to them who daub it with untempered mortar, that it shall fall: there shall be an overflowing shower; and ye, O great hailstones, shall fall; and a stormy wind shall rend it.
13:12 Lo, when the wall hath fallen, shall it not be said to you, Where is the daubing with which ye have daubed it?
13:13 Therefore thus saith the Lord GOD; I will even rend it with a stormy wind in my fury; and there

shall be an overflowing shower in my anger, and great hailstones in my fury to consume it.
13:14 So will I break down the wall that ye have daubed with untempered mortar, and bring it down to the ground, so that its foundation shall be made bare, and it shall fall, and ye shall be consumed in the midst of it: and ye shall know that I am the LORD.
13:15 Thus will I accomplish my wrath upon the wall, and upon them that have daubed it with untempered mortar, and will say to you, The wall is no more, neither they that daubed it;
13:16 To wit, the prophets of Israel who prophesy concerning Jerusalem, and who see visions of peace for her, and there is no peace, saith the Lord GOD.
13:17 Likewise, thou son of man, set thy face against the daughters of thy people, who prophesy out of their own heart; and prophesy thou against them,
13:18 And say, Thus saith the Lord GOD; Woe to the women that sew pillows to all arm-holes, and make kerchiefs upon the head of every stature to hunt souls! Will ye hunt the souls of my people, and will ye save the souls alive that come to you?
13:19 And will ye profane me among my people for handfuls of barley and for pieces of bread, to slay the souls that should not die, and to save the souls alive that should not live, by your lying to my people that hear your lies?
13:20 Wherefore thus saith the Lord GOD; Behold, I am against your pillows, with which ye there hunt the souls to make them fly, and I will tear them from your arms, and will let the souls go, even the souls that ye hunt to make them fly.
13:21 Your kerchiefs also will I tear, and deliver my people out of your hand, and they shall no more be in your hand to be hunted; and ye shall know that I am the LORD.
13:22 Because with lies ye have made the heart of the righteous sad, whom I have not made sad; and strengthened the hands of the wicked, that he should not return from his wicked way, by promising him life:
13:23 Therefore ye shall see no more vanity, nor divine divinations: for I will deliver my people out of your hand: and ye shall know that I am the LORD.

14

14:1 Then came certain of the elders of Israel to me, and sat before me.
14:2 And the word of the LORD came to me, saying,
14:3 Son of man, these men have set up their idols in their heart, and put the stumbling-block of their iniquity before their face: should I be inquired of at all by them?
14:4 Therefore speak to them, and say to them, Thus saith the Lord GOD; Every man of the house of Israel that setteth up his idols in his heart, and putteth the stumbling-block of his iniquity before his face, and cometh to the prophet; I the LORD will answer him that cometh according to the multitude of his idols;
14:5 That I may take the house of Israel in their own heart, because they are all estranged from me through their idols.
14:6 Therefore say to the house of Israel, Thus saith the Lord GOD; Repent, and turn yourselves from your idols; and turn away your faces from all your abominations.
14:7 For every one of the house of Israel, or of the stranger that sojourneth in Israel, who separateth himself from me, and setteth up his idols in his heart, and putteth the stumbling-block of his iniquity before his face, and cometh to a prophet to inquire of him concerning me; I the LORD will answer him by myself:
14:8 And I will set my face against that man, and will make him a sign and a proverb, and I will cut him off from the midst of my people; and ye shall know that I am the LORD.
14:9 And if the prophet be deceived when he hath spoken a thing, I the LORD have deceived that prophet, and I will stretch out my hand upon him, and will destroy him from the midst of my people Israel.
14:10 And they shall bear the punishment of their iniquity: the punishment of the prophet shall be even as the punishment of him that seeketh to him;
14:11 That the house of Israel may no more go astray from me, neither be polluted any more with all their transgressions; but that they may be my people, and I may be their God, saith the Lord GOD.
14:12 The word of the LORD came again to me, saying,
14:13 Son of man, when the land sinneth against me by trespassing grievously, then will I stretch out my hand upon it, and will break the staff of the bread thereof, and will send famine upon it, and will cut off man and beast from it:

14:14 Though these three men, Noah, Daniel, and Job, were in it, they should deliver their own souls only by their righteousness, saith the Lord GOD.
14:15 If I cause noisome beasts to pass through the land, and they lay it waste, so that it be desolate, that no man may pass through because of the beasts:
14:16 Though these three men were in it, as I live, saith the Lord GOD, they shall deliver neither sons nor daughters; they only shall be delivered, but the land shall be desolate.
14:17 Or if I bring a sword upon that land, and say, Sword, go through the land; so that I cut off man and beast from it:
14:18 Though these three men were in it, as I live, saith the Lord GOD, they shall deliver neither sons nor daughters, but they only shall be delivered themselves.
14:19 Or if I send a pestilence into that land, and pour out my fury upon it in blood, to cut off from it man and beast:
14:20 Though Noah, Daniel, and Job, were in it, as I live, saith the Lord GOD, they shall deliver neither son nor daughter; they shall deliver their own souls only by their righteousness.
14:21 For thus saith the Lord GOD; How much more when I send my four severe judgments upon Jerusalem, the sword, and the famine, and the noisome beast, and the pestilence, to cut off from it man and beast?
14:22 Yet behold, therein shall be left a remnant that shall be brought forth, both sons and daughters: behold, they shall come forth to you, and ye shall see their way and their doings: and ye shall be comforted concerning the evil that I have brought upon Jerusalem, even concerning all that I have brought upon it.
14:23 And they shall comfort you, when ye see their ways and their doings: and ye shall know that I have not done without cause all that I have done in it, saith the Lord GOD.

15

15:1 And the word of the LORD came to me, saying,
15:2 Son of man, What is the vine-tree more than any tree, or than a branch which is among the trees of the forest?
15:3 Shall wood be taken of it to do any work? or will men take a pin of it to hang any vessel upon it?
15:4 Behold, it is cast into the fire for fuel; the fire devoureth both the ends of it, and the midst of it is burned. Is it suitable for any work?
15:5 Behold, when it was whole, it was fit for no work: how much less then shall it be fit for any work, when the fire hath devoured it, and it is burned?
15:6 Therefore thus saith the Lord GOD; As the vine-tree among the trees of the forest, which I have given to the fire for fuel, so will I give the inhabitants of Jerusalem.
15:7 And I will set my face against them; they shall go out from one fire, and another fire shall devour them; and ye shall know that I am the LORD, when I set my face against them.
15:8 And I will make the land desolate, because they have committed a trespass, saith the Lord GOD.

16

16:1 Again the word of the LORD came to me, saying,
16:2 Son of man, cause Jerusalem to know her abominations,
16:3 And say, Thus saith the Lord GOD to Jerusalem; Thy birth and thy nativity is of the land of Canaan; thy father was an Amorite, and thy mother a Hittite.
16:4 And as for thy nativity, in the day thou wast born thy navel was not cut, neither wast thou washed in water to supple thee; thou wast not salted at all, nor swaddled at all.
16:5 No eye pitied thee, to do any of these to thee, to have compassion upon thee; but thou wast cast out in the open field, to the lothing of thy person, in the day that thou wast born.
16:6 And when I passed by thee, and saw thee polluted in thy own blood, I said to thee when thou wast in thy blood, Live; yes, I said to thee when thou wast in thy blood, Live.
16:7 I have caused thee to multiply as the bud of the field, and thou hast increased and become great, and thou art come to excellent ornaments: thy breasts are fashioned, and thy hair is grown, whereas thou wast naked and bare.
16:8 Now when I passed by thee, and looked upon thee, behold, thy time was the time of love; and I spread my skirt over thee, and covered thy nakedness: yes, I swore to thee, and entered into a covenant

with thee, saith the Lord GOD, and thou becamest mine.
16:9 Then I washed thee with water; yes, I thoroughly washed away thy blood from thee, and I anointed thee with oil.
16:10 I clothed thee also with broidered work, and shod thee with badgers' skin, and I girded thee with fine linen, and I covered thee with silk.
16:11 I decked thee also with ornaments, and I put bracelets upon thy hands, and a chain on thy neck.
16:12 And I put a jewel on thy forehead, and ear-rings in thy ears, and a beautiful crown upon thy head.
16:13 Thus wast thou decked with gold and silver; and thy raiment was of fine linen, and silk, and broidered work; thou didst eat fine flour, and honey, and oil: and thou wast exceeding beautiful, and thou didst prosper into a kingdom.
16:14 And thy renown went forth among the heathen for thy beauty: for it was perfect through my comeliness, which I had put upon thee, saith the Lord GOD.
16:15 But thou didst trust in thy own beauty, and playedst the harlot because of thy renown, and pouredst out thy fornications on every one that passed by; his it was.
16:16 And of thy garments thou didst take, and deck thy high places with divers colors, and play the harlot upon them: the like things shall not come, neither shall it be so.
16:17 Thou hast also taken thy fair jewels of my gold and of my silver, which I had given thee, and hast made to thyself images of men, and hast committed lewdness with them.
16:18 And hast taken thy broidered garments, and covered them: and thou hast set my oil and my incense before them.
16:19 My provisions also which I gave thee, fine flour, and oil, and honey, with which I fed thee, thou hast even set before them for a sweet savor: and thus it was, saith the Lord GOD.
16:20 Moreover thou hast taken thy sons and thy daughters, whom thou hast borne to me, and these hast thou sacrificed to them to be devoured. Is this of thy lewdness a small matter,
16:21 That thou hast slain my children, and delivered them to cause them to pass through the fire for them?
16:22 And in all thy abominations and thy deeds of lewdness thou hast not remembered the days of thy youth, when thou wast naked and bare, and wast polluted in thy blood.
16:23 And it came to pass after all thy wickedness, (woe, woe to thee! saith the Lord GOD;)
16:24 That thou hast also built to thee an eminent place, and hast made thee a high place in every street.
16:25 Thou hast built thy high place at every head of the way, and hast made thy beauty to be abhorred, and hast prostituted thyself to every one that passed by, and multiplied thy lewd deeds.
16:26 Thou hast also committed fornication with the Egyptians thy neighbors, great of flesh; and hast multiplied thy lewd deeds, to provoke me to anger.
16:27 Behold, therefore I have stretched out my hand over thee, and have diminished thy ordinary food, and delivered thee to the will of them that hate thee, the daughters of the Philistines, who are ashamed of thy lewd way.
16:28 Thou hast played the harlot also with the Assyrians, because thou wast insatiable; yes, thou hast played the harlot with them, and yet couldst not be satisfied.
16:29 Thou hast moreover multiplied thy fornication in the land of Canaan to Chaldea; and yet with this thou wast not satisfied.
16:30 How weak is thy heart, saith the Lord GOD, seeing thou doest all these things, the work of an imperious lewd woman;
16:31 In that thou buildest thy eminent place in the head of every way, and makest thy high place in every street; and hast not been as a harlot, in that thou scornest hire;
16:32 But as a wife that committeth adultery, who taketh strangers instead of her husband!
16:33 They give gifts to all lewd women: but thou givest thy gifts to all thy lovers, and hirest them, that they may come to thee on every side for thy lewdness.
16:34 And the contrary is in thee from other women in thy unlawful commerce, whereas none followeth thee to commit lewdness: and in that thou givest a reward, and no reward is given to thee, therefore thou art contrary.
16:35 Wherefore, O harlot, hear the word of the LORD:
16:36 Thus saith the Lord GOD; Because thy filthiness was poured out, and thy nakedness exposed through thy carnal connection with thy lovers, and with all the idols of thy abominations, and by the blood of thy children, which thou didst give to them;
16:37 Behold therefore, I will gather all thy lovers, with whom thou hast taken pleasure, and all them that thou hast loved, with all them that thou hast hated; I will even gather them on every side against thee, and will uncover thy nakedness to them, that they may see all thy nakedness.
16:38 And I will judge thee, as women that break wedlock and shed blood are judged; and I will give

thee blood in fury and jealousy.
16:39 And I will also give thee into their hand, and they shall throw down thy eminent place, and shall break down thy high places: they shall strip thee also of thy clothes, and shall take thy fair jewels, and leave thee naked and bare.
16:40 They shall also bring up a company against thee, and they shall stone thee with stones, and thrust thee through with their swords.
16:41 And they shall burn thy houses with fire, and execute judgments upon thee in the sight of many women: and I will cause thee to cease from playing the harlot, and thou also shalt give no hire any more.
16:42 So will I make my fury towards thee to rest, and my jealousy shall depart from thee, and I will be quiet, and will be no more angry.
16:43 Because thou hast not remembered the days of thy youth, but hast provoked me in all these things; behold therefore, I also will recompense thy way upon thy head, saith the Lord GOD: and thou shalt not commit this lewdness above all thy abominations.
16:44 Behold, every one that useth proverbs shall use this proverb against thee, saying, As is the mother, so is her daughter.
16:45 Thou art thy mother's daughter, that lotheth her husband and her children; and thou art the sister of thy sisters, who lothed their husbands and their children: your mother was a Hittite, and your father an Amorite.
16:46 And thy elder sister is Samaria, she and her daughters that dwell at thy left hand: and thy younger sister, that dwelleth at thy right hand, is Sodom and her daughters.
16:47 Yet hast thou not walked after their ways, nor done after their abominations: but as if that were a very little thing, thou wast corrupted more than they in all thy ways.
16:48 As I live, saith the Lord GOD, Sodom thy sister hath not done, she nor her daughters, as thou hast done, thou and thy daughters.
16:49 Behold, this was the iniquity of thy sister Sodom, pride, fullness of bread, and abundance of idleness was in her and in her daughters, neither did she strengthen the hand of the poor and needy.
16:50 And they were haughty, and committed abomination before me: therefore I took them away as I saw good.
16:51 Neither hath Samaria committed half of thy sins; but thou hast multiplied thy abominations more than they, and hast justified thy sisters in all thy abominations which thou hast done.
16:52 Thou also, who hast judged thy sisters, bear thy own shame for thy sins that thou hast committed more abominable than they: they are more righteous than thou: yes, be thou confounded also, and bear thy shame, in that thou hast justified thy sisters.
16:53 When I shall bring again their captivity, the captivity of Sodom and her daughters, and the captivity of Samaria and her daughters, then will I bring again the captivity of thy captives in the midst of them:
16:54 That thou mayest bear thy own shame, and mayest be confounded in all that thou hast done, in that thou art a comfort to them.
16:55 When thy sisters, Sodom and her daughters, shall return to their former state, and Samaria and her daughters shall return to their former state, then thou and thy daughters shall return to your former state.
16:56 For thy sister Sodom was not mentioned by thy mouth in the day of thy pride,
16:57 Before thy wickedness was disclosed, as at the time of thy reproach of the daughters of Syria, and all that are around her, the daughters of the Philistines, who despise thee on every side.
16:58 Thou hast borne thy lewdness and thy abominations, saith the LORD.
16:59 For thus saith the Lord GOD; I will even deal with thee as thou hast done, who hast despised the oath in breaking the covenant.
16:60 Nevertheless I will remember my covenant with thee in the days of thy youth, and I will establish to thee an everlasting covenant.
16:61 Then thou shalt remember thy ways, and be ashamed, when thou shalt receive thy sisters, thy elder and thy younger: and I will give them to thee for daughters, but not by thy covenant.
16:62 And I will establish my covenant with thee; and thou shalt know that I am the LORD:
16:63 That thou mayest remember, and be confounded, and never open thy mouth any more because of thy shame, when I am pacified towards thee for all that thou hast done, saith the Lord GOD.

17

17:1 And the word of the LORD came to me, saying,

17:2 Son of man, put forth a riddle, and speak a parable to the house of Israel;
17:3 And say, Thus saith the Lord GOD; A great eagle with great wings, long-winged, full of feathers, which had divers colors, came to Lebanon, and took the highest branch of the cedar:
17:4 He cropped off the top of its young twigs, and carried it into a land of traffick; he set it in a city of merchants.
17:5 He took also of the seed of the land, and planted it in a fruitful field; he placed it by great waters, and set it as a willow tree.
17:6 And it grew, and became a spreading vine of low stature, whose branches turned towards him, and its roots were under him: so it became a vine, and brought forth branches, and shot forth sprigs.
17:7 There was also another great eagle with great wings and many feathers: and behold, this vine did bend her roots towards him, and shot forth her branches towards him, that he might water it by the furrows of her plantation.
17:8 It was planted in a good soil by great waters, that it might bring forth branches, and that it might bear fruit, that it might be a goodly vine.
17:9 Say thou, Thus saith the Lord GOD; Shall it prosper? shall he not pull up its roots, and cut off its fruit, that it may wither? it shall wither in all the leaves of her spring, even without great power or many people to pluck it up by its roots.
17:10 Yes, behold, being planted, shall it prosper? shall it not utterly wither, when the east wind toucheth it? it shall wither in the furrows where it grew.
17:11 Moreover the word of the LORD came to me, saying,
17:12 Say now to the rebellious house, Know ye not what these things mean? tell them, Behold, the king of Babylon hath come to Jerusalem, and hath taken its king, and its princes, and led them with him to Babylon;
17:13 And hath taken of the king's seed, and made a covenant with him, and hath taken an oath from him: he hath also taken the mighty of the land:
17:14 That the kingdom might be base, that it might not lift itself up, but that by keeping his covenant it might stand.
17:15 But he rebelled against him in sending his embassadors into Egypt, that they might give him horses and many people. Shall he prosper? shall he escape that doeth such things? or shall he break the covenant, and be delivered?
17:16 As I live, saith the Lord GOD, surely in the place where the king dwelleth that made him king, whose oath he despised, and whose covenant he broke, even with him in the midst of Babylon he shall die.
17:17 Neither shall Pharaoh with his mighty army and great company make for him in the war, by casting up mounts, and building forts, to cut off many persons:
17:18 Seeing he despised the oath by breaking the covenant, when lo, he had given his hand, and hath done all these things, he shall not escape.
17:19 Therefore thus saith the Lord GOD; As I live, surely my oath that he hath despised, and my covenant that he hath broken, even that will I recompense upon his own head.
17:20 And I will spread my net upon him, and he shall be taken in my snare, and I will bring him to Babylon, and will plead with him there for his trespass that he hath trespassed against me.
17:21 And all his fugitives with all his bands shall fall by the sword, and they that remain shall be scattered towards all winds: and ye shall know that I the LORD have spoken it.
17:22 Thus saith the Lord GOD, I will also take of the highest branch of the high cedar, and will set it; I will crop off from the top of its young twigs a tender one, and will plant it upon a high mountain and eminent:
17:23 In the mountain of the hight of Israel will I plant it: and it shall bring forth boughs, and bear fruit, and be a goodly cedar: and under it shall dwell all fowl of every wing; in the shade of its branches shall they dwell.
17:24 And all the trees of the field shall know that I the LORD have brought down the high tree, have exalted the low tree, have dried up the green tree, and have made the dry tree to flourish: I the LORD have spoken and have done it.

18

18:1 The word of the LORD came to me again, saying,
18:2 What mean ye, that ye use this proverb concerning the land of Israel, saying, The fathers have eaten sour grapes, and the children's teeth are set on edge?

18:3 As I live, saith the Lord GOD, ye shall not have occasion any more to use this proverb in Israel.
18:4 Behold, all souls are mine; as the soul of the father, so also the soul of the son is mine: the soul that sinneth, it shall die.
18:5 But if a man is just, and doeth that which is lawful and right,
18:6 And hath not eaten upon the mountains, neither hath lifted up his eyes to the idols of the house of Israel, neither hath defiled his neighbor's wife, neither hath come near to a polluted woman,
18:7 And hath not oppressed any, but hath restored to the debtor his pledge, hath stripped none by violence, hath given his bread to the hungry, and hath covered the naked with a garment:
18:8 He that hath not given forth upon interest, neither hath taken any increase, that hath withdrawn his hand from iniquity, hath executed true judgment between man and man,
18:9 Hath walked in my statutes, and hath kept my judgments, to deal truly; he is just, he shall surely live, saith the Lord GOD.
18:10 If he begetteth a son that is a robber, a shedder of blood, and that doeth the like to any one of these things,
18:11 And that doeth not any of those duties, but even hath eaten upon the mountains, and defiled his neighbor's wife,
18:12 Hath oppressed the poor and needy, hath stripped by violence, hath not restored the pledge, and hath lifted up his eyes to the idols, hath committed abomination.
18:13 Hath given forth upon interest, and hath taken increase: shall he then live? he shall not live: he hath done all these abominations; he shall surely die; his blood shall be upon him.
18:14 Now lo, if he begetteth a son, that seeth all his father's sins which he hath done, and considereth, and doeth not such like,
18:15 That hath not eaten upon the mountains, neither hath lifted up his eyes to the idols of the house of Israel, hath not defiled his neighbor's wife,
18:16 Neither hath oppressed any, hath not withheld the pledge, neither hath stripped by violence, but hath given his bread to the hungry, and hath covered the naked with a garment,
18:17 That hath taken off his hand from the poor, that hath not received interest nor increase, hath executed my judgments, hath walked in my statutes; he shall not die for the iniquity of his father, he shall surely live.
18:18 As for his father, because he cruelly oppressed, stripped his brother by violence, and did that which is not good among his people, lo, even he shall die in his iniquity.
18:19 Yet say ye, Why? doth not the son bear the iniquity of the father? When the son hath done that which is lawful and right, and hath kept all my statutes, and hath done them, he shall surely live.
18:20 The soul that sinneth, it shall die. The son shall not bear the iniquity of the father, neither shall the father bear the iniquity of the son: the righteousness of the righteous shall be upon him, and the wickedness of the wicked shall be upon him.
18:21 But if the wicked will turn from all his sins that he hath committed, and keep all my statutes, and do that which is lawful and right, he shall surely live, he shall not die.
18:22 All his transgressions that he hath committed, they shall not be mentioned to him: in his righteousness that he hath done he shall live.
18:23 Have I any pleasure at all that the wicked should die? saith the Lord GOD: and not that he should return from his ways, and live?
18:24 But when the righteous turneth away from his righteousness, and committeth iniquity, and doeth according to all the abominations that the wicked man doeth, shall he live? All his righteousness that he hath done shall not be mentioned: in his trespass that he hath trespassed, and in his sin that he hath sinned, in them shall he die.
18:25 Yet ye say, The way of the Lord is not equal. Hear now, O house of Israel; Is not my way equal? are not your ways unequal?
18:26 When a righteous man turneth away from his righteousness, and committeth iniquity, and dieth in them; for his iniquity that he hath done shall he die.
18:27 Again, when a wicked man turneth away from his wickedness that he hath committed, and doeth that which is lawful and right, he shall save his soul alive.
18:28 Because he considereth and turneth away from all his transgressions that he hath committed, he shall surely live, he shall not die.
18:29 Yet saith the house of Israel, The way of the Lord is not equal. O house of Israel, are not my ways equal? are not your ways unequal?
18:30 Therefore I will judge you, O house of Israel, every one according to his ways, saith the Lord GOD. Repent, and turn yourselves from all your transgressions; so iniquity shall not be your ruin.
18:31 Cast away from you all your transgressions, by which ye have transgressed; and make you a new

heart and a new spirit: for why will ye die, O house of Israel?
18:32 For I have no pleasure in the death of him that dieth, saith the Lord GOD: wherefore turn ye, and live.

19

19:1 Moreover take thou up a lamentation for the princes of Israel,
19:2 And say, What is thy mother: A lioness: she lay down among lions, she nourished her whelps among young lions.
19:3 And she brought up one of her whelps: it became a young lion, and it learned to catch the prey; it devoured men.
19:4 The nations also heard of him; he was taken in their pit, and they brought him with chains to the land of Egypt.
19:5 Now when she saw that she had waited, and her hope was lost, then she took another of her whelps, and made him a young lion.
19:6 And he went up and down among the lions, he became a young lion, and learned to catch the prey, and devoured men.
19:7 And he knew their desolate palaces, and he laid waste their cities; and the land was desolate, and the fullness of it, by the noise of his roaring.
19:8 Then the nations set against him on every side from the provinces, and spread their net over him: he was taken in their pit.
19:9 And they put him in custody in chains, and brought him to the king of Babylon: they brought him into holds, that his voice should no more be heard upon the mountains of Israel.
19:10 Thy mother is like a vine in thy blood, planted by the waters: she was fruitful and full of branches by reason of many waters.
19:11 And she had strong rods for the scepters of them that bore rule, and her stature was exalted among the thick branches, and she appeared in her hight with the multitude of her branches.
19:12 But she was plucked up in fury, she was cast down to the ground, and the east wind dried up her fruit: her strong rods were broken and withered; the fire consumed them.
19:13 And now she is planted in the wilderness, in a dry and thirsty ground.
19:14 And fire hath gone out of a rod of her branches, which hath devoured her fruit, so that she hath no strong rod to be a scepter to rule. This is a lamentation, and shall be for a lamentation.

20

20:1 And it came to pass in the seventh year, in the fifth month, the tenth day of the month, that certain of the elders of Israel came to inquire of the LORD, and sat before me.
20:2 Then came the word of the LORD to me, saying,
20:3 Son of man, speak to the elders of Israel, and say to them, Thus saith the Lord GOD; Are ye come to inquire of me? As I live, saith the Lord GOD, I will not be inquired of by you.
20:4 Wilt thou judge them, son of man, wilt thou judge them? cause them to know the abominations of their fathers:
20:5 And say to them, Thus saith the Lord GOD; In the day when I chose Israel, and lifted up my hand to the seed of the house of Jacob, and made myself known to them in the land of Egypt, when I lifted up my hand to them, saying, I am the LORD your God;
20:6 In the day that I lifted up my hand to them, to bring them forth from the land of Egypt into a land that I had espied for them, flowing with milk and honey, which is the glory of all lands:
20:7 Then said I to them, Cast ye away every man the abominations of his eyes, and defile not yourselves with the idols of Egypt: I am the LORD your God.
20:8 But they rebelled against me, and would not hearken to me: they did not every man cast away the abominations of their eyes, neither did they forsake the idols of Egypt: then I said, I will pour out my fury upon them, to accomplish my anger against them in the midst of the land of Egypt.
20:9 But I wrought for my name's sake, that it should not be profaned before the heathen, among whom they were, in whose sight I made myself known to them, in bringing them forth from the land of Egypt.
20:10 Wherefore I caused them to go forth from the land of Egypt, and brought them into the wilderness.
20:11 And I gave them my statutes, and showed them my judgments, which if a man doeth, he shall

even live in them.

20:12 Moreover also I gave them my sabbaths, to be a sign between me and them, that they might know that I am the LORD that sanctify them.

20:13 But the house of Israel rebelled against me in the wilderness: they walked not in my statutes, and they despised my judgments, which if a man doeth, he shall even live in them; and my sabbaths they greatly profaned: then I said, I would pour out my fury upon them in the wilderness, to consume them.

20:14 But I wrought for my name's sake, that it should not be profaned before the heathen, in whose sight I brought them out.

20:15 Yet also I lifted up my hand to them in the wilderness, that I would not bring them into the land which I had given them, flowing with milk and honey, which is the glory of all lands;

20:16 Because they despised my judgments, and walked not in my statutes, but profaned my sabbaths: for their heart went after their idols.

20:17 Nevertheless my eye spared them from destroying them, neither did I make an end of them in the wilderness.

20:18 But I said to their children in the wilderness, Walk ye not in the statutes of your fathers, neither observe their judgments, nor defile yourselves with their idols:

20:19 I am the LORD your God; walk in my statutes, and keep my judgments, and do them;

20:20 And hallow my sabbaths; and they shall be a sign between me and you, that ye may know that I am the LORD your God.

20:21 Notwithstanding the children rebelled against me: they walked not in my statutes, neither kept my judgments to do them, which if a man doeth, he shall even live in them: they profaned my sabbaths: then I said, I would pour out my fury upon them, to accomplish my anger against them in the wilderness.

20:22 Nevertheless I withdrew my hand, and wrought for my name's sake, that it should not be profaned in the sight of the heathen, in whose sight I brought them forth.

20:23 I lifted up my hand to them also in the wilderness, that I would scatter them among the heathen, and disperse them through the countries;

20:24 Because they had not executed my judgments, but had despised my statutes, and had profaned my sabbaths, and their eyes were after their fathers' idols.

20:25 Wherefore I gave them also statutes that were not good, and judgments by which they should not live;

20:26 And I polluted them in their own gifts, in that they caused to pass through the fire all the first-born, that I might make them desolate, to the end that they might know that I am the LORD.

20:27 Therefore, son of man, speak to the house of Israel, and say to them, Thus saith the Lord GOD; Yet in this your fathers have blasphemed me, in that they have committed a trespass against me.

20:28 For when I had brought them into the land, for which I lifted up my hand to give it to them, then they saw every high hill, and all the thick trees, and they offered there their sacrifices, and there they presented the provocation of their offering: there also they made their sweet savor, and poured out there their drink-offerings.

20:29 Then I said to them, What is the high place to which ye go? and its name is called Bamah to this day.

20:30 Wherefore say to the house of Israel, Thus saith the Lord GOD; Are ye polluted after the manner of your fathers? and commit ye lewd deeds after their abominations?

20:31 For when ye offer your gifts, when ye make your sons to pass through the fire, ye pollute yourselves with all your idols, even to this day: and shall I be inquired of by you, O house of Israel? As I live, saith the Lord GOD, I will not be inquired of by you.

20:32 And that which cometh into your mind shall not be at all, that ye say, We will be as the heathen, as the families of the countries, to serve wood and stone.

20:33 As I live, saith the Lord GOD, surely with a mighty hand, and with an out-stretched arm, and with fury poured out, will I rule over you:

20:34 And I will bring you out from the people, and will gather you out of the countries in which ye are scattered, with a mighty hand, and with an out-stretched arm, and with fury poured out.

20:35 And I will bring you into the wilderness of the people, and there will I plead with you face to face.

20:36 As I pleaded with your fathers in the wilderness of the land of Egypt, so will I plead with you, saith the Lord GOD.

20:37 And I will cause you to pass under the rod, and I will bring you into the bond of the covenant.

20:38 And I will purge out from among you the rebels, and them that transgress against me: I will bring them forth out of the country where they sojourn, and they shall not enter into the land of Israel: and ye shall know that I am the LORD.

20:39 As for you, O house of Israel, thus saith the Lord GOD; Go ye, serve ye every one his idols, and hereafter also, if ye will not hearken to me: but profane ye my holy name no more with your gifts, and with your idols.
20:40 For on my holy mountain, on the mountain of the hight of Israel, saith the Lord GOD, there shall all the house of Israel, all of them in the land, serve me: there will I accept them, and there will I require your offerings, and the first fruits of your oblations, with all your holy things.
20:41 I will accept you with your sweet savor, when I bring you out from the people, and gather you out of the countries in which ye have been scattered; and I will be sanctified in you before the heathen.
20:42 And ye shall know that I am the LORD, when I shall bring you into the land of Israel, into the country for which I lifted up my hand to give it to your fathers.
20:43 And there shall ye remember your ways, and all your doings in which ye have been defiled; and ye shall lothe yourselves in your own sight for all your evils that ye have committed.
20:44 And ye shall know that I am the LORD, when I have wrought with you for my name's sake, not according to your wicked ways, nor according to your corrupt doings, O ye house of Israel, saith the Lord GOD.
20:45 Moreover the word of the LORD came to me, saying,
20:46 Son of man, set thy face towards the south, and drop thy word towards the south, and prophesy against the forest of the south field;
20:47 And say to the forest of the south, Hear the word of the LORD; Thus saith the Lord GOD; Behold, I will kindle a fire in thee, and it shall devour every green tree in thee, and every dry tree: the flaming flame shall not be quenched, and all faces from the south to the north shall be burned therein.
20:48 And all flesh shall see that I the LORD have kindled it: it shall not be quenched.
20:49 Then said I, Ah Lord GOD! they say of me, Doth he not speak parables?

21

21:1 And the word of the LORD came to me, saying,
21:2 Son of man, set thy face towards Jerusalem, and drop thy word towards the holy places, and prophesy against the land of Israel,
21:3 And say to the land of Israel, Thus saith the LORD; Behold, I am against thee, and will draw forth my sword out of its sheath, and will cut off from thee the righteous and the wicked.
21:4 Seeing then that I will cut off from thee the righteous and the wicked, therefore shall my sword go forth from its sheath against all flesh from the south to the north:
21:5 That all flesh may know that I the LORD have drawn my sword out of its sheath: it shall not return any more.
21:6 Sigh therefore, thou son of man, with the breaking of thy loins; and with bitterness sigh before their eyes.
21:7 And it shall be, when they say to thee, Why sighest thou? that thou shalt answer, For the tidings; because it cometh: and every heart shall melt, and all hands shall be feeble, and every spirit shall faint, and all knees shall be weak as water: behold, it cometh, and shall be brought to pass, saith the Lord GOD.
21:8 Again the word of the LORD came to me, saying,
21:9 Son of man, prophesy, and say, Thus saith the LORD; Say, A sword, a sword is sharpened, and also furbished:
21:10 It is sharpened to make a grievous slaughter; it is furbished that it may glitter: should we then make mirth? it contemneth the rod of my son, as every tree.
21:11 And he hath given it to be furbished, that it may be handled: the sword is sharpened, and it is furbished, to give it into the hand of the slayer.
21:12 Cry and howl, son of man: for it shall be upon my people, it shall be upon all the princes of Israel: terrors by reason of the sword shall be upon my people: smite therefore upon thy thigh.
21:13 Because it is a trial, and what if the sword contemneth even the rod? it shall be no more, saith the Lord GOD.
21:14 Thou therefore, son of man, prophesy, and smite thy hands together, and let the sword be doubled the third time, the sword of the slain: it is the sword of the great men that are slain, which entereth into their private chambers.
21:15 I have set the point of the sword against all their gates, that their heart may faint, and their ruins be multiplied: ah! it is made bright, it is sharpened for the slaughter.
21:16 Go thee one way or other, either on the right hand, or on the left, whithersoever thy face is set.

21:17 I will also smite my hands together, and I will cause my fury to rest: I the LORD have said it.
21:18 The word of the LORD came to me again, saying,
21:19 Also, thou son of man, appoint thee two ways, that the sword of the king of Babylon may come: both ways shall come forth from one land: and choose thou a place, choose it at the head of the way to the city.
21:20 Appoint a way, that the sword may come to Rabbah of the Ammonites, and to Judah in Jerusalem the fortified.
21:21 For the king of Babylon stood at the parting of the way, at the head of the two ways, to use divination; he made his arrows bright, he consulted with images, he looked in the liver.
21:22 At his right hand was the divination for Jerusalem, to appoint captains, to open the mouth in the slaughter, to lift up the voice with shouting, to appoint battering rams against the gates, to cast a mount, and to build a fort.
21:23 And it shall be to them as a false divination in their sight, to them that have sworn oaths: but he will call to remembrance the iniquity, that they may be taken.
21:24 Therefore thus saith the Lord GOD; Because ye have made your iniquity to be remembered, in that your transgressions are disclosed, so that in all your doings your sins do appear; because, I say, that ye are come to remembrance, ye shall be taken with the hand.
21:25 And thou, profane wicked prince of Israel, whose day is come, when iniquity shall have an end,
21:26 Thus saith the Lord GOD; Remove the diadem, and take off the crown: this shall not be the same: exalt him that is low, and abase him that is high.
21:27 I will overturn, overturn, overturn it: and it shall be no more, until he cometh whose right it is; and I will give it him.
21:28 And thou, son of man, prophesy and say, Thus saith the Lord GOD concerning the Ammonites, and concerning their reproach; even say thou, The sword, the sword is drawn: for the slaughter it is furbished, to consume because of the glittering:
21:29 While they see vanity to thee, while they divine a lie to thee, to bring thee upon the necks of them that are slain, of the wicked, whose day is come, when their iniquity shall have an end.
21:30 Shall I cause it to return into its sheath? I will judge thee in the place where thou wast created, in the land of thy nativity.
21:31 And I will pour out my indignation upon thee, I will blow against thee in the fire of my wrath, and deliver thee into the hand of brutish men, and skillful to destroy.
21:32 Thou shalt be for fuel to the fire; thy blood shall be in the midst of the land; thou shalt be no more remembered: for I the LORD have spoken it.

22

22:1 Moreover the word of the LORD came to me, saying,
22:2 Now, thou son of man, wilt thou judge, wilt thou judge the bloody city? yes, thou shalt show her all her abominations.
22:3 Then say thou, Thus saith the Lord GOD; The city sheddeth blood in the midst of it, that her time may come, and maketh idols against herself to defile herself.
22:4 Thou art become guilty in thy blood that thou hast shed; and hast defiled thyself by thy idols which thou hast made; and thou hast caused thy days to draw near, and art come even to thy years: therefore have I made thee a reproach to the heathen, and a mocking to all countries.
22:5 Those that are near, and those that are far from thee, shall mock thee, who art infamous and much troubled.
22:6 Behold, the princes of Israel, every one were in thee to their power to shed blood.
22:7 In thee have they set light by father and mother: in the midst of thee have they dealt by oppression with the stranger: in thee have they oppressed the fatherless and the widow.
22:8 Thou hast despised my holy things, and hast profaned my sabbaths.
22:9 In thee are men that carry tales to shed blood: and in thee they eat upon the mountains: in the midst of thee they commit lewdness.
22:10 In thee have they uncovered their fathers' nakedness: in thee have they humbled her that was set apart for pollution.
22:11 And one hath committed abomination with his neighbor's wife; and another hath lewdly defiled his daughter-in-law; and another in thee hath humbled his sister, his father's daughter.
22:12 In thee have they taken gifts to shed blood; thou hast taken interest and increase, and thou hast greedily gained from thy neighbors by extortion, and hast forgotten me, saith the Lord GOD.

22:13 Behold, therefore I have smitten my hand at thy dishonest gain which thou hast made, and at thy blood which hath been in the midst of thee.
22:14 Can thy heart endure, or can thy hands be strong, in the days that I shall deal with thee? I the LORD have spoken it, and will do it.
22:15 And I will scatter thee among the heathen, and disperse thee in the countries, and will consume thy filthiness out of thee.
22:16 And thou shalt take thy inheritance in thyself in the sight of the heathen, and thou shalt know that I am the LORD.
22:17 And the word of the LORD came to me, saying,
22:18 Son of man, the house of Israel is to me become dross: all they are brass, and tin, and iron, and lead, in the midst of the furnace; they are even the dross of silver.
22:19 Therefore thus saith the Lord GOD, Because ye are all become dross, behold, therefore I will gather you into the midst of Jerusalem.
22:20 As they gather silver, and brass, and iron, and lead, and tin, into the midst of the furnace, to blow the fire upon it, to melt it; so will I gather you in my anger and in my fury, and I will leave you there, and melt you.
22:21 Yes, I will gather you, and blow upon you in the fire of my wrath, and ye shall be melted in the midst of it.
22:22 As silver is melted in the midst of the furnace, so shall ye be melted in the midst of it; and ye shall know that I the LORD have poured out my fury upon you.
22:23 And the word of the LORD came to me, saying,
22:24 Son of man, say to her, Thou art the land that is not cleansed, nor rained upon in the day of indignation.
22:25 There is a conspiracy of her prophets in the midst of her, like a roaring lion ravening the prey; they have devoured souls; they have taken the treasure and precious things; they have made her many widows in the midst of her.
22:26 Her priests have violated my law, and have profaned my holy things: they have put no difference between the holy and profane, neither have they shown difference between the unclean and the clean, and have hid their eyes from my sabbaths, and I am profaned among them.
22:27 Her princes in the midst of her are like wolves ravening the prey, to shed blood, and to destroy souls, to get dishonest gain.
22:28 And her prophets have daubed them with untempered mortar, seeing vanity, and divining lies to them, saying, Thus saith the Lord GOD, when the LORD hath not spoken.
22:29 The people of the land have used oppression, and exercised robbery, and have oppressed the poor and needy: yes, they have oppressed the stranger wrongfully.
22:30 And I sought for a man among them, that should make up the hedge, and stand in the gap before me for the land, that I should not destroy it: but I found none.
22:31 Therefore have I poured out my indignation upon them; I have consumed them with the fire of my wrath: their own way have I recompensed upon their heads, saith the Lord GOD.

23

23:1 The word of the LORD came again to me, saying,
23:2 Son of man, there were two women, the daughters of one mother:
23:3 And they committed lewd deeds in Egypt; they committed lewd deeds in their youth: there were their breasts pressed, and there they were first corrupted.
23:4 And the names of them were Aholah the elder, and Aholibah her sister: and they were mine, and they bore sons and daughters. Thus were their names; Samaria is Aholah, and Jerusalem Aholibah.
23:5 And Aholah played the harlot when she was mine; and she doted on her lovers, on the Assyrians her neighbors.
23:6 Who were clothed with blue, captains and rulers, all of them desirable young men, horsemen riding upon horses.
23:7 Thus she committed her lewd deeds with them, with all them that were the chosen men of Assyria, and with all on whom she doted: with all their idols she defiled herself.
23:8 Neither left she her lewd deeds brought from Egypt: for in her youth they lay with her, and they first corrupted her, and poured their impurities upon her.
23:9 Wherefore I have delivered her into the hand of her lovers, into the hand of the Assyrians, upon whom she doted.

23:10 These uncovered her nakedness: they took her sons and her daughters, and slew her with the sword: and she became famous among women; for they had executed judgment upon her.
23:11 And when her sister Aholibah saw this, she was more corrupt in her inordinate love than she, and in her prostitutions more than her sister in her prostitutions.
23:12 She doted upon the Assyrians her neighbors, captains and rulers clothed most gorgeously, horsemen riding upon horses, all of them desirable young men.
23:13 Then I saw that she was defiled, that they took both one way.
23:14 And that she increased her prostitutions: for when she saw men pourtrayed upon the wall, the images of the Chaldeans pourtrayed with vermilion.
23:15 Girded with girdles upon their loins, exceeding in dyed attire upon their heads, all of them princes to look to, after the manner of the Babylonians of Chaldea, the land of their nativity:
23:16 And as soon as she saw them with her eyes she doted upon them, and sent messengers to them into Chaldea.
23:17 And the Babylonians came to her into the bed of love, and they defiled her with their lewdness, and she was polluted with them, and her mind was alienated from them.
23:18 So she disclosed her lewd deeds, and exposed her nakedness: then my mind was alienated from her, as my mind was alienated from her sister.
23:19 Yet she multiplied her prostitutions, in calling to remembrance the days of her youth, in which she had played the harlot in the land of Egypt.
23:20 For she doted upon their paramours, whose flesh is as the flesh of asses, and whose issue is like the issue of horses.
23:21 Thus thou calledst to remembrance the lewdness of thy youth, by being corrupted by the Egyptians in thy youth.
23:22 Therefore, O Aholibah, thus saith the Lord GOD; Behold, I will raise up thy lovers against thee, from whom thy mind is alienated, and I will bring them against thee on every side;
23:23 The Babylonians, and all the Chaldeans, Pekod, and Shoa, and Koa, and all the Assyrians with them: all of them desirable young men, captains and rulers, great lords and renowned, all of them riding upon horses.
23:24 And they shall come against thee with chariots, wagons, and wheels, and with an assembly of people, which shall set against thee buckler and shield and helmet on every side: and I will set judgment before them, and they shall judge thee according to their judgments.
23:25 And I will set my jealousy against thee, and they shall deal furiously with thee: they shall take away thy nose and thy ears; and thy remnant shall fall by the sword: they shall take thy sons and thy daughters; and thy residue shall be devoured by the fire.
23:26 They shall also strip thee of thy clothes, and take away thy fair jewels.
23:27 Thus will I make thy lewdness to cease from thee, and thy adultery brought from the land of Egypt: so that thou shalt not lift up thy eyes to them, nor remember Egypt any more.
23:28 For thus saith the Lord GOD; Behold, I will deliver thee into the hand of them whom thou hatest, into the hand of them from whom thy mind is alienated:
23:29 And they shall treat thee with hatred, and shall take away all thy labor, and shall leave thee naked and bare: and the nakedness of thy prostitutions shall be disclosed, both thy lewdness and thy prostitutions.
23:30 I will do these things to thee, because thou hast gone astray after the heathen, and because thou art polluted with their idols.
23:31 Thou hast walked in the way of thy sister; therefore will I give her cup into thy hand.
23:32 Thus saith the Lord GOD; Thou shalt drink of thy sister's cup deep and large: thou shalt be treated with scorn and had in derision; it containeth much.
23:33 Thou shalt be filled with drunkenness and sorrow, with the cup of astonishment and desolation, with the cup of thy sister Samaria.
23:34 Thou shalt even drink it, and empty it to the dregs, and thou shalt break its pieces, and pluck off thy own breasts: for I have spoken it, saith the Lord GOD.
23:35 Therefore thus saith the Lord GOD; Because thou hast forgotten me, and cast me behind thy back, therefore bear thou also thy lewdness and thy prostitutions.
23:36 The LORD said moreover to me; Son of man, wilt thou judge Aholah and Aholibah? yes, declare to them their abominations;
23:37 That they have committed adultery, and blood is in their hands, and with their idols have they committed adultery, and have also caused their sons, whom they bore to me, to pass for them through the fire, to devour them.
23:38 Moreover this they have done to me: they have defiled my sanctuary in the same day, and have

profaned my sabbaths.
23:39 For when they had slain their children to their idols, then they came the same day into my sanctuary to profane it; and lo, thus have they done in the midst of my house.
23:40 And furthermore, that ye have sent for men to come from far, to whom a messenger was sent; and lo, they came: for whom thou didst wash thyself, paint thy eyes, and deck thyself with ornaments,
23:41 And sattest upon a stately bed and a table prepared before it, upon which thou hast set my incense and my oil.
23:42 And a voice of a multitude being at ease was with her: and with the men of the common sort were brought Sabeans from the wilderness, who put bracelets upon their hands, and beautiful crowns upon their heads.
23:43 Then said I to her that was old in adulteries, Will they now commit lewd deeds with her, and she with them?
23:44 Yet they went in to her, as they go in to a woman that playeth the harlot: so they went in to Aholah and to Aholibah, the lewd women.
23:45 And the righteous men, they shall judge them after the manner of adulteresses, and after the manner of women that shed blood; because they are adulteresses, and blood is in their hands.
23:46 For thus saith the Lord GOD; I will bring up a company upon them, and will give them to be removed and plundered.
23:47 And the company shall stone them with stones, and dispatch them with their swords; they shall slay their sons and their daughters, and burn their houses with fire.
23:48 Thus will I cause lewdness to cease out of the land, that all women may be taught not to do after your lewdness.
23:49 And they shall recompense your lewdness upon you, and ye shall bear the sins of your idols: and ye shall know that I am the Lord GOD.

24

24:1 Again in the ninth year, in the tenth month, in the tenth day of the month, the word of the LORD came to me, saying,
24:2 Son of man, Write for thee the name of the day, even of this same day: the king of Babylon set himself against Jerusalem this same day.
24:3 And utter a parable to the rebellious house, and say to them, Thus saith the Lord GOD; Set on a pot, set it on, and also pour water into it:
24:4 Gather its pieces into it, even every good piece, the thigh, and the shoulder; fill it with the choice bones.
24:5 Take the choice of the flock, and burn also the bones under it, and make it boil well, and let them boil its bones in it.
24:6 Wherefore thus saith the Lord GOD; Woe to the bloody city, to the pot whose scum is therein, and whose scum is not gone out of it! bring it out piece by piece; let no lot fall upon it.
24:7 For her blood is in the midst of her; she set it upon the top of a rock; she poured it not upon the ground, to cover it with dust;
24:8 That it might cause fury to come up to take vengeance; I have set her blood upon the top of a rock, that it should not be covered.
24:9 Therefore thus saith the Lord GOD; Woe to the bloody city! I will even make the pile for fire great.
24:10 Heap on wood, kindle the fire, consume the flesh, and spice it well, and let the bones be burned.
24:11 Then set it empty upon its coals, that the brass of it may be hot, and may burn, and that the filthiness of it may be melted in it, that the scum of it may be consumed.
24:12 She hath wearied herself with lies, and her great scum went not forth out of her: her scum shall be in the fire.
24:13 In thy filthiness is lewdness: because I have purged thee, and thou wast not purged, thou shalt not be purged from thy filthiness any more, till I have caused my fury to rest upon thee.
24:14 I the LORD have spoken it; it shall come to pass, and I will do it; I will not go back, neither will I spare, neither will I repent; according to thy ways, and according to thy doings, shall they judge thee, saith the Lord GOD.
24:15 Also the word of the LORD came to me, saying,
24:16 Son of man, behold, I take away from thee the desire of thy eyes with a stroke: yet neither shalt

thou mourn nor weep, neither shall thy tears run down.
24:17 Forbear to cry, make no mourning for the dead, bind the tire of thy head upon thee, and put on thy shoes upon thy feet, and cover not thy lips, and eat not the bread of men.
24:18 So I spoke to the people in the morning: and at evening my wife died; and I did in the morning as I was commanded.
24:19 And the people said to me, Wilt thou not tell us what these things are to us, that thou doest so?
24:20 Then I answered them, the word of the LORD came to me, saying,
24:21 Speak to the house of Israel, Thus saith the Lord GOD; Behold, I will profane my sanctuary, the excellence of your strength, the desire of your eyes, and that which your soul pitieth; and your sons and your daughters whom ye have left shall fall by the sword.
24:22 And ye shall do as I have done: ye shall not cover your lips, nor eat the bread of men.
24:23 And your tires shall be upon your heads, and your shoes upon your feet: ye shall not mourn nor weep; but ye shall pine away for your iniquities, and mourn one towards another.
24:24 Thus Ezekiel is to you a sign: according to all that he hath done shall ye do: and when this cometh, ye shall know that I am the Lord GOD.
24:25 Also, thou son of man, shall it not be in the day when I take from them their strength, the joy of their glory, the desire of their eyes, and that on which they set their minds, their sons and their daughters,
24:26 That he that escapeth in that day shall come to thee, to cause thee to hear it with thy ears?
24:27 In that day shall thy mouth be opened to him who hath escaped, and thou shalt speak, and be no more dumb: and thou shalt be a sign to them; and they shall know that I am the LORD.

25

25:1 The word of the LORD came again to me, saying,
25:2 Son of man, set thy face against the Ammonites, and prophesy against them;
25:3 And say to the Ammonites, Hear the word of the Lord GOD; Thus saith the Lord GOD; Because thou saidst, Aha, against my sanctuary, when it was profaned; and against the land of Israel, when it was desolate; and against the house of Judah, when they went into captivity;
25:4 Behold, therefore I will deliver thee to the men of the east for a possession, and they shall set their palaces in thee, and make their dwellings in thee: they shall eat thy fruit, and they shall drink thy milk.
25:5 And I will make Rabbah a stable for camels, and the Ammonites a couching-place for flocks: and ye shall know that I am the LORD.
25:6 For thus saith the Lord GOD; Because thou hast clapped thy hands, and stamped with the feet, and rejoiced in heart with all thy despite against the land of Israel;
25:7 Behold, therefore I will stretch out my hand upon thee, and will deliver thee for a spoil to the heathen; and I will cut thee off from the people, and I will cause thee to perish out of the countries: I will destroy thee; and thou shalt know that I am the LORD.
25:8 Thus saith the Lord GOD; Because that Moab and Seir do say, Behold, the house of Judah is like all the heathen;
25:9 Therefore behold, I will open the side of Moab from the cities, from his cities which are on his frontiers, the glory of the country, Beth-jeshimoth, Baal-meon, and Kiriathaim,
25:10 To the men of the east with the Ammonites, and will give them in possession, that the Ammonites may not be remembered among the nations.
25:11 And I will execute judgments upon Moab; and they shall know that I am the LORD.
25:12 Thus saith the Lord GOD; Because Edom hath dealt against the house of Judah by taking vengeance, and hath greatly offended, and revenged himself upon them;
25:13 Therefore thus saith the Lord GOD; I will also stretch out my hand upon Edom, and will cut off man and beast from it; and I will make it desolate from Teman; and they of Dedan shall fall by the sword.
25:14 And I will lay my vengeance upon Edom by the hand of my people Israel: and they shall do in Edom according to my anger and according to my fury; and they shall know my vengeance, saith the Lord GOD.
25:15 Thus saith the Lord GOD; Because the Philistines have dealt by revenge, and have taken vengeance with a despiteful heart, to destroy it for the old hatred;
25:16 Therefore thus saith the Lord GOD; Behold, I will stretch out my hand upon the Philistines, and I will cut off the Cherethims, and destroy the remnant of the sea coast.
25:17 And I will execute great vengeance upon them with furious rebukes; and they shall know that I am the LORD, when I shall lay my vengeance upon them.

26

26:1 And it came to pass in the eleventh year, in the first day of the month, that the word of the LORD came to me, saying,
26:2 Son of man, because that Tyre hath said against Jerusalem, Aha, she is broken that was the gates of the people: she is turned to me: I shall be replenished, now she is laid waste:
26:3 Therefore thus saith the Lord GOD; Behold, I am against thee, O Tyre, and will cause many nations to come up against thee, as the sea causeth its waves to come up.
26:4 And they shall destroy the walls of Tyre, and break down her towers: I will also scrape her dust from her, and make her like the top of a rock.
26:5 It shall be a place for the spreading of nets in the midst of the sea: for I have spoken it, saith the Lord GOD: and it shall become a spoil to the nations.
26:6 And her daughters who are in the field shall be slain by the sword; and they shall know that I am the LORD.
26:7 For thus saith the Lord GOD; Behold, I will bring upon Tyre Nebuchadrezzar king of Babylon, a king of kings, from the north, with horses, and with chariots, and with horsemen, and companies, and much people.
26:8 He shall slay with the sword thy daughters in the field: and he shall make a fort against thee, and cast a mount against thee, and lift up the buckler against thee.
26:9 And he shall set engines of war against thy walls, and with his axes he shall break down thy towers.
26:10 By reason of the abundance of his horses their dust shall cover thee: thy walls shall shake at the noise of the horsemen, and of the wheels, and of the chariots, when he shall enter into thy gates, as men enter into a city in which is made a breach.
26:11 With the hoofs of his horses shall he tread down all thy streets: he shall slay thy people by the sword, and thy strong garrisons shall go down to the ground.
26:12 And they shall make a spoil of thy riches, and make a prey of thy merchandise: and they shall break down thy walls, and destroy thy pleasant houses: and they shall lay thy stones and thy timber and thy dust in the midst of the water.
26:13 And I will cause the noise of thy songs to cease; and the sound of thy harps shall be no more heard.
26:14 And I will make thee like the top of a rock: thou shalt be a place to spread nets upon; thou shalt be built no more: for I the LORD have spoken it, saith the Lord GOD.
26:15 Thus saith the Lord GOD to Tyre; Shall not the isles shake at the sound of thy fall, when the wounded cry, when the slaughter is made in the midst of thee?
26:16 Then all the princes of the sea shall come down from their thrones, and lay away their robes, and put off their broidered garments: they shall clothe themselves with trembling; they shall sit upon the ground, and shall tremble at every moment, and be astonished at thee.
26:17 And they shall take up a lamentation for thee, and say to thee, How art thou destroyed, that wast inhabited by sea-faring men, the renowned city, which wast strong in the sea, she and her inhabitants, who cause their terror to be on all that haunt it!
26:18 Now shall the isles tremble in the day of thy fall; yes, the isles that are in the sea shall be disturbed at thy departure.
26:19 For thus saith the Lord GOD; When I shall make thee a desolate city, like the cities that are not inhabited; when I shall bring up the deep upon thee, and great waters shall cover thee;
26:20 When I shall bring thee down with them that descend into the pit, with the people of old time, and shall set thee in the low parts of the earth, in places desolate of old, with them that go down to the pit, that thou be not inhabited; and I shall set glory in the land of the living;
26:21 I will make thee a terror, and thou shalt be no more: though thou shalt be sought for, yet shalt thou never be found again, saith the Lord GOD.

27

27:1 The word of the LORD came again to me, saying,
27:2 Now, thou son of man, take up a lamentation for Tyre;
27:3 And say to Tyre, O thou that art situated at the entry of the sea, which art a merchant of the people for many isles, Thus saith the Lord GOD; O Tyre, thou hast said, I am of perfect beauty.

27:4 Thy borders are in the midst of the seas, thy builders have perfected thy beauty.
27:5 They have made all thy ship-boards of fir-trees of Senir: they have taken cedars from Lebanon to make masts for thee.
27:6 Of the oaks of Bashan have they made thy oars; the company of the Ashurites have made thy benches of ivory, brought out of the isles of Chittim.
27:7 Fine linen with broidered work from Egypt was that which thou spreadest forth to be thy sail; blue and purple from the isles of Elishah was that which covered thee.
27:8 The inhabitants of Zidon and Arvad were thy mariners: thy wise men, O Tyre, that were in thee, were thy pilots.
27:9 The ancients of Gebal and its wise men were in thee thy calkers: all the ships of the sea with their mariners were in thee to occupy thy merchandise.
27:10 They of Persia and of Lud and of Phut were in thy army, thy military men: they hung the shield and helmet in thee; they set forth thy comeliness.
27:11 The men of Arvad with thy army were upon thy walls on all sides, and the Gammadims were in thy towers: they hung their shields upon thy walls on every side; they have made thy beauty perfect.
27:12 Tarshish was thy merchant by reason of the multitude of all kind of riches; with silver, iron, tin, and lead, they traded in thy fairs.
27:13 Javan, Tubal, and Meshech, they were thy merchants: they traded in the persons of men and vessels of brass in thy market.
27:14 They of the house of Togarmah traded in thy fairs with horses and horsemen and mules.
27:15 The men of Dedan were thy merchants; many isles were the merchandise of thy hand: they brought thee for a present horns of ivory and ebony.
27:16 Syria was thy merchant by reason of the multitude of the wares of thy making: they occupied in thy fairs with emeralds, purple, and broidered work, and fine linen, and coral, and agate.
27:17 Judah, and the land of Israel, they were thy merchants: they traded in thy market in wheat of Minnith, and Pannag, and honey, and oil, and balm.
27:18 Damascus was thy merchant in the multitude of the wares of thy making, for the multitude of all riches; in the wine of Helbon, and white wool.
27:19 Dan also and Javan going to and fro occupied in thy fairs: bright iron, cassia, and calamus, were in thy market.
27:20 Dedan was thy merchant in precious clothes for chariots.
27:21 Arabia, and all the princes of Kedar, they occupied with thee in lambs, and rams, and goats: in these were they thy merchants.
27:22 The merchants of Sheba and Raamah, they were thy merchants: they occupied in thy fairs with chief of all spices, and with all precious stones, and gold.
27:23 Haran, and Canneh, and Eden, the merchants of Sheba, Asshur, and Chilmad, were thy merchants.
27:24 These were thy merchants in all sorts of things, in blue clothes, and broidered work, and in chests of rich apparel, bound with cords, and made of cedar, among thy merchandise.
27:25 The ships of Tarshish did sing of thee in thy market; and thou wast replenished, and made very glorious in the midst of the seas.
27:26 Thy rowers have brought thee into great waters: the east wind hath broken thee in the midst of the seas.
27:27 Thy riches, and thy fairs, thy merchandise, thy mariners, and thy pilots, thy calkers, and the occupiers of thy merchandise, and all thy military men, that are in thee, and in all thy company which is in the midst of thee, shall fall into the midst of the seas in the day of thy ruin.
27:28 The suburbs shall shake at the sound of the cry of thy pilots.
27:29 And all that handle the oar, the mariners, and all the pilots of the sea, shall come down from their ships, they shall stand upon the land;
27:30 And shall cause their voice to be heard against thee, and shall cry bitterly, and shall cast up dust upon their heads, they shall wallow themselves in the ashes:
27:31 And they shall make themselves utterly bald for thee, and gird themselves with sackcloth, and they shall weep for thee with bitterness of heart and bitter wailing.
27:32 And in their wailing they shall take up a lamentation for thee, and lament over thee, saying, What city is like Tyre, like the destroyed in the midst of the sea?
27:33 When thy wares went forth out of the seas, thou filledst many people; thou didst enrich the kings of the earth with the multitude of thy riches and of thy merchandise.
27:34 In the time when thou shalt be broken by the seas in the depths of the waters, thy merchandise and all thy company in the midst of thee shall fall.

27:35 All the inhabitants of the isles shall be astonished at thee, and their kings shall be terribly afraid, they shall be troubled in their countenance.
27:36 The merchants among the people shall hiss at thee; thou shalt be a terror, and never shalt be any more.

28

28:1 The word of the LORD came again to me, saying,
28:2 Son of man, say to the prince of Tyre, Thus saith the Lord GOD; Because thy heart is lifted up, and thou hast said, I am a god, I sit in the seat of God, in the midst of the seas; yet thou art a man, and not God, though thou settest thy heart as the heart of God:
28:3 Behold, thou art wiser than Daniel; there is no secret that they can hide from thee:
28:4 With thy wisdom and with thy understanding thou hast gained for thee riches, and hast gained gold and silver into thy treasures:
28:5 By thy great wisdom and by thy traffick hast thou increased thy riches, and thy heart is lifted up because of thy riches:
28:6 Therefore thus saith the Lord GOD; Because thou hast set thy heart as the heart of God;
28:7 Behold, therefore I will bring strangers upon thee, the terrible of the nations: and they shall draw their swords against the beauty of thy wisdom, and they shall defile thy brightness.
28:8 They shall bring thee down to the pit, and thou shalt die the deaths of them that are slain in the midst of the seas.
28:9 Wilt thou yet say before him that slayeth thee, I am God? but thou shalt be a man, and no god, in the hand of him that slayeth thee.
28:10 Thou shalt die the deaths of the uncircumcised by the hand of strangers: for I have spoken it, saith the Lord GOD.
28:11 Moreover the word of the LORD came to me, saying,
28:12 Son of man, take up a lamentation upon the king of Tyre, and say to him, Thus saith the Lord GOD; Thou sealest up the sum, full of wisdom, and perfect in beauty.
28:13 Thou hast been in Eden the garden of God; every precious stone was thy covering, the sardius, topaz, and the diamond, the beryl, the onyx, and the jasper, the sapphire, the emerald, and the carbuncle, and gold: the workmanship of thy tabrets and of thy pipes was prepared in thee in the day that thou wast created.
28:14 Thou art the anointed cherub that covereth; and I have set thee so: thou wast upon the holy mountain of God; thou hast walked up and down in the midst of the stones of fire.
28:15 Thou wast perfect in thy ways from the day that thou wast created, till iniquity was found in thee.
28:16 By the multitude of thy merchandise they have filled the midst of thee with violence, and thou hast sinned: therefore I will cast thee as profane out of the mountain of God: and I will destroy thee, O covering cherub, from the midst of the stones of fire.
28:17 Thy heart was lifted up because of thy beauty, thou hast corrupted thy wisdom by reason of thy brightness: I will cast thee to the ground, I will lay thee before kings, that they may behold thee.
28:18 Thou hast defiled thy sanctuaries by the multitude of thy iniquities, by the iniquity of thy traffick; therefore will I bring forth a fire from the midst of thee, it shall devour thee, and I will bring thee to ashes upon the earth in the sight of all them that behold thee.
28:19 All they that know thee among the people shall be astonished at thee: thou shalt be a terror, and never shalt thou be any more.
28:20 Again the word of the LORD came to me, saying,
28:21 Son of man, set thy face against Zidon, and prophesy against it,
28:22 And say, Thus saith the Lord GOD; Behold, I am against thee, O Zidon; and I will be glorified in the midst of thee: and they shall know that I am the LORD, when I shall have executed judgments in her, and shall be sanctified in her.
28:23 For I will send into her pestilence, and blood into her streets; and the wounded shall be judged in the midst of her by the sword upon her on every side; and they shall know that I am the LORD.
28:24 And there shall be no more a pricking brier to the house of Israel, nor any grieving thorn of all that are around them, that despised them; and they shall know that I am the Lord GOD.
28:25 Thus saith the Lord GOD; When I shall have gathered the house of Israel from the people among whom they are scattered, and shall be sanctified in them in the sight of the heathen, then shall they dwell in their land that I have given to my servant Jacob.
28:26 And they shall dwell safely therein, and shall build houses, and plant vineyards; yes, they shall

dwell with confidence, when I have executed judgments upon all those that despise them around them; and they shall know that I am the LORD their God.

29

29:1 In the tenth year, in the tenth month, in the twelfth day of the month, the word of the LORD came to me, saying,
29:2 Son of man, set thy face against Pharaoh king of Egypt, and prophesy against him, and against all Egypt:
29:3 Speak, and say, Thus saith the Lord GOD; Behold, I am against thee, Pharaoh king of Egypt, the great dragon that lieth in the midst of his rivers, which hath said, My river is my own, and I have made it for myself.
29:4 But I will put hooks in thy jaws, and I will cause the fish of thy rivers to stick to thy scales, and I will bring thee out of the midst of thy rivers, and all the fish of thy rivers shall stick to thy scales.
29:5 And I will leave thee thrown into the wilderness, thee and all the fish of thy rivers: thou shalt fall upon the open fields; thou shalt not be brought together, nor gathered: I have given thee for food to the beasts of the field and to the fowls of heaven.
29:6 And all the inhabitants of Egypt shall know that I am the LORD, because they have been a staff of reed to the house of Israel.
29:7 When they took hold of thee by thy hand, thou didst break, and rend all their shoulder: and when they leaned upon thee, thou didst break, and make all their loins to be at a stand.
29:8 Therefore thus saith the Lord GOD; Behold, I will bring a sword upon thee, and cut off man and beast out of thee.
29:9 And the land of Egypt shall be desolate and waste; and they shall know that I am the LORD: because he hath said, The river is mine, and I have made it.
29:10 Behold, therefore, I am against thee, and against thy rivers, and I will make the land of Egypt utterly waste and desolate, from the tower of Syene even to the border of Cush.
29:11 No foot of man shall pass through it, nor foot of beast shall pass through it, neither shall it be inhabited forty years.
29:12 And I will make the land of Egypt desolate in the midst of the countries that are desolate, and her cities among the cities that are laid waste shall be desolate forty years: and I will scatter the Egyptians among the nations, and will disperse them through the countries.
29:13 Yet thus saith the Lord GOD; At the end of forty years will I gather the Egyptians from the people whither they were scattered:
29:14 And I will bring again the captivity of Egypt, and will cause them to return into the land of Pathros, into the land of their habitation; and they shall be there a base kingdom.
29:15 It shall be the basest of the kingdoms; neither shall it exalt itself any more above the nations: for I will diminish them, that they shall no more rule over the nations.
29:16 And it shall be no more the confidence of the house of Israel, which bringeth their iniquity to remembrance, when they shall look after them: but they shall know that I am the Lord GOD.
29:17 And it came to pass in the seven and twentieth year, in the first month, in the first day of the month, the word of the LORD came to me, saying,
29:18 Son of man, Nebuchadrezzar king of Babylon caused his army to serve a great service against Tyre: every head was made bald, and every shoulder was peeled: yet had he no wages, nor his army, for Tyre, for the service that he had served against it:
29:19 Therefore thus saith the Lord GOD; Behold, I will give the land of Egypt to Nebuchadrezzar king of Babylon; and he shall take her multitude, and take her spoil, and take her prey; and it shall be the wages for his army.
29:20 I have given him the land of Egypt for his labor with which he served against it, because they wrought for me, saith the Lord GOD.
29:21 In that day will I cause the horn of the house of Israel to bud forth, and I will give thee the opening of the mouth in the midst of them; and they shall know that I am the LORD.

30

30:1 The word of the LORD came again to me, saying,
30:2 Son of man, prophesy and say, Thus saith the Lord GOD; Howl ye, Alas the day!

30:3 For the day is near, even the day of the LORD is near, a cloudy day; it shall be the time of the heathen.
30:4 And the sword shall come upon Egypt, and great pain shall be in Cush, when the slain shall fall in Egypt, and they shall take away her multitude, and her foundations shall be broken down.
30:5 Cush, and Libya, and Lydia, and all the mingled people, and Kub, and the men of the land that is in league, shall fall with them by the sword.
30:6 Thus saith the LORD; They also that uphold Egypt shall fall; and the pride of her power shall come down: from the tower of Syene shall they fall in it by the sword, saith the Lord GOD.
30:7 And they shall be desolate in the midst of the countries that are desolate, and her cities shall be in the midst of the cities that are wasted.
30:8 And they shall know that I am the LORD, when I have set a fire in Egypt, and when all her helpers shall be destroyed.
30:9 In that day shall messengers go forth from me in ships to make the careless Cushites afraid, and great pain shall come upon them, as in the day of Egypt: for lo, it cometh.
30:10 Thus saith the Lord GOD; I will also make the multitude of Egypt to cease by the hand of Nebuchadrezzar king of Babylon.
30:11 He and his people with him, the terrible of the nations, shall be brought to destroy the land: and they shall draw their swords against Egypt, and fill the land with the slain.
30:12 And I will make the rivers dry, and sell the land into the hand of the wicked: and I will make the land waste, and all that is in it, by the hand of strangers: I the LORD have spoken it.
30:13 Thus saith the Lord GOD; I will also destroy the idols, and I will cause their images to cease out of Noph; and there shall be no more a prince of the land of Egypt: and I will put a fear in the land of Egypt.
30:14 And I will make Pathros desolate, and will set fire in Zoan, and will execute judgments in No.
30:15 And I will pour my fury upon Sin, the strength of Egypt; and I will cut off the multitude of No.
30:16 And I will set fire in Egypt: Sin shall have great pain, and No shall be rent asunder, and Noph shall have distresses daily.
30:17 The young men of Aven and of Pibeseth shall fall by the sword: and these cities shall go into captivity.
30:18 At Tehaphnehes also the day shall be darkened, when I shall break there the yokes of Egypt: and the pomp of her strength shall cease in her: as for her, a cloud shall cover her, and her daughters shall go into captivity.
30:19 Thus will I execute judgments in Egypt: and they shall know that I am the LORD.
30:20 And it came to pass in the eleventh year, in the first month, in the seventh day of the month, that the word of the LORD came to me, saying,
30:21 Son of man, I have broken the arm of Pharaoh king of Egypt; and lo, it shall not be bound up to be healed, to put a roller to bind it, to make it strong to hold the sword.
30:22 Therefore thus saith the Lord GOD; Behold, I am against Pharaoh king of Egypt, and will break his arms, the strong, and that which was broken; and I will cause the sword to fall out of his hand.
30:23 And I will scatter the Egyptians among the nations, and will disperse them through the countries.
30:24 And I will strengthen the arms of the king of Babylon, and put my sword in his hand: but I will break Pharaoh's arms, and he shall groan before him with the groanings of a deadly wounded man.
30:25 But I will strengthen the arms of the king of Babylon, and the arms of Pharaoh shall fall down; and they shall know that I am the LORD, when I shall put my sword into the hand of the king of Babylon, and he shall stretch it out upon the land of Egypt.
30:26 And I will scatter the Egyptians among the nations, and disperse them among the countries; and they shall know that I am the LORD.

31

31:1 And it came to pass in the eleventh year, in the third month, in the first day of the month, that the word of the LORD came to me, saying,
31:2 Son of man, speak to Pharaoh king of Egypt, and to his multitude; Whom art thou like in thy greatness?
31:3 Behold, the Assyrian was a cedar in Lebanon with fair branches, and with a shady cover, and of a high stature; and his top was among the thick boughs.
31:4 The waters made him great, the deep set him up on high with her rivers running round his plants, and sent out her little rivers to all the trees of the field.

31:5 Therefore his hight was exalted above all the trees of the field, and his boughs were multiplied, and his branches became long because of the multitude of waters, when he shot forth.
31:6 All the fowls of heaven made their nests in his boughs, and under his branches did all the beasts of the field bring forth their young, and under his shade dwelt all great nations.
31:7 Thus was he fair in his greatness, in the length of his branches: for his root was by great waters.
31:8 The cedars in the garden of God could not hide him: the fir-trees were not like his boughs, and the chesnut-trees were not like his branches; not any tree in the garden of God was like to him in his beauty.
31:9 I have made him fair by the multitude of his branches: so that all the trees of Eden, that were in the garden of God, envied him.
31:10 Therefore thus saith the Lord GOD; Because thou hast lifted up thyself in hight, and he hath shot up his top among the thick boughs, and his heart is lifted up in his hight;
31:11 I have therefore delivered him into the hand of the mighty one of the heathen; he shall surely deal with him: I have driven him out for his wickedness.
31:12 And strangers, the terrible of the nations, have cut him off, and have left him: upon the mountains and in all the valleys his branches are fallen, and his boughs are broken by all the rivers of the land; and all the people of the earth have gone down from his shade, and have left him.
31:13 Upon his ruin shall all the fowls of the heaven remain, and all the beasts of the field shall be upon his branches:
31:14 To the end that none of all the trees by the waters exalt themselves for their hight, neither shoot up their top among the thick boughs, neither their trees stand up in their hight, all that drink water: for they are all delivered to death, to the nether parts of the earth, in the midst of the children of men, with them that go down to the pit.
31:15 Thus saith the Lord GOD; In the day when he went down to the grave I caused a mourning: I covered the deep for him, and I restrained its floods, and the great waters were stayed: and I caused Lebanon to mourn for him, and all the trees of the field fainted for him.
31:16 I made the nations to shake at the sound of his fall, when I cast him down to the grave with them that descend into the pit: and all the trees of Eden, the choice and best of Lebanon, all that drink water, shall be comforted in the nether parts of the earth.
31:17 They also went down into the grave with him to them that are slain with the sword; and they that were his arm, that dwelt under his shade in the midst of the heathen.
31:18 To whom art thou thus like in glory and in greatness among the trees of Eden? yet shalt thou be brought down with the trees of Eden to the nether parts of the earth: thou shalt lie in the midst of the uncircumcised with them that are slain by the sword. This is Pharaoh and all his multitude, saith the Lord GOD.

32

32:1 And it came to pass in the twelfth year, in the twelfth month, in the first day of the month, that the word of the LORD came to me, saying,
32:2 Son of man, take up a lamentation for Pharaoh king of Egypt, and say to him, Thou art like a young lion of the nations, and thou art as a whale in the seas: and thou didst come forth with thy rivers, and disturb the waters with thy feet, and render their rivers foul.
32:3 Thus saith the Lord GOD; I will therefore spread out my net over thee with a company of many people; and they shall bring thee up in my net.
32:4 Then will I leave thee upon the land, and I will cast thee forth upon the open field, and will cause all the fowls of the heaven to remain upon thee, and I will fill the beasts of the whole earth with thee.
32:5 And I will lay thy flesh upon the mountains, and fill the valleys with thy hight.
32:6 I will also water with thy blood the land in which thou swimmest, even to the mountains; and the rivers shall be full of thee.
32:7 And when I shall extinguish thee, I will cover the heaven, and make the stars thereof dark; I will cover the sun with a cloud, and the moon shall not give her light.
32:8 All the bright lights of heaven will I make dark over thee, and set darkness upon thy land, saith the Lord GOD.
32:9 I will also vex the hearts of many people, when I shall bring thy destruction among the nations, into the countries which thou hast not known.
32:10 Yes, I will make many people amazed at thee, and their kings shall be horribly afraid for thee, when I shall brandish my sword before them; and they shall tremble at every moment, every man for his own life, in the day of thy fall.

32:11 For thus saith the Lord GOD; The sword of the king of Babylon shall come upon thee.
32:12 By the swords of the mighty will I cause thy multitude to fall, the terrible of the nations, all of them: and they shall lay waste the pomp of Egypt, and all its multitude shall be destroyed.
32:13 I will destroy also all its beasts from beside the great waters; neither shall the foot of man disturb them any more, nor the hoofs of beasts disturb them.
32:14 Then will I make their waters deep, and cause their rivers to run like oil, saith the Lord GOD.
32:15 When I shall make the land of Egypt desolate, and the country shall be destitute of that of which it was full, when I shall smite all them that dwell in it, then shall they know that I am the LORD.
32:16 This is the lamentation with which they shall lament her: the daughters of the nations shall lament her: they shall lament for her, even for Egypt, and for all her multitude, saith the Lord GOD.
32:17 It came to pass also in the twelfth year, in the fifteenth day of the month, that the word of the LORD came to me, saying,
32:18 Son of man, wail for the multitude of Egypt, and cast them down, even her, and the daughters of the famous nations, to the nether parts of the earth, with them that go down into the pit.
32:19 Whom dost thou pass in beauty? go down, and be thou laid with the uncircumcised.
32:20 They shall fall in the midst of them that are slain by the sword: she is delivered to the sword: draw her and all her multitudes.
32:21 The strong among the mighty shall speak to him out of the midst of the grave with them that help him: they are gone down, they lie uncircumcised, slain by the sword.
32:22 Asshur is there and all her company: his graves are about him: all of them slain, fallen by the sword:
32:23 Whose graves are set in the sides of the pit, and her company is around her grave: all of them slain, fallen by the sword, who caused terror in the land of the living.
32:24 There is Elam and all her multitude around her grave, all of them slain, fallen by the sword, who are gone down uncircumcised into the nether parts of the earth, who caused their terror in the land of the living; yet have they borne their shame with them that go down to the pit.
32:25 They have set her a bed in the midst of the slain with all her multitude: her graves are around him: all of them uncircumcised, slain by the sword: though their terror was caused in the land of the living, yet have they borne their shame with them that go down to the pit: he is put in the midst of them that are slain.
32:26 There is Meshech, Tubal, and all her multitude: her graves are around him: all of them uncircumcised, slain by the sword, though they caused their terror in the land of the living.
32:27 And they shall not lie with the mighty that are fallen of the uncircumcised, who are gone down to the grave, with their weapons of war: and they have laid their swords under their heads, but their iniquities shall be upon their bones, though they were the terror of the mighty in the land of the living.
32:28 Yes, thou shalt be broken in the midst of the uncircumcised, and shalt lie with them that are slain with the sword.
32:29 There is Edom, her kings, and all her princes, who with their might are laid by them that were slain by the sword: they shall lie with the uncircumcised, and with them that go down to the pit.
32:30 There are the princes of the north, all of them, and all the Zidonians, who are gone down with the slain; with their terror they are ashamed of their might; and they lie uncircumcised with them that are slain by the sword, and bear their shame with them that go down to the pit.
32:31 Pharaoh shall see them, and shall be comforted over all his multitude, even Pharaoh and all his army slain by the sword, saith the Lord GOD.
32:32 For I have caused my terror in the land of the living: and he shall be laid in the midst of the uncircumcised with them that are slain with the sword, even Pharaoh and all his multitude, saith the Lord GOD.

33

33:1 Again the word of the LORD came to me, saying,
33:2 Son of man, speak to the children of thy people, and say to them, When I bring the sword upon a land, if the people of the land take a man of their borders, and set him for their watchman:
33:3 If when he seeth the sword come upon the land, he shall blow the trumpet, and warn the people;
33:4 Then whoever heareth the sound of the trumpet, and taketh not warning; if the sword shall come and take him away, his blood shall be upon his own head.
33:5 He heard the sound of the trumpet, and took not warning; his blood shall be upon him. But he that taketh warning shall deliver his soul.

33:6 But if the watchman shall see the sword come, and blow not the trumpet, and the people be not warned; if the sword shall come, and take any person from among them, he is taken away in his iniquity; but his blood will I require at the watchman's hand.
33:7 So thou, O son of man, I have set thee a watchman to the house of Israel; therefore thou shalt hear the word at my mouth, and warn them from me.
33:8 When I say to the wicked, O wicked man, thou shalt surely die; if thou dost not speak to warn the wicked from his way, that wicked man shall die in his iniquity; but his blood will I require at thy hand.
33:9 Nevertheless, if thou shalt warn the wicked of his way to turn from it; if he shall not turn from his way, he shall die in his iniquity; but thou hast delivered thy soul.
33:10 Therefore, O thou son of man, speak to the house of Israel; Thus ye speak, saying, If our transgressions and our sins are upon us, and we pine away in them, how should we then live?
33:11 Say to them, As I live, saith the Lord GOD, I have no pleasure in the death of the wicked; but that the wicked should turn from his way and live: turn ye, turn ye from your evil ways; for why will ye die, O house of Israel?
33:12 Therefore, thou son of man, say to the children of thy people, The righteousness of the righteous shall not deliver him in the day of his transgression: as for the wickedness of the wicked, he shall not fall by it in the day that he turneth from his wickedness; neither shall the righteous be able to live for his righteousness in the day that he sinneth.
33:13 When I shall say to the righteous, that he shall surely live; if he shall trust to his own righteousness, and commit iniquity, all his righteousnesses shall not be remembered; but for his iniquity that he hath committed, he shall die for it.
33:14 Again, when I say to the wicked, Thou shalt surely die; if he shall turn from his sin, and do that which is lawful and right;
33:15 If the wicked shall restore the pledge, give again that which he had robbed, walk in the statutes of life, without committing iniquity; he shall surely live, he shall not die.
33:16 None of his sins that he hath committed shall be mentioned to him: he hath done that which is lawful and right; he shall surely live.
33:17 Yet the children of thy people say, The way of the Lord is not equal: but as for them, their way is not equal.
33:18 When the righteous turneth from his righteousness, and committeth iniquity, for that he shall even die.
33:19 But if the wicked shall turn from his wickedness, and do that which is lawful and right, for that he shall live.
33:20 Yet ye say, The way of the Lord is not equal. O ye house of Israel, I will judge you every one after his ways.
33:21 And it came to pass in the twelfth year of our captivity, in the tenth month, in the fifth day of the month, that one that had escaped out of Jerusalem came to me, saying, The city is smitten.
33:22 Now the hand of the LORD was upon me in the evening, before he that had escaped came; and had opened my mouth, until he came to me in the morning; and my mouth was opened, and I was no more dumb.
33:23 Then the word of the LORD came to me, saying,
33:24 Son of man, they that inhabit those wastes of the land of Israel speak, saying, Abraham was one, and he inherited the land: but we are many; the land is given to us for inheritance.
33:25 Wherefore say to them, Thus saith the Lord GOD; Ye eat with the blood, and lift up your eyes towards your idols, and shed blood: and shall ye possess the land?
33:26 Ye stand upon your sword, ye work abomination, and ye defile every one his neighbor's wife: and shall ye possess the land?
33:27 Say thou thus to them, Thus saith the Lord GOD; As I live, surely they that are in the wastes shall fall by the sword, and him that is in the open field will I give to the beasts to be devoured, and they that are in the forts and in the caves shall die by the pestilence.
33:28 For I will lay the land most desolate, and the pomp of her strength shall cease; and the mountains of Israel shall be desolate, that none shall pass through.
33:29 Then shall they know that I am the LORD, when I have laid the land most desolate because of all their abominations which they have committed.
33:30 Also, thou son of man, the children of thy people still are talking against thee by the walls and in the doors of the houses, and speak one to another, every one to his brother, saying, Come, I pray you, and hear what is the word that cometh forth from the LORD.
33:31 And they come to thee as the people come, and they sit before thee as my people, and they hear thy words, but they will not do them: for with their mouth they show much love, but their heart goeth

after their covetousness.
33:32 And lo, thou art to them as a very lovely song of one that hath a pleasant voice, and can play well on an instrument: for they hear thy words, but they do not perform them.
33:33 And when this cometh to pass, (lo, it will come,) then shall they know that a prophet hath been among them.

34

34:1 And the word of the LORD came to me, saying,
34:2 Son of man, prophesy against the shepherds of Israel, prophesy, and say to them, Thus saith the Lord GOD to the shepherds; Woe be to the shepherds of Israel that do feed themselves! should not the shepherds feed the flocks?
34:3 Ye eat the fat, and ye clothe yourselves with the wool, ye kill them that are fed: but ye feed not the flock.
34:4 The diseased ye have not strengthened, neither have ye healed that which was sick, neither have ye bound up that which was broken, neither have ye brought again that which was driven away, neither have ye sought that which was lost; but with force and with cruelty have ye ruled them.
34:5 And they were scattered, because there is no shepherd: and they became food to all the beasts of the field, when they were scattered.
34:6 My sheep wandered through all the mountains, and upon every high hill: yes, my flock was scattered upon all the face of the earth, and none did search or seek for them.
34:7 Therefore, ye shepherds, hear the word of the LORD;
34:8 As I live, saith the Lord GOD, surely because my flock became a prey, and my flock became food to every beast of the field, because there was no shepherd, neither did my shepherds search for my flock, but the shepherds fed themselves, and fed not my flock;
34:9 Therefore, O ye shepherds, hear the word of the LORD;
34:10 Thus saith the Lord GOD; Behold, I am against the shepherds; and I will require my flock at their hand, and cause them to cease from feeding the flock; neither shall the shepherds feed themselves any more; for I will deliver my flock from their mouth, that they may not be food for them.
34:11 For thus saith the Lord GOD; Behold, I even I, will both search for my sheep, and seek them out.
34:12 As a shepherd seeketh out his flock in the day that he is among his sheep that are scattered; so will I seek out my sheep, and will deliver them out of all places where they have been scattered in the cloudy and dark day.
34:13 And I will bring them out from the people, and gather them from the countries, and will bring them to their own land, and feed them upon the mountains of Israel by the rivers, and in all the inhabited places of the country.
34:14 I will feed them in a good pasture, and upon the high mountains of Israel shall their fold be: there shall they lie in a good fold, and in a fat pasture shall they feed upon the mountains of Israel.
34:15 I will feed my flock, and I will cause them to lie down, saith the Lord GOD.
34:16 I will seek that which was lost, and bring again that which was driven away, and will bind up that which was broken, and will strengthen that which was sick: but I will destroy the fat and the strong; I will feed them with judgment.
34:17 And as for you, O my flock, Thus saith the Lord GOD; Behold, I judge between cattle and cattle, between the rams and the he-goats.
34:18 Seemeth it a small thing to you to have eaten up the good pasture, but ye must tread down with your feet the residue of your pastures? and to have drank of the deep waters, but ye must foul the residue with your feet?
34:19 And as for my flock, they eat that which ye have trodden with your feet; and they drink that which ye have fouled with your feet.
34:20 Therefore thus saith the Lord GOD to them; Behold, I, even I, will judge between the fat cattle and between the lean cattle.
34:21 Because ye have thrust with side and with shoulder, and pushed all the diseased with your horns, till ye have scattered them abroad;
34:22 Therefore will I save my flock, and they shall no more be a prey; and I will judge between cattle and cattle.
34:23 And I will set up one shepherd over them, and he shall feed them, even my servant David; he shall feed them, and he shall be their shepherd.
34:24 And I the LORD will be their God, and my servant David a prince among them; I the LORD

have spoken it.
34:25 And I will make with them a covenant of peace, and will cause the evil beasts to cease out of the land: and they shall dwell safely in the wilderness, and sleep in the woods.
34:26 And I will make them and the places around my hill a blessing; and I will cause the shower to come down in its season; there shall be showers of blessing.
34:27 And the tree of the field shall yield her fruit, and the earth shall yield her increase, and they shall be safe in their land, and shall know that I am the LORD, when I have broken the bands of their yoke, and delivered them out of the hand of those that subjected them to service.
34:28 And they shall no more be a prey to the heathen, neither shall the beast of the land devour them; but they shall dwell safely, and none shall make them afraid.
34:29 And I will raise up for them a plant of renown, and they shall be no more consumed with hunger in the land, neither bear the shame of the heathen any more.
34:30 Thus shall they know that I the LORD their God am with them, and that they, even the house of Israel, are my people, saith the Lord GOD.
34:31 And ye my flock, the flock of my pasture, are men, and I am your God, saith the Lord GOD.

35

35:1 Moreover the word of the LORD came to me, saying,
35:2 Son of man, set thy face against mount Seir, and prophesy against it,
35:3 And say to it, Thus saith the Lord GOD; Behold, O mount Seir, I am against thee, and I will stretch out my hand against thee, and I will make thee most desolate.
35:4 I will lay thy cities waste, and thou shalt be desolate, and thou shalt know that I am the LORD.
35:5 Because thou hast had a perpetual hatred, and hast shed the blood of the children of Israel by the force of the sword in the time of their calamity, in the time that their iniquity had an end:
35:6 Therefore, as I live, saith the Lord GOD, I will prepare thee to blood, and blood shall pursue thee: since thou hast not hated blood, even blood shall pursue thee.
35:7 Thus will I make mount Seir most desolate, and cut off from it him that passeth out and him that returneth.
35:8 And I will fill his mountains with his slain men: in thy hills, and in thy valleys, and in all thy rivers, shall they fall that are slain with the sword.
35:9 I will make thee perpetual desolations, and thy cities shall not return: and ye shall know that I am the LORD.
35:10 Because thou hast said, These two nations and these two countries shall be mine, and we will possess it; whereas the LORD was there:
35:11 Therefore, as I live, saith the Lord GOD, I will even do according to thy anger, and according to thy envy which thou hast used out of thy hatred against them; and I will make myself known among them, when I have judged thee.
35:12 And thou shalt know that I am the LORD, and that I have heard all thy blasphemies which thou hast spoken against the mountains of Israel, saying, They are laid desolate, they are given us to consume.
35:13 Thus with your mouth ye have boasted against me, and have multiplied your words against me: I have heard them.
35:14 Thus saith the Lord GOD; When the whole earth rejoiceth, I will make thee desolate.
35:15 As thou didst rejoice at the inheritance of the house of Israel, because it was desolate, so will I do to thee: thou shalt be desolate, O mount Seir, and all Edom, even all of it: and they shall know that I am the LORD.

36

36:1 Also thou son of man, prophesy to the mountains of Israel, and say, Ye mountains of Israel, hear the word of the LORD:
36:2 Thus saith the Lord GOD; Because the enemy had said against you, Aha, even the ancient high places are ours in possession:
36:3 Therefore prophesy and say, Thus saith the Lord GOD; Because they have made you desolate, and swallowed you up on every side, that ye might be a possession to the residue of the heathen, and ye are taken up in the lips of talkers, and are an infamy of the people:
36:4 Therefore, ye mountains of Israel, hear the word of the Lord GOD; Thus saith the Lord GOD to

the mountains, and to the hills, to the rivers, and to the valleys, to the desolate wastes, and to the cities
that are forsaken, which became a prey and derision to the residue of the heathen that are around;
36:5 Therefore thus saith the Lord GOD; Surely in the fire of my jealousy have I spoken against the
residue of the heathen, and against all Edom, who have appointed my land into their possession with
the joy of all their heart, with despiteful minds, to cast it out for a prey.
36:6 Prophesy therefore concerning the land of Israel, and say to the mountains, and to the hills, to the
rivers, and to the valleys, Thus saith the Lord GOD; Behold, I have spoken in my jealousy and in my
fury, because ye have borne the shame of the heathen:
36:7 Therefore thus saith the Lord GOD; I have lifted up my hand, Surely the heathen that are about
you, they shall bear their shame.
36:8 But ye, O mountains of Israel, ye shall shoot forth your branches, and yield your fruit to my people
of Israel; for they are at hand to come.
36:9 For behold, I am for you, and I will turn to you, and ye shall be tilled and sown:
36:10 And I will multiply men upon you, all the house of Israel, even all of it: and the cities shall be
inhabited, and the wastes shall be built.
36:11 And I will multiply upon you man and beast; and they shall increase and bring fruit: and I will
settle you after your old states, and will do better to you than at your beginnings: and ye shall know that
I am the LORD.
36:12 Yes, I will cause men to walk upon you, even my people Israel; and they shall possess thee, and
thou shalt be their inheritance, and thou shalt no more henceforth bereave them of men.
36:13 Thus saith the Lord GOD; Because they say to you, Thou land devourest men, and hast bereaved
thy nations;
36:14 Therefore thou shalt devour men no more, neither bereave thy nations any more, saith the Lord
GOD.
36:15 Neither will I cause men to hear in thee the shame of the heathen any more, neither shalt thou
bear the reproach of the people any more, neither shalt thou cause thy nations to fall any more, saith the
Lord GOD.
36:16 Moreover the word of the LORD came to me, saying,
36:17 Son of man, when the house of Israel dwelt in their own land, they defiled it by their own way and
by their doings: their way was before me as the uncleanness of a removed woman.
36:18 Wherefore I poured my fury upon them for the blood that they had shed upon the land, and for
their idols with which they had polluted it:
36:19 And I scattered them among the heathen, and they were dispersed through the countries:
according to their way and according to their doings I judged them.
36:20 And when they entered among the heathen, whither they went, they profaned my holy name,
when they said to them, These are the people of the LORD, and are gone forth out of his land.
36:21 But I had pity for my holy name, which the house of Israel had profaned among the heathen,
whither they went.
36:22 Therefore say to the house of Israel, Thus saith the Lord GOD; I do not this for your sakes, O
house of Israel, but for my holy name's sake, which ye have profaned among the heathen, whither ye
went.
36:23 And I will sanctify my great name, which was profaned among the heathen, which ye have
profaned in the midst of them; and the heathen shall know that I am the LORD, saith the Lord GOD,
when I shall be sanctified in you before their eyes.
36:24 For I will take you from among the heathen, and gather you out of all countries, and will bring
you into your own land.
36:25 Then will I sprinkle clean water upon you, and ye shall be clean: from all your filthiness, and from
all your idols, will I cleanse you.
36:26 A new heart also will I give you, and a new spirit will I put within you: and I will take away the
stony heart out of your flesh, and I will give you a heart of flesh.
36:27 And I will put my spirit within you, and cause you to walk in my statutes, and ye shall keep my
judgments, and do them.
36:28 And ye shall dwell in the land that I gave to your fathers; and ye shall be my people, and I will be
your God.
36:29 I will also save you from all your uncleannesses: and I will call for the corn, and will increase it,
and lay no famine upon you.
36:30 And I will multiply the fruit of the tree, and the increase of the field, that ye shall receive no more
reproach of famine among the heathen.
36:31 Then shall ye remember your own evil ways, and your doings that were not good, and shall lothe

yourselves in your own sight for your iniquities, and for your abominations.
36:32 Not for your sakes do I this, saith the Lord GOD, be it known to you: be ashamed and confounded for your own ways, O house of Israel.
36:33 Thus saith the Lord GOD; In the day that I shall have cleansed you from all your iniquities I will also cause you to dwell in the cities, and the wastes shall be built.
36:34 And the desolate land shall be tilled, whereas it lay desolate in the sight of all that passed by.
36:35 And they shall say, This land that was desolate is become like the garden of Eden; and the waste and desolate and ruined cities are become fortified, and are inhabited.
36:36 Then the heathen that are left around you shall know that I the LORD build the ruined places, and plant that which was desolate: I the LORD have spoken it, and I will do it.
36:37 Thus saith the Lord GOD; I will yet for this be inquired of by the house of Israel, to do it for them; I will increase them with men like a flock.
36:38 As the holy flock, as the flock of Jerusalem in her solemn feasts; so shall the waste cities be filled with flocks of men: and they shall know that I am the LORD.

37

37:1 The hand of the LORD was upon me, and carried me out in the spirit of the LORD, and set me down in the midst of the valley which was full of bones,
37:2 And caused me to pass by them around: and behold, there were very many in the open valley; and lo, they were very dry.
37:3 And he said to me, Son of man, can these bones live? and I answered, O Lord GOD, thou knowest.
37:4 Again he said to me, Prophesy upon these bones, and say to them, O ye dry bones, hear the word of the LORD.
37:5 Thus saith the Lord GOD to these bones; Behold, I will cause breath to enter into you, and ye shall live:
37:6 And I will lay sinews upon you, and will bring up flesh upon you, and cover you with skin, and put breath in you, and ye shall live; and ye shall know that I am the LORD.
37:7 So I prophesied as I was commanded: and as I prophesied, there was a noise, and behold a shaking, and the bones came together, bone to his bone.
37:8 And when I beheld, lo, the sinews and the flesh came up upon them, and the skin covered them above: but there was no breath in them.
37:9 Then said he to me, Prophesy to the wind, prophesy, son of man, and say to the wind, Thus saith the Lord GOD; Come from the four winds, O breath, and breathe upon these slain, that they may live.
37:10 So I prophesied as he commanded me, and the breath came into them, and they lived, and stood up upon their feet, an exceeding great army.
37:11 Then he said to me, Son of man, these bones are the whole house of Israel: behold, they say, Our bones are dried, and our hope is lost: we are cut off for our parts.
37:12 Therefore prophesy and say to them, Thus saith the Lord GOD; Behold, O my people, I will open your graves, and cause you to come out of your graves, and bring you into the land of Israel.
37:13 And ye shall know that I am the LORD, when I have opened your graves, O my people, and brought you out of your graves,
37:14 And shall put my spirit in you, and ye shall live, and I shall place you in your own land: then shall ye know that I the LORD have spoken it, and performed it, saith the LORD.
37:15 The word of the LORD came again to me, saying,
37:16 Moreover, thou son of man, take thee one stick, and write upon it, For Judah, and for the children of Israel his companions: then take another stick, and write upon it, For Joseph, the stick of Ephraim, and for all the house of Israel his companions:
37:17 And join them one to another into one stick; and they shall become one in thy hand.
37:18 And when the children of thy people shall speak to thee, saying, Wilt thou not show us what thou meanest by these?
37:19 Say to them, Thus saith the Lord GOD; Behold, I will take the stick of Joseph, which is in the hand of Ephraim, and the tribes of Israel his fellows, and will put them with him, even with the stick of Judah, and make them one stick, and they shall be one in my hand.
37:20 And the sticks on which thou writest shall be in thy hand before their eyes.
37:21 And say to them, Thus saith the Lord GOD; Behold, I will take the children of Israel from among the heathen, whither they are gone, and will gather them on every side, and bring them into their own

land:
37:22 And I will make them one nation in the land upon the mountains of Israel; and one king shall be king to them all: and they shall be no more two nations, neither shall they be divided into two kingdoms any more at all:
37:23 Neither shall they defile themselves any more with their idols, nor with their detestable things, nor with any of their transgressions: but I will save them out of all their dwelling-places, in which they have sinned, and will cleanse them: so shall they be my people, and I will be their God.
37:24 And David my servant shall be king over them; and they all shall have one shepherd: they shall also walk in my judgments, and observe my statutes, and do them.
37:25 And they shall dwell in the land that I have given to Jacob my servant, in which your fathers have dwelt, and they shall dwell in it, even they, and their children, and their children's children for ever: and my servant David shall be their prince for ever.
37:26 Moreover I will make a covenant of peace with them; it shall be an everlasting covenant with them: and I will place them, and multiply them, and will set my sanctuary in the midst of them for evermore.
37:27 My tabernacle also shall be with them: and I will be their God, and they shall be my people.
37:28 And the heathen shall know that I the LORD do sanctify Israel, when my sanctuary shall be in the midst of them for ever.

38

38:1 And the word of the LORD came to me, saying,
38:2 Son of man, set thy face against Gog, the land of Magog, the chief prince of Meshech and Tubal, and prophesy against him.
38:3 And say, Thus saith the Lord GOD: Behold, I am against thee, O Gog, the chief prince of Meshech and Tubal:
38:4 And I will turn thee back, and put hooks into thy jaws, and I will bring thee forth, and all thy army, horses and horsemen, all of them clothed with all sorts of armor, even a great company with bucklers and shields, all of them handling swords:
38:5 Persia, Cush, and Phut with them; all of them with shield and helmet:
38:6 Gomer, and all his bands; the house of Togarmah of the north quarters, and all his bands: and many people with thee.
38:7 Be thou prepared, and prepare for thyself, thou, and all thy company that are assembled to thee, and be thou a guard to them.
38:8 After many days thou shalt be visited: in the latter years thou shalt come into the land that is brought back from the sword, and is gathered out of many people, against the mountains of Israel, which have been always waste: but it is brought forth out of the nations, and they shall all dwell in safety.
38:9 Thou shalt ascend and come like a storm, thou shalt be like a cloud to cover the land, thou, and all thy bands, and many people with thee.
38:10 Thus saith the Lord GOD; It shall also come to pass, that at the same time shall things come into thy mind, and thou shalt think an evil thought:
38:11 And thou shalt say, I will go up to the land of unwalled villages; I will go to them that are at rest, that dwell safely, all of them dwelling without walls, and having neither bars nor gates,
38:12 To take a spoil, and to take a prey; to turn thy hand upon the desolate places that are now inhabited, and upon the people that are gathered out of the nations, which have gotten cattle and goods, that dwell in the midst of the land.
38:13 Sheba, and Dedan, and the merchants of Tarshish, with all its young lions, shall say to thee, Art thou come to take a spoil? hast thou gathered thy company to take a prey? to carry away silver and gold, to take away cattle and goods, to take a great spoil?
38:14 Therefore, son of man, prophesy and say to Gog, Thus saith the Lord GOD; In that day when my people of Israel dwelleth safely, shalt thou not know it?
38:15 And thou shalt come from thy place out of the north parts, thou, and many people with thee, all of them riding upon horses, a great company, and a mighty army:
38:16 And thou shalt come against my people of Israel, as a cloud to cover the land; it shall be in the latter days, and I will bring thee against my land, that the heathen may know me, when I shall be sanctified in thee, O Gog, before their eyes.
38:17 Thus saith the Lord GOD; Art thou he of whom I have spoken in old time by my servants the

prophets of Israel, who prophesied in those days many years, that I would bring thee against them?
38:18 And it shall come to pass at the same time when Gog shall come against the land of Israel, saith the Lord GOD, that my fury shall come up in my face.
38:19 For in my jealousy and in the fire of my wrath have I spoken, Surely in that day there shall be a great shaking in the land of Israel.
38:20 So that the fishes of the sea, and the fowls of the heaven, and the beasts of the field, and all creeping animals that creep upon the earth, and all the men that are upon the face of the earth, shall shake at my presence, and the mountains shall be overturned, and the steep places shall fall, and every wall shall fall to the ground.
38:21 And I will call for a sword against him throughout all my mountains, saith the Lord GOD: every man's sword shall be against his brother.
38:22 And I will plead against him with pestilence and with blood; and I will rain upon him, and upon his bands, and upon the many people that are with him, an overflowing rain, and great hailstones, fire, and brimstone.
38:23 Thus will I magnify myself, and sanctify myself; and I will be known in the eyes of many nations, and they shall know that I am the LORD.

39

39:1 Therefore, thou son of man, prophesy against Gog, and say, Thus saith the Lord GOD; Behold, I am against thee, O Gog, the chief prince of Meshech and Tubal:
39:2 And I will turn thee back, and leave but the sixth part of thee, and will cause thee to come from the north parts, and will bring thee upon the mountains of Israel:
39:3 And I will strike thy bow out of thy left hand, and I will cause thy arrows to fall from thy right hand.
39:4 Thou shalt fall upon the mountains of Israel, thou, and all thy bands, and the people that are with thee: I will give thee to the ravenous birds of every sort, and to the beasts of the field to be devoured.
39:5 Thou shalt fall upon the open field: for I have spoken it, saith the Lord GOD.
39:6 And I will send a fire on Magog, and among them that dwell carelessly in the isles: and they shall know that I am the LORD.
39:7 So will I make my holy name known in the midst of my people Israel; and I will not let them profane my holy name any more: and the heathen shall know that I am the LORD, the Holy One in Israel.
39:8 Behold, it is come, and it is done, saith the Lord GOD; this is the day of which I have spoken.
39:9 And they that dwell in the cities of Israel shall go forth, and shall set on fire and burn the weapons, both the shields and the bucklers, the bows and the arrows, and the handstaffs, and the spears, and they shall burn them with fire seven years:
39:10 So that they shall take no wood out of the field, neither cut down any out of the forests; for they shall burn the weapons with fire: and they shall lay waste those that wasted them, and rob those that robbed them, saith the Lord GOD.
39:11 And it shall come to pass in that day, that I will give to Gog a place there of graves in Israel, the valley of the passengers on the east of the sea: and it shall stop the noses of the passengers: and there shall they bury Gog and all his multitude: and they shall call it The valley of Hamon-gog.
39:12 And seven months shall the house of Israel be in burying them, that they may cleanse the land.
39:13 Yes, all the people of the land shall bury them: and it shall be to them a renown in the day that I shall be glorified, saith the Lord GOD.
39:14 And they shall sever out men of continual employment, passing through the land to bury with the passengers those that remain upon the face of the earth, to cleanse it: after the end of seven months shall they search.
39:15 And as passengers pass through the land, when any seeth a man's bone, then shall he set up a sign by it, till the buriers have buried it in the valley of Hamon-gog.
39:16 And also the name of the city shall be Hamonah. Thus shall they cleanse the land.
39:17 And, thou son of man, thus saith the Lord GOD; Speak to every feathered fowl, and to every beast of the field, Assemble yourselves, and come; gather yourselves on every side to my sacrifice that I do sacrifice for you, even a great sacrifice upon the mountains of Israel, that ye may eat flesh, and drink blood.
39:18 Ye shall eat the flesh of the mighty, and drink the blood of the princes of the earth, of rams, of lambs, and of goats, of bullocks, all of them fatlings of Bashan.

39:19 And ye shall eat fat till ye are full, and drink blood till ye are drunken, of my sacrifice which I have sacrificed for you.
39:20 Thus ye shall be filled at my table with horses and chariots, with mighty men, and with all men of war, saith the Lord GOD.
39:21 And I will set my glory among the heathen, and all the heathen shall see my judgment that I have executed, and my hand that I have laid upon them.
39:22 So the house of Israel shall know that I am the LORD their God from that day and forward.
39:23 And the heathen shall know that the house of Israel went into captivity for their iniquity: because they trespassed against me, therefore I hid my face from them, and gave them into the hand of their enemies: so they all fell by the sword.
39:24 According to their uncleanness and according to their transgressions have I done to them, and hid my face from them.
39:25 Therefore thus saith the Lord GOD; Now will I bring again the captivity of Jacob, and have mercy upon the whole house of Israel, and will be jealous for my holy name;
39:26 After they have borne their shame, and all their trespasses by which they have trespassed against me, when they dwelt safely in their land, and none made them afraid.
39:27 When I have brought them again from the people, and gathered them out of the lands of their enemies, and am sanctified in them in the sight of many nations;
39:28 Then shall they know that I am the LORD their God, who caused them to be led into captivity among the heathen: but I have gathered them to their own land, and have left none of them there any more.
39:29 Neither will I hide my face any more from them: for I have poured out my spirit upon the house of Israel, saith the Lord GOD.

40

40:1 In the five and twentieth year of our captivity, in the beginning of the year, in the tenth day of the month, in the fourteenth year after the city was smitten, in the same day the hand of the LORD was upon me, and brought me thither.
40:2 In the visions of God he brought me into the land of Israel, and set me upon a very high mountain, by which was as the frame of a city on the south.
40:3 And he brought me thither, and behold, there was a man, whose appearance was like the appearance of brass, with a line of flax in his hand, and a measuring reed; and he stood in the gate.
40:4 And the man said to me, Son of man, behold with thy eyes, and hear with thy ears, and set thy heart upon all that I shall show thee; for, to the intent that I might show them to thee art thou brought hither: declare all that thou seest to the house of Israel.
40:5 And behold a wall on the outside of the house around, and in the man's hand a measuring reed of six cubits long by the cubit and a hand-breadth: so he measured the breadth of the building, one reed: and the hight, one reed.
40:6 Then he came to the gate which looketh towards the east, and ascended its stairs, and measured the threshhold of the gate, which was one reed broad; and the other threshhold of the gate, which was one reed broad.
40:7 And every little chamber was one reed long, and one reed broad; and between the little chambers were five cubits; and the threshhold of the gate by the porch of the gate within was one reed.
40:8 He measured also the porch of the gate within, one reed.
40:9 Then he measured the porch of the gate, eight cubits; and its posts, two cubits; and the porch of the gate was inward.
40:10 And the little chambers of the gate eastward were three on this side, and three on that side; they three were of one measure: and the posts had one measure on this side and on that side.
40:11 And he measured the breadth of the entry of the gate, ten cubits; and the length of the gate, thirteen cubits.
40:12 The space also before the little chambers was one cubit on this side, and the space was one cubit on that side: and the little chambers were six cubits on this side, and six cubits on that side.
40:13 He measured then the gate from the roof of one little chamber to the roof of another: the breadth was five and twenty cubits, door against door.
40:14 He made also posts of sixty cubits; even to the post of the court around the gate.
40:15 And from the face of the gate of the entrance to the face of the porch of the inner gate were fifty cubits.

40:16 And there were narrow windows to the little chambers, and to their posts within the gate around, and likewise to the arches: and windows were around inward: and upon each post were palm-trees.
40:17 Then he brought me into the outward court, and lo, there were chambers, and a pavement made for the court around: thirty chambers were upon the pavement.
40:18 And the pavement by the side of the gates over against the length of the gates was the lower pavement.
40:19 Then he measured the breadth from the front of the lower gate to the front of the inner court without, a hundred cubits eastward and northward.
40:20 And the gate of the outward court that looked towards the north, he measured its length, and its breadth.
40:21 And the little chambers of it were three on this side and three on that side; and its posts and its arches were after the measure of the first gate; its length was fifty cubits, and its breadth five and twenty cubits.
40:22 And their windows, and their arches, and their palm-trees, were after the measure of the gate that looketh towards the east; and they went up to it by seven steps; and its arches were before them.
40:23 And the gate of the inner court was over against the gate towards the north, and towards the east; and he measured from gate to gate a hundred cubits.
40:24 After that he brought me towards the south, and behold a gate towards the south: and he measured its posts and its arches according to these measures.
40:25 And there were windows in it and in its arches around, like those windows: the length was fifty cubits, and the breadth five and twenty cubits.
40:26 And there were seven steps to go up to it, and its arches were before them: and it had palm-trees, one on this side, and another on that side, upon its posts.
40:27 And there was a gate in the inner court towards the south: and he measured from gate to gate towards the south a hundred cubits.
40:28 And he brought me to the inner court by the south gate; and he measured the south gate according to these measures;
40:29 And its little chambers, and its posts, and its arches, according to these measures; and there were windows in it and in its arches around: it was fifty cubits long, and five and twenty cubits broad.
40:30 And the arches around were five and twenty cubits long, and five cubits broad.
40:31 And its arches were towards the outer court; and palm-trees were upon its posts: and the ascent to it had eight steps.
40:32 And he brought me into the inner court towards the east: and he measured the gate according to these measures.
40:33 And its little chambers, and its posts, and its arches, were according to these measures; and there were windows in it and in its arches around: it was fifty cubits long, and five and twenty cubits broad.
40:34 And its arches were towards the outward court; and palm-trees were upon its posts, on this side, and on that side: and the ascent to it had eight steps.
40:35 And he brought me to the north gate, and measured it according to these measures;
40:36 Its little chambers, its posts, and its arches, and the windows to it around: the length was fifty cubits, and the breadth five and twenty cubits.
40:37 And its posts were towards the outer court; and palm-trees were upon its posts, on this side, and on that side: and the ascent to it had eight steps.
40:38 And the chambers and its entries were by the posts of the gates, where they washed the burnt-offering.
40:39 And in the porch of the gate were two tables on this side, and two tables on that side, to slay upon it the burnt-offering and the sin-offering and the trespass-offering.
40:40 And at the side without, as one goeth up to the entry of the north gate, were two tables; and on the other side, which was at the porch of the gate, were two tables.
40:41 Four tables were on this side, and four tables on that side, by the side of the gate; eight tables, upon which they slew their sacrifices.
40:42 And the four tables were of hewn stone for the burnt-offering, of a cubit and a half long, and a cubit and a half broad, and one cubit high: upon which also they laid the instruments with which they slew the burnt-offering and the sacrifice.
40:43 And within were hooks, a hand broad, fastened around: and upon the tables was the flesh of the offering.
40:44 And without the inner gate were the chambers of the singers in the inner court, which was at the side of the north gate; and their prospect was towards the south: one at the side of the east gate having the prospect towards the north.

40:45 And he said to me, This chamber, whose prospect is towards the south, is for the priests, the keepers of the charge of the house.
40:46 And the chamber whose prospect is towards the north is for the priests, the keepers of the charge of the altar: these are the sons of Zadok among the sons of Levi, who come near to the LORD to minister to him.
40:47 So he measured the court, a hundred cubits long, and a hundred cubits broad, foursquare; and the altar that was before the house.
40:48 And he brought me to the porch of the house, and measured each post of the porch, five cubits on this side, and five cubits on that side: and the breadth of the gate was three cubits on this side, and three cubits on that side.
40:49 The length of the porch was twenty cubits, and the breadth eleven cubits; and he brought me by the steps by which they went up to it: and there were pillars by the posts, one on this side, and another on that side.

41

41:1 Afterward he brought me to the temple, and measured the posts, six cubits broad on the one side, and six cubits broad on the other side, which was the breadth of the tabernacle.
41:2 And the breadth of the door was ten cubits; and the sides of the door were five cubits on the one side, and five cubits on the other side: and he measured the length of it forty cubits: and the breadth, twenty cubits.
41:3 Then he went inward, and measured the post of the door, two cubits; and the door, six cubits; and the breadth of the door, seven cubits.
41:4 So he measured the length of it twenty cubits; and the breadth, twenty cubits, before the temple: and he said to me, This is the most holy place.
41:5 Afterward he measured the wall of the house, six cubits; and the breadth of every side-chamber, four cubits, round the house on every side.
41:6 And the side-chambers were three, one over another, and thirty in order; and they entered into the wall which was of the house for the side-chambers around, that they might have hold, but they had not hold in the wall of the house.
41:7 And there was an enlarging, and a winding about still upward to the side-chambers: for the winding about of the house went still upward around the house; therefore the breadth of the house was still upward, and so increased from the lowest chamber to the highest by the midst.
41:8 I saw also the hight of the house around: the foundations of the side-chambers were a full reed of six great cubits.
41:9 The thickness of the wall, which was for the side-chamber without, was five cubits: and that which was left was the place of the side-chambers that were within.
41:10 And between the chambers was the width of twenty cubits around the house on every side.
41:11 And the doors of the side-chambers were towards the place that was left, one door towards the north, and another door towards the south: and the breadth of the place that was left was five cubits around.
41:12 Now the building that was before the separate place at the end towards the west was seventy cubits broad; and the wall of the building was five cubits thick around, and its length ninety cubits.
41:13 So he measured the house, a hundred cubits long; and the separate place, and the building, with its walls, a hundred cubits long;
41:14 Also the breadth of the face of the house, and of the separate place towards the east, a hundred cubits.
41:15 And he measured the length of the building over against the separate place which was behind it, and its galleries on the one side and on the other side, a hundred cubits, with the inner temple, and the porches of the court;
41:16 The door posts, and the narrow windows, and the galleries around on their three stories, over against the door, ceiled with wood around, and from the ground up to the windows, and the windows were covered;
41:17 To that above the door, even to the inner house, and without, and by all the wall around within and without, by measure.
41:18 And it was made with cherubim and palm-trees, so that a palm-tree was between a cherub and a cherub; and every cherub had two faces;
41:19 So that the face of a man was towards the palm-tree on the one side, and the face of a young lion

towards the palm-tree on the other side: it was made through all the house around.
41:20 From the ground to above the door were cherubim and palm-trees made, and on the wall of the temple.
41:21 The posts of the temple were squared, and the face of the sanctuary; the appearance of the one as the appearance of the other.
41:22 The altar of wood was three cubits high, and its length two cubits; and its corners, and its length, and its walls, were of wood: and he said to me, This is the table that is before the LORD.
41:23 And the temple and the sanctuary had two doors.
41:24 And the doors had two leaves each, two turning leaves; two leaves for the one door, and two leaves for the other door.
41:25 And there were made on them, on the doors of the temple, cherubim and palm-trees, as were made upon the walls; and there were thick planks upon the face of the porch without.
41:26 And there were narrow windows and palm-trees on the one side and on the other side, on the sides of the porch, and upon the side-chambers of the house, and thick planks.

42

42:1 Then he brought me forth into the outer court, the way towards the north: and he brought me into the chamber that was over against the separate place, and which was before the building towards the north.
42:2 Before the length of a hundred cubits was the north door, and the breadth was fifty cubits.
42:3 Over against the twenty cubits which were for the inner court, and over against the pavement which was for the outer court, was gallery against gallery in three stories.
42:4 And before the chambers was a walk of ten cubits breadth inward, a way of one cubit; and their doors towards the north.
42:5 Now the upper chambers were shorter: for the galleries were higher than these, than the lower, and than the middlemost of the building.
42:6 For they were in three stories, but had not pillars as the pillars of the courts: therefore the building was straitened more than the lowest and the middlemost from the ground.
42:7 And the wall that was without over against the chambers, towards the outer court on the forepart of the chambers, the length of it was fifty cubits.
42:8 For the length of the chambers that were in the outer court was fifty cubits: and lo, before the temple were a hundred cubits.
42:9 And from under these chambers was the entry on the east side, as one goeth into them from the outer court.
42:10 The chambers were in the thickness of the wall of the court towards the east, over against the separate place, and over against the building.
42:11 And the way before them was like the appearance of the chambers which were towards the north, as long as they, and as broad as they: and all their goings out were both according to their fashions, and according to their doors.
42:12 And according to the doors of the chambers that were towards the south was a door in the head of the way, even the way directly before the wall towards the east, as one entereth into them.
42:13 Then said he to me, The north chambers and the south chambers which are before the separate place, they are holy chambers, where the priests that approach to the LORD shall eat the most holy things: there shall they lay the most holy things, and the meat-offering, and the sin-offering, and the trespass-offering; for the place is holy.
42:14 When the priests enter therein, then shall they not go out of the holy place into the outer court, but there they shall lay their garments in which they minister; for they are holy; and shall put on other garments, and shall approach to those things which are for the people.
42:15 Now when he had made an end of measuring the inner house, he brought me forth towards the gate whose prospect is towards the east, and measured it around.
42:16 He measured the east side with the measuring reed, five hundred reeds, with the measuring reed around.
42:17 He measured the north side, five hundred reeds, with the measuring reed around.
42:18 He measured the south side, five hundred reeds, with the measuring reed.
42:19 He turned about to the west side, and measured five hundred reeds, with the measuring reed.
42:20 He measured it by the four sides: it had a wall around, five hundred reeds long, and five hundred broad, to make a separation between the sanctuary and the profane place.

43

43:1 Afterward he brought me to the gate, even the gate that looketh towards the east:

43:2 And behold, the glory of the God of Israel came from the way of the east: and his voice was like a noise of many waters: and the earth shined with his glory.

43:3 And it was according to the appearance of the vision which I saw, even according to the vision that I saw when I came to destroy the city: and the visions were like the vision that I saw by the river Kebar; and I fell upon my face.

43:4 And the glory of the LORD came into the house by the way of the gate whose prospect is towards the east.

43:5 So the spirit took me up, and brought me into the inner court; and behold, the glory of the LORD filled the house.

43:6 And I heard him speaking to me out of the house; and the man stood by me.

43:7 And he said to me, Son of man, the place of my throne, and the place of the soles of my feet, where I will dwell in the midst of the children of Israel for ever, and my holy name, shall the house of Israel no more defile, neither they, nor their kings, by their lewd deeds, nor by the carcasses of their kings in their high places.

43:8 In their setting of their threshhold by my threshholds, and their post by my posts, and the wall between me and them, they have even defiled my holy name by their abominations that they have committed: wherefore I have consumed them in my anger.

43:9 Now let them put away their lewd deeds, and the carcasses of their kings, far from me, and I will dwell in the midst of them for ever.

43:10 Thou son of man, show the house to the house of Israel, that they may be ashamed of their iniquities: and let them measure the pattern.

43:11 And if they shall be ashamed of all that they have done, show them the form of the house, and the fashion of it, and its goings out, and its comings in, and all its forms, and all its ordinances, and all its forms, and all its laws: and write it in their sight, that they may keep the whole form of it, and all its ordinances, and do them.

43:12 This is the law of the house; Upon the top of the mountain, the whole limit of it around shall be most holy. Behold, this is the law of the house.

43:13 And these are the measures of the altar after the cubits: The cubit is a cubit and a hand-breadth; even the bottom shall be a cubit, and the breadth a cubit, and the border of it by its edge around shall be a span: and this shall be the higher place of the altar.

43:14 And from the bottom upon the ground even to the lower settle shall be two cubits, and the breadth one cubit; and from the lesser settle even to the greater settle shall be four cubits, and the breadth one cubit.

43:15 So the altar shall be four cubits; and from the altar and upward shall be four horns.

43:16 And the altar shall be twelve cubits long, twelve broad, square in the four squares of it.

43:17 And the settle shall be fourteen cubits long and fourteen broad in its four squares; and the border about it shall be half a cubit; and the bottom of it shall be a cubit about; and its stairs shall look towards the east.

43:18 And he said to me, Son of man, thus saith the Lord GOD; These are the ordinances of the altar in the day when they shall make it, to offer burnt-offerings upon it, and to sprinkle blood upon it.

43:19 And thou shalt give to the priests the Levites that are of the seed of Zadok, who approach to me, to minister to me, saith the Lord GOD, a young bullock for a sin-offering.

43:20 And thou shalt take of his blood, and put it on the four horns of it, and on the four corners of the settle, and upon the border around: thus shalt thou cleanse and purge it.

43:21 Thou shalt take the bullock also of the sin-offering, and he shall burn it in the appointed place of the house, without the sanctuary.

43:22 And on the second day thou shalt offer a kid of the goats without blemish for a sin-offering; and they shall cleanse the altar, as they cleansed it with the bullock.

43:23 When thou hast made an end of cleansing it, thou shalt offer a young bullock without blemish, and a ram out of the flock without blemish.

43:24 And thou shalt offer them before the LORD, and the priests shall cast salt upon them, and they shall offer them for a burnt-offering to the LORD.

43:25 Seven days shalt thou prepare every day a goat for a sin-offering: they shall also prepare a young bullock, and a ram out of the flock, without blemish.

43:26 Seven days shall they purge the altar and purify it; and they shall consecrate themselves.
43:27 And when these days have expired, it shall be, that upon the eighth day, and so forward, the priests shall make your burnt-offerings upon the altar, and your peace-offerings: and I will accept you, saith the Lord GOD.

44

44:1 Then he brought me back the way of the gate of the outward sanctuary which looketh towards the east; and it was shut.
44:2 Then said the LORD to me; This gate shall be shut, it shall not be opened, and no man shall enter in by it; because the LORD the God of Israel hath entered in by it, therefore it shall be shut.
44:3 It is for the prince; the prince, he shall sit in it to eat bread before the LORD; he shall enter by the way of the porch of that gate, and shall go out by the way of the same.
44:4 Then he brought me the way of the north gate before the house: and I looked, and behold, the glory of the LORD filled the house of the LORD: and I fell upon my face.
44:5 And the LORD said to me, Son of man mark well, and behold with thy eyes, and hear with thy ears all that I say to thee concerning all the ordinances of the house of the LORD, and all its laws; and mark well the entrance of the house, with every going forth of the sanctuary;
44:6 And thou shalt say to the rebellious, even to the house of Israel, Thus saith the Lord GOD; O ye house of Israel, let it suffice you of all your abominations;
44:7 In that ye have brought into my sanctuary strangers, uncircumcised in heart, and uncircumcised in flesh, to be in my sanctuary, to pollute it, even my house, when ye offer my bread, the fat and the blood, and they have broken my covenant because of all your abominations.
44:8 And ye have not kept the charge of my holy things: but ye have set keepers of my charge in my sanctuary for yourselves.
44:9 Thus saith the Lord GOD; No stranger, uncircumcised in heart, nor uncircumcised in flesh, shall enter into my sanctuary, of any stranger that is among the children of Israel.
44:10 And the Levites that have gone away far from me, when Israel went astray, who went astray from me after their idols; they shall even bear their iniquity.
44:11 Yet they shall be ministers in my sanctuary, having charge at the gates of the house, and ministering to the house: they shall slay the burnt-offering and the sacrifice for the people, and they shall stand before them to minister to them.
44:12 Because they ministered to them before their idols, and caused the house of Israel to fall into iniquity; therefore have I lifted up my hand against them, saith the Lord GOD, and they shall bear their iniquity.
44:13 And they shall not come near to me, to do the office of a priest to me, nor to come near to any of my holy things, in the most holy place: but they shall bear their shame, and their abominations which they have committed.
44:14 But I will make them keepers of the charge of the house, for all its service, and for all that shall be done therein.
44:15 But the priests the Levites, the sons of Zadok, that kept the charge of my sanctuary when the children of Israel went astray from me, they shall come near to me to minister to me, and they shall stand before me to offer to me the fat and the blood, saith the Lord GOD:
44:16 They shall enter into my sanctuary, and they shall come near to my table, to minister to me, and they shall keep my charge.
44:17 And it shall come to pass, that when they enter in at the gates of the inner court, they shall be clothed with linen garments; and no wool shall come upon them, while they minister in the gates of the inner court, and within.
44:18 They shall have linen bonnets upon their heads, and shall have linen breeches upon their loins; they shall not gird themselves with any thing that causeth sweat.
44:19 And when they go forth into the outer court, even into the outer court to the people, they shall put off their garments in which they ministered, and lay them in the holy chambers, and they shall put on other garments; and they shall not sanctify the people with their garments.
44:20 Neither shall they shave their heads, nor suffer their locks to grow long; they shall only poll their heads.
44:21 Neither shall any priest drink wine, when they enter into the inner court.
44:22 Neither shall they take for their wives a widow, nor her that is put away: but they shall take maidens of the seed of the house of Israel, or a widow that had a priest before.

44:23 And they shall teach my people the difference between the holy and profane, and cause them to discern between the unclean and the clean.
44:24 And in controversy they shall stand in judgment; and they shall judge it according to my judgments: and they shall keep my laws and my statutes in all my assemblies; and they shall hallow my sabbaths.
44:25 And they shall come at no dead person to defile themselves: but for father, or for mother, or for son, or for daughter, for brother, or for sister that hath had no husband, they may defile themselves.
44:26 And after he is cleansed, they shall reckon to him seven days.
44:27 And in the day that he goeth into the sanctuary, to the inner court, to minister in the sanctuary, he shall offer his sin-offering, saith the Lord GOD.
44:28 And it shall be to them for an inheritance: I am their inheritance: and ye shall give them no possession in Israel: I am their possession.
44:29 They shall eat the meat-offering, and the sin-offering, and the trespass-offering; and every dedicated thing in Israel shall be theirs.
44:30 And the first of all the first-fruits of all things, and every oblation of all, of every sort of your oblations, shall be the priest's: ye shall also give to the priest the first of your dough, that he may cause the blessing to rest in thy house.
44:31 The priests shall not eat of any thing that is dead of itself, or torn, whether of fowl or beast.

45

45:1 Moreover, when ye shall divide by lot the land for inheritance, ye shall offer an oblation to the LORD, a holy portion of the land: the length shall be the length of five and twenty thousand reeds, and the breadth shall be ten thousand. This shall be holy in all its borders on every side.
45:2 Of this there shall be for the sanctuary five hundred in length, with five hundred in breadth, square around; and fifty cubits around for the suburbs of it.
45:3 And of this measure shalt thou measure the length of five and twenty thousand, and the breadth of ten thousand: and in it shall be the sanctuary and the most holy place.
45:4 The holy portion of the land shall be for the priests the ministers of the sanctuary, who shall come near to minister to the LORD: and it shall be a place for their houses, and a holy place for the sanctuary.
45:5 And the five and twenty thousand of length, and the ten thousand of breadth, shall also the Levites, the ministers of the house, have for themselves, for a possession for twenty chambers.
45:6 And ye shall appoint the possession of the city five thousand broad, and five and twenty thousand long, over against the oblation of the holy portion: it shall be for the whole house of Israel.
45:7 And a portion shall be for the prince on the one side and on the other side of the oblation of the holy portion, and of the possession of the city, before the oblation of the holy portion, and before the possession of the city, from the west side westward, and from the east side eastward: and the length shall be over against one of the portions, from the west border to the east border.
45:8 In the land shall be his possession in Israel: and my princes shall no more oppress my people; and the rest of the land shall they give to the house of Israel according to their tribes.
45:9 Thus saith the Lord GOD; Let it suffice you, O princes of Israel: remove violence and spoil, and execute judgment and justice, take away your exactions from my people, saith the Lord GOD.
45:10 Ye shall have just balances, and a just ephah, and a just bath.
45:11 The ephah and the bath shall be of one measure, that the bath may contain the tenth part of a homer, and the ephah the tenth part of a homer: the measure of it shall be after the homer.
45:12 And the shekel shall be twenty gerahs: twenty shekels, five and twenty shekels, fifteen shekels, shall be your maneh.
45:13 This is the oblation that ye shall offer; the sixth part of an ephah of a homer of wheat, and ye shall give the sixth part of an ephah of a homer of barley;
45:14 Concerning the ordinance of oil, the bath of oil, ye shall offer the tenth part of a bath out of the cor, which is a homer of ten baths: for ten baths are a homer:
45:15 And one lamb out of the flock, out of two hundred, out of the fat pastures of Israel; for a meat-offering, and for a burnt-offering, and for peace-offerings, to make reconciliation for them, saith the Lord GOD.
45:16 All the people of the land shall give this oblation for the prince in Israel.
45:17 And it shall be the prince's part to give burnt-offerings, and meat-offerings, and drink-offerings, in the feasts, and in the new moons, and in the sabbaths, in all solemnities of the house of Israel: he shall prepare the sin-offering, and the meat-offering, and the burnt-offering, and the peace-offerings, to make

reconciliation for the house of Israel.
45:18 Thus saith the Lord GOD; In the first month, in the first day of the month, thou shalt take a young bullock without blemish, and cleanse the sanctuary:
45:19 And the priest shall take of the blood of the sin-offering, and put it upon the posts of the house, and upon the four corners of the settle of the altar, and upon the posts of the gate of the inner court.
45:20 And so thou shalt do the seventh day of the month for every one that erreth, and for him that is simple: so shall ye reconcile the house.
45:21 In the first month, in the fourteenth day of the month, ye shall have the passover, a feast of seven days; unleavened bread shall be eaten.
45:22 And upon that day shall the prince prepare for himself and for all the people of the land a bullock for a sin-offering.
45:23 And seven days of the feast he shall prepare a burnt-offering to the LORD, seven bullocks and seven rams without blemish daily the seven days; and a kid of the goats daily for a sin-offering.
45:24 And he shall prepare a meat-offering of an ephah for a bullock, and an ephah for a ram, and a hin of oil for an ephah.
45:25 In the seventh month, in the fifteenth day of the month, shall he do the like in the feast of the seven days, according to the sin-offering, according to the burnt-offering, and according to the meat-offering, and according to the oil.

46

46:1 Thus saith the Lord GOD; The gate of the inner court that looketh towards the east shall be shut the six working days; but on the sabbath it shall be opened, and in the day of the new moon it shall be opened.
46:2 And the prince shall enter by the way of the porch of that gate without, and shall stand by the post of the gate, and the priest shall prepare his burnt-offering and his peace-offerings, and he shall worship at the threshhold of the gate: then he shall go forth; but the gate shall not be shut until the evening.
46:3 Likewise the people of the land shall worship at the door of this gate before the LORD in the sabbaths and in the new moons.
46:4 And the burnt-offering that the prince shall offer to the LORD in the sabbath day shall be six lambs without blemish, and a ram without blemish.
46:5 And the meat-offering shall be an ephah for a ram, and the meat-offering for the lambs as he shall be able to give, and a hin of oil to an ephah.
46:6 And in the day of the new moon it shall be a young bullock without blemish, and six lambs, and a ram: they shall be without blemish.
46:7 And he shall prepare a meat-offering, an ephah for a bullock, and an ephah for a ram, and for the lambs according as his hand shall be able, and a hin of oil to an ephah.
46:8 And when the prince shall enter, he shall go in by the way of the porch of that gate, and he shall go forth by the way of it.
46:9 But when the people of the land shall come before the LORD in the solemn feasts, he that entereth in by the way of the north gate to worship shall go out by the way of the south gate; and he that entereth by the way of the south gate shall go forth by the way of the north gate: he shall not return by the way of the gate by which he came in, but shall go forth over against it.
46:10 And the prince in the midst of them, when they go in, shall go in; and when they go forth, shall go forth.
46:11 And in the feasts and in the solemnities the meat-offering shall be an ephah to a bullock, and an ephah to a ram, and to the lambs as he is able to give, and a hin of oil to an ephah.
46:12 Now when the prince shall prepare a voluntary burnt-offering or peace-offerings voluntarily to the LORD, one shall then open to him the gate that looketh towards the east, and he shall prepare his burnt-offering and his peace-offerings, as he did on the sabbath-day: then he shall go forth; and after his going forth one shall shut the gate.
46:13 Thou shalt daily prepare a burnt-offering to the LORD of a lamb of the first year without blemish: thou shalt prepare it every morning.
46:14 And thou shalt prepare a meat-offering for it every morning, the sixth part of an ephah, and the third part of a hin of oil, to temper with the fine flour; a meat-offering continually by a perpetual ordinance to the LORD.
46:15 Thus shall they prepare the lamb, and the meat-offering, and the oil, every morning for a continual burnt-offering.

46:16 Thus saith the Lord GOD; If the prince shall give a gift to any of his sons, the inheritance of it shall be to his sons; it shall be their possession by inheritance.
46:17 But if he shall give a gift of his inheritance to one of his servants, then it shall be his to the year of liberty; afterward it shall return to the prince: but his inheritance shall be to his sons for them.
46:18 Moreover the prince shall not take of the people's inheritance by oppression, to thrust them out of their possession; but he shall give his sons' inheritance out of his own possession: that my people be not scattered every man from his possession.
46:19 Afterward he brought me through the entry, which was at the side of the gate, into the holy chambers of the priests, which looked towards the north: and behold, there was a place on the two sides westward.
46:20 Then said he to me, This is the place where the priests shall boil the trespass-offering and the sin-offering, where they shall bake the meat-offering; that they bear them not out into the outer court, to sanctify the people.
46:21 Then he brought me forth into the outer court, and caused me to pass by the four corners of the court; and behold, in every corner of the court there was a court.
46:22 In the four corners of the court there were courts joined of forty cubits long and thirty broad: these four corners were of one measure.
46:23 And there was a row of building around in them, around them four, and it was made with boiling places under the rows around.
46:24 Then said he to me, These are the places of them that boil, where the ministers of the house shall boil the sacrifice of the people.

47

47:1 Afterward he brought me again to the door of the house; and behold, waters issued out from under the threshhold of the house eastward: for the front of the house stood towards the east, and the waters came down from under from the right side of the house, at the south side of the altar.
47:2 Then he brought me out of the way of the gate northward, and led me about the way without to the outer gate by the way that looketh eastward; and behold, there ran out waters on the right side.
47:3 And when the man that had the line in his hand went forth eastward, he measured a thousand cubits, and he brought me through the waters; the waters were to the ankles.
47:4 Again he measured a thousand, and brought me through the waters; the waters were to the knees. Again he measured a thousand, and brought me through; the waters were to the loins.
47:5 Afterward he measured a thousand; and it was a river that I could not pass over: for the waters had risen, waters to swim in, a river that could not be passed over.
47:6 And he said to me, Son of man, hast thou seen this? Then he brought me, and caused me to return to the brink of the river.
47:7 Now when I had returned, behold, at the bank of the river were very many trees on the one side and on the other.
47:8 Then said he to me, These waters issue out towards the east country, and go down into the desert, and go into the sea: which being brought forth into the sea, the waters shall be healed.
47:9 And it shall come to pass, that every thing that liveth, which moveth, whithersoever the rivers shall come, shall live: and there shall be a very great multitude of fish, because these waters shall come thither: for they shall be healed; and every thing shall live whither the river cometh.
47:10 And it shall come to pass, that the fishers shall stand upon it from En-gedi even to En-eglaim; they shall be a place to spread forth nets; their fish shall be according to their kinds, as the fish of the great sea, very numerous.
47:11 But its miry places and its marshes shall not be healed; they shall be given to salt.
47:12 And by the river upon its bank, on this side and on that side, shall grow all trees for food, whose leaf shall not fade, neither shall its fruit be consumed: it shall bring forth new fruit according to its months, because their waters they issued out of the sanctuary: and its fruit shall be for food, and its leaf for medicine.
47:13 Thus saith the Lord GOD; This shall be the border, by which ye shall inherit the land according to the twelve tribes of Israel: Joseph shall have two portions.
47:14 And ye shall inherit it, one as well as another: concerning which I lifted up my hand to give it to your fathers: and this land shall fall to you for inheritance.
47:15 And this shall be the border of the land towards the north side, from the great sea, the way of Hethlon, as men go to Zedad;

47:16 Hamath, Berothah, Sibraim, which is between the border of Damascus and the border of Hamath; Hazar-hatticon, which is by the border of Hauran.
47:17 And the border from the sea shall be Hazar-enan, the border of Damascus, and the north northward, and the border of Hamath. And this is the north side.
47:18 And the east side ye shall measure from Hauran, and from Damascus, and from Gilead, and from the land of Israel by Jordan, from the border to the east sea. And this is the east side.
47:19 And the south side southward, from Tamar even to the waters of strife in Kadesh, the river to the great sea. And this is the south side southward.
47:20 The west side also shall be the great sea from the border, till a man cometh over against Hamath. This is the west side.
47:21 So shall ye divide this land to you according to the tribes of Israel.
47:22 And it shall come to pass, that ye shall divide it by lot for an inheritance to you, and to the strangers that sojourn among you, which shall beget children among you: and they shall be to you as born in the country among the children of Israel; they shall have inheritance with you among the tribes of Israel.
47:23 And it shall come to pass, that in what tribe the stranger sojourneth, there shall ye give him his inheritance, saith the Lord GOD.

48

48:1 Now these are the names of the tribes. From the north end to the border of the way of Hethlon, as one goeth to Hamath, Hazar-enan, the border of Damascus northward, to the limit of Hamath; for these are his sides east and west; a portion for Dan.
48:2 And by the border of Dan, from the east side to the west side, a portion for Asher.
48:3 And by the border of Asher, from the east side even to the west side, a portion for Naphtali.
48:4 And by the border of Naphtali, from the east side to the west side, a portion for Manasseh.
48:5 And by the border of Manasseh, from the east side to the west side, a portion for Ephraim.
48:6 And by the border of Ephraim, from the east side even to the west side, a portion for Reuben.
48:7 And by the border of Reuben, from the east side to the west side, a portion for Judah.
48:8 And by the border of Judah, from the east side to the west side, shall be the offering which ye shall offer of five and twenty thousand reeds in breadth, and in length as one of the other parts, from the east side to the west side: and the sanctuary shall be in the midst of it.
48:9 The oblation that ye shall offer to the LORD shall be of five and twenty thousand in length, and of ten thousand in breadth.
48:10 And for them, even for the priests, shall be this holy oblation; towards the north five and twenty thousand in length, and towards the west ten thousand in breadth, and towards the east ten thousand in breadth, and towards the south five and twenty thousand in length: and the sanctuary of the LORD shall be in the midst of it.
48:11 It shall be for the priests that are sanctified of the sons of Zadok; who have kept my charge, who went not astray when the children of Israel went astray, as the Levites went astray.
48:12 And this oblation of the land that is offered shall be to them a thing most holy, by the border of the Levites.
48:13 And over against the border of the priests the Levites shall have five and twenty thousand in length, and ten thousand in breadth: all the length shall be five and twenty thousand, and the breadth ten thousand.
48:14 And they shall not sell of it, neither exchange, nor alienate the first-fruits of the land: for it is holy to the LORD.
48:15 And the five thousand, that are left in the breadth over against the five and twenty thousand, shall be a profane place for the city, for dwelling, and for suburbs, and the city shall be in the midst of it.
48:16 And these shall be the measures of it; the north side four thousand and five hundred, and the south side four thousand and five hundred, and on the east side four thousand and five hundred, and the west side four thousand and five hundred.
48:17 And the suburbs of the city shall be towards the north two hundred and fifty, and towards the south two hundred and fifty, and towards the east two hundred and fifty, and towards the west two hundred and fifty.
48:18 And the residue in length over against the oblation of the holy portion shall be ten thousand eastward, and ten thousand westward: and it shall be over against the oblation of the holy portion; and its increase shall be for food to them that serve the city.

48:19 And they that serve the city shall serve it out of all the tribes of Israel.
48:20 All the oblation shall be five and twenty thousand by five and twenty thousand: ye shall offer the holy oblation foursquare, with the possession of the city.
48:21 And the residue shall be for the prince, on the one side and on the other of the holy oblation, and of the possession of the city, over against the five and twenty thousand of the oblation towards the east border, and westward over against the five and twenty thousand towards the west border, over against the portions for the prince: and it shall be the holy oblation; and the sanctuary of the house shall be in the midst of it.
48:22 Moreover from the possession of the Levites, and from the possession of the city, being in the midst of that which is the prince's, between the border of Judah and the border of Benjamin, shall be for the prince.
48:23 As for the rest of the tribes, from the east side to the west side, Benjamin shall have a portion.
48:24 And by the border of Benjamin, from the east side to the west side, Simeon shall have a portion.
48:25 And by the border of Simeon, from the east side to the west side, Issachar a portion.
48:26 And by the border of Issachar, from the east side to the west side, Zebulun a portion.
48:27 And by the border of Zebulun, from the east side to the west side, Gad a portion.
48:28 And by the border of Gad, at the south side southward, the border shall be even from Tamar to the waters of strife in Kadesh, and to the river towards the great sea.
48:29 This is the land which ye shall divide by lot to the tribes of Israel for inheritance, and these are their portions, saith the Lord GOD.
48:30 And these are the goings out of the city on the north side, four thousand and five hundred measures.
48:31 And the gates of the city shall be after the names of the tribes of Israel: three gates northward; one gate of Reuben, one gate of Judah, one gate of Levi.
48:32 And at the east side four thousand and five hundred: and three gates; one gate of Joseph, one gate of Benjamin, one gate of Dan.
48:33 And at the south side four thousand and five hundred measures: and three gates; one gate of Simeon, one gate of Issachar, one gate of Zebulun.
48:34 And the west side four thousand and five hundred, with their three gates: one gate of Gad, one gate of Asher, one gate of Naphtali.
48:35 The circuit was eighteen thousand measures: and the name of the city from that day shall be, The LORD is there.

COMMENTARY

BY MATTHEW HENRY

Introduction to Ezekiel

Ezekiel was one of the priests; he was carried captive to Chaldea with Jehoiachin. All his prophecies appear to have been delivered in that country, at some place north of Babylon. Their chief object appears to have been to comfort his brethren in captivity.

He is directed to warn of the dreadful calamities coming upon Judea, particularly upon the false prophets, and the neighbouring nations. Also to announce the future restoration of Israel and Judah from their several dispersions, and their happy state in their latter days, under the Messiah. Much of Christ will be found in this book, especially in the conclusion.

Ezekiel 1

Chapter Contents

Ezekiel's vision of God, and of the angelic host. (1-14) The conduct of Divine Providence. (15-25) A revelation of the Son of man upon his heavenly throne. (26-28)

Commentary on Ezekiel 1:1-14

It is a mercy to have the word of God brought to us, and a duty to attend to it diligently, when we are in affliction. The voice of God came in the fulness of light and power, by the Holy Spirit. These visions seem to have been sent to possess the prophet's mind with great and high thoughts of God. To strike terror upon sinners. To speak comfort to those that feared God, and humbled themselves. In verses 4-14, is the first part of the vision, which represents God as attended and served by a vast company of angels, who are all his messengers, his ministers, doing his commandments. This vision would impress the mind with solemn awe and fear of the Divine displeasure, yet raise expectations of blessings. The fire is surrounded with a glory. Though we cannot by searching find out God to perfection, yet we see the brightness round about it. The likeness of the living creatures came out of the midst of the fire; angels derive their being and power from God. They have the understanding of a man, and far more. A lion excels in strength and boldness. An ox excels in diligence and patience, and unwearied discharge of the work he has to do. An eagle excels in quickness and piercing sight, and in soaring high; and the angels, who excel man in all these respects, put on these appearances.

The angels have wings; and whatever business God sends them upon, they lose no time. They stood straight, and firm, and steady. They had not only wings for motion, but hands for action. Many persons are quick, who are not active; they hurry about, but do nothing to purpose; they have wings, but no hands. But wherever the angels' wings carried them, they carried hands with them, to be doing what duty required. Whatever service they went about, they went every one straight forward. When we go straight, we go forward; when we serve God with one heart, we perform work. They turned not when they went. They made no mistakes; and their work needed not to be gone over again. They turned not from their business to trifle with any thing. They went whithersoever the Spirit of God would have them go. The prophet saw these living creatures by their own light, for their appearance was like burning coals of fire; they are seraphim, or "burners;" denoting the ardour of their love to God, and fervent zeal in his service. We may learn profitable lessons from subjects we cannot fully enter into or understand. But let us attend to the things which relate to our peace and duty, and leave secret things to the Lord, to whom alone they belong.

Commentary on Ezekiel 1:15-25

Providence, represented by the wheels, produces changes. Sometimes one spoke of the wheel is uppermost, sometimes another; but the motion of the wheel on its own axletree is regular and steady. We need not despond in adversity; the wheels are turning round and will raise us in due time, while those who presume in prosperity know not how soon they may be cast down. The wheel is near the living creatures; the angels are employed as ministers of God's providence. The spirit of the living creatures was in the wheels; the same wisdom, power, and holiness of God, that guide and govern the angels, by them order all events in this lower world. The wheel had four faces, denoting that the providence of God exerts itself in all parts. Look every way upon the wheel of providence, it has a face toward you. Their appearance and work were as a wheel in the middle of a wheel. The disposals of Providence seem to us dark, perplexed, and unaccountable, yet are all wisely ordered for the best. The motion of these wheels was steady, regular, and constant. They went as the Spirit directed, therefore returned not. We should not have to undo that by repentance which we have done amiss, if we followed the guidance of the Spirit. The rings, or rims of the wheels were so vast, that when put in motion the prophet was afraid to look upon them. The consideration of the height and depth of God's counsel should awe us. They were full of eyes round about. The motions of Providence are all directed by infinite Wisdom. All events are determined by the eyes of the Lord, which are in every place beholding the evil and the good; for there is no such thing as chance or fortune. The firmament above was a crystal, glorious, but terribly so. That which we take to be a dark cloud, is to God clear as crystal, through which he looks upon all the inhabitants of the earth. When the angels had roused a careless world, they let down their wings, that God's voice might be plainly heard. The voice of Providence is to open men's ears to the voice of the word. Sounds on earth should awaken our attention to the voice from heaven; for how shall we escape, if we turn away from Him that speaks from thence.

Commentary on Ezekiel 1:26-28

The eternal Son, the second Person in the Trinity, who afterwards took the human nature, is here denoted. The first thing observed was a throne. It is a throne of glory, a throne of grace, a throne of triumph, a throne of government, a throne of judgment. It is good news to men, that the throne above the firmament is filled with One who appears, even there, in the likeness of a man. The throne is surrounded with a rainbow, the well-known emblem of the covenant, representing God's mercy and covenanted love to his people. The fire of God's wrath was breaking out against Jerusalem, but bounds should be set to it; he would look upon the bow, and remember the covenant. All the prophet saw was only to prepare him for what he was to hear. When he fell on his face, he heard the voice of One that spake. God delights to teach the humble. Let sinners, then, humble themselves before him. And let believers think upon his glory, that they may be gradually changed into his image by the Spirit of the Lord.

Ezekiel 2

Chapter Contents

The prophet is directed what he is to do. (1-5) And encouraged to be resolute, faithful, and devoted. (6-10)

Commentary on Ezekiel 2:1-5

Lest Ezekiel should be lifted up with the abundance of the revelations, he is put in mind that still he is a son of man, a weak, mortal creature. As Christ usually called himself the Son of man, it was also an honourable distinction. Ezekiel's posture showed reverence, but his standing up would be a posture of greater readiness and fitness for business. God will speak to us, when we stand ready to do what he commands us. As Ezekiel had not strength of his own, the Spirit entered into him. God is graciously pleased to work in us whatever he requires of us. The Holy Spirit sets us upon our feet, by inclining our wills to our duty. Thus, when the Lord calls upon the sinner to awake, and attend to the concerns of his soul, the Spirit of life and grace comes with the call. Ezekiel is sent with a message to the children of Israel. Many might treat his message with contempt, yet they should know by the event that a prophet had been sent to them. God will be glorified, and his word made honourable, whether it be a savour of life unto life, or of death unto death.

Commentary on Ezekiel 2:6-10

Those who will do any thing to purpose in the service of God, must not fear men. Wicked men are as briers and thorns; but they are nigh unto cursing, and their end is to be burned. The prophet must be faithful to the souls of those to whom he was sent. All who speak from God to others, must obey his voice. The discoveries of sin, and the warnings of wrath, should be matter of lamentation. And those acquainted with the word of God, will clearly perceive it is filled with woe to impenitent sinners; and that all the precious promises of the gospel are for the repenting, believing servants of the Lord.

Ezekiel 3

Chapter Contents

The preparation of the prophet for his work. (1-11) His office, as that of a watchman. (12-2) The restraining and restoring his speech. (22-27)

Commentary on Ezekiel 3:1-11

Ezekiel was to receive the truths of God as the food for his soul, and to feed upon them by faith, and he would be strengthened. Gracious souls can receive those truths of God with delight, which speak terror to the wicked. He must speak all that, and that only, which God spake to him. How can we better speak God's mind than with his words? If disappointed as to his people, he must not be offended. The Ninevites were wrought upon by Jonah's preaching, when Israel was unhumbled and unreformed. We must leave this unto the Divine sovereignty, and say, Lord, thy judgments are a great deep. They will not regard the word of the prophet, for they will not regard the rod of God. Christ promises to strengthen him. He must continue earnest in preaching, whatever the success might be.

Commentary on Ezekiel 3:12-21

This mission made the holy angels rejoice. All this was to convince Ezekiel, that the God who sent him had power to bear him out in his work. He was overwhelmed with grief for the sins and miseries of his people, and overpowered by the glory of the vision he had seen. And however retirement, meditation, and communion with God may be sweet, the servant of the Lord must prepare to serve his generation. The Lord told the prophet he had appointed him a watchman to the house of Israel. If we warn the wicked, we are not chargeable with their ruin. Though such passages refer to the national covenant made with Israel, they are equally to be applied to the final state of all men under every dispensation. We are not only to encourage and comfort those who appear to be righteous, but they are to be warned, for many have grown high-minded and secure, have fallen, and even died in their sins. Surely then the hearers of the gospel should desire warnings, and even reproofs.

Commentary on Ezekiel 3:22-27

Let us own ourselves for ever indebted to the mediation of Christ, for the blessed intercourse between God and man; and a true believer will say, I am never less alone than when thus alone. When the Lord opened Ezekiel's mouth, he was to deliver his message boldly, to place life and death, the blessing and the curse, before the people, and leave them to their choice.

Ezekiel 4

Chapter Contents
The siege of Jerusalem. (1-8) The famine the inhabitants would suffer. (9-17)
Commentary on Ezekiel 4:1-8
The prophet was to represent the siege of Jerusalem by signs. He was to lie on his left side for a number of days, supposed to be equal to the years from the establishment of idolatry. All that the prophet sets before the children of his people, about the destruction of Jerusalem, is to show that sin is the provoking cause of the ruin of that once flourishing city.

Commentary on Ezekiel 4:9-17

The bread which was Ezekiel's support, was to be made of coarse grain and pulse mixed together, seldom used except in times of urgent scarcity, and of this he was only to take a small quantity. Thus was figured the extremity to which the Jews were to be reduced during the siege and captivity. Ezekiel does not plead, Lord, from my youth I have been brought up delicately, and never used to any thing like this; but that he had been brought up conscientiously, and never had eaten any thing forbidden by the law. It will be comfortable when we are brought to suffer hardships, if our hearts can witness that we have always been careful to keep even from the appearance of evil. See what woful work sin makes, and acknowledge the righteousness of God herein. Their plenty having been abused to luxury and excess, they were justly punished by famine. When men serve not God with cheerfulness in the abundance of all things, God will make them serve their enemies in the want of all things.

Ezekiel 5

Chapter Contents
A type of hair, showing the judgments about to come upon the Jews. (1-4) These awful judgments are declared. (5-17)

Commentary on Ezekiel 5:1-4

The prophet must shave off the hair of his head and beard, which signifies God's utter rejecting and abandoning that people. One part must be burned in the midst of the city, denoting the multitudes that should perish by famine and pestilence. Another part was to be cut in pieces, representing the many who were slain by the sword. Another part was to be scattered in the wind, denoting the carrying away of some into the land of the conqueror, and the flight of others into the neighbouring countries for shelter. A small quantity of the third portion was to be bound in his shirts, as that of which he is very careful. But few were reserved. To whatever refuge sinners flee, the fire and sword of God's wrath will consume them.

Commentary on Ezekiel 5:5-17

The sentence passed upon Jerusalem is very dreadful, the manner of expression makes it still more so. Who is able to stand in God's sight when he is angry? Those who live and die impenitent, will perish for ever unpitied; there is a day coming when the Lord will not spare. Let not persons or churches, who change the Lord's statutes, expect to escape the doom of Jerusalem. Let us endeavour to adorn the doctrine of God our Saviour in all things. Sooner or later God's word will prove itself true.

Ezekiel 6

Chapter Contents
The Divine judgments for idolatry. (1-7) A remnant shall be saved. (8-10) The calamities are to be lamented. (11-14)

Commentary on Ezekiel 6:1-7.

War desolates persons, places, and things esteemed most sacred. God ruins idolatries even by the hands of idolaters. It is just with God to make that a desolation, which we make an idol. The superstitions to which many trust for safety, often cause their ruin. And the day is at hand, when idols and idolatry will be as thoroughly destroyed from the professedly Christian church as they were from among the Jews.

Commentary on Ezekiel 6:8-10

A remnant of Israel should be left; at length they should remember the Lord, their obligations to him, and rebellion against him. True penitents see sin to be that abominable thing which the Lord hates. Those who truly loathe sin, loathe themselves because of sin. They give glory to God by their repentance. Whatever brings men to remember Him, and their sins against him, should be regarded as a blessing.

Commentary on Ezekiel 6:11-14

It is our duty to be affected, not only with our own sins and sufferings, but to look with compassion upon the miseries wicked people bring upon themselves. Sin is a desolating thing; therefore, stand in awe, and sin not. If we know the worth of souls, and the danger to which unbelievers are exposed, we shall deem every sinner who takes refuge in Jesus from the wrath to come, an abundant recompence for all contempt or opposition we may meet with.

Ezekiel 7

Chapter Contents

The desolation of the land. (1-15) The distress of the few who should escape. (16-22) The captivity. (23-27)

Commentary on Ezekiel 7:1-15

The abruptness of this prophecy, and the many repetitions, show that the prophet was deeply affected by the prospect of these calamities. Such will the destruction of sinners be; for none can avoid it. Oh that the wickedness of the wicked might end before it bring them to an end! Trouble is to the impenitent only an evil, it hardens their hearts, and stirs up their corruptions; but there are those to whom it is sanctified by the grace of God, and made a means of much good. The day of real trouble is near, not a mere echo or rumour of troubles. Whatever are the fruits of God's judgments, our sin is the root of them. These judgments shall be universal. And God will be glorified in all. Now is the day of the Lord's patience and mercy, but the time of the sinner's trouble is at hand.

Commentary on Ezekiel 7:16-22

Sooner or later, sin will cause sorrow; and those who will not repent of their sin, may justly be left to pine away in it. There are many whose wealth is their snare and ruin; and the gaining the world is the losing of their souls. Riches profit not in the day of wrath. The wealth of this world has not that in it which will answer the desires of the soul, or be any satisfaction to it in a day of distress. God's temple shall stand them in no stead. Those are unworthy to be honoured with the form of godliness, who will not be governed by its power.

Commentary on Ezekiel 7:23-27

Whoever break the bands of God's law, will find themselves bound and held by the chains of his judgments. Since they encouraged one another to sin, God would dishearten them. All must needs be in trouble, when God comes to judge them according to their deserts. May the Lord enable us to seek that good part which shall not be taken away.

Ezekiel 8

Chapter Contents

The idolatries committed by the Jewish rulers. (1-6) The superstitions to which the Jews were then devoted, the Egyptian. (7-12) The Phoenician. (13,14) The Persian. (15,16) The heinousness of their sin. (17,18)

Commentary on Ezekiel 8:1-6

The glorious personage Ezekiel beheld in vision, seemed to take hold upon him, and he was conveyed in spirit to Jerusalem. There, in the inner court of the temple, was prepared a place for some base idol. The whole was presented in vision to the prophet. If it should please God to give any man a clear view of his glory and majesty, and of all the abominations committing in any one city, he would then admit the justice of the severest punishments God should inflict thereon.

Commentary on Ezekiel 8:7-12

A secret place was, as it were, opened, where the prophet saw creatures painted on the walls, and a number of the elders of Israel worshipped before them. No superiority in worldly matters will preserve men from lust, or idolatries, when they are left to their own deceitful hearts; and those who are soon wearied in the service of God, often grudge no toil nor expense when following their superstitions. When hypocrites screen themselves behind the wall of an outward profession, there is some hole or other left in the wall, something that betrays them to those who look diligently. There is a great deal of secret wickedness in the world. They think themselves out of God's sight. But those are ripe indeed for ruin, who lay the blame of their sins upon the Lord.

Commentary on Ezekiel 8:13-18

The yearly lamenting for Tammuz was attended with infamous practices; and the worshippers of the sun here described, are supposed to have been priests. The Lord appeals to the prophet concerning the heinousness of the crime; "and lo, they put the branch to their nose," denoting some custom used by idolaters in honour of the idols they served. The more we examine human nature and our own hearts, the more abominations we shall discover; and the longer the believer searches himself, the more he will humble himself before God, and the more will he value the fountain open for sin, and seek to wash therein.

Ezekiel 9

Chapter Contents
A vision denoting the destruction of the inhabitants of Jerusalem, and the departure of the symbol of the Divine presence.
Commentary on Ezekiel 9:1-4
It is a great comfort to believers, that in the midst of destroyers and destructions, there is a Mediator, a great High Priest, who has an interest in heaven, and in whom saints on earth have an interest. The representation of the Divine glory from above the ark, removed to the threshold, denoted that the Lord was about to leave his mercy-seat, and to pronounce judgment on the people. The distinguishing character of this remnant that is to be saved, is such as sigh and cry to God in prayer, because of the abominations in Jerusalem. Those who keep pure in times of general wickedness, God will keep safe in times of general trouble and distress.
Commentary on Ezekiel 9:5-11
The slaughter must begin at the sanctuary, that all may see and know that the Lord hates sin most in those nearest to him. He who was appointed to protect, reported the matter. Christ is faithful to the trust reposed in him. Is he commanded by his Father to secure eternal life to the chosen remnant? He says, Of all that thou hast given me, I have lost none. If others perish, and we are saved, we must ascribe the difference wholly to the mercy of our God, for we too have deserved wrath. Let us still continue to plead in behalf of others. But where the Lord shows no mercy he does no injustice; he only recompenses men's ways.

Ezekiel 10

Chapter Contents
A vision of the burning of the city. (1-7) The Divine glory departing from the temple. (8-22)
Commentary on Ezekiel 10:1-7

The fire being taken from between the wheels, under the cherubim, 13, seems to have signified the wrath of God to be executed upon Jerusalem. It intimated that the fire of Divine wrath, which kindles judgment upon a people, is just and holy; and in the great day, the earth, and all the works that are therein, will be burnt up.

Commentary on Ezekiel 10:8-22

Ezekiel sees the working of Divine providence in the government of the lower world, and the affairs of it. When God is leaving a people in displeasure, angels above, and all events below, further his departure. The Spirit of life, the Spirit of God, directs all creatures, in heaven and on earth, so as to make them serve the Divine purpose. God removes by degrees from a provoking people; and, when ready to depart, would return to them, if they were a repenting, praying people. Let this warn sinners to seek the Lord while he may be found, and to call on him while he is near, and cause us all to walk humbly and watchfully with our God.

Ezekiel 11

Chapter Contents
Divine judgments against the wicked at Jerusalem. (1-13) Divine favour towards those in captivity. (14-21) The Divine presence forsakes the city. (22-25)

Commentary on Ezekiel 11:1-13

Where Satan cannot persuade men to look upon the judgment to come as uncertain, he gains his point by persuading them to look upon it as at a distance. These wretched rulers dare to say, We are as safe in this city as flesh in a boiling pot; the walls of the city shall be to us as walls of brass, we shall receive no more damage from the besiegers than the caldron does from the fire. When sinners flatter themselves to their own ruin, it is time to tell them they shall have no peace if they go on. None shall remain in possession of the city but those who are buried in it. Those are least safe who are most secure. God is often pleased to single out some sinners for warning to others. Whether Pelatiah died at that time in Jerusalem, or when the fulfilment of the prophecy drew near, is uncertain. Like Ezekiel, we ought to be much affected with the sudden death of others, and we should still plead with the Lord to have mercy on those who remain.

Commentary on Ezekiel 11:14-21

The pious captives in Babylon were insulted by the Jews who continued in Jerusalem; but God made gracious promises to them. It is promised, that God will give them one heart; a heart firmly fixed for God, and not wavering. All who are made holy have a new spirit, a new temper and dispositions; they act from new principles, walk by new rules, and aim at new ends. A new name, or a new face, will not serve without a new spirit. If any man be in Christ, he is a new creature. The carnal heart, like a stone, cannot be made to feel. Men live among the dead and dying, and are neither concerned nor humbled. He will make their hearts tender and fit to receive impressions: this is God's work, it is his gift by promise; and a wonderful and happy change is wrought by it, from death to life. Their practices shall be agreeable to those principles. These two must and will go together. When the sinner feels his need of these blessings, let him present the promises as prayers in the name of Christ, they will be performed.

Commentary on Ezekiel 11:22-25

Here is the departure of God's presence from the city and temple. It was from the Mount of Olives that the vision went up, typifying the ascension of Christ to heaven from that very mountain. Though the Lord will not forsake his people, yet he may be driven away from any part of his visible church by their sins, and woe will be upon them when He withdraws his presence, glory, and protection.

Ezekiel 12

Chapter Contents

The approaching captivity. (1-16) An emblem of the consternation of the Jews. (17-20) Answers to the objections of scoffers. (21-28)
Commentary on Ezekiel 12:1-16

By the preparation for removal, and his breaking through the wall of his house at evening, as one desirous to escape from the enemy, the prophet signified the conduct and fate of Zedekiah. When God has delivered us, we must glorify him and edify others, by acknowledging our sins. Those who by afflictions are brought to this, are made to know that God is the Lord, and may help to bring others to know him.

Commentary on Ezekiel 12:17-20

The prophet must eat and drink in care and fear, with trembling, that he might express the condition of those in Jerusalem during the siege. When ministers speak of the ruin coming upon sinners, they must speak as those that know the terrors of the Lord. Afflictions are happy ones, however grievous to flesh and blood, that improve us in the knowledge of God.

Commentary on Ezekiel 12:21-28

From that forbearance of God, which should have led them to repent, the Jews hardened themselves in sin. It will not serve for an excuse in speaking evil, to plead that it is a common saying. There is but a step between us and an awful eternity; therefore it concerns us to get ready for a future state. No one will be able to put from himself the evil day, unless by seeking peace with the Lord.

Ezekiel 13

Chapter Contents

Heavy judgments against lying prophets. (1-9) The insufficiency of their work. (10-16) Woes against false prophetesses. (17-23)

Commentary on Ezekiel 13:1-9

Where God gives a warrant to do any thing, he gives wisdom. What they delivered was not what they had seen or heard, as that is which the ministers of Christ deliver. They were not praying prophets, had no intercourse with Heaven; they contrived how to please people, not how to do them good; they stood not against sin. They flattered people into vain hopes. Such widen the breach, by causing men to think themselves deserving of eternal life, when the wrath of God abides upon them.

Commentary on Ezekiel 13:10-16

One false prophet built the wall, set up the notion that Jerusalem should be victorious, and made himself acceptable by it. Others made the matter yet more plausible and promising; they daubed the wall which the first had built; but they would, ere long, be undeceived when their work was beaten down by the storm of God's just wrath; when the Chaldean army desolated the land. Hopes of peace and happiness, not warranted by the word of God, will cheat men; like a wall well daubed, but ill built.

Commentary on Ezekiel 13:17-23

It is ill with those who had rather hear pleasing lies than unpleasing truths. The false prophetesses tried to make people secure, signified by laying them at ease, and to make them proud, signified by the finery laid on their heads. They shall be confounded in their attempts, and God's people shall be delivered out of their hands. It behoves Christians to keep close to the word of God, and in every thing to seek the teaching of the Holy Spirit. Let us so trust the promises of God as to keep his commandments.

Ezekiel 14

Chapter Contents

Threatenings against hypocrites. (1-11) God's purpose to punish the guilty Jews, but a few should be saved. (12-23)
Commentary on Ezekiel 14:1-11

No outward form or reformation can be acceptable to God, so long as any idol possesses the heart; yet how many prefer their own devices and their own righteousness, to the way of salvation! Men's corruptions are idols in their hearts, and are of their own setting up; God will let them take their course. Sin renders the sinner odious in the eyes of the pure and holy God; and in his own eyes also, whenever conscience is awakened. Let us seek to be cleansed from the guilt and pollution of sins, in that fountain which the Lord has opened.

Commentary on Ezekiel 14:12-23

National sins bring national judgments. Though sinners escape one judgment, another is waiting for them. When God's professing people rebel against him, they may justly expect all his judgments. The faith, obedience, and prayers of Noah prevailed to the saving of his house, but not of the old world. Job's sacrifice and prayer in behalf of his friends were accepted, and Daniel had prevailed for the saving his companions and the wise men of Babylon. But a people that had filled the measure of their sins, was not to expect to escape for the sake of any righteous men living among them; not even of the most eminent saints, who could be accepted in their own case only through the sufferings and righteousness of Christ. Yet even when God makes the greatest desolations by his judgments, he saves some to be monuments of his mercy. In firm belief that we shall approve the whole of God's dealings with ourselves, and with all mankind, let us silence all rebellious murmurs and objections.

Ezekiel 15

Chapter Contents

Jerusalem like an unfruitful vine.

If a vine be fruitful, it is valuable. But if not fruitful, it is worthless and useless, it is cast into the fire. Thus man is capable of yielding a precious fruit, in living to God; this is the sole end of his existence; and if he fails in this, he is of no use but to be destroyed. What blindness then attaches to those who live in the total neglect of God and of true religion! This similitude is applied to Jerusalem. Let us beware of an unfruitful profession. Let us come to Christ, and seek to abide in him, and to have his words abide in us.

Ezekiel 16

Chapter Contents

A parable showing the first low estate of the Jewish nation, its prosperity, idolatries, and punishment.

Commentary on Ezekiel 16:1-58

In this chapter God's dealings with the Jewish nation, and their conduct towards him, are described, and their punishment through the surrounding nations, even those they most trusted in. This is done under the parable of an exposed infant rescued from death, educated, espoused, and richly provided for, but afterwards guilty of the most abandoned conduct, and punished for it; yet at last received into favour, and ashamed of her base conduct. We are not to judge of these expressions by modern ideas, but by those of the times and places in which they were used, where many of them would not sound as they do to us. The design was to raise hatred to idolatry, and such a parable was well suited for that purpose.

Commentary on Ezekiel 16:59-63

After a full warning of judgments, mercy is remembered, mercy is reserved. These closing verses are a precious promise, in part fulfilled at the return of the penitent and reformed Jews out of Babylon, but to have fuller accomplishment in gospel times. The Divine mercy should be powerful to melt our hearts into godly sorrow for sin. Nor will God ever leave the sinner to perish, who is humbled for his sins, and comes to trust in His mercy and grace through Jesus Christ; but will keep him by his power, through faith unto salvation.

Ezekiel 17

Chapter Contents

A parable relative to the Jewish nation. (1-10) to which an explanation is added. (11-21) A direct promise of the Messiah. (22-24)

Commentary on Ezekiel 17:1-10

Mighty conquerors are aptly likened to birds or beasts of prey, but their destructive passions are overruled to forward God's designs. Those who depart from God, only vary their crimes by changing one carnal confidence for another, and never will prosper.

Commentary on Ezekiel 17:11-21

The parable is explained, and the particulars of the history of the Jewish nation at that time may be traced. Zedekiah had been ungrateful to his benefactor, which is a sin against God. In every solemn oath, God is appealed to as a witness of the sincerity of him that swears. Truth is a debt owing to all men. If the professors of the true religion deal treacherously with those of a false religion, their profession makes their sin the worse; and God will the more surely and severely punish it. The Lord will not hold those guiltless who take his name in vain; and no man shall escape the righteous judgment of God who dies under unrepented guilt.

Commentary on Ezekiel 17:22-24

The unbelief of man shall not make the promise of God of none effect. The parable of a tree, used in the threatening, is here presented in the promise. It appears only applicable to Jesus, the Son of David, the Messiah of God. The kingdom of Satan, which has borne so long, so large a sway, shall be broken, and the kingdom of Christ, which was looked upon with contempt, shall be established. Blessed be God, our Redeemer is seen even by the ends of the earth. We may find refuge from the wrath to come, and from every enemy and danger, under his shadow; and believers are fruitful in him.

Ezekiel 18

Chapter Contents

God has no respect of persons. (1-20) The Divine providence is vindicated. (21-29) A gracious invitation to repentance. (30-32)
Commentary on Ezekiel 18:1-20

The soul that sinneth it shall die. As to eternity, every man was, is, and will be dealt with, as his conduct shows him to have been under the old covenant of works, or the new covenant of grace. Whatever outward sufferings come upon men through the sins of others, they deserve for their own sins all they suffer; and the Lord overrules every event for the eternal good of believers. All souls are in the hand of the great Creator: he will deal with them in justice or mercy; nor will any perish for the sins of another, who is not in some sense worthy of death for his own. We all have sinned, and our souls must be lost, if God deal with us according to his holy law; but we are invited to come to Christ. If a man who had shown his faith by his works, had a wicked son, whose character and conduct were the reverse of his parent's, could it be expected he should escape the Divine vengeance on account of his father's piety? Surely not. And should a wicked man have a son who walked before God as righteous, this man would not perish for his father's sins. If the son was not free from evils in this life, still he should be partaker of salvation. The question here is not about the meritorious ground of justification, but about the Lord's dealings with the righteous and the wicked.

Commentary on Ezekiel 18:21-29

The wicked man would be saved, if he turned from his evil ways. The true penitent is a true believer. None of his former transgressions shall be mentioned unto him, but in the righteousness which he has done, as the fruit of faith and the effect of conversion, he shall surely live. The question is not whether the truly righteous ever become apostates. It is certain that many who for a time were thought to be righteous, do so, while verses 26,27 speaks the fulness of pardoning mercy: when sin is forgiven, it is blotted out, it is remembered no more. In their righteousness they shall live; not for their righteousness, as if that were an atonement for their sins, but in their righteousness, which is one of the blessings purchased by the Mediator. What encouragement a repenting, returning sinner has to hope for pardon and life according to this promise! In verse 28 is the beginning and progress of repentance. True believers watch and pray, and continue to the end, and they are saved. In all our disputes with God, he is in the right, and we are in the wrong.

Commentary on Ezekiel 18:30-32

Book of Ezekiel

The Lord will judge each of the Israelites according to his ways. On this is grounded an exhortation to repent, and to make them a new heart and a new spirit. God does not command what cannot be done, but admonishes us to do what is in our power, and to pray for what is not. Ordinances and means are appointed, directions and promises are given, that those who desire this change may seek it from God.

Ezekiel 19

Chapter Contents
A parable lamenting the ruin of Jehoahaz and Jehoiakim. (1-9) Another describing the desolation of the people. (10-14)

Commentary on Ezekiel 19:1-9

Ezekiel is to compare the kingdom of Judah to a lioness. He must compare the kings of Judah to a lion's whelps; they were cruel and oppressive to their own subjects. The righteousness of God is to be acknowledged, when those who have terrified and enslaved others, are themselves terrified and enslaved. When professors of religion form connexions with ungodly persons, their children usually grow up following after the maxims and fashions of a wicked world. Advancement to authority discovers the ambition and selfishness of men's hearts; and those who spend their lives in mischief, generally end them by violence.

Commentary on Ezekiel 19:10-14

Jerusalem was a vine, flourishing and fruitful. This vine is now destroyed, though not plucked up by the roots. She has by wickedness made herself like tinder to the sparks of God's wrath, so that her own branches serve as fuel to burn her. Blessed be God, one Branch of the vine here alluded to, is not only become a strong rod for the sceptre of those that rule, but is Himself the true and living Vine. This shall be for a rejoicing to all the chosen people of God throughout all generations.

Ezekiel 20

Chapter Contents

The elders of Israel are reminded of the idolatry in Egypt. (1-9) In the wilderness. (10-26) In Canaan. (27-32) God promises to pardon and restore them. (33-44) Prophecy against Jerusalem. (45-49)
Commentary on Ezekiel 20:1-9.
Those hearts are wretchedly hardened which ask God leave to go on in sin, and that even when suffering for it; see verse 32. God is justly angry with those who are resolved to go on still in their trespasses. Cause the people to know the evil deeds of their fathers, that they may see how righteous it was with God to cut them off.

Commentary on Ezekiel 20:10-26.

The history of Israel in the wilderness is referred to in the new Testament as well as in the Old, for warning. God did great things for them. He gave them the law, and revived the ancient keeping of the sabbath day. Sabbaths are privileges; they are signs of our being his people. If we do the duty of the day, we shall find, to our comfort, it is the Lord that makes us holy, that is, truly happy, here; and prepares us to be happy, that is, perfectly holy, hereafter. The Israelites rebelled, and were left to the judgments they brought upon themselves. God sometimes makes sin to be its own punishment, yet he is not the Author of sin: there needs no more to make men miserable, than to give them up to their own evil desires and passions.

Commentary on Ezekiel 20:27-32

The Jews persisted in rebellion after they settled in the land of Canaan. And these elders seem to have thought of uniting with the heathen. We make nothing by our profession if it be but a profession. There is nothing got by sinful compliances; and the carnal projects of hypocrites will stand them in no stead.

Commentary on Ezekiel 20:33-44

The wicked Israelites, notwithstanding they follow the sinful ways of other nations, shall not mingle with them in their prosperity, but shall be separated from them for destruction. There is no shaking off God's dominion; and those who will not yield to the power of his grace, shall sink under the power of his wrath. But not one of God's jewels shall be lost in the lumber of this world. He will bring the jews to the land of Israel again; and will give them true repentance. They will be overcome with his kindness: the more we know of God's holiness, the more we see the hateful nature of sin. Those who remain unaffected amidst means of grace, and would live without Christ, like the world around them, may be sure it is the way to destruction.

Commentary on Ezekiel 20:45-49

Judah and Jerusalem had been full of people, as a forest of trees, but empty of fruit. God's word prophesies against those who bring not forth the fruits of righteousness. When He will ruin a nation, who or what can save it? The plainest truths were as parables to the people. It is common for those who will not be wrought upon by the word, to blame it.

Ezekiel 21

Chapter Contents
The ruin of Judah under the emblem of a sharp sword. (1-17) The approach of the king of Babylon described. (18-27) The destruction of the Ammonites. (28-32)

Commentary on Ezekiel 21:1-17

Here is an explanation of the parable in the last chapter. It is declared that the Lord was about to cut off Jerusalem and the whole land, that all might know it was his decree against a wicked and rebellious people. It behoves those who denounce the awful wrath of God against sinners, to show that they do not desire the woful day. The example of Christ teaches us to lament over those whose ruin we declare. Whatever instruments God uses in executing his judgments, he will strengthen them according to the service they are employed in. The sword glitters to the terror of those against whom it is drawn. It is a sword to others, a rod to the people of the Lord. God is in earnest in pronouncing this sentence, and the prophet must show himself in earnest in publishing it.

Commentary on Ezekiel 21:18-27

By the Spirit of prophecy Ezekiel foresaw Nebuchadnezzar's march from Babylon, which he would determine by divination. The Lord would overturn the government of Judah, till the coming of Him whose right it is. This seems to foretell the overturnings of the Jewish nation to the present day, and the troubles of states and kingdoms, which shall make way for establishing the Messiah's kingdom throughout the earth. The Lord secretly leads all to adopt his wise designs. And in the midst of the most tremendous warnings of wrath, we still hear of mercy, and some mention of Him through whom mercy is shown to sinful men.

Commentary on Ezekiel 21:28-32

The diviners of the Ammonites made false prophecies of victory. They would never recover their power, but in time would be wholly forgotten. Let us be thankful to be employed as instruments of mercy; let us use our understandings in doing good; and let us stand aloof from men who are only skilful to destroy.

Ezekiel 22

Chapter Contents

The sins of Jerusalem. (1-16) Israel is condemned as dross. (17-22) As the corruption is general, so shall be the punishment. (23-31)

Commentary on Ezekiel 22:1-16

The prophet is to judge the bloody city; the city of bloods. Jerusalem is so called, because of her crimes. The sins which Jerusalem stands charged with, are exceeding sinful. Murder, idolatry, disobedience to parents, oppression and extortion, profanation of the sabbath and holy things, seventh commandment sins, lewdness and adultery. Unmindfulness of God was at the bottom of all this wickedness. Sinners provoke God because they forget him. Jerusalem has filled the measure of her sins. Those who give up themselves to be ruled by their lusts, will justly be given up to be portioned by them. Those who resolve to be their own masters, let them expect no other happiness than their own hands can furnish; and a miserable portion it will prove.

Commentary on Ezekiel 22:17-22

Israel, compared with other nations, had been as the gold and silver compared with baser metals. But they were now as the refuse that is consumed in the furnace, or thrown away when the silver is refined. Sinners, especially backsliding professors, are, in God's account, useless and fit for nothing. When God brings his own people into the furnace, he sits by them as the refiner by his gold, to see that they are not continued there any longer than is fitting and needful. The dross shall be wholly separated, and the good metal purified. Let those who suffer pains, or lingering sickness, and find that their hearts can scarcely bear these light and momentary afflictions, take warning to flee from the wrath to come; for if these trials are not sanctified by the power of the Holy Spirit, to the cleansing their hearts and hands from sin, far worse things will come upon them.

Commentary on Ezekiel 22:23-31

All orders and degrees of men had helped to fill the measure of the nation's guilt. The people that had any power abused it, and even the buyers and sellers find some way to oppress one another. It bodes ill to a people when judgments are breaking in upon them, and the spirit of prayer is restrained. Let all who fear God, unite to promote his truth and righteousness; as wicked men of every rank and profession plot together to run them down.

Ezekiel 23

Chapter Contents

A history of the apostacy of God's people from him, and the aggravation thereof.
In this parable, Samaria and Israel bear the name Aholah, "her own tabernacle;" because the places of worship those kingdoms had, were of their own devising. Jerusalem and Judah bear the name of Aholibah, "my tabernacle is in her," because their temple was the place which God himself had chosen, to put his name there. The language and figures are according to those times. Will not such humbling representations of nature keep open perpetual repentance and sorrow in the soul, hiding pride from our eyes, and taking us from self-righteousness? Will it not also prompt the soul to look to God continually for grace, that by his Holy Spirit we may mortify the deeds of the body, and live in holy conversation and godliness?

Ezekiel 24

Chapter Contents

The fate of Jerusalem. (1-14) The extent of the sufferings of the Jews. (15-27)
Commentary on Ezekiel 24:1-14

The pot on the fire represented Jerusalem besieged by the Chaldeans: all orders and ranks were within the walls, prepared as a prey for the enemy. They ought to have put away their transgressions, as the scum, which rises by the heat of the fire, is taken from the top of the pot. But they grew worse, and their miseries increased. Jerusalem was to be levelled with the ground. The time appointed for the punishment of wicked men may seem to come slowly, but it will come surely. It is sad to think how many there are, on whom ordinances and providences are all lost.

Commentary on Ezekiel 24:15-27

Though mourning for the dead is a duty, yet it must be kept under by religion and right reason: we must not sorrow as men that have no hope. Believers must not copy the language and expressions of those who know not God. The people asked the meaning of the sign. God takes from them all that was dearest to them. And as Ezekiel wept not for his affliction, so neither should they weep for theirs. Blessed be God, we need not pine away under our afflictions; for should all comforts fail, and all sorrows be united, yet the broken heart and the mourner's prayer are always acceptable before God.

Ezekiel 25

Chapter Contents

Judgments against the Ammonites. (1-7) Against the Moabites, Edomites, and Philistines. (8-17)
Commentary on Ezekiel 25:1-7.

It is wicked to be glad at the calamities of any, especially of God's people; it is a sin for which he will surely reckon. God will make it appear that he is the God of Israel, though he suffers them for a time to be captives in Babylon. It is better to know Him, and to be poor, than to be rich and ignorant of him.

Commentary on Ezekiel 25:8-17.

Though one event seem to the righteous and wicked, it is vastly different. Those who glory in any other defence and protection than the Divine power, providence, and promise, will, sooner or later, be ashamed of their glorying. Those who will not leave it to God to take vengeance for them, may expect that he will take vengeance on them. The equity of the Lord's judgments is to be observed, when he not only avenges injuries upon those that did them, but by those against whom they were done. Those who treasure up old hatred, and watch for the opportunity of manifesting it, are treasuring up for themselves wrath against the day of wrath.

Ezekiel 26

Chapter Contents
A prophecy against Tyre.
Commentary on Ezekiel 26:1-14

To be secretly pleased with the death or decay of others, when we are likely to get by it; or with their fall, when we may thrive upon it, is a sin that easily besets us, yet is not thought so bad as really it is. But it comes from a selfish, covetous principle, and from that love of the world as our happiness, which the love of God expressly forbids. He often blasts the projects of those who would raise themselves on the ruin of others. The maxims most current in the trading world, are directly opposed to the law of God. But he will show himself against the money-loving, selfish traders, whose hearts, like those of Tyre, are hardened by the love of riches. Men have little cause to glory in things which stir up the envy and rapacity of others, and which are continually shifting from one to another; and in getting, keeping, and spending which, men provoke that God whose wrath turns joyous cities into ruinous heaps.

Commentary on Ezekiel 26:15-21

See how high, how great Tyre had been. See how low Tyre is made. The fall of others should awaken us out of security. Every discovery of the fulfilment of a Scripture prophecy, is like a miracle to confirm our faith. All that is earthly is vanity and vexation. Those who now have the most established prosperity, will soon be out of sight and forgotten.

Ezekiel 27

Commentary on Ezekiel 27:1-25

Those who live at ease are to be lamented, if they are not prepared for trouble. Let none reckon themselves beautified, any further than they are sanctified. The account of the trade of Tyre intimates, that God's eye is upon men when employed in worldly business. Not only when at church, praying and hearing, but when in markets and fairs, buying and selling. In all our dealings we should keep a conscience void of offence. God, as the common Father of mankind, makes one country abound in one commodity, and another in another, serviceable to the necessity or to the comfort and ornament of human life. See what a blessing trade and merchandise are to mankind, when followed in the fear of God. Besides necessaries, an abundance of things are made valuable only by custom; yet God allows us to use them. But when riches increase, men are apt to set their hearts upon them, and forget the Lord, who gives power to get wealth.

Commentary on Ezekiel 27:26-36

The most mighty and magnificent kingdoms and states, sooner or later, come down. Those who make creatures their confidence, and rest their hopes upon them, will fall with them: happy are those who have the God of Jacob for their Help, and whose hope is in the Lord their God, who lives for ever. Those who engage in trade should learn to conduct their business according to God's word. Those who possess wealth should remember they are the Lord's stewards, and should use his goods in doing good to all. Let us seek first the kingdom of God and his righteousness.

Ezekiel 28

Chapter Contents

The sentence against the prince or king of Tyre. (1-19) The fall of Zidon. (20-23) The restoration of Israel. (24-26)
Commentary on Ezekiel 28:1-19

Ethbaal, or Ithobal, was the prince or king of Tyre; and being lifted up with excessive pride, he claimed Divine honours. Pride is peculiarly the sin of our fallen nature. Nor can any wisdom, except that which the Lord gives, lead to happiness in this world or in that which is to come. The haughty prince of Tyre thought he was able to protect his people by his own power, and considered himself as equal to the inhabitants of heaven. If it were possible to dwell in the garden of Eden, or even to enter heaven, no solid happiness could be enjoyed without a humble, holy, and spiritual mind. Especially all spiritual pride is of the devil. Those who indulge therein must expect to perish.
Commentary on Ezekiel 28:20-26.
The Zidonians were borderers upon the land of Israel, and they might have learned to glorify the Lord; but, instead of that, they seduced Israel to the worship of their idols. War and pestilence are God's messengers; but he will be glorified in the restoring his people to their former safety and prosperity. God will cure them of their sins, and ease them of their troubles. This promise will at length fully come to pass in the heavenly Canaan: when all the saints shall be gathered together, every thing that offends shall be removed, all griefs and fears for ever banished. Happy, then, is the church of God, and every living member of it, though poor, afflicted, and despised; for the Lord will display his truth, power, and mercy, in the salvation and happiness of his redeemed people.

Ezekiel 29

Chapter Contents

The desolation of Egypt. (1-16) Also a promise of mercy to Israel. (17-21)
Commentary on Ezekiel 29:1-16

Worldly, carnal minds pride themselves in their property, forgetting that whatever we have, we received it from God, and should use it for God. Why, then, do we boast? Self is the great idol which all the world worships, in contempt of God and his sovereignty. God can force men out of that in which they are most secure and easy. Such a one, and all that cleave to him, shall perish together. Thus end men's pride, presumption, and carnal security. The Lord is against those who do harm to his people, and still more against those who lead them into sin. Egypt shall be a kingdom again, but it shall be the basest of the kingdoms; it shall have little wealth and power. History shows the complete fulfilment of this prophecy. God, not only in justice, but in wisdom and goodness to us, breaks the creature-stays on which we lean, that they may be no more our confidence.

Commentary on Ezekiel 29:17-21

The besiegers of Tyre obtained little plunder. But when God employs ambitious or covetous men, he will recompense them according to the desires of their hearts; for every man shall have his reward. God had mercy in store for the house of Israel soon after. The history of nations best explains ancient prophecies. All events fulfil the Scriptures. Thus, in the deepest scenes of adversity, the Lord sows the seed of our future prosperity. Happy are those who desire his favour, grace, and image; they will delight in his service, and not covet any earthly recompence; and the blessings they have chosen shall be sure to them for ever.

Ezekiel 30

Chapter Contents

A prophecy against Egypt. (1-19) Another. (20-26)
Commentary on Ezekiel 30:1-19

The prophecy of the destruction of Egypt is very full. Those who take their lot with God's enemies, shall be with them in punishment. The king of Babylon and his army shall be instruments of this destruction. God often makes one wicked man a scourge to another. No place in the land of Egypt shall escape the fury of the Chaldeans. The Lord is known by the judgments he executes. Yet these are only present effects of the Divine displeasure, not worthy of our fear, compared with the wrath to come, from which Jesus delivers his people.
Commentary on Ezekiel 30:20-26

Egypt shall grow weaker and weaker. If lesser judgments do not prevail to humble and reform sinners, God will send greater. God justly breaks that power which is abused, either to put wrongs upon people, or to put cheats upon them. Babylon shall grow stronger. In vain do men endeavour to bind up the arm the Lord is pleased to break, and to strengthen those whom he will bring down. Those who disregard the discoveries of his truth and mercy, shall know his power and justice, in the punishment for their sins.

Ezekiel 31

Chapter Contents

The glory of Assyria. (1-9) Its fall, and the like for Egypt. (10-18)
Commentary on Ezekiel 31:1-9

The falls of others, both into sin and ruin, warn us not to be secure or high-minded. The prophet is to show an instance of one whom the king of Egypt resembled in greatness, the Assyrian, compared to a stately cedar. Those who excel others, make themselves the objects of envy; but the blessings of the heavenly paradise are not liable to such alloy. The utmost security that any creature can give, is but like the shadow of a tree, a scanty and slender protection. But let us flee to God for protection, there we shall be safe. His hand must be owned in the rising of the great men of the earth, and we must not envy them. Though worldly people may seem to have firm prosperity, yet it only seems so.

Commentary on Ezekiel 31:10-18

The king of Egypt resembled the king of Assyria in his greatness: here we see he resembles him in his pride. And he shall resemble him in his fall. His own sin brings his ruin. None of our comforts are ever lost, but what have been a thousand times forfeited. When great men fall, many fall with them, as many have fallen before them. The fall of proud men is for warning to others, to keep them humble. See how low Pharaoh lies; and see what all his pomp and pride are come to. It is best to be a lowly tree of righteousness, yielding fruit to the glory of God, and to the good of men. The wicked man is often seen flourishing like the cedar, and spreading like the green bay tree, but he soon passes away, and his place is no more found. Let us then mark the perfect man, and behold the upright, for the end of that man is peace.

Ezekiel 32

Chapter Contents
The fall of Egypt. (1-16) It is like that of other nations. (17-32)
Commentary on Ezekiel 32:1-16

It becomes us to weep and tremble for those who will not weep and tremble for themselves. Great oppressors are, in God's account, no better than beasts of prey. Those who admire the pomp of this world, will wonder at the ruin of that pomp; which to those who know the vanity of all things here below, is no surprise. When others are ruined by sin, we have to fear, knowing ourselves guilty. The instruments of the desolation are formidable. And the instances of the desolation are frightful. The waters of Egypt shall run like oil, which signifies there should be universal sadness and heaviness upon the whole nation. God can soon empty those of this world's goods who have the greatest fulness of them. By enlarging the matters of our joy, we increase the occasions of our sorrow. How weak and helpless, as to God, are the most powerful of mankind! The destruction of Egypt was a type of the destruction of the enemies of Christ.

Commentary on Ezekiel 32:17-32

Divers nations are mentioned as gone down to the grave before Egypt, who are ready to give her a scornful reception; these nations had been lately ruined and wasted. But though Judah and Jerusalem were about this time ruined and laid waste, yet they are not mentioned here. Though they suffered the same affliction, and by the same hand, yet the kind design for which they were afflicted, and the mercy God reserved for them, altered its nature. It was not to them a going down to the pit, as it was to the heathen. Pharaoh shall see, and be comforted; but the comfort wicked ones have after death, is poor comfort, not real, but only in fancy. The view this prophecy gives of ruined states shows something of this present world, and the empire of death in it. Come and see the calamitous state of human life. As if men did not die fast enough, they are ingenious at finding out ways to destroy one another. Also of the other world; though the destruction of nations as such, seems chiefly intended, here is plain allusion to the everlasting ruin of impenitent sinners. How are men deceived by Satan! What are the objects they pursue through scenes of bloodshed, and their many sins? Surely man disquiets himself in vain, whether he pursues wealth, fame, power, or pleasure. The hour cometh, when all that are in their graves shall hear the voice of Christ, and shall come forth; those that have done good to the resurrection of life, and those that have done evil to the resurrection of damnation.

Ezekiel 33

Chapter Contents

Ezekiel's duty as a watchman. (1-9) He is to vindicate the Divine government. (10-20) The desolation of Judea. (21-29) Judgments on the mockers of the prophets. (30-33)
Commentary on Ezekiel 33:1-9

The prophet is a watchman to the house of Israel. His business is to warn sinners of their misery and danger. He must warn the wicked to turn from their way, that they may live. If souls perish through his neglect of duty, he brings guilt upon himself. See what those have to answer for, who make excuses for sin, flatter sinners, and encourage them to believe they shall have peace, though they go on. How much wiser are men in their temporal than in their spiritual concerns! They set watchmen to guard their houses, and sentinels to warn of the enemies' approach, but where the everlasting happiness or misery of the soul is at stake, they are offended if ministers obey their Master's command, and give a faithful warning; they would rather perish, listening to smooth things.

Commentary on Ezekiel 33:10-20

Those who despaired of finding mercy with God, are answered with a solemn declaration of God's readiness to show mercy. The ruin of the city and state was determined, but that did not relate to the final state of persons. God says to the righteous, that he shall surely live. But many who have made profession, have been ruined by proud confidence in themselves. Man trusts to his own righteousness, and presuming on his own sufficiency, he is brought to commit iniquity. If those who have lived a

wicked life repent and forsake their wicked ways, they shall be saved. Many such amazing and blessed changes have been wrought by the power of Divine grace. When there is a settled separation between a man and sin, there shall no longer be a separation between him and God.
Commentary on Ezekiel 33:21-29

Those are unteachable indeed, who do not learn their dependence upon God, when all creature-comforts fail. Many claim an interest in the peculiar blessings to true believers, while their conduct proves them enemies of God. They call this groundless presumption strong faith, when God's testimony declares them entitled to his threatenings, and nothing else.

Commentary on Ezekiel 33:30-33

Unworthy and corrupt motives often lead men to the places where the word of God is faithfully preached. Many come to find somewhat to oppose: far more come of curiosity or mere habit. Men may have their hearts changed. But whether men hear or forbear, they will know by the event that a servant of God has been among them. All who will not know the worth of mercies by the improvement of them, will justly be made to know their worth by the want of them.

Ezekiel 34

Chapter Contents

The rulers reproved. (1-6) The people are to be restored to their own land. (7-16) The kingdom of Christ. (17-31)

Commentary on Ezekiel 34:1-6

The people became as sheep without a shepherd, were given up as a prey to their enemies, and the land was utterly desolated. No rank or office can exempt from the reproofs of God's word, men who neglect their duty, and abuse the trust reposed in them.

Commentary on Ezekiel 34:7-16

The Lord declared that he intended mercy towards the scattered flock. Doubtless this, in the first place, had reference to the restoration of the Jews. It also represented the good Shepherd's tender care of the souls of his people. He finds them in their days of darkness and ignorance, and brings them to his fold. He comes to their relief in times of persecution and temptation. He leads them in the ways of righteousness, and causes them to rest on his love and faithfulness. The proud and self-sufficient, are enemies of the true gospel and of believers; against such we must guard. He has rest for disquieted saints, and terror for presumptuous sinners.

Commentary on Ezekiel 34:17-31

The whole nation seemed to be the Lord's flock, yet they were very different characters; but he knew how to distinguish between them. By good pastures and deep waters, are meant the pure word of God and the dispensing of justice. The latter verses, 23-31, prophesy of Christ, and of the most glorious times of his church on earth. Under Him, as the good Shepherd, the church would be a blessing to all around. Christ, though excellent in himself, was as a tender plant out of a dry ground. Being the Tree of life, bearing all the fruits of salvation, he yields spiritual food to the souls of his people. Our constant desire and prayer should be, that there may be showers of blessings in every place where the truth of Christ is preached; and that all who profess the gospel may be filled with fruits of righteousness.

Ezekiel 35

Chapter Contents

A prophecy against Edom.
Commentary on Ezekiel 35:1-9
All who have God against them, have the word of God against them. Those that have a constant hatred

to God and his people, as the carnal mind has, can only expect to be made desolate for ever.
Commentary on Ezekiel 35:10-15

When we see the vanity of the world in the disappointments, losses, and crosses, which others meet with, instead of showing ourselves greedy of worldly things, we should sit more loose to them. In the multitude of words, not one is unknown to God; not the most idle word; and the most daring is not above his rebuke. In the destruction of the enemies of the church, God designs his own glory; and we may be sure that he will not come short of his design. And when the fulness of the Jews and Gentiles shall come into the church, all antichristian opposers shall be destroyed.

Ezekiel 36

Chapter Contents

The land shall be delivered from heathen oppressors. (1-15) The people are reminded of former sins, and promised deliverance. (16-24) Also holiness, and gospel blessings. (25-38)

Commentary on Ezekiel 36:1-15

Those who put contempt and reproach on God's people, will have them turned on themselves. God promises favour to his Israel. We have no reason to complain, if the more unkind men are, the more kind God is. They shall come again to their own border. It was a type of the heavenly Canaan, of which all God's children are heirs, and into which they all shall be brought together. And when God returns in mercy to a people who return to him in duty, all their grievances will be set right. The full completion of this prophecy must be in some future event.

Commentary on Ezekiel 36:16-24
The restoration of that people, being typical of our redemption by Christ, shows that the end aimed at in our salvation is the glory of God. The sin of a people defiles their land; renders it abominable to God, and uncomfortable to themselves. God's holy name is his great name; his holiness is his greatness, nor does any thing else make a man truly great.

Commentary on Ezekiel 36:25-38

Water is an emblem of the cleansing our polluted souls from sin. But no water can do more than take away the filth of the flesh. Water seems in general the sacramental sign of the sanctifying influences of the Holy Ghost; yet this is always connected with the atoning blood of Christ. When the latter is applied by faith to the conscience, to cleanse it from evil works, the former is always applied to the powers of the soul, to purify it from the pollution of sin. All that have an interest in the new covenant, have a new heart and a new spirit, in order to their walking in newness of life. God would give a heart of flesh, a soft and tender heart, complying with his holy will. Renewing grace works as great a change in the soul, as the turning a dead stone into living flesh. God will put his Spirit within, as a Teacher, Guide, and Sanctifier. The promise of God's grace to fit us for our duty, should quicken our constant care and endeavour to do our duty. These are promises to be pleaded by, and will be fulfilled to, all true believers in every age.

Ezekiel 37

Chapter Contents

God restores dried bones to life. (1-14) The whole house of Israel is represented as enjoying the blessings of Christ's kingdom. (15-28)
Commentary on Ezekiel 37:1-14

No created power could restore human bones to life. God alone could cause them to live. Skin and flesh covered them, and the wind was then told to blow upon these bodies; and they were restored to life. The wind was an emblem of the Spirit of God, and represented his quickening powers. The vision was to encourage the desponding Jews; to predict both their restoration after the captivity, and also their recovery from their present and long-continued dispersion. It was also a clear intimation of the resurrection of the dead; and it represents the power and grace of God, in the conversion of the most hopeless sinners to himself. Let us look to Him who will at last open our graves, and bring us forth to judgment, that He may now deliver us from sin, and put his Spirit within us, and keep us by his power, through faith, unto salvation.

Commentary on Ezekiel 37:15-28

This emblem was to show the people, that the Lord would unite Judah and Israel. Christ is the true David, Israel's King of old; and those whom he makes willing in the day of his power, he makes to walk in his judgments, and to keep his statutes. Events yet to come will further explain this prophecy. Nothing has more hindered the success of the gospel than divisions. Let us study to keep the unity of the Spirit in the bond of peace; let us seek for Divine grace to keep us from detestable things; and let us pray that all nations may be obedient and happy subjects of the Son of David, that the Lord may be our God, and we may be his people for evermore.

Ezekiel 38

Chapter Contents
The army and malice of Gog. (1-13) God's judgments. (14-23)
Commentary on Ezekiel 38:1-13

These events will be in the latter days. It is supposed these enemies will come together to invade the land of Judea, and God will defeat them. God not only sees who are now the enemies of his church, but he foresees who will be so, and lets them know by his word that he is against them; though they join together, the wicked shall not be unpunished.

Commentary on Ezekiel 38:14-23

The enemy should make a formidable descent upon the land of Israel. When Israel dwell safely under the Divine protection, shalt not thou be made to know it by finding that endeavours to destroy them are made in vain? Promises of security are treasured up in the word of God, against the troubles and dangers the church may be brought into in the latter days. In the destruction of sinners, God makes it appear that he is a great and holy God. We should desire and pray daily. Father, glorify thine own name.

Ezekiel 39

Chapter Contents

The destruction of Gog. (1-10) Its extent. (11-22) Israel again favoured. (23-29)

Commentary on Ezekiel 39:1-10

The Lord will make the most careless and hardened transgressors know his holy name, either by his righteous anger, or by the riches of his mercy and grace. The weapons formed against Zion shall not prosper. Though this prophecy is to be fulfilled in the latter days, it is certain. From the language used, it seems that the army of Gog will be destroyed by miracle.

Commentary on Ezekiel 39:11-22

How numerous the enemies which God destroyed for the defence of his people Israel! Times of great deliverances should be times of reformation. Every one should help the utmost he can, toward cleansing the land from reproach. Sin is an enemy every man should strive against. Those engaged in public work, especially of cleansing and reforming a land, ought to be men who will go through with what they undertake, who will be always employed. When good work is to be done, every one should further it. Having received special favours from God, let us cleanse ourselves from all evil.
It is a work which will require persevering diligence, that search may be made into the secret recesses of sin. The judgments of the Lord, brought upon sin and sinners, are a sacrifice to the justice of God, and a feast to the faith and hope of God's people. See how evil pursues sinners, even after death. After all that ambitious and covetous men do and look for, "a place of graves" is all the Lord gives them on earth,

while their guilty souls are doomed to misery in another world.

Commentary on Ezekiel 39:23-29

When the Lord shall have mercy on the whole house of Israel, by converting them to Christianity, and when they shall have borne the shame of being cast off for their sins, then the nations shall learn to know, worship, and serve him. Then Israel also shall know the Lord, as revealed in and by Christ. Past events do not answer to these predictions. The pouring out of the Spirit is a pledge that God's favour will continue. He will hide his face no more from those on whom he has poured out his Spirit. When we pray that God would never cast us from his presence, we must as earnestly pray that, in order thereto, he would never take his Holy Spirit from us.

Ezekiel 40

Chapter Contents

The Vision of the Temple.

Here is a vision, beginning at ch. 40, and continued to the end of the book, ch. 48, which is justly looked upon to be one of the most difficult portions in all the book of God. When we despair to be satisfied as to any difficulty we meet with, let us bless God that our salvation does not depend upon it, but that things necessary are plain enough; and let us wait till God shall reveal even this unto us. This chapter describes two outward courts of the temple. Whether the personage here mentioned was the Son of God, or a created angel, is not clear. But Christ is both our Altar and our Sacrifice, to whom we must look with faith in all approaches to God; and he is Salvation in the midst of the earth, Psalm 74:12, to be looked unto from all quarters.

Ezekiel 41

Chapter Summary

After the prophet had observed the courts, he was brought to the temple. If we attend to instructions in the plainer parts of religion, and profit by them, we shall be led further into an acquaintance with the mysteries of the kingdom of heaven.

Ezekiel 42

Chapter Summary

In this chapter are described the priests' chambers, their use, and the dimensions of the holy mount on which the temple stood. These chambers were many. Jesus said, In my Father's house are many mansions: in his house on earth there are many; multitudes, by faith, are lodging in his sanctuary, and yet there is room. These chambers, though private, were near the temple. Our religious services in our chambers, must prepare for public devotions, and further us in improving them, as our opportunities are.

Ezekiel 43

After Ezekiel had surveyed the temple of God, he had a vision of the glory of God. When Christ crucified, and the things freely given to us of God, through Him, are shown to us by the Holy Ghost, they make us ashamed for our sins. This frame of mind prepares us for fuller discoveries of the mysteries of redeeming love; and the whole of the Scriptures should be opened and applied, that men may see their sins, and repent of them. We are not now to offer any atoning sacrifices, for by one offering Christ has perfected for ever those that are sanctified, Hebrews 10:14; but the sprinkling of his blood is needful in all our approaches to God the Father. Our best services can be accepted only as sprinkled with the blood which cleanses from all sin.

Ezekiel 44

This chapter contains ordinances relative to the true priests. The prince evidently means Christ, and the words in verse 2, may remind us that no other can enter heaven, the true sanctuary, as Christ did; namely, by virtue of his own excellency, and his personal holiness, righteousness, and strength. He who is the Brightness of Jehovah's glory entered by his own holiness; but that way is shut to the whole human race, and we all must enter as sinners, by faith in his blood, and by the power of his grace.

Ezekiel 45

Chapter Summary

In the period here foretold, the worship and the ministers of God will be provided for; the princes will rule with justice, as holding their power under Christ; the people will live in peace, ease, and godliness. These things seem to be represented in language taken from the customs of the times in which the prophet wrote. Christ is our Passover that is sacrificed for us: we celebrate the memorial of that sacrifice, and feast upon it, triumphing in our deliverance out of the Egyptian slavery of sin, and our preservation from the destroying sword of Divine justice, in the Lord's supper, which is our passover feast; as the whole Christian life is, and must be, the feast of the unleavened bread of sincerity and truth.

Ezekiel 46

Chapter Summary

The ordinances of worship for the prince and for the people, are here described, and the gifts the prince may bestow on his sons and servants. Our Lord has directed us to do many duties, but he has also left many things to our choice, that those who delight in his commandments may abound therein to his glory, without entangling their own consciences, or prescribing rules unfit for others; but we must never omit our daily worship, nor neglect to apply the sacrifice of the Lamb of God to our souls, for pardon, peace, and salvation.

Ezekiel 47

These waters signify the gospel of Christ, which went forth from Jerusalem, and spread into the countries about; also the gifts and powers of the Holy Ghost which accompanied it, by virtue of which is spread far, and produced blessed effects. Christ is the Temple; and he is the Door; from him the living waters flow, out of his pierced side. They are increasing waters. Observe the progress of the gospel in the world, and the process of the work of grace in the heart; attend the motions of the blessed Spirit under Divine guidance. If we search into the things of God, we find some things plain and easy to be understood, as the waters that were but to the ankles; others more difficult, which require a deeper search, as the waters to the knees, or the loins; and some quite beyond our reach, which we cannot penetrate; but must, as St. Paul did, adore the depth, Romans 11. It is wisdom to begin with that which is most easy, before we proceed to that which is dark and hard to be understood. The promises of the sacred word, and the privileges of believers, as shed abroad in their souls by the quickening Spirit, abound where the gospel is preached; they nourish and delight the souls of men; they never fade nor wither, nor are exhausted. Even the leaves serve as medicines to the soul: the warnings and reproofs of the word, though less pleasant than Divine consolations, tend to heal the diseases of the soul. All who believe in Christ, and are united to him by his sanctifying Spirit, will share the privileges of Israelites. There is room in the church, and in heaven, for all who seek the blessings of that new covenant of which Christ is Mediator.

Ezekiel 48

Chapter Summary

Here is a description of the several portions of the land belonging to each tribe. In gospel times, behold all things are become new. Much is wrapped up in emblems and numbers. This method God has used to state mysterious truths in his word, not to be more clearly revealed till the proper time and season. But into the church of Christ, both in its state of warfare and triumph, there is free access by faith, from every side. Christ has opened the kingdom of heaven for all believers. Whoever will, may come, and take of the water of life, of the tree of life, freely. The Lord is there, in his church, to be nigh unto them in all they call upon him for. This is true of every real Christian; whatever soul has in it a living principle of grace, it may truly be said, The Lord is there. May we be found citizens of this holy city, and act agreeably to that character; and have the benefit of the Lord's presence with us, in life, in death, and for evermore.

Made in the USA
Middletown, DE
31 March 2024